SCHAUM'S OUTLINE OF

THEORY AND PROBLEMS

of

PROGRAMMING

with

BASIC

including expanded MICROCOMPUTER BASIC section

•

Third Edition

•

BYRON S. GOTTFRIED, Ph. D.

Professor of Industrial Engineering
Engineering Management and Operations Research
University of Pittsburgh

SCHAUM'S OUTLINE SERIES
McGRAW-HILL PUBLISHING COMPANY

New York St. Louis San Francisco Auckland Bogotá Caracas
Hamburg Lisbon London Madrid Mexico Milan Montreal
New Delhi Oklahoma City Paris San Juan São Paulo
Singapore Sydney Tokyo Toronto

BYRON S. GOTTFRIED is a Professor of Industrial Engineering, Engineering Management and Operations Research at the University of Pittsburgh. He received his Ph.D. from Case-Western Reserve University (1962) and has been a member of the Pitt faculty since 1970. His primary interests are in the development of complex technical and business applications of computers. Dr. Gottfried is the author of several textbooks, including *Introduction to Engineering Calculations* and *Programming with Pascal* in the Schaum's Outline Series.

Schaum's Outline of Theory and Problems of
PROGRAMMING WITH BASIC

4 5 6 7 8 9 10 11 12 13 14 15 16 17 18 19 20 SHP SHP 8 9

ISBN 0-07-023875-8

Sponsoring Editor, John Aliano
Editing Supervisor, Marthe Grice
Production Manager, Nick Monti

Library of Congress Cataloging in Publication Data

Gottfried, Byron S., date
Schaum's Outline of programming with BASIC.

(Schaum's outline series)
Rev. ed. of: Schaum's Outline of theory and problems of programming with BASIC, including microcomputer BASIC, 2nd ed. c1982.
Includes index.
1. Basic (Computer program language) I. Gottfried, Byron S. Schaum's Outline of theory and problems of programming with BASIC, including microcomputer BASIC. II. Title. III. Title: Outline of programming with BASIC.
QA76.73.B3G67 1986 001.64'24 85-7749
ISBN 0-07-023875-8

To Marcia, Sharon, Gail and Susan

Preface

Of the many programming languages that are currently in common use, none is easier to learn or to use than BASIC. Yet this remarkably simple language contains enough power and versatility to be used by people in many different occupations for a wide variety of applications. Consequently, BASIC programming courses have become common in many high schools and junior high schools as well as most colleges and universities. Even elementary schools now offer introductory BASIC courses to select groups of students!

Another reason for BASIC's popularity is its widespread availability. The language is now available on practically every large computer, and it is supported by virtually all commercial timesharing services. Moreover, in recent years BASIC has become the standard language for most microcomputer applications. Hence the language can be used on both large and small computers, in all types of different programming environments.

This book offers instruction in computer programming using the standard features of BASIC and the commonly used features of microcomputer BASIC. All the principal features of BASIC are discussed. In addition, the book stresses the development of programs that are logical, efficient and orderly. Thus, the reader is exposed to the principles of good programming practice as well as the specific rules of BASIC.

The style of writing is deliberately elementary. This enables the book to be easily understood by a wide reader audience, ranging from high school students to practicing professionals. The book is particularly well suited to the advanced secondary or beginning college level, either as a textbook for an elementary programming course, as a supplementary text for a more comprehensive course in analytical techniques or as an effective self-study guide. For the most part, the required mathematical level does not go beyond high school algebra.

In this third edition, the material on microcomputer BASIC has been greatly expanded. The text is now organized into three major parts: Elementary BASIC, Advanced BASIC and Microcomputer BASIC. Part I presents the commonly used features of the language. A brief programming course can be taught from this material alone. Part II is concerned with more specialized features, such as subroutines, matrix statements and file manipulation. Part III concentrates on the enhancements typically available in microcomputer BASIC, with particular emphasis on Microsoft BASIC as implemented on the IBM Personal Computer. This material includes a brief chapter on user-friendly programming and a longer chapter on microcomputer graphics.

The material is presented in such a manner that the reader can write complete, though elementary, BASIC programs as soon as possible. It is very important that the reader write such programs and run them on a computer concurrently with reading the text. This greatly enhances the beginning programmer's self-confidence and stimulates his or her interest in the subject. (Learning to program a computer is like learning to play a musical instrument; it cannot be learned simply by studying a textbook!)

A large number of examples are included as an integral part of the text. These include a number of comprehensive programming problems as well as the customary drill type of exercises. In addition, a set of solved problems is included at the end of most chapters. These examples and solved problems should be studied carefully as the reader progresses through each chapter and begins to write his or her own programs.

Sets of review questions, supplementary problems and programming problems are also included at the end of each chapter. The review questions enable the reader to test his or her recall of the material presented within the chapter. They also provide an effective chapter summary. Most of the supplementary problems and programming problems require no special mathematical or technological background. The student should solve as many of these problems as possible. (Answers to some of the supplementary problems are provided at the end of the text.) When using this book as a course text, it may also be advisable for the instructor to supplement the programming problems with additional assignments that reflect particular disciplinary interests.

The principal features of the language are summarized on the inside back cover and in five appendixes, for the reader's convenience. This material should be used frequently for ready reference and quick recall. It will be particularly helpful when writing or debugging a new program.

Finally, the reader who completes this book will have learned quite a lot about general computer-programming concepts as well as the specific rules of BASIC. He or she should be completely convinced that programming with BASIC is not only *easy* but also *fun*!

BYRON S. GOTTFRIED

Contents

Complete Programming Examples

Software for these examples is available; see last page for details.

COMPLETE PROGRAMMING EXAMPLES

PART I: *Elementary BASIC*

Chapter 1

Introductory Concepts

This book offers instruction in computer programming using a popular, easily learned programming language called BASIC (Beginner's All-purpose Symbolic Instruction Code). We will see how a problem that is initially described in words can be analyzed, outlined and finally transformed into a well-organized BASIC program. These concepts are demonstrated in detail by the many sample problems that are included in the text.

1.1 INTRODUCTION TO COMPUTERS

Today's computers come in a variety of shapes, sizes and costs. Huge, general-purpose computers are used by many large corporations, universities, hospitals and government agencies to carry out sophisticated scientific and business calculations. These computers are generally referred to as

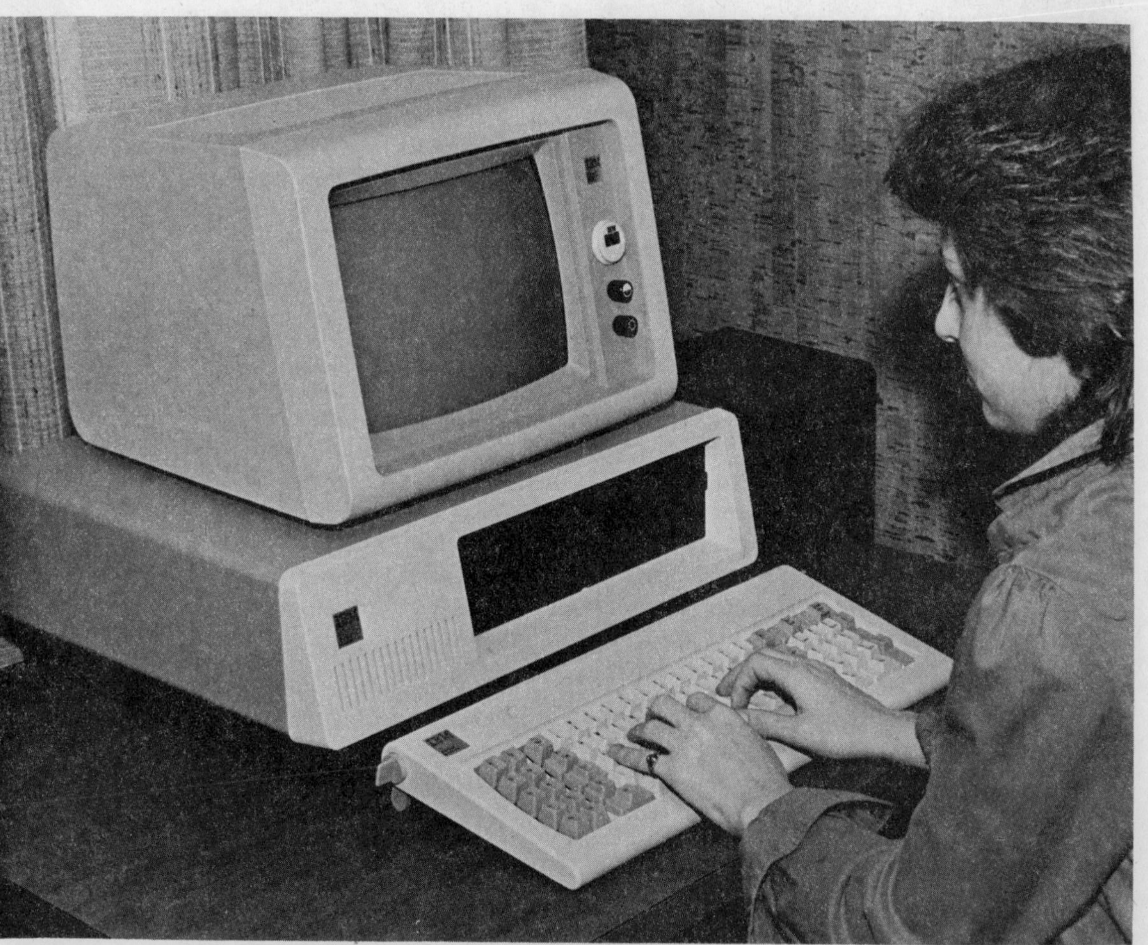

Fig. 1.1

mainframes. They are very expensive (some cost millions of dollars), and they require a carefully controlled environment (temperature, humidity, etc.). As a rule, they are not physically accessible to the people who use them.

Mainframes have been available since the early 1950s, though relatively few people knew how to use them in the earlier years. Those privileged persons who did use them were generally highly trained scientists, engineers and accountants. Thus it is not surprising that computers were viewed both with awe and with suspicion by the general public. During the 1960s it became increasingly common for students at large universities to learn to program mainframe computers (usually via BASIC or some other high-level programming language). As a result, some of the mystery associated with the use of computers began to disappear.

The late 1960s and early 1970s witnessed the development of smaller, less expensive *minicomputers.* These machines offered the performance of earlier mainframes at a fraction of the cost. Many schools and businesses that could not afford mainframes therefore acquired minicomputers as they became increasingly available.

By the mid-1970s, advances in integrated-circuit technology (silicon "chips") resulted in the development of still smaller and less expensive computers called *microcomputers.* Because these machines are built entirely of integrated circuits, they are not much larger (and not much more expensive) than a conventional office typewriter.

Microcomputers are often referred to as *personal computers* because most of them are intended to be used by only one person at a time. Figure 1.1 shows a student utilizing a personal computer.

Many modern microcomputers approach minicomputers in computing power, and their performance continues to improve dramatically as their cost continues to drop. Thus, they can be used for a wide variety of personal, educational, commercial and technical applications. Microcomputers are therefore very prevalent in many schools and businesses, and it appears likely that they will soon become common household items.

Many large organizations utilize microcomputers as *terminals* or *workstations* that are connected to larger computers or to other microcomputers through a communications network. When used in this manner, microcomputers tend to *complement,* rather than replace, the use of larger computers.

1.2 COMPUTER CHARACTERISTICS

All digital computers, regardless of their size, are basically electronic devices that can transmit, store and manipulate *information,* or *data.* There are basically two different types of data: *numerical* data and *character-type* data (e.g., names, addresses, etc.). Scientific and technical applications primarily require the processing of numerical data, whereas business applications usually involve the processing of both numerical and character data. Some computers are used only to process textual-type character data (e.g., letters, book manuscripts, etc.); this is known as *word processing.*

In order to process a particular set of data, the computer must be given an appropriate set of instructions, called a *program.* These instructions are entered into the computer and then stored in a portion of the computer's *memory.*

A stored program can be *executed* at any time. This causes the following things to happen.

1. A set of information, called the *input data,* is entered into the computer (from a terminal, card reader, etc.) and stored in another portion of the computer's memory.
2. The input data is then processed to produce certain desired results, known as the *output data.*
3. The output data (and perhaps some of the input data) are printed onto a sheet of paper or displayed on a monitor (i.e., a video-type display device).

This three-step procedure can be repeated many times if desired, thus causing a large quantity of data to be processed in rapid sequence. It should be understood, however, that each of these steps, particularly steps 2 and 3, can be lengthy and complicated.

EXAMPLE 1.1

A computer has been programmed to calculate the area of a circle using the formula $A = \pi r^2$, given a numerical value for the radius r as input data. The following steps are required.

1. Read the numerical value for the radius of the circle.
2. Calculate the value of the area, using the above formula. (This value will be stored, along with the input data, in the computer's memory.)
3. Print (display) the values of the radius and the corresponding area.
4. Stop.

Each of these steps will require one or more instructions in a computer program.

We can represent the entire procedure pictorially, as shown in Fig. 1.2. This is known as a *flowchart*. Flowcharts can be very helpful in assisting the reader to visualize the flow of logic within a program.

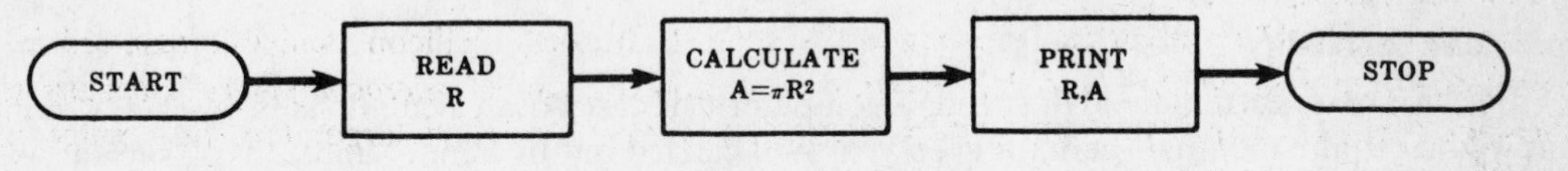

Fig. 1.2

The foregoing discussion illustrates two important characteristics of a digital computer: *memory* and *capability to be programmed.* A third important characteristic is its *speed and reliability.* We will say more about memory, speed and reliability in the next few paragraphs. Programmability will be discussed at length throughout the remainder of this book.

Memory

Every piece of information that is stored within the computer's memory is encoded as some unique combination of zeros and ones. These zeros and ones are called *bits* (*bi*nary digi*ts*). Each bit is represented by an electronic device that is, in some sense, either "off" (zero) or "on" (one).

Small computers have memories that are organized into 8-bit multiples called *bytes.* Normally 1 byte will represent a single character (i.e., a letter, a single digit or a punctuation symbol); an instruction may occupy 1, 2 or 3 bytes, and a single numerical quantity may occupy anywhere from 2 to 8 bytes, depending on the precision and type of number.

The size of a computer's memory is usually expressed as some multiple of $2^{10} = 1024$ bytes. This is referred to as *1K*. Small computers have memories whose sizes typically range from 64K to 1024K (1M) bytes.

EXAMPLE 1.2

The memory of a small personal computer has a capacity of 256K bytes. Thus, as many as $256 \times 1024 = 262{,}144$ characters and/or instructions can be stored in the computer's memory. If the entire memory is used to represent character data, then over 3200 names and addresses can be stored within the computer at any one time (assuming 80 characters for each name and address).

If the memory is used to represent numerical data rather than names and addresses, then over 65,000 individual quantities can be stored at any one time (assuming 4 bytes per number).

Large computers have memories that are organized into *words* rather than bytes. Each word will consist of a relatively large number of bits—typically 32 or 36. This allows one numerical quantity or a small *group* of characters (typically four or five) to be represented within a single word of memory. Large computer memories are usually expressed as some multiple of 1K (i.e., $2^{10} = 1024$) words. A large computer may have several million words of memory.

EXAMPLE 1.3

The memory of a large general-purpose computer has a capacity of 2048K, which is equivalent to $2048 \times 1024 = 2{,}097{,}152$ words. If the entire memory is used to represent numerical data, then more than 2 million numbers can be stored within the computer at any one time.

If the memory is used to represent characters rather than numerical data, then about 8 million characters can be stored at any one time. This is more than enough memory to store the contents of an entire book.

Most computers also employ *auxiliary memory devices* (e.g., magnetic tapes, disks, solid-state memory devices) in addition to their primary memories. These devices typically range from a few hundred thousand bytes (for a small computer) to several million words (for a larger computer). Moreover, they allow for the permanent recording of information, since they can be physically mounted or dismounted from the computer and stored when not in use. However the access time (i.e., the time required to store or retrieve information) is considerably greater for these auxiliary devices than for primary memory.

Speed and Reliability

Because of its extremely high speed, a computer can carry out calculations in just a few minutes that would require months—perhaps even years—if carried out by hand. Simple tasks, such as adding two numbers, can be carried out in a fraction of a *microsecond* ($1\ \mu\text{sec} = 10^{-6}$ sec). On a more practical level, the end-of-semester grades for all students in a large university can typically be processed in just a few minutes of computer time.

This very high speed is accompanied by an equally high level of reliability. Thus a computer practically never makes a mistake of its own accord. Highly publicized "computer" errors, such as a person's receiving a monthly bill of over a million dollars from a local department store, are virtually always the result of a programming error or an error in data transmission rather than an error caused by the computer itself.

1.3 MODES OF OPERATION

There are two different ways that a large digital computer facility can be utilized by a large number of users. These are the *batch mode* and the *interactive mode.* Each has its own advantages for certain types of problems.

Batch Processing

In the early days of computing, all jobs were processed via *batch processing.* This mode of operation is still in use in some schools and businesses, though it is much less common than it once was.

In batch processing a number of jobs are read into the computer, stored internally and then processed sequentially. (A *job* refers to a computer program and its associated sets of input data that are to be processed.) Classical batch processing requires that the program and the data be recorded on punched cards. This information is read into the computer by means of a mechanical cardreader and then processed. After the job is processed, the output, along with a listing of the computer program, is printed on large sheets of paper by a high-speed printer. This form of batch processing is now largely obsolete.

Modern batch processing is generally tied into a timesharing system (see below). In this system the program and the data are typed into the computer via a *timesharing terminal* or a microcomputer. The information is then stored within the computer's memory and processed in its proper sequence. This form of batch processing is preferable to classical batch processing since it eliminates the need for punched cards and allows the input information (program and data) to be edited while it is being entered.

Large quantities of information (both programs and data) can be transmitted into and out of the computer very quickly in batch processing. Furthermore, the user need not be present while the job is being processed. Therefore this mode of operation is well suited to jobs that require large amounts of computer time or are physically lengthy. On the other hand, the total time required for a job to be processed in this manner may vary from several minutes to several hours, even though the job may have required only a second or two of actual computer time. (The job must wait its turn before it can be read, processed and printed out.) Thus batch processing can be undesirable when it is necessary to process many small, simple jobs and return the results as quickly as possible.

Interactive Computing

Interactive computing is carried out either with a personal computer, such as the one shown in Fig. 1.1, or with a computer *terminal*, as illustrated in Fig. 1.3. In either case the user provides the computer with input information through a keyboard, which resembles an ordinary typewriter. The corresponding output information is then either printed onto large sheets of paper or displayed on a video-type *monitor.* (Printed output may be more desirable for some types of applications, since it provides a "hard copy" of the interactive session; however, the use of a monitor is usually more convenient.) Interactive computer terminals are sometimes referred to as *consoles.*

Fig. 1.3

A significant feature of interactive computing is that the user and the computer are able to *converse* with each other during the computational session. Thus the user may periodically be asked to provide certain information that will determine what subsequent actions are to be taken by the computer.

EXAMPLE 1.4

A student wishes to use a personal computer to calculate the radius of a circle, the area of which has a value of 100. A program is available which will calculate the area of a circle, given the radius. (Note that this is just the opposite of what the student wishes to do.) This program isn't exactly what is needed, but it does allow the student to proceed by trial and error. The procedure will be to guess a value for the radius and then calculate a corresponding area. This trial-and-error procedure continues until the student has found a value for the radius that yields an area sufficiently close to 100.

Once the desired program has been entered, the message

RADIUS=?

will be printed. The student then enters a value for the radius. Let us assume that the student enters a value of 5 for the radius. The computer will respond by printing

AREA=78.5398

DO YOU WISH TO REPEAT THE CALCULATION?

The student then types either YES or NO. If the student types YES, then the message

RADIUS=?

will again be printed, and the entire procedure will be repeated. If the student types NO, then the message

GOODBYE

is printed and the computation is terminated.

In Fig. 1.4 we see the information that is printed during a typical interactive session, using the program described above. The information typed by the student has been underlined. An approximate value of $r = 5.6$ was determined after only three calculations.

```
RADIUS=? 5
AREA= 78.5398

DO YOU WISH TO REPEAT THE CALCULATION? YES

RADIUS=? 6
AREA= 113.097

DO YOU WISH TO REPEAT THE CALCULATION? YES

RADIUS=? 5.6
AREA= 98.5204

DO YOU WISH TO REPEAT THE CALCULATION? NO

GOODBYE
```

Fig. 1.4

Notice the manner in which the student and the computer appear to be conversing with one another. Also, note that the student waits until he or she sees the calculated value of the area before deciding whether or not to carry out another calculation. If another calculation is initiated, the new value for the radius that the student supplies will depend on the previously calculated results.

Programs that are designed for interactive-type applications are sometimes said to be *conversational* in nature. Computerized games, such as Adventure, checkers and chess, are excellent examples of such interactive applications. So are the fast-action, graphical arcade games, such as Space Invaders, Pac-Man and Defender.

Timesharing

Timesharing is a form of interactive computing in which many different users are able to use a single computer simultaneously. Each user will communicate with the computer through a terminal, such as the one shown in Fig. 1.3. The terminals may be wired directly to the computer, or they may be connected to the computer over telephone lines or a microwave circuit. Thus a timesharing terminal can be located far away—perhaps several hundred miles away—from its host computer.

Microcomputers, such as that shown in Fig. 1.1, are often used in place of timesharing terminals. Such interconnections are becoming particularly common with telephone line connections. This arrangement allows a person working at home on his or her own personal computer to access a remote computer at school or at the office.

Since a computer operates much faster than a human sitting at a terminal, one large computer can support many terminals at essentially the same time. Therefore each user will be unaware of the presence of any other users and will seem to have the remote computer at his or her own disposal.

Timesharing is best suited for processing relatively simple jobs that do not require extensive data transmission or large amounts of computer time. Many of the computer applications that arise in schools and commercial offices have these characteristics. Using timesharing, such applications can be processed quickly, easily and at minimum expense.

EXAMPLE 1.5

A large university has a computer timesharing capability consisting of 100 timesharing terminals and 80 separate telephone connections. The timesharing terminals, which are located at various places around the campus, are wired directly to a large central computer. Each terminal is able to transmit information to or from the main computer at a maximum speed of 120 characters per second.

The telephone connections allow students who are not on campus to connect their personal computers to the main computer. Each personal computer can transmit data to or from the computer at a maximum speed of 120 characters per second. Thus all 180 terminals and microcomputers can interact with the main computer at the same time. However, each student will be unaware that others are also using the computer.

1.4 TYPES OF PROGRAMMING LANGUAGES

There are many different languages that can be used to program a computer. The most basic of these is *machine language*, a collection of very detailed, cryptic instructions that control the computer's internal circuitry. This is the natural dialect of the computer. Very few computer programs are actually written in machine language, however, for two significant reasons: first, because machine language is very cumbersome to work with, and second, because most computers have their own unique instruction sets. Thus a machine-language program written for one type of computer cannot be run on another type of computer without significant alterations.

Usually, a computer program will be written in some *high-level language*, the instruction set of which is more compatible with human languages and human thought processes. Most of these high-level languages are *general-purpose* languages, such as BASIC. (Other commonly used general-purpose languages are Pascal, C, PL/1, Fortran and Cobol.) There are also various high-level *special-purpose* languages whose instruction sets are specifically designed for some particular type of application.

As a rule, a single instruction in a high-level language will be equivalent to several instructions in machine language. Moreover, a program that is written in a high-level language can generally be run on many different computers with little or no modification. Therefore the use of a high-level language offers us some very significant advantages over the use of machine language—namely, *simplicity*, *uniformity* and *portability* (i.e., machine independence).

A program that is written in a high-level language must, however, be translated into machine language before it can be executed. This is known as *compilation* or *interpretation*, depending on how it is carried out. (Most versions of BASIC are interpreted rather than compiled.)

It is generally more convenient to develop a new program using an interpreter rather than a compiler, though compiled programs execute much faster than interpreted programs. (The reasons for this are beyond the scope of our present discussion.) In either case, however, the translation is carried out automatically within the computer. In fact, an inexperienced programmer may not even be aware that this procedure is taking place, since he or she typically sees only the original program, the input data and the resulting output data.

The compiler or interpreter is itself a *computer program* that accepts a high-level program (e.g., a BASIC program) as input data and generates a corresponding machine-language program as output. Accordingly, the original high-level program is called the *source* program, and the resulting machine-language program is called the *object* program. Every computer must have its own compiler or interpreter for a given high-level language. It is this use of compilers and interpreters that allows us to achieve uniformity and machine independence with high-level languages such as BASIC.

1.5 INTRODUCTION TO BASIC

BASIC is an easy-to-use, "friendly" language whose instructions resemble elementary algebraic formulas, augmented by certain English keywords such as LET, READ, PRINT, GO TO, IF, THEN, etc. Most other high-level languages have similar features though they are generally more complicated, which makes them more difficult to learn and to use. Thus, BASIC is particularly well suited for persons learning to program for the first time. In fact, many high schools and junior high schools now offer courses in BASIC programming. Some elementary schools even introduce the subject to select groups of students.

The use of BASIC is by no means restricted, however, to elementary applications. It is often used for a variety of more advanced applications in such areas as business, science, engineering and mathematics. BASIC is also the principal language that is used with microcomputers. Hence BASIC can be used for many novel applications, for example, computer games requiring the use of graphics and sound generation, as well as more traditional applications such as personal finance and database management. We will see a representative sampling of these different types of programming applications in the examples that are included within this book.

History of BASIC

BASIC was originally developed at Dartmouth College by John Kemeny and Thomas Kurtz in the mid-1960s. Because of its simplicity, it was quickly adopted by several commercial timesharing services, which caused it to receive a broad exposure among thousands of computer users. Each of the major computer manufacturers, wishing to remain competitive, soon offered a version of BASIC for its own line of computers. Thus, BASIC rapidly became the most widely used timesharing language in the United States and Canada.

As microcomputers began to evolve in the mid-1970s, microcomputer manufacturers adopted BASIC as their standard programming language. In fact, the convenience and simplicity of BASIC has been a major contributor to the rapid proliferation of these devices. The language is now provided automatically with the purchase of virtually every new microcomputer. Many microcomputers even include a BASIC interpreter as a part of their internal circuitry.

In 1978 the American National Standards Institute (ANSI) standardized an essential subset of BASIC* in order to promote uniformity from one version of BASIC to another. Virtually all versions

---

* *American National Standard for Minimal BASIC,* ANSI X3.60-1978, American National Standards Institute, New York, 1978.

of BASIC include these standard features, though most include numerous other features as well. Unfortunately, the 1978 standard was too small to provide effective standardization within the commercial marketplace. A more comprehensive standard is currently under development, though it redefines the language to such an extent that its practical influence appears questionable.

Variations in BASIC

Most versions of BASIC that are implemented on large computers or supported by commercial timesharing services are reasonably similar to one another. They all include the features described in the 1978 ANSI standard, plus a number of additional commonly used features. (Many also include certain special features that are unique to each particular version of the language.) Such implementations are often referred to as variants of "Dartmouth BASIC," since they closely resemble the version of the language that was originally developed at Dartmouth College. Programs that are confined to the features of the original Dartmouth BASIC can usually be run on many different computers with little or no modification.

In the microcomputer marketplace, the competition between computer manufacturers discourages any attempts at official standardization. Most versions of microcomputer BASIC are highly enhanced with special instructions customized for the hardware capabilities of their respective computers. Thus, there are special instructions for carrying out graphics, for generating sounds and for controlling various microcomputer peripherals, such as floppy-disk drives, printers, light pens and joysticks. There are, nonetheless, similarities in these instructions from one version of microcomputer BASIC to another. Thus, many BASIC programs that are written for one microcomputer can be modified to run on another without undue effort.

This book describes all of the commonly used features of BASIC, beginning with the more elementary and traditional features of the language and progressing to more specialized material, including features that are available only on microcomputers. Specifically, the material in Chapters 2 through 6 applies to practically all versions of BASIC. Many mainframe versions of the language also include the features described in Chapter 7 (Vectors and Matrices). The material in Chapter 8 (Data Files) applies to many versions of BASIC, though there is considerable variation in the exact manner in which these features are implemented. Chapters 9 through 12 describe many of the special features and techniques that are available in microcomputer BASIC, with particular emphasis on Microsoft BASIC as implemented on the IBM Personal Computer. The book also contains five appendixes which summarize most of the material presented earlier.

The reader who has mastered this material should have little difficulty in utilizing the features that are available in any particular version of BASIC or in altering a program so that it will run under a different version of the language.

Structure of a BASIC Program

Each instruction in a BASIC program is written as a separate *statement.* Thus a complete BASIC program will be composed of a sequence of statements. These statements will be executed in the order in which they appear unless a deliberate "jump" (i.e., a transfer of control) is indicated.

The following rules apply to the older, more traditional versions of BASIC.

1. Every statement must appear on a separate line.*
2. A statement cannot exceed one line in length (i.e., cannot be "continued" from one line to the next).
3. Each statement must begin with a positive integer quantity known as a *statement number* (or *line number*). No two statements can have the same statement number.

* On most timesharing terminals a line is equivalent to 80 characters, though some terminals allow 132 characters per line.

4. Successive statements must have increasing statement numbers.
5. Each statement number must be followed by a BASIC *keyword*, which indicates the type of instruction that is to be carried out.
6. Blank spaces may be inserted wherever desired in order to improve the readability of the statement.

It is also possible to include empty lines in a BASIC program. Every empty line must include at least one character, which may be a blank space. (If a line number is followed immediately by a carriage return, then that line will be *deleted* from the program. We will discuss this further in Chapter 3.)

These six rules will be observed in the programming examples presented in the first eight chapters of this book. When we reach Chapter 9 we will see that these rules can be relaxed considerably in some versions of microcomputer BASIC. However, programs which adhere to these rules will still be valid.

EXAMPLE 1.6 Area of a Circle

Figure 1.5 presents a simple BASIC program to calculate the area of a circle whose radius is specified. The logic used to carry out the computation has already been discussed in Example 1.1. The program is so elementary, however, that its logical basis can be determined by simple inspection.

```
10 INPUT R
20 LET A=3.14159*R^2
30 PRINT R,A
40 END
```

Fig. 1.5

We see that the program consists of four statements, each of which appears on a separate line. Every statement has its own statement number (line number). These numbers increase successively from the beginning (top) to the end (bottom) of the program. The statements contain the BASIC keywords INPUT, LET, PRINT and END, respectively.

The purpose of the first statement (INPUT R) is to enter a numerical value for the radius (R) from the terminal The second statement (LET A=3.14159*R↑2) causes the quantity πR^2 to be evaluated. This quantity will then be represented by the letter A (for area). The third statement (PRINT R,A) causes the numerical values for R and A to be transmitted to the terminal, where they are printed or displayed. Finally, the last statement (END) is required in order to identify the end of the program.

Notice the symbols that are used in line 20 to represent arithmetic operations. Multiplication is indicated by an asterisk (*), and an upward-pointing arrow (↑) is used to raise a quantity to a power. [This latter operation is known as *exponentiation.* Some terminals use an upper caret (^) to indicate exponentiation, as seen in Fig. 1.5.] The remaining arithmetic operations, namely addition, subtraction and division, are represented in BASIC by a plus sign (+), a minus sign (−) and a slash (/), respectively.

Some Advantages of BASIC

1. BASIC is "friendly," i.e., it is "people-oriented." It is easy to learn and fun to use. Any well-organized person can learn to program in BASIC. An extensive background in mathematics is not necessary.
2. BASIC is very flexible, allowing the programmer to develop new programs and to alter existing programs with relatively little effort.
3. BASIC is well suited for use in an interactive environment. This includes dedicated microcomputer applications as well as large-computer timesharing applications.
4. BASIC is universally available, on both large and small computers. It has become the standard programming language for most microcomputer applications.
5. The commonly used features of BASIC are relatively standard, though there are some differences between one version of BASIC and another. Many BASIC programs can be run on a variety of different computers with little or no modification.

Review Questions

1.1 What is meant by a mainframe computer? Where can mainframes be found? What are they generally used for?

1.2 What is a minicomputer? How do minicomputers differ from mainframes?

1.3 What is a microcomputer? How do microcomputers differ from mainframes and minicomputers?

1.4 Name two different types of data.

1.5 What is meant by a computer program? What, in general, happens when a computer program is executed?

1.6 What is a computer memory? What kinds of information are stored in a computer's memory?

1.7 What is a bit? What is a byte? What is the difference between a byte and a word of memory?

1.8 What terms are used to describe the size of a computer's memory? What are some typical memory sizes?

1.9 Name some typical auxiliary memory devices. How does this type of memory differ from the computer's main memory?

1.10 What time unit is used to express the speed with which elementary tasks are carried out by a computer?

1.11 What is the difference between the batch mode and the interactive mode? What are their advantages and disadvantages?

1.12 What is meant by timesharing? For what types of applications is timesharing best suited?

1.13 What is machine language? How does machine language differ from high-level languages?

1.14 Name some commonly used high-level languages. What are the advantages in the use of high-level languages?

1.15 What is meant by compilation? What is meant by interpretation? How do these two processes differ?

1.16 What is a source program? An object program? Why are these concepts important?

1.17 What does the acronym "BASIC" stand for?

1.18 What are the general characteristics of the BASIC language?

1.19 Where was BASIC originally developed and by whom was it developed?

1.20 To what extent do individual versions of BASIC differ from one another? Has the language been standardized?

1.21 What is a BASIC statement? In what order must the statements appear in a BASIC program?

1.22 Summarize six rules that apply to older, more traditional versions of the language. Do these rules also apply to most versions of microcomputer BASIC?

1.23 In BASIC, what symbols are used to indicate addition, subtraction, multiplication and division?

1.24 What is meant by exponentiation? What symbol is used in BASIC to represent exponentiation?

1.25 Summarize the principal advantages of BASIC.

Solved Problems

1.26 Several elementary BASIC programs are presented below. Explain the purpose of each program.

(*a*)
```
10 INPUT L,W
20 LET A=L*W
30 PRINT L,W,A
40 END
```

To calculate the area of a rectangle whose length and width are given.

(*b*)
```
10 INPUT A,B,C,D,E
20 LET S=A+B+C+D+E
30 PRINT A,B,C,D,E
40 PRINT S
50 END
```

To calculate the sum of five numbers. Note that the five numbers will be printed on one line and the calculated sum on the next line. (Each PRINT statement begins on a new line.)

(*c*)
```
10 INPUT A,B,C
20 LET X1=(-B+(B↑2-4*A*C)↑.5)/(2*A)
30 LET X2=(-B-(B↑2-4*A*C)↑.5)/(2*A)
40 PRINT A,B,C,X1,X2
50 END
```

To calculate values for x_1 and x_2 from the formulas

$$x_1 = \frac{-b + \sqrt{b^2 - 4ac}}{2a}$$

$$x_2 = \frac{-b - \sqrt{b^2 - 4ac}}{2a}$$

where the values for a, b and c are specified.

1.27 Write an elementary BASIC program for each of the situations described below.

(*a*) Calculate the radius of a circle whose area is known (see Example 1.7).

Since $A = \pi r^2$ we can solve for r, which yields

$$r = \sqrt{A/\pi}$$

Hence the desired program is

```
10 INPUT A
20 LET R=(A/3.141593)↑.5
30 PRINT A,R
40 END
```

(*b*) Calculate the length of a rectangle whose area and width are known [see Problem 1.26(*a*)].

```
10 INPUT A,W
20 LET L=A/W
30 PRINT A,W,L
40 END
```

(*c*) Calculate the product of five given numbers [see Problem 1.26(*b*)].

```
10 INPUT A,B,C,D,E
20 LET P=A*B*C*D*E
30 PRINT A,B,C,D,E
40 PRINT P
50 END
```

Supplementary Problems

1.28 Several elementary BASIC programs are presented below. Explain the purpose of each program.

(*a*)
```
10 INPUT B,H
20 LET A=(B*H)/2
30 PRINT B,H,A
40 END
```

(*b*)
```
10 INPUT L,W
20 LET C=2*(L+W)
30 PRINT L,W,C
40 END
```

(*c*)
```
10 INPUT U,V
20 LET W=U+V
30 LET X=U-V
40 LET Y=U*V
50 LET Z=U/V
60 PRINT U,V
70 PRINT W,X,Y,Z
80 END
```

(*d*)
```
10 INPUT X
20 LET Y=1+X+(X↑2)/2+(X↑3)/6
30 PRINT X,Y
40 END
```

1.29 Write an elementary BASIC program for each of the situations described below.

(*a*) Calculate the circumference of a circle whose radius is given (see Example 1.7).

(*b*) Calculate the length of the hypotenuse of a right triangle whose base and height are given [see Problem 1.28(*a*)].

(*c*) Evaluate the formula

$$w = \frac{u - v}{u + v}$$

where u and v are given [see Problem 1.28(*c*)].

(*d*) Evaluate the formula

$$y = 100(1 + x + 2x^2 + 3x^3)$$

where x is specified [see Problem 1.28(*d*)].

1.30 Shown below is a BASIC program to calculate the area and perimeter of a rectangle and the length of the diagonal. Some of the statements are written incorrectly. Identify all errors.

```
10 INPUT L,W
20 LET A=L*W          30 LET P=2*(L+W)
35 D=(L↑2+W↑2)↑.5
25 PRINT L,W,A,P,D
40 END
```

Chapter 2

Getting Started with BASIC

In this chapter we will examine several fundamental concepts of the BASIC language, such as numbers, variables and formulas. Then we will consider the six most commonly used BASIC statements, which allow us to do input/output and data manipulation operations and jump to other parts of a program whenever we wish. After completing this chapter the reader will be able to write BASIC programs for a variety of problem situations.

2.1 NUMBERS (CONSTANTS)

Numerical quantities are referred to in BASIC as *numbers* (or *constants*). Numbers can be expressed two different ways: as integer quantities (whole numbers without a decimal point) or as decimal quantities (numbers that have a decimal point). The following rules apply to the writing of numbers:

1. Commas cannot appear anywhere in a number.
2. A number can be preceded by a + or − sign. (The number is understood to be positive if a sign does not appear.)
3. A number can contain an exponent, if desired. Exponential notation is similar to scientific notation, except that the base 10 is replaced by the letter E. (Thus the quantity 1.2×10^{-3} could be written in BASIC as 1.2E−3.) The exponent can be either positive or negative but cannot have a decimal point.
4. Most versions of BASIC allow a number to have as many as eight or nine significant figures.
5. Typically the magnitude of a number can be as large as 10^{38} and as small as 10^{-38}. (These values vary from one version of BASIC to another.) A value of zero is also permissible.

EXAMPLE 2.1

The numerical quantities below are expressed as valid BASIC numbers. Note that each quantity (each row) can be written in several different ways.

0	+0	−0
1	+1	0.1E+1
−5280	−5.280E+3	−.5280E4
+1492	1492	1.492E+3
−.0000613	−6.13 E−5	−613 E−7
3000000	3E6	3 E+6

2.2 STRINGS

A *string* is a sequence of characters (i.e., letters, numbers and certain special characters, such as +, −, /, *, =, $, ., etc.). Blank spaces may be included in a string but not quotation marks. The maximum number of characters that can be included in a string will vary from one version of BASIC to another. In some versions a string cannot exceed 15 characters, while others allow as many as 4095 characters.

Strings are used to represent nonnumeric information—names, addresses, etc. They are also used to label numerical output data and print out textual messages (applications that we will see later in the book).

EXAMPLE 2.2

Here are several strings.

```
SANTA CLAUS                    TYPE A VALUE FOR C:
APOLLO-17                      $19.95
X1=                            3730425
DO YOU WISH TO TRY AGAIN?      THE ANSWER IS
```

Note that a sequence of integers, such as 3730425, *does not* represent a numerical quantity when written as a string.

2.3 VARIABLES

A *variable* is a name that represents a number or a string. In the older, more traditional versions of BASIC, a *numeric variable* must consist of a letter or a letter followed by an integer, and a *string variable* must be written as a letter followed by a dollar sign. Most versions of BASIC also allow a string variable to be written as a letter, followed by an integer, followed by a dollar sign.

EXAMPLE 2.3

Each of the following variables can represent a numerical quantity:

```
A    K    X    C1    X5
```

Any of the following variables can represent a string:

```
A$    K$    X$    C$    T$
```

In many versions of BASIC a string can also be represented by any of the following variables:

```
A2$    K9$    X0$    C1$    X5$
```

2.4 OPERATORS AND FORMULAS (EXPRESSIONS)

In BASIC we use special symbols, called *operators*, to indicate the arithmetic operations of addition, subtraction, multiplication, division and exponentiation. These operators are

Addition:	+	(plus sign)
Subtraction:	−	(minus sign)
Multiplication:	*	(asterisk)
Division:	/	(slash)
Exponentiation:	↑	(upward-pointing arrow)
	^	(some terminals use the upper caret)

The operators are used to connect numbers and numerical variables, thus forming *formulas* (or *expressions*).

The indicated operations are carried out on the numeric terms in a formula, resulting in a single numerical value. Hence *a formula represents a specific numerical quantity.*

EXAMPLE 2.4

Several BASIC formulas are presented below:

```
J+1
A+B−C
(2*X−3*Y)/(U+V)
3.141593*R↑2
B↑2−4*A*C
```

Each formula represents a numerical quantity. Thus if the variables A, B and C represent the numerical quantities 2, 5 and 3, respectively, the formula A+B−C will represent the quantity 4.

Strictly speaking, a formula can be composed of a single number or a single numeric variable as well as some combination of numbers, numeric variables and operators. It is important to understand, however, that *a numeric variable must be assigned some numerical quantity before it can appear in a formula.* Otherwise the formula could not be evaluated to yield a numerical value.

2.5 HIERARCHY OF OPERATIONS

Questions in meaning may arise when we have two or more operators in a formula. For example, does the formula 2*X–3*Y correspond to the algebraic term $(2x)-(3y)$ or to $2(x-3y)$? Similarly, does A/B*C correspond to $a/(bc)$ or to $(a/b)c$? These questions can easily be answered once we have become familiar with the *hierarchy of operations* and the *order of execution* within a given hierarchical group.

The hierarchy of operations is

1. *Exponentiation.* All exponentiation operations are performed first.
2. *Multiplication and division.* These operations are carried out after all exponentiation operations have been performed. Multiplication does not necessarily precede division.
3. *Addition and subtraction.* These operations are the last to be carried out. Addition does not necessarily precede subtraction.

Within a given hierarchical group the operations are carried out from left to right.

EXAMPLE 2.5

The formula

```
A/B*C
```

is equivalent to the mathematical expression $(a/b)c$, since the operations are carried out from left to right.

Similarly, the formula

```
B↑2−4*A*C
```

is equivalent to the mathematical expression $b^2-(4ac)$. In this case the quantity B↑2 is formed initially, followed by the product 4*A*C [first 4*A, then (4*A)*C]. The subtraction is performed last, resulting in the quantity (B↑2)−(4*A*C).

2.6 USE OF PARENTHESES

There are many situations in which we will want to alter the normal hierarchy of operations in a formula. This is easily accomplished by inserting pairs of parentheses at the proper places within the formula. The operations within the innermost pairs of parentheses will then be performed first, followed by the operations within the second innermost pairs, and so on. Within a given pair of parentheses the natural hierarchy of operations will apply unless specifically altered by other pairs of parentheses embedded inside the given pair.

We must remember always to use *pairs* of parentheses. A careless imbalance of right and left parentheses is a common error.

EXAMPLE 2.6

Suppose we want to evaluate the term

$$[2(a+b)^2+(3c)^2]^{m/(n+1)}$$

A BASIC formula that corresponds to this algebraic term is

```
(2*(A+B)↑2+(3*C)↑2)↑(M/(N+1))
```

If there is some uncertainty in the order in which the operations are carried out, we can introduce additional pairs of parentheses, giving

```
((2*((A+B)↑2))+((3*C)↑2))↑(M/(N+1))
```

Both formulas are correct. The first formula may be preferable, however, since it is less cluttered with parentheses and is therefore easier to read.

2.7 SPECIAL RULES CONCERNING FORMULAS

Special problems can arise if a formula is not correctly written. They can be avoided by applying these rules.

1. Preceding a variable by a minus sign is equivalent to multiplication by −1.

EXAMPLE 2.7

The formula

```
-X↑N
```

is equivalent to −(X↑N) or −1*(X↑N), since exponentiation has precedence over multiplication. Hence if X and N are assigned values of 3 and 2, respectively, then −X↑N will yield a value of −9.

2. Except for the condition just described, operations cannot be implied.

EXAMPLE 2.8

The algebraic expression $2(x_1+3x_2)$ must be written in BASIC as

```
2*(X1+3*X2)
```

with the multiplication operators shown explicitly. The formulas 2(X1+3*X2) and 2*(X1+3X2) are incorrect.

3. A negative quantity can be raised to a power only if the exponent is an integer. (Do not confuse the exponent in an *exponentiation formula* with the exponent that is a part of a *decimal number.*)

   To understand this restriction, we must see how exponentiation is carried out. If the exponent is an *integer* quantity, then the quantity to be exponentiated is multiplied by itself an appropriate number of times.

   On the other hand, suppose the exponent is a *decimal* quantity. The procedure used with a decimal exponent is to compute the *logarithm* of the quantity being exponentiated, multiply this logarithm by the exponent and then compute the antilog. Since the logarithm of a negative number is not defined, we see that the operation is invalid if the quantity being exponentiated is negative.

EXAMPLE 2.9

Consider the formula

```
(C1+C2)↑3
```

The quantity represented by (C1+C2) is multiplied by itself twice, thus forming the cubic expression. Notice that it does not matter whether the quantity (C1+C2) is positive or negative.

However, the formula

```
(B↑2−4*A*C)↑.5
```

will be valid only if B↑2−4*A*C represents a positive quantity.

Finally, consider what happens when either A or N in the expression

```
A↑N
```

is zero. If N has a value of zero, then A↑N will be assigned a value of 1, regardless of the value of A. If A has a value of zero and N is nonzero, however, A↑N will be evaluated as zero.

4. Numerical operations cannot be performed on strings or string variables. However, some versions of BASIC allow strings and string variables to be *concatenated* (i.e., combined, one behind the other).

EXAMPLE 2.10

Suppose that the string variables X$ and Y$ have been assigned the following values:

```
X$="TEN"
Y$="THOUSAND"
```

The formula

```
X$+Y$+" DOLLARS"
```

is not a valid formula, since it is not meaningful to perform numerical operations on strings. In some versions of BASIC, however, the expression

```
X$+" "+Y$+" DOLLARS"
```

will cause the three strings to be concatenated, resulting in the single string

```
TEN THOUSAND DOLLARS
```

2.8 ASSIGNING VALUES—THE LET STATEMENT

The *LET statement* is used to assign a numerical or a string value to a variable. We can *define* a particular variable in a program by establishing its value in this manner.

A LET statement is composed of a statement number, followed by the keyword LET, followed by an *assignment* term that resembles a mathematical equation. The assignment term must consist of a variable, an equal sign and a formula, as shown in the examples below.

EXAMPLE 2.11

```
10 LET X=12.5
20 LET C1=F3
30 LET A=3.141593*R↑2
40 LET N$="NAME"
50 LET T$=N$
```

In each of these statements the value of the term on the right of the equal sign is assigned to the variable on the left.

Note that the variable to the left of the equal sign and the term to the right must be of the same type (either numeric or string). In other words, a numerical value cannot be assigned to a string variable, and vice versa. Also, note that a string must be enclosed in quotation marks if it appears in a LET statement.

It is important to understand the difference between the assignment term that appears in the LET statement and an algebraic equation. Many assignment terms look like algebraic equations. On the other hand, there are certain legitimate assignment terms that would make no sense if viewed as algebraic equations.

EXAMPLE 2.12

Consider the following LET statement, which is both correct and meaningful:

```
5 LET J=J+1
```

The assignment term J=J+1 obviously does not correspond to an algebraic equation, since the equation $j = j + 1$ makes no sense. What we are doing here is to increase the value of the numeric variable J by one unit. Thus the assignment term is entirely logical if we interpret it as follows: add one to the value represented by the variable J, and assign this new value to J. Note that this new value of J will replace the old value.

We will see that LET statements of this type are used quite often in BASIC.

Some versions of BASIC allow greater flexibility in writing LET statements than others. For example, in some versions of BASIC it is possible to assign the same value to two or more variables in a single LET statement. Moreover, the keyword LET can be omitted in certain versions of BASIC.

EXAMPLE 2.13

The following LET statements would be permitted in *some* versions of BASIC:

```
10 LET A=B=C=5.089
20 A=L*W
30 X1=X2=(A+B)/(C+D)
40 LET A$=K$="TERMINATE"
```

Notice that the first, third and fourth statements involve multiple assignments and that the keyword LET has been omitted from the second and third statements.

2.9 READING INPUT—THE INPUT STATEMENT

The *INPUT statement* is used to enter numerical or string data into the computer during program execution. The statement consists of a statement number, the keyword INPUT and a list of variables. Both numeric and string variables can be included in the list. The variables must be separated by commas.

EXAMPLE 2.14

```
5 INPUT A,B,C
10 INPUT N$,M$,X0,F5
15 INPUT P(I),Q(I),T$(I)
```

The variables shown in the last statement are called *subscripted variables.* We will discuss subscripted variables in Chapter 5.

When an INPUT statement is encountered during program execution, a question mark (?) is printed on the console, indicating a request for data. Normally the question mark appears at the start of a new line. Further execution of the program is suspended until the requested data have been supplied.

Once the question mark appears, the programmer (or program user) must supply the requested information by typing the appropriate data into the console, followed by a carriage return. The data will then be transmitted to the computer's memory, and program execution will resume. Thus the INPUT statement can be particularly useful in conversational-mode programming.

The following rules must be observed when entering the required input data:

1. The data items must correspond in number and in type to the variables listed in the INPUT statement (i.e., numbers must be supplied for numeric variables, strings for string variables). Extra data items will be ignored.
2. The data items must be separated by commas.
3. The data items must consist of numbers and strings. Formulas are not permitted.
4. Strings containing commas or beginning with blank spaces must be enclosed in quotation marks. Other strings may be enclosed in quotation marks if desired.

EXAMPLE 2.15

Suppose that the statement

```
60 INPUT X,Y,C$
```

is encountered during execution of a BASIC program. This will cause a question mark to be printed at the start of a new line on the console. Further program execution will be temporarily suspended.

Upon seeing the question mark, the user proceeds to enter the required input data. Suppose the appropriate values for X, Y and C$ are 5, -1.2×10^{-3} and NOVEMBER 27, 1937. The line of input would then appear as

```
? 5,-1.2E-3,"NOVEMBER 27, 1937"
```

After the data have been typed, the user depresses the carriage return, causing the data to be transmitted to the computer's memory. Execution of the remainder of the program then proceeds in the normal manner.

The INPUT statement is quite useful for elementary programs not requiring large quantities of input data. The entering of data via an INPUT statement, however, is relatively time-consuming, and data entered in this manner cannot be stored for subsequent use. (In most BASIC systems a *program* can be stored indefinitely and rerun whenever desired.) We will see another method for defining data in Chapter 5.

2.10 PRINTING OUTPUT—THE PRINT STATEMENT

The *PRINT statement* is used to transmit numerical or string output data from the computer. The statement consists of a statement number, the keyword PRINT and a list of output items. The output items can be numbers, formulas or strings. Successive items must be separated by either commas or semicolons.

EXAMPLE 2.16

Several typical PRINT statements are shown below.

```
100 PRINT A,B,C
110 PRINT "X=";X,"Y=";Y
120 PRINT "NAME:";N$,"ADDRESS:";A$
130 PRINT
140 PRINT K;C$(K);5*X0↑2/2;U(I)+V(I);P$
```

The variables C$(K), U(I) and V(I) in the last statement are called *subscripted variables.* We will discuss subscripted variables in Chapter 5.

The following rules must be followed when writing a PRINT statement.

Line Spacing

1. Each PRINT statement begins a new line of output (an exception is discussed in rules 5 and 6 below). However, two or more lines of output will be generated by a single PRINT statement if the list of data items has a large number of entries.

EXAMPLE 2.17

The PRINT statement

```
50 PRINT C1,C2,C3,C4,C5,C6,C7,C8
```

will cause the values of C1 through C5 to be printed on one line and the values of C6 through C8 to be printed on the second line. Suppose, for example, that C1 through C8 represent the following values:

```
C1=3
C2=-12
C3=6.5
C4=5000
C5=0
C6=0.0047
C7=-8
C8=7.2E-15
```

The output would appear as

```
3              -12               6.5            5000          0
0.0047         -8                7.20000E-15
```

2. If a PRINT statement does not contain any data items, then a blank line will appear. This is a useful way to control the vertical spacing of output data.

EXAMPLE 2.18

The PRINT statements

```
40 PRINT C1,C2,C3,C4
50 PRINT
60 PRINT C5,C6,C7,C8
```

will cause the values of C1 through C4 to be printed on one line and C5 through C8 to be printed on another line, with a blank line between them.

If C1 through C8 have the same values as indicated in Example 2.17, then the output result from the above three print statements will appear as

```
3              -12              6.5             5000

0              0.0047           -8              7.20000E-15
```

Significant Figures

3. Numerical output quantities will appear as follows:

   In most versions of BASIC, an integer quantity that contains eight or fewer digits will be printed as an integer number. If an integer quantity exceeds eight digits, it will be rounded to six significant figures and printed as a decimal number with an exponent.

   A decimal quantity will be printed as a decimal number. If the quantity contains more than six digits (including any leading zeros to the right of the decimal point), it will be rounded to six digits. An exponent will be shown if the magnitude of the number exceeds 999999 or is less than 0.1 and contains more than six significant figures.

EXAMPLE 2.19

Suppose a BASIC program contains the variables A, B, C, D, E and F, which have been assigned the following values:

A=1234567
B=123456789
C=−0.001234
D=0.000012345
E=−1234.5
F=1234567.89

The statements

```
100 PRINT A,B,C
110 PRINT D,E,F
```

would generate the following two lines of output:

```
1234567          1.23457E+8     -0.001234
1.23450E-5      -1234.5          1.23457E+6
```

Strings

4. Strings must be enclosed in quotation marks. (See Example 2.20, below.)

Spacing of Output Items Within a Line

5. If the data items in the output list are separated by commas, then each line of output will be divided into five zones of equal length, and one output value will be printed in each zone.

EXAMPLE 2.20

A BASIC program contains the statement

```
65 PRINT "NAME",N$,X,.5*(C1+C2)
```

If the variables have been assigned the values

N$=CINNAMON   C1=7
X=39   C2=11

then the above PRINT statement will generate the following line of output:

```
NAME          CINNAMON          39          9
```

Other illustrations of the use of commas in a PRINT statement are shown in Examples 2.17, 2.18 and 2.19.

If a comma follows the *last* item in the data list, then the next output quantity (i.e., the first output quantity in a subsequent PRINT statement) will be printed on the same line providing sufficient space is available. (Note that this produces an exception to rule 1 on page 22.)

EXAMPLE 2.21

The statements

```
100 PRINT A,B,C,
110 PRINT D,E,F
```

will cause the values of A, B, C, D and E to be printed on one line, followed by the value of F on the next line.

If A, B, C, D, E and F have been assigned the same numerical values as in Example 2.19, the output resulting from the above PRINT statements will appear as follows:

```
1234567          1.23457E+8     -0.001234        1.23450E-5     -1234.5
1.23457E+6
```

(Compare with the results in Example 2.19.)

As many as four commas can appear consecutively if desired. The effect of each comma is to move to the start of the next zone. Thus it is possible to print widely spaced data in this manner.

EXAMPLE 2.22

A BASIC program contains the statements

```
120 PRINT A,B,C,D,E
130 PRINT F,,,,G
```

If the variables have been assigned the following values

```
A=1    C=3    E=5    G=7
B=2    D=4    F=6
```

then the above statements will generate the following lines of output:

```
 1              2              3              4              5
 6                                                           7
```

6. If semicolons are used rather than commas to separate numerical data items in an output list, then the output values will be spaced more closely together. The particular spacing will depend on the number of digits or characters in each output item. By using semicolons in this manner it is possible to print more than five output quantities on each line.

EXAMPLE 2.23

A BASIC program contains the statement

```
100 PRINT A1;A2;A3;A4;A5;A6;A7;A8
```

If the variables have been assigned the following values

```
A1=11    A5=15
A2=12    A6=16
A3=13    A7=17
A4=14    A8=18
```

then the above PRINT statement will generate the following line of output

```
 11  12  13  14  15  16  17  18
```

If a semicolon follows a string or a string variable in an output list, then the string will be printed without any trailing spaces and the next output item will be printed immediately beyond the string.

EXAMPLE 2.24

A BASIC program contains the statement

```
200 PRINT "X=";X,"Y=";Y
```

If the variables are assigned the values X=12 and Y=−5, then the above statement will generate the following line of output:

```
X= 12          Y=-5
```

In many BASIC programs an INPUT statement is preceded by a PRINT statement that contains a string. The purpose of the PRINT statement is to produce a *prompt* message requesting the required input data. If the string is followed by a semicolon, then the question mark generated by the INPUT statement will appear at the end of the printed message.

EXAMPLE 2.25

A BASIC program has been written to compute the area and circumference of a circle. The first step in executing the program is to read in a value of the radius. Hence the program will contain the statements

```
10 PRINT "RADIUS=";
20 INPUT R
```

These two statements will cause the following line of output to be printed:

```
RADIUS=?
```

The user then enters a value for R (the radius), as shown in Example 1.4.

Finally, it should be understood that the effect of placing a semicolon after the last entry in the data list is the same as the placement of a comma in this position (i.e., the next printed quantity will appear on the same line). We have just seen an illustration of this in Example 2.25.

2.11 THE END STATEMENT

The *END statement* indicates the end of a BASIC program. The statement consists simply of a statement number followed by the keyword END. This statement is required in the older, more traditional versions of BASIC (it is optional in some of the newer versions). If it is required, it must be the last statement in the program, and it must have the highest statement number.

One use of the END statement is shown in Example 1.6. For another such illustration, see Example 2.26.

2.12 WRITING COMPLETE BASIC PROGRAMS

By now we have learned how to read data into the computer, perform arithmetic calculations and write out the results. Hence we can carry out all of the major steps in a complete (though simple) BASIC program.

In Chapter 3, we will discuss the mechanics of entering a program into the computer, editing the program and executing the program. For now we will be concerned only with writing simple programs. Example 2.26 illustrates such a program. Readers are urged to write a few other programs of this nature on their own. (Several suggestions are given at the end of this chapter.)

EXAMPLE 2.26 Roots of a Quadratic Equation

We wish to calculate the roots of a quadratic equation, using the well-known formulas

$$x_1 = \frac{-b + \sqrt{b^2 - 4ac}}{2a} \qquad x_2 = \frac{-b - \sqrt{b^2 - 4ac}}{2a}$$

Let us assume that the values of a, b and c are such that $b^2 - 4ac$ will always be positive. Therefore we need not worry about calculating the square root of a negative number.

The steps to be followed are these:

1. Read numerical values for a, b and c.
2. Calculate a value for $\sqrt{b^2 - 4ac}$.
3. Calculate values for x_1 and x_2, using the above formulas.
4. Print the values for a, b, c, x_1 and x_2.
5. Stop.

A corresponding flowchart is shown in Fig. 2.1.

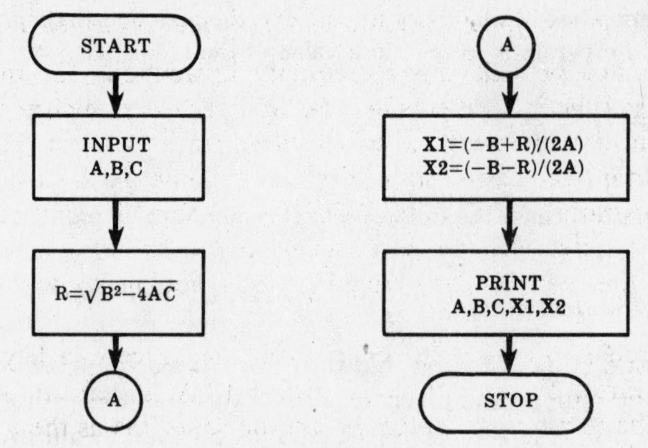

Fig. 2.1

If we make use of the material presented earlier in this chapter, it is quite simple to write a complete BASIC program to carry out the calculations. Step 1 can be implemented by means of a PRINT and an INPUT statement, and Steps 2 and 3 can be accompanied by LET statements. PRINT statements will be required for Step 4 and an END statement for Step 5. The desired BASIC program is shown in Fig. 2.2. Note that the input data are underlined.

```
10 PRINT "ENTER VALUES FOR A, B AND C"
20 INPUT A,B,C
30 LET R=(B^2-4*A*C)^.5
40 LET X1=(-B+R)/(2*A)
50 LET X2=(-B-R)/(2*A)
60 PRINT
70 PRINT "A=";A,"B=";B,"C=";C
80 PRINT "X1=";X1,"X2=";X2
90 END

>RUN

ENTER VALUES FOR A, B AND C
 ?2,5,3

A= 2            B= 5            C= 3
X1=-1           X2=-1.5
```

Fig. 2.2

At the bottom of Fig. 2.2 is the output generated by the program for $a = 2$, $b = 5$ and $c = 3$. (We will discuss the method for executing a BASIC program in Chapter 3.) We see that x_1 has a value of -1, and x_2 a value of -1.5.

2.13 PROGRAM COMMENTS—THE REM STATEMENT

The most common way to introduce remarks (comments) into a BASIC program is to make use of the *REM (REMARK) statement.* This statement consists of a statement number followed by the keyword REM and a textual message. REM statements can be inserted anywhere in a BASIC program.

EXAMPLE 2.27

A typical REM statement is shown below:

```
5 REM PROGRAM TO CALCULATE THE ROOTS OF A QUADRATIC EQUATION
```

This statement would provide an appropriate heading for the program presented in Example 2.26.

REM statements do not provide any executable instructions for the computer. They are, however, listed with all the other statements in a BASIC program, in correct sequential order. Thus they offer the programmer a convenient means to *document* a program (i.e., to provide a program heading, to identify important variables and to distinguish the major logical segments of a program). We will see numerous illustrations of the use of REM statements in subsequent examples.

Surrounding the REM statement with blank lines causes the remarks of the REM statement to stand out clearly from the rest of the program, thus adding to the clarity of the program documentation.

Sometimes it is desirable to add a comment explaining a certain key statement in a BASIC program. This can, of course, be accomplished with a REM statement. An even more desirable method, however, might be to place the comment on the same line as the statement. A comment of this type must be preceded by an apostrophe in order to distinguish it from the end of the statement. Such a comment cannot exceed the remaining length of the line.

EXAMPLE 2.28

Add the comments CALCULATE FIRST ROOT and CALCULATE SECOND ROOT to the fourth and fifth statements, respectively, of the program shown in Fig. 2.2.

The fourth and fifth statements will appear as

```
40 LET X1=(-B+R)/(2*A) 'CALCULATE FIRST ROOT
50 LET X2=(-B-R)/(2*A) 'CALCULATE SECOND ROOT
```

2.14 TRANSFERRING CONTROL—THE GO TO STATEMENT

Normally the statements in a BASIC program are executed in the same order as they appear, one after another. Sometimes, however, it is necessary to "jump" to some other part of the program, thus altering the normal sequence of execution. This can be accomplished by means of the *GO TO statement.* We usually refer to such a jump as an *unconditional branching* operation, or as a *transfer of control.* Hence the GO TO statement allows us to transfer control to any other statement in a BASIC program (including a REM statement).

The GO TO statement consists of a statement number, followed by the keywords GO TO and the number of the statement to which control will be transferred.

EXAMPLE 2.29

A BASIC program contains the following GO TO statement

```
100 GO TO 10
```

Thus the computer is instructed to execute statement number 10 next.

We will consider branching operations in much more detail in Chapter 4. For now we will restrict our attention to one simple but important application of the GO TO statement.

2.15 REPETITIOUS PROGRAM EXECUTION

Many situations arise that require the use of a BASIC program to process several sets of data, one after the other. This can easily be accomplished by ending the program with a transfer of control back to the "read input" statements, thus causing successive sets of input data to be read into the computer and then processed. (Note that we are referring to the *logical* ending of the program, not the *physical* ending. The last *physical* statement in the program must still be the END statement.) This procedure continues until all of the input data have been processed, at which time the user terminates the connection to the computer.

The transfer of control is usually carried out by means of a GO TO statement. Example 2.30 illustrates.

EXAMPLE 2.30 Roots of a Quadratic Equation

Let us modify the BASIC program presented in Example 2.26 so that we can process several sets of input data (i.e., several different radii) sequentially. If we examine the program shown in Fig. 2.2 we see that the modification can easily be carried out if we add a "GO TO 10" statement immediately before the END statement.

The modified program is shown in Fig. 2.3. Note that we have added an empty PRINT statement and a GO TO 10 statement near the end of the program. The purpose of the empty PRINT statement is to separate the output data from the successive input messages. Also, note that we have added a REM statement at the beginning of the program and that comments have been added to lines 40 and 50.

Notice that the information supplied by the user has been underlined.

```
5  REM PROGRAM TO CALCULATE THE ROOTS OF A QUADRATIC EQUATION
10 PRINT "ENTER VALUES FOR A, B AND C"
20 INPUT A,B,C
30 LET R=(B^2-4*A*C)^.5
40 LET X1=(-B+R)/(2*A)     'CALCULATE FIRST ROOT
50 LET X2=(-B-R)/(2*A)     'CALCULATE SECOND ROOT
60 PRINT
70 PRINT "A=";A,"B=";B,"C=";C
80 PRINT "X1=";X1,"X2=";X2
90 PRINT
100 GOTO 10
110 END

>RUN

ENTER VALUES FOR A, B AND C
 ?2,6,1

A= 2           B= 6           C= 1
X1=-0.177124   X2=-2.82288

ENTER VALUES FOR A, B AND C
 ?3,3,0

A= 3           B= 3           C= 0
X1=-9.93411E-9                X2=-1.

ENTER VALUES FOR A, B AND C
 ?1,3,1

A= 1           B= 3           C= 1
X1=-0.381966   X2=-2.61803
```

Fig. 2.3

At the bottom of Fig. 2.3 we see the output resulting from three different sets of values for a, b and c. (Notice that the second value for x_1 is calculated as -9.9×10^{-9} rather than zero, which is the exact answer.) The connection to the computer was terminated after processing the third set of data, though the procedure could have been continued as long as we had wished.

2.16 CLOSING REMARKS

By now we have learned enough about BASIC so that readers can organize and write complete, though elementary, programs of their own. Later chapters will show how to write programs that are more interesting, challenging and sophisticated.

Review Questions

2.1 Name two different ways that numbers (constants) can be written in BASIC.

2.2 Summarize the grammatical rules for writing numbers.

2.3 Present a detailed comparison between a number written in scientific notation and a number written in BASIC as a decimal quantity with an exponent.

2.4 What is a string? What are strings used for?

2.5 Summarize the grammatical rules for writing numeric and string variables.

2.6 What are the arithmetic operators used in BASIC? What is their natural hierarchy? In what order are operations carried out within a hierarchical group?

2.7 What is a formula (expression) in BASIC? What does a formula represent?

2.8 How can the natural hierarchy of operations be altered in a formula?

2.9 Cite a particular problem that can arise in exponentiation operations. Present the reason for the problem, and describe how the problem can be avoided.

2.10 What is the purpose of the LET statement?

2.11 Summarize the grammatical rules for writing a LET statement.

2.12 Discuss the similarities and differences between a LET statement and an algebraic equation.

2.13 In what ways are the rules for writing a LET statement relaxed in some versions of BASIC?

2.14 What is the purpose of the INPUT statement?

2.15 What happens when an INPUT statement is encountered during execution of a BASIC program?

2.16 Summarize the grammatical rules for writing an INPUT statement.

2.17 Cite two disadvantages in the use of INPUT statements for entering data into the computer.

2.18 What is the purpose of the PRINT statement?

2.19 Summarize the grammatical rules that apply to each of the following aspects of the PRINT statement:

(*a*) The generation and spacing of lines of output.
(*b*) The appearance of numerical output quantities and the maximum number of significant figures.
(*c*) The treatment of strings.
(*d*) The spacing of numerical quantities and strings within a line of output.

2.20 In what way can a PRINT statement be used in conjunction with an INPUT statement when reading data into the computer?

2.21 What is the purpose of the END statement? What are the rules associated with its use?

2.22 What is the purpose of the REM statement? What rules govern its use?

2.23 What is meant by program documentation? How can program documentation be carried out in BASIC?

2.24 What is the purpose of the GO TO statement? How is it written?

2.25 Name one statement that *must* be present in every BASIC program when using an older, more traditional version of BASIC. Where will this statement appear? What can be said about its statement number?

2.26 Exactly what advantage is there in writing a BASIC program that can be executed repetitiously? Is a significant amount of programming effort required to write a program in this manner?

Solved Problems

2.27 Express each of the following quantities as a BASIC number.

Quantity	*BASIC Number*
7,350	7350 or 7.35E+3
−12	−12
10^6	1000000 or 1E+6
$-2{,}053.18 \times 10^3$	−2053180 or −2.05318E+6
0.00008291	0.00008291 or 8.291E−5
9.563×10^{12}	9.563E+12
1/6	0.16666667

2.28 Each of the following BASIC numbers is written incorrectly. Identify the errors.

Number	*Error*
7,104	comma not allowed
−+4920	double sign not allowed
2.665E+42	exponent is too large in magnitude
0.333333333333	too many significant figures
4.63E−0.8	exponent cannot contain a decimal point

2.29 Each of the following items represents a BASIC string. Identify which, if any, are written incorrectly.

String	*Error*
TWENTY-SEVEN	correct
2+5=7	correct
ENTER ALL INPUT DATA	too long for some versions of BASIC
75.50	correct
SYMBOL IS "X"	quotation marks are not allowed within the string

2.30 Each of the following represents a numeric variable. Identify which, if any, are written incorrectly.

Variable	*Error*
XR	second character, if present, must be an integer
Q	correct
C23	too many characters
8C	first character must be a letter; second character, if present, must be an integer
BIGC	too many characters
J8	correct
A$	second character, if present, must be an integer

2.31 Each of the following represents a string variable. Identify, which, if any, are written incorrectly.

Variable	*Error*
N$	correct
C	dollar sign is missing
Z$3	last character must be a dollar sign; some versions of BASIC allow only two characters
Z3$	may be correct, though some versions of BASIC allow only two characters
E$	correct

2.32 Write a BASIC formula that corresponds to each of the following algebraic expressions.

Algebraic Expression	*BASIC Formula*
$3x+5$	3*X+5
$i+j-2$	I+J−2
x^2+y^2	X↑2+Y↑2
$(x+y)^2$	(X+Y)↑2
$a/b+c/d$	A/B+C/D or (A/B)+(C/D)
$(u+v)^{k-1}$	(U+V)↑(K−1)
$(4t)^{1/6}$	(4*T)↑.16666667 or (4*T)↑(1/6)

2.33 Write a LET statement for each of the following situations.

(*a*) Assign a value of 2.54 to the variable C.

```
10 LET C=2.54
```

(*b*) Assign a value of 12 to the variable X.

```
20 LET X=12
```

(*c*) Assign the value represented by the variable N to the variable N1.

```
30 LET N1=N
```

(*d*) Assign the string JANUARY 31 to the variable A$.

```
40 LET A$="JANUARY 31"
```

(*e*) Assign the string represented by the variable S$ to the variable T$.

```
50 LET T$=S$
```

(*f*) Assign the value represented by the formula (A↑2+B↑2+C↑2) to the variable F.

```
60 LET F=A↑2+B↑2+C↑2
```

(*g*) Increase the value assigned to the variable C7 by 0.01.

```
70 LET C7=C7+.01
```

(*h*) Assign the value represented by the formula (I+J) to the variable I.

```
80 LET I=I+J
```

2.34 Write a multiple LET statement for each of the following situations.

(*a*) Assign a value of −37.5 to the variables C1, C2 and C3.

```
10 LET C1=C2=C3=-37.5
```

(*b*) Assign the string *****ERROR***** to the variables P5$ and P7$.

```
20 LET P5$=P7$="*****ERROR*****"
```

(*c*) Assign the value represented by the formula (I+J)/K to the variables M and N.

```
30 LET M=N=(I+J)/K
```

Note that multiple LET statements are not available in all versions of BASIC. In some versions of BASIC, the keyword LET can be omitted, i.e.

```
30 M=N=(I+J)/K
```

2.35 Write a LET statement that corresponds to each of the following algebraic equations.

(*a*) $z = (x/y) + 3$

```
10 LET Z=X/Y+3
```

(*b*) $z = x/(y + 3)$

```
20 LET Z=X/(Y+3)
```

(*c*) $w = (u + v)/(s + t)$

```
30 LET W=(U+V)/(S+T)
```

(*d*) $f = \left[\dfrac{2ab}{c+1} - \dfrac{t}{3(p+q)}\right]^{1/3}$

```
40 LET F=(2*A*B/(C+1)-T/(3*(P+Q)))↑.33333333
```

(*e*) $r = \dfrac{6.8(a+b)^2/c - 7.2a/\sqrt{b+c}}{(a+c)^{1/n}}$

```
50 LET R=(6.8*(A+B)↑2/C-7.2*A/(B+C)↑.5)/(A+C)↑(1/N)
```

2.36 Two complicated algebraic equations are shown below. Replace each equation with several simple equations and write the corresponding LET statements.

(*a*) $t = \left[\dfrac{2ab}{c+1} - \dfrac{r}{7(p+q)}\right]^{1/n}$

$t_1 = \dfrac{2ab}{c+1}$	10 LET T1=2*A*B/(C+1)
$t_2 = \dfrac{r}{7(p+q)}$	20 LET T2=R/(7*(P+Q))
$t = (t_1 - t_2)^{1/n}$	30 LET T=(T1-T2)↑(1/N)

(*b*) $f = \dfrac{[6.8(a-b)^2/c - 7.2a/\sqrt{b+c}]^{1/7}}{[(c-a)^m + b^n]^{1/3}}$

$f_1 = 6.8(a-b)^2/c$	10 LET F1=6.8*(A-B)↑2/C
$f_2 = 7.2a/\sqrt{b+c}$	20 LET F2=7.2*A/(B+C)↑.5
$f_3 = (c-a)^m + b^n$	30 LET F3=(C-A)↑M+B↑N
$f = (f_1 - f_2)^{1/7}/f_3^{1/3}$	40 LET F=(F1-F2)↑(1/7)/F3↑(1/3) or
	40 LET F=(F1-F2)↑.14285714/F3↑.33333333

2.37 Write an appropriate statement, or set of statements, for each situation described below.

(*a*) Enter numerical values for X1, X2 and X3 and a string value of X$. All of the data are to be typed on one line.

```
10 INPUT X1,X2,X3,X$
```

(*b*) Enter numerical values for X1, X2 and X3 on one line and a string value for X$ on the next line.

```
10 INPUT X1,X2,X3
15 INPUT X$
```

(*c*) Enter numerical values for X1 and X2 on one line and a numerical value for X3, followed by a string value for X$, on the next line.

```
10 INPUT X1,X2
15 INPUT X3,X$
```

(*d*) Print the values of C1, C2, C3, C4 and C5 all on one line.

```
50 PRINT C1,C2,C3,C4,C5
```

(*e*) Print the values of A1, A2 and A3 on one line and the values of B1, B2 and B3 on another line, with a blank line separating them.

```
60 PRINT A1,A2,A3
65 PRINT
70 PRINT B1,B2,B3
```

(*f*) Print the values of A1, A2, A3, B1, B2 and B3 all on one line, as closely spaced as possible.

```
50 PRINT A1;A2;A3;B1;B2;B3
```

(*g*) Print the values of X, Y and Z on one line. Precede each numerical value with an appropriate label.

```
100 PRINT "X=";X,"Y=";Y,"Z=";Z
```

or

```
100 PRINT "X=";X;"Y=";Y;"Z=";Z
```

(*h*) Print the values of N$ and N next to one another, followed by the value of the formula A↑2+B↑2.

```
120 PRINT N$;N;A↑2+B↑2
```

or

```
120 PRINT N$;N,A↑2+B↑2
```

(*i*) Print the strings LEFT and RIGHT near the left and right edges.

```
150 PRINT "LEFT",,,,"RIGHT"
```

(*j*) Print the message ROOTS OF SIMULTANEOUS EQUATIONS on one line, centered as closely as possible.

```
200 PRINT, "ROOTS OF SIMULTANEOUS EQUATIONS"
```

(*k*) Print a message indicating a request for the numerical value of *C*, then enter a numerical value for C.

```
5 PRINT "C=";
10 INPUT C
```

2.38 Show how the input data will appear in each of the following situations.

(*a*) 10 INPUT X1,X2,X3,X$

where X1 $= 4.83 \times 10^{-3}$ X3=941.55
X2=−537 X$=BUCS

```
?4.83E-3,-537,941.55,BUCS
```

or

```
?.00483,-537,941.55,BUCS
```

(*b*) 10 INPUT X$,X1
20 INPUT X2,X3

where the variables have the same values as in part (*a*).

```
?BUCS,4.83E-3
?-537,941.55
```

(*c*) 30 INPUT A,A$,A1

where A=350 A1=−8.05
A$=APRIL 12, 1969

```
?350,"APRIL 12, 1969",-8.05
```

2.39 Show how the printed output will appear in each of the following situations.

(*a*) 10 PRINT "NAME",N$,(X+Y)↑2/3,T4

where N$=GEORGE Y=8.2
X=27.6 T4 $= -5.83 \times 10^{-4}$

```
NAME            GEORGE          427.213         -0.000583
```

(*b*) 10 PRINT "NAME";N$;(X+Y)↑2/3;T4

where the variables have the same values as in part (*a*).

```
NAME GEORGE 427.213 -0.000583
```

(*c*) 12 PRINT A1,A2,A3,A4
14 PRINT B1,B2,B3,B4

where A1 $= 7.43 \times 10^{3}$ B1 $= -2.55 \times 10^{-8}$
A2=−4373665.8 B2 $= 0.843 \times 10^{7}$
A3=0.0006066183 B3=400.33
A4=−3136687 B4 $= 10^{-3}$

```
 7430            -4.37367E+6      6.06618E-4      -3136687
-2.55000E-8       8430000         400.33           0.001
```

(*d*) 12 PRINT A1;A2;A3;A4;
14 PRINT B1;B2;B3;B4

where the variables have the same values as in part (*c*).

```
7430 -4.37367E+6  6.06618E-4 -3136687 -2.55000E-8  8430000  400.33
0.001
```

2.40 In each of the following cases show how the comment (or remark) can be placed in a BASIC program.

(*a*) Add the program heading AREA AND CIRCUMFERENCE OF A CIRCLE

```
10 REM AREA AND CIRCUMFERENCE OF A CIRCLE
```

(*b*) Add the comments AREA and CIRCUMFERENCE to the statements

40 LET A=P*R↑2

and

50 LET C=2*P*R

```
40 LET A=P*R↑ 'AREA
50 LET C=2*P*R 'CIRCUMFERENCE
```

2.41 Several GO TO statements are shown below. Identify which, if any, are written incorrectly.

Statement	*Error*
10 GO TO 50	correct
120 GO TO M	the statement number to which control is transferred must be a positive integer, not a variable
80 GO TO 25	correct
50 GO TO 50	a GO TO statement cannot transfer control to itself.

Supplementary Problems

2.42 Answer the following questions for the version of BASIC that is used at your particular school or office.

(*a*) How many significant figures can be included in a number?

(*b*) How many characters can appear in a string (i.e., what is the maximum string length)?

(*c*) Can a string variable be written as a letter followed by a digit and a dollar sign (e.g., C1$)?

(*d*) Can the keyword LET be omitted from a LET statement (e.g., 10 A=B+C)?

(*e*) Are multiple assignments permitted in a single LET statement (e.g., 10 LET X=Y=Z=13)?

2.43 Express each of the following quantities as a BASIC number.

(*a*) 5
(*b*) 8000
(*c*) -1.8033×10^{-9}
(*d*) 1/3
(*e*) −7,328,500
(*f*) 0.2851×10^{4}
(*g*) 0.2851×10^{10}
(*h*) −16,752.47

2.44 Some of the following constants are written incorrectly. Identify all errors.

(*a*) +0.250
(*b*) 5076
(*c*) 3 E−2
(*d*) 3.8822E−7.3
(*e*) −77777777
(*f*) 1,000,000
(*g*) 2.53E+99
(*h*) 64E+6
(*i*) 0.833333333333E−2
(*j*) −00263
(*k*) 4.48E
(*l*) 0.83333333−E2

2.45 Some of the following strings are written incorrectly. Identify all errors.

(*a*) $1,995.00
(*b*) JULY 4, 1776
(*c*) BEGINNER'S ALL-PURPOSE SYMBOLIC INSTRUCTION CODE
(*d*) 4 O'CLOCK
(*e*) "NUTS!"
(*f*) 2X+4Y=Z

2.46 Each of the following represents either a numeric or a string variable. Some are written incorrectly. Determine the type of variable in each correct case, and identify all errors.

(*a*) J	(*c*) J$	(*e*) $J6	(*g*) XSTAR	(*i*) PI	(*k*) 5T	(*m*) Z0
(*b*) J6	(*d*) J$6	(*f*) J6$	(*h*) C10	(*j*) N$	(*l*) Y*	(*n*) M 5

2.47 Write a BASIC formula that corresponds to each of the following algebraic terms.

(*a*) t^{n+1}
(*b*) $(x+3)^{1/k}$
(*c*) $2(a/b)^{1/3}$
(*d*) $1.87(u+v)-5.088(x/y+2z^2)$
(*e*) $1-x+x^2/2-x^3/6+x^4/24-x^5/120$
(*f*) $\dfrac{2(p/q)^{k-1}}{(r-3t)^{1/m}}$
(*g*) $(i+j-1)^2/5$
(*h*) $\left[\dfrac{(x_1+x_2)^m(y_1+y_2)^n}{(x_1/y_1)^{m+n}(x_2/y_2)^{m-n}}\right]^{1/mn}$

2.48 In your version of BASIC, can a variable that has not been defined (i.e., that has not been assigned a value) appear on the right side of the equal sign in a LET statement? If so, what is the effect of doing this?

2.49 Write a LET statement for each of the following situations.

(*a*) Assign a value of 758.33 to the variable P.
(*b*) Assign the value represented by the variable A to the variable B.
(*c*) Assign the string PITTSBURGH, PA. to the variable F$.
(*d*) Assign the string represented by the variable M$ to the variable N$.
(*e*) Assign the value of the formula X/(A+B−C) to the variable Y3.
(*f*) Decrease the value assigned to the variable K by 2.
(*g*) Double the value assigned to the variable C5.
(*h*) Assign the value of the formula (A↑2+B↑2)↑.5 to the variables B and C.

2.50 Write a LET statement that corresponds to each of the following algebraic equations.

(*a*) $w=\dfrac{(a+3)b^n}{2.7(c-d/b)+1}$

(*b*) $f=\left\{\dfrac{(a/b)^n/(c-d)^m}{[d/(b+a)^{n+m}]}\right\}^{1/(n+m)}$

(*c*) $y=\dfrac{a_1-a_2x+a_3x^2-a_4x^3+a_5x^4}{c_1-c_2x+c_3x^2-c_4x^3}$

(*d*) $P=rA(1+r)^n/[(1+r)^n-1]$

2.51 Each of the equations in Problem 2.50 above will have resulted in a lengthy LET statement. Replace each statement with an equivalent sequence of short, simple LET statements.

2.52 Write an algebraic equation that corresponds to each of the following LET statements.

(*a*) 10 LET F=A+2*B/C↑.5

(*b*) 20 LET F=A+(2*B/C)↑.5

(*c*) 30 LET F=(A+2)*(B/C)↑.5

(*d*) 40 LET F=((A+2)*B/C)↑.5

(*e*) 50 LET G=P*Q/R*S/T

2.53 What particular difficulty might be experienced in executing the statement

15 LET X=(Y−Z)↑.25

2.54 Consider the statement

25 LET P=−Q↑4

If Q=2, what value will be assigned to P?

2.55 Consider the statement

35 LET P=Q↑4

If Q=−2, what value will be assigned to P? (Compare with the answer to Problem 2.54 above.)

2.56 Write an appropriate statement, or set of statements for each situation described below.

(*a*) Enter numerical values for A, B and C and string values for M$ and N$. All of the data are to be typed on one line of a typewriter terminal.

(*b*) Enter the values for A, N$ and B on one line and the values for M$ and C on the next line.

(*c*) Enter numerical values for A, B and C and string values for M$ and N$. Each value is to be typed at the start of a new line.

(*d*) Print a message saying

ENTER VALUES FOR A,B,C,M$ AND N$

and then enter the requested data on the same line as the printed message.

(*e*) Print the message described in part (*d*). Then enter the requested data on the next line.

(*f*) Print the values of A, B, C, M$ and N$ on one line, with normal spacing between each item.

(*g*) Print the values of A, B, C, M$ and N$ on one line, spacing the items as closely as possible.

(*h*) Print the values of A, B and C on one line, spacing the items as closely as possible. Allow for subsequent output to begin on the same line, immediately after the value for C.

(*i*) Print the values of A, B, C, (A+B+C)/3, (A*B*C)↑(1/3) and (A↑2+B↑2+C↑2)↑.5 all on one line. Follow this with a blank line, then a third line with the value of M$ printed near the left margin and the value of N$ printed near the right.

(*j*) Print the numerical values of A, B and C all on one line. Precede each number with an appropriate descriptive label.

(*k*) Print the values of M$ and N$ on separate lines, with a blank line between them. Precede the value of M$ with the label NAME, and precede N$ with the label SOCIAL SECURITY NUMBER. Center the output as closely as possible.

2.57 Show how the input data will appear in each of the following situations.

(*a*) 5 INPUT A,B,C
10 INPUT M$,N$

where A = 0.0000062   M$ = SHARON
B = 27.5×10^{-2} N$ = GAIL
C = −1000

(*b*) 20 INPUT P1,P2,T$

where P1 = −743.08 T$ = SUSAN
P2 = 0.00987

(*c*) 25 INPUT A$,B$,C$

where A$ = NEW YORK C$ = SAN FRANCISCO
B$ = CHICAGO

(*d*) 15 INPUT P,P$,Q,Q$

where P = 2,770,543 $Q = 48.8 \times 10^9$
P$ = DECEMBER 29, 1963 Q$ = ELEVEN O'CLOCK

2.58 Show how the output will appear in each of the following situations.

(*a*) 100 PRINT A;B;C;P;P1;P2;Q

where A = 0.0000062 P1 = −743.08
$B = 27.5 \times 10^{-12}$ P2 = 0.00987
C = −1000 $Q = 48.8 \times 10^9$
P = 2,770,543

(*b*) 110 PRINT A,B,C,P,P1,P2,Q

where the variables have the same values as in part (*a*).

(*c*) 120 PRINT A+B*C,P/Q,P1/P2

where the variables have the same values as in part (*a*).

(*d*) 130 PRINT M$,P$,Q$

where M$ = SHARON
P$ = DECEMBER 29, 1963
Q$ = ELEVEN O'CLOCK

2.59 In each of the following cases show how the comment (or remark) can be placed in a BASIC program.

(*a*) Add the program heading AVERAGING OF AIR POLLUTION DATA.

(*b*) Insert the remark BEGIN LOOP TO CALCULATE CUMULATIVE SUM.

(*c*) Add the comment CALCULATE AVERAGE VALUE to the statement

```
80 LET A=S/N
```

(*d*) Add the comment READ A DATA POINT to the statement

```
20 INPUT X,T
```

2.60 Several GO TO statements are shown below. Identify which, if any, are written incorrectly.

(*a*) 100 GO TO 12 (*d*) 55 GO TO 400

(*b*) 75 GO TO K+1 (*e*) 20 GO TO "60"

(*c*) 30 GO TO 30

Programming Problems

2.61 Prepare a flowchart for the program shown in Example 2.30. Compare with the flowchart for Example 2.26, shown in Fig. 2.1.

2.62 Write a complete BASIC program for each of the following problem situations.

(*a*) Print HELLO! in the middle of a line.

(*b*) Have the computer print

HI, WHAT'S YOUR NAME?

on one line. The user then enters his or her name immediately after the question mark. The computer then skips two lines and prints

WELCOME (name)!
LET'S BE FRIENDS!

on two consecutive lines.

2.63 Write a complete conversational-type BASIC program for each of the following problem situations.

(*a*) A temperature reading, in Fahrenheit degrees, is to be read into the computer and converted into Celsius degrees, using the formula

$$°C = \frac{5}{9}(°F - 32)$$

(*b*) A piggy bank contains n_1 half-dollars, n_2 quarters, n_3 dimes, n_4 nickels and n_5 pennies. How much money is in the bank, in terms of dollars?

2.64 Develop an outline, draw a flowchart and then write a complete BASIC program for each of the following problems. Write each program in such a manner that it can be used to process several sets of data sequentially. Be sure that all output data is clearly labeled.

(*a*) Calculate the volume and area of a sphere using the formulas

$$V = 4\pi r^3/3$$
$$A = 4\pi r^2$$

where r is the radius of the sphere.

(*b*) The pressure, volume and temperature of a mass of air are related by the formula

$$PV = 0.37m(T + 460)$$

where P = pressure, pounds per square inch
V = volume, cubic feet
m = mass of air, pounds
T = temperature, °F

If an automobile tire containing 2 cubic feet of air is inflated to 28 pounds per square inch at room temperature, how much air is in the tire?

(*c*) If a, b and c represent the three sides of a triangle, then the area of the triangle is

$$A = \sqrt{s(s-a)(s-b)(s-c)}$$

where $s = (a + b + c)/2$. Also, the radius of the *largest inscribed* circle is given by

$$r_i = A/s$$

and the radius of the *smallest circumscribed* circle is

$$r_c = abc/(4A)$$

Calculate the area of the triangle, the area of the largest inscribed circle and the area of the smallest circumscribed circle for each of the following sets of data:

a	11.88	5.55	10.00	13.75	12.00	20.42	7.17	173.67
b	8.06	4.54	10.00	9.89	8.00	27.24	2.97	87.38
c	12.75	7.56	10.00	11.42	12.00	31.59	6.66	139.01

(*d*) Suppose that P dollars are invested at an annual interest rate of i (expressed as a decimal). If the interest is reinvested, after n years the total amount of money, F, can be determined as $F = P(1+i)^n$. (This is known as the *law of compound interest.*)

If \$5000 is invested at 6%, compounded annually, how much will have accumulated after 10 years?

If the interest is compounded quarterly rather than annually the above equation must be changed to read $F = P(1+i/4)^{4n}$.

If the same \$5000 is invested at an annual rate of 6%, compounded quarterly, how much will have accumulated after 10 years? Compare this answer with the result obtained earlier (for interest compounded annually).

(*e*) The increase in population of a bacteria culture with time is directly proportional to the size of the population. Thus the larger the population, the faster the bacteria will increase in number. Mathematically the population at any time can be expressed as

$$P = P_0\left[1 + 0.0289t + \frac{(0.0289t)^2}{2} + \frac{(0.0289t)^3}{6} + \frac{(0.0289t)^4}{24} + \cdots + \frac{(0.0289t)^n}{n!}\right]$$

where t = time in hours beyond a reference time
P_0 = bacteria population at the reference time
P = bacteria population at time t

Calculate the population multiplication factor (P/P_0) at 2, 5, 10, 20 and 50 hours beyond the reference time. Include the first 10 terms of the series (i.e., let $n = 9$).

Chapter 3

Running a BASIC Program

Now that we have learned how to write simple BASIC programs, let us see how these programs can be entered into the computer, edited, saved, listed and executed. We will also consider some methods for detecting and correcting various types of errors that can occur in improperly written programs.

In this chapter our attention will be directed toward the use of a large mainframe computer within a timesharing environment. We will assume that a "hard-copy" terminal, similar to that shown in Fig. 1.3, is used to communicate with the host computer (i.e., the mainframe). The use of a video-type terminal is essentially the same, except that old information will "scroll" off the top of the screen as new information is generated at the bottom.

Running a BASIC program on a microcomputer is similar, though the details are somewhat different. (Actually, the procedures for running BASIC are somewhat different on all computers, regardless of their size.) Representative examples that illustrate how BASIC programs can be listed, edited, saved and executed on a microcomputer are included in Chapter 10 (see Sections 10.2 and 10.7).

3.1 THE TIMESHARING TERMINAL

We have already learned that a programmer must communicate with a computer through a *timesharing terminal* (i.e., a *console*) when operating in a timesharing environment. These devices can be "hard wired" directly to the computer, or they can be used with a *modem* (i.e., a *mo*dulator-*dem*odulator) to establish a connection via a telephone line. In fact, some timesharing terminals include a built-in modem with telephone dialup capability. Moreover, some terminals are able to store programs, edit programs and transfer programs to and from the host computer. Such devices are referred to as *intelligent* ("*smart*") *terminals.*

Figure 3.1 shows a closeup of the keyboard for the terminal presented in Fig. 1.3. Other terminals have keyboards that are quite similar, if not identical. We will refer to certain of these keys in subsequent sections of this chapter.

Fig. 3.1

3.2 LOGGING IN

The first step in communicating with a computer through a timesharing terminal is to establish a connection to the computer. This is accomplished by means of the *login* (or *logon*) procedure. The following description is representative of a login procedure, though there are some variations from one version of BASIC to another.*

If the connection is to be made via a telephone line, the login procedure begins by the user dialing a specified telephone number (after turning on the power to the terminal). The computer will then respond by typing a brief message and requesting that the user "log in" (i.e., identify himself or herself by specifying a project number, etc.). The user must then type LOGIN (or LOGON, or simply LOG), followed by the desired information. It may then be necessary for the user to type BASIC, indicating that the user wishes to work with BASIC rather than some other language.

The procedure is similar, though simpler, when the terminal is wired directly to the computer, thus not requiring a telephone line connection. In this case the procedure normally begins when the user types LOGIN, followed by the project number.

EXAMPLE 3.1

A student at a large university wishes to run a BASIC program from a telephone-dialup terminal. The student's assigned project number is 123456. The login procedure is described below.

1. The student turns on the power switch of the terminal. (On the terminal shown in Fig. 1.3, the power switch is located near the left front of the keyboard.)
2. The student then dials the appropriate telephone number, and the computer responds by typing

   ```
   PLEASE LOGIN.
   ```

3. The student types the word LOG after the period and then depresses the RETURN key. The computer responds by typing

   ```
   JOB 27  TTY42
   #
   ```

4. The student then enters the project number, 123456, after the # sign and again depresses the RETURN key. The computer then types

   ```
   08-FEB          THUR  21:11:46
   ```

   indicating the date, day and time, respectively.
5. The word BASIC is then typed by the student after the period. This causes the BASIC system to be accessed from the computer's library of programming languages.
6. The computer types

   ```
   NEW OR OLD-->
   ```

   and the student must respond accordingly. If trying to access a BASIC program that had previously been stored in the computer's library, the student would type OLD. In this case, however, the student wishes to enter a new program and, therefore, types the word NEW after the arrow.
7. Finally, the computer types

   ```
   NEW FILE NAME-->
   ```

   and the user responds by typing the name of the new program—in this case, SAMPLE. (Typically, a program name will consist of one to six characters, beginning with a letter.) The student is now ready to begin typing in the program.

A listing of the entire login procedure is shown in Fig. 3.2. Those items that were typed by the student have been underlined.

---

* The procedures described in this chapter apply specifically to the DECsystem-10 computer, as currently implemented at the University of Pittsburgh. For simplicity, some of the detail has been omitted from the narrative text.

```
PLEASE LOGIN.

.LOG
JOB 27     TTY42
#123456
08-FEB        THUR     21:11:46

.BASIC

NEW OR OLD-->NEW
NEW FILE NAME-->SAMPLE
```

Fig. 3.2

If an error is made in transmitting the required information to the computer during the login procedure, then an appropriate message will be typed and the user will be asked to enter the information again.

EXAMPLE 3.2

Referring to the situation described in Example 3.1, suppose the student had typed BASIV instead of BASIC during the login procedure (the V key is next to the C key). The computer would respond by typing

?BASIV

The student would then type BASIC after the period, and the login procedure would be continued. The entire login procedure is shown in Fig. 3.3. Again, the student responses are underlined.

```
PLEASE LOGIN.

.LOG
JOB 32      TTY42
#123456
08-FEB         THUR      21:37:07

.BASIV

?BASIV

.BASIC

NEW OR OLD-->NEW
NEW FILE NAME-->SAMPLE
```

Fig. 3.3

```
PITT DEC-1055/A   54A.31 21:11:46

PLEASE LOGIN OR ATTACH.

.LOG
JOB 27 PITT DEC-1055/A   54A.31 TTY42
#115421/160531
PASSWORD:
ALLOCATION REMAINING: 9.8 UNITS
2111     08-FEB              THUR

.R BASIC

NEW OR OLD-->NEW
NEW FILE NAME-->EX3.1
```

Fig. 3.4

Many timesharing systems issue each user a separate *password* that must be supplied with the project number. The password is keyed in, but the typing is suppressed by the computer, thus maintaining confidentiality. The user will not be allowed to log in if the correct password for a given project number is not supplied.

A listing of a login procedure requiring a password is shown in Fig. 3.4. As before, the user-supplied responses have been underscored.

3.3 ENTERING A PROGRAM

Once the login procedure has been completed, the user may type in the program, one statement (one line) at a time. To do so, the user must wait for the computer to type the symbol

>

at the start of a line. (This is known as *prompting*.) The user then types in a BASIC statement, starting with the statement number (line number). The typed information will not be transmitted to the computer, however, until the RETURN key has been depressed. Once this is done the printing head will move to the start of the next line, and the computer will request the next statement by printing another > symbol.

This procedure is continued until all of the program statements have been entered and transmitted to the computer. When the computer generates the symbol > after the last statement, the user may respond with a command specifying what should be done with the program (e.g., RUN, LIST, SAVE, etc.). We will discuss these commands later in this chapter.

When typing a program into the computer, the instructions need not be entered in the same order that they will be executed. The computer will rearrange the instructions by increasing statement numbers once the entire program has been entered. (Remember that it is the ordering of the statement numbers that determines the sequence with which the statements will be executed.)

EXAMPLE 3.3

A programmer who has just completed the login procedure wishes to enter a program into the computer. In the rush to enter and run the complete program, the programmer forgot to type the first two statements. Realizing the mistake before finishing, however, the programmer then typed in the missing statements. This is entirely permissible, since the program will be properly rearranged within the computer's memory.

A listing of the statements, in the order that they were entered, is shown in Fig. 3.5.

```
>20 PRINT "RADIUS=";
>30 INPUT R
>40 LET A=P*R^2
>50 LET C=2*P*R
>60 PRINT "R=";R,"A=";A,"C=";C
>70 GOTO 20
>80 END
>5  REM PROGRAM TO CALCULATE AREA AND CIRCUMFERENCE OF A CIRCLE
>10 LET P=3.1415927
>
```

Fig. 3.5

3.4 CORRECTING ERRORS

It is practically impossible for a programmer to write a complete program and enter it into the computer without making an occasional mistake. Therefore we must have a way to correct typing errors and to add, delete or change a statement once it has been transmitted to the computer. In this section we will see that all of these operations can easily be accomplished in BASIC.

Incorrectly typed characters can be deleted by depressing the DELETE key (on some terminals, the RUBOUT key). The most recent character will be deleted by depressing the DELETE key once; depressing it twice will cause the two most recent characters to be deleted, and so on. Such deletions must, however, be made before the line containing the errors is transmitted to the computer (by depressing the RETURN key). After the desired characters have been deleted, the programmer may proceed to type in the correct characters.

EXAMPLE 3.4

A programmer wishes to enter the BASIC program shown in Fig. 3.5 into the computer. While typing the first statement, however, the programmer accidentally types a U in place of an I. Thus the line appears as follows:

```
>20 PRU
```

Realizing the mistake immediately, the programmer depresses the DELETE key once and then proceeds to type in the remainder of the statement.

The entire typed line will appear as

```
>20 PRU\U\INT "RADIUS=";
```

Note that the deleted character (U) is shown between a pair of backward slashes. The backward slashes are typed automatically when the DELETE key is first used and when its use is first discontinued. It is important to understand, however, that the backward slashes and the deleted character will not be transmitted to the computer. Thus the computer will interpret the line of type as

```
20 PRINT "RADIUS=";
```

as desired.

EXAMPLE 3.5

Let us again consider the typing error discussed in the previous example. Now, however, we assume that the programmer has not noticed the error until a few more characters have been typed. Thus the typed line will appear as

```
>20 PRUNT "RA
```

when the error is discovered. The programmer must therefore depress the DELETE key seven times in order to delete everything from (and including) the letter U and then retype the rest of the statement correctly.

The first typed line will appear as follows:

```
>20 PRUNT "RA\AR" TNU\INT "RADIUS=";
```

Again we see that the deleted characters are enclosed by a pair of backward slashes. The slashes are printed automatically when the DELETE key is first used and when it is first discontinued. Note that the deletions run "backward," i.e., the first character to be deleted is the letter A, followed by the letter R, etc., until the U has been deleted. Since these characters are not transmitted to the computer, the typed line will be stored in the computer as

```
20 PRINT "RADIUS=";
```

Sometimes a typing error is not noticed until an entire line (or most of it) has been typed. In such a situation it may be very cumbersome to delete one character at a time with the DELETE (or RUBOUT) key. A better procedure is to delete the entire line, replacing it with a new line. If the line has not been transmitted to the computer it can be deleted by depressing the ALTMODE or ESCAPE key (labeled ESC in Fig. 3.1). If the line has been transmitted, it can be replaced simply by entering a new line having the same statement number as the old line.

EXAMPLE 3.6

In entering the program shown in Fig. 3.5, suppose that the programmer had typed

```
>20 PRUNT "RA
```

and then realized the mistake (typing a U instead of an I). He or she could delete the incorrect line by depressing the ESC key and then retype the line correctly.

Alternatively, the programmer could depress the RETURN key, thus entering the incorrect, incomplete statement into the computer. The correct statement would then be typed as follows:

```
>20 PRINT "RADIUS=";
```

When the RETURN key is again depressed, the new statement will be entered into the computer, thus replacing the previous (incorrect) statement having the same statement number.

An entire statement can be deleted from a BASIC program simply by typing the statement number and then depressing the RETURN key.

EXAMPLE 3.7

Suppose that the program shown in Fig. 3.5 has been entered into the computer and the programmer then decides to delete the REM statement. It is only necessary to type

```
>5
```

and then depress the RETURN key. This deletes statement number 5 (the REM statement).

3.5 PROCESSING A PROGRAM

A program is ready to be processed once it has been entered into the computer and all known mistakes have been corrected. Usually we will want to type out (i.e., *list*) the program, store (i.e., *save*) the program for later use and, of course, execute (i.e., *run*) the program. These operations are easily carried out by typing the words LIST, SAVE and RUN. The programmer can issue these commands in whatever order desired.

EXAMPLE 3.8 Area and Circumference of a Circle

A program similar to the one shown in Fig. 3.5 has been entered into the computer, and the programmer then wishes to print out, store and execute the program. The programmer therefore types the word LIST after the *original* program listing (which may contain error corrections, statements out of order, etc.). This causes the corrected statements to be listed in the proper order.

Once the complete listing has been printed out by the computer, the programmer types the words SAVE and RUN in order to store and execute the program. Finally, the programmer types BYE after the execution has terminated, thus terminating the connection to the computer.

A listing of the entire timesharing session is shown in Fig. 3.6. The information provided by the programmer has been underlined as before. Notice that the original program statements contain error corrections in statements 10 and 20, and that the initial statement 20 has been replaced with a later, corrected statement. Also, we see that the statements have not been typed in the sequence in which they will be executed.

Once the programmer types LIST we see that the title of the program (which happens to be CIRCLE) is printed, followed by a properly sequenced listing of the program statements. The input and output data associated with the execution of the program are shown after the command RUN. Finally, the last few lines contain statistical information that is provided by the logout procedure resulting from the BYE command (we will say more about this in Section 3.6).

After the programmer has logged out it is no longer possible to communicate with the computer (unless, of course, he or she subsequently logs in again). The program CIRCLE will be stored for subsequent use, however, as a result of the SAVE command. (The program will be stored on a magnetic disk or tape rather than in the computer's main memory, though the programmer need not be concerned with this.)

If a previously stored program is to be processed rather than a newly entered program, then the programmer must type OLD rather than NEW after the login procedure. The computer will respond with

```
OLD FILE NAME-->
```

The programmer will then type in the name of the stored program. From this point on the program can be processed in the manner described earlier.

EXAMPLE 3.9

Suppose that the program CIRCLE, discussed in Example 3.8, is to be executed after having previously been stored. Figure 3.7 below shows a listing of the complete timesharing session, including the login and logout procedures. Notice that the commands are very similar to those shown in Fig. 3.6, the only difference being the use of the word OLD instead of NEW.

In order to replace an old program with a newly edited version (keeping the same name as before), the programmer simply types REPLACE followed by the program name. (Note that this will

```
PITT DEC-1055/A  54B.01B 18:21:29

PLEASE LOGIN OR ATTACH.

.LOGIN
JOB 42 PITT DEC-1055/A  54B.01B TTY42
#115421/160531
PASSWORD:
ALLOCATION REMAINING: 9.8 UNITS
1821     15-FEB            THUR

.R BASIC

NEW OR OLD-->NEW
NEW FILE NAME-->CIRCLE

>20 PRUNT\TNU\INT RADIUS
>30 INPUT R
>40 LET A=P*R^2
>50 LET C=2*P*R
>60 PRINT "R=";R,"A=";A,"C=";C
>70 GOTO 20
>80 END
>5  REM PROGRAM TO CALCULATE AREA AND CIRCUMFERENCE OF A CIRCLE
>10 LET P=3.1416\6\5927
>65 PRINT
>20 PRINT "RADIUS=";
>35 IF R=0 THEN 80
>LIST

CIRCLE          18:27          15-FEB

5  REM PROGRAM TO CALCULATE AREA AND CIRCUMFERENCE OF A CIRCLE
10 LET P=3.141593
20 PRINT "RADIUS=";
30 INPUT R
35 IF R=0 THEN 80
40 LET A=P*R^2
50 LET C=2*P*R
60 PRINT "R=";R,"A=";A,"C=";C
65 PRINT
70 GOTO 20
80 END

>SAVE

>RUN

CIRCLE          18:28          15-FEB

RADIUS= ?15
R= 15           A= 706.858     C= 94.2478

RADIUS= ?6.82
R= 6.82         A= 146.123     C= 42.8513

RADIUS= ?37.4
R= 37.4         A= 4394.33     C= 234.991

RADIUS= ?0

TIME:  0.21 SECS.

>BYE
Job 42, USER[115421,160531]  LOGGED OFF TTY42    1829  15-FEB
SAVED ALL FILES (25 BLOCKS)
CPUTIME 0:01   DISK R+W=77+15  CONNECT=8 MIN   UNITS=0.0101
```

Fig. 3.6

```
PITT DEC-1055/A  54B.01B 20:13:09

PLEASE LOGIN OR ATTACH.

.LOGIN
JOB 62 PITT DEC-1055/A  54B.01B TTY42
#115421/160531
PASSWORD:
ALLOCATION REMAINING: 9.8 UNITS
2013     15-FEB              THUR

.R BASIC


NEW OR OLD-->OLD
OLD FILE NAME-->CIRCLE

>RUN

CIRCLE            20:14            15-FEB


RADIUS= ?17.45
R= 17.45          A= 956.623       C= 109.642

RADIUS= ?12.7
R= 12.7           A= 506.707       C= 79.7965

RADIUS= ?32.6
R= 32.6           A= 3338.76       C= 204.832

RADIUS= ?0


TIME:   0.20 SECS.

>BYE
JOB 62, USER[115421,160531]  LOGGED OFF TTY42      2015   15-FEB
SAVED ALL FILES (25 BLOCKS)
CPUTIME 0:01    DISK R+W=98+6   CONNECT=3 MIN    UNITS=0.0078
```

Fig. 3.7

cause the old version of the program to be destroyed, since it will be written over by the newer version.)

The BASIC language also allows us to process a program in other ways. For example, we can delete a previously stored program by typing UNSAVE, or we can obtain a listing of the names of all stored programs by typing CATALOG. Collectively, the commands used to process a program are called *system commands* (or *editing commands*). Although the number of available editing commands will differ from one version of BASIC to another, virtually all versions of the language contain the essential features described above. A summary of the more commonly used system commands is presented in Appendix C.

3.6 LOGGING OUT

We have already seen that the procedure required to terminate the connection to the computer (i.e., the logout procedure) is initiated by typing the word GOODBYE (or simply BYE). Once this command has been issued the computer will respond by typing some summary statistics for the current timesharing session. Included in the statistics are the date, the number of *files* (i.e., programs and data sets) that have been saved, the length of the connection (timewise), the amount of actual computer time used and, usually, the cost. The logout procedure is illustrated in Examples 3.8 and 3.9 (see Figs. 3.6 and 3.7) as well as in Example 3.10 below.

EXAMPLE 3.10

A programmer has just completed processing a program and has therefore typed the word BYE. The computer responds by typing the three lines of information shown in Fig. 3.8 and then breaking the connection to the terminal immediately thereafter.

```
>BYE
JOB 27, USER[115421,160531]  LOGGED OFF TTY42     2128  8-FEB
SAVED ALL FILES (15 BLOCKS)
CPUTIME 0:07   DISK R+W=856+8  CONNECT=17 MIN   UNITS=0.0240
```

Fig. 3.8

The first line of output states that the user whose account number is 115421, 160531 has logged out from terminal number 42 at 9:28 p.m. (i.e., 2128 hours) on February 8. The second line shows that 15 "blocks" of information have been saved (where one block contains 640 characters in this particular version of BASIC). In line 3 we see that 0.07 seconds of computer time (actually, central processor time) were required to process this program; that information was read from a magnetic disk storage device 856 times and written onto the disk 8 times; and that the timesharing session lasted 17 minutes at a charge of 0.0240 "units."

3.7 ERROR DIAGNOSTICS

Programming errors often remain undetected until an attempt is made to execute the program. Once the RUN command has been issued, however, the presence of certain errors will become readily apparent, since such errors will prevent the program from being interpreted, i.e., transformed into a machine-language program. Some particularly common errors of this type are a reference to an undefined variable or an undefined statement number, right- and left-hand parentheses that do not balance, failure to terminate the program with an END statement, etc. Such errors are called *grammatical* (or *syntactical*) errors.

Most versions of BASIC will generate a diagnostic message when a grammatical error has been detected. These messages are not always completely straightforward in their meaning, but they are nevertheless helpful in identifying the nature and location of the error.

EXAMPLE 3.11

Figure 3.9 shows a BASIC program similar to that presented in Fig. 3.6, except that several grammatical errors have deliberately been introduced. The diagnostic messages that are generated by issuing the RUN command are clearly shown. Notice that the errors in lines 40 and 80 and the omission of the END statement have been found. However, the error in line 50 (reference to the variable B rather than P) has gone undetected.

Grammatical and typing errors are usually very obvious when they occur. Much more insidious, however, are *logical* errors. Here the program correctly conveys the programmer's instructions, free of grammatical or typing errors, but the programmer has supplied the computer with a logically incorrect set of instructions.

Sometimes a logical error will result in a condition that can be recognized by the computer. Such a situation might result from the generation of an excessively large numerical quantity (exceeding the largest permissible number that can be stored in the computer), or from an attempt to compute the square root of a negative number, etc. Diagnostic messages will be generated in situations of this type, making it easy to identify and correct the errors. These diagnostic messages are called *execution* diagnostics to distinguish them from the *interpretation* diagnostics described earlier.

```
5  REM PROGRAM TO CALCULATE AREA AND CIRCUMFERENCE OF A CIRCLE
10 LET P=3.1415927
20 PRINT "RADIUS=";
30 INPUT R
40 LET A=(P*R^2
50 LET C=2*B*R
60 PRINT "R=";R,"A=";A,"C=";C
70 PRINT
80 GO TO 15

>RUN

EX3.11          22:19          18-FEB

? ILLEGAL FORMULA IN LINE 40
? UNDEFINED LINE NUMBER 15 IN LINE 80

? NO END INSTRUCTION

TIME:  0.18 SECS.
```

Fig. 3.9

```
EX3.12          22:05          22-FEB

10 REM REAL ROOTS OF A QUADRATIC EQUATION
20 INPUT A,B,C
30 IF A=0 THEN 90
40 LET D=B^2-4*A*C
50 LET X1=(-B+D^.5)/(2*A)
60 LET X2=(-B-D^.5)/(2*A)
70 PRINT "A=";A,"B=";B,"C=";C,"X1=";X1,"X2=";X2
80 GO TO 20
90 END

>RUN

EX3.12          22:05          22-FEB

? 1,2,3

% ABSOLUTE VALUE RAISED TO POWER IN LINE 50

% ABSOLUTE VALUE RAISED TO POWER IN LINE 60
A= 1            B= 2           C= 3           X1= 0.414214  X2=-2.41421
? 1E-30,1E10,1E36

% OVERFLOW IN LINE 60
A= 1.00000E-30                 B= 1.00000E+10                  C=
 1.00000E+36  X1=-8.32000E+32                 X2=-1.70141E+38
? 0,0,0

TIME:  0.50 SECS.
```

Fig. 3.10

EXAMPLE 3.12

Figure 3.10 shows a BASIC program for computing the real roots of the quadratic equation

$$ax^2 + bx + c = 0$$

using the quadratic formula

$$x = \frac{-b \pm \sqrt{b^2 - 4ac}}{2a}$$

The program is completely free of grammatical errors. However, the program is unable to accommodate negative values for $b^2 - 4ac$ (see rule 3, Section 2.7). Furthermore, numerical difficulties may be encountered if the variable a has a very small or a very large numerical value (see rule 5, Section 2.1).

Following the listing of the program we see the output that is generated for $a = 1$, $b = 2$ and $c = 3$, and for $a = 10^{-30}$, $b = 10^{10}$ and $c = 10^{36}$. In the first case we obtain a negative value for $b^2 - 4ac$. This is the reason for the first two diagnostic messages (notice that the computation proceeds using the absolute value of $b^2 - 4ac$). The second set of data results in an excessively large value for x_2, thus causing the overflow message. (Note that the information supplied by the user is underlined.)

3.8 LOGICAL DEBUGGING

We have just seen that grammatical errors and certain types of logical errors will cause diagnostic messages to be generated when compiling or executing a program. Errors of this type are very easy to find and correct. Usually, however, logical errors are much more difficult to detect, since the output resulting from a logically incorrect program may appear to be error-free. Moreover, logical errors are often hard to find even when they are known to exist (as, for example, when the computed output is obviously incorrect). Thus a good bit of "detective work" may be required in order to find and correct errors of this type. Such detective work is known as *logical debugging*.

Detecting Errors

The first step in attacking logical errors is to find out if they are present. This can sometimes be accomplished by testing a new program with data that will yield a known answer. If the correct results are not obtained, then the program obviously contains errors. Even if the correct results are obtained, however, one cannot be absolutely certain that the program is error-free, since some errors cause incorrect results only under certain circumstances (as, for example, with certain values of the input data or with certain program options). Therefore a new program should receive thorough testing before it is considered to be debugged. This is especially true of complicated programs or programs that will be used extensively by others.

As a rule, a calculation will have to be carried out by hand, with the aid of a calculator, in order to obtain a known answer. For some problems, however, the amount of work involved in carrying out a hand calculation is prohibitive. (A problem requiring a few seconds of time on a large computer may require several weeks to solve by hand!) Therefore a sample problem cannot always be developed to test a new program. Though logical debugging of such programs can be particularly difficult, the programmer can often detect logical errors by studying the computed results carefully to see if they are reasonable.

Correcting Errors

Once it has been established that a program contains a logical error, some resourcefulness and ingenuity may be required to find the error. Error detection should always begin with the programmer carefully reviewing each logical group of statements in the program. Armed with the knowledge that an error exists somewhere, the programmer can often spot the error by such careful study. If the error cannot be found, it sometimes helps to set the program aside for a while. It is not unusual for an overly intent programmer to miss an obvious error the first time around.

If an error has not been found after repeated inspection of the program, then the programmer should proceed to rerun the program, printing out a large quantity of intermediate output. This is referred to as *tracing*. Often the source of error will become evident once the intermediate calculations have been carefully examined.

When a programmer has tried all known tricks and still has not found an error, there may be an inclination to suspect either a machine error or a compilation error. Though rare, such errors do occur. (Machine errors are sometimes intermittent, whereas a compilation error will be consistent and therefore reproducible.) In most instances, however, a suspected compilation or machine error will turn out to be a logical programming error once the problem has finally been resolved.

Finally, the reader should recognize the fact that logical errors are inescapable in computer programming, though a conscientious programmer should make every attempt to minimize their occurrence. Thus the programmer should anticipate that a certain amount of debugging will be required as a part of the overall effort in writing a realistic, meaningful BASIC program.

EXAMPLE 3.13

A student has written a BASIC program to evaluate the formula

$$y = \left(\frac{x-1}{x}\right) + \frac{1}{2}\left(\frac{x-1}{x}\right)^2 + \frac{1}{3}\left(\frac{x-1}{x}\right)^3 + \frac{1}{4}\left(\frac{x-1}{x}\right)^4 + \frac{1}{5}\left(\frac{x-1}{x}\right)^5$$

To simplify the programming, the student has defined a new variable, u, as

$$u = \left(\frac{x-1}{x}\right)$$

so that the formula becomes

$$y = u + \tfrac{1}{2}u^2 + \tfrac{1}{3}u^3 + \tfrac{1}{4}u^4 + \tfrac{1}{5}u^5$$

The complete BASIC program is shown in Fig. 3.11.

```
10 PRINT "X=";
20 INPUT X
30 LET U=X-1/X
40 LET Y=U+(U/2)^2+(U/3)^3+(U/4)^4+(U/5)^5
50 PRINT "Y=";Y
60 END

>RUN


EX3.13          21:25          05-MAY

X= ?2
Y= 2.20971


TIME:   0.08 SECS.
```

Fig. 3.11

The student knows that y should have a value of about 0.69 when $x = 2$. However, the program results in a calculated value of $y = 2.20971$ when $x = 2$, as seen in Fig. 3.11. The student concludes, therefore, that the program contains logical errors, which must be found and corrected.

By carefully inspecting the program, the student became aware that statement number 30 results in a value of $u = 1.5$ when $x = 2$, whereas the correct value should be $u = 0.5$. The reason for the error is the omission of parentheses in statement 30, which *should* read

30 LET U=(X−1)/X

The student then corrected the program and reran it for a value of $x = 2$. The PRINT statement (line 50) was also changed so that the calculated value of u is printed out along with the calculated value of y.

When the program was executed, the value of u was calculated correctly, but the value of y was still incorrect, as seen in Fig. 3.12. Therefore the student concluded that the program contains an additional error, which must be located somewhere in statement number 40.

```
10 PRINT "X=";
20 INPUT X
30 LET U=(X-1)/X
40 LET Y=U+(U/2)^2+(U/3)^3+(U/4)^4+(U/5)^5
50 PRINT "U=";U,"Y=";Y
60 END

>RUN


EX3.13            21:27            05-MAY

X= ?2
U= 0.5            Y= 0.567384


TIME:   0.07 SECS.
```

Fig. 3.12

After some additional study, the student discovered that statement number 40 is indeed incorrect. This statement should be written

40 LET Y=U+(U↑2)/2+(U↑3)/3+(U↑4)/4+(U↑5)/5

(Note that the pairs of parentheses are actually not necessary because of the natural hierarchy of operations.) The program was then corrected, as shown in Fig. 3.13. At the bottom of Fig 3.13 we see that the value of y corresponding to $x = 2$ is correctly calculated as $y = 0.688542$.

```
10 PRINT "X=";
20 INPUT X
30 LET U=(X-1)/X
40 LET Y=U+(U^2)/2+(U^3)/3+(U^4)/4+(U^5)/5
50 PRINT "U=";U,"Y=";Y
60 END

>RUN


EX3.13            21:29            05-MAY

X= ?2
U= 0.5            Y= 0.688542


TIME:   0.08 SECS.
```

Fig. 3.13

3.9 CLOSING REMARKS

The reader is again reminded that BASIC programming is a skill, much like learning to play a musical instrument. It cannot be learned simply by reading a book. Rather, the reader must become actively involved in writing, editing, saving, listing, executing and debugging his or her own programs. Several appropriate programs are suggested in the programming problems listed at the end of this chapter. The reader is urged to solve as many of these problems as possible.

Although the material in this chapter is oriented toward the use of a large mainframe computer operating in a timesharing mode, it should be helpful to all beginning programmers, regardless of their particular computing environment. However, microcomputer programmers are encouraged to study the examples in Sections 10.2 and 10.7, in addition to the material in this chapter, before attempting to run their own BASIC programs.

Review Questions

3.1 What is a console? A timesharing terminal? A modem? An intelligent ("smart") terminal?

3.2 Describe, in general terms, the login and logout procedures used with BASIC.

3.3 What is meant by prompting? How is prompting indicated on a terminal when entering or processing a BASIC program?

3.4 How is a line of information that has been typed on a terminal transmitted to the computer?

3.5 Suppose a BASIC program is entered into the computer with certain of the statements in the wrong places. How can this situation be corrected?

3.6 How can one or more characters be deleted from a line of text on a terminal? How can an entire line be deleted?

3.7 How can an incorrect statement be changed once it has been transmitted to the computer?

3.8 How can a statement be deleted from a BASIC program once it has been transmitted to the computer?

3.9 How can a BASIC program be listed on a terminal?

3.10 How can a BASIC program be stored on a magnetic device for later use?

3.11 How is a BASIC program executed?

3.12 Suppose a BASIC program has been stored on a magnetic storage device and is to be retrieved for subsequent processing. How can the program be accessed?

3.13 Describe the purpose of each of the following system commands: BYE, CATALOG, GOODBYE, LIST, NEW, OLD, REPLACE, RUN, SAVE, UNSAVE.

3.14 What is meant by a syntactical error?

3.15 How do grammatical errors and logical errors differ from one another?

3.16 Name some common grammatical errors.

3.17 Name some common logic errors.

3.18 What is meant by diagnostic messages? How can interpretation diagnostics be distinguished from execution diagnostics?

3.19 Are diagnostic messages generated in response to logical programming errors?

3.20 What is meant by logical debugging? Name some common debugging procedures.

3.21 In what way is learning to program with BASIC like learning to play a musical instrument?

Supplementary Problems

The following "problems" are concerned with information gathering rather than actual problem solving.

3.22 Familiarize yourself with the timesharing terminals used at your school or office.

(*a*) Where is the ON/OFF switch?

(*b*) Does the unit have a built-in modem? If so, how does it operate?

(*c*) Does the unit have built-in intelligence?

(*d*) Which key causes one or more characters to be deleted from a line of text? An entire line to be deleted?

(*e*) Which key causes a typed line to be transmitted to the computer?

(*f*) Can the unit be operated in a LOCAL mode (i.e., as a stand-alone device, disconnected from a computer)? If so, how is this done?

3.23 Determine the exact login and logout procedures that are used at your particular school or office. Exactly what information is required to log in? What is the meaning of the information provided by the computer during the login and logout procedures?

3.24 What are the BASIC system commands in use at your school or office? Familiarize yourself with those that were not discussed in this chapter.

3.25 How can interpretation diagnostics be distinguished from execution diagnostics in the version of BASIC used at your particular school or office?

3.26 How are timesharing costs determined at your particular school or office? What is the actual cost of one timesharing unit? (*Note*: It is especially important that this question be answered by the student who receives free access to a computer through an educational institution. Most students have no idea of the equivalent commercial cost of using a large computer!)

Programming Problems

3.27 Log in to your computer system, determine the names of any programs that may have been saved under your account number and log out.

3.28 Enter the program shown in Fig. 3.6 for calculating the area and circumference of a circle. Be sure to correct any typing errors. List the program after it has been read into the computer. When you are sure that it is correct, execute the program several times using whatever values you wish for the radius. Verify that the computed answers are correct by comparing them with hand calculations. (Note that the execution is terminated by entering a value of zero for the radius.)

3.29 Enter, correct, list, save and then execute the programs for a few of the following problems:

(*a*) The "hello" problem described in Problem 2.62(*a*).

(*b*) The "what's your name?" problem described in Problem 2.62(*b*).

(*c*) The temperature conversion problem described in Problem 2.63(*a*).

(*d*) The piggy-bank problem described in Problem 2.63(*b*).

(*e*) Computation of the volume and area of a sphere, as described in Problem 2.64(*a*).

(*f*) Computation of the mass of air in an automobile tire, as described in Problem 2.64(*b*).

(*g*) Computation of the area of a triangle, areas of the largest inscribed circle and the smallest circumscribed circle, as described in Problem 2.64(*c*).

(*h*) The compound-interest problem, as described in Problem 2.64(*d*).

(*i*) Computation of the growth of a bacteria culture, as described in Problem 2.64(*e*).

Chapter 4

Branching and Looping

The programming problems we have considered so far have been sequential in nature. That is, the calculations were always carried out in a fixed order. However, the remarkable versatility of the digital computer lies not in its ability to carry out a fixed sequence of calculations in a short period of time. Rather, it is the ability of the computer to make logical decisions and then carry out an appropriate set of orders, based on the outcome of those decisions, that renders the computer so useful. Let us now turn our attention to this important topic.

We have already learned that *unconditional branching* operations (i.e., a transfer of control, or "jump," from one part of a program to another) can be carried out in BASIC by means of the GO TO statement (see Section 2.14). Another situation that arises frequently is a transfer to one of two different portions of a program, depending on the outcome of a comparison between two quantities. Such an operation, called a *conditional branch*, allows logical decisions to be carried out within the computer.

Looping is another operation that is often required in a computer program. This involves repeating some portion of the program either a specified number of times or until some particular condition has been satisfied. The repeated portion of the program (the loop) may contain a conditional branching operation that determines whether the loop will be terminated or executed at least one more time. If the loop is to be executed again, then control is transferred back to the start of the loop. Hence the instructions in the repeated portion of the program need not be written more than once.

In this chapter we will see how branching and looping operations can be carried out in BASIC. This opens the door to a much broader and more interesting class of programming problems.

4.1 RELATIONAL OPERATORS

In order to carry out a conditional branching operation in BASIC we must have a way to express conditions of equality and inequality. This is accomplished through the use of the *relational operators.* These operators are

Equal to:	=
Not equal to:	<>
Less than:	<
Less than or equal to:	<=
Greater than:	>
Greater than or equal to:	>=

The relational operators are used to connect numerical quantities (i.e., numbers, variables or formulas) or strings, thus forming conditions that are either satisfied or unsatisfied.

EXAMPLE 4.1

Several conditions involving numerical quantities are shown below. Each condition will be either satisfied or unsatisfied, depending on the numerical values of the variables.

```
X=27
N<=0.001
C>(C1+C2)↑2
A+B<C+D
P<>Q
Z>=X*Y
```

Thus the last condition will be satisfied if the value of Z is greater than or equal to the value of X*Y; otherwise it will be unsatisfied.

Inequality conditions involving strings are interpreted as "comes before" or "comes after" rather than "less than" or "greater than." Moreover, trailing blanks are ignored when comparing strings.

EXAMPLE 4.2

Several conditions involving strings are presented below. Each condition will be either satisfied or unsatisfied, depending on the particular strings that are assigned to the string variables.

```
N$="SMITH"
P$<>Q$
C$<G$
```

The first condition will be satisfied if the string assigned to N$ is SMITH; otherwise it will be unsatisfied. The second condition will be satisfied only if the string assigned to P$ is different from that assigned to Q$. In order for the last condition to be satisfied, the string assigned to C$ must come earlier in an alphabetized list than the string assigned to G$.

4.2 CONDITIONAL BRANCHING—THE IF-THEN STATEMENT

The *IF-THEN statement* is used to carry out a conditional branching operation. The statement consists of the words IF and THEN, separated by a relation and followed by the number of a remote statement. When executing the IF-THEN statement, control will be transferred to the remote statement if the relation is satisfied; otherwise, the statement following IF-THEN will be executed next. (Note that control can be transferred to *any* remote statement within a program, including a REM statement.)

EXAMPLE 4.3

Shown below is a portion of a BASIC program which includes an IF-THEN statement.

```
15...
...
50 IF I>=100 THEN 80
55 LET I=I+1
60 GO TO 15
...
80...
```

The manner in which the program is executed will depend on the relation

```
I>=100
```

contained in the IF-THEN statement. If the relation is satisfied (i.e., if the value of I is greater than or equal to 100), then statement number 80 will be executed next. If the relation is not satisfied (i.e., if the value of I is less than 100), then statement number 55 will be executed next.

Notice the way the IF-THEN statement is used in conjunction with the GO TO statement in this example to form a loop.

Many versions of BASIC allow use of the words GO TO rather than THEN.

EXAMPLE 4.4

Shown below is an IF-GO TO statement involving strings.

```
45 IF N$="SHARON" GO TO 120
```

(It should be clear that the use of GO TO rather than THEN has nothing to do with the type of relation, i.e., numerical vs. string.)

EXAMPLE 4.5 Roots of an Algebraic Equation

Computers are frequently used to solve algebraic equations that cannot be solved by elementary methods. Consider, for example, the equation

$$x^5 + 3x^2 - 10 = 0$$

This equation cannot be rearranged to yield an exact solution for x. Hence we will determine the solution by a repeated trial-and-error procedure (i.e., an *iterative* procedure) that successively refines an initially crude guess.

Computational Procedure

We begin by rearranging the equation into the form

$$x = \sqrt[5]{10 - 3x^2}$$

Our procedure will then be to guess a value for x, substitute this value into the right-hand side of the rearranged equation and thus calculate a new value for x. This new value will then be substituted into the right-hand side, and still another value obtained for x, and so on. The procedure will continue until either the successive values of x have become sufficiently close (i.e., the method has *converged*) or a specified number of iterations has been exceeded (thus preventing the computation from continuing indefinitely in the event that the computed results do not converge).

To see how the method works, suppose we choose an initial value of $x = 1.0$. Substituting this value into the right side of the equation, we obtain

$$x = \sqrt[5]{10 - 3(1.0)^2} = 1.47577$$

We then substitute this new value of x into the equation, resulting in

$$x = \sqrt[5]{10 - 3(1.47577)^2} = 1.28225$$

Continuing the procedure, we obtain

$$x = \sqrt[5]{10 - 3(1.28225)^2} = 1.38344$$
$$x = \sqrt[5]{10 - 3(1.38344)^2} = 1.33613$$

and so on. Note that the successive values for x appear to be converging to some final answer.

The Program Outline

In order to write a BASIC program outline, let us define the following symbols.

X = the value of x substituted in the right-hand side of the equation

X1 = the newly calculated value of x

I = an iteration counter (I will increase by one unit at each successive iteration)

N = the maximum permissible number of iterations.

We will continue the computation until either (a) the difference in successive values of x becomes less than 0.00001, or (b) the iteration counter (I) has reached its maximum allowable value (N).

We can now write an outline of our BASIC program as follows:

1. Read X, N
2. Initialize the counter (set I=1).
3. Compute a value for X1 using the formula

```
X1=(10-3*X↑2)↑.2
```

4. Print the newly calculated values for I and X1. (By printing out the results of each iteration in this manner, we can actually see whether or not the computation is converging.)
5. Test to see if |X−X1| (i.e., the absolute value of successive differences in the values of x) is less than 0.00001.
   (*a*) If |X−X1|<0.00001, then go to step 7 (print final answers).
   (*b*) If |X−X1|≥0.00001, then proceed to step 6 below.
6. Test to see if I=N (note that the value of I will be less than N in the early stages of the computation).
   (*a*) If I=N, then go to step 8 (print a message indicating that the computation has not converged).
   (*b*) If I<N, then increase I by one unit (i.e., I=I+1), let the recently calculated value for X1 be called X and go back to step 3, thus beginning the next iteration.
7. Print the final values of X1 and I, and then go to step 9 (stop).
8. Print a message indicating that the computation has not converged, followed by the most recent value for I and N.
9. Stop.

A flowchart of the computational procedure is shown in Fig. 4.1.

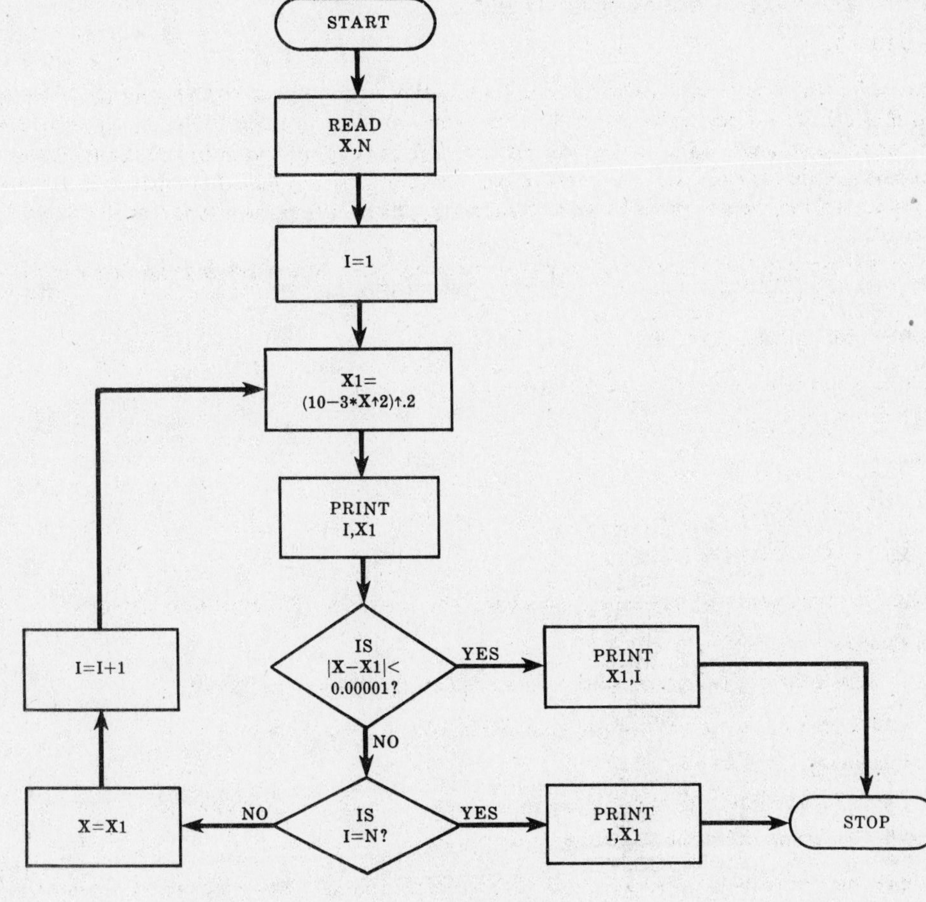

Fig. 4.1

The BASIC Program

In Fig. 4.2 we see a complete BASIC program that corresponds to the above outline and flowchart. The program contains two IF statements, in lines 60 and 70. (For illustrative purposes both the IF-THEN and the IF-GO TO forms have been used.) Notice that the program reads in an initial value for X and a value for N, but the convergence criterion (i.e., the value 0.00001) is a fixed constant within the program. The convergence criterion could have been treated as an input quantity if we had wished. Also, notice the use of the letters ABS in line 60. This refers to a BASIC library function that determines the absolute value of the quantity (X−X1). (We will discuss library functions in Chapter 5, Section 5.1) Finally, we see that we could have experienced some difficulty with this program if the formula

10−3*X↑2

in line 40 resulted in a negative quantity. A test for such a condition could have been included in the program.

Notice that the input information is underlined.

```
>LIST

EX4.5            17:51         03-MAR

10 REM AN ITERATIVE METHOD FOR COMPUTING ROOTS OF AN EQUATION
20 INPUT X,N
25 PRINT
30 LET I=1
40 LET X1=(10-3*X^2)^.2
50 PRINT "I=";I,"X1=";X1
60 IF ABS(X-X1)<.00001 THEN 110
70 IF I=N GOTO 160
80 LET X=X1
90 LET I=I+1
100 GOTO 40
110 PRINT
120 PRINT "THE FINAL ANSWER IS X =";X1
130 PRINT
140 PRINT "NUMBER OF ITERATIONS REQUIRED =";I
150 GOTO 190
160 PRINT
165 PRINT "COMPUTATION HAS NOT CONVERGED AFTER ";I;" ITERATIONS"
170 PRINT
180 PRINT "LAST VALUE OF X =";X1
190 END

>RUN

EX4.5            17:52         03-MAR

?1, 25
I= 1             X1= 1.47577
I= 2             X1= 1.28225
I= 3             X1= 1.38344
I= 4             X1= 1.33613
I= 5             X1= 1.35951
I= 6             X1= 1.34826
I= 7             X1= 1.35375
I= 8             X1= 1.35109
I= 9             X1= 1.35238
I= 10            X1= 1.35175
I= 11            X1= 1.35206
I= 12            X1= 1.35191
I= 13            X1= 1.35198
I= 14            X1= 1.35195
I= 15            X1= 1.35196
I= 16            X1= 1.35195

THE FINAL ANSWER IS X = 1.35195

NUMBER OF ITERATIONS REQUIRED = 16

TIME:   0.36 SECS.
```

Fig. 4.2

Following the program listing we see a set of output that is generated for an initial guess of $x = 1.0$. Notice that the computation has converged to the solution $x = 1.35195$ after 16 iterations. From the printed output we can actually see the successive values of x become closer and closer, leading to the final converged solution.

Figure 4.3 shows the output that is generated when convergence is not obtained. In this case we have specified a maximum value of only 10 iterations (N=10), which is not sufficient to obtain a converged solution from the starting value $x = 1.0$. The lack of convergence is clearly indicated by the printed message.

```
>RUN

EX4.5           17:53           03-MAR

?1, 10

I= 1            X1= 1.47577
I= 2            X1= 1.28225
I= 3            X1= 1.38344
I= 4            X1= 1.33613
I= 5            X1= 1.35951
I= 6            X1= 1.34826
I= 7            X1= 1.35375
I= 8            X1= 1.35109
I= 9            X1= 1.35238
I= 10           X1= 1.35175

COMPUTATION HAS NOT CONVERGED AFTER  10  ITERATIONS

LAST VALUE OF X = 1.35175


TIME:   0.26 SECS.
```

Fig. 4.3

4.3 MULTIPLE BRANCHING—THE ON-GO TO STATEMENT

Multiple branching can be carried out in BASIC by means of the *ON-GO TO statement.* This statement contains a numeric variable or formula and two or more numbers of remote statements. Control will be transferred to the first remote statement if the variable or formula has a value of 1, to the second remote statement if the variable or formula has a value of 2, etc.

EXAMPLE 4.6

A typical ON-GO TO statement is shown below.

```
30 ON K GO TO 15,40,25,40,60
```

Control will be transferred to statement number 15 if K has a value of 1, to statement 40 if K has a value of 2 or 4, to statement 25 if K equals 3 and to statement 60 if K equals 5.

If the variable or formula has a value that is not integral, then the decimal portion of the number will be ignored (i.e., the number will be *truncated*).

EXAMPLE 4.7

Suppose the variable K in Example 4.6 had been assigned a value of 3.67. The .67 would be ignored, and K would be considered to have a value of 3. Hence control would be transferred to statement number 25.

Notice that the value originally assigned to K has been *truncated—not rounded.*

Most versions of BASIC allow the use of the word THEN in place of GO TO.

EXAMPLE 4.8

A typical ON-GO TO statement is shown below.

```
50 ON A↑2+B↑2 GO TO 20,150,180
```

In most versions of BASIC the above statement could also be written as

```
50 ON A↑2+B↑2 THEN 20,150,180
```

4.4 THE STOP STATEMENT

The *STOP statement* is used to terminate the computation at any point in the program. It is equivalent to a GO TO statement that transfers control to the END statement. The statement consists simply of a statement number followed by the word STOP.

It is important to understand the distinction between the STOP and END statements. The STOP statement can appear *anywhere* in a BASIC program except at the very end. More than one STOP statement may appear. On the other hand, the END statement *cannot* appear anywhere *except* at the end of the program, hence it cannot be used more than once in any given program. (Recall that every BASIC program *must* end with an END statement.)

The use of the STOP statement, as well as the ON-GO TO statement, is illustrated in Example 4.9 below.

EXAMPLE 4.9 Calculating Depreciation

Let us consider how to calculate the yearly depreciation for a depreciable item (e.g., a building, piece of machinery, etc.). There are three different methods for calculating depreciation, known as the *straight-line* method, the *double declining balance* method and the *sum-of-the-years'-digits* method. We wish to write a BASIC program that will allow us to select any one of these methods for each set of calculations.

Computational Procedure

The computation will begin by reading in the original (undepreciated) value of the item, the life of the item (the number of years over which it will be depreciated) and an integer that indicates which method of depreciation will be used. The yearly depreciation and the remaining (depreciated) value of the item will then be calculated and printed out for each year.

The *straight-line* method is the simplest to use. In this method the original value of the item is divided by its life (total number of years). The resulting quotient will be the amount by which the item depreciates each year. For example, if an $8000 item is to be depreciated over 10 years, then the annual depreciation would be $8000 ÷ 10 = $800, and the item would decrease by $800 every year. Notice that the annual depreciation is the same each year.

When using the *double declining balance* method, the value of the item will decrease by a constant *percentage* each year. (Hence the *actual amount* of the depreciation, in dollars, will vary from one year to the next.) To obtain the depreciation factor we divide 2 by the life of the item. This factor is multiplied by the value of the item at the beginning of each year (*not the original* value of the item) to obtain the annual depreciation.

Suppose, for example, that we wish to depreciate an $8000 item over 10 years, using the double declining balance method. The depreciation factor will be 2 ÷ 10 = 0.20. Hence the depreciation for the first year will be 0.20 × $8000 = $1600. The second year's depreciation will be 0.20 × ($8000 − $1600) = 0.20 × ($6400) = $1280; the third year's depreciation will be 0.20 × $5120 = $1024; and so on.

In the *sum-of-the-years'-digits* method the value of the item will decrease by a percentage that is different each year. The depreciation factor will be a fraction whose denominator is the sum of the digits from 1 to N, where N represents the life of the item (e.g., for a 10-year lifetime the denominator will be $1+2+3+\cdots+9+10=55$). For the first year the numerator will be N, for the second year it will be (N − 1), for the third year (N − 2), and so on. The yearly depreciation is obtained by multiplying the depreciation factor by the *original* value of the item.

To see how the sum-of-the-years'-digits method works, we again depreciate an $8000 item over 10 years. The depreciation for the first year will be (10/55) × $8000 = $1454.55; for the second year it will be (9/55) × $8000 = $1309.09, and so on.

The Program Outline

We begin by defining the following symbols.

V = the value of the item

N = the number of years over which the item will be depreciated (the lifetime)

I = an integer that indicates which methods will be used to calculate the depreciation

- (a) I=1 indicates straight-line depreciation
- (b) I=2 indicates the double declining balance method
- (c) I=3 indicates the sum-of-the-years'-digits method

J = a counter that indicates which year is currently being considered

D1,D2,D3 = the annual depreciation calculated by each of the three methods

Our BASIC program will follow the outline presented below.

1. Read V,N,I
2. Print a message indicating which method will be used to calculate the depreciation.
3. Set J=0
4. Calculate D1=V/N

$$F1=\frac{V}{N*(N+1)/2}$$

[F1 is used in the sum-of-the-years'-digits method. Note that the sum of the digits $1+2+3+\cdots+N$ is equal to N*(N+1)/2.]

5. Increment J (i.e., J=J+1).
6. Calculate the yearly depreciation and the new value for the item by the appropriate method, and print the results.
   - (a) If I=1, then:
     - (i) Calculate V=V−D1
     - (ii) Print J,D1,V
     - (iii) If J<N, go to step 5; otherwise, stop.
   - (b) If I=2, then:
     - (i) Calculate D2=(2/N)*V
V=V−D2
     - (ii) Print J,D2,V
     - (iii) If J<N, go to step 5; otherwise, stop.
   - (c) If I=3, then:
     - (i) Calculate F2=N−J+1
D3=F1*F2
V=V−D3
     - (ii) Print J,D3,V
     - (iii) If J<N, go to step 5; otherwise, stop.

A corresponding flowchart is shown in Fig. 4.4.

The BASIC Program

In Fig. 4.5 we see a complete BASIC program for carrying out the computation. Notice that the program contains two ON-GO TO statements, in lines 90 and 210. (We could just as easily have used ON-THEN; the logic would have been identical.) Each of these statements provides us with a conditional three-way branch in this particular problem. We also see the use of the STOP statement in lines 340 and 450. As an alternative we could have written GO TO 560 in place of the STOP statements.

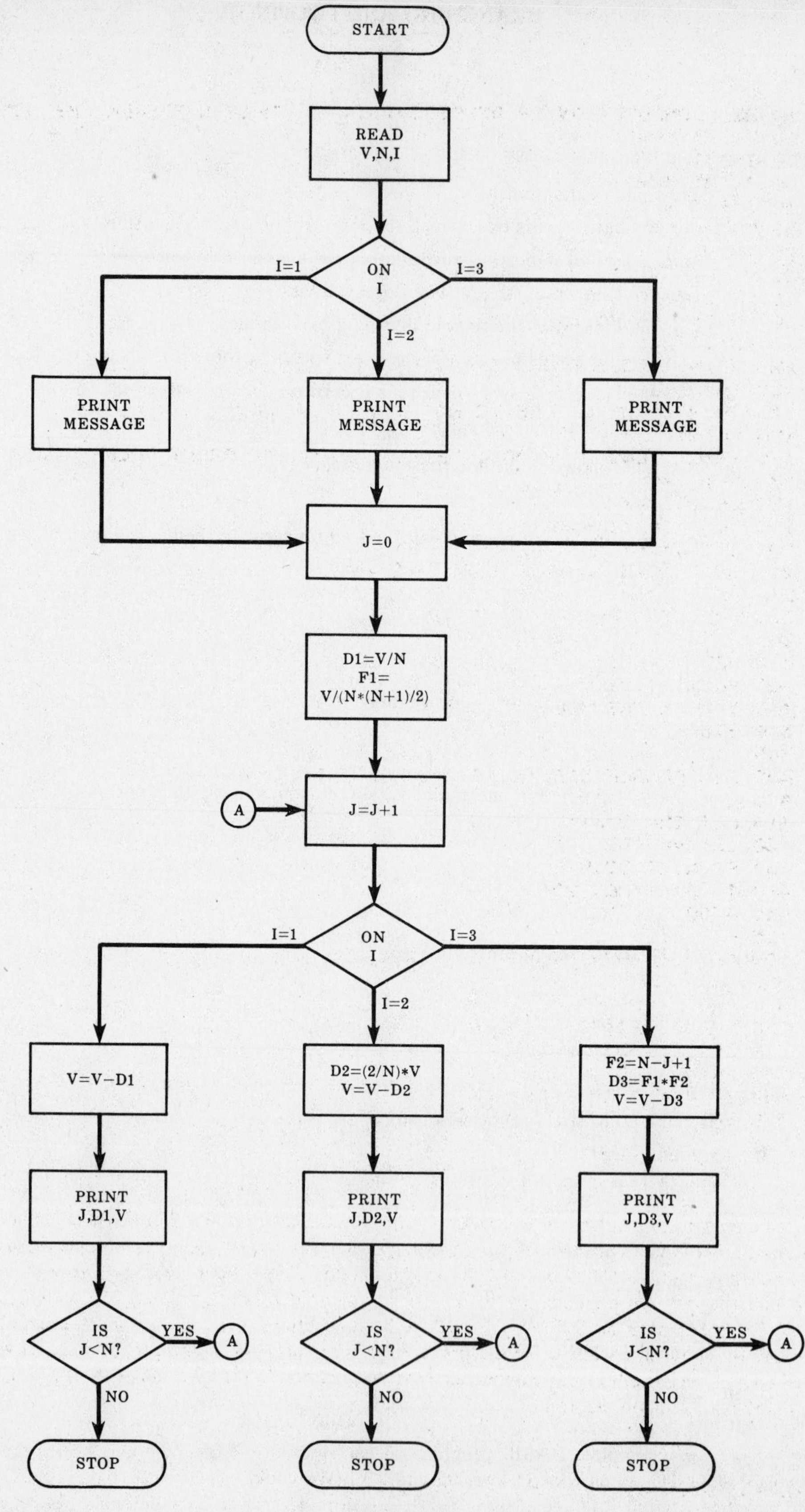
START
READ
V,N,I
ON
I
I=1
I=2
I=3
PRINT
MESSAGE
PRINT
MESSAGE
PRINT
MESSAGE
J=0
D1=V/N
F1=
V/(N*(N+1)/2)
A
J=J+1
ON
I
I=1
I=2
I=3
V=V−D1
D2=(2/N)*V
V=V−D2
F2=N−J+1
D3=F1*F2
V=V−D3
PRINT
J,D1,V
PRINT
J,D2,V
PRINT
J,D3,V
IS
J<N?
YES
NO
A
STOP
IS
J<N?
YES
NO
A
STOP
IS
J<N?
YES
NO
A
STOP

Fig. 4.4

```
10 REM COMPUTATION OF DEPRECIATION BY THREE DIFFERENT METHODS
20 PRINT "V=";
30 INPUT V
40 PRINT "N=";
50 INPUT N
60 PRINT "I=";
70 INPUT I
80 PRINT
90 ON I GOTO 100,120,140
100 PRINT "STRAIGHT-LINE METHOD"
110 GOTO 150
120 PRINT "DOUBLE DECLINING BALANCE METHOD"
130 GOTO 150
140 PRINT "SUM-OF-THE-YEARS'-DIGITS METHOD"
150 PRINT
160 PRINT "END OF YEAR","DEPRECIATION","CURRENT VALUE"
170 LET J=0
180 LET D1=V/N
190 LET F1=V/(N*(N+1)/2)
200 LET J=J+1
210 ON I GOTO 300,400,500
215
300 REM STRAIGHT-LINE METHOD
305
310 LET V=V-D1
320 PRINT J,D1,V
330 IF J<N THEN 200
340 STOP
345
400 REM DOUBLE DECLINING BALANCE METHOD
405
410 LET D2=(2/N)*V
420 LET V=V-D2
430 PRINT J,D2,V
440 IF J<N THEN 200
450 STOP
455
500 REM SUM-OF-THE-YEARS'-DIGITS METHOD
505
510 LET F2=N-J+1
520 LET D3=F1*F2
530 LET V=V-D3
540 PRINT J,D3,V
550 IF J<N THEN 200
560 END
```

Fig. 4.5

Figures 4.6(*a*), (*b*) and (*c*) show the output that is obtained with the straight-line method, the double declining balance method and the sum-of-the-years'-digits method, respectively. In each case we are depreciating an item whose initial value is $8000 over a 10-year lifetime. (The input data are underlined.)

Notice that the last two methods results in a large annual depreciation during the early years but a very small annual depreciation in the last few years of the item's lifetime. Also, we see that the item has a value of zero at the end of its lifetime when using the first and third methods, but a finite value remains when using the double declining balance method. (The appearance of the number 2.47955E–5 rather than zero in Fig. 4.6(*c*) is caused by numerical roundoff errors.)

4.5 BUILDING A LOOP—THE FOR-TO STATEMENT

We have already seen that a loop can be built in BASIC by using the IF-THEN and the GO TO statements. This is convenient when it is not known in advance how many times the loop must be repeated. Often, however, we do know in advance how many times a loop should be executed.

```
V= ?8000
N= ?10
I= ?1

STRAIGHT-LINE METHOD

END OF YEAR    DEPRECIATION   CURRENT VALUE
 1               800            7200
 2               800            6400
 3               800            5600
 4               800            4800
 5               800            4000
 6               800            3200
 7               800            2400
 8               800            1600
 9               800            800
 10              800            0

TIME:  0.45 SECS.
```

(*a*)

```
V= ?8000
N= ?10
I= ?2

DOUBLE DECLINING BALANCE METHOD

END OF YEAR    DEPRECIATION   CURRENT VALUE
 1               1600           6400
 2               1280           5120
 3               1024           4096
 4               819.2          3276.8
 5               655.36         2621.44
 6               524.288        2097.15
 7               419.43         1677.72
 8               335.544        1342.18
 9               268.435        1073.74
 10              214.748        858.993

TIME:  0.43 SECS.
```

(*b*)

```
V= ?8000
N= ?10
I= ?3

SUM-OF-THE-YEARS'-DIGITS METHOD

END OF YEAR    DEPRECIATION   CURRENT VALUE
 1               1454.55        6545.45
 2               1309.09        5236.36
 3               1163.64        4072.73
 4               1018.18        3054.55
 5               872.727        2181.82
 6               727.273        1454.55
 7               581.818        872.727
 8               436.364        436.364
 9               290.909        145.455
 10              145.455        2.47955E-5

TIME:  0.31 SECS.
```

(*c*)

Fig. 4.6

Under these circumstances the loop can be built most easily by using the FOR-TO and the NEXT statements.

The *FOR-TO statement* specifies how many times the loop will be executed. It must always be the first statement in the loop. Included in the FOR-TO statement is a nonsubscripted (ordinary) numeric variable, called the *running variable*, whose value changes each time the loop is executed. The number of executions is determined by specifying initial and final values for the running variable.

EXAMPLE 4.10

A typical FOR-TO statement is shown below.

```
50 FOR I=1 TO 10
```

In this example I is the running variable. The first time the loop is executed, I will be assigned a value of 1. I will increase by one unit each time the loop is repeated, until it has reached its final value of 10 during the last execution. The execution will be terminated once I has exceeded its final value of 10. Hence the loop defined by the above FOR-TO statement will be executed 10 times.

The running variable will always increase by one unit if the FOR-TO statement contains no instructions to the contrary. We can, however, increment the running variable by some value other than 1 if we wish. This is accomplished by adding a STEP clause to the FOR-TO statement, as illustrated in the next example.

EXAMPLE 4.11

Suppose we want to execute a loop 50 times, and we require that the running variable increase by two units after each successive execution. We could write

```
75 FOR J=1 TO 99 STEP 2
```

Thus the running variable J would be assigned a value of 1 during the first pass, a value of 3 during the second pass, 5 during the third pass, etc., until J would take on a value of 99 during the 50th (last) pass.

The running variable need not be restricted to positive integer values; it can take on negative and fractional values if desired. Furthermore, the running variable can be made to *decrease* with each successive execution of the loop. (This is accomplished by specifying a negative quantity in the STEP clause.) Finally, the initial, final and STEP values assigned to the running variable can be expressed as variables or formulas as well as numbers.

EXAMPLE 4.12

Shown below are several illustrations of valid FOR-TO statements.

```
30 FOR X=-1.5 TO 2.7 STEP 0.1
15 FOR I=N TO 0 STEP -1
55 FOR K=N1 TO N2 STEP N3
80 FOR F=A/2 TO (B+C)↑2 STEP K+1
```

Some versions of BASIC allow use of the word BY rather than STEP.

EXAMPLE 4.13

In some versions of BASIC the FOR-TO statement shown in Example 4.11 could also be written as

```
75 FOR J=1 TO 99 BY 2
```

4.6 CLOSING A LOOP—THE NEXT STATEMENT

Just as a loop always begins with a FOR-TO statement, it always ends with a *NEXT statement.* The complete loop comprises all statements included between the FOR-TO and the NEXT statements.

The NEXT statement consists of a statement number followed by the keyword NEXT, followed by a running variable name. This running variable must be the same as the running variable that appears in the corresponding FOR-TO statement.

EXAMPLE 4.14

Shown below is the skeletal structure of a loop that is built using the FOR-TO and NEXT statements.

```
50 FOR I=1 TO 10
...
90 NEXT I
```

The loop will consist of all statements from statement number 50 to statement number 90, and it will be executed 10 times.

Several rules must be kept in mind when constructing a FOR-TO . . . NEXT loop. These rules are summarized below.

1. The running variable can appear in a statement inside the loop, but its value cannot be altered.
2. If the initial and final values of the running variable are equal and the step size is nonzero, then the loop will be executed once.
3. The loop will not be executed at all under the following three special conditions.
   (*a*) The initial and final values of the running variable are equal, and the step size is zero.
   (*b*) The final value of the running variable is less than the original value, and the step size is positive.
   (*c*) The final value of the running variable is greater than the original value, and the step size is negative.

   (Usually the conditions described in rules 2 and 3 occur only by accident.)
4. Control can be transferred out of a loop but not in. (The transfer out can be accomplished by a GO TO, IF-THEN or ON-GO TO statement.)

EXAMPLE 4.15

Consider the skeletal structure of the loop shown below.

```
120 FOR X=0 TO 0.5 STEP 0.01
          ...
165       LET Z=X+Y
170       IF Z>Z1 THEN 250
          ...
195 NEXT X
    ...
250 PRINT X,Y,Z
```

This example illustrates the use of the running variable (X) within the loop (specifically, in statement 165). We also see that statement 170 causes control to be transferred outside the loop if the value of Z is greater than the value of Z1. Finally, we see that the running variable that appears in the NEXT statement (X) is the same as the running variable in the FOR-TO statement, as required.

Notice that the statements within the loop, between FOR-TO and NEXT, are indented to the right. This is not required but it is good programming practice, since the indentation allows the statements within the loop to be easily identified.

The FOR-TO . . . NEXT loop structure is frequently used in many different types of problem situations. A typical problem involving the use of such a loop is shown in the example below.

EXAMPLE 4.16 Averaging of Air Pollution Data

The level of air pollution can be expressed in terms of the air quality, i.e., the number of particles of a particular pollutant per cubic centimeter of air. Hence the higher the value for air quantity, the greater the pollution level. Measurements of air quality are made several times a day in most large cities.

Suppose we are given a table containing N measurements of air quality at different times during the day, as shown in Table 4.1. (Note that the time is given in 24-hour cycles, i.e., 13:00 refers to 1:00 p.m. Also, note that N=20 in this example.) We would like to calculate an average (mean) value of air quality for the entire period. This can be accomplished by first calculating an average value for each time interval (i.e., the time period between successive readings) and then calculating a weighted overall average from the individual averages.

Table 4.1

Time	Air Quality	Time	Air Quality
0:00	12.2	13:00	46.6
2:00	12.5	14:00	43.1
4:00	11.9	15:00	39.2
6:00	13.5	16:00	44.7
7:00	22.4	17:00	62.9
8:00	31.4	18:00	88.0
9:00	57.7	19:00	71.4
10:00	84.4	20:00	59.0
11:00	68.0	22:00	43.5
12:00	51.6	24:00	28.7

Computational Procedure

Let us first introduce the following symbols.

T1 = the time at the start of a given time interval

T2 = the time at the end of the given time interval

Q1 = the air quality at the start of the given time interval

Q2 = the air quality at the end of the given time interval

Q3 = the average air quality within the given time interval

The computation will proceed as follows.

1. Calculate the average air quality within each time interval using the formula

   Q3=(Q1+Q2)/2

2. Multiply each average air quality by the corresponding time interval (T2–T1) and add up all of these products, i.e.,

   $$S=[Q3*(T2-T1)]_1+[Q3*(T2-T1)]_2+\cdots+[Q3*(T2-T1)]_{N-1}$$

   In the above formula S refers to the sum of the individual products, and the subscripts 1, 2, . . . , N−1 refer to the various time intervals. (Note that there will be N−1 time intervals, since there are N values of Q and T.)

3. Divide this sum by the *overall* time interval (the time of the last reading minus the time of the first reading) to obtain the time-averaged value.

   A=S/(T9−T0)

   where A refers to the time-averaged air quality, and T0 and T9 refer to the times of the first and last readings, respectively.

(The reader who has studied numerical calculus will recognize this problem as an elementary exercise in numerical integration. The method is known as the *trapezoidal rule.*)

The Program Outline

We can now write the following detailed outline of the computational procedure.

1. Read N.
2. Set S equal to zero before reading any of the actual data.
3. Read the first set of data (i.e., the initial values for T1 and Q1).
4. Set T0 equal to T1. (This is a way of "tagging" the time of the first reading. We will need this value in step 7 below.)
5. Perform the following calculations (N−1) times.
   (*a*) Read T2 and Q2.
   (*b*) Calculate Q3.
   (*c*) Add the product Q3*(T2−T1) to S.
   (*d*) Set T1 equal to T2 and Q1 equal to Q2 in preparation for the next time interval. (In other words, the values for T and Q at the *end* of a *given* time interval become the values for T and Q at the *start* of the *next* time interval.)
6. Set T9 equal to the last value of T2.
7. Calculate A.
8. Print A and the overall time interval, (T9−T0).
9. Stop.

A flowchart corresponding to the above outline is shown in Fig. 4.7. Notice that the FOR-TO . . . NEXT loop is enclosed within a dashed rectangle.

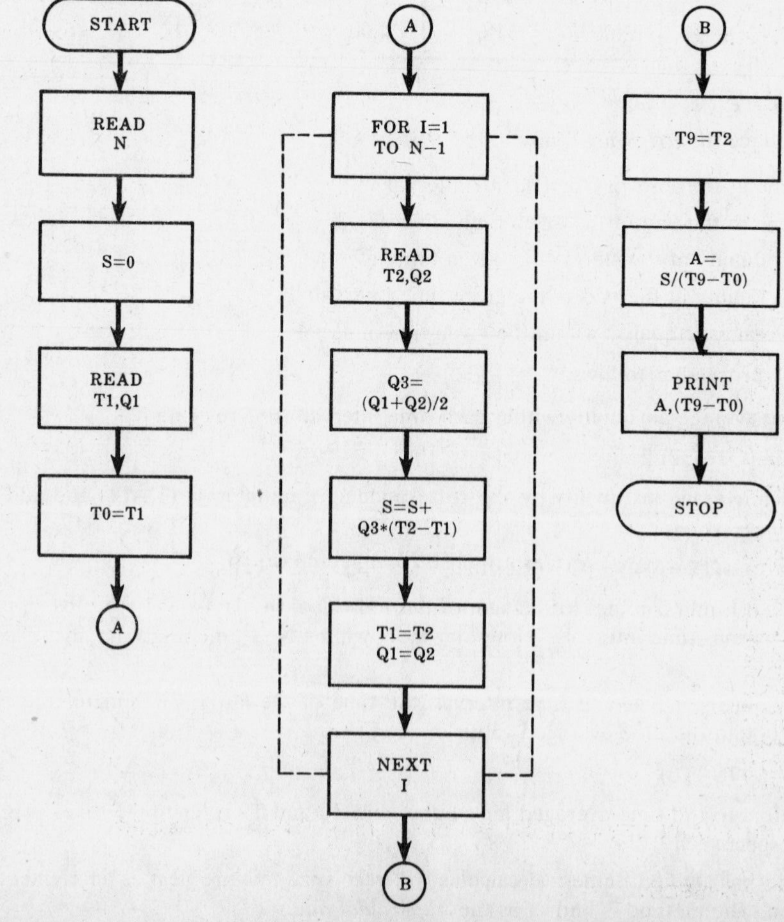

Fig. 4.7

The Basic Program

Figure 4.8 shows a complete BASIC program that corresponds to the outline presented above. We see that the cumulative sum S is formed by the FOR-TO . . . NEXT loop consisting of statements 100 through 160. Notice that the program does not require that the complete list of input data be stored internally in order to calculate this cumulative sum. (We will see a convenient way to store a complete list, if we should choose to do so, in the next chapter.)

```
10 REM AVERAGING OF AIR POLLUTION DATA
20 PRINT "N=";
30 INPUT N
40 LET S=0
50 PRINT
60 PRINT "  T    Q"
70 PRINT
80 INPUT T1,Q1
90 LET T0=T1
100 FOR I=1 TO N-1
110     INPUT T2,Q2
120     LET Q3=(Q1+Q2)/2
130     LET S=S+Q3*(T2-T1)
140     LET T1=T2
150     LET Q1=Q2
160 NEXT I
170 LET T9=T2
180 LET A=S/(T9-T0)
190 PRINT
200 PRINT "AVERAGE AIR QUALITY=";A;"TIME INTERVAL=";T9-T0;"HOURS"
210 END

>RUN


EX4.16         21:58          14-MAR

N= ?20

  T   Q

 ?0,  12.2
 ?2,  12.5
 ?4,  11.9
 ?6,  13.5
 ?7,  22.4
 ?8,  31.4
 ?9,  57.7
 ?10, 84.4
 ?11, 68.0
 ?12, 51.6
 ?13, 46.6
 ?14, 43.1
 ?15, 39.2
 ?16, 44.7
 ?17, 62.9
 ?18, 88.0
 ?19, 71.4
 ?20, 59.0
 ?22, 43.5
 ?24, 28.7

AVERAGE AIR QUALITY= 41.5354 TIME INTERVAL= 24 HOURS

TIME:  0.63 SECS.
```

Fig. 4.8

The lower portion of Fig. 4.8 shows the input values and the calculated results corresponding to the data in Table 4.1. We see that the overall average air quality is 41.5 for the given 24-hour period. (Note that the answer will not be accurate to more than three significant figures, since this is the accuracy of the input data.) The input information is underlined.

4.7 NESTED LOOPS

One loop can be embedded with another (i.e., *nested*) if desired. In fact, there can be several levels of nesting. The rules for writing single loops also apply to nested loops. In addition, the following restrictions must be observed.

1. Each nested loop must begin with its own FOR-TO statement and end with its own NEXT statement.
2. An outer loop and an inner (nested) loop cannot have the same running variable.
3. Each inner (nested) loop must be *completely* imbedded within an outer loop (i.e., the loops cannot overlap).
4. Control can be transferred from an inner (nested) loop to a statement in an outer loop or to a statement outside of the entire nest. However, control cannot be transferred to a statement within a nest from a point outside the nest.

EXAMPLE 4.17

Shown below is the skeletal structure of a program containing a nested loop.

```
100 FOR I=0 TO N STEP 2
        . . .
120     FOR J=I TO N
            . . .
160     NEXT J
        . . .
200 NEXT I
```

Notice that the inner loop (statements 120 through 160) is completely imbedded within the outer loop (statements 100 through 200). Each loop begins and ends with its own FOR-TO and NEXT statements, and each loop has its own running variable. Note, however, that the running variable of the outer loop (I) is used as the *initial value* for the running variable of the inner loop (J). This is permissible, since the value of I is not altered within the inner loop.

A nest of loops provides a convenient means of carrying out repeated sets of calculations. An example follows.

EXAMPLE 4.18 Generation of Fibonacci Numbers and Search for Primes

The Fibonacci numbers are members of an interesting sequence in which each number is equal to the sum of the previous two numbers. In other words

$$F_i = F_{i-1} + F_{i-2}$$

where F_i refers to the *i*th Fibonacci number. The first two Fibonacci numbers are defined to equal 1, i.e.,

$$F_1 = 1$$
$$F_2 = 1$$

Hence

$$F_3 = F_2 + F_1 = 1 + 1 = 2$$
$$F_4 = F_3 + F_2 = 2 + 1 = 3$$
$$F_5 = F_4 + F_3 = 3 + 2 = 5$$

and so on.

All of the Fibonacci numbers are positive integer quantities, and some of them will be *primes.* A prime number is a positive integer that is divisible, without a remainder, only by 1 or by itself. For example, 5 is a prime number because the only quantities that can be divided evenly into 5 are 1 and 5. On the other hand, 8 is not a prime because 8 is divisible by 2 and 4 as well as by 1 and 8.

Computational Procedure

It is very easy to calculate the first N Fibonacci numbers using the above formula. However, the procedure for determining whether or not a number is prime requires some explanation.

Suppose we want to determine if a given integer whose value is greater than 2 can be divided evenly by a smaller integer. Let us call the given integer F and the divisor J. The procedure is to calculate a quotient, Q, as

Q=F/J

We then calculate a *truncated* quotient, Q1, as

Q1=INT(Q)

The letters INT refer to a BASIC library function that will determine the largest integer that does not exceed Q. (We will say more about BASIC library functions in the next chapter.) Thus if Q has a value of 5.3, then Q1 will have a value of 5.

If Q and Q1 have the same value, then F is evenly divisible by J. Furthermore, if F is evenly divisible by *any* value of J, from J=2 to J=INT($\sqrt{F}$), then F cannot be prime. Hence F will be a prime number only if Q and Q1 *are not equal* for J=2, 3, . . . , INT($\sqrt{F}$).

The Program Outline

Let us refer to F as a given Fibonacci number (i.e., F_i), F1 as the previous Fibonacci number (F_{i-1}) and F2 as the second previous Fibonacci number (F_{i-2}). We can now write an outline of our program as follows.

1. Read N.
2. Set F1 and F2 equal to 1.
3. Print F1 and F2, identifying each as a prime.
4. Do the following calculations for I=3, 4, . . . , N.
   (*a*) Calculate a value for F using the formula

   F=F1+F2

   (*b*) Do the following for J=2, 3, . . . , R, where R is the largest integer that does not exceed $\sqrt{F}$. (Test for a prime number.)
      (i) Calculate values for Q and Q1, and test to see if they are equal.
      (ii) If Q and Q1 are equal for any value of J, then F cannot be a prime number. Hence print I and F, and proceed directly to step 4(*c*) below.
      (iii) If Q and Q1 are unequal for *all* values of J, then F must be a prime number. Hence print I and F, identifying F as a prime, and proceed to step 4(*c*) below.

   (*c*) Update F1 and F2 (i.e., assign the current value of F1 to F2, then assign the current value of F to F1), in preparation for calculating a new Fibonacci number (i.e., a new value for F).
5. Stop.

A corresponding flowchart is shown in Fig. 4.9.

The BASIC Program

A complete BASIC program corresponding to the above outline is shown in Fig. 4.10. Notice that the program contains a nest of loops. The purpose of the inner loop (statements 130–170) is to determine whether or not each Fibonacci number is a prime, whereas the outer loop (statements 110–230) causes the desired sequence of

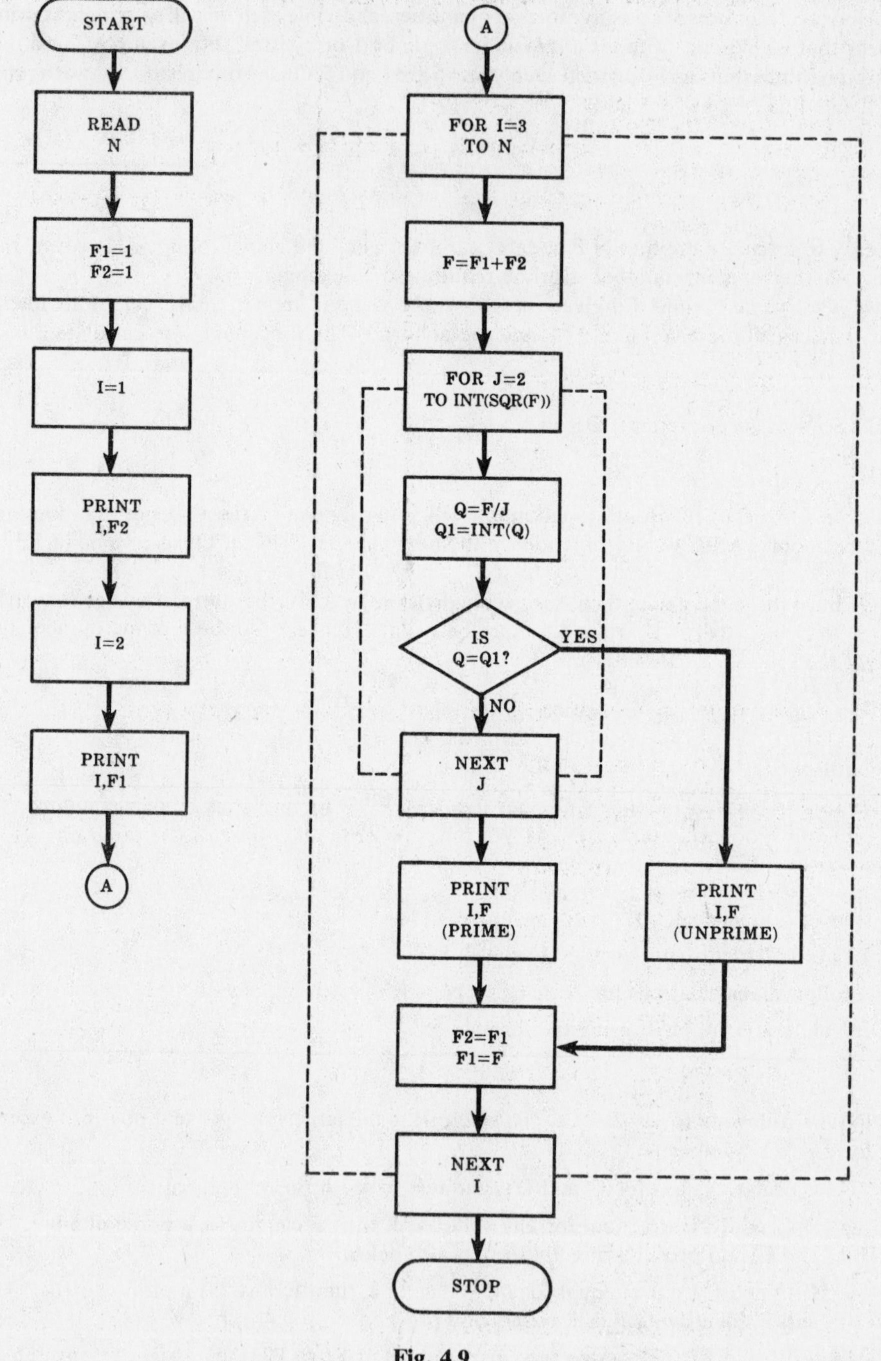

Fig. 4.9

Fibonacci numbers to be generated. Notice the use of the library function SQR (in line 130), which is used to obtain the square root of F (see Section 5.1). Also, note the conditional transfer of control out of the inner loop when Q = Q1 (statement 160).

The lower portion of Fig. 4.10 shows the output that is generated when the program is executed for a value of N = 30. We see that 11 of the first 30 Fibonacci numbers are primes. (Note that the user's responses are underlined.)

```
10 REM GENERATION OF FIBONACCI NUMBERS AND SEARCH FOR PRIMES
20 PRINT "N=";
30 INPUT N
40 PRINT
50 PRINT "GENERATION OF FIBONACCI NUMBERS AND SEARCH FOR PRIMES"
60 PRINT
70 LET F1=1
80 LET F2=1
90 PRINT "I=";1,"F=";1;" (PRIME)"
100 PRINT "I=";2,"F=";1;" (PRIME)"
110 FOR I=3 TO N     '(GENERATE FIBONACCI NUMBERS)
120     LET F=F1+F2
130     FOR J=2 TO INT(SQR(F))     '(TEST FOR A PRIME NUMBER)
140         LET Q=F/J
150         LET Q1=INT(Q)
160         IF Q=Q1 THEN 200
170     NEXT J
180     PRINT "I=";I,"F=";F;" (PRIME)"
190     GOTO 210
200     PRINT "I=";I,"F=";F
210     LET F2=F1
220     LET F1=F
230 NEXT I
240 END

>RUN

EX4.18          09:26          15-MAR

N= ?30

GENERATION OF FIBONACCI NUMBERS AND SEARCH FOR PRIMES

I= 1            F= 1  (PRIME)
I= 2            F= 1  (PRIME)
I= 3            F= 2  (PRIME)
I= 4            F= 3  (PRIME)
I= 5            F= 5  (PRIME)
I= 6            F= 8
I= 7            F= 13  (PRIME)
I= 8            F= 21
I= 9            F= 34
I= 10           F= 55
I= 11           F= 89  (PRIME)
I= 12           F= 144
I= 13           F= 233  (PRIME)
I= 14           F= 377
I= 15           F= 610
I= 16           F= 987
I= 17           F= 1597  (PRIME)
I= 18           F= 2584
I= 19           F= 4181
I= 20           F= 6765
I= 21           F= 10946
I= 22           F= 17711
I= 23           F= 28657  (PRIME)
I= 24           F= 46368
I= 25           F= 75025
I= 26           F= 121393
I= 27           F= 196418
I= 28           F= 317811
I= 29           F= 514229  (PRIME)
I= 30           F= 832040

TIME:  0.35 SECS.
```

Fig. 4.10

Review Questions

4.1 Is logical decision making an important attribute of a digital computer? Explain the reasons for your answer.

4.2 What is meant by a transfer of control within a BASIC program?

4.3 What is a conditional branching operation? How does this operation differ from an unconditional branching operation?

4.4 What is a looping operation? What is the purpose of such an operation?

4.5 Name the six relational operators used in BASIC. What is their purpose?

4.6 What is the purpose of the IF-THEN statement?

4.7 Summarize the rules for writing an IF-THEN statement, and explain what happens when this statement is executed.

4.8 How does the IF-THEN statement differ from the GO TO statement? Can these two statements be used together to carry out a common logical operation?

4.9 What is meant by an iterative procedure?

4.10 What is the purpose of the ON-GO TO statement?

4.11 How does the ON-GO TO statement differ from the IF-THEN statement?

4.12 Summarize the rules for writing an ON-GO TO statement, and explain what happens when this statement is executed.

4.13 Exactly what happens to a number when it is truncated?

4.14 What is the purpose of the STOP statement? How does this statement differ from an END statement?

4.15 What is the purpose of the FOR-TO statement? What is the purpose of the running variable? The STEP clause?

4.16 Can the running variable in a FOR-TO statement take on fractional or negative values?

4.17 Can the running variable be made to decrease in value with each successive execution of the loop?

4.18 What is the purpose of the NEXT statement? What is required of the running variable that appears in this statement?

4.19 Indicate two different ways that a loop can be structured in BASIC. For what kind of situation is each type of loop best suited?

4.20 Can the running variable appear in a statement that is contained within a FOR-TO . . . NEXT loop? Can the value of the running variable be altered in such a statement?

4.21 Under what conditions will a FOR-TO . . . NEXT loop be executed only once? Not at all?

4.22 What restrictions apply to a transfer of control into or out of a FOR-TO . . . NEXT loop?

4.23 Why are the statements that appear in a FOR-TO . . . NEXT loop frequently indented? Is such indentation necessary?

4.24 What is meant by nested loops?

4.25 Summarize the rules that apply to a nest of FOR-TO . . . NEXT loops. Compare with the rules that apply to a single such loop.

Solved Problems

4.26 Each of the following is a condition that involves the use of relational operators. Identify which, if any, are written incorrectly.

Condition	*Error*
X="DATE"	A numeric variable cannot be compared with a string.
K↑2>=100	Correct.
N$<>A+B	A string variable cannot be compared with a numeric quantity.
P$="123456"	Correct.
T$=R$*S$	Arithmetic formulas involving strings or string variables are not allowed.

4.27 Several IF-THEN statements are shown below. Identify which, if any, are written incorrectly.

Statement	*Error*
20 IF K↑2>=100 THEN 50	Correct.
20 IF (K↑2>=100) THEN 50	Correct.
20 IF K↑2>=100 GO TO 50	Not all versions of BASIC allow use of GO TO in place of THEN.
65 IF X+Y<>Z THEN M	The statement number to which control is transferred must be a positive integer, not a variable.
100 IF G$="MAY 13" THEN 45	Correct.
35 GO TO 150 IF J=3	Incorrect grammatical structure (statement must begin with IF).
50 IF X1<=50 THEN X=X+5	Possible incorrect grammatical structure. (In the older, more traditional versions of BASIC, THEN must be followed by a line number. However, most current versions of BASIC allow THEN to be followed by other statements, as shown. Thus, the statement may be correct.)

4.28 The skeletal structures of several IF-THEN . . . GO TO loops are shown below. Identify which, if any, are written incorrectly.

(*a*)
```
20...
...
60 IF N>N1 THEN 110
...
85 LET N=N+1
90 GO TO 20
...
110...
```

Correct.

(*b*)
```
35 LET P=0
. . .
50 . . .
. . .
75 IF P<=0 THEN 125
80 GO TO 50
. . .
125 . . .
```

Control will always be transferred to statement 125, since P is initially assigned a value of zero and this value is not subsequently altered.

(*c*)
```
15 . . .
. . .
45 INPUT X
50 IF X<50 THEN 90
. . .
85 STOP
90 . . .
. . .
110 GO TO 15
```

Correct.

(*d*)
```
110 C=5
. . .
130 . . .
. . .
160 IF C<=0 THEN 200
170 C=C+5
180 GO TO 130
. . .
200 . . .
```

The loop will continue indefinitely, since C will never be less than or equal to zero.

4.29 Several ON-GO TO statements are shown below. Identify which, if any, are written incorrectly.

Statement	*Error*
15 ON X3 GO TO 25,15,25,40	Correct.
100 ON 2*(C1+C2)/N GO TO K1,K2,K3	The statement numbers to which control is transferred must be positive integers, not variables.
55 ON J+K THEN 120,90,150	Not all versions of BASIC allow use of THEN in place of GO TO.
80 ON T GO TO 25	At least two different statement numbers must be given.
20 ON N$ GO TO 50,70,50,90	A string variable cannot appear in an ON-GO TO statement.
60 ON P(I) GO TO 10,120	Correct. (Note that P(I) is a *subscripted* variable. We will discuss subscripted variables in Chapter 5.)

4.30 Several FOR-TO statements are shown below. Identify which, if any, are written incorrectly.

Statement	*Error*
20 FOR N=J TO 3*(K+1) STEP J1	Correct.
50 FOR N=0 TO −100 STEP −5	Correct.
75 FOR X(I)=1 TO 100	A subscripted variable cannot be used as a running variable.
35 FOR K=K1 TO 100 STEP K1	Correct.
65 FOR N$=1 TO 19 STEP 2	A string variable cannot be used as a running variable.
100 FOR I=J TO K STEP I	The running variable cannot appear in the STEP clause.

4.31 The skeletal structures of several FOR-TO . . . NEXT loops are shown below. Identify which, if any, are written incorrectly.

(*a*)
```
20 FOR I=1 TO 100 STEP J
...
80 NEXT J
```

The running variable in the NEXT statement (J) is not the same as the running variable in the FOR-TO statement (I).

(*b*)
```
50 FOR N=N1 TO N2
...
75...
...
90 NEXT N
...
120 IF N=10 THEN 75
```

Control cannot be transferred into a loop.

(*c*)
```
100 FOR K=3 TO -3 STEP -1
...
130 PRINT X↑K
...
150 NEXT K
```

Correct, provided a value has been assigned to X. (Notice that the running variable appears within the PRINT statement, but its value is not altered.)

(*d*)
```
25 FOR X=0 TO 1 STEP 0.05
      ...
50      FOR Y=0 TO 10 STEP 0.1
           ...
75      NEXT X
      ...
100 NEXT Y
```

The loops overlap.

(*e*)
```
100 FOR I=1 TO M
       . . .
125     FOR J=1 TO N
           . . .
135        FOR K=1 TO M+N
              . . .
160        NEXT K
           . . .
180     NEXT J
        . . .
200     FOR J=1 TO N
           . . .
225     NEXT J
        . . .
235     FOR K=1 TO M+N
           . . .
240     NEXT K
        . . .
250 NEXT I
```

Correct.

Supplementary Problems

4.32 Each of the following is a condition that involves the use of a relational operator. Identify which, if any, are written incorrectly.

(*a*) J>=J1+J2
(*b*) C=C+1
(*c*) N$="END"
(*d*) X<.01
(*e*) P2<>T$
(*f*) A/B<=C/D

4.33 In order that the condition

P$<Q$

be satisfied, what is required of the strings represented by the variables P$ and Q$?

4.34 Several IF-THEN statements are shown below. Identify which, if any, are written incorrectly.

(*a*) 30 IF K<>K1 THEN 10
(*b*) 50 IF J<100 THEN J=J+1
(*c*) 120 IF X>=Y+Z GO TO 200
(*d*) 75 IF M$="DATE" THEN 50
(*e*) 150 IF P=P1 THEN K
(*f*) 100 IF B↑2<>(4*A*C) THEN 150
(*g*) 45 IF X↑2<0 THEN 20

4.35 Write one or more BASIC statements to accommodate each situation described below.

(*a*) If K has a value less than 15, then transfer control to statement number 50; otherwise execute the next statement.

(*b*) If N$ represents the string "OPTION A," then transfer control to statement number 70; otherwise transfer control to statement number 150.

(*c*) If X has a value equal to or greater than 100, then transfer control ahead to statement 200; otherwise increment J by one unit, read a new value for X, and return to statement 60.

(*d*) If J has a value of zero, then transfer control to statement 150; otherwise add the value of J to the value of S and return to statement 20.

4.36 The skeletal structures of several IF-THEN . . . GO TO loops are shown below. Identify which, if any, are written incorrectly.

(*a*)
```
20...
...
120 IF K$="END" THEN 200
130 PRINT A,B,C
140 GO TO 20
...
200 STOP
```

(*b*)
```
10 INPUT N
20 LET T=0
30 LET J = 1
40 INPUT T1
50 LET T=T+T1
60 IF J=N THEN 150
70 LET J=J+1
80 GO TO 30
...
150 PRINT J,T
160 END
```

(*c*)
```
10 LET X=100
...
50...
...
100 IF X>=100 THEN 200
110 LET X=X-5
120 GO TO 50
...
200...
```

(*d*)
```
10 LET X=100
...
50...
...
100 IF X>100 THEN 200
110 LET X=X-5
120 GO TO 50
...
200...
```

(*e*)
```
10 LET X=100
...
50...
...
100 IF X=0 THEN 200
110 LET X=X-5
120 GO TO 50
...
200...
```

4.37 Several ON-GO TO statements are shown below. Identify which, if any, are written incorrectly.

(*a*) 50 ON N$ GO TO 10,70,120

(*b*) 100 ON A GO TO 50,20,50,200,120

(*c*) 75 ON X1 GO TO 100,25,75,150

(*d*) 100 ON N GO TO N1,N2,N3,N4,N5

(*e*) 150 ON ((A+B)/C)↑2 GO TO 170,190,225

(*f*) 45 ON K−3 THEN 65,90

(*g*) 80 GO TO 50,120,150 ON (X+Y)

4.38 Consider the following ON-GO TO statement (which is grammatically correct):

75 ON J−K GO TO 100,50,20,150

What will happen when this statement is executed if

(*a*) J=2 and K=3?

(*b*) J=4.5 and K=0.75?

(*c*) J=1 and K=−1?

(*d*) J=5 and K=0?

(*e*) J=−1 and K=−2.8?

4.39 Several FOR-TO statements are shown below. Identify which, if any, are written incorrectly.

(*a*) 100 FOR C=.1*A TO .25*(A+B) STEP P/2

(*b*) 65 FOR X↑2=0 TO 100 STEP 20

(*c*) 80 FOR K$=P$ TO Q$

(*d*) 125 FOR X=V(1) TO V(2) STEP V(3)

(*e*) 30 FOR J1=25 TO −25 STEP −5

(*f*) 45 FOR A=12 TO 0 STEP 0.1

4.40 Write an appropriate pair of FOR-TO and NEXT statements (i.e., write the skeletal structure of a FOR-TO . . . NEXT loop) for each situation described below.

(*a*) A loop is to be repeated 200 times.

(*b*) A loop is to be repeated 200 times, except that control will be transferred out of the loop to statement 175 if the value of the variable X becomes less than 0.001.

(*c*) A loop will be repeated as many times as necessary for the running variable to increase from 1 to 73, assuming that the running variable is increased by three units each time the loop is executed.

(*d*) A loop will be repeated as many times as necessary for the running variable to increase from 0.5 to a value given by the formula A↑3−10. Each time the loop is executed, the running variable will increase by the value given by the formula A+B.

4.41 The skeletal structures of several FOR-TO . . . NEXT loops are shown below. Identify which, if any, are written incorrectly.

(a)
```
10 FOR K=K1 TO K2
      . . .
50      K=K+1
      . . .
90 NEXT K
```

(*b*)
```
10 FOR C1=0 TO 50 STEP 5
      . . .
35      FOR C2=0 TO C1
           . . .
65      NEXT C2
      . . .
100 NEXT C1
```

(*c*)
```
10 FOR J=1 TO N
      . . .
40      FOR K=1 TO M
      . . .
70      NEXT J
      . . .
120 NEXT K
```

(*d*)
```
100 FOR X=0 TO 1 STEP .02
      . . .
150 FOR X=0 TO 5 STEP .05
      . . .
200 NEXT X
```

(*e*)
```
50 FOR P=1 TO 50
      . . .
80      FOR Q=2 TO 100 STEP 2
           . . .
100          IF T>=T1 THEN 160
           . . .
120      NEXT Q
      . . .
160 PRINT "T=";T
      . . .
200 NEXT P
```

(*f*)
```
75 FOR X=A TO (A+B) STEP C
      . . .
125 NEXT C
```

Programming Problems

4.42 The equation

$$x^5 + 3x^2 - 10 = 0$$

which was presented in Example 4.5, can be rearranged into the form

$$x = \sqrt{(10 - x^5)/3}$$

Rewrite the BASIC program presented in Example 4.5 to make use of the above form of the equation. Run the program, printing out the value of x calculated during each iteration. Compare the calculated results with those presented in Example 4.5.

4.43 Rewrite the program presented in Example 4.5 so that it makes use of a FOR-TO . . . NEXT loop rather than an IF-THEN . . . GO TO loop.

4.44 Rewrite the program presented in Example 4.9 so that the ON-GO TO statements are replaced by IF-THEN statements. What conveniences have been achieved by using the ON-GO TO statements?

4.45 Rewrite the program presented in Example 4.16 so that it makes use of an IF-THEN . . . GO TO loop rather than a FOR-TO . . . NEXT loop.

4.46 Write a conversational-style program that will read in a positive integer value and determine the following.

(*a*) If the integer is a prime number

(*b*) If the integer is a Fibonacci number

Write the program in such a manner that it will execute repeatedly (loop), until a zero value is detected for the input quantity.

4.47 Several simple programming exercises are presented below. Prepare a detailed outline, a corresponding flowchart and a complete BASIC program for each exercise. Execute (RUN) the program using the data provided.

(*a*) Calculate the average of a list of n numbers. Test your program with the following set of data ($n = 10$):

27.5	87.0
13.4	39.9
53.8	47.7
29.2	8.1
74.5	63.2

(*b*) Calculate the *weighted average* of a list of n numbers, using the formula

$$x_{avg} = f_1x_1 + f_2x_2 + \cdots + f_nx_n$$

where the f's are fractional *weighting factors*, i.e., $0 \le f_i < 1$ and $f_1 + f_2 + \cdots + f_n = 1$. Test your program with the data given in part (*a*) above, and the following weighting factors ($n = 10$):

$i = 1$	$f = 0.06$	$i = 6$	$f = 0.10$
2	0.08	7	0.12
3	0.08	8	0.12
4	0.10	9	0.12
5	0.10	10	0.12

(*c*) Calculate the cumulative product of a list of n numbers. Test your program with the following set of data ($n = 6$): 6.2, 12.3, 5.0, 18.8, 7.1, 12.8.

(*d*) Calculate the geometric average of a list of numbers, using the formula

$$x_{avg} = [x_1x_2x_3 \cdots x_n]^{1/n}$$

Test your program using the data given in part (*c*) above. Compare the result obtained with the arithmetic average of the same data. Which average is larger?

4.48 Prepare a detailed outline, a corresponding flowchart and a complete BASIC program for each of the problems presented below.

(*a*) Calculate the sum of the first 100 odd integers (i.e., $1 + 3 + 5 + \cdots + 199$). Write the program two different ways:

(i) Write a sequence of statements that will add the next integer to the sum each time the sequence is repeated. Let the decision to repeat the sequence or to terminate depend on the outcome of an IF-THEN statement.

(ii) Use a FOR-TO . . . NEXT loop.

What advantages and disadvantages characterize each method?

(*b*) Calculate the sum of the first N multiples of an integer K. (For example, if K=3 and N=10, then calculate the sum of $1\times3+2\times3+\cdots+10\times3$.) Make the program completely general by reading in values for N and K each time the program is run. Test the program by calculating the sum of the first 1000 multiples of the integer 3.

(*c*) Compute the value of K!, where K represents an integer whose value is read into the computer each time the program is run. Test the program by calculating the value of 10! (Note that K! is defined as $1\times2\times3\times\cdots\times K$.)

(*d*) The sine of x can be calculated approximately by summing the first N terms of the infinite series

$$\sin x = x - \frac{x^3}{3!} + \frac{x^5}{5!} - \frac{x^7}{7!} + \cdots \quad (x \text{ in radians})$$

Write a complete BASIC program that will read in a value for x and then calculate its sine. Write the program two different ways:

(i) Sum the first N terms, where N represents a positive integer that is read into the computer along with the numerical value for x.

(ii) Continue adding successive terms in the series until the value of a term becomes smaller (in magnitude) than 10^{-5}.

Test the program for $x = 1$, $x = 2$ and $x = -3$. In each case write out the number of terms used along with the final answer.

(*e*) Suppose you place a given sum of money, A, into a savings account at the beginning of each year for n years. If the account earns interest at the rate of i percent annually, then the amount of money that will have accumulated after n years, F, is given by

$$F = A[(1+i/100)+(1+i/100)^2+(1+i/100)^3+\cdots+(1+i/100)^n]$$

Write a conversational-style BASIC program to determine the following.

(i) How much money will accumulate after 30 years if $1000 is deposited at the beginning of each year and the interest rate is 6 percent per year (annual compounding)?

(ii) How much money must be deposited at the beginning of each year in order to accumulate $100,000 after 30 years (again assuming that the interest rate is 6 percent per year, compounded annually)?

In each case, first determine the unknown amount of money. Then create a table showing the total amount of money that will have accumulated at the end of each year.

(*f*) Modify the above program to accommodate quarterly rather than annual compounding of interest. Compare the calculated results with those obtained in part (*e*). *Hint*: The proper formula is

$$F = A[(1+i/100m)^m+(1+i/100m)^{2m}+(1+i/100m)^{3m}+\cdots+(1+i/100m)^{nm}]$$

where m represents the number of interest periods per year.

(*g*) A class of students earned the following grades for the six examinations taken in a BASIC programming course.

Name	*Exam Scores (percent)*					
Adams	45	80	80	95	55	75
Brown	60	50	70	75	55	80
Davis	40	30	10	45	60	55
Fisher	0	5	5	0	10	5
Hamilton	90	85	100	95	90	90
Jones	95	90	80	95	85	80
Ludwig	35	50	55	65	45	70
Osborne	75	60	75	60	70	80
Prince	85	75	60	85	90	100
Richards	50	60	50	35	65	70
Smith	70	60	75	70	55	75
Thomas	10	25	35	20	30	10
Wolfe	25	40	65	75	85	95
Zorba	65	80	70	100	60	95

Write a conversational-style BASIC program that will accept each student's name and grades as input and determine an average grade for each student. Make the program as general as possible.

(*h*) Modify the program written for part (*g*) above to allow for unequal weighting of the individual exam grades. In particular, assume that each of the first four exams contributes 15 percent to the final score and each of the last two exams contributes 20 percent.

(*i*) Extend the program written for part (*h*) above so that an overall class average is determined in addition to the individual student averages.

(*j*) Write a BASIC program that will allow the console to be used as a desk calculator. Consider only the common arithmetic operations (addition, subtraction, multiplication and division).

(*k*) Write a BASIC program to calculate the roots of the quadratic equation

$$ax^2 + bx + c = 0$$

(See Examples 2.26 and 2.30.) Allow for the possibility that one of the constants has a value of zero and that the quantity $b^2 - 4ac$ is less than or equal to zero.

Chapter 5

Some Additional Features of BASIC

This chapter presents some additional frequently used features of BASIC. We begin with a discussion of the built-in library functions, which simplify such common operations as calculating the absolute value of a number, log of a number, etc. Then we will consider the use of lists and tables, which allow us to manipulate collections of numerical quantities or strings as though they were single variables. Finally we present two additional statements for entering data, thus providing us with an alternative to the use of the INPUT statement.

5.1 LIBRARY FUNCTIONS

The BASIC *library functions* (also called *standard functions* or *elementary functions*) provide a quick and easy way to evaluate many mathematical functions and to carry out certain logical operations. These library functions are prewritten routines that are included as an integral part of the language. Each function is accessed simply by stating its name, followed by whatever information must be supplied to the function, enclosed in parentheses. (A numeric quantity or a string that is passed to a function in this manner is called an *argument.*) Once the library function has been accessed the desired operation will be carried out automatically, without the need for detailed, explicit programming.

EXAMPLE 5.1

Suppose we wanted to calculate the square root of the value represented by the variable X. We could write

```
50 LET Y=SQR(X)
```

This would cause the variable Y to be assigned a value equal to the square root of X. The name of the square root function is SQR, and its argument, in this example, is the variable X.

Of course, we could have written

```
50 LET Y=X↑.5
```

Thus the use of the square root function is not required; it is merely a convenience. (It should be pointed out, however, that calculating the square root of a number by means of the square root function may require less computer time than the corresponding exponentiation operation.)

Table 5.1 presents several of the commonly used library functions. A more extensive list, including the entries contained in Table 5.1, is shown in Appendix B.

The use of all of the functions in Table 5.1 should be readily apparent except for INT and TAB, which are discussed below. Notice that some of the functions (e.g., LOG and SQR) require a positive argument. If any such function is supplied a negative argument, the minus sign will be ignored and the calculation will be based on the absolute value of the argument. Usually, however, an error message will be printed when the function is evaluated, indicating that a negative argument has been supplied.

The INT function requires some additional explanation. This function causes an argument having a *positive* value to be *truncated* (i.e., the decimal portion of the number will be dropped). Thus the INT function will generate a positive integer whose magnitude is less than that of its argument. On the other hand, if the argument has a negative value, the INT function will produce a negative integer whose magnitude is *greater* than that of its argument. This is illustrated in Example 5.2 below.

Table 5.1 Commonly Used Library Functions

Function	Application	Description
ABS	10 LET Y=ABS(X)	Calculate the absolute value of x; $y = \|x\|$.
ATN	10 LET Y=ATN(X)	Calculate the arctangent of x; $y = \arctan(x)$.
COS	10 LET Y=COS(X)	Calculate the cosine of x; $y=\cos(x)$, x in radians.
COT	10 LET Y=COT(X)	Calculate the cotangent of x; $y = \cot(x)$, x in radians.
EXP	10 LET Y=EXP(X)	Raise e to the x power; $y = e^{x\dagger}$.
INT	10 LET Y=INT(X)	Assign to y the largest integer that algebraically does not exceed x.
LOG	10 LET Y=LOG(X)	Calculate the natural logarithm of x; $y = \log_e x$, $x > 0$.
SGN	10 LET Y=SGN(X)	Determine the sign of x ($y = +1$ if x is positive, $y = 0$ if $x = 0$, $y = -1$ if x is negative).
SIN	10 LET Y=SIN(X)	Calculate the sine of x; $y = \sin(x)$, x in radians.
SQR	10 LET Y=SQR(X)	Calculate the square root of x; $y = \sqrt{x}$, $x > 0$.
TAB	20 PRINT TAB(N);X	Causes the value of x to be printed or displayed at column n. (Left column is considered column 0.)
TAN	10 LET Y=TAN(X)	Calculate the tangent of x; $y = \tan(x)$, x in radians.

† The symbol e represents the base of the natural (Naperian) system of logarithms. It is an irrational number whose approximate value is 2.718282.

EXAMPLE 5.2

Consider the statement

```
10 LET Y=INT(X)
```

If X (the argument) represents the value 12.9, then Y will be assigned the value 12. On the other hand, if X represents −4.2, then Y will be assigned a value of −5.

The TAB function permits the programmer to specify the exact positioning of each output item listed in a PRINT statement. This allows greater flexibility in the spacing of output data than the methods described in Section 2.10. Each time the TAB function appears in an output list, the print head or cursor of the console will move to the right until the specified column has been reached. (Note that the leftmost column is considered column 0.) If the print head is already positioned beyond (i.e., to the right of) the indicated column, however, then the TAB function will be ignored.

EXAMPLE 5.3

Suppose we wanted to print the values of A, B and C on one line, with the first value beginning in column number 9, the second in column 29 and the third in column 47. (Note that these are actually the 10th, 30th and 48th columns, respectively.) This is accomplished by writing

```
100 PRINT TAB(9);A;TAB(29);B;TAB(47);C
```

On the other hand, consider the statement

```
150 PRINT "NAME AND ADDRESS";TAB(12);N$
```

In this case the TAB function will be ignored, since the print head (or cursor) will already be positioned at column number 16 after the string NAME AND ADDRESS has been printed. Hence the string represented by N$ will begin in column 16. If the argument of the TAB function were greater than 16, however, then the print head (cursor) would be positioned as desired.

Use of a library function is not confined to a LET or a PRINT statement—a library function may appear wherever a variable might ordinarily be present. Moreover, the arguments need not be simple variables. Constants, subscripted variables, formulas—even references to other functions—can be used as valid function arguments. Truncation will be performed automatically if necessary for those functions that require integer-valued arguments (as, for example, the TAB function).

EXAMPLE 5.4

Each of the following statements is a valid example of the use of a library function.

```
40 LET X1=(-B+SQR(D))/(2*A)
60 IF ABS(X-X1)<.00001 THEN 110
100 PRINT SIN(T), COS(T), TAN(T), LOG(T), EXP(T)
200 FOR J=0 TO INT(Y)
75 LET A=LOG(SQR(ABS(P)))
```

The use of library functions is demonstrated in the following example. (Note that library functions were used in Figs. 4.2 and 4.10.)

EXAMPLE 5.5 A Table of Functions

Suppose we wish to generate a table of values for sin (x), cos (x), tan (x), log (x) and e^x for 21 values of x ranging from 0 to π. This is easily accomplished with a FOR-TO loop, with the calculated data displayed in columnar form.

The Program Outline

The computation will proceed as follows.

1. Print the following six column headings.

   X SIN(X) COS(X) TAN(X) LOG(X) EXP(X)

2. Print the value of x, sin (x), cos (x), tan (x), log (x) and e^x for each value of x ranging from $x = 0$ to $x = 3.1416$, with a step size of 0.15708 (which is equal to $3.1416 \div 20$). This will generate 21 lines of output.
3. Stop.

A corresponding flowchart is shown in Fig. 5.1.

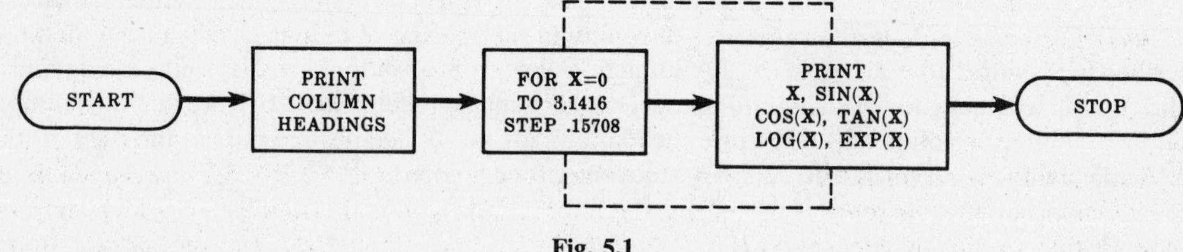

Fig. 5.1

The BASIC Program

A complete BASIC program, followed by the calculated output data, is shown in Fig. 5.2. The program is straightforward and requires no special explanation. It should be pointed out, however, that some care must be used in assigning arguments to the TAB functions so that the six columns of output are spaced evenly across the page. The program may have to be executed several times, with intermittent adjustments of the TAB arguments after each execution, before the columns are spaced correctly.

The output data clearly show the calculated values of sin (x), cos (x), tan (x), log (x) and e^x for each specified value of x. Notice that an error message is produced when we attempt to calculate the log of zero. This is followed by the number −1.70141E+38, which is the largest (in magnitude) negative number that the computer can accommodate. (Actually, the log of zero is defined to have a negative infinite value.) We could have avoided this situation by including an appropriate IF statement in the program.

```
10 REM GENERATION OF A TABLE OF MATHEMATICAL FUNCTIONS
20 PRINT TAB(7);"X";TAB(15);"SIN(X)";TAB(27);"COS(X)";
30 PRINT TAB(39);"TAN(X)";TAB(51);"LOG(X)";TAB(63);"EXP(X)"
40 PRINT
50 FOR X=0 TO 3.1416 STEP .15708
60     PRINT TAB(3);X;TAB(13);SIN(X);TAB(25);COS(X);
70     PRINT TAB(37);TAN(X);TAB(49);LOG(X);TAB(61);EXP(X)
80 NEXT X
90 END

>RUN

EX5.5          09:28          15-MAR

      X        SIN(X)        COS(X)       TAN(X)       LOG(X)       EXP(X)

  0          0           1            0
% LOG OF ZERO IN LINE 70
          -1.70141E+38                                             1
  0.15708    0.156435    0.987688     0.158385     -1.851          1.17009
  0.31416    0.309018    0.951056     0.324921     -1.15785        1.36911
  0.47124    0.453991    0.891006     0.509527     -0.752388       1.60198
  0.62832    0.587786    0.809016     0.726545     -0.464706       1.87446
  0.7854     0.707108    0.707105     1.           -0.241562       2.19328
  0.94248    0.809018    0.587783     1.37639      -5.92406E-2     2.56634
  1.09956    0.891008    0.453988     1.96262       9.49101E-2     3.00284
  1.25664    0.951057    0.309014     3.07771       0.228441       3.5136
  1.41372    0.987689    0.156431     6.31389       0.346225       4.11122
  1.5708     1          -3.65144E-6  -273864.       0.451585       4.81049
  1.72788    0.987688   -0.156438    -6.31359       0.546895       5.62871
  1.88496    0.951055   -0.309021    -3.07764       0.633907       6.58609
  2.04204    0.891004   -0.453995    -1.96259       0.713949       7.70631
  2.19912    0.809014   -0.587789    -1.37637       0.788057       9.01707
  2.3562     0.707103   -0.707111    -0.999989      0.85705        10.5508
  2.51328    0.587781   -0.80902     -0.726534      0.921589       12.3454
  2.67036    0.453985   -0.891009    -0.509518      0.982213       14.4452
  2.82744    0.309011   -0.951059    -0.324912      1.03937        16.9021
  2.98452    0.156428   -0.987689    -0.158377      1.09344        19.777
  3.1416    -7.25607E-6 -1            7.25607E-6    1.14473        23.1409

 TIME:  0.18 SECS.
```

Fig. 5.2

Virtually all versions of BASIC include the library functions shown in Table 5.1 and Appendix B. Many versions of the language also include additional library functions, some of which may be unique to that particular version. Most of these are of a numeric nature, but some accept string arguments or return string values (or both). This is especially true of microcomputer versions of BASIC (see Section 9.3). The reader should consult a reference manual to determine exactly what library functions are available at his or her particular installation.

5.2 LISTS AND TABLES (ARRAYS)

When writing a complete program, it is often convenient to refer to an entire collection of items at one time. Such a collection is usually referred to as an *array.* We may, for example, be concerned with a complete *list* of items (also known as a *one-dimensional array*) or with all of the entries in a *table* (a *two-dimensional array*). BASIC allows us to refer to the elements of lists and tables as though they were ordinary variables, thus making array manipulation as simple as possible.

The elements in a list or table can be either numerical quantities or strings. (Some versions of BASIC allow string lists but not string tables.) However, all of the elements in a given array must be of the same type (i.e., all numeric or all string). If an array contains numeric elements, it must be named with a single letter, whereas a string array is referred to with a letter followed by a dollar sign. Note that array names consisting of a letter followed by an integer, or of a letter followed by an integer and a dollar sign, are not allowed in traditional BASIC.

Within a given program each array name must be unique, i.e., no two arrays can have the same name. On the other hand, an array and an ordinary variable can be assigned the same name. Such duplication of names within a program can be logically confusing, however, and is therefore not recommended.

EXAMPLE 5.6

A program is to contain a list of names and a table of numbers. The list will be called L$ and the table T.

It is also possible to include in the program an ordinary string variable called L$ and an ordinary numeric variable called T. These variables would be separate and distinct from the arrays L$ and T. It would probably be wiser, however, to name these variables differently (e.g., L1$ and T9), thus avoiding any possible confusion between the arrays and other program variables.

5.3 SUBSCRIPTED VARIABLES

The individual elements within an array are known as *subscripted variables.* Any such element can be referred to by stating the array name, followed by the value of the subscript, enclosed in parentheses. In the case of a table, two subscripts must be specified, separated by a comma. Thus P(3) is an element of the list P, and T(8,5) is an element of the table T. The subscripts must be integer-valued and cannot be negative.

EXAMPLE 5.7

Ten names (strings) are to be placed in a single list. The list will be called L$, and the individual names will be referred to as L$(1), L$(2), . . . , L$(10). Notice that the subscript takes on integer values ranging from 1 to 10.

Similarly, forty numbers are to be arranged in a table having five rows and eight columns. We will refer to the table as T. The first subscript (representing the row number) will take on integer values ranging from 1 to 5, and the second subscript (representing the column number) will range from 1 to 8. Thus the number in the third row, fourth column will be referred to as T(3,4), etc.

A subscript need not necessarily be written as a constant. Variables, formulas and function names can also be used. However, the value that a subscript takes on must be either zero or a positive integer. If a formula or a function reference results in a noninteger value for a subscript, then that value will be truncated, thus resulting in an integer-valued subscript. Execution will be suppressed and an error message written if a negative value is generated for a subscript or if too large a positive value is generated.

EXAMPLE 5.8

All the subscripted variables shown below are written correctly.

```
P(3)                T(8,5)
P(K)                T(J1,J2)
P(C(J))             T(6,N)
P(2*A−B)            T(A1+B1, A2+B2)
P(SQR(X↑2+Y↑2))     T(ABS(X+Y),ABS(X−Y))
```

Consider the subscripted variable P(2*A−B). Suppose the formula 2*A−B has a value of 2.8. This value will be truncated, and the subscripted variable will be interpreted as P(2). If this formula has a value of −3.6, however, then an error message will be written and program execution will terminate.

Subscripted variables can be used within a program in the same manner as ordinary variables. This is illustrated in the following example.

EXAMPLE 5.9 Word Unscrambling

An interesting problem involving the manipulation of subscripted variables is that of rearranging a group of letters to form all possible words. Suppose, for example, we are given four letters, such as OPST. We would like to form all possible combinations of these four letters and then write out each combination. Thus we can find all possible four-letter words that can be formed from the original four letters (viz., POST, POTS, TOPS, STOP, SPOT).

Computational Procedure

In order to do this, let us place the given letters in a list that we will call L$. Each letter will be represented by a subscripted variable L$(1), L$(2), ... Hence our objective will be to write out all possible combinations of the subscripted variables.

Let us print out the given four letters in the order designated by the indices I1, I2, I3 and I4, where I1 is the subscript of the first letter to be printed, I2 refers to the second letter to be printed, and so on. For example, if I1=3, I2=2, I3=4 and I4=1, we would print the letters in the order

L$(3)   L$(2)   L$(4)   L$(1)

We wish to write a BASIC program that will allow I1, I2, I3 and I4 to take on all possible values, with the restriction that each index have a unique numerical value. That is, no two indices will be allowed to represent the same number.

In addition to the INPUT and PRINT statements, the BASIC program will consist essentially of a nest of three FOR-TO loops. The outermost loop will assign a value to I1; the next loop will assign a value to I2, testing to make sure that I2 differs from I1. The innermost loop will establish a value for I3, again testing to see that I3 has a different value than I1 or I2. Finally, we can obtain a value for I4 by noting that the sum of the first four integers is 10. Therefore once I1, I2 and I3 have each been assigned a unique value, we can calculate I4 from the formula

I4=10−(I1+I2+I3)

The Program Outline

We can outline the entire procedure as follows:

1. Read L$(1), L$(2), L$(3) and L$(4).
2. Do the following, for I1=1,2,3,4.
   (*a*) Assign a value to I1.
   (*b*) Do the following, letting I2=1,2,3,4.
      (i) Assign a value to I2.
      (ii) Test to see if I2 differs from I1. If not, increase I2 by one unit and test again.
      (iii) For each value of I1 and I2 do the following, letting I3=1,2,3,4.
         (1) Assign a value to I3.
         (2) Test to see that I3 differs from both I1 and I2. If not, increase I3 by one unit and test again.
         (3) Calculate a value for I4 from the formula I4=10−(I1+I2+I3).
         (4) Print out L$(I1), L$(I2), L$(I3) and L$(I4).
3. Stop.

A flowchart of the procedure is shown in Fig. 5.3.

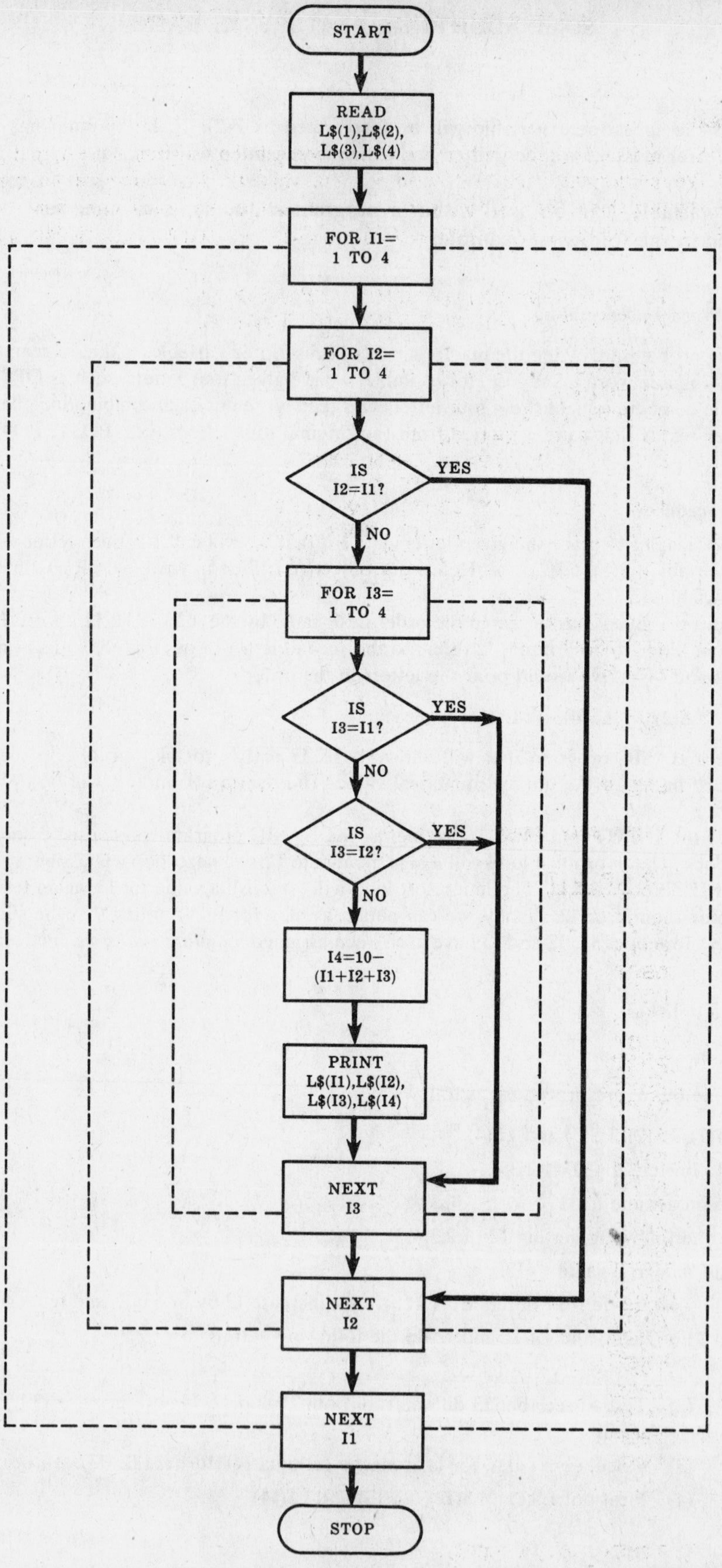

START

READ L$(1),L$(2), L$(3),L$(4)

FOR I1= 1 TO 4

FOR I2= 1 TO 4

IS I2=I1?

YES

NO

FOR I3= 1 TO 4

IS I3=I1?

YES

NO

IS I3=I2?

YES

NO

I4=10−(I1+I2+I3)

PRINT L$(I1),L$(I2), L$(I3),L$(I4)

NEXT I3

NEXT I2

NEXT I1

STOP

Fig. 5.3

The BASIC Program

The actual BASIC program appears in Fig. 5.4. Shown beneath the program is the output generated for the four letters OPST. We see that there are 24 different ways in which the four letters can be combined. It can be proven mathematically that this is the correct number of combinations. By visual inspection we can find the five recognizable words POST, POTS, SPOT, STOP and TOPS. These words have been circled in Fig. 5.4.

```
10 REM FOUR-LETTER WORD UNSCRAMBLER
20 PRINT "TYPE ANY FOUR LETTERS:"
30 PRINT
40 INPUT L$(1),L$(2),L$(3),L$(4)
50 PRINT
60 FOR I1=1 TO 4
70    FOR I2=1 TO 4
80       IF I2=I1 THEN 150
90       FOR I3=1 TO 4
100         IF I3=I1 THEN 140
110         IF I3=I2 THEN 140
120         LET I4=10-(I1+I2+I3)
130         PRINT L$(I1);L$(I2);L$(I3);L$(I4)
140      NEXT I3
150   NEXT I2
160 NEXT I1
170 END

>RUN


EX5.9          09:30          15-MAR

TYPE ANY FOUR LETTERS:

 ?O,P,S,T

OPST
OPTS
OSPT
OSTP
OTPS
OTSP
POST
POTS
PSOT
PSTO
PTOS
PTSO
SOPT
SOTP
SPOT
SPTO
STOP
STPO
TOPS
TOSP
TPOS
TPSO
TSOP
TSPO


TIME:  0.11 SECS.
```

Fig. 5.4

5.4 DEFINING ARRAYS—THE DIM STATEMENT

BASIC automatically assigns 11 elements to every list and 121 elements (11 rows and 11 columns) to every table appearing in a program. Thus each subscript is allowed to range from 0 to 10. Of course we need not make use of all these array elements—a subscript can begin with some integer value greater than zero and end with an integer less than 10. (In Example 5.9, for instance, the subscript ranged only from 1 to 4.)

We can also make use of larger arrays if we wish. To do so, however, we must *define* the size of each array, i.e., we must specify the maximum number of elements in each array. This is accomplished by means of the *DIM (DIMENSION) statement.*

The DIM statement consists of a statement number, followed by the keyword DIM, followed by one or more array names separated by commas. Each array name must be followed by one or two integer constants (one for a list, two for a table) enclosed in parentheses and, if two integers are shown, separated by a comma. These integers indicate the maximum value of each subscript that is permitted in an array.

EXAMPLE 5.10

A program is to contain a numeric table called A, two numeric lists called B and C and a string list called F$. The table is to have 50 rows and 100 columns, B and C will have 100 elements and 50 elements respectively, and F$ will contain 65 elements. Hence the program may contain the following DIM statement.

```
20 DIM  A(50,100), B(100), C(50), F$(65)
```

This statement actually reserves 51 rows and 101 columns for A, 101 elements for B, 51 elements for C and 66 elements for F$. Thus the arrays are slightly larger than necessary. However, many programmers prefer to have a subscript begin with a value of 1 rather than 0, as though they were working with a subscripted algebraic variable. Under these circumstances it is easiest to write the DIM statement as shown above.

A DIM statement can appear anywhere in a BASIC program. However, it is good programming practice to place the DIM statement at the beginning of a program where its presence will be readily apparent. This allows a programmer or user to determine maximum array sizes easily and quickly.

Lists having fewer than 11 elements and tables having fewer than 121 elements can also be included in a DIM statement, even though it may not be necessary to do so. This will cause fewer words of storage to be reserved in the computer's memory. Some care is required with tables, however, because one of the subscripts may exceed a value of 10 even though the total number of elements is less than 121. When this happens a DIM statement *must* be used. We will see such a situation in the next example.

EXAMPLE 5.11

A program contains the following DIM statement.

```
30 DIM  P(6), Q(10), R(5,15)
```

This results in 7 words of storage being reserved for the 7 elements of P, 11 words for Q and 96 words (6 rows, 16 columns) for the table R.

The inclusion of P and Q in the DIM statement was really not necessary, since adequate storage would have been assigned automatically. Note, however, that by including P in the DIM statement we have saved 4 words of storage. On the other hand, the table R *must* be included in the DIM statement since the second subscript exceeds 10. This is true despite the fact that the total number of words required by R is less than 121.

We will see an example of a complete program requiring the presence of a DIM statement later in this chapter.

5.5 ENTERING INPUT DATA—THE READ AND DATA STATEMENTS

Many BASIC programs require that a large number of data items be entered into the computer. This can be accomplished with the INPUT statement, though it may be somewhat cumbersome to do so. Usually it is more convenient to enter such data by means of the *READ* and *DATA statements.* These statements are also used to enter data when a program is run in the batch rather than the timesharing mode.

The READ statement specifies the variables whose values are to be entered into the computer. This statement consists of a statement number, followed by the keyword READ, followed by a list of input variables. The list can contain both ordinary and subscripted variables, representing numeric and/or string values. If the list contains two or more variables, they must be separated by commas.

The purpose of the DATA statement is to assign appropriate values to the variables listed in the READ statement. The DATA statement comprises a statement number, followed by the keyword DATA, followed by a set of numbers and/or strings separated by commas. Each number and/or string in a DATA statement must correspond to a variable of the same type in a READ statement.

EXAMPLE 5.12

A BASIC program contains the statements

```
30 READ K,N$,Z(1)
  . . .
120 DATA 12,SEVENTEEN,-5
```

These statements cause the number 12 to be assigned to the variable K, the string SEVENTEEN to be assigned to N$, and −5 to be assigned to Z(1).

Each DATA statement need not correspond to a particular READ statement, although such one-to-one correspondence is permitted if desired (as we have seen in the last example). The important point is that *all* of the DATA statements in a program collectively form a *block* of data values. Each element in the data block must correspond to a variable in a READ statement. This correspondence must be with respect to both order and type.

EXAMPLE 5.13

The following statements are included in a BASIC program.

```
40 READ A,B,C
50 READ P$,Q$
60 READ F(1),F(2),F(3)
  . . .
210 DATA 3,-2,11,AB
220 DATA CD,-8,0,10
```

These statements cause the numbers 3, −2 and 11 to be assigned to A, B and C, the strings AB and CD to be assigned to P$ and Q$ and the numbers −8, 0, 10 to be assigned to the subscripted variables F(1), F(2) and F(3). Notice that the READ statements do not correspond to the DATA statements on a one-to-one basis, but the variables in the three READ statements do correspond, in order and in type, to the elements in the data block.

The two DATA statements could just as well be combined, yielding the single statement

```
210 DATA 3,-2,11,AB,CD,-8,0,10
```

The results would be the same as above.

It should be pointed out that data specified via READ-DATA statements are a part of the program, in contrast to data entered via INPUT statements. Therefore the data contained in a data block are stored whenever the program is stored and are assigned to the appropriate set of variables whenever the program is executed. Hence such data are relatively permanent; they can be changed only by altering one or more DATA statements within the program.

The following rules must be observed when placing data items in a data block.

1. The data items must correspond in order and in type to the variables listed in the READ statements. There must be at least as many elements in the data block as there are variables in the READ statements. Extra data items will be ignored.
2. The data items within a DATA statement must be separated by commas. However, the last data item in a DATA statement should not be followed by a comma.
3. The data items must consist of numbers or strings. Variables and formulas are not permitted.
4. Strings containing commas or beginning with blank spaces must be enclosed in quotation marks. Other strings *may* be enclosed in quotation marks if desired.

DATA statements may appear anywhere in a BASIC program. However, it is good programming practice to place all DATA statements consecutively near the end of the program. Thus the location and composition of the data block will be readily apparent.

The following example illustrates the assignment of numeric data values to a set of subscripted variables and the manipulation of those subscripted variables. Use of the DIM statement is also demonstrated.

EXAMPLE 5.14 Reordering a List of Numbers

Consider the well-known problem of rearranging a list of N numbers into a sequence of increasing magnitudes. The program is to be written in such a manner that unnecessary storage will not be used. Therefore the program will contain only one array, which will be rearranged one element at a time.

Computational Procedure

The procedure will be first to scan the entire list for the smallest number and interchange this number with the first number in the list. Next the remaining N−1 numbers are scanned for the smallest of these numbers, and this smallest number is interchanged with the second number. Then the last N−2 numbers are scanned for the smallest numbers, which is interchanged with the third number, and so on, until the entire list has been rearranged. This will require a total of N−1 passes through the list, though the list will decrease by one number for each subsequent scan.

In order to find the smallest number for each pass, we sequentially compare each number in the list with the starting number (the ith number). If the ith number is larger than, say, the jth number, then we interchange the two numbers; otherwise we leave the two numbers in their original positions. Once this procedure has been applied to the entire list, the first number in the list will be the smallest. We then repeat the entire procedure N−2 times, for a total of N−1 passes ($i = 1, 2, \ldots, N-1$).

The only remaining question is how the ith number and the jth number are interchanged. We first "set aside" the ith number for future reference; that is, we save the original value of the ith subscripted variable. Then we assign the value of the jth subscripted variable to the ith subscripted variable. Finally we assign the *original* value of the ith subscripted variable, which had been set aside, to the jth subscripted variable. The interchange is now complete.

The Program Outline

The entire computational procedure can be carried out with a double FOR-TO loop. To see how this is accomplished, consider the following outline:

1. Read in the size of the list (N).
2. Read in and then print out the list of N integer constants.
3. Perform the following calculations N−1 times, letting $i = 1, 2, \ldots, N-1$: Compare the ith number, which will be the starting number in the list, with each successive number (each jth number, where $j = i+1, i+2, \ldots, N$). Whenever the ith number is larger than the jth number, interchange the two numbers.

4. Print out the rearranged list of numbers.
5. Stop.

A flowchart of the procedure is shown in Fig. 5.5.

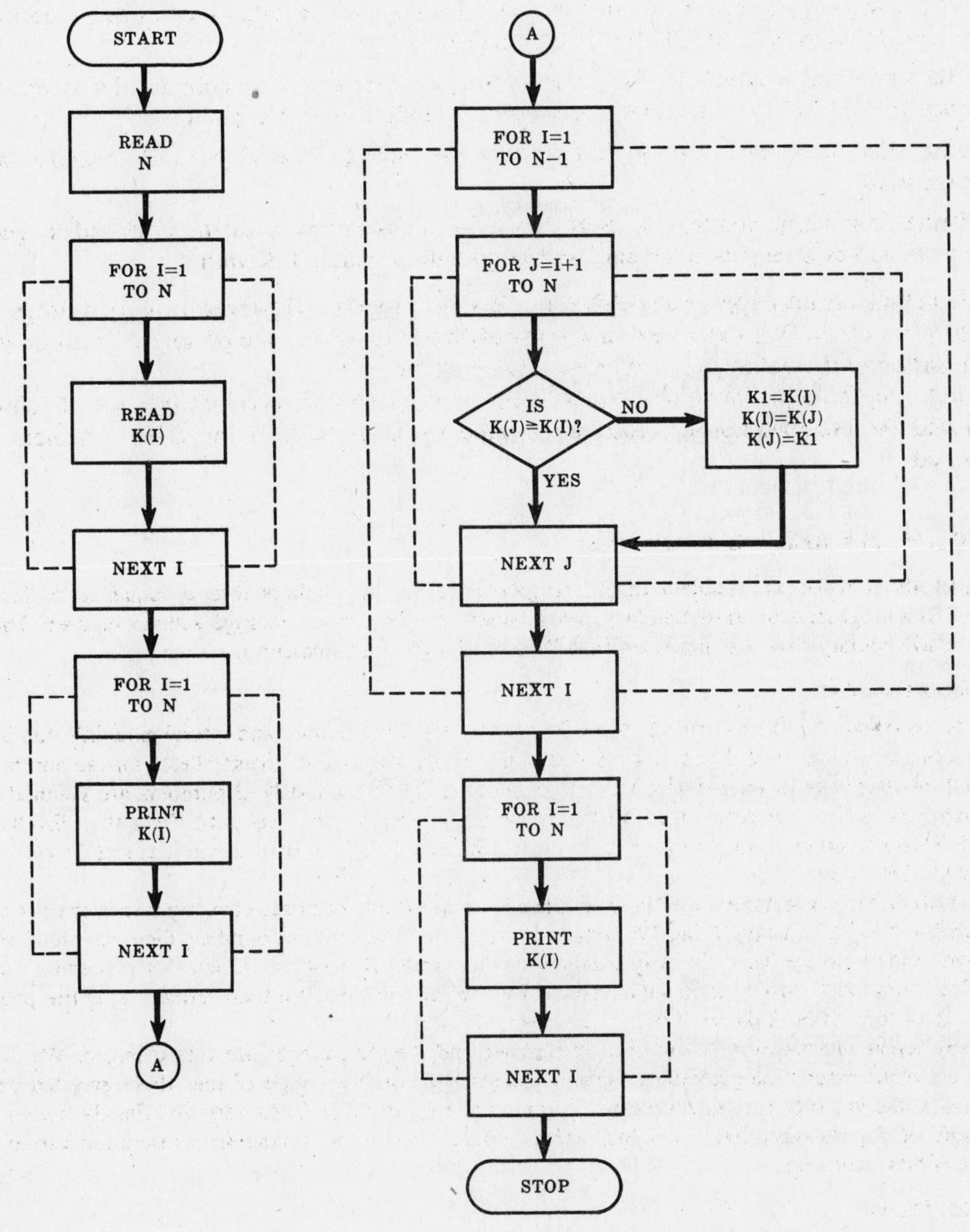

Fig. 5.5

The BASIC Program

When writing the actual BASIC program, let us refer to the list of integer constants as K. We will assume that K will never consist of more than 101 elements. Hence we will set the maximum permissible value of the subscript at 100.

The BASIC program is shown in Fig. 5.6. Notice the DIM statement near the start of the program (line 20), which establishes that K can contain as many as 101 elements. Observe also the use of FOR-TO loops in order to read in and print out the elements of K (e.g., see lines 40–60, 90–110 and 330–350).

```
10 REM PROGRAM TO REARRANGE A LIST OF NUMBERS INTO ASCENDING ORDER
20 DIM K(100)
30 READ N
40 FOR I=1 TO N
50    READ K(I)
60 NEXT I
70 PRINT "ORIGINAL LIST OF NUMBERS:"
80 PRINT
90 FOR I=1 TO N
100    PRINT K(I);
110 NEXT I
120 PRINT
130
140 REM          REPEAT INTERCHANGE N-1 TIMES
150
160 FOR I=1 TO N-1
170
180    REM       FIND SMALLEST NUMBER IN LIST AND INTERCHANGE
190
200    FOR J=I+1 TO N
210       IF K(J)>=K(I) THEN 280
220
230       REM   INTERCHANGE K(J) AND K(I)
240
250       LET K1=K(I)
260       LET K(I)=K(J)
270       LET K(J)=K1
280    NEXT J
290 NEXT I
300 PRINT
310 PRINT "REORDERED LIST OF NUMBERS:"
320 PRINT
330 FOR I=1 TO N
340    PRINT K(I);
350 NEXT I
360 DATA 20,595,78,1505,891,29,7,18,191,36,68,7051,509,212,46,726,1806
370 DATA 289,401,1488,710
380 END
>RUN

EX5.14        09:32          15-MAR

ORIGINAL LIST OF NUMBERS:

 595  78  1505  891  29  7  18  191  36  68  7051  509  212  46  726
 1806  289  401  1488  710

REORDERED LIST OF NUMBERS:

 7  18  29  36  46  68  78  191  212  289  401  509  595  710  726
 891  1488  1505  1806  7051

TIME:  0.09 SECS.
```

Fig. 5.6

The actual rearrangement is carried out with a double FOR-TO loop, as described above (lines 140–290). Three REM statements are included in the sequence. These statements help to clarify the logic of the double FOR-TO loop.

Finally, note that two DATA statements, containing 21 data values, are included near the end of the program (lines 360 and 370). The first of these (the constant 20) is the value for N, which indicates that 20 elements of K will be utilized in this particular example. Following are the 20 values of K, in their original order [i.e., K(1)=595, K(2)=78, K(3)=1505, . . . , K(20)=710].

At the bottom of Fig. 5.6 is the output generated by this particular example. We see the original list of numbers at the top of the output, followed by the list of rearranged numbers immediately thereafter.

The elements of a table are manipulated in much the same manner as the elements of a list. Double FOR-TO loops are frequently required for table input/output operations and for manipulation of the table elements. We will see an illustration of this in the next example.

EXAMPLE 5.15 Table Manipulation

Consider the table of numbers shown in Table 5.2. Suppose we wish to sum all the elements in each row of the table, as well as all the elements in each column. Let us write a BASIC program which will allow us to carry out these elementary calculations.

Table 5.2

6	0	−12	4	17	21
−8	15	5	5	−18	0
11	3	1	−17	12	7
13	2	13	−9	24	4
−27	−3	0	14	8	−10

The Program Outline

The computation will proceed in accordance with the following outline.

1. Read the values for the number of rows (M) and the number of columns (N).
2. Read the elements of the table (T) on a row-by-row basis by proceeding as follows for each value of I (the row counter) ranging from 1 to M: For a given value of I, let J (the column counter) range from 1 to N. Read a value of T(I,J) for each value of I and J.
3. Print the elements of T on a row-by-row basis. Hence for each value of I ranging from 1 to M, proceed as follows: For a given value of I, let J range from 1 to N. Print the value of T(I,J) for each value of I and J.
4. Calculate and print the sum of the elements in each row and the sum of all individual row sums (i.e., the cumulative sum for all rows) as follows.
   (*a*) Set the initial value of the cumulative sum (S1) equal to zero.
   (*b*) Do the following for each value of I ranging from 1 to M.
      (i) Set the initial value of the row sum, S(I), equal to zero.
      (ii) For each value of J ranging from 1 to N, add T(I,J) to S(I), i.e., let

      S(I)=S(I)+T(I,J)

      (iii) Print the current value for I and the corresponding value for S(I).
      (iv) Add the value of S(I) to S1, i.e., let

      S1=S1+S(I)

   (*c*) Print the final value for S1 (i.e., the cumulative sum of all previously calculated row sums).
5. Calculate and print the sum of the elements in each column, and the sum of all individual column sums (i.e., the cumulative sum for all columns) as follows.
   (*a*) Set the initial value of the cumulative sum (S1) equal to zero.
   (*b*) Do the following for each value of J ranging from 1 to N.
      (i) Set the initial value of the column sum, S(J), equal to zero.
      (ii) For each value of I ranging from 1 to M, add T(I,J) to S(J), i.e., let

      S(J)=S(J)+T(I,J)

      (iii) Print the current value for J and the corresponding value for S(J).
      (iv) Add the value for S(J) to S1, i.e., let

      S1=S1+S(J)

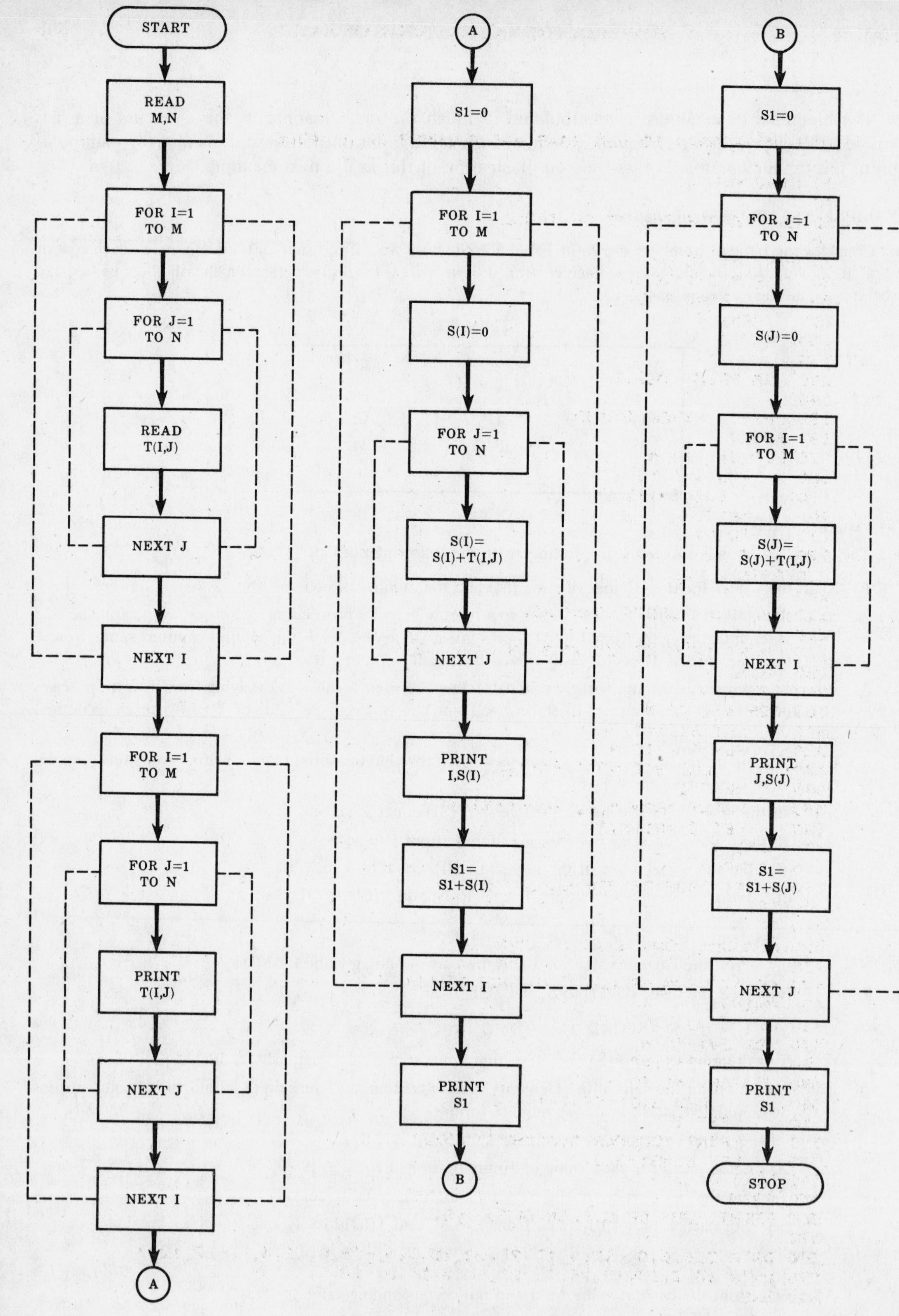
START
READ M,N
FOR I=1 TO M
FOR J=1 TO N
READ T(I,J)
NEXT J
NEXT I
FOR I=1 TO M
FOR J=1 TO N
PRINT T(I,J)
NEXT J
NEXT I
A
A
S1=0
FOR I=1 TO M
S(I)=0
FOR J=1 TO N
S(I)= S(I)+T(I,J)
NEXT J
PRINT I,S(I)
S1= S1+S(I)
NEXT I
PRINT S1
B
B
S1=0
FOR J=1 TO N
S(J)=0
FOR I=1 TO M
S(J)= S(J)+T(I,J)
NEXT I
PRINT J,S(J)
S1= S1+S(J)
NEXT J
PRINT S1
STOP

Fig. 5.7

```
10 REM PROGRAM TO SUM ROWS AND COLUMNS OF A TABLE
20
30 READ M,N
40 '
50 REM READ ELEMENTS OF TABLE
60
70 FOR I=1 TO M
80    FOR J=1 TO N
90       READ T(I,J)
100    NEXT J
110 NEXT I
120
130 REM PRINT TABLE
140
150 PRINT "GIVEN TABLE:"
160 PRINT
170 FOR I=1 TO M
180    FOR J=1 TO N
190       PRINT T(I,J);
200    NEXT J
210    PRINT
220 NEXT I
230 PRINT
240
250 REM SUM ACROSS EACH ROW
260
270 PRINT "SUM OF COLUMNS IN EACH ROW:"
280 PRINT
290 LET S1=0
300 FOR I=1 TO M
310    LET S(I)=0
320    FOR J=1 TO N
330       LET S(I)=S(I)+T(I,J)
340    NEXT J
350    PRINT "ROW ";I,"SUM=";S(I)
360    LET S1=S1+S(I)
370 NEXT I
380 PRINT
390 PRINT "SUM OF ROW SUMS=";S1
400 PRINT
410
420 REM SUM DOWN EACH COLUMN
430
440 PRINT "SUM OF ROWS IN EACH COLUMN:"
450 PRINT
460 LET S1=0
470 FOR J=1 TO N
480    LET S(J)=0
490    FOR I=1 TO M
500       LET S(J)=S(J)+T(I,J)
510    NEXT I
520    PRINT "COLUMN ";J,"SUM=";S(J)
530    LET S1=S1+S(J)
540 NEXT J
550 PRINT
560 PRINT "SUM OF COLUMN SUMS=";S1
570
580 DATA 5,6,6,0,-12,4,17,21,-8,15,5,5,-18,0,11,3,1,-17,12,7
590 DATA 13,2,13,-9,24,4,-27,-3,0,14,8,-10
600 END
```

Fig. 5.8

(c) Print the final value for S1 (i.e., the cumulative sum of all previously calculated column sums). Note that the cumulative column sum should equal the cumulative row sum; hence this value of S1 should equal the value printed in step 4. This serves as a check.

6. Stop.

Figure 5.7 contains a flowchart that corresponds to the above outline.

The BASIC Program

Figure 5.8 presents a complete BASIC program for this problem. Notice the nested FOR-TO loops that are used to read and print the elements of the table (see lines 70–110 and 170–220). Double FOR-TO loops are also used to form the row sums (lines 290–370) and the column sums (lines 460–540).

The DATA statements at the bottom of the program (lines 580 and 590) establish a data block having 32 elements. The first two numbers are the values for M and N, which indicate that this particular table will have five rows and six columns. The remaining 30 numbers are the values for the elements of T, on a row-by-row basis (thus requiring the second subscript, J, to increase most rapidly when reading the data).

We see that a DIM statement is not included in this program, since none of the subscripts take on values exceeding 10. If the array sizes were to be increased, then a DIM statement would, of course, be necessary. Finally, note that the program contains a number of REM statements and blank lines, which increase its readability and provide some indication of program logic.

In Fig. 5.9 we see the output which is generated for this example. The given table is printed first, followed by the sum of the columns (elements) for each row and the cumulative sum of the row sums. Following these values are the individual column sums and the cumulative column sum. Notice that the cumulative row sum equals the cumulative column sum (81), as expected.

```
GIVEN TABLE:

  6   0 -12   4  17  21
 -8  15   5   5 -18   0
 11   3   1 -17  12   7
 13   2  13  -9  24   4
-27  -3   0  14   8 -10

SUM OF COLUMNS IN EACH ROW:

ROW   1        SUM= 36
ROW   2        SUM=-1
ROW   3        SUM= 17
ROW   4        SUM= 47
ROW   5        SUM=-18


SUM OF ROW SUMS= 81


SUM OF ROWS IN EACH COLUMN:

COLUMN   1     SUM=-5
COLUMN   2     SUM= 17
COLUMN   3     SUM= 7
COLUMN   4     SUM=-3
COLUMN   5     SUM= 43
COLUMN   6     SUM= 22


SUM OF COLUMN SUMS= 81
```

Fig. 5.9

5.6 REREADING DATA—THE RESTORE STATEMENT

In the last section we saw that a correspondence is always maintained between the variables whose values are to be read (i.e., the variables listed in the READ statements) and the individual data items in a data block (the numbers and strings in the DATA statements). This is accomplished by means of an internal "pointer" which indicates the next data item to be read. In fact, two pointers are maintained if the data block contains both numeric and string data—one for the numeric constants, the other for the strings. Each time a data item is read the pointer is automatically advanced to the next data item of the same type.

There are certain kinds of problems that require some, perhaps all, of the data to be read more than once. To do this we must reset one or both pointers to the start of the data block. The *RESTORE statement* is used for this purpose.

The RESTORE statement consists of a statement number followed by the keyword RESTORE. The appearance of this statement causes each pointer to be reset to the first data item of the proper type within the data block.

EXAMPLE 5.16

A BASIC program contains the statements

```
30 READ A,B,C
   . . .
60 RESTORE
70 READ W,X,Y,Z
   . . .
200 DATA 1,3,5,7,9,11,13
```

Statement number 30 causes the variable A to be assigned a value of 1, B a value of 3 and C a value of 5. When statement number 60 is encountered, the pointer is reset to the first number in the data block. Hence statement number 70 causes the variable W to be assigned a value of 1, X a value of 3, Y a value of 5 and Z a value of 7. If the RESTORE statement were not present, then W would be assigned a value of 7, X a value of 9, and so on.

Notice that we have been concerned with only one pointer in this example since the data block contains only numeric constants.

Some versions of BASIC permit the keyword RESTORE to be followed by an asterisk (*) or a dollar sign ($). If an asterisk is present then only the numeric pointer will be reset, whereas only the string pointer will be reset if the dollar sign is shown. Both an asterisk and a dollar sign are, however, not permitted in the same statement.

EXAMPLE 5.17

A BASIC program contains the statements

```
50 READ A,B,M$,N$
   . . .
150 RESTORE*
160 READ C1,C2,F1$,F2$
   . . .
250 DATA 2,4,RED,GREEN,6,8,BLUE,WHITE
```

Statement number 50 causes the variables A and B to be assigned the values 2 and 4, and the variables M$ and N$ will be assigned the strings RED and GREEN. The numeric pointer is reset by statement number 150. Hence statement 160 causes C1 and C2 to be assigned the values 2 and 4, whereas F1$ and F2$ will represent the strings BLUE and WHITE.

If statement number 150 were changed to

```
150 RESTORE$
```

then the string pointer would be reset rather than the numeric pointer. Therefore C1 and C2 would be assigned the values 6 and 8, but the strings RED and GREEN would be assigned to F1$ and F2$, respectively.

Now suppose that statement 150 were changed to

```
150 RESTORE
```

Then both pointers would be reset, resulting in C1=2, C2=4, F1$=RED and F2$=GREEN. Finally, if statement number 150 were deleted entirely, then statement 160 would result in C1=6, C2=8, F1$=BLUE and F2$=WHITE.

It should be clear that the values assigned to A, B, M$ and N$ will be unaffected by the subsequent RESTORE and READ statements in this example.

5.7 CLOSING REMARKS

With this chapter we conclude our discussion of the elementary features of BASIC. We have seen that use of the library functions allows the programmer to carry out certain programming operations (e.g., truncation, spacing of output data, etc.) as well as the more common mathematical operations. Collections of numbers and strings can be stored and manipulated by using lists and tables, and large quantities of data can be conveniently stored and assigned to program variables or array elements through the use of the READ and DATA statements. These features simplify the programming of a great many different problem situations.

Review Questions

5.1 What are library functions? What useful purpose do they serve?

5.2 What other names are sometimes used for library functions?

5.3 Name several of the more common library functions. State the purpose of each library function.

5.4 What is meant by an argument? Do all library functions require arguments?

5.5 How is a library function used in a BASIC program?

5.6 What happens if a negative value is supplied to a library function that requires a positive argument?

5.7 What is meant by truncation? Present an example illustrating truncation.

5.8 What is the purpose of the INT function? What happens when the INT function receives a positive argument? A negative argument?

5.9 What is the purpose of the TAB function? In which statement is it used?

5.10 Can a formula be used as a library function argument? Can a reference to another library function be used for this purpose?

5.11 What happens if a library function requiring an integer argument is supplied with an argument having a noninteger value?

5.12 What is meant by a list? A table?

5.13 What is meant by a one-dimensional array? A two-dimensional array? Compare your answer with the answer to the previous question.

5.14 What is meant by the elements of a list or table? What do these elements represent?

5.15 Can a single array contain both numbers and strings?

5.16 What is a subscripted variable? How do we refer to a particular subscripted variable?

5.17 Can a formula be used as a subscript? Can a reference to a library function be used for this purpose?

5.18 What restriction applies to the values that a subscript can take on?

5.19 What is the purpose of a DIM statement? When *must* this statement appear in a BASIC program?

5.20 Summarize the rules for writing a DIM statement.

5.21 Can a formula or a reference to a library function appear in a DIM statement?

5.22 Is there any purpose in specifying the size of a *small* array in a DIM statement? Explain.

5.23 What is the purpose of the READ and DATA statements?

5.24 Summarize the rules for writing a READ statement.

5.25 Summarize the rules for writing a DATA statement.

5.26 Does each READ statement require its own data statement? Explain.

5.27 What is meant by a data block? How is a data block formed?

5.28 Are data entered via an INPUT statement as permanent as data entered via READ-DATA statements? Explain.

5.29 Summarize the rules that must be observed when placing data items in a data block.

5.30 Where are DATA statements usually placed in a BASIC program? Why?

5.31 How are list and table input/output operations usually carried out in BASIC?

5.32 Discuss the purpose and use of pointers in connection with a data block.

5.33 What is the purpose of the RESTORE statement? Cite three different ways that this statement can be written.

Solved Problems

5.34 Write a BASIC statement that corresponds to each of the following algebraic equations.

(*a*) $z = \tan t$

```
10 LET Z=TAN(T)
```

(*b*) $w = \log_e (v)$

```
10 LET W=LOG(V)
```

(*c*) $y = ae^{bx} \sin cx$

```
10 LET Y=A*EXP(B*X)*SIN(C*X)
```

(*d*) $x_1 = \dfrac{-b + \sqrt{b^2 - 4ac}}{2a}$

```
10 LET X1=(-B+SQR(B↑2-4*A*C))/(2*A)
```

5.35 Write a BASIC statement for each of the following situations.

(*a*) Determine the absolute value of the difference between the variables U and V. Assign this value to the variable W.

```
10 LET W=ABS(U-V)
```

(*b*) Determine the sign of x. If x is negative, go to statement 50; if x equals zero, go to statement 20; and if x is positive, go to statement 170.

```
100 ON SGN(X)+2 GO TO 50,20,170
```

(*c*) Determine the largest integer which algebraically does not exceed z, where $z = x^2 - y^2$. Assign this integer to the variable I.

```
10 LET I=INT(X↑2-Y↑2)
```

(*d*) In (*c*) above, if $x = 2.5$ and $y = 6.3$, what value will be assigned to the variable I?

$x^2 - y^2 = -33.44$, hence $I = -34$.

(*e*) Print the values of X$, X, Y$ and Y on one line. Let the string represented by X$ begin in the 10th column, followed immediately by the value of X. Similarly, let Y$ begin in the 46th column, followed immediately by Y.

```
100 PRINT TAB(9);X$;X;TAB(45);Y$;Y
```

5.36 Each example below shows a reference to one or more subscripted variables. Describe the type of array referred to in each case.

(*a*) 10 DIM C1(100),N$(100,3)

C1 is a numeric list; N$ is a string table.

(*b*) 50 LET P(I)=P(I)+Q(I,J)

P is a numeric list; Q is a numeric table.

(*c*) 100 IF A$(5)=G$ THEN 220

A$ is a string list.

(*d*) 150 ON X(K(I),J(I)) GO TO 100,20,180,20,250

X is a numeric table; K and J are numeric lists.

(*e*) 200 PRINT X$(K),N1(K),N2(K)

X$ is a string list; N1 and N2 are numeric lists.

5.37 Write one or more statements to carry out each of the following operations.

(*a*) Sum the first 100 elements of the numeric list T.

```
10 LET S=0
20 FOR I=0 TO 99
30      LET S=S+T(I)
40 NEXT I
```

(*b*) Print the even elements of the numeric list T for values of the subscript ranging from 0 to 100, i.e., print T(0), T(2), T(4), . . . , T(100).

```
10 FOR I=0 TO 100 STEP 2
20      PRINT T(I):
30 NEXT I
```

(*c*) Calculate the sum of all elements of the numeric table P. Let M indicate the number of rows and N the number of columns.

```
10 LET S=0
20 FOR I=1 TO M
30      FOR J=1 TO N
40           LET S=S+P(I,J)
50      NEXT J
60 NEXT I
```

(*d*) Print the elements in the third column of the string table K$. Display the output in columnar form, beginning in column number 12 (the column number here refers to the location on the console).

```
10 FOR I=1 TO M
20      PRINT TAB(12);K$(I,3)
30 NEXT I
```

5.38 Write appropriate READ and DATA statements for each situation described below.

(*a*) Assign the values −1.6E−6, −500, .4077, MAY, OCTOBER, 100, 110, 120, 130, 140 and 150 to the variables C1, C2, C3, X$, Y$, Z(1), Z(2), Z(3), Z(4), Z(5), and Z(6). List each subscripted variable separately in the READ statement.

```
10 READ C1,C2,C3,X$,Y$,Z(1),Z(2),Z(3),Z(4),Z(5),Z(6)
   ...
200 DATA -1.6E-6,-500,.4077,MAY,OCTOBER,100,110,120,130,140,150
```

The READ and DATA statements can also be broken up if desired, e.g.,

```
10 READ C1,C2,C3,X$,Y$
20 READ Z(1),Z(2),Z(3),Z(4),Z(5),Z(6)
   ...
200 DATA -1.6E-6,-500,.4077
210 DATA MAY,OCTOBER,100,110
220 DATA 120,130,140,150
```

(*b*) Assign the values given in part (*a*) above to their respective variables. Use a FOR-TO loop for the array elements.

```
10 READ C1,C2,C3,X$,Y$
20 FOR I=1 TO 6
30     READ Z(I)
40 NEXT I
   ...
200 DATA -1.6E-6,-500,.4077,MAY,OCTOBER
210 DATA 100,110,120,130,140,150
```

(*c*) Assign the values given in part (*a*) above to their respective variables, as in part (*b*). At a later point in the program, reset the string pointer and assign the strings MAY and OCTOBER to the variables F$ and G$.

```
10 READ C1,C2,C3,X$,Y$
20 FOR I=1 TO 6
30     READ Z(I)
40 NEXT I
   ...
100 RESTORE$
110 READ F$,G$
   ...
200 DATA -1.6E-6,-500,.4077,MAY,OCTOBER
210 DATA 100,110,120,130,140,150
```

Supplementary Problems

5.39 Find out which library functions are available at your particular installation. (Refer to the BASIC reference manual published by the manufacturer of your computer.) Specify the purpose of each library function. Determine exactly how each function is referenced.

5.40 Write a BASIC statement that corresponds to each of the following algebraic equations.

(*a*) $y = \sqrt{\sin x - \cos x}$

(*b*) $p = qe^{-qt}$

(*c*) $c = \log_e \sqrt{|a + b|} + \log_e \sqrt{|a - b|}$

(*d*) $w = \| u - v| - |u + v \|$

(*e*) $z = \cos(x + \arctan y)$

5.41 Write a BASIC statement for each of the following situations.

(*a*) Determine the sign of the quantity $(ab - cd)/(f + g)$. Go to statement number 75 if the quantity is positive, to statement 260 if the quantity is zero, and to statement 135 if the quantity is negative.

(*b*) Print the following on one line of the console: "X=", followed by the value of the variable X; "Y=", followed by the value of Y; and "Z=", followed by the value of Z. Begin printing in columns 4, 28 and 52, respectively.

(*c*) Determine if the value of the variable N is even or odd, assuming that N has a positive integer value. (*Hint*: Compare the value of N/2 with the truncated value of N/2.)

(*d*) In part (*c*) above, what will happen if N has a negative integer value?

5.42 Each example below shows a reference to one or more subscripted variables. Describe the type of array referred to in each case.

(*a*) 75 LET N$(3)="ERROR-CHECK"

(*b*) 20 DIM A(12,25),A$(12,25),B(12),C$(25)

(*c*) 100 PRINT P$(I),P(I,J)

(*d*) 50 IF Z(J1,J2)<10 THEN 185

5.43 Shown below are several BASIC statements and sequences of statements containing subscripted variables. Some of the examples are written incorrectly. Identify all errors.

(*a*) 50 LET C(I,J)=(3*X↑2−2*Y↑3)/(17*Z)

(*b*) 75 LET P(K,5)=Q(K+1,J)+R(K,J+1)

(*c*) 20 INPUT M,N
30 DIM A(M,N),X(N),Y(M)

(*d*) 10 DIM K(100),W(10,20),C1,C2,K(100)

(*e*) 150 LET S=S+T(K,−3)

(*f*) 200 LET X(K(I))=Y(K(I+1))+Z(K(I−1))

5.44 Write one or more statements to carry out each of the following operations.

(*a*) Calculate the square root of the sum of the squares of the first 100 odd elements of the numeric list X, i.e., calculate $[X(1)^2+X(3)^2+X(5)^2+\cdots+X(199)^2]^{1/2}$.

(*b*) Calculate the elements of the numeric table H which has 8 rows and 12 columns. Each element of H is determined by the formula

$$h_{ij} = \frac{1}{i+j-1}$$

(*c*) A numeric list K has N elements. Print the value of each subscript and each corresponding element for those elements whose value does not exceed 15. Display the output in two columns, with the value of the subscript in the first column and the corresponding subscripted variable in the second column. Label each column. Start the first column of output in column number 8 (the column number here refers to the location on the console) and the second column of output in column number 44.

(*d*) A numeric table W has K rows and K columns. Calculate the product of the terms on the main diagonal of W, where the main diagonal runs from upper left to lower right, i.e., calculate W(1,1)*W(2,2)*W(3,3)* . . . *W(K,K).

(*e*) Print the elements in the fourth column of the string table M$. Display the output in columnar form, beginning in column number 10 (the column number here refers to the location on the console). Assume that M$ contains M rows.

(*f*) Repeat problem (*e*) above, displaying the output in row form with one blank space between each element.

(*g*) Print the elements in the fifth row of the string table M$. Display the output in row form with one blank space between each element. Assume that M$ contains N columns.

5.45 Write appropriate READ and DATA statements for each situation described below.

(*a*) The following values are to be assigned to the list L$, the variables P,Q,R and H$, and the table T.

L$(1)=WHITE	P=2.25E+5	T(1,1)=1	T(2,1)=−2
L$(2)=YELLOW	Q=6.08E−9	T(1,2)=−3	T(2,2)=4
L$(3)=ORANGE	R=−1.29E+12	T(1,3)=5	T(2,3)=−6
L$(4)=RED	H$=RESTART	T(1,4)=−7	T(2,4)=8

List each subscripted variable separately in the READ statements.

(*b*) Repeat part (*a*) above, using FOR-TO loops for the array elements.

(*c*) Repeat part (*a*) above, using FOR-TO loops for the array elements, as in part (*b*). At a later point in the program, reset the numeric pointer and assign the values 2.25E+5, 6.08E−9 and −1.29E+12 to the variables P1, Q1 and R1.

(*d*) Repeat part (*a*) above, using FOR-TO loops for the array elements, as in part (*b*). At a later point in the program, reset the pointer and assign the strings WHITE, YELLOW, ORANGE and RED to the variables A1$, A2$, A3$ and A4$.

Programming Problems

5.46 Alter the program shown in Example 5.5 so that the logarithm is not calculated when x has a value of zero. Include a provision for printing eight successive asterisks for the log of zero, thus indicating an overflow condition.

5.47 Write a BASIC program similar to the one in Example 5.5 that will generate a table of x, $\sin^2 x$, $\cos^2 x$, $\tan^2 x$, $\text{cotan}^2\, x$, $\sec^2 x$ and $\text{cosec}^2\, x$. (Note that $\sec x = 1/\cos x$, and $\text{cosec}\, x = 1/\sin x$.) Generate 101 entries for evenly spaced values of x between 0 and π. (That is, let $x = 0, \pi/100, 2\pi/100, \ldots, 99\pi/100, \pi$.) Be sure that the output is adequately labeled.

5.48 Write a BASIC program which will produce a table of values of the equation

$$y = 2e^{-0.1t} \sin 0.5\, t$$

where t varies between 0 and 60. Allow the size of the t increment to be entered as an input parameter.

5.49 Extend the word unscrambler program in Example 5.9 so that it prints out all possible two-letter, three-letter and four-letter combinations of any given four letters. Select a set of four letters and execute the program. Identify all valid English words by inspecting the output visually. Can you determine, without running the program, how many different combinations of two or more letters will be generated?

5.50 Extend the program in Example 5.14 so that a list of numbers can be rearranged in any one of the following four ways.

(*a*) Smallest to largest, algebraically (that is, largest negative to largest positive values)

(*b*) Smallest to largest in magnitude (ignoring signs)

(*c*) Largest to smallest, algebraically

(*d*) Largest to smallest in magnitude

(Note that the elements of the list need not necessarily have positive values.)

Write the program in such a manner that only one rearrangement is carried out each time the program is executed. Include in the program a variable whose value is entered via an INPUT statement each time the program is executed. Let the particular rearrangement of the list of numbers be determined by the value assigned to this variable (e.g., if A=1 then rearrange from smallest to largest, algebraically; if A=2 rearrange from smallest to largest in magnitude; etc.).

Use the program to rearrange the numbers given in Table 5.3. Rearrange the numbers all four ways.

Table 5.3

43	−85	−4	65
−83	10	−71	−59
61	−51	−45	−32
14	49	19	23
−94	−34	−50	86

5.51 Write a BASIC program that will rearrange a list of words into alphabetical order. To do so, enter the words in a list, with each element representing one complete word. The list of words can then be alphabetized in the same manner that a list of numbers is rearranged from smallest to largest (see Example 5.14).

Use the program to rearrange the names given in Table 5.4. Be careful with the first initials.

Table 5.4

Washington	Arthur
Adams, J.	Cleveland
Jefferson	Harrison, B.
Madison	McKinley
Monroe	Roosevelt, T.
Adams, J. Q.	Taft
Jackson	Wilson
Van Buren	Harding
Harrison, W. H.	Coolidge
Tyler	Hoover
Polk	Roosevelt, F. D.
Taylor	Truman
Fillmore	Eisenhower
Pierce	Kennedy
Buchanan	Johnson, L. B.
Lincoln	Nixon
Johnson, A.	Ford
Grant	Carter
Hayes	Reagan
Garfield	

5.52 Rewrite the BASIC program in Example 5.15 so that the *product* of the elements in each row and each column will be calculated.

5.53 Write a BASIC program that will generate a table of compound interest factors, F/P, where

$$F/P = [1 + (i/100)]^n$$

In this formula i represents the annual interest rate, expressed as a percentage, and n represents the number of years.

Let each row in the table correspond to a different value of n, with n ranging from 1 to 30 (hence 30 rows). Let each column represent a different interest rate. Include the following interest rates; 4, 4.5, 5, 5.5, 6, 6.5, 7, 7.5, 8, 8.5, 9, 9.5, 10, 11, 12 and 15 percent (hence a total of 16 columns). Be sure to label the rows and columns appropriately.

5.54 Write a BASIC program that will read in a set of temperatures, determine an average and then calculate the deviation of each temperature about the average.

The deviation is defined as

$$D = T(I) - A$$

where A represents the average temperature. Notice that the deviation will be positive if the temperature is above the average and negative if the temperature is below the average.

Print out the average temperature, followed by three columns containing the values for I, $T(I)$, and D, respectively. Be sure that everything is clearly labeled.

Test the program using the following set of temperatures: 28.2, 29.3, 33.7, 42.0, 58.4, 71.3, 84.1, 83.8, 74.5, 53.9, 41.6, 34.4.

5.55 Extend the program to calculate student grade averages [Problem 4.48(*i*)] so that the deviation of each student's average about the overall class average will be determined. Print out the class average, followed by each student's name, exam grades, final score and deviation about the class average. Be sure that the output is logically organized and clearly labeled.

5.56 Consider the following list of countries and their capitals

Country	Capital
Canada	Ottawa
England	London
France	Paris
India	New Delhi
Israel	Jerusalem
Italy	Rome
Japan	Tokyo
Mexico	Mexico City
People's Republic of China	Peking
United States	Washington
U.S.S.R.	Moscow
West Germany	Bonn

Write a conversational-style BASIC program that will accept the name of a country as input and print out the corresponding capital, and vice versa.

5.57 Several different types of technical problems are described below. Prepare a detailed outline, a corresponding flowchart, and a complete BASIC program for each problem.

(*a*) Suppose we are given a numeric table A having M rows and N columns and a numeric list X having N elements. We wish to generate a numeric list Y by carrying out the following operations.

```
Y(1)=A(1,1)*X(1)+A(1,2)*X(2)+ ··· +A(1,N)*X(N)
Y(2)=A(2,1)*X(1)+A(2,2)*X(2)+ ··· +A(2,N)*X(N)
...
Y(M)=A(M,1)*X(1)+A(M,2)*X(2)+ ··· +A(M,N)*X(N)
```

Print out the input data (i.e., the values for the elements of A and X), followed by the computed values for the elements of Y.

Use the program to process the following set of data.

$$A = \begin{bmatrix} 1 & 2 & 3 & 4 & 5 & 6 & 7 & 8 \\ 2 & 3 & 4 & 5 & 6 & 7 & 8 & 9 \\ 3 & 4 & 5 & 6 & 7 & 8 & 9 & 10 \\ 4 & 5 & 6 & 7 & 8 & 9 & 10 & 11 \\ 5 & 6 & 7 & 8 & 9 & 10 & 11 & 12 \\ 6 & 7 & 8 & 9 & 10 & 11 & 12 & 13 \end{bmatrix}$$

$$X = \begin{bmatrix} 1 \\ -8 \\ 3 \\ -6 \\ 5 \\ -4 \\ 7 \\ -2 \end{bmatrix}$$

(*b*) Suppose that A is a numeric table having K rows and M columns and that B is a numeric table having M rows and N columns. We wish to calculate the elements of the numeric table C, where each element of C is determined by

C(I,J)=A(I,1)*B(1,J)+A(I,2)*B(2,J)+ · · · +A(I,M)*B(M,J)

for I = 1, 2, . . . , K and J = 1, 2, . . . , N. Print out the elements of A, B and C.
Use the program to process the following set of data.

$$A = \begin{bmatrix} 2 & -1/3 & 0 & 2/3 & 4 \\ 1/2 & 3/2 & 4 & -2 & 1 \\ 0 & 3 & -9/7 & 6/7 & 4/3 \end{bmatrix}$$

$$B = \begin{bmatrix} 6/5 & 0 & -2 & 1/3 \\ 5 & 7/2 & 3/4 & -3/2 \\ 0 & -1 & 1 & 0 \\ 9/2 & 3/7 & -3 & 3 \\ 4 & -1/2 & 0 & 3/4 \end{bmatrix}$$

(*c*) The *Legendre polynomials* can be calculated by means of the formulas

$$P_0 = 1$$
$$P_1 = x$$
$$\cdots$$
$$P_n = \left(\frac{2n-1}{n}\right)xP_{n-1} - \left(\frac{n-1}{n}\right)P_{n-2}$$

where $n = 2, 3, 4, \ldots$ and x is any number between -1 and $+1$.

Write a BASIC program that will generate a table of P_n vs. x for any specified value of n up to and including $n = 10$. Generate 201 values of P_n in each table, based upon evenly spaced values of x. (That is, let $x = -1.00, -0.99, -0.98, \ldots, -0.01, 0, 0.01, \ldots, 0.98, 0.99, 1.00$.) Output the results in a legible, columnar form.

(*d*) Consider a sequence of real numbers, x_i, $i = 1, 2, \ldots, M$. The mean is defined as

$$\bar{x} = \frac{x_1 + x_2 + \cdots + x_M}{M}$$

the deviation about the mean is

$$d_i = x_i - \bar{x}$$

and the standard deviation is

$$\sigma = \left(\frac{d_1^2 + d_2^2 + \cdots + d_M^2}{M}\right)^{1/2}$$

Read in the first M elements of a one-dimensional array. Calculate the sum of these elements, the mean, the deviations, the standard deviation, the algebraic maximum and the algebraic minimum. Apply the program to the temperature data given in Problem 5.54.

Repeat the computation for K different arrays. Calculate the overall mean, the overall standard deviation, the absolute (largest) maximum and the absolute (algebraically smallest) minimum.

(*e*) Write a BASIC program to calculate the variance, $\bar{v}$, of a list of numbers in two ways, using the formulas

$$\bar{v} = \frac{1}{M}[(x_1 - \bar{x})^2 + (x_2 - \bar{x})^2 + \cdots + (x_M - \bar{x})^2]$$

and

$$\bar{v} = \frac{1}{M}(x_1^2 + x_2^2 + \cdots + x_M^2) - \bar{x}^2$$

In these formulas $\bar{x}$ is the mean (average) value, calculated as

$$\bar{x} = \frac{1}{M}(x_1 + x_2 + \cdots + x_M)$$

and M is the number of values in the list.

Mathematically the two formulas for $\bar{v}$ can be shown to be identical. When the given numbers have values that are very close together, however, then the value obtained for $\bar{v}$ using the second formula can be considerably in error. The reason for this is that we must calculate the difference between two values that are very nearly equal. Such calculated differences can be highly inaccurate. The first formula for the variance yields much more accurate results under these conditions.

Demonstrate that the above statements are true by calculating the variance of the data given in Table 5.5. (The correct value is $\bar{v} = 0.00339966$.)

Table 5.5

99.944	100.054	100.059	100.061
100.039	100.066	100.029	100.098
99.960	99.936	100.085	100.038
100.093	99.932	100.079	100.024
99.993	99.913	100.095	100.046

(*Note*: This example disproves the common misconception that a computer always yields answers that are absolutely correct.)

(*f*) Home mortgage costs are determined in such a manner that the borrower pays the same amount of money to the lending institution each month throughout the life of the mortgage. The fraction of the total monthly payment which is required as an interest payment on the outstanding balance of the loan varies, however, from month to month. Early in the life of the mortgage most of the monthly payment is required to pay interest, and only a small fraction of the total monthly payment is applied toward reducing the amount of the loan. Gradually, the outstanding balance becomes smaller, which causes the monthly interest payment to decrease, and the amount that is used to reduce the outstanding balance therefore increases. Hence the balance of the loan is reduced at an accelerated rate.

Typically the prospective home buyer knows how much money to borrow and the time required for repayment. He or she then asks a lending institution how much the monthly payment will be at the prevailing interest rate. The home buyer should also be concerned with how much of each monthly payment is charged to interest, how much total interest has been paid since first borrowing the money, and how much money is still owed the lending institution at the end of each month.

Write a BASIC program that can be used by a lending institution to provide a potential customer with this information. Assume that the amount of the loan, the annual interest rate and the duration of the loan are specified. The amount of the monthly payment is calculated by means of the formula

$$A = iP\left[\frac{(1+i)^n}{(1+i)^n - 1}\right]$$

where A = monthly payment, dollars
P = total amount of the loan, dollars
i = monthly interest rate expressed as a decimal, e.g., $\frac{1}{2}$% would be written 0.005
n = total number of monthly payments

The monthly interest payment can be calculated from the formula

$$I = iB$$

where I = monthly interest payment, dollars
B = outstanding balance of the loan, dollars

The outstanding balance is simply equal to the original amount of the loan, less the sum of the previous payments toward principal. The monthly payment toward principal, i.e., the amount which is used to reduce the outstanding balance, is simply

$$T = A - I$$

where T = monthly payment toward principal

Use the program to calculate the cost of a 25-year, $30,000 mortgage at an annual rate of interest of 8 percent. Then repeat the calculations for an annual interest rate of 8.5 percent. How significant is the additional half percent in the interest rate over the entire life of the mortgage?

(*g*) The method used to calculate the cost of a home mortgage in Problem 5.57(*f*) above is known as a *constant payment* method, since each monthly payment is the same. Suppose instead that the monthly payments were computed by the method of simple interest. That is, suppose that each month the same amount is paid toward reducing the loan. Hence

$$T = P/n$$

In addition, interest is paid each month, the amount depending on the size of the outstanding balance; that is,

$$I = iB$$

Thus the monthly payment $A = T + I$ will decrease each month, as the outstanding balance diminishes.

Write a BASIC program to calculate the cost of a home mortgage using this method of repayment. Label the output clearly. Use the program to calculate the cost of a 25-year, $30,000 loan at 8 percent annual interest. Compare the results with those obtained in Problem 5.57(*f*).

(*h*) Suppose we are given a set of tabulated values for y vs. x, i.e.,

y_0	y_1	y_2	$\cdots$	y_n
x_0	x_1	x_2	$\cdots$	x_n

and we wish to obtain a value of y at some x that lies between two of the tabulated values. This problem is commonly solved by *interpolation*, i.e., by passing a polynomial $y(x)$ through the n points such that $y(x_0) = y_0$, $y(x_1) = y_1, \ldots, y(x_n) = y_n$ and then evaluating y at the desired value of x.

A common way to carry out the interpolation is to use the *Lagrange form* of the interpolating polynomial. To do this we write

$$y(x) = f_0(x) \cdot y_0 + f_1(x) \cdot y_1 + \cdots + f_n(x) \cdot y_n$$

where $f_i(x)$ is a polynomial such that

$$f_i(x) = \frac{(x - x_0)(x - x_1)\cdots(x - x_{i-1})(x - x_{i+1})\cdots(x - x_n)}{(x_i - x_0)(x_i - x_1)\cdots(x_i - x_{i-1})(x_i - x_{i+1})\cdots(x_i - x_n)}$$

Notice that $f_i(x_i) = 1$ and $f_i(x_j) = 0$, where x_j is a tabulated value of x different from x_i. Therefore we are assured that $y(x_i) = y_i$.

Write a BASIC program to read in n pairs of data, where n does not exceed 10, and then obtain an interpolated value of y at one or more specified values of x. Use the program to obtain interpolated values of y at $x = 13.7$, $x = 37.2$, $x = 112$ and $x = 147$ from the data listed in Table 5.6. Determine how many tabulated pairs of data are required in each calculation in order to obtain a reasonably accurate interpolated value for y.

Table 5.6

y	0.21073	0.37764	0.45482	0.49011	0.50563	0.49245	0.47220	0.43433	0.33824	0.19390
x	0	10	20	30	40	50	60	80	120	180

(*i*) Example 4.5 describes the *method of successive substitutions* for solving an algebraic equation of the form $x = F(x)$ by means of an iterative technique employing the recursive formula $x_{i+1} = F(x_i)$.

Another method, usually more efficient, for solving equations of this type is *Newton-Raphson iteration* (sometimes called *Newton's method*). To use this method the algebraic equation must be written in the form $f(x) = 0$. The recursive formula

$$x_{i+1} = x_i - \frac{f(x_i)}{f'(x_i)}$$

is then employed, where $f'(x_i)$ represents the first derivative of $f(x)$ evaluated at x_i.

The iteration is carried out in the same manner as the method of successive substitutions. That is, a value of x_{i+1} is calculated from the recursive formula and compared with x_i. If the two values are not sufficiently close, then the value for x_{i+1} is substituted into the right-hand side of the recursive equation and the computation is repeated.

Write a BASIC program to solve a nonlinear algebraic equation by either of the above techniques. Determine which method will be used by assigning an appropriate numerical value to some input variable.

Use the program to solve the equation $x + \cos x = 1 + \sin x$ for some value of x bounded between $\pi/2$ and π. Solve using both techniques. Which method seems to be the best?

(*j*) Suppose we are given a number of discrete points $(x_1, y_1), (x_2, y_2), \ldots, (x_n, y_n)$ which are read from a curve $y = f(x)$, where x is bounded between x_1 and x_n. We wish to approximate the area under the curve by breaking up the curve into a number of small rectangles and calculating the area of these rectangles. (This is known as the *trapezoidal rule.*) Use the formula

$$A = \tfrac{1}{2}(y_1 + y_2)(x_2 - x_1) + \tfrac{1}{2}(y_2 + y_3)(x_3 - x_2) + \cdots + \tfrac{1}{2}(y_{n-1} + y_n)(x_n - x_{n-1})$$

Notice that the average height of each rectangle is given by $\frac{1}{2}(y_i + y_{i+1})$ and that the width of each rectangle is equal to $(x_{i+1} - x_i)$, $i = 1, 2, \ldots, (n-1)$.

Use the program to calculate the area under the curve $y = x^3$ between the limits $x = 1$ and $x = 4$. Solve this problem first with 16 evenly spaced points, then with 61 points, and finally with 301 points. Note that the accuracy of the solution will improve as the number of points increases. (The exact answer to this problem is 63.75.)

(*k*) Problem 5.57(*j*) above describes a method known as the *trapezoidal rule* for calculating the area under a curve $y(x)$, where a set of tabulated values $(y_1, x_1), (y_2, x_2), \ldots, (y_n, x_n)$ is used to describe the curve. If the tabulated values of x are equally spaced, then the equation given in Problem 5.57(j) can be simplified to read

$$A = \tfrac{1}{2}(y_1 + 2y_2 + 2y_3 + 2y_4 + \cdots + 2y_{n-1} + y_n)\,\Delta x$$

where Δx is the distance between successive values of x.

Another technique that applies when there is an even number of equally spaced intervals, i.e., an odd number of data points, is *Simpson's rule.* The computational equation for implementing Simpson's rule is

$$A = \tfrac{1}{3}(y_1 + 4y_2 + 2y_3 + 4y_4 + 2y_5 + \cdots + 4y_{n-1} + y_n)\,\Delta x$$

For a given value of Δx, Simpson's rule will yield a more accurate result than the trapezoidal rule.

Write a BASIC program for calculating the area under a curve using either of the above techniques, assuming an odd number of equally spaced data points. Determine which method will be used by assigning an appropriate numerical value to some input variable. Allow for as many as 101 sets of data, where the tabulated data points can either be read into the computer or calculated internally using an algebraic equation.

Use the program to compute the area under the curve.

$$y = e^{-x^2}$$

where x ranges from 0 to 1. Calculate the area using each computational technique, and compare the results with the correct answer of A=0.7468241.

(l) A first-order differential equation with a known initial condition can be written as

$$\frac{dy}{dx} = f(x, y), \quad x \geq x_0$$

with $y(x_0) = y_0$, where y_0 represents a known numerical value. When solving a differential equation the objective is to obtain an equation, or a set of tabulated values, for y as a function of x.

A differential equation of this type can be solved by successively "stepping ahead" a small distance in the x direction. In other words, beginning with the known value $y(x_0)$, a value is calculated for $y(x_1)$, where $x_1 = x_0 + \Delta x$ and Δx is some prescribed small number (the step size). Then a value is obtained for $y(x_2)$, where $x_2 = x_1 + \Delta x$; then $y(x_3)$, where $x_3 = x_2 + \Delta x$; and so on, until a sufficient number of points have been calculated.

The easiest way to calculate a value for $y(x_{i+1})$, given a value for $y(x_i)$, is to use *Euler's method*:

$$y_{i+1} = y_i + f(x_i, y_i)\,\Delta x$$

where y_i represents $y(x_i)$, y_{i+1} represents $y(x_{i+1})$ and $f(x_i, y_i)$ represents dy/dx evaluated at (x_i, y_i). Euler's method is very easy to work with, but it results in a rather inaccurate approximation for the curve $y(x)$ unless Δx is chosen to be very small. Therefore a great many points may be required in order to calculate $y(x)$ over some reasonably large interval of x, $x_0 \leq x \leq x_n$.

A method that results in much more accurate values for y_{i+1} is the fourth order *Runge-Kutta method*:

$$y_{i+1} = y_i + \tfrac{1}{6}(k_1 + 2k_2 + 2k_3 + k_4)$$

where
$$k_1 = f(x_i, y_i)\,\Delta x$$
$$k_2 = f(x_i + \Delta x/2,\ y_i + k_1/2)\,\Delta x$$
$$k_3 = f(x_i + \Delta x/2,\ y_i + k_2/2)\,\Delta x$$
$$k_4 = f(x_i + \Delta x,\ y_i + k_3)\,\Delta x$$

Thus for a given point (x_i, y_i), the procedure is to calculate $x_{i+1} = x_i + \Delta x$, then calculate values for k_1, k_2, k_3 and k_4, and finally obtain a value for y_{i+1}.

Write a BASIC program which will solve a first-order differential equation with a known initial condition using either of the above two techniques. Determine which method will be used by assigning an appropriate numerical value to an input variable. Specify the step size (Δx) and the total number of steps (n) as input parameters.

Use the program to solve the differential equation

$$\frac{dy}{dx} = x - y, \quad 0 \le x \le 2$$

where $y(0) = 1$. Obtain a solution using each of the above methods. Compare the results obtained with the correct solution, which is given by the equation $y = 2e^{-x} + x - 1$. Determine how small the step size must be for each method in order to obtain a solution which is accurate to three significant figures.

PART II: *Advanced BASIC*

Chapter 6

Functions and Subroutines

6.1 DEFINING A FUNCTION—THE DEF STATEMENT

To avoid repeated programming of the same calculations, the programmer will want to write his or her own functions, to be used along with the library functions. A single-line function is defined by means of the *DEF (DEFINE) statement.* This statement is composed of a statement number, the keyword DEF and the function definition. The function definition itself consists of the function name, followed by an equal sign, followed by an appropriate constant, variable or formula. If the function requires arguments, then they must appear immediately after the function name, enclosed in parentheses and separated by commas. Only nonsubscripted variables are permitted as arguments in a function definition.

Both numeric and string functions can be defined with the DEF statement. (A numeric function returns a numeric value; a string function returns a string value.) If the function is numeric, then the function name must consist of three letters, the first two of which must be FN. Thus there can be as many as 26 separate numeric functions in a single program (FNA, FNB, FNC, . . .).

The name of a string function must consist of three letters followed by a dollar sign. Again the first two letters must be FN. As many as 26 separate string functions can be defined in a single program (FNA$, FNB$, FNC$, . . .). A numeric and a string function having the same three letters (e.g., FNP and FNP$) are separate entities and may therefore appear in the same program.

EXAMPLE 6.1

Three typical single-line function definitions are shown below.

```
10 DEF FNA(X)=X↑3+2*X↑2-3*X+4
20 DEF FNC$="NAME AND ADDRESS:"
30 DEF FNR(A,B,C)=SQR(A↑2+B↑2+C↑2)
```

The first and third statements define the numeric functions FNA and FNR, and the second statement defines the string function FNC$. Notice that the second function does not contain an argument. Also, note that the third function makes use of the library function SQR in the function definition.

Some versions of BASIC require that function definitions precede the corresponding function references; other versions allow function definitions to appear anywhere in a BASIC program. In either event, it is good programming practice to group together all function definitions and place them near the beginning of a program. This contributes to an orderly and legible program structure.

It should be clear that the presence of a DEF statement serves only to *define* a function. In order to *evaluate* the function it is necessary to refer to the function name elsewhere in the program, just as we would do with a library function. We will see how this is accomplished in the next section.

6.2 REFERENCING A FUNCTION

A function is referenced (evaluated) by specifying the name of the function within a BASIC statement, as though the function name were an ordinary variable. The function name must be followed by an appropriate set of arguments, enclosed in parentheses and separated by commas.

When a function is evaluated, the values of the arguments are specified by the function *reference,* not the function *definition.* For this reason the arguments appearing in a DEF statement are called *dummy arguments.* The names of the arguments in the function reference need not be the same as those in the function definition. However, the *number* of arguments must be the same, and the arguments must be of the correct *type* (i.e., numeric or string).

EXAMPLE 6.2

Shown below is the skeletal structure of a BASIC program containing two references to a programmer-defined function.

```
10 DEF FNA(X)=X↑3+2*X↑2-3*X+4
...
50 LET W=FNA(Y)+Z
...
90 IF FNA(C)>=C1 THEN 140
```

Statement number 50 causes the function FNA to be evaluated using the current value of the variable Y as an input parameter. (Hence the function will return the value of Y↑3+2*Y↑2−3*Y+4.) In statement 90 the same function is evaluated using the current value of C (thus returning the value of C↑3+2*C↑2−3*C+4).

The arguments in a function reference must correspond to the dummy arguments on a one-to-one (argument-for-argument) basis when two or more arguments are required. Again the correspondence must be with respect to the number of arguments and the type of each argument but not with respect to the names of the arguments.

EXAMPLE 6.3

A BASIC program contains the following statements.

```
20 DEF FNR(A,B,C)=SQR(A↑2+B↑2+C↑2)
...
80 LET A=FNR(C,X,Y)
```

The LET statement (line 80) will cause the function SQR(C↑2+X↑2+Y↑2) to be evaluated and the value assigned to the variable A.

Notice that the function definition (line 20) and the function reference (line 80) contain three numeric arguments each, but the names of the arguments do not correspond.

Recall from Section 6.1 that the arguments appearing in a function *definition* (the dummy arguments) must be nonsubscripted variables. We have much more freedom, however, in a function *reference*. Here the arguments can be written as constants, subscripted variables, formulas or references to other functions. It is the *value* of each argument that is actually used in the calculation.

EXAMPLE 6.4

A BASIC program contains the statements

```
30 DEF FNR(A,B,C)=SQR(A↑2+B↑2+C↑2)
...
170 LET X3=FNR(K(I),5*(P+Q),LOG(T))
```

Notice that the function definition contains only nonsubscripted variables as arguments. In the function reference, however, we see that the arguments are expressed as a subscripted variable, a formula and a reference to a library function. Execution of the program will cause the function

```
SQR(K(I)↑2+(5*(P+Q))↑2+LOG(T)↑2)
```

to be evaluated. The resulting value will then be assigned to the variable X3.

The variables used in a function definition need not be confined to the arguments. Other program variables (including subscripted variables) may also appear. When the function is evaluated, the most recently assigned values of these variables will be used.

EXAMPLE 6.5

The skeletal structure of a BASIC program is shown below.

```
30 DEF FNZ(X,Y)=(C1*X+C2*Y)/(C1+C2)
   . . .
60 LET C1=10
70 LET C2=20
80 LET R=FNZ(P,Q)
```

Execution of statement number 80 will cause the function

```
(10*P+20*Q)/(10+20)
```

to be evaluated. Notice that the values of C1 and C2 are not supplied as arguments. The most recently assigned values for C1 and C2 (i.e. C1=10 and C2=20) are used when the function is evaluated.

In Example 6.6 below we see a more comprehensive illustration of the use of a programmer-defined function.

EXAMPLE 6.6 Search for a Maximum

Suppose we wish to find the particular value of x which causes the function

$$y = x \cos x$$

to be maximized within the interval bounded by $x = 0$ on the left and $x = \pi$ on the right. We will require that the maximizing value of x be known quite accurately. We will also require that the search scheme be relatively efficient in the sense that the function $y = x \cos x$ should be evaluated as few times as possible.

An obvious way to solve this problem would be to generate a large number of closely spaced trial functions (that is, evaluate the function at $x = 0$, $x = 0.0001$, $x = 0.0002, \ldots, x = 3.1415$ and $x = 3.1416$) and determine the largest of these by visual inspection. This would not be very efficient, however, and it would require human intervention to obtain the final result. Instead let us use the following *elimination scheme*, which is a highly efficient computational procedure for all functions which have only one "peak" within the search interval.

Computational Procedure

Suppose we place two search points at the center of the interval, located a very small distance from each other, as shown in Fig. 6.1, where

X1 = left end of the search interval
X2 = left-hand interior search point
X3 = right-hand interior search point
X4 = right end of the search interval
D = distance between X2 and X3

If X1, X4 and D are known, then the interior points can be calculated as

```
X2=X1+.5*(X4-X1-D)
X3=X1+.5*(X4-X1+D)=X2+D
```

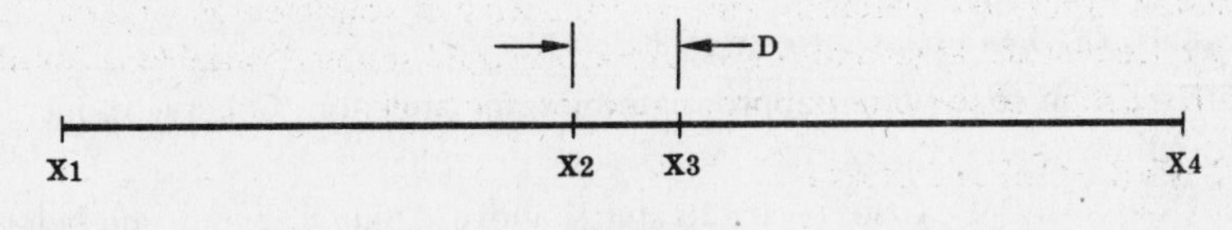

Fig. 6.1

Let us evaluate the function $y = x \cos x$ at X2 and at X3, and let us call these values Y2 and Y3, respectively. Suppose Y2 turns out to be greater than Y3. Then we know that the maximum that we are seeking will lie somewhere between X1 and X3. Hence we retain only that portion of the search interval which ranges from $x = \text{X1}$ to $x = \text{X3}$ (we will now refer to the old point X3 as X4, since it is now the right end of the new search interval), and generate two *new* search points, X2 and X3. These points will be located at the center of the new search interval, a distance D apart, as shown in Fig. 6.2.

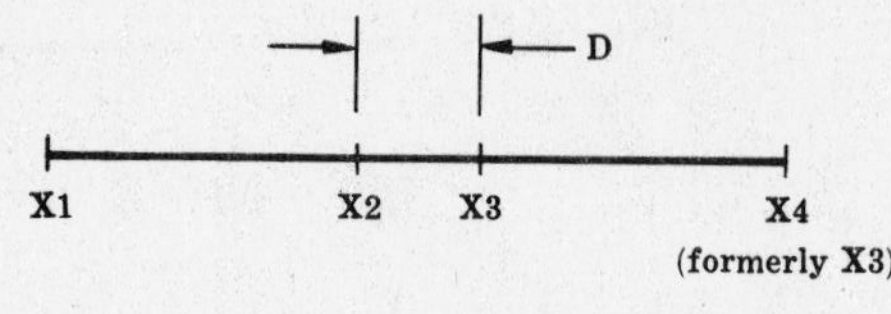

Fig. 6.2

D
X1
(formerly X2)
X2
X3
X4

Fig. 6.3

On the other hand, suppose now that in our *original* search interval the value of Y3 turned out to be greater than Y2. This would indicate that our new search interval should lie between X2 and X4. Hence we rename the point which was originally called X2 to be X1 and we generate two *new* search points, X2 and X3, at the center of the new search interval, as shown in Fig. 6.3.

We continue to generate a new pair of search points at the center of each new interval, compare the respective values of y and eliminate a portion of the search interval until the search interval becomes smaller than 3*D. Once this happens we cannot distinguish the interior points from the boundaries. Hence the search is ended.

Each time we make a comparison between Y2 and Y3 we eliminate that portion of the search interval which contains the smaller value of y. If both interior values of y should happen to be identical (which can happen, though it is unusual), then the search procedure stops, and the maximum is assumed to occur at the center of the two search points.

Once the search has ended, either because the search interval has become sufficiently small or because the two interior points yield identical values of y, we can calculate the approximate location of the maximum as

X5=.5*(X2+X3)

The corresponding maximum value of the function can then be obtained as X5*COS(X5).

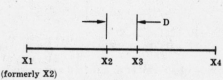

The Program Outline

1. Define the function $y = x \cos x$.
2. Read the initial values of X1 and X4 and a value for D.
3. Set I=1 (where I is an iteration counter).
4. Calculate a pair of interior points.
5. Write out the values of x at the ends of the interval and at the interior points, and write out the corresponding values for y.
6. Compare Y2 and Y3
   (*a*) If Y2 is greater than Y3, let X3 be called X4, thus defining a new search interval, and proceed to step 7.
   (*b*) If Y3 is greater than Y2, let X2 be called X1, thus defining a new search interval, and proceed to step 7.
   (*c*) If Y2 equals Y3, then proceed to step 9 below.
7. Test to see if I=100. If so, write an appropriate message and stop. Otherwise, increment the iteration counter and continue.
8. Test to see if (X4−X1)>3*D. If so, return to step 4 above. Otherwise, proceed below.
9. Calculate X5=.5*(X2+X3)
   Y5=X5*COS(X5)

   then write out the final results and stop.

A flowchart of the procedure is given in Fig. 6.4.

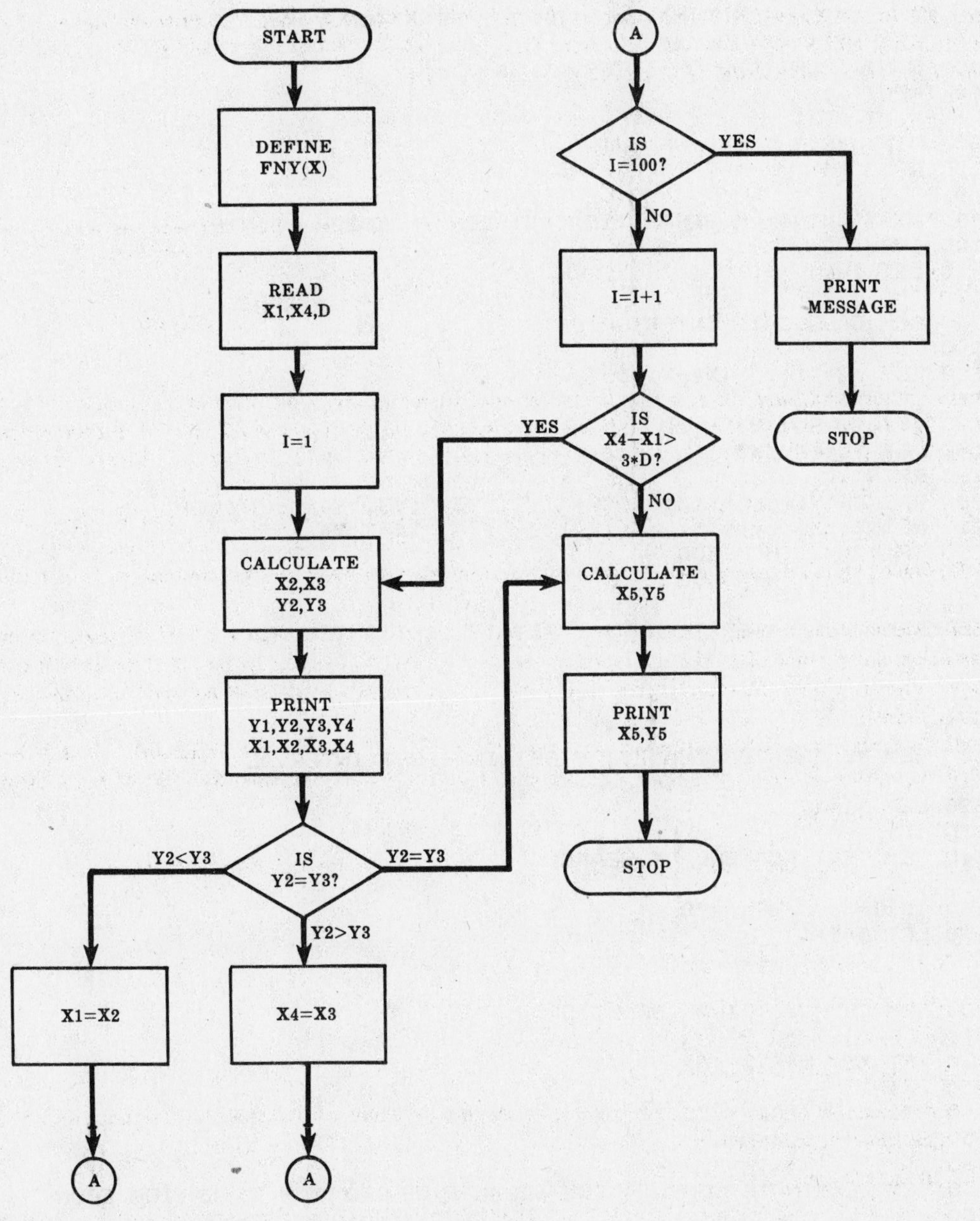

Fig. 6.4

The BASIC Program

The actual BASIC program appears in Fig. 6.5. For simplicity we have included a function definition to evaluate the quantity $y = x \cos x$. (Note that a reference to the library function COS is contained within the function definition.) We see that the function is referenced in lines 170, 180, 200 and 440. A different value for the argument (i.e., a different value of x) is supplied in each function reference.

Figure 6.6 shows the output generated by the program for the case X1=0, X4=3.14159 and D=0.0001. We see that the maximum value of y is approximately 0.5611, occurring at $x = 0.8604$. Notice that this result has been obtained to a high degree of accuracy with only 14 pairs of search points!

```
10 REM SEARCH FOR A MAXIMUM OF THE FUNCTION Y=X*COS(X)
20 DEF FNY(X)=X*COS(X)
30 PRINT "LEFT END OF INTERVAL (X1) =";
40 INPUT X1
50 PRINT
60 PRINT "RIGHT END OF INTERVAL (X4) =";
70 INPUT X4
80 PRINT
90 PRINT "MINIMUM SEPARATION BETWEEN INTERIOR POINTS (D) =";
100 INPUT D
110 LET I=1
120
130 REM CALCULATE INTERIOR POINTS
140
150 LET X2=X1+.5*(X4-X1-D)
160 LET X3=X2+D
170 LET Y2=FNY(X2)
180 LET Y3=FNY(X3)
190 PRINT
200 PRINT "Y1=";FNY(X1),"Y2=";Y2,"Y3=";Y3,"Y4=";FNY(X4)
210 PRINT "X1=";X1,"X2=";X2,"X3=";X3,"X4=";X4
220 IF Y2<Y3 THEN 300
230 IF Y2=Y3 THEN 400
240
250 REM Y2 GREATER THAN Y3 - RETAIN LEFT INTERVAL
260
270 LET X4=X3
280 GOTO 340
290
300 REM Y3 GREATER THAN Y2 - RETAIN RIGHT INTERVAL
310
320 LET X1=X2
330
340 REM TEST FOR END OF SEARCH
350
360 IF I=100 THEN 470
370 LET I=I+1
380 IF (X4-X1)>3*D THEN 130
390
400 REM COMPUTE FINAL SOLUTION
410
420 LET X5=.5*(X2+X3)
430 PRINT
440 PRINT ,"XMAX=";X5,"YMAX=";FNY(X5)
450 STOP
460
470 REM TERMINATE COMPUTATION BECAUSE OF MAXIMUM ITERATION COUNT
480
490 PRINT "MAXIMUM NUMBER OF ITERATIONS EXCEEDED - COMPUTATION ENDS"
500 END
```

Fig. 6.5

The procedure given in this example can also be used to *minimize* a function of x. In fact, the same program can be used, given some very minor modification. Such a minimization procedure can provide us with a highly effective technique for calculating the roots of a nonlinear algebraic equation. For example, suppose we want to find the particular value of x which causes some function $f(x)$ to equal zero. A typical function of this nature might be $f(x) = x - \sin x + \cos x - 1$. If we let $y(x) = f(x)^2$, then the function $y(x)$ will always be positive except for those values of x which are roots of the given function, i.e., for which $y(x)$ will equal zero. Thus any value of x which causes $y(x)$ to be minimized will also be a root of the equation $f(x) = 0$.

```
LEFT END OF INTERVAL (X1) = ?0

RIGHT END OF INTERVAL (X4) = ?3.14159

MINIMUM SEPARATION BETWEEN INTERIOR POINTS (D) = ?.0001

Y1= 0          Y2= 8.06277E-5                 Y3=-7.64780E-5
Y4=-3.14159
X1= 0          X2= 1.57075    X3= 1.57085     X4= 3.14159

Y1= 0          Y2= 0.555356   Y3= 0.555372    Y4=-7.64780E-5
X1= 0          X2= 0.785372   X3= 0.785473    X4= 1.57085

Y1= 0.555356   Y2= 0.450865   Y3= 0.450795    Y4=-7.64780E-5
X1= 0.785372   X2= 1.17806    X3= 1.17816     X4= 1.57085

Y1= 0.555356   Y2= 0.545438   Y3= 0.545412    Y4= 0.450795
X1= 0.785372   X2= 0.981716   X3= 0.981816    X4= 1.17816

Y1= 0.555356   Y2= 0.560534   Y3= 0.560529    Y4= 0.545412
X1= 0.785372   X2= 0.883544   X3= 0.883644    X4= 0.981816

Y1= 0.555356   Y2= 0.560405   Y3= 0.56041     Y4= 0.560529
X1= 0.785372   X2= 0.834458   X3= 0.834558    X4= 0.883644

Y1= 0.560405   Y2= 0.561094   Y3= 0.561095    Y4= 0.560529
X1= 0.834458   X2= 0.859001   X3= 0.859101    X4= 0.883644

Y1= 0.561094   Y2= 0.560972   Y3= 0.560969    Y4= 0.560529
X1= 0.859001   X2= 0.871273   X3= 0.871373    X4= 0.883644

Y1= 0.561094   Y2= 0.561072   Y3= 0.561071    Y4= 0.560969
X1= 0.859001   X2= 0.865137   X3= 0.865237    X4= 0.871373

Y1= 0.561094   Y2= 0.561093   Y3= 0.561093    Y4= 0.561071
X1= 0.859001   X2= 0.862069   X3= 0.862169    X4= 0.865237

Y1= 0.561094   Y2= 0.561096   Y3= 0.561096    Y4= 0.561093
X1= 0.859001   X2= 0.860535   X3= 0.860635    X4= 0.862169

Y1= 0.561094   Y2= 0.561096   Y3= 0.561096    Y4= 0.561096
X1= 0.859001   X2= 0.859768   X3= 0.859868    X4= 0.860635

Y1= 0.561096   Y2= 0.561096   Y3= 0.561096    Y4= 0.561096
X1= 0.859768   X2= 0.860152   X3= 0.860252    X4= 0.860635

Y1= 0.561096   Y2= 0.561096   Y3= 0.561096    Y4= 0.561096
X1= 0.860152   X2= 0.860343   X3= 0.860443    X4= 0.860635

               XMAX= 0.860393                 YMAX= 0.561096
```

Fig. 6.6

6.3 MULTILINE FUNCTIONS

There are many calculations that cannot be carried out using a single statement. This is especially true of computations that involve lengthy arithmetic formulas or conditional branching operations. Some versions of BASIC support a multiline function feature, which is well suited for calculations of this type.

A multiline function, like a single-line function, can have any number of dummy input arguments but returns only one value. The first statement must be a DEF statement. Unlike a single-line function, however, the function definition is not included in the DEF statement. The last statement must be a *FNEND (FUNCTION END) statement*, which consists simply of a statement number followed by the keyword FNEND.

Between the DEF and FNEND statements there can be any number of statements which define the function. One of these statements must assign a value to the function name. Usually this is accomplished with a LET statement in which the function name appears to the left of the equal sign. The same naming convention is used as with single-line functions.

EXAMPLE 6.7

The skeletal structure of a multiline function is shown below.

```
200 DEF FNA(X,Y,Z)
    . . .
250 LET FNA=. . .
260 FNEND
```

This function is called FNA, and it makes use of the dummy input arguments X, Y and Z. The value returned by the function is computed in statement number 250.

The grammatical rules that apply to multiline functions are the same as those for single-line functions (e.g., a function definition can appear anywhere in a program; a function is referenced by specifying its name, followed by a list of arguments enclosed in parentheses and separated by commas; etc.). In addition, control cannot be transferred between a statement within a function and a point exterior to the function.

EXAMPLE 6.8

Shown below is a part of a BASIC program containing a multiline function definition and a reference to that function. The purpose of the function is to determine the smaller of a pair of numbers.

```
20 DEF FNM(A,B)
30 LET FNM=A
40 IF A<=B THEN 60
50 LET FNM=B
60 FNEND
   . . .
150 PRINT FNM(FNM(C1,C2),FNM(C2,C3))
```

Notice that the function FNM is nested within itself in statement number 150. This statement causes the smallest of the three quantities represented by C1, C2 and C3 to be printed.

Variables other than those specified as arguments may appear in a multiline function, just as in a single-line function. This includes subscripted as well as nonsubscripted variables. The currently assigned values of these variables will be used each time the function is evaluated.

EXAMPLE 6.9

A BASIC program contains the following multiline function definition.

```
100 DEF FNY(X)
110 IF X>300 THEN 140
120 LET FNY=A+B*X+C*X↑2
130 GO TO 150
140 LET FNY=D+E*X+F*X↑2
150 FNEND
```

Notice that the value of X is supplied via an argument when the function is referenced. However, the values of A, B, C, D, E and F are not supplied as arguments. Thus the most recently assigned values for these variables will be used whenever the function is evaluated.

It should be understood that a function having arguments of a given type can result in a value which is of a different type (e.g., a function having string arguments can be used to determine a numeric value). Furthermore, the arguments themselves need not be of the same type (i.e., both numeric and string arguments can be present). This is true for both multiline and single-line functions. Remember, however, that the arguments in a function reference must correspond in number and in type with the dummy arguments in the function definition.

EXAMPLE 6.10

Presented below is the skeletal structure of a multiline function which requires both a numeric and a string argument. The function itself returns a string value (hence the dollar sign in the function name).

```
100 DEF FNW$(C,N$)
    . . .
140 LET FNW$=. . .
150 FNEND
```

When referencing this function it will be necessary to supply a numeric and a string argument, in that order. The names of the arguments need not, of course, be the same as the names of the dummy arguments. Hence an appropriate function reference might be

```
250 LET N$=FNW$(X,T$)
```

Examples 6.15 and 6.20 illustrate the use of multiline functions in complete BASIC programs.

6.4 ENCODING AND DECODING DATA—THE CHANGE STATEMENT

When a string is represented within a computer, the characters that make up the string are stored not as characters but as an encoded sequence of numbers. Each digit, letter and special character is represented by its own unique number.

There are several different numerical coding schemes which are used with various computers. The most common of these is the 7-bit ASCII Code[†], in which the letter A is represented by the (decimal) number 65, B by the number 66, and so on. Table 6.1 shows the complete ASCII character set.

The conversions from characters to numbers, and vice versa, are carried out automatically within the computer. Usually the programmer is not even aware of the fact that such conversion takes place. Sometimes, however, it is desirable to work with the numerical equivalent of the characters in a string. This allows each character to be manipulated individually. The *CHANGE statement* allows us to carry out this conversion.

There are two different ways that the CHANGE statement can be written. The first of these consists of a statement number, the keyword CHANGE, a string variable, the keyword TO and a numeric list, in that order. This statement causes each character in a string to be converted to its numerical equivalent and stored in a numeric list. The first element in the list (for which the subscript has a value of zero) will indicate the number of encoded characters contained in the list.

[†] American Standard Code for Information Interchange, a widely used code supported by the American National Standards Institute.

Table 6.1 The ASCII Character Set

ASCII Value	Character	ASCII Value	Character	ASCII Value	Character	ASCII Value	Character
000	NUL	032	blank	064	@	096	`
001	SOH	033	!	065	A	097	a
002	STX	034	"	066	B	098	b
003	ETX	035	#	067	C	099	c
004	EOT	036	$	068	D	100	d
005	ENQ	037	%	069	E	101	e
006	ACK	038	&	070	F	102	f
007	BEL	039	'	071	G	103	g
008	BS	040	(	072	H	104	h
009	HT	041	)	073	I	105	i
010	LF	042	*	074	J	106	j
011	VT	043	+	075	K	107	k
012	FF	044	,	076	L	108	l
013	CR	045	–	077	M	109	m
014	SO	046	.	078	N	110	n
015	SI	047	/	079	O	111	o
016	DLE	048	0	080	P	112	p
017	DC1	049	1	081	Q	113	q
018	DC2	050	2	082	R	114	r
019	DC3	051	3	083	S	115	s
020	DC4	052	4	084	T	116	t
021	NAK	053	5	085	U	117	u
022	SYN	054	6	086	V	118	v
023	ETB	055	7	087	W	119	w
024	CAN	056	8	088	X	120	x
025	EM	057	9	089	Y	121	y
026	SUB	058	:	090	Z	122	z
027	ESC	059	;	091	[	123	{
028	FS	060	<	092	\	124	|
029	GS	061	=	093	]	125	}
030	RS	062	>	094	↑	126	~
031	US	063	?	095	_	127	DEL

Note: The first 32 characters and the last character are control characters. They cannot be printed.

EXAMPLE 6.11

A BASIC program contains the statement

```
100 CHANGE N$ TO N
```

where N is the name of a numeric list. Suppose that N$ represents the string MONDAY and that the ASCII code shown in Table 6.1 is applicable. Then execution of the CHANGE statement will cause the elements of N to be assigned the following values.

N(0)= 6 (indicating six characters in the string)
N(1)=77 (the numerical equivalent of the letter M)
N(2)=79 (the numerical equivalent of the letter O)
N(3)=78 (the numerical equivalent of the letter N)
N(4)=68 (the numerical equivalent of the letter D)
N(5)=65 (the numerical equivalent of the letter A)
N(6)=89 (the numerical equivalent of the letter Y)

It is now possible to access the numerical equivalent of any character in the given string simply by referring to the appropriate subscripted variable.

The position of the string variable and the numeric list can be interchanged in the CHANGE statement. That is, the statement can be written as a statement number, followed by the keyword CHANGE, a numeric list, the keyword TO and a string variable. In this form the statement causes the elements of the numeric list to be converted into a string of characters. The character conversion begins with the second element of the list (for which the subscript has a value of one); the first element in the list (subscript equal to zero) will indicate the number of characters in the string, as before.

EXAMPLE 6.12

A BASIC program contains the statement

```
225 CHANGE L TO A$
```

where L is the name of a numeric list. Suppose that the elements of L have the following values, which represent 7-bit ASCII characters.

L(0)=11 L(6)=32
L(1)=83 L(7)=67
L(2)=65 L(8)=76
L(3)=78 L(9)=65
L(4)=84 L(10)=85
L(5)=65 L(11)=83

When the CHANGE statement is executed, each element of L, beginning with L(1), will be converted to its corresponding character and the resulting string will be assigned to A$. Hence A$ will represent the string SANTA CLAUS.

In Example 6.15 we will see a complete BASIC program that makes use of the CHANGE statement.

6.5 THE ASC AND CHR$ FUNCTIONS

Closely associated with the CHANGE statement are the library functions ASC and CHR$. The first of these, ASC, converts any single character to its ASCII equivalent. This function will therefore accept only a single character as an argument.

EXAMPLE 6.13

Consider the statement

```
50 LET C=ASC(P)
```

This statement will cause a value of 80 to be assigned to the variable C, since 80 is the ASCII equivalent of the letter P.

Similarly, the statement

```
70 IF L(I)=ASC( ) THEN 110
```

will result in a transfer of control to statement number 110 if the subscripted variable L(I) represents the value 32, since 32 is the ASCII representation for a blank space.

The purpose of the library function CHR$ is just the opposite of ASC. That is, CHR$ is used to convert the ASCII representation of a single character into that character. In this case the value of the argument must be a recognized ASCII integer quantity. Noninteger values will automatically be truncated.

EXAMPLE 6.14

Consider the statement

```
75 LET A$=CHR$(X)
```

If the variable X has a value of 42, then A$ will represent the character *, since 42 is the ASCII representation for an asterisk.

In a similar vein, the statement

```
310 PRINT CHR$(L(I));
```

will cause the letter P to be printed if L(I) has a value of 80.

The ASC and CHR$ functions, as well as the CHANGE statement, are included in the following programming example.

EXAMPLE 6.15 A Piglatin Generator

Piglatin is an encoded form of English that is often used by children as a game. A piglatin word is formed from an English word by transposing the first sound (usually the first letter) to the end of the word and then adding the letter "a". Thus the word "cat" becomes "atca", "BASIC" becomes "ASICBA", "piglatin" becomes "iglatinpa" (or "igpa atinla", if spelled as two separate words), and so on.

We wish to write a BASIC program which will accept a line of English text and then print out the text in piglatin.

Computational Procedure

We will assume that each textual message can be typed on one line of a 72-character timesharing terminal, with a space between successive words. The computational procedure will then be straightforward, consisting of a means of extracting each word from the textual message, rearranging the word, adding the letter "a" and then printing the rearranged word. In principle it is quite simple to extract each word from the line of text, since the blank spaces allow us to distinguish one word from another.

The detailed computation is somewhat tricky, however, since the characters in the line of text can be manipulated individually only if they are first changed to their ASCII-encoded numerical equivalents. Before printing each rearranged word, it will be necessary to change the ASCII numbers back into characters. The CHANGE statement and the CHR$ function will be used for this purpose.

The extraction of the ASCII quantities representing a single word from the entire list of ASCII numbers must be carried out carefully. Two "pointers" (numeric variables) will be used for this purpose. The first pointer will indicate the location of the ASCII equivalent of the first letter in the word, and the second pointer will indicate where the ASCII equivalent of the last letter can be found. These pointers will have to be reset after each word has been rearranged.

We will use a multiline function in order to extract each word, i.e., to position the pointers. There will be no problem in positioning the first pointer, since we know that the first word will start in location 1, and each successive word will begin two places beyond the end of the previous word. In order to position the second pointer, however, we will have to examine each ASCII-encoded character beyond the first pointer until we find a blank space. The second pointer will then be positioned one place before the blank space.

The Program Outline

In order to write a detailed outline of the computational procedure let us first define the following symbols.

N$ = the given line of text (a string)

L = a numeric list containing the ASCII equivalents of the characters in the line of text (note that L will consist of 72 individual encoded quantities)

P1 = the location in L of the ASCII equivalent of the first letter of a particular word (a number between 1 and 72)

P2 = the location in L of the ASCII equivalent of the last letter of a particular word (a number between 1 and 72 but not less than the value of P1)

Consider the multiline function FNP, which will return a value for P2, given a value for P1. The computation will proceed as follows.

1. For each value of the subscript I beginning with I=P1+1, test to see if the subscripted variable L(I) contains the ASCII equivalent of a blank space.
   (*a*) If some L(I) represents a blank space (indicating the end of a word), let P2=I−1.
   (*b*) If all of the L(I) represent something other than a blank space, set P2=72 (the end of a line).
2. Return the value of P2 to the function reference point. Figure 6.7 shows a flowchart of the above procedure.

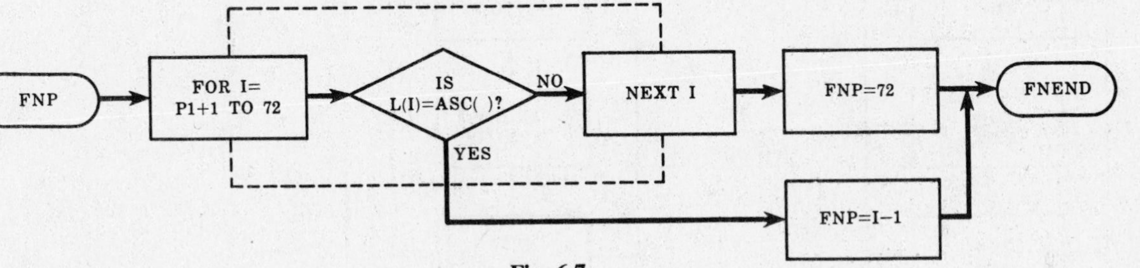

Fig. 6.7

The remainder of the program will proceed in the following manner.

1. Read N$.
2. Test to see if N$ represents the word END. If so, terminate the computation; otherwise, proceed with step 3 below.
3. Assign to each element in L the ASCII equivalent of a blank space (thus "erasing" whatever may have been stored in L before).
4. Change N$ to L.
5. Let P1=1.
6. Reference the function FNP to establish a value for P2.
7. Rearrange and print the characters in the word as follows.
   (*a*) If the word contains only one letter, then P2 will coincide with P1. Hence proceed directly to step 7(*c*) below.
   (*b*) Print the characters represented by L(P1+1) through L(P2) consecutively.
   (*c*) Print the character represented by L(P1), followed immediately by the letter "a" and a blank space.
8. Establish the beginning of the next word as follows.
   (*a*) Let P1=P2+2.
   (*b*) If the new value of P1 exceeds 72, then the line of text has been exceeded. Therefore go back to step 1 and read a new line of text.

(*c*) If L(P1) represents a blank space (even though P1 does not exceed 72), then the end of the textual message has been reached. Therefore go back to step 1 and read a new line of text.

(*d*) Go back to step 6 and establish a new value for P2.

Note that this strategy will continue to read successive lines of text until the word END has been encountered (see steps 1 and 2 above).

A flowchart corresponding to the above steps is shown in Fig. 6.8.

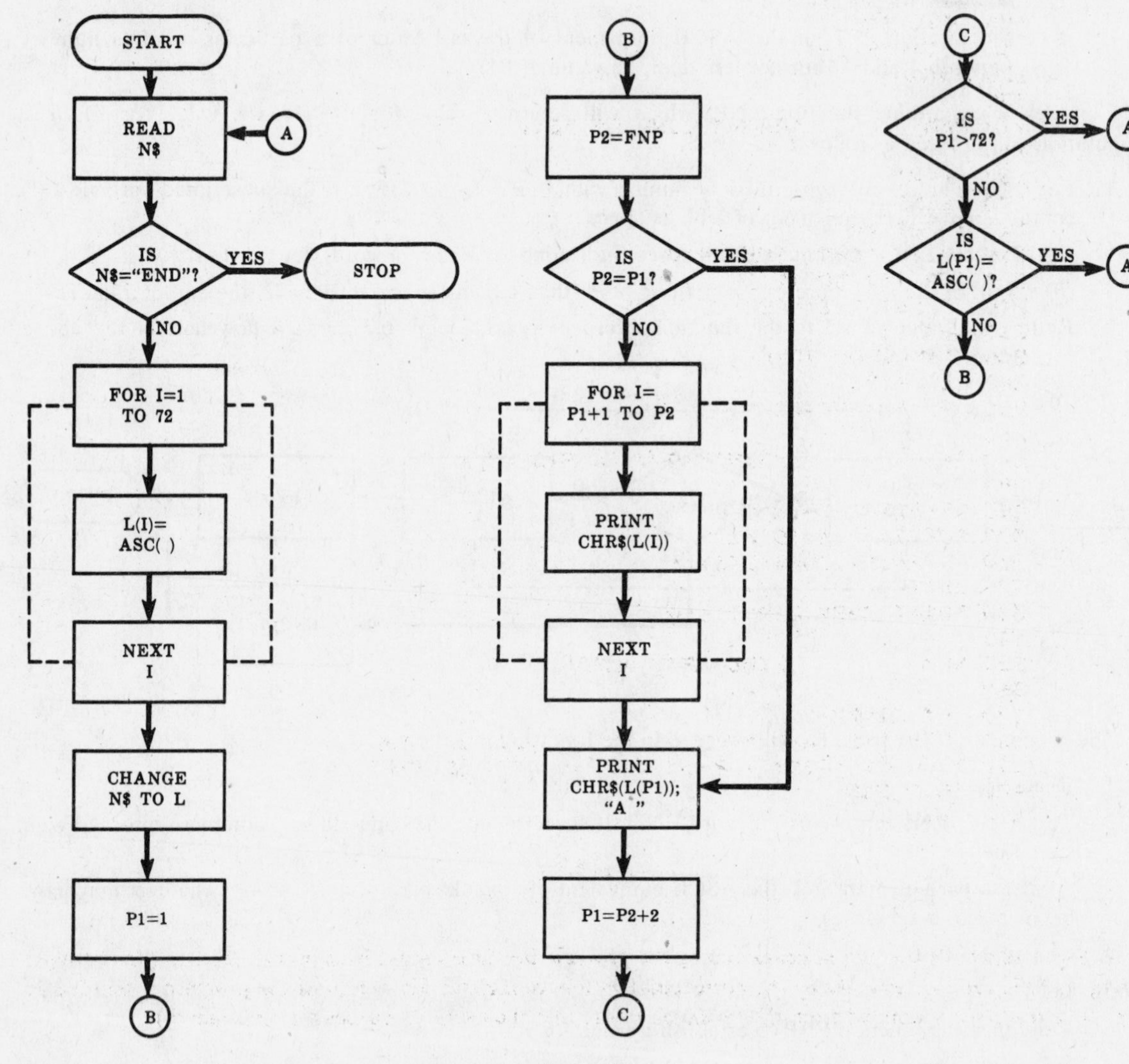

Fig. 6.8

The BASIC Program

Figure 6.9 contains the actual BASIC program for this problem. Notice the use of the ASC library function in lines 70, 210 and 390 and the CHR$ function in lines 310 and 330. These functions are used to convert single characters to and from their ASCII equivalents.

The computation of P2 for a given value of P1 is programmed as a multiline function in lines 40–120. It should be pointed out that this particular program could just as easily have been written without the use of a programmer-defined function. The purpose of the function, in this case, is to structure a relatively self-contained part of the computational strategy as an equally self-contained program element. Hence the advantage of the function is *organizational* rather than *computational*. In many other programs, however, the presence of a programmer-defined function will eliminate the need for repeated programming of the same set of calculations.

```
10 REM          PIGLATIN GENERATOR
20 DIM L(72)
30
40 DEF FNP(P1)
50 REM          THIS FUNCTION FINDS THE END OF A SINGLE WORD
60 FOR I=P1+1 TO 72
70     IF L(I)=ASC( ) THEN 110
80 NEXT I
90 LET FNP = 72
100 GOTO 120
110 LET FNP=I-1
120 FNEND
130
140 REM          READ A LINE OF TEXT
150
160 PRINT
170 PRINT
180 INPUT N$
190 IF N$="END" THEN 410
200 FOR I=1 TO 72
210     LET L(I)=ASC( )
220 NEXT I
230 CHANGE N$ TO L
240 LET P1=1
250 LET P2=FNP(P1)
260
270 REM          PRINT WORD IN PIGLATIN
280
290 IF P2=P1 THEN 330
300 FOR I=P1+1 TO P2
310     PRINT CHR$(L(I));
320 NEXT I
330 PRINT CHR$(L(P1));"A ";
340
350 REM          FIND NEXT WORD
360
370 LET P1=P2+2
380 IF P1>72 THEN 140            'END OF LINE
390 IF L(P1)=ASC( ) THEN 140     'END OF TEXT
400 GOTO 250
410 END
```

Fig. 6.9

In Fig. 6.10 we see the output generated by the program for three typical lines of text. Each single-line input message is followed immediately by the corresponding line of piglatin. Execution of the program is terminated after the word END is entered from the terminal. (Note that the user's responses are underlined.)

```
 ?THIS IS A PIGLATIN GENERATOR
HISTA SIA AA IGLATINPA ENERATORGA

 ?WHAT SORT OF GARBLED MESSAGE IS THIS ANYHOW
HATWA ORTSA FOA ARBLEDGA ESSAGEMA SIA HISTA NYHOWAA

 ?NOW IS THE TIME FOR ALL GOOD MEN TO COME TO THE AID OF THEIR COUNTRY
OWNA SIA HETA IMETA ORFA LLAA OODGA ENMA OTA OMECA OTA HETA IDAA FOA HEI
RTA OUNTRYCA

 ?END
```

Fig. 6.10

6.6 GENERATING RANDOM NUMBERS—THE RND FUNCTION

Many interesting computer applications are based upon the generation of random numbers. In BASIC it is very easy to generate a random number by means of the RND library function. This function returns a different random number with a value between zero and one each time the function is referenced. An argument is not required.

EXAMPLE 6.16

A BASIC program contains the statements

```
20 DIM X(100)
    . . .
50 FOR I=1 TO 100
60       LET X(I)=RND
70 NEXT I
```

These statements will cause 100 random numbers to be generated and stored in the list X. Each random number will be a decimal quantity whose value lies between zero and one.

EXAMPLE 6.17

Suppose we wish to generate a random number having a value between 3 and 7. This can be accomplished by writing

```
100 LET X=3+(7-3)*RND
```

or simply

```
100 LET X=3+4*RND
```

EXAMPLE 6.18

The statement shown below will generate an integer-valued random number between 1 and 6. Each digit will occur with equal likelihood.

```
100 LET X=1+INT(6*RND)
```

In interpreting this statement it should be understood that the RND function can return a function very close to 1 but not exactly 1. Thus if RND returns a value of 0.99999999, then 6*RND will yield a value of 5.9999994, and INT(6*RND) will result in a value of 5. Hence X will be assigned a value of 6.

We will see a complete BASIC program that makes use of the RND function in Example 6.20.

6.7 THE RANDOMIZE STATEMENT

The numbers obtained from the RND function are not truly random, since they are generated by using a fixed computational procedure. However, such numbers *appear* to be random, and they have the same statistical properties as numbers which are truly random. Therefore these numbers are often referred to as *pseudo-random* numbers.

Every time a program containing the RND function is executed the same sequence of pseudo-random numbers will be generated. This reproducibility of the random number sequence is very helpful when debugging a program. On the other hand, it is often desirable to generate a different sequence of pseudo-random numbers each time a debugged program is executed. This can be accomplished by means of the *RANDOMIZE statement.*

The RANDOMIZE statement consists simply of a line number followed by the keyword RANDOMIZE. Its purpose is to provide a different starting point for the random number generator. Therefore the RANDOMIZE statement must precede the first reference to the RND function in a program.

EXAMPLE 6.19

A BASIC program contains the statements

```
20 DIM X(100)
30 RANDOMIZE
 . . .
50 FOR I=1 TO 100
60     LET X(I)=RND
70 NEXT I
```

These statements will cause a sequence of 100 pseudo-random numbers to be generated and stored in the list X, just as in Example 6.16. Unlike Example 6.16 however, a different sequence of random numbers will be generated each time the program is executed.

EXAMPLE 6.20 A Game of Chance (Shooting Craps)

In this example we will simulate a game of "craps" on a computer. Craps is a popular dice game in which a player throws a pair of dice one or more times until he either wins or loses. The game can be computerized by substituting the generation of random numbers for the actual throwing of the dice.

Rules of the Game

There are two ways a player can win in craps. The player can throw the dice once and obtain a score of either 7 or 11, or he can obtain a 4, 5, 6, 8, 9 or 10 on the first throw and then come up with the same score on a subsequent throw before obtaining a score of 7. Conversely, there are two ways to lose. Either the player can throw the dice once and obtain a score of 2, 3 or 12, or he can obtain a 4, 5, 6, 8, 9 or 10 on the first throw and then obtain a score of 7 on a subsequent throw before coming up with the same score as on the first throw.

Computational Procedure

Let us computerize the game in a conversational manner so that one throw of the dice will be simulated each time the player depresses the carriage return on the console. A message will then appear indicating the outcome of each throw. The game will continue until the player types the word END. In addition, we will include a provision for printing the rules of the game if the player enters the word RULES.

In order to simulate one throw of the dice we will generate two random numbers, each having an integer value between 1 and 6. The sum of these two numbers will represent the score obtained by throwing the dice. It is convenient to use a programmer-defined function for this purpose, since each reference to the function will simulate a different throw of the dice.

The main part of the program will examine the score obtained from each throw and determine if the player has won or lost the game, or whether another throw is required. An appropriate message, along with the simulated score, will be printed in each case. Also included will be a block of PRINT statements which will cause the rules to be printed in response to the player typing RULES.

The Program Outline

1. Initialize the random number generator.
2. Read a value for the string variable N$.
   (*a*) Stop the execution if N$=END.
   (*b*) If N$=RULES, print the rules of the game and then repeat this step (i.e., read a new value for N$).
   (*c*) If N$ represents some string other than the words END or RULES, then proceed to step 3 below. (Note that any single character can be assigned to N$ for this purpose. A carriage return may be most convenient, since the carriage return key is particularly conspicuous on a console.)
3. Simulate one throw of the dice, calling the resulting score K.
   (*a*) A value of K = 2, 3 or 12 indicates a loss; hence, print an appropriate message and return to step 2.
   (*b*) A value of K = 7 or 11 indicates a win; hence, print an appropriate message and return to step 2.
   (*c*) A value of K = 4, 5, 6, 8, 9 or 10 will require additional throws of the dice; hence, print an appropriate message and proceed with step 4 below.

4. Let K1=K. (This will allow subsequent values of K to be compared with the original value, which will now be called K1.)
5. Read a new value for N$ and then simulate another throw of the dice, thus generating a new value for K. (Note that the dice will not be thrown until the player signals to do so by entering some character, such as a carriage return, for N$.)
6. Compare K with K1.
   (*a*) A value of K=K1 indicates a win; hence, print an appropriate message and return to step 2.
   (*b*) A value of K = 7 indicates a loss; hence, print an appropriate message and return to step 2.
   (*c*) If K does not equal either K1 or 7, then return to step 5 and generate a new value for K.

A flowchart of the procedure is shown in Fig. 6.11.

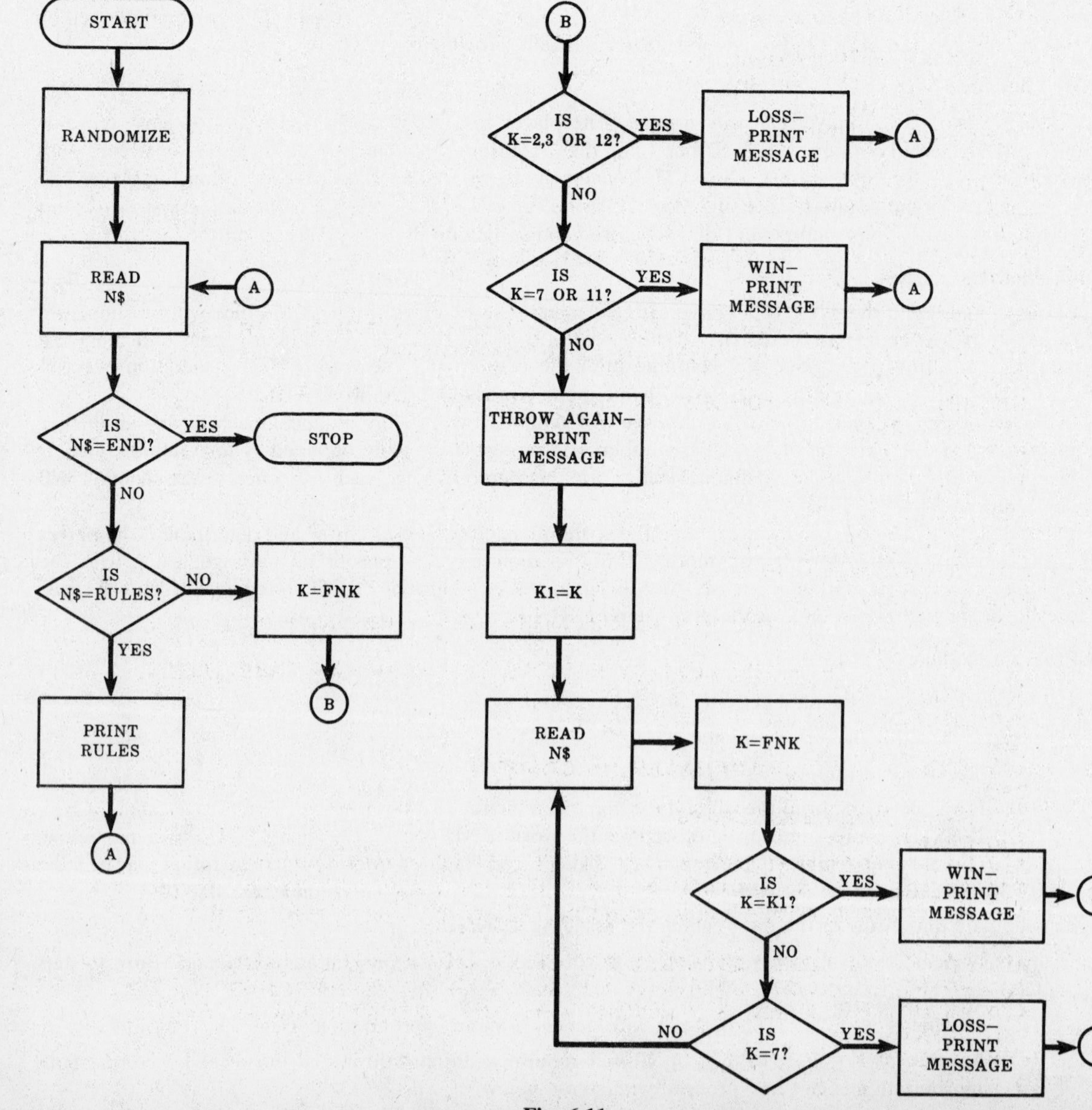

Fig. 6.11

The simulation of one throw of the dice will be carried out in a programmer-defined function as follows.

1. Let K2=1+INT(6*RND).
   (See Example 6.18 for an explanation of this statement.)
2. Let K3=1+INT(6*RND).
3. Let K=K2+K3.
4. Return the current value for K to the function reference point.

A corresponding flowchart is shown in Fig. 6.12. Note that the calculated value of K is called FNK within the function.

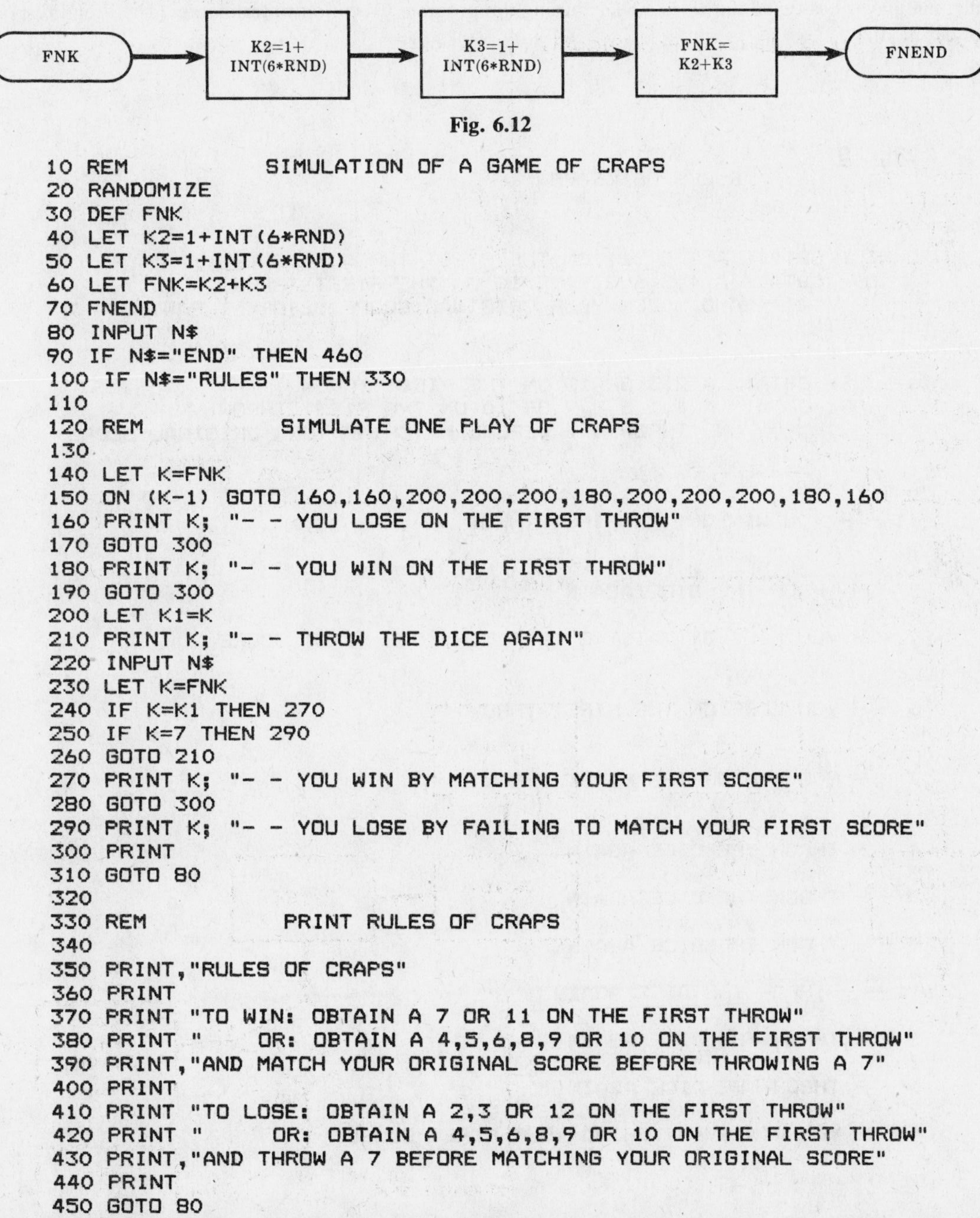

Fig. 6.12

```
10 REM          SIMULATION OF A GAME OF CRAPS
20 RANDOMIZE
30 DEF FNK
40 LET K2=1+INT(6*RND)
50 LET K3=1+INT(6*RND)
60 LET FNK=K2+K3
70 FNEND
80 INPUT N$
90 IF N$="END" THEN 460
100 IF N$="RULES" THEN 330
110
120 REM          SIMULATE ONE PLAY OF CRAPS
130
140 LET K=FNK
150 ON (K-1) GOTO 160,160,200,200,200,180,200,200,200,180,160
160 PRINT K; "- - YOU LOSE ON THE FIRST THROW"
170 GOTO 300
180 PRINT K; "- - YOU WIN ON THE FIRST THROW"
190 GOTO 300
200 LET K1=K
210 PRINT K; "- - THROW THE DICE AGAIN"
220 INPUT N$
230 LET K=FNK
240 IF K=K1 THEN 270
250 IF K=7 THEN 290
260 GOTO 210
270 PRINT K; "- - YOU WIN BY MATCHING YOUR FIRST SCORE"
280 GOTO 300
290 PRINT K; "- - YOU LOSE BY FAILING TO MATCH YOUR FIRST SCORE"
300 PRINT
310 GOTO 80
320
330 REM          PRINT RULES OF CRAPS
340
350 PRINT,"RULES OF CRAPS"
360 PRINT
370 PRINT "TO WIN: OBTAIN A 7 OR 11 ON THE FIRST THROW"
380 PRINT "     OR: OBTAIN A 4,5,6,8,9 OR 10 ON THE FIRST THROW"
390 PRINT,"AND MATCH YOUR ORIGINAL SCORE BEFORE THROWING A 7"
400 PRINT
410 PRINT "TO LOSE: OBTAIN A 2,3 OR 12 ON THE FIRST THROW"
420 PRINT "      OR: OBTAIN A 4,5,6,8,9 OR 10 ON THE FIRST THROW"
430 PRINT,"AND THROW A 7 BEFORE MATCHING YOUR ORIGINAL SCORE"
440 PRINT
450 GOTO 80
460 END
```

Fig. 6.13

The BASIC Program

Figure 6.13 contains a complete BASIC program for carrying out the computation. Notice that lines 30 through 70 define the multiline function FNK, which simulates the throw of a pair of dice. This function is referenced at two different points within the program—namely, lines 140 and 230.

Within the programmer-defined function FNK we see two references to the library function RND. Also, notice that statement number 20 is a RANDOMIZE statement, which is used to initialize the random number generator each time the program is executed. It is significant that the RANDOMIZE statement precedes the first reference to the RND function (through reference to function FNK).

In Fig. 6.14 we see a representative listing of output data. First we see the rules printed out in response to the player typing in the word RULES. Following this we see five typical plays (three wins and two losses). Finally, the player has typed the word END, causing the program execution to terminate. (The user's responses are underlined.)

```
?RULES
              RULES OF CRAPS


TO WIN: OBTAIN A 7 OR 11 ON THE FIRST THROW
    OR: OBTAIN A 4,5,6,8,9 OR 10 ON THE FIRST THROW
              AND MATCH YOUR ORIGINAL SCORE BEFORE THROWING A 7


TO LOSE: OBTAIN A 2,3 OR 12 ON THE FIRST THROW
     OR: OBTAIN A 4,5,6,8,9 OR 10 ON THE FIRST THROW
              AND THROW A 7 BEFORE MATCHING YOUR ORIGINAL SCORE

?
11 - - YOU WIN ON THE FIRST THROW

?
5 - - THROW THE DICE AGAIN
?
7 - - YOU LOSE BY FAILING TO MATCH YOUR FIRST SCORE

?
3 - - YOU LOSE ON THE FIRST THROW

?
7 - - YOU WIN ON THE FIRST THROW

?
4 - - THROW THE DICE AGAIN
?
8 - - THROW THE DICE AGAIN
?
9 - - THROW THE DICE AGAIN
?
11 - - THROW THE DICE AGAIN
?
6 - - THROW THE DICE AGAIN
?
5 - - THROW THE DICE AGAIN
?
4 - - YOU WIN BY MATCHING YOUR FIRST SCORE

?END
```

Fig. 6.14

6.8 DEFINING A SUBROUTINE

Sometimes it is more convenient to structure a sequence of statements as a *subroutine* than as a function. Subroutines are similar to functions in the sense that they can be referenced from other places in a program. Unlike a function, however, a subroutine is not given a name, and it can be used to determine more than one numeric and/or string quantity. Furthermore, arguments are not used. Hence a subroutine can exchange information with the rest of the program in a very general manner.

A subroutine need not begin with any special statement. Thus a subroutine may begin with a REM statement, a LET statement, a FOR-TO statement, an INPUT statement, etc. The last statement, however, must be a *RETURN statement,* which consists simply of a statement number followed by the keyword RETURN. This statement causes control to be transferred back to the statement following the point of reference. (It should be understood that control *cannot* be transferred by some other type of branching statement, such as GO TO, IF-THEN or ON-GO TO.)

EXAMPLE 6.21

A typical subroutine is shown below.

```
300 REM SUBROUTINE TO CALCULATE CRITICAL CONSTANTS
310 LET C1=(A+B+C)/3
320 LET C2=SQR(A↑2+B↑2+C↑2)
330 LET C3=SQR(A*B*C)
340 RETURN
```

Notice that the subroutine begins with a REM statement and ends with a RETURN statement. The variables A, B and C must be assigned numerical values before the subroutine is first referenced.

A subroutine may contain several RETURN statements if desired. This is often necessary if the subroutine contains a conditional branch or a multiple branch. When the subroutine is executed, the first RETURN statement to be encountered will cause control to be transferred from the subroutine.

EXAMPLE 6.22

The skeletal structure of a subroutine containing multiple RETURN statements is shown below.

```
500 REM SAMPLE SUBROUTINE WITH MULTIPLE RETURNS
510 ON N 520,580,650
520 LET X=...
    ...
570 RETURN
580 LET Y=...
    ...
640 RETURN
650 LET Z=...
    ...
690 RETURN
```

This subroutine contains a multiple branch, with control being transferred to statement 520, 580 or 650 (all of which are contained within the subroutine), depending on the value of N. Control will then be transferred back to the statement following the subroutine reference when any one of the RETURN statements is encountered.

6.9 REFERENCING A SUBROUTINE—THE GOSUB STATEMENT

A subroutine is referenced by means of the *GOSUB statement.* This statement consists of a statement number, the keyword GOSUB and the number of the first statement in the subroutine. Execution of this statement will cause a transfer of control to the subroutine. Control will then be transferred back to the statement following GOSUB when a RETURN statement is encountered within the subroutine.

EXAMPLE 6.23

A BASIC program contains the following statements.

```
120 GOSUB 300
130 PRINT "Z=";Z
 . . .
300 LET X=A+B ⎫
 . . .        ⎬ Subroutine
380 RETURN    ⎭
```

When statement number 120 (GOSUB) is encountered during program execution, control will be transferred to statement number 300 and the subroutine will be executed. Upon reaching statement number 380 (RETURN), control will be transferred back to statement number 130, which is the first statement after GOSUB.

A program may contain more than one reference to the same subroutine. Control will always be returned from the subroutine to the statement following the particular GOSUB statement that referenced the subroutine.

EXAMPLE 6.24

A BASIC program contains the following statements.

```
120 GOSUB 300
130 PRINT "Z=";Z
 . . .
180 GOSUB 300
190 IF Z<10 THEN 250
 . . .
300 LET X=A+B ⎫
 . . .        ⎬ Subroutine
380 RETURN    ⎭
```

Statements 300 through 380 define a subroutine, as in Example 6.23. If the subroutine is referenced by statement number 120, then control will be returned to statement 130 following execution of the subroutine. Similarly, if the subroutine is referenced by statement 180, then control will return to statement 190 after the subroutine has been executed.

It is possible for one subroutine to contain a reference to another subroutine. Subroutines that are structured in this manner are said to be *nested*. (Recall that we have encountered this term in Chapter 4, where we discussed nested FOR-TO loops.)

EXAMPLE 6.25

The following statements are contained in a BASIC program.

```
50 GOSUB 200
 . . .
200 LET C=A+B ⎫
 . . .        ⎪
240 GOSUB 300 ⎬ First subroutine
 . . .        ⎪
270 RETURN    ⎭
 . . .
300 LET P=Q+R ⎫
 . . .        ⎬ Second subroutine
350 RETURN    ⎭
```

This program contains two subroutines. The first subroutine consists of statements 200 through 270, and the second is made up of statements 300 through 350. Notice that the second subroutine is referenced from a point within the first subroutine (line 240); hence the subroutines are nested.

When statement number 350 is encountered during program execution, control is transferred back to the statement following line 240. Hence control is transferred from the second subroutine to the first. Similarly, statement number 270 will return control to the statement following line 50, thus transferring control from the first subroutine to the initial reference point.

Nested subroutines must maintain a strict hierarchical ordering. That is, if subroutine A references subroutine B, then subroutine B cannot reference subroutine A. On the other hand, subroutine B can be referenced from the main part of the program as well as from subroutine A.

Examples 6.26 and 6.28 illustrate the use of subroutines in complete BASIC programs.

EXAMPLE 6.26 A Monthly Payroll

In this example we will determine the amount of federal, state and local income tax to be withheld, given an employee's gross salary, marital status and number of exemptions. A more complete payroll computation will not be attempted, since the program structure can become quite complicated.

Table 6.2 indicates the amount of federal income tax to be withheld on a monthly basis for both single and married employees.

Table 6.2 Federal Income Tax Withholding Rates

MONTHLY Payroll Period

(*a*) SINGLE person—including head of household:				(*b*) MARRIED person—			
If the amount of wages is: Not over $88		*The amount of income tax to be withheld shall be:* 0		*If the amount of wages is:* Not over $88		*The amount of income tax to be withheld shall be:* 0	
Over—	*But not over—*		*of excess over—*	*Over—*	*But not over—*		*of excess over—*
$88	−$133	14%	−$88	$88	−$183	14%	−$88
$133	−$217	$6.30 plus 17%	−$133	$183	−$333	$13.30 plus 17%	−$183
$217	−$433	$20.58 plus 20%	−$217	$333	−$708	$38.80 plus 16%	−$333
$433	−$583	$63.78 plus 18%	−$433	$708	−$1167	$98.80 plus 19%	−$708
$583	−$917	$90.78 plus 21%	−$583	$1167	−$1667	$186.01 plus 21%	−$1167
$917	—	$160.92 plus 24%	−$917	$1667	—	$291.01 plus 25%	−$1667

In order to use this table it is necessary to calculate an adjusted monthly gross income, which is equal to the gross monthly income less $54.20 for each exemption. The particular tax rate that is applicable will depend on which tax bracket the adjusted gross income falls into. Notice that there are two different sets of tax brackets—one for single employees and one for married persons.

The state tax will be calculated as 1 percent of all gross income up to $600 a month, $1\frac{1}{2}$ percent of any additional income up to $2000 a month, and 2 percent of any excess over $2000. The local tax will be levied at a rate of 1 percent of the first $800 of gross income. Monthly earnings in excess of $800 will not be taxed at the local level.

Computational Procedure

Let us calculate the adjusted monthly gross income, the state tax and the local tax in one subroutine and federal tax within another subroutine. This allows us to segregate the program into separate computational packages. The subroutines will be nested, with the federal tax subroutine being referenced by the other subroutine. The remainder of the program will simply read in the required data (i.e., name, employee number, gross monthly salary, marital status and number of exemptions); reference the subroutines; compute the net monthly salary and print out the desired results (namely, the amount of federal, state and local tax to be withheld and the net monthly salary) for each employee.

Within the federal tax subroutine we will refer to the numbers in the left-hand columns of the tax table, which determine the various income brackets, as elements of the array C. We will define C to be a two-dimensional, 6×2 array. If the second subscript (J) is equal to 1 we will refer to the data for single persons, whereas J=2 will indicate the data for married persons. Hence C(1,1)=88, C(2,1)=133, . . . , C(6,1)=917, C(1,2)=88, C(2,2)=183, . . . , C(6,2)=1667.

In a similar manner let T be a two-dimensional, 6×2 array which contains the amount of the base tax in each income bracket, and let R be a two-dimensional, 6×2 array which represents the tax rate (expressed as a decimal) for each income bracket. Thus T(1,1)=0, T(2,1)=6.30, . . . , T(6,1)=160.92, T(1,2)=0, T(2,2)=13.30, . . . , T(6,2)=291.01; and R(1,1)=0.14, R(2,1)=0.17, . . . , R(6,1)=0.24, R(1,2)=0.14, R(2,2)=0.17, . . . , R(6,2)=0.25.

The Program Outline

Let us define the following symbols.

N$ = employee's name	P2 = adjusted gross monthly salary
M$ = marital status (M for married, S for single)	P3 = net monthly salary
N = employee number	T1 = state tax withheld
E = number of exemptions	T2 = local tax withheld
P1 = gross monthly salary	T3 = federal tax withheld

The computation will be carried out as indicated below.

1. Assign numerical values to the 6×2 arrays C, R and T by means of READ and DATA statements. (A nest of double FOR-TO loops will be required for each array, as discussed in Chapter 5.)
2. Read an appropriate string value for N$.
   (*a*) If N$=END then terminate the computation.
   (*b*) Otherwise proceed with step 3 below.
3. Read an appropriate string or numeric value for N, P1, M$ and E.
4. Compute numeric values for T1, T2 and T3 by referencing the appropriate subroutines.
5. Calculate a value for P3 using the formula

   P3=P1−(T1+T2+T3)

6. Print the current values for T3, T1, T2 and P3.
7. Return to step 2 and begin to process data for the next employee.

The subroutine that is referenced directly in step 4 above will proceed as follows.

1. Examine the value of P1.
   (*a*) If P1 does not exceed $600, then calculate a value for T1 (state tax)

   T1=0.01*P1

   and proceed to step 2 below
   (*b*) If P1 exceeds $600 but does not exceed $2000, then calculate a value for T1 using the formula

   T1=6+0.015*(P1−600)

   and proceed to step 2 below.
   (*c*) If P1 exceeds $2000, then evaluate T1 as

   T1=27+0.02*(P1−2000)

   and proceed with step 2 below.
2. Again examine the value of P1.
   (*a*) If P1 does not exceed $800, then calculate a value for T2 (local tax) as

   T2=0.01*P1

   and proceed to step 3 below.
   (*b*) If P1 exceeds $800, then set T2=8 and proceed with step 3 below.

3. Calculate a value for P2 (adjusted gross monthly salary) using the formula

   P2=P1−54.20*E

   (*a*) If P2 is less than or equal to zero, then set T3 (federal tax) equal to zero and return to the main part of the program.

   (*b*) If P2 has a positive value, then reference the subroutine that will determine a value for T3 and return to the main part of the program.

The subroutine that computes a value for T3 (federal tax) will proceed in the following manner.

1. Determine whether the employee is single or married by examining the string M$.

   (*a*) If M$=S, assign a value of 1 to the subscript J and proceed to step 2 below.

   (*b*) If M$=M, then let J=2 and proceed with step 2 below.

2. Assign an initial value of zero to T3.

3. Compare P2 with C(I,J) for all values of I ranging from 1 to 6.

   (*a*) If P2 does not exceed C(1,J), then retain the value of T3=0 and return to the reference point.

   (*b*) If P2 exceeds C(1,J), then proceed through the loop until a value of C(I,J) is found that exceeds P2. If such a value is found, then calculate a value for T3 as

   T3=T(I−1,J)+R(I−1,J)*(P2−C(I−1,J))

   and return to the reference point.

   (*c*) If P2 exceeds C(I,J) at the end of the loop (i.e., when I=6), then calculate a value for T3 using the formula

   T3=T(6,J)+R(6,J)*(P2−C(6,J))

   and return to the reference point.

Figure 6.15 contains a detailed flowchart corresponding to the above outline.

The BASIC Program

A complete BASIC program is shown in Fig. 6.16. Notice that the first subroutine, which computes the adjusted gross income and the state and local tax, is composed of statements 400 through 580. Two separate RETURN statements are included (lines 560 and 580). The subroutine is referenced by statement number 310 in the main part of the program.

Statements 600 through 730 make up the second subroutine, which is used to calculate the federal tax. We see that this subroutine contains only one RETURN statement (line 730) and is referenced by statement number 570 in the first subroutine. (Hence the subroutines are nested.) Note that a FOR-TO loop (lines 660 through 710) is included within this second subroutine.

It is also interesting to observe that this program contains both READ and INPUT statements. The READ statements are used to assign values to the arrays C, R and T at the start of the program execution, whereas the INPUT statements are used to enter the information required for each employee.

The reader should understand that this program could just as easily have been written without making use of subroutines. Hence the purpose of the subroutines, in this example, is to organize the program into several well-defined, self-contained "packages." We have seen a similar situation with regard to programmer-defined functions in Example 6.15. There are some situations, however, in which the programming effort is simplified significantly through the use of subroutines. This is especially true of programs that contain several references to the same subroutine.

Finally, Fig. 6.17 shows a typical set of output for seven different employees. Notice that all of the data (both input and output data) for each employee are shown in a well-organized and neatly labeled block. The input data are underlined.

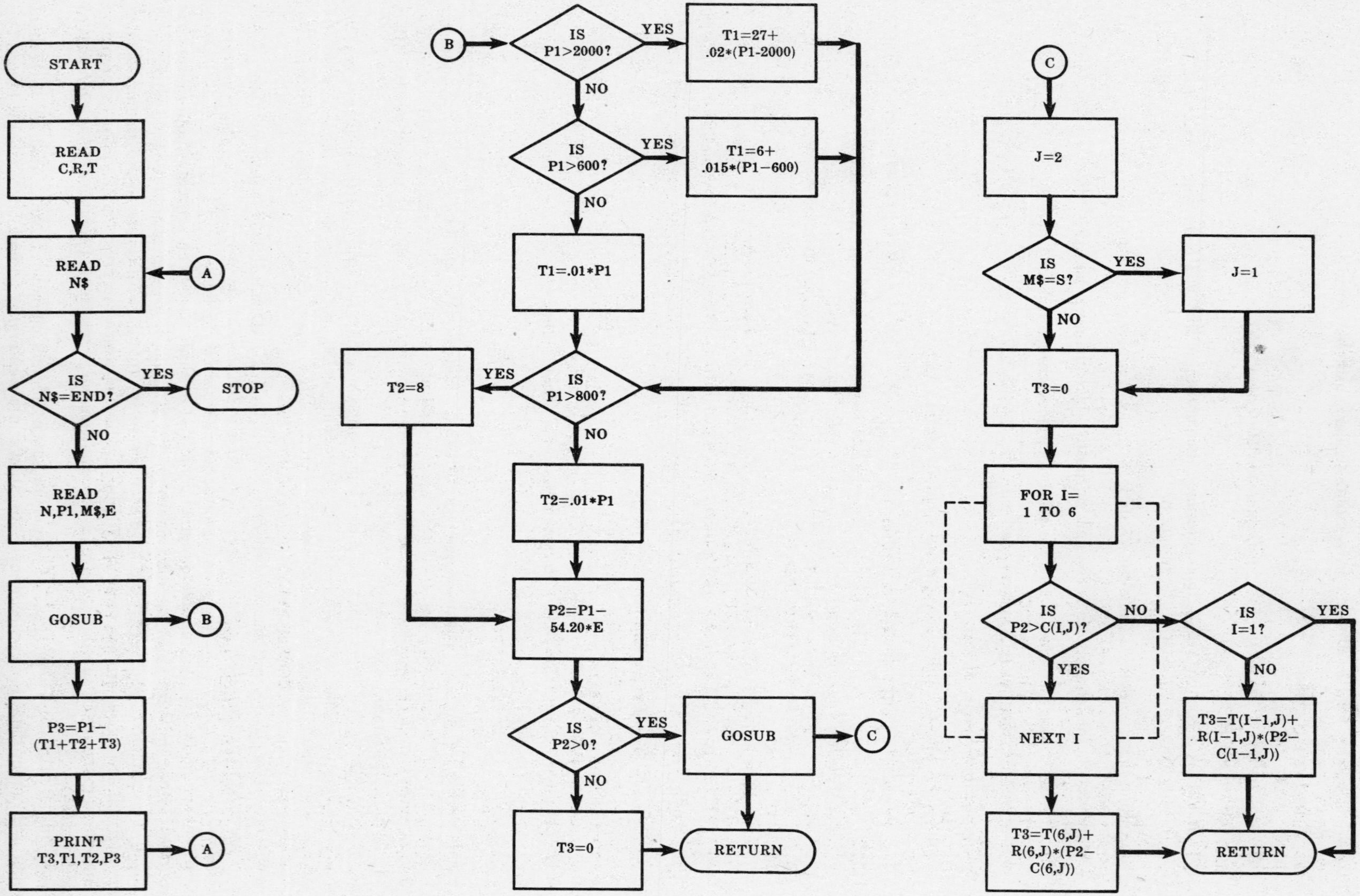

START
READ C,R,T
READ N$
A
IS N$=END?
YES
STOP
NO
READ N,P1,M$,E
GOSUB
B
P3=P1− (T1+T2+T3)
PRINT T3,T1,T2,P3
A

B
IS P1>2000?
YES
T1=27+ .02*(P1-2000)
NO
IS P1>600?
YES
T1=6+ .015*(P1−600)
NO
T1=.01*P1
IS P1>800?
YES
T2=8
NO
T2=.01*P1
P2=P1− 54.20*E
IS P2>0?
YES
GOSUB
C
NO
T3=0
RETURN

C
J=2
IS M$=S?
YES
J=1
NO
T3=0
FOR I= 1 TO 6
IS P2>C(I,J)?
NO
IS I=1?
YES
NO
T3=T(I−1,J)+ R(I−1,J)*(P2− C(I−1,J))
YES
NEXT I
T3=T(6,J)+ R(6,J)*(P2− C(6,J))
RETURN

Fig. 6.15

```
10 REM           COMPUTATION OF A MONTHLY PAYROLL
20 DIM C(6,2),R(6,2),T(6,2)
30 FOR J=1 TO 2
40    FOR I=1 TO 6
50       READ C(I,J)
60    NEXT I
70 NEXT J
80 FOR J=1 TO 2
90    FOR I=1 TO 6
100      READ R(I,J)
110   NEXT I
120 NEXT J
130 FOR J=1 TO 2
140    FOR I=1 TO 6
150       READ T(I,J)
160    NEXT I
170 NEXT J
180 PRINT,"MONTHLY PAYROLL"
190 PRINT
200 PRINT "NAME";
210 INPUT N$
220 IF N$="END" THEN 800
230 PRINT "EMPLOYEE NUMBER";
240 INPUT N
250 PRINT "GROSS SALARY";
260 INPUT P1
270 PRINT "MARITAL STATUS (M OR S)";
280 INPUT M$
290 PRINT "NUMBER OF EXEMPTIONS";
300 INPUT E
310 GOSUB 400
320 LET P3=P1-(T1+T2+T3)
330 PRINT "FEDERAL TAX=$";T3,"STATE TAX=$";T1,"LOCAL TAX=$";T2
340 PRINT "NET SALARY=$";P3
350 GOTO 190
360 DATA 88,133,217,433,583,917,88,183,333,708,1167,1667
370 DATA .14,.17,.20,.18,.21,.24,.14,.17,.16,.19,.21,.25
380 DATA 0,6.3,20.58,63.78,90.78,160.92,0,13.3,38.8,98.8,186.01,291.01
390
400 REM COMPUTATION OF STATE TAX, LOCAL TAX AND ADJUSTED GROSS SALARY
410
420 IF P1>2000 THEN 480
430 IF P1>600 THEN 460
440 LET T1=.01*P1
450 GOTO 490
460 LET T1=6+.015*(P1-600)
470 GOTO 490
480 LET T1=27+.02*(P1-2000)
490 IF P1>800 THEN 520
500 LET T2=.01*P1
510 GOTO 530
520 LET T2=8
530 LET P2=P1-54.2*E
540 IF P2>0 THEN 570
550 LET T3=0
560 RETURN
570 GOSUB 600
580 RETURN
590
600 REM          COMPUTATION OF FEDERAL TAX
610
620 LET J=2
630 IF M$="M" THEN 650
640 LET J=1
650 LET T3=0
660 FOR I=1 TO 6
670    IF P2>C(I,J) THEN 710
680    IF I=1 THEN 730
690    LET T3=T(I-1,J)+R(I-1,J)*(P2-C(I-1,J))
700    GOTO 730
710 NEXT I
720 LET T3=T(I,J)+R(I,J)*(P2-C(I,J))
730 RETURN
800 END
```

Fig. 6.16

```
                MONTHLY PAYROLL

NAME ?ANDREWS, J J
EMPLOYEE NUMBER ?2717
GROSS SALARY ?870.00
MARITAL STATUS (M OR S) ?M
NUMBER OF EXEMPTIONS ?2
FEDERAL TAX=$ 108.984       STATE TAX=$ 10.05       LOCAL TAX=$ 8
NET SALARY=$ 742.966

NAME ?COHEN, A M
EMPLOYEE NUMBER ?5375
GROSS SALARY ?1250.00
MARITAL STATUS (M OR S) ?M
NUMBER OF EXEMPTIONS ?3
FEDERAL TAX=$ 170.886       STATE TAX=$ 15.75       LOCAL TAX=$ 8
NET SALARY=$ 1055.36

NAME ?DIPASQUALE, G V
EMPLOYEE NUMBER ?4660
GROSS SALARY ?2075.00
MARITAL STATUS (M OR S) ?S
NUMBER OF EXEMPTIONS ?1
FEDERAL TAX=$ 425.832       STATE TAX=$ 28.5        LOCAL TAX=$ 8
NET SALARY=$ 1612.67

NAME ?HOLLAND, C J
EMPLOYEE NUMBER ?0892
GROSS SALARY ?520.00
MARITAL STATUS (M OR S) ?S
NUMBER OF EXEMPTIONS ?2
FEDERAL TAX=$ 59.5          STATE TAX=$ 5.2         LOCAL TAX=$
 5.2
NET SALARY=$ 450.1

NAME ?JONES, D M
EMPLOYEE NUMBER ?6839
GROSS SALARY ?1120.00
MARITAL STATUS (M OR S) ?M
NUMBER OF EXEMPTIONS ?2
FEDERAL TAX=$ 156.484       STATE TAX=$ 13.8        LOCAL TAX=$ 8
NET SALARY=$ 941.716

NAME ?KOWALSKI, S
EMPLOYEE NUMBER ?8462
GROSS SALARY ?1100.00
MARITAL STATUS (M OR S) ?M
NUMBER OF EXEMPTIONS ?3
FEDERAL TAX=$ 142.386       STATE TAX=$ 13.5        LOCAL TAX=$ 8
NET SALARY=$ 936.114

NAME ?LOWE, H G
EMPLOYEE NUMBER ?9587
GROSS SALARY ?1075.00
MARITAL STATUS (M OR S) ?M
NUMBER OF EXEMPTIONS ?5
FEDERAL TAX=$ 117.04        STATE TAX=$ 13.125      LOCAL TAX=$ 8
NET SALARY=$ 936.835

NAME ?END
```

Fig. 6.17

6.10 GRAPHICAL OUTPUT

Many computer programs generate a list of numeric output data that is eventually plotted on graph paper. In such cases it is often very effective to have the computer generate the graph directly on a hard-copy terminal, in addition to the regular numerical output data. This allows the user to see the general appearance of the graph and then refer to the more precise tabulation of the data if necessary.

It is very easy to produce a graph on a hard-copy terminal. To do so we must make use of a FOR-TO loop which includes a PRINT statement containing the TAB function. A graph produced in this manner will run vertically down the printed page, with the actual curve being represented by a number of closely spaced discrete points, as shown in Fig. 6.18.

The detailed mechanics of producing the graph are best described by means of an example.

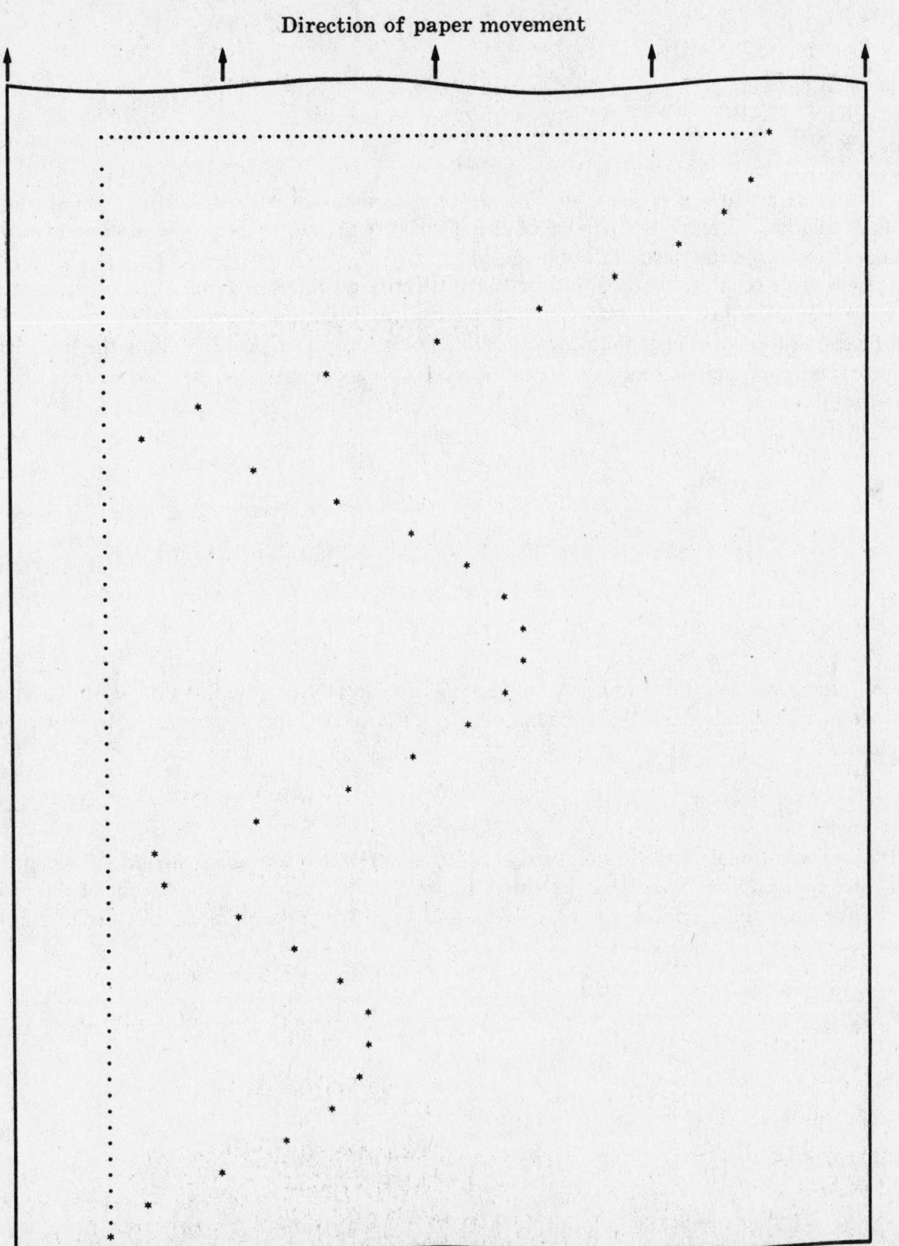

Fig. 6.18

EXAMPLE 6.27

A BASIC program has generated two numeric lists, Y and T, which describe the position of a projectile at various times. (The elements of Y represent the height of the projectile, and the elements of T represent the corresponding times.) We wish to produce a graph of Y against T, thus indicating the trajectory of the projectile, on a 72-character hard-copy terminal. In order to generate the graph as clearly as possible we will double space the points on the curve; i.e., we will place a blank line between each asterisk, as shown in Fig. 6.18.

Since the graph will be positioned vertically along the page, the Y axis will be generated by a single line of dots (periods). The T axis will run perpendicular to the printed line (i.e., down the page). Hence one dot of the T axis will be printed on each line of output.

Let us first print out the Y axis, showing the position of the projectile at the top of the axis (at time zero). To do this we print a dot (period) in each of the first 71 positions and then place an asterisk in the 72d position. Hence we can write

```
580 FOR J=0 TO 70
590       PRINT TAB(J);".";
600 NEXT J
610 PRINT TAB(71);"*"
620 PRINT "."
```

Statements 580 through 610 will produce the Y axis, as described above. A subsequent line, containing only a dot in the first column (to represent a part of the T axis), will be generated by statement 620. This line is required in order to obtain the desired double spacing.

Next we will want to print the position of the projectile at different times. Let us generate two lines of output for each time. The first of these will contain a dot (representing the T axis) in the first column and an asterisk (representing the position of the projectile) at some appropriate position along the line. The second line will be a spacer, containing only a dot in the first position. To accomplish this we can write

```
630 FOR I=2 TO I1
640       LET J=INT(71*Y(I)/Y(1))
650       IF J=0 THEN 680
660       PRINT ".";TAB(J);"*"
670       GO TO 690
680       PRINT "*"
690       PRINT "."
700 NEXT I
```

where I1 is an integer variable that indicates the last point to be plotted (the last time). Notice that the first line of output is produced by statements 640 through 680, and the second line is generated by statement 690.

The statement

```
640       LET J=INT(71*Y(I)/Y(1))
```

may require some additional clarification. First, note that Y(1) is the original height of the projectile. If we assume that this represents the *maximum* height of the projectile, then Y(I), the height of the projectile at the Ith time, will be some number bounded between zero and Y(1). We are seeking a value for J, an integer which is bounded between 0 and 71. The value for J will indicate the position of the asterisk on the graph, i.e., J=0 corresponds to Y(I)=0, and J=71 corresponds to Y(I)=Y(1). Hence by direct proportion,

$$\frac{J}{71}=\frac{Y(I)}{Y(1)} \quad \text{or} \quad J=71*Y(I)/Y(1)$$

Since J can take on only integer values, we write

```
J=INT(71*Y(I)/Y(1))
```

In Example 6.28 we will see a complete BASIC program that generates both numerical and graphical outputs.

EXAMPLE 6.28 Simulation of a Bouncing Ball

In this example we would like to calculate the movement of a rubber ball as it bounces up and down under the force of gravity, while at the same time traveling in the horizontal direction with a constant velocity. We will assume that the initial vertical displacement (that is, the original height above the ground) is specified (H), along with the horizontal velocity (V) and the number of times the ball bounces (N). Also known will be the bounce coefficient (C), which is the ratio of the vertical velocity just after impact to the vertical velocity just before impact

Computational Procedure

In order to calculate the position of the ball at various times, we will first select a small increment of time (D) and then make use of the following laws of physics, which apply within each time increment:

```
T(I+1)=T(I)+D
X(I+1)=X(I)+V*D
Z(I+1)=Z(I)-G*D
Y(I+1)=Y(I)+.5*(Z(I)+Z(I+1))*D
```

where X refers to the horizontal displacement (originally zero at the start of the problem), Z is the vertical velocity (also zero at the start of the problem), Y is the height above the ground and G is the acceleration due to gravity (32.2 ft/sec^2). The subscripts I and I+1 refer to the values of the different variables at the start and end of the time increment, respectively.

If a bounce occurs during the time increment, the computational formulas must be modified somewhat. A bounce condition is signified by a negative value for Y(I+1), which is physically impossible. When this condition occurs we recalculate Z(I+1) and Y(I+1) as follows. First calculate the time required for the ball to hit the ground, starting from its position at the start of the Ith time increment. If we call this time D1, then, from simple proportionality,

$$\frac{D1}{D} = \frac{Y(I)-0}{Y(I)-Y(I+1)}$$

which can be written in BASIC as

```
D1=D*Y(I)/(Y(I)-Y(I+1))
```

We can compute the vertical velocity immediately *before* impact as

```
Z=Z(I)-G*D1
```

so that the vertical velocity immediately *after* impact will be

```
Z1=-C*(Z(I)-G*D1)
```

Now the vertical velocity at the end of the time increment will be

```
Z(I+1)=Z1-G*(D-D1)
```

and the vertical displacement at the end of the time increment can be written as

```
Y(I+1)=.5*(Z1+Z(I+1))*(D-D1)
```

The Program Outline

We now have enough information at our disposal to write an outline of a complete BASIC program. Specifically,

1. Read H, V, N, C and D.
   (*a*) If H=0, then terminate the computation.
   (*b*) If H is assigned some positive value, then proceed below.
2. Initialize all parameters:

I=1 (I is the increment counter)	X(1)=0
B=0 (B is the bounce counter)	Z(1)=0
T(1)=0	Y(1)=H

3. Compute the horizontal and vertical displacement and the vertical velocity for each time increment, using the formulas given above.
4. If the ball hits the ground during the time increment, test to see whether this is a bounce condition or a program termination.
   (*a*) Bounce condition (B<N)—recalculate the vertical velocity and the vertical displacement to account for the bounce, increment the bounce counter (i.e., B=B+1) and then continue to the next time increment.
   (*b*) Terminal condition (B=N)—obtain the final time and the horizontal displacement when the ball hits the ground.

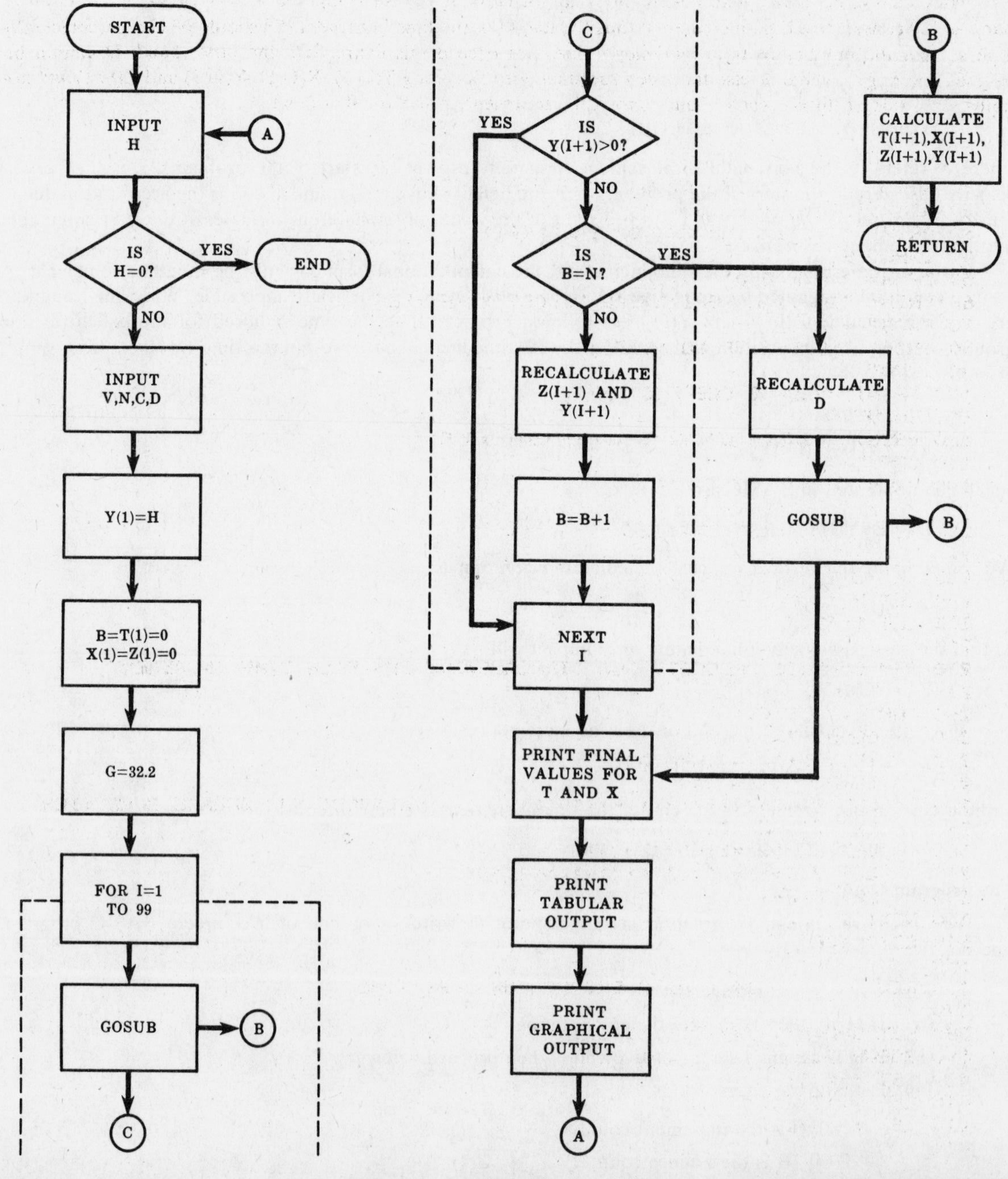

Fig. 6.19

5. Print the final values for X and T, followed by a complete tabulation of T, X, Y and Z.
6. Plot Y against T, using the method discussed in Example 6.27.
7. Return to step 1.

An overall flowchart of the computation is shown in Fig. 6.19. Notice that the computation of T(I+1), X(I+1), Z(I+1) and Y(I+1) is shown within the structure of a subroutine.

The reader who has studied numerical calculus should recognize that we are integrating the second-order differential equation $d^2y/dt^2 = -g$ in this example. The integration technique is known as a *modified Euler method.*

The BASIC Program

Figure 6.20 shows a complete BASIC program for carrying out the computation. The program allows for as many as 100 consecutive time increments; thus the length of the time increment (D) should be chosen sufficiently large so that the number of time increments does not exceed this figure. [On the other hand, D cannot be assigned too large a value or else the given formulas for calculating T(I+1), X(I+1), Y(I+1) and Z(I+1) will not apply. As a rule of thumb, each bounce should be represented by 8 to 20 points.]

```
10 REM          SIMULATION OF A BOUNCING BALL
20 DIM X(100),Y(100),Z(100),T(100)
30 PRINT "INITIAL HEIGHT OF BALL (FT)";
40 INPUT H
50 IF H=0 THEN 810
60 PRINT "INITIAL HORIZONTAL VELOCITY (FT/SEC)";
70 INPUT V
80 PRINT "NUMBER OF BOUNCES";
90 INPUT N
100 PRINT "BOUNCE COEFFICIENT";
110 INPUT C
120 PRINT "LENGTH OF TIME INCREMENT (SEC)";
130 INPUT D
140 PRINT
150
160 REM          INITIALIZE PARAMETERS
170
180 LET B=T(1)=X(1)=Z(1)=0
190 LET Y(1)=H
200 LET G=32.2
210
220 REM COMPUTE VELOCITY AND DISPLACEMENT FOR EACH TIME INCREMENT
230
240 FOR I=1 TO 99
250    GOSUB 730
260    IF Y(I+1)>0 THEN 330
270    IF B=N THEN 360
280    LET D1=D*Y(I)/(Y(I)-Y(I+1))          'CORRECT FOR BOUNCE CONDITION
290    LET Z1=-C*(Z(I)-G*D1)
300    LET Z(I+1)=Z1-G*(D-D1)
310    LET Y(I+1)=.5*(Z1+Z(I+1))*(D-D1)
320    LET B=B+1
330 NEXT I
340 GOTO 400
350
360 REM          BALL HITS GROUND FOR LAST TIME
370
380 LET D=D*Y(I)/(Y(I)-Y(I+1))
390 GOSUB 730
400 LET I1=I+1
410 LET T1=T(I1)
420 LET X1=X(I1)
430
```

Fig. 6.20 (*Program continues on next page*)

```
440 REM          PRINT NUMERICAL OUTPUT
450
460 PRINT "HORIZONTAL DISTANCE TRAVELED=";X1;"FT"
470 PRINT "TIME REQUIRED=";T1;"SECS"
480 PRINT
490 FOR I=1 TO I1
500    PRINT "T=";T(I),"X=";X(I),"Y=";Y(I),"Z=";Z(I)
510 NEXT I
520 PRINT
530
540 REM          PRINT GRAPHICAL OUTPUT
550
560 PRINT "GRAPHICAL SOLUTION TO BOUNCING BALL PROBLEM"
570 PRINT
580 FOR J=0 TO 70
590    PRINT TAB(J);".";
600 NEXT J
610 PRINT TAB(71);"*"
620 PRINT "."
630 FOR I=2 TO I1          'GENERATE SUCCESSIVE POINTS OF CURVE
640    LET J=INT(71*Y(I)/Y(1))
650    IF J=0 THEN 680
660    PRINT ".";TAB(J);"*"
670    GOTO 690
680    PRINT "*"
690    PRINT "."
700 NEXT I
710 GOTO 30
720
730 REM SUBROUTINE TO CALCULATE VELOCITY AND DISPLACEMENT AT END
740 REM          OF TIME INCREMENT
750
760 LET T(I+1)=T(I)+D
770 LET X(I+1)=X(I)+V*D
780 LET Z(I+1)=Z(I)-G*D
790 LET Y(I+1)=Y(I)+.5*(Z(I+1)+Z(I))*D
800 RETURN
810 END
```

Fig. 6.20 *(continued)*

The subroutine which is used to evaluate T(I+1), X(I+1), Z(I+1) and Y(I+1) is made up of statements 730–800. It should be understood that the subroutine structure is not at all essential for carrying out these calculations. Use of a subroutine is desirable, however, since this block of statements is referenced from two different places within the program (namely statements 250 and 390).

The generation of the tabular output data is carried out in a straightforward manner by means of a FOR-TO loop (statements 490 through 510). Although the method used to generate the graph (statements 560 through 700) is less obvious, we see that this portion of the program is identical to the material discussed in Example 6.27. Hence the logic used should be readily apparent.

Figure 6.21(*a*) contains the numerical output which is generated for the following input data. (The input data are underlined.)

H = 2.00 ft

V = 1.20 ft/sec

N = 3

C = 0.80

D = 0.05 sec

We see that a distance of 2.06 feet is required for the ball to experience three complete bounces. The corresponding time is 1.72 seconds.

```
INITIAL HEIGHT OF BALL (FT) ?2.00
INITIAL HORIZONTAL VELOCITY (FT/SEC) ?1.20
NUMBER OF BOUNCES ?3
BOUNCE COEFFICIENT ?0.80
LENGTH OF TIME INCREMENT (SEC) ?0.05


HORIZONTAL DISTANCE TRAVELED= 2.06344 FT
TIME REQUIRED= 1.71953 SECS


T= 0          X= 0            Y= 2            Z= 0
T= 0.05       X= 6.00000E-2   Y= 1.95975      Z=-1.61
T= 0.1        X= 0.12         Y= 1.839        Z=-3.22
T= 0.15       X= 0.18         Y= 1.63775      Z=-4.83
T= 0.2        X= 0.24         Y= 1.356        Z=-6.44
T= 0.25       X= 0.3          Y= 0.99375      Z=-8.05
T= 0.3        X= 0.36         Y= 0.551        Z=-9.66
T= 0.35       X= 0.42         Y= 2.77500E-2   Z=-11.27
T= 0.4        X= 0.48         Y= 0.396269     Z= 7.5392
T= 0.45       X= 0.54         Y= 0.732979     Z= 5.9292
T= 0.5        X= 0.6          Y= 0.989189     Z= 4.3192
T= 0.55       X= 0.66         Y= 1.1649       Z= 2.7092
T= 0.6        X= 0.72         Y= 1.26011      Z= 1.0992
T= 0.65       X= 0.78         Y= 1.27482      Z=-0.5108
T= 0.7        X= 0.84         Y= 1.20903      Z=-2.1208
T= 0.75       X= 0.9          Y= 1.06274      Z=-3.7308
T= 0.8        X= 0.96         Y= 0.835949     Z=-5.3408
T= 0.85       X= 1.02         Y= 0.528659     Z=-6.9508
T= 0.9        X= 1.08         Y= 0.140869     Z=-8.5608
T= 0.95       X= 1.14         Y= 0.233292     Z= 6.1104
T= 1.         X= 1.2          Y= 0.498562     Z= 4.5004
T= 1.05       X= 1.26         Y= 0.683332     Z= 2.8904
T= 1.1        X= 1.32         Y= 0.787602     Z= 1.2804
T= 1.15       X= 1.38         Y= 0.811372     Z=-0.329597
T= 1.2        X= 1.44         Y= 0.754642     Z=-1.9396
T= 1.25       X= 1.5          Y= 0.617413     Z=-3.5496
T= 1.3        X= 1.56         Y= 0.399683     Z=-5.1596
T= 1.35       X= 1.62         Y= 0.101453     Z=-6.7696
T= 1.4        X= 1.68         Y= 0.189303     Z= 4.58198
T= 1.45       X= 1.74         Y= 0.378152     Z= 2.97198
T= 1.5        X= 1.8          Y= 0.486501     Z= 1.36198
T= 1.55       X= 1.86         Y= 0.514351     Z=-0.248016
T= 1.6        X= 1.92         Y= 0.4617       Z=-1.85802
T= 1.65       X= 1.98         Y= 0.328549     Z=-3.46802
T= 1.7        X= 2.04         Y= 0.114898     Z=-5.07802
T= 1.71953    X= 2.06344      Y= 9.58086E-3   Z=-5.7069
```

(*a*)

Fig. 6.21 (*continues on p. 156*)

In Fig. 6.21(*b*) we see a computer-prepared graph showing the position of the ball at various times. The individual bounces can be seen very clearly in this figure.

Finally, the bottom of Fig. 6.21(*b*) shows a request for a new set of input data. The computation is terminated by supplying a zero value for H.

We will say much more about the generation of graphical output in Chapter 12, which is concerned with microcomputer graphics.

```
GRAPHICAL SOLUTION TO BOUNCING BALL PROBLEM
```

```
INITIAL HEIGHT OF BALL (FT) ?0
```

(*b*)

Fig. 6.21 (*continued*)

Review Questions

6.1 What are the differences between a function and a subroutine?

6.2 Are functions and/or subroutines ever *required* in a BASIC program? What are the advantages in their use?

6.3 In what way can functions and subroutines be helpful in improving the organization of a BASIC program?

6.4 Summarize the rules for naming functions. How are numeric functions distinguished from string functions?

6.5 What is the purpose of the DEF statement? How is it written?

6.6 What are the rules that govern the use of arguments in a function? Can a function make use of variables that are not specified as arguments?

6.7 What is the difference between a function definition and a function reference? How is a function referenced?

6.8 What are dummy arguments? What correspondence must exist between a set of arguments in a function reference and the associated dummy arguments?

6.9 Can an argument consist of something other than a nonsubscripted variable (e.g., a constant, subscripted variable or formula)? Is this also true of a dummy argument?

6.10 How is a DEF statement written for a multiline function?

6.11 Cite two places where the function name must appear in a multiline function.

6.12 What is the purpose of the FNEND statement? How is it written?

6.13 Can control be transferred out of a multiline function by means of a GO TO statement? A RETURN statement?

6.14 Must the value returned by a function be of the same type as the function's arguments?

6.15 Is it necessary that all of the arguments in a function be of the same type?

6.16 How are characters stored within a computer?

6.17 What is the 7-bit ASCII code?

6.18 What is the purpose of the CHANGE statement? Cite two different ways that it can be written.

6.19 What is the purpose of the ASC function? How is it used?

6.20 What is the purpose of the CHR$ function? How is it used?

6.21 What is the purpose of the RND function? How is it used? Does this function require an argument?

6.22 What is meant by pseudo-random numbers? How do pseudo-random numbers differ from numbers that are truly random?

6.23 What is the purpose of the RANDOMIZE statement? How is it written?

6.24 Summarize the rules for defining a subroutine. Must a subroutine begin with any particular statement?

6.25 Can arguments be included in a subroutine?

6.26 Can a subroutine end with an FNEND statement? A RETURN statement? An END statement?

6.27 What is the purpose of the RETURN statement? How is it written? What happens when a RETURN statement is encountered during program execution?

6.28 Can a subroutine contain more than one RETURN statement? Explain.

6.29 What is the purpose of a GOSUB statement? How is it written? Can a program which has only one subroutine contain more than one GOSUB statement?

6.30 Can a FOR-TO loop be included in a subroutine or a multiline function?

6.31 Can control be transferred out of a subroutine by means of a GO TO statement? An IF-THEN statement?

6.32 Describe the hierarchical ordering that must be observed when subroutines are nested.

6.33 What advantage is there in the graphical display of output data?

6.34 Which library functions are used to produce graphical output? In what type of programming structure are these functions usually included?

Solved Problems

6.35 Write a BASIC function for each of the situations described below.

(*a*) Evaluate the algebraic formula $z = \dfrac{(u/v)+(x/y)}{2}$

```
10 DEF FNZ(U,V,X,Y)=(U/V+X/Y)/2
```

(*b*) If X represents a positive decimal quantity, obtain a rounded value for X with two digits to the right of the decimal point.

```
20 DEF FNY(X)=.01*INT(100*(X+.005))
```

(*c*) Evaluate the algebraic formula $p = \begin{cases} \log(t^2 - a) & \text{for } t^2 > a \\ \log(t^2) & \text{for } t^2 \leq a \end{cases}$

```
30 DEF FNP(T,A)
40 IF T<=SQR(A) THEN 70
50 LET FNP=LOG(T↑2-A)
60 GO TO 80
70 LET FNP=LOG(T↑2)
80 FNEND
```

(*d*) Calculate the sum of the first N elements of the numeric list L; i.e., compute the sum L(1)+L(2)+ · · · +L(N).

```
100 DEF FNS(N)
110 LET S=0
120 FOR I=1 TO N
130       LET S=S+L(I)
140 NEXT I
150 LET FNS=S
160 FNEND
```

(*e*) Suppose that M$ and N$ each represent a single letter. Construct a single string containing the two letters, arranged in alphabetical order.

```
200 DEF FNN$(M$,N$)
210 LET L(0)=2
220 IF M$>N$ THEN 260
230 LET L(1)=ACS(M$)
240 LET L(2)=ASC(N$)
250 GO TO 280
260 LET L(1)=ASC(N$)
270 LET L(2)=ASC(M$)
280 CHANGE L TO L$
290 LET FNN$=L$
300 FNEND
```

(*f*) Calculate the average of two random numbers, each having a value between A and B.

```
100 DEF FNR(A,B)
110 LET R1=A+(B-A)*RND
120 LET R2=A+(B-A)*RND
130 LET FNR=(R1+R2)/2
140 FNEND
```

This function can also be written as simply

```
100 DEF FNR=A+(B-A)*(RND+RND)/2
```

6.36 Each of the situations described below requires a reference to one of the functions defined in Problem 6.35. Write an appropriate BASIC statement, or a sequence of statements, in each case.

(*a*) Print a value for *f*, where

$$f = \frac{(a/b) + (c/d)}{2}$$

[See Problem 6.35(*a*).]

```
100 PRINT FNZ(A,B,C,D)
```

(*b*) Suppose T represents some positive quantity whose value may exceed 1. Calculate a value for T1, where T1 has the same value as T except that the decimal portion of T1 is rounded to two digits. [See Problem 6.35(*b*).]

```
110 LET T1=INT(T)+FNY(T-INT(T))
```

(*c*) Let P1 represent the quantity

$$\log[(a+b)^2 - c] \quad \text{if} \quad (a+b)^2 > c$$

and

$$\log[(a+b)^2] \quad \text{if} \quad (a+b)^2 \le c$$

[See Problem 6.35(*c*).]

```
30 LET P1=FNP((A+B),C)
```

(*d*) A numeric list L contains 101 elements. Beginning with L(1), determine how many consecutive elements can be added without the sum exceeding a value of 25. [See Problem 6.35(*d*).]

```
40 FOR J=1 TO 100
50      IF FNS(J)>25 THEN 80
60 NEXT J
70 LET J=101
80 PRINT "N=";J-1
```

(*e*) The variables M and N each represent the ASCII equivalent of a single letter (character). Form a string consisting of the two letters, in alphabetical order. [See Problem 6.35(*e*).]

```
80 LET L$=FNN$(CHR$(M),CHR$(N))
```

(*f*) Determine the average of two random numbers, each having a value between 1 and 10. Transfer control to statement number 250 if this average value exceeds 5. [See Problem 6.35(*f*).]

```
100 IF FNR(1,10)>5 THEN 250
```

6.37 Each of the following problems contains a function definition and/or function reference which is incorrectly written. Identify all errors.

(*a*) DEF FNW(A,B,C↑2,3)=((A+B)*C↑2)/3

Constants and formulas cannot be used as dummy arguments.

(*b*)
```
10 DEF FNC(T1,T2,N)=((T1-T2)/T2)↑N
 . . .
60 LET V=C*FNC(2*A,F$)
```

The arguments in the function reference do not agree in number or in type with the dummy arguments in the function definition.

(*c*)
```
10 DEF FN4(X(1),X(2),X(3))=X(1)+2*X(2)-3*X(3)
```

This statement contains two errors:

(i) The function is named incorrectly.

(ii) Subscripted variables cannot appear as dummy arguments.

(*d*)
```
10 DEF FNG(A,B,C)
20 LET P=A+B*X+C*X↑2
30 LET Q=B+C*X
40 LET G=P+Q*X+C*X↑2
50 FNEND
```

The function name (FNG) is not assigned a value within the function.

(*e*)
```
100 DEF FNC(X,Y,Z)
110 IF X+Y>=Z THEN 140
120 LET FNC=LOG(Z-(X+Y))
130 RETURN
140 LET FNC=LOG(Z)
150 FNEND
```

Control cannot be transferred out of a function by means of a RETURN statement.

6.38 The following groups of statements represent portions of BASIC programs that contain one or more subroutines. Each example is written correctly.

(*a*)
```
10 DIM L(100)
   . . .
60 GOSUB 200
   . . .
120 GOSUB 200
   . . .
160 GOSUB 200
   . . .
190 STOP
200 LET S=0              )
210 FOR I=1 TO N         |
220       LET S=S+L(I)   } Subroutine
230 NEXT I               |
240 RETURN               )
250 END
```

Notice that the subroutine is referenced from three different points within the program.

(*b*)
```
50 GOSUB 120
   . . .
120 IF A>B THEN 150               )
130 LET C=SQR((B-A)↑N)            |
140 RETURN                        } Subroutine
150 LET C=SQR(((A+B)/(A-B))↑N)    |
160 RETURN                        )
```

The subroutine in this example contains two RETURN statements.

(*c*)
```
10 DEF FNZ(X,Y)=X↑2+Y↑2
   . . .
70 GOSUB 180
   . . .
180 REM SAMPLE SUBROUTINE    )
   . . .                     |
210 LET W=FNZ(A,B+C)         } Subroutine
   . . .                     |
250 RETURN                   )
```

Notice that the subroutine references the programmer-defined function FNZ.

(*d*)

```
75 GOSUB 300
   . . .
125 GOSUB 200
   . . .
200 LET Z=C1*X+C2*Y  ⎫
   . . .             ⎪
250 GOSUB 300        ⎬ First subroutine
   . . .             ⎪
290 RETURN           ⎭
300 LET W=(U+V)/Z    ⎫
   . . .             ⎬ Second subroutine
370 RETURN           ⎭
380 END
```

This example makes use of nested subroutines. Notice that the second subroutine is referenced by both the first subroutine and the main part of the program.

6.39 The following groups of statements represent portions of BASIC programs that contain subroutines. Each example contains one or more errors. Identify all errors.

(*a*)

```
45 GOSUB 165
   . . .
165 LET C=C1+C2+C3   ⎫
   . . .             ⎪
190 GO TO 60         ⎪
   . . .             ⎬ Subroutine
225 RETURN           ⎪
230 FNEND            ⎭
235 END
```

This example contains two errors:

(i) Control cannot be transferred out of a subroutine by means of a GO TO statement.

(ii) A subroutine cannot end with an FNEND statement.

(*b*)

```
60 GOSUB 200
   . . .
120 IF X<Y THEN 225
   . . .
200 REM START OF SUBROUTINE  ⎫
   . . .                     ⎬ Subroutine
300 RETURN                   ⎭
```

Control cannot be transferred into a subroutine by an IF-THEN statement.

(*c*)

```
30 GOSUB 100
   . . .
100 REM SUBROUTINE A  ⎫
   . . .              ⎪
120 GOSUB 200         ⎬ Subroutine A
   . . .              ⎪
160 RETURN            ⎭
200 REM SUBROUTINE B  ⎫
   . . .              ⎪
225 GOSUB 100         ⎬ Subroutine B
   . . .              ⎪
245 RETURN            ⎭
```

The subroutines are not nested properly. (Subroutine A references subroutine B, which in turn references subroutine A.)

6.40 Write a portion of a program to generate a graph of the function $y = \sin t$. Generate 130 points, double-spaced, with the t axis running down the center of the printed page. Let the time increment be 0.1 second.

```
10 FOR J=0 TO 70
20     IF J=35 THEN 50
30     PRINT TAB(J);".";
40     GO TO 60
50     PRINT TAB(J);"*";
60 NEXT J
70 PRINT
80 PRINT TAB(35);"."
90 LET T=0
100 FOR I=2 TO 130
110     LET T=T+.1
120     LET J=35+INT(35*SIN(T))
130     IF J>35 THEN 190
140     IF J=35 THEN 170
150     PRINT TAB(J);"*";TAB(35);"."
160     GO TO 200
170     PRINT TAB(J);"*"
180     GO TO 200
190     PRINT TAB(35);".";TAB(J);"*"
200     PRINT TAB(35);"."
210 NEXT I
220 END
```

Supplementary Problems

6.41 Write a BASIC function to evaluate each of the algebraic formulas shown below.

(*a*) $y = ax^b$

(*b*) $q = c_0 + c_1 r + c_2 r^2 + c_3 r^3 + c_4 r^4$

(*c*) $i = (j + k)^{j+k}$

(*d*) $r = \begin{cases} \sqrt{b^2 - 4ac} & \text{if } b^2 > 4ac \\ \sqrt{4ac - b^2} & \text{if } b^2 < 4ac \end{cases}$

6.42 Write a BASIC function for each of the situations described below.

(*a*) If Z represents some positive quantity whose value may exceed 1, obtain a rounded integer value.

(*b*) Calculate the product of the first N elements of the numeric list T; i.e., compute the product T(1)*···*T(N).

(*c*) Generate five random numbers, each having a value between A and B, where A and B represent positive quantities and B>A. Return the value of the largest number.

(*d*) Examine the sign of the number represented by some variable X. If X is negative, return the string NEGATIVE; if X is positive, return the string POSITIVE; and if X has a value of zero, return the string ZERO.

(*e*) Suppose N$ represents a multiletter word. Examine each of the letters and return the letter that comes first in the alphabet.

6.43 Each of the situations described below requires a reference to a function defined in Problem 6.41 or 6.42. Write an appropriate BASIC statement, or a sequence of statements, in each case.

(*a*) Evaluate $t = (c_1 + c_2)(x + y)^3$ [see Problem 6.41(*a*)].

(*b*) Evaluate $q = c_0 + c_1 \log(x) + c_2 [\log(x)]^2 + c_3 [\log(x)]^3 + c_4 [\log(x)]^4$ [see Problem 6.41(*b*)].

(*c*) Print the value of $f = (a - b + c)^{a-b+c}$ [see Problem 6.41(*c*)].

(*d*) Calculate the difference between a given number, represented by the variable X, and its closest integer. Express this difference as a positive quantity. [See Problem 6.42(*a*).]

(*e*) A numeric list T contains 61 elements. Beginning with T(1), determine how many consecutive elements must be multiplied together in order that the product will exceed 1000. Assume that all of the quantities are positive. [See Problem 6.42(*b*).]

(*f*) Generate 20 sets of 5 random numbers, each having a value between 2 and 5. Print the largest random number obtained in each set of 5. [See Problem 6.42(*c*).]

6.44 Each of the following problems shows a part of a BASIC program involving a function or a subroutine. At least one error is present in every case. Identify all errors.

(*a*)
```
10 DEF FNK(J,K)=(C1*J+C2*K)/(J+K)
...
60 LET T=FNK(A,B,C)
```

(*b*)
```
10 DEF FNC(X,Y)
20 IF X<Y THEN 50
30 LET C=SQR((X-Y)/2)
40 RETURN
50 LET C=SQR(X/(X+Y))
60 RETURN
70 FNEND
```

(*c*)
```
50 GOSUB 200
...
80 GO TO 230
...
200 REM SUBROUTINE A  ⎫
...                   ⎪
230 LET Z=X+Y         ⎬ Subroutine
...                   ⎪
250 RETURN            ⎭
260 FNEND
```

(*d*)
```
10 DEF FNZ1(A↑2,B↑2)
...
50 LET FNZ1=(A↑2-B↑2)/(A↑2+B↑2)
60 FNEND
```

(*e*)
```
10 DEF FNK(J,K)=(C1*J+C2*K)/(J+K)
...
80 PRINT J,K,FNK
```

(*f*)
```
100 GOSUB 200
...
200 REM SUBROUTINE A  ⎫
...                   ⎪
240 IF D<.01 THEN 150 ⎬ Subroutine
...                   ⎪
270 RETURN            ⎭
```

(*g*)

```
10 DEF FNX(A,B,C)
 . . .
50 GOSUB 300
 . . .
80 FNEND
 . . .
300 REM FIRST SUBROUTINE   ⎫
 . . .                      ⎪
330 LET Y=FNX(U,V,W)        ⎬ Subroutine
 . . .                      ⎪
350 RETURN                  ⎭
```

Programming Problems

6.45 Modify the program shown in Example 6.6 to *minimize* a given function. Use the program to obtain the roots of the following equations, using the method described at the end of Example 6.6.

(*a*) $x + \cos x = 1 + \sin x,\ \pi/2 < x < \pi$

(*b*) $x^5 + 3x^2 = 10,\ 0 \le x \le 3$ (see Example 4.5)

6.46 Modify the program shown in Example 6.15 so that the function FNP is replaced by a subroutine.

6.47 Modify the program shown in Example 6.20 so that a sequence of craps games will be simulated automatically, in a nonconversational manner. Include a counter that will determine the total number of wins and an input variable whose value will specify how many games will be simulated.

Use the program to simulate some large number of games (e.g., 1000). Estimate the probability of coming out ahead when playing craps. (This value, expressed as a decimal, is equal to the number of wins divided by the total number of games played. If the probability exceeds .500, it favors the player; otherwise it favors the "house.")

6.48 Modify the program shown in Example 6.26 to process a weekly payroll. Use a function rather than a subroutine to calculate the amount of federal tax withheld.

The amount of federal income tax to be withheld on a weekly basis is shown in Table 6.3. These figures are based upon an adjusted weekly gross income equal to the weekly gross income less $35.58 for each exemption.

Table 6.3 Federal Income Tax Withholding Rates

WEEKLY Payroll Period							
(*a*) SINGLE person—including head of household:				(*b*) MARRIED person—			
If the amount of wages is:		*The amount of income tax to be withheld shall be:*		*If the amount of wages is:*		*The amount of income tax to be withheld shall be:*	
Not over $20		0		Not over $20		0	
Over—	*But not over—*		*of excess over—*	*Over—*	*But not over—*		*of excess over—*
$20	−$31	14%	−$20	$20	−$42	14%	−$20
$31	−$50	$1.54 plus 17%	−$31	$42	−$77	$3.08 plus 17%	−$42
$50	−$100	$4.77 plus 20%	−$50	$77	−$163	$9.03 plus 16%	−$77
$100	−$135	$14.77 plus 18%	−$100	$163	−$269	$22.79 plus 19%	−$163
$135	−$212	$21.07 plus 21%	−$135	$269	−$385	$42.93 plus 21%	−$269
$212	—	$37.24 plus 24%	−$212	$385	—	$67.29 plus 25%	−$385

The state tax will be calculated as 1 percent of all gross income up to \$150 a week, $1\frac{1}{2}$ percent of any additional income up to \$500 and 2 percent of any excess over \$500. The local tax will be computed as 1 percent of the first \$200 of gross income. Weekly earnings in excess of \$200 will not be taxed at the local level.

6.49 Modify the bouncing ball program in Example 6.28 to solve the following problem. A target is located a distance L feet from the origin (L is an input parameter). Determine by trial and error what horizontal velocity the ball should have so that it hits the target after the second bounce. Assume the target is a small circle that rests on the ground. Show the location of the target on the output graph.

6.50 Write a BASIC program that will generate a hard-copy graph of each of the following functions.

(*a*) $y = 2\sqrt{x}$, for values of x varying from 0 to 10

(*b*) $y = x^3$, for values of x varying from -1 to $+1$

(*c*) $y = 2e^{-0.1t} \sin 0.5t$, for values of t varying from 0 to 60 (see Problem 5.48)

In each case plot enough points so that the curve can be seen clearly.

6.51 Write a BASIC program that will generate a picture of the American flag. Use an asterisk to denote each star. Represent each stripe by several lines of repeated R's or W's, depending on the color of the stripe.

6.52 Prepare a detailed outline, a corresponding flowchart and a complete BASIC program for each of the problems presented below. Include functions and subroutines wherever it is practicable to do so.

(*a*) Calculate the average of a set of N numbers. Carry out the calculations within a programmer-defined function. Use the program to process the temperature data given in Problem 5.54.

(*b*) Extend the program in Problem 6.52(*a*) to calculate the deviation of each number from the average. Use the program to process the temperature data given in Problem 5.54. Can a programmer-defined function be used for this purpose?

(*c*) Calculate the area under a curve, using the methods described in Problems 5.57(*j*) and 5.57(*k*). Use the program to calculate the area under the curve $y = x^3$ between the limits $x = 1$ and $x = 4$.

(*d*) Another way to calculate the area under a curve is to employ the *Monte Carlo* method, which makes use of randomly generated numbers. Suppose that the curve $y = f(x)$ is positive for any value of x between the specified lower and upper limits $x = a$ and $x = b$. Let the largest value of y be y^*. The Monte Carlo method proceeds as follows:

(i) Begin with a counter set equal to zero.

(ii) Generate a random number, r_x, whose value lies between a and b.

(iii) Evaluate $y(r_x)$.

(iv) Generate a second random number, r_y, whose value lies between 0 and y^*.

(v) Compare r_y with $y(r_x)$. If r_y is less than or equal to $y(r_x)$, then this point will fall under or on the given curve. Hence the counter is incremented by 1.

(vi) Steps (ii) through (v) are repeated a large number of times. Each time will be called a *cycle.*

(vii) When a specified number of cycles has been completed, the fraction of points which fell on or under the curve, F, is computed as the value of the counter divided by the total number of cycles. The area under the curve is then obtained as $A = Fy^*(b - a)$.

Write a BASIC program to implement this strategy. Use the program to find the area under the curve $y = e^{-x^2}$ between the limits $x = 0$ and $x = 1$. Determine how many cycles are required to obtain an answer which is accurate to three significant figures. Compare the computer time required for this problem with the time required for Problem 5.57(*k*).

(*e*) Calculate an average score for each student in a class, and then calculate a class average of the individual averages. [See Problems 4.48(*g*) through 4.48(*i*).] Determine the *median* of the individual averages (a value which is equalled or exceeded by half of the individual averages). Use a function to calculate the averages and a different function to compute the median. Apply the program to the data given in Problem 4.48(*g*). Can subroutines be used rather than functions?

(*f*) A normally distributed random variate x, with mean μ and standard deviation σ, can be generated from the formula

$$x = \mu + \sigma \frac{\sum_{i=1}^{N} r_i - N/2}{\sqrt{N/12}}$$

where r_i is a uniformly distributed random number whose value lies between 0 and 1. A value of $N = 12$ is frequently selected when using this formula. The underlying basis for the formula is the *central limit theorem*, which states that a set of mean values of uniformly distributed random variables will be normally distributed.

Write a BASIC program that will generate a specified number of normally distributed random variates with a given mean and a given standard deviation. Let the number of random variates, the mean and the standard deviation be input parameters.

Use the program to generate a histogram of a normal distribution with $\mu = 2.5$ and $\sigma = 1.5$.

(*g*) Write a BASIC program that will allow a person to play a game of tic-tac-toe against the computer. Write the program in such a manner that the computer can be either the first or the second player. If the computer is to be the first player, let the first move be generated randomly. Write out the complete status of the game after each move. Have the computer acknowledge a win by either party when it occurs.

(*h*) Write a BASIC program which will simulate a game of blackjack between two players. Note that the computer will not be a participant in this game but will simply deal the cards to each player and provide each player with one or more "hits" (additional cards) when requested.

The cards are dealt in order, first one card to each player, then a second card to each player. Additional hits may then be requested.

The object of the game is to obtain 21 points, or as many points as possible without exceeding 21 points, on each hand. A player is automatically disqualified if his or her hand exceeds 21 points. Face cards count 10 points, and an ace can count either 1 point or 11 points. Thus a player can obtain 21 points with the first two cards (blackjack!) if dealt an ace and either a 10 or a picture card. If the player has a low score with the first two cards, he may ask for one or more hits.

A random number generator should be used to simulate the dealing of the cards. Be sure to include a provision that the same card is not dealt more than once.

(*i*) Roulette is played with a wheel containing 38 different squares along its circumference. Two of these squares, numbered 0 and 00, are green; 18 squares are red; and 18 are black. The red and black squares alternate in color and are numbered 1 through 36 in random order.

A small marble is spun within the wheel. Eventually, the marble comes to rest in a groove beneath one of the squares. The game is played by betting on the outcome of each spin in any one of the following ways.

1. By selecting a single red or black square, at 35-to-1 odds. (Thus, if a player were to bet $1.00 and win, he or she would receive a total of $36.00—the original $1.00 plus an additional $35.00.)
2. By selecting a color (either red or black) at 1-to-1 odds. (Thus, if a player chose red on a $1.00 bet, he or she would receive $2.00 if the marble came to rest beneath any red square.)
3. By selecting either the odd or the even numbers (excluding 0 and 00) at 1-to-1 odds.
4. By selecting either the low 18 or the high 18 numbers at 1-to-1 odds.

The player will automatically lose if the marble comes to rest beneath one of the green squares (0 or 00).

Write a conversational-style BASIC program that will simulate a roulette game. Allow the players to select whatever type of play they wish. Then print the outcome of each game followed by an appropriate message indicating whether each player has won or lost.

(*j*) Write a BASIC program that will encode or decode a line of text (a string). To encode a line of text, proceed as follows.

1. Convert each character (including blank spaces) to its ASCII equivalent.
2. Generate a positive random integer. Add this integer to the ASCII equivalent of each character. (The same integer will be used for the entire line of text.)

3. Suppose that N1 represents the lowest permissible value in the ASCII code, and N2 represents the highest permissible value. If the number obtained in step 2 above (i.e., the original ASCII equivalent plus the random integer) exceeds N2, then subtract the largest possible multiple of N2 from this number and add the remainder to N1. Hence the encoded number will always fall between N1 and N2 and will therefore always represent some character.
4. Print the characters that correspond to the encoded ASCII values.

The procedure is reversed when decoding a line of text. Be certain, however, that the same random number is used in decoding as was used in encoding.

(*k*) Write a complete BASIC program that will simulate a game of BINGO. Print each letter-number combination as it is drawn. Be sure that no combination is drawn more than once. Remember that each of the letters B-I-N-G-O corresponds to a certain range of numbers, as indicated below.

B: 1–15
I: 16–30
N: 31–45
G: 46–60
O: 61–75

Chapter 7

Vectors and Matrices

In Chapter 5 we learned that all of the elements in an array can be referred to collectively by specifying a common array name. When carrying out array manipulations, however, it was necessary to work individually with each element of the array (i.e., each subscripted variable). Usually this was accomplished by means of a FOR-TO loop.

Some versions of BASIC contain a collection of special statements, known as *matrix statements*, for carrying out the more common array operations. Usually a single matrix statement will be used for a given operation. Thus it is possible to perform an operation on all of the elements in an array without making use of a FOR-TO loop. We will see how this is accomplished in this chapter.

7.1 VECTOR AND MATRIX OPERATIONS

Vector and *matrix* are mathematical terms that refer to a list and a table, respectively. Thus a vector is a one-dimensional array, and a matrix is a two-dimensional array. Since a vector is actually a special kind of matrix, most of the general rules that apply to matrices are also valid for vectors.

As before, we will use subscripted variables to represent the individual array elements. In the case of a matrix we will let the first subscript represent the row, and the second subscript will indicate the column. Thus A(3,2) will represent the element in the third row, second column of the matrix A. Moreover, we will refer to a matrix having m rows and n columns as an $m \times n$ matrix. (Remember that the size of a vector or matrix must be specified by a DIM statement if the value of a subscript exceeds 10.)

The most common vector and matrix operations are addition, subtraction, scalar multiplication and vector multiplication. A special BASIC statement is available for each of these operations. The language also contains a matrix assignment statement. Each of these statements is discussed separately below.

Assignment

The matrix assignment statement is of the form

```
10 MAT C=A
```

This statement causes each element of A to be assigned to the corresponding element of C.

EXAMPLE 7.1

Suppose that A represents the following 2×3 matrix.

$$A = \begin{bmatrix} 3 & 5 & -9 \\ 2 & -6 & 7 \end{bmatrix}$$

The matrix statement

```
10 MAT C=A
```

will cause C to be a 2×3 matrix whose elements are

$$C = \begin{bmatrix} 3 & 5 & -9 \\ 2 & -6 & 7 \end{bmatrix}$$

Subscripted variables are used to refer to the individual matrix elements. Hence C(1,1)=3, C(1,2)=5, C(1,3)=−9, C(2,1)=2, C(2,2)=−6 and C(2,3)=7.

Addition

Matrix addition is carried out by a statement of the form

```
10 MAT C=A+B
```

The result of this statement is that each element of C is assigned the sum of the corresponding elements of A and B, i.e., C(I,J)=A(I,J)+B(I,J). The matrices A and B must have the same number of rows and the same number of columns.

EXAMPLE 7.2

Suppose that A and B are 2×3 matrices whose elements have the following values.

$$A = \begin{bmatrix} 3 & 5 & -9 \\ 2 & -6 & 7 \end{bmatrix} \qquad B = \begin{bmatrix} 2 & 2 & 0 \\ -4 & 5 & 1 \end{bmatrix}$$

The matrix statement

```
10 MAT C=A+B
```

will cause C to be a 2×3 matrix whose elements are as follows.

$$C = \begin{bmatrix} (3+2) & (5+2) & (-9+0) \\ (2-4) & (-6+5) & (7+1) \end{bmatrix} = \begin{bmatrix} 5 & 7 & -9 \\ -2 & -1 & 8 \end{bmatrix}$$

A matrix can be updated with a matrix addition statement, e.g., a statement of the form

```
10 MAT A=A+B
```

is permissible. However multiple sums, such as

```
10 MAT D=A+B+C
```

are not allowed.

Subtraction

The matrix subtraction statement is very similar to the matrix addition statement except that the plus sign is replaced by a minus sign. Thus the statement

```
10 MAT C=A-B
```

will cause each element of C to be assigned the difference of the corresponding values of A and B, i.e., C(I,J)=A(I,J)−B(I,J). The matrices A and B must have the same number of rows and the same number of columns.

EXAMPLE 7.3

Suppose that A and B are 2×3 matrices having the same elements as in Example 7.2. The matrix statement

```
10 MAT C=A-B
```

will cause the following values to be assigned to C.

$$C = \begin{bmatrix} (3-2) & (5-2) & (-9-0) \\ (2+4) & (-6-5) & (7-1) \end{bmatrix} = \begin{bmatrix} 1 & 3 & -9 \\ 6 & -11 & 6 \end{bmatrix}$$

As with the matrix addition statement, a matrix can be updated via matrix subtraction. Thus a statement such as

```
10 MAT A=A-B
```

is permissible. On the other hand, statements such as

```
10 MAT D=A-B-C
```

and

```
10 MAT D=A+B-C
```

are not allowed.

Scalar Multiplication

In scalar multiplication all of the elements in a matrix are multiplied by a given constant. This is accomplished in BASIC with a statement of the form

```
10 MAT C=(K)*A
```

where A and C are matrices and K is an ordinary variable. Each element of C will be obtained as C(I,J)=(K)*A(I,J).

EXAMPLE 7.4

Suppose that A is the same 2×3 matrix given in Examples 7.1 and 7.2 and that K is a variable whose value is 3.5. The statement

```
10 MAT C=(K)*A
```

will cause the elements of C to have the following values.

$$C = (3.5)*\begin{bmatrix} 3 & 5 & -9 \\ 2 & -6 & 7 \end{bmatrix} = \begin{bmatrix} 10.5 & 17.5 & -31.5 \\ 7 & -21 & 24.5 \end{bmatrix}$$

The term contained in parentheses need not be a single variable. Constants, subscripted variables, formulas and function references may also appear. The point is, this term must represent a single numerical quantity. The scalar term must always be enclosed in parentheses.

EXAMPLE 7.5

Shown below are several examples of valid scalar multiplication statements.

```
10 MAT C=(100)*A
10 MAT C=(2*X+Y)*A
10 MAT C=(SQR(P↑2+Q↑2))*A
```

In these examples A and C are matrices, X, Y, P and Q are ordinary numeric variables, and SQR represents the square root library function.

A vector can be updated with the scalar multiplication statement. Thus the statement

```
10 MAT A=(10)*A
```

is permissible. As with matrix addition and subtraction, however, statements such as

```
10 MAT C=(10)*A*B
```

and

```
10 MAT C=(10)*A+B
```

are not allowed.

Matrix Multiplication

Two matrices can be multiplied if the number of columns in the first matrix is the same as the number of rows in the second matrix. The result will be a matrix having the same number of rows as the first matrix and the same number of columns as the second. Thus if A is a $k \times m$ matrix and B is an $m \times n$ matrix, then the matrix operation C=A*B will generate a new matrix, C, having k rows and n columns. Each element of C will be obtained as

C(I,J)=A(I,1)*B(1,J)+A(I,2)*B(2,J)+ · · · +A(I,K)*B(K,J)

Matrix multiplication can be carried out in BASIC by means of a statement of the form

```
10 MAT C=A*B
```

where A, B and C are matrices and A has the same number of columns as B has rows.

EXAMPLE 7.6

Suppose that we are given the following two matrices.

$$A = \begin{bmatrix} 1 & 2 & 3 & 4 \\ 5 & 6 & 7 & 8 \end{bmatrix} \qquad B = \begin{bmatrix} 9 & 5 & 1 \\ 8 & 4 & 0 \\ 7 & 3 & 9 \\ 6 & 2 & 8 \end{bmatrix}$$

The matrix statement

```
10 MAT C=A*B
```

will result in the 2×3 matrix

$$C = \begin{bmatrix} 70 & 30 & 60 \\ 190 & 86 & 132 \end{bmatrix}$$

where the individual elements were obtained as follows.

C(1,1)=(1×9)+(2×8)+(3×7)+(4×6)=70
C(1,2)=(1×5)+(2×4)+(3×3)+(4×2)=30
C(1,3)=(1×1)+(2×0)+(3×9)+(4×8)=60
C(2,1)=(5×9)+(6×8)+(7×7)+(8×6)=190
C(2,2)=(5×5)+(6×4)+(7×3)+(8×2)=86
C(2,3)=(5×1)+(6×0)+(7×9)+(8×8)=132

Unlike the matrix statements presented earlier, a matrix *cannot* be updated by means of the matrix multiplication statement. Nor can more than two matrices appear in a matrix product. Thus statements of the form

```
10 MAT A=A*C
```

and

```
10 MAT D=A*B*C
```

are not allowed. It is possible, however, to multiply a matrix by itself, i.e., to write

```
10 MAT C=A*A
```

provided A is a *square* matrix (i.e., A must have the same number of rows and columns).

7.2 VECTOR AND MATRIX INPUT/OUTPUT

Matrix input/output operations are carried out in much the same manner as ordinary input/output operations. BASIC provides us with three matrix I/O statements—*MAT READ, MAT PRINT* and *MAT INPUT.* Each is discussed individually below.

MAT READ

The purpose of the MAT READ statement is to enter values for the elements of a vector or a matrix. This statement is used in conjunction with one or more DATA statements (see Section 5.5). A typical MAT READ statement might appear as

```
10 MAT READ A
```

where A represents a vector or a matrix whose dimensions have been specified.

Execution of the MAT READ statement causes a set of values contained in a data block to be assigned to the appropriate elements of the vector or matrix. The assignment always begins with the subscript (or subscripts) equal to 1, i.e., the zeroth elements are ignored. In the case of a matrix, the data will be assigned on a row-by-row basis.

EXAMPLE 7.7

A portion of a BASIC program is shown below.

```
10 DIM A(5,3)
...
40 MAT READ A
...
200 DATA 1,3,5,7,9,11,13,15,17,19,21,23,25,27,29
```

Execution of this program will cause the following values to be assigned to the elements of A.

```
A(1,1)=1     A(1,2)=3     A(1,3)=5
A(2,1)=7     A(2,2)=9     A(2,3)=11
A(3,1)=13    A(3,2)=15    A(3,3)=17
A(4,1)=19    A(4,2)=21    A(4,3)=23
A(5,1)=25    A(5,2)=27    A(5,3)=29
```

Observe that the data are assigned row-by-row.

Notice that A actually contains 24 elements, since the subscripts range from 0 to 5 and 0 to 3, respectively. Only 15 elements of A are assigned values, however, because the zeroth elements are ignored.

If the DIM statement were not present, then A would automatically consist of 121 elements (each subscript ranging from 0 to 10). Therefore 100 values would be required in the data block. An error would result if only 15 values were supplied, as in the above DATA statement.

A single MAT READ statement can contain several vectors and matrices if desired. The successive vectors and matrices must be separated by commas. All elements of the first vector/matrix will be read in before any elements of the second vector/matrix, and so on. As before, the elements of each matrix will be assigned row-by-row.

EXAMPLE 7.8

A portion of a BASIC program is presented below.

```
10 DIM X(2,2),Y(5),Z(2,3)
50 MAT READ X,Y,Z
150 DATA 1,2,3,4,5,6,7,8,9,10,11,12,13,14,15
```

When the program is executed, the following values will be assigned to the elements of X, Y and Z.

```
X(1,1)=1    Y(1)=5    Z(1,1)=10
X(1,2)=2    Y(2)=6    Z(1,2)=11
X(2,1)=3    Y(3)=7    Z(1,3)=12
X(2,2)=4    Y(4)=8    Z(2,1)=13
            Y(5)=9    Z(2,2)=14
                      Z(2,3)=15
```

Thus we see that the first four values in the data block are assigned to X, the next five values are assigned to Y and the last six values to Z. Each matrix is assigned values by rows.

MAT PRINT

The MAT PRINT statement is used to print the elements of a vector or a matrix. A typical MAT PRINT statement can be written as

10 MAT PRINT A

where A represents either a vector or a matrix. The elements of A will be printed in columnar form if A is a vector and in a tabular, row-by-row form if A is a matrix. As with the MAT READ statement, the zeroth elements will be ignored.

The elements of each row of a matrix will be widely separated, with a maximum of five elements on each printed line. Hence several lines may be required for each row. A blank line will appear between successive rows, thus distinguishing one row from another.

EXAMPLE 7.9

Consider the following BASIC program.

```
10 DIM X(3,8),Y(6)
20 MAT READ X,Y
30 MAT PRINT X
40 MAT PRINT Y
50 DATA 1,2,3,4,5,6,7,8,9,10,11,12,13,14,15
60 DATA 16,17,18,19,20,21,22,23,24,25,26,27,28,29,30
70 END
```

Execution of this program will produce the following output.

```
1              2              3              4              5
6              7              8

9              10             11             12             13
14             15             16

17             18             19             20             21
22             23             24


25
26
27
28
29
30
```

Notice that each row of X requires two lines, since only five elements can be printed in each line. A blank line separates each successive row. Also, notice that Y is printed in columnar form, since it is a vector.

The spacing between successive array elements can be altered by placing a comma or a semicolon after the array name in the MAT PRINT statement. Vectors are handled somewhat differently than matrices. The rules governing the spacing of array elements are given below.

1. Vectors

   (*a*) If a vector name is followed by a comma, then the elements are printed in row form rather than columnar form. Wide spacing (not more than five elements per line) will be used.

   (*b*) If a vector name is followed by a semicolon, then the elements are printed in row form with minimum spacing between them.

2. Matrices

Following a matrix name with a comma will have no effect on the spacing of the output. If the matrix name is followed by a semicolon, however, then the matrix will be printed row-by-row, with minimum spacing between the elements. Successive rows will still be separated by a blank line.

EXAMPLE 7.10

Let us again consider the BASIC program presented in Example 7.9. If the MAT PRINT statements are changed to

```
30 MAT PRINT X,
40 MAT PRINT Y,
```

then the following output will be generated when the program is executed.

```
1              2              3              4              5
6              7              8

9              10             11             12             13
14             15             16

17             18             19             20             21
22             23             24



25             26             27             28             29
30
```

We see that the matrix X is printed in the same manner as before, but the vector Y now appears in row form.

On the other hand, suppose we replace the commas in the MAT PRINT statement with semicolons, i.e., let us write

```
30 MAT PRINT X;
40 MAT PRINT Y;
```

The output will now appear as follows.

```
1  2  3  4  5  6  7  8

9  10  11  12  13  14  15  16

17  18  19  20  21  22  23  24



25  26  27  28  29  30
```

The elements within each row are now spaced much more closely.

Several vectors and matrices can appear in the same MAT PRINT statement if desired. The successive entries must be separated by commas or semicolons. The appearance of the output for each vector or matrix will be determined by the type of punctuation mark following that vector or matrix.

EXAMPLE 7.11

The two MAT PRINT statements in Example 7.9 can be replaced by the single statement

```
30 MAT PRINT X,Y
```

When the program is executed, the output will be spaced as shown in Example 7.9.

On the other hand, suppose that this MAT PRINT statement is changed to

```
30 MAT PRINT X,Y,
```

(note the addition of the last comma). Execution of the program will now generate a set of widely spaced output, with the vector elements displayed in row form as shown at the beginning of Example 7.10.

If the commas are replaced with semicolons, i.e.,

```
30 MAT PRINT X;Y;
```

then the output will be closely spaced, as in the second part of Example 7.10.

Finally, it should be pointed out that the MAT PRINT statement can contain only vector and matrix names. Formulas, function references, etc., are not permitted. Thus a statement of the form

```
100 MAT PRINT A+B,C*D,(K)*X
```

would not be allowed.

MAT INPUT

The MAT INPUT statement is used to enter vector elements directly from the console. A typical MAT INPUT statement might appear as

```
10 MAT INPUT A
```

where A represents a vector name. Most versions of BASIC allow only one vector to appear in a MAT INPUT statement.

When the MAT INPUT statement is executed, a question mark (?) appears at the beginning of a new line, indicating a request for data. Further execution of the program will be halted temporarily while the user types in the required vector elements, separated by commas. The first data value will be assigned to A(1), the second to A(2), and so on (where A is the vector name). The zeroth vector element will be ignored.

After the last element has been typed, the user must depress the RETURN key, thus causing the data to be transmitted to the computer. Execution of the program will then be resumed.

It is important to note that *any number* of data values can be entered (provided, of course, that the number of data values does not exceed the maximum permissible number of vector elements as specified by a DIM statement). Hence it is possible to enter only a *partial set* of vector elements via the MAT INPUT statement. This feature accounts for the frequent use of the MAT INPUT statement in many BASIC programs.

EXAMPLE 7.12

A BASIC program contains the following two statements.

```
10 DIM A(100)
 . . .
50 MAT INPUT A
```

When statement number 50 is encountered during program execution, a question mark will be printed at the start of a new line. Further execution of the program will temporarily be suspended.

Suppose that the following line of data is entered in response to the question mark.

```
?12,-3,17,10,62,-87,49,5,39,9,-7,-22
```

When the RETURN key is depressed, the data will be transmitted to the computer, causing the following values to be assigned to the vector A.

```
A(1)=12     A(4)=10     A(7)=49     A(10)=9
A(2)=-3     A(5)=62     A(8)=5      A(11)=-7
A(3)=17     A(6)=-87    A(9)=39     A(12)=-22
```

Notice that the vector element A(0) and the elements A(13) through A(100) are not affected.

Sometimes there are too many data values to be entered on a single line of the console. When this happens the data values may be entered on subsequent lines. An ampersand (&) must be used to indicate that a subsequent line of data will be entered. The ampersand must appear after the final data value in every line except the last. A new question mark will be printed at the start of each line.

EXAMPLE 7.13

Suppose that the following two lines of input data have been typed in response to the MAT INPUT statement shown in Example 7.12.

```
?3,6,9,12,15,18,21,24,27,30&
?33,36,39,42,45,48,51,54,57,60
```

The question mark at the start of the second line, indicating a request for more data, was generated by the ampersand at the end of the first line. This procedure could have been continued if necessary (i.e., an ampersand could have been typed at the end of the second line, generating a request for a third line of data, and so on).

Execution of the program will be resumed after the second carriage return (following the second line of data). The 100-element vector A will then have the following values for its first 20 elements; A(1)=3, A(2)=6, A(3)=9, . . . , A(19)=57, A(20)=60. The remaining elements of A will be unaffected.

It is sometimes desirable to know how many values have been entered from the console. The NUM library function allows us to answer this question. Whenever the NUM function is referenced, it returns the number of data values entered in the most recent MAT INPUT statement. Arguments are not required.

EXAMPLE 7.14

A portion of a BASIC program is shown below.

```
10 DIM A(100)
 . . .
50 MAT INPUT A
60 LET A(0)=NUM
 . . .
150 PRINT "THE LIST CONTAINS"; A(0); " VALUES"
```

When the program is executed, an unspecified number of data values will be entered and assigned to the elements of A. Statement 60 causes the number of data values to be determined and stored in the zeroth element of A. Execution of statement 150 causes a message to be printed which indicates the effective size of the vector A.

Suppose, for example, that A had been assigned 20 values (as in Example 7.13). Then statement 150 would generate the message

```
THE LIST CONTAINS 20 VALUES
```

since A(0) was assigned a value of 20 in statement 60.

In some versions of BASIC the MAT INPUT statement can be used to enter matrix elements as well as vector elements. With a matrix, however, the number of elements to be entered must always be specified within the statement. (We will see how this is accomplished in Section 7.4.) Thus the MAT INPUT statement is less useful for entering matrix elements than for vector elements, since a *partial* set of matrix elements cannot be entered. For this reason, and because many versions of BASIC do not allow the MAT INPUT statement to be used at all with a matrix, we will not discuss this topic any further.

The next example illustrates the use of several matrix statements, including MAT READ and MAT PRINT, in a complete BASIC program. We will see a complete program that makes use of the MAT INPUT statement in Example 7.22 of this chapter.

EXAMPLE 7.15 Matrix Manipulation

Suppose that A and B are 3×3 matrices whose elements are assigned the following values.

$$A = \begin{bmatrix} 1 & 3 & 5 \\ 7 & 9 & 11 \\ 13 & 15 & 17 \end{bmatrix} \qquad B = \begin{bmatrix} 2 & 4 & 6 \\ 8 & 10 & 12 \\ 14 & 16 & 18 \end{bmatrix}$$

We wish to evaluate the matrix formula

F=5*(A+B)*(A−B)

This can be accomplished very easily by means of the matrix statements presented earlier in this chapter. (This problem can also be solved without using matrix statements, though the programming would be more complicated.)

Computational Procedure

Since the given formula cannot be evaluated with a single matrix statement, we must construct a sequence of simple matrix operations that will yield the desired result. This can be accomplished as follows.

C=A+B
D=A−B
E=C*D
F=(5)*E

Each operation can be carried out with a single matrix statement.

The Program Outline

Let us print out the elements of each matrix as soon as they are either read or calculated. This allows us to observe the outcome of each step in the overall computational procedure. Also, the results of the individual matrix statements will be readily apparent.

The computation will proceed as follows.

1. Read the elements of A and B.
2. Print the elements of A, followed by the elements of B.
3. Calculate the elements of C.
4. Print the elements of C.
5. Calculate the elements of D.
6. Print the elements of D.
7. Calculate the elements of E.
8. Print the elements of E.
9. Calculate the elements of F.
10. Print the elements of F.
11. Stop.

A corresponding flowchart is shown in Fig. 7.1.

The BASIC Program

In Fig. 7.2 we see a complete BASIC program for carrying out the computation. Notice that several different matrix statements are included. Also, note that a DIM statement is included, though its presence is not really necessary since this program requires only 3×3 arrays.

Figure 7.3 contains the output that is generated by this program. The elements of each matrix defined in the program are printed out in closely spaced, tabular form. We see the desired results (the calculated elements of the F-matrix) at the bottom of the figure.

Finally, we again remark that the matrix statements were not essential—we could have accomplished the same thing by including several FOR-TO loops in our program. (A program written in this manner is shown in Example 5.15.) However, the use of the matrix statements simplifies the programming considerably.

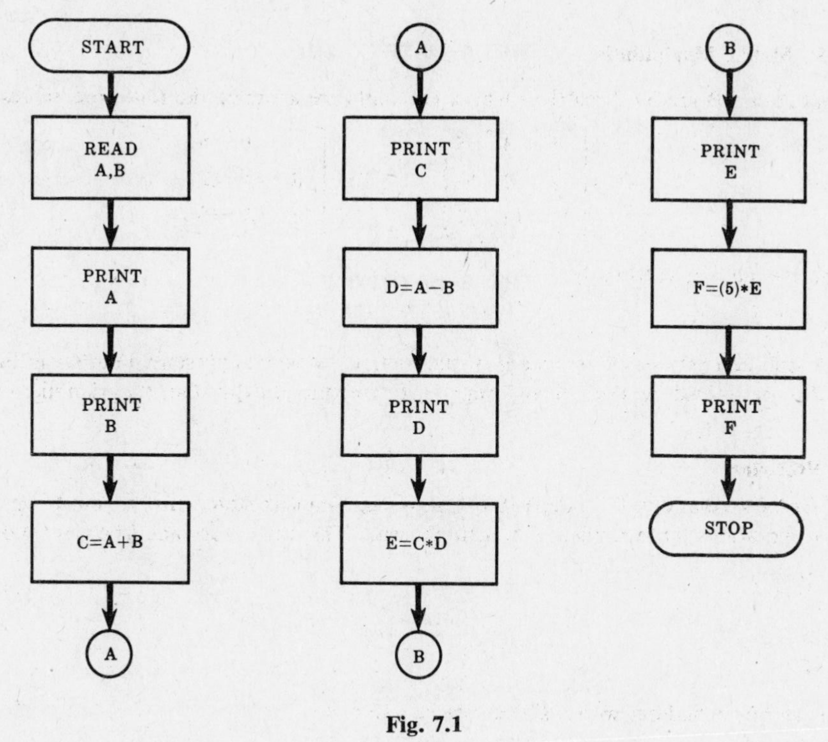

Fig. 7.1

```
10 REM EVALUATION OF THE MATRIX FORMULA F=(5)*(A+B)*(A-B)
20 DIM A(3,3),B(3,3),C(3,3),D(3,3),E(3,3),F(3,3)
30 MAT READ A,B
40 PRINT "THE A-MATRIX IS:"
50 MAT PRINT A;
60 PRINT "THE B-MATRIX IS:"
70 MAT PRINT B;
80 MAT C=A+B
90 PRINT "THE C-MATRIX IS:"
100 MAT PRINT C;
110 MAT D=A-B
120 PRINT "THE D-MATRIX IS:"
130 MAT PRINT D;
140 MAT E=C*D
150 PRINT "THE E-MATRIX IS:"
160 MAT PRINT E;
170 MAT F=(5)*E
180 PRINT "THE F-MATRIX IS:"
190 MAT PRINT F;
200 DATA 1,3,5,7,9,11,13,15,17,2,4,6,8,10,12,14,16,18
210 END
```

Fig. 7.2

```
THE A-MATRIX IS:

 1  3  5

 7  9  11

 13  15  17
THE B-MATRIX IS:

 2  4  6

 8  10  12

 14  16  18
THE C-MATRIX IS:

 3  7  11

 15  19  23

 27  31  35
THE D-MATRIX IS:

-1 -1 -1

-1 -1 -1

-1 -1 -1
THE E-MATRIX IS:

-21 -21 -21

-57 -57 -57

-93 -93 -93
THE F-MATRIX IS:

-105 -105 -105

-285 -285 -285

-465 -465 -465
```

Fig. 7.3

7.3 SPECIAL MATRICES

When carrying out matrix operations, we must sometimes make use of certain special matrices, such as the *identity* matrix, the *transpose* of a matrix or the *inverse* of a matrix. BASIC contains a number of matrix statements that allow these special matrices to be formed. Let us consider each of these statements individually.

MAT ZER

The MAT ZER statement is used to assign 0s to the elements of a given matrix. A typical MAT ZER statement might appear as

```
10 MAT A=ZER
```

where A represents a matrix whose dimensions have been specified.

MAT CON

The purpose of this statement is to assign 1s to the elements of a given matrix. A MAT CON statement might typically be written as

```
10 MAT B=CON
```

where B represents a matrix whose dimensions have been specified.

MAT IDN

This statement causes 0s to be assigned to all of the elements of a square matrix except those on the *principal diagonal* (i.e., the diagonal running from upper left to lower right), where 1s will be assigned. A matrix whose elements are assigned these values is known as an *identity matrix.*

The MAT IDN statement might typically be written as

```
10 MAT C=IDN
```

where C represents a square matrix whose dimensions have been specified. (Note that C must have the same number of rows and columns if it is to be a square matrix.)

The identity matrix has the following important characteristic: If a square matrix D is multiplied by the identity matrix C, then the product will be simply the given matrix D. In other words,

```
C*D=D*C=D
```

(provided C and D conform to the rules of matrix multiplication). Hence we see that matrix multiplication involving the identity matrix is analogous to ordinary multiplication where one of the factors is the constant 1.

EXAMPLE 7.16

A portion of a BASIC program is shown below.

```
10 DIM A(2,3),B(4,2),C(3,3)
   . . .
70 MAT A=ZER
80 MAT B=CON
90 MAT C=IDN
```

Execution of this program will cause the matrices A, B and C to be defined as follows.

$$A = \begin{bmatrix} 0 & 0 & 0 \\ 0 & 0 & 0 \end{bmatrix} \qquad B = \begin{bmatrix} 1 & 1 \\ 1 & 1 \\ 1 & 1 \\ 1 & 1 \end{bmatrix} \qquad C = \begin{bmatrix} 1 & 0 & 0 \\ 0 & 1 & 0 \\ 0 & 0 & 1 \end{bmatrix}$$

MAT TRN

The MAT TRN statement causes the rows and columns of a given matrix to be transposed (i.e., interchanged). The statement might appear as

```
10 MAT B=TRN(A)
```

Thus if A is an $m \times n$ matrix, then B will be an $n \times m$ matrix whose elements are determined as

B(I,J) = A(J,I)

The matrix B is called the *transpose* of A.

EXAMPLE 7.17

Consider a BASIC program that contains the following statements

```
10 DIM A(2,3),B(3,2)
20 MAT READ A
. . .
50 MAT B=TRN(A)
. . .
80 DATA 1,3,5,7,9,11
```

Statement number 20 causes the elements of A to be assigned the values shown below.

$$A = \begin{bmatrix} 1 & 3 & 5 \\ 7 & 9 & 11 \end{bmatrix}$$

Statement number 50 will therefore assign the following values to the elements of B.

$$B = \begin{bmatrix} 1 & 7 \\ 3 & 9 \\ 5 & 11 \end{bmatrix}$$

Notice that B has three rows and two columns, whereas A has two rows and three columns.

MAT INV

The *inverse* of a square matrix is itself a square matrix having the following important property: The product of a matrix and its inverse is equal to the identity matrix. In other words, if A is a square matrix and B is its inverse, then

A*B=B*A=C

where C is the identity matrix. A matrix must be square for its inverse to be defined. For some square matrices, however, it is not possible to calculate an inverse. Thus an inverse matrix may or may not exist for a given square matrix.

A matrix inverse may be calculated (if it exists) by means of the MAT INV statement. This statement might appear as

```
10 MAT B=INV(A)
```

where A and B are square matrices whose dimensions have been established.

Once the inverse of a matrix has been determined, we may obtain the *determinant* of the original matrix by means of the DET library function. This function returns a single numerical value and does not require an argument.

Among other things the DET function may be used to determine whether a given matrix has an inverse, since the determinant will be zero if the inverse does not exist. Remember, however, that the DET function can only be referenced *after* a MAT INV statement. If the DET function returns a value of zero for a given matrix, then the inverse determined by the preceding MAT INV statement will not be meaningful. Moreover, the computation of both the inverse and the determinant may be inaccurate under certain conditions, e.g., if the original matrix is large (many rows and columns) or if it is nearly *singular* (the true value of its determinant is close to zero).

EXAMPLE 7.18 Matrix Inversion

Shown below is a simple BASIC program that computes the inverse of a matrix, the determinant of the matrix and the product of the matrix and its inverse.

```
10 DIM A(3,3),B(3,3),C(3,3)
20 MAT READ A
30 MAT B=INV(A)
40 MAT C=A*B
50 MAT PRINT A,B,C
60 PRINT "DETERMINANT=";DET
70 DATA 5,3,1,3,7,4,1,4,9
80 END
```

Execution of this program should result in the following values for the elements of A, B and C:

$$A=\begin{bmatrix}5 & 3 & 1\\ 3 & 7 & 4\\ 1 & 4 & 9\end{bmatrix} \qquad B=\begin{bmatrix}0.274854 & -0.134503 & 0.0292398\\ -0.134503 & 0.25731 & -0.0994152\\ 0.0292398 & -0.0994152 & 0.152047\end{bmatrix} \qquad C=\begin{bmatrix}1 & 0 & 0\\ 0 & 1 & 0\\ 0 & 0 & 1\end{bmatrix}$$

Also, the determinant of A should equal 171.

The actual output produced by this program is shown below.

```
 5              3              1

 3              7              4

 1              4              9

 0.274854      -0.134503       2.92398E-2

-0.134503       0.25731       -9.94152E-2

 2.92398E-2    -9.94152E-2     0.152047

 1.             8.38190E-9     3.72529E-9

 5.58794E-9     1.             7.45058E-9

 0              7.45058E-9     1.

DETERMINANT= 171
```

Notice that some of the elements of C are only approximately correct, owing to numerical errors that occur in the calculation of C. These errors result when we compute the difference between numbers that are very nearly equal.

Solution of Simultaneous Equations

The MAT INV statement allows us to solve a system of simultaneous, linear algebraic equations very easily. To understand how the method works, we must utilize the properties of both the inverse and the identity matrices. Suppose, for example, that we are given the system of n equations

$$\begin{aligned} c_{11}x_1 + c_{12}x_2 + \cdots + c_{1n}x_n &= d_1 \\ c_{21}x_1 + c_{22}x_2 + \cdots + c_{2n}x_n &= d_2 \\ \cdots\cdots\cdots\cdots\cdots\cdots & \\ c_{n1}x_1 + c_{n2}x_2 + \cdots + c_{nn}x_n &= d_n \end{aligned}$$

where the c's and d's represent known values and the x's are the unknown quantities.

We can write the given equations in matrix form as follows.

C*X=D

where C is a matrix containing the values of the coefficients, that is,

$$C = \begin{bmatrix} c_{11} & c_{12} & \cdots & c_{1n} \\ c_{21} & c_{22} & \cdots & c_{2n} \\ \cdots & \cdots & \cdots & \cdots \\ c_{n1} & c_{n2} & \cdots & c_{nn} \end{bmatrix}$$

and D is a vector containing the right-hand values, i.e.,

$$D = \begin{bmatrix} d_1 \\ d_2 \\ \vdots \\ d_n \end{bmatrix}$$

and X is a vector containing the unknown quantities,

$$X = \begin{bmatrix} x_1 \\ x_2 \\ \vdots \\ x_n \end{bmatrix}$$

Let us multiply our given matrix equation by E, where E represents the inverse of C. Then we have

E*C*X=E*D

However, the matrix product E*C is simply the identity matrix, which we will call I. Therefore we can write

I*X=E*D

Since I*X=X, our matrix equation simplifies to

X=E*D

which is the desired result.

The significance of this result is the following. *The solution to a system of simultaneous, linear algebraic equations is equal to the product of the inverse of the coefficient matrix and the right-hand side vector.* Example 7.19 illustrates how easily this idea can be incorporated into a BASIC program.

EXAMPLE 7.19 Simultaneous Equations

Suppose we are given the following system of five equations and five unknowns.

$$\begin{aligned} 11x_1 + 3x_2 \qquad\quad + x_4 + 2x_5 &= 51 \\ 4x_2 + 2x_3 \qquad\quad + x_5 &= 15 \\ 3x_1 + 2x_2 + 7x_3 + x_4 \qquad &= 15 \\ 4x_1 \qquad + 4x_3 + 10x_4 + x_5 &= 20 \\ 2x_1 + 5x_2 + x_3 + 3x_4 + 13x_5 &= 92 \end{aligned}$$

We wish to determine the values for the unknowns x_1, x_2, x_3, x_4 and x_5.

Computational Procedure

Let us rewrite the equations in matrix form as

C*X=D

where

$$C = \begin{bmatrix} 11 & 3 & 0 & 1 & 2 \\ 0 & 4 & 2 & 0 & 1 \\ 3 & 2 & 7 & 1 & 0 \\ 4 & 0 & 4 & 10 & 1 \\ 2 & 5 & 1 & 3 & 13 \end{bmatrix} \qquad D = \begin{bmatrix} 51 \\ 15 \\ 15 \\ 20 \\ 92 \end{bmatrix}$$

and X will contain the values for x_1, x_2, x_3, x_4 and x_5. We can obtain these values simply by calculating the matrix product

X=E*D

where E is the inverse of C.

Once we have determined the values for x_1 through x_5, we can check the accuracy of our solution by calculating the product

F=C*X

If the elements of X have been determined correctly, then the vector F will be the same as the specified vector D. Any differences in magnitude between the elements of F and the corresponding elements of D therefore provide a measure of the errors involved in calculating X.

The Program Outline

The computation can be carried out as follows.

1. Read the elements of C and D.
2. Print the elements of C and D.
3. Calculate E (the inverse of C).
4. Determine X by forming the matrix product E*D.
5. Print the elements of X.
6. Determine F by forming the product C*X.
7. Calculate the error vector G=D−F.
8. Print the elements of G.
9. Stop.

A corresponding flowchart is shown in Fig. 7.4.

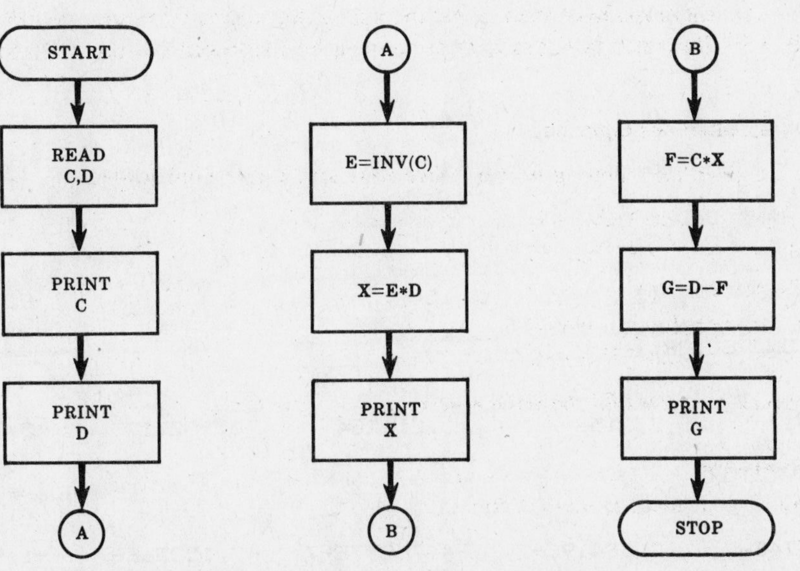

Fig. 7.4

The BASIC Program

A complete BASIC program is shown in Fig. 7.5. The structure of the program is very straightforward, since branches and loops are not required. This simplicity results from the use of the matrix statements, which free the programmer from considering the logical details of matrix manipulation.

```
10 REM SOLUTION OF SIMULTANEOUS LINEAR ALGEBRAIC EQUATIONS
20 DIM C(5,5),D(5),E(5,5),F(5),G(5),X(5)
30 MAT READ C,D
40 PRINT "COEFFICIENT MATRIX:"
50 MAT PRINT C
60 PRINT "RIGHT HAND SIDE:"
70 MAT PRINT D,
80 MAT E=INV(C)
90 MAT X=E*D
100 PRINT "SOLUTION VECTOR:"
110 MAT PRINT X,
120 MAT F=C*X
130 MAT G=D-F
140 PRINT "ERROR VECTOR:"
150 MAT PRINT G,
160 DATA 11,3,0,1,2,0,4,2,0,1,3,2,7,1,0
170 DATA 4,0,4,10,1,2,5,1,3,13,51,15,15,20,92
180 END
```

Fig. 7.5

In Fig. 7.6 we see the output that is generated by the program, providing us with a solution to our system of five equations in five unknowns. Our desired solution is approximately $x_1 = 3.0$, $x_2 = 2.2$, $x_3 = 0.21$, $x_4 = 0.15$ and $x_5 = 5.7$. Notice also that the elements of the error vector, G, are all smaller (in magnitude) than 10^{-6}. This assures us that the solution is reasonably accurate.

```
COEFFICIENT MATRIX:

 11           3            0            1            2

 0            4            2            0            1

 3            2            7            1            0

 4            0            4            10           1

 2            5            1            3            13

RIGHT HAND SIDE:

 51           15           15           20           92

SOLUTION VECTOR:

 2.97917      2.2156       0.211284     0.152317     5.71503

ERROR VECTOR:

-9.53674E-7  -2.38419E-7  -4.76837E-7  -7.15256E-7  -1.90735E-6
```

Fig. 7.6

7.4 CHANGING DIMENSIONS

We have already seen that the MAT INPUT statement allows us to enter an unspecified number of vector elements from the console, thus providing us with a variable dimension feature. In addition, several of the matrix statements allow us to alter the dimensions of an array during program execution. In fact we can, if we wish, change the effective size of an array at different places within a program. This capability can be used to extend the generality of many BASIC programs that involve vectors and matrices.

The matrix statements that permit an array to be redimensioned are MAT READ, MAT ZER, MAT CON and MAT IDN. (Note that the MAT PRINT statement *is not* included.) This feature is implemented by enclosing the effective dimensions in parentheses, following the array name. In the case of a matrix the dimensions must be separated by a comma.

EXAMPLE 7.20

A BASIC program contains the statements

```
10 DIM  A(24,24),B(24,24)
   . . .
50 MAT  A=IDN(20,20)
60 MAT  B=CON(8,12)
```

When the program is executed, a total of 625 elements (including the zeroth row and the zeroth column) will be reserved for each of the matrices A and B. Statement 50, however, will define A to be a 20×20 identity matrix, and statement 60 will establish B as an 8×12 matrix each of whose elements has a value of 1.

Either constants or variables can be used to represent the effective dimensions of an array. However, the dimensions must be expressed as positive integer values, and they cannot exceed the maximum array sizes specified in a DIM statement. (If a DIM statement is not present, then each effective dimension cannot exceed 10.)

EXAMPLE 7.21

A portion of a BASIC program is shown below.

```
10 DIM  P(35),Q(50,50),R(50,50)
   . . .
50 INPUT  M,N
   . . .
80 MAT  READ  P(M),Q(N,N)
90 MAT  R=INV(Q)
   . . .
200 DATA . . .
```

Statement 50 will cause values of M and N (the effective array sizes) to be entered from the console. Any positive integer values can be entered, provided they do not exceed 35 and 50, respectively.

When statement 80 is encountered, the first M values in the data block will be assigned to the elements of P, and the next N × N (i.e., the next N↑2) values will be assigned to the elements of Q. In statement 90 the matrix R will *implicitly* be redimensioned as an N × N matrix, since the inverse of a matrix must have the same dimensionality as the given matrix.

Finally, statement 200 must be present in order to define the data block (there may actually be several DATA statements). Notice that the data block must contain at least N↑2+M data values (extra data values will be ignored). Also, note that a given value in the data block may be assigned to an element of P, an element of Q, or it may not be read at all—depending on the values assigned to M and N.

In the following example we will see that the generality of a BASIC program can be enhanced considerably by making use of the variable dimension feature.

EXAMPLE 7.22 Least Squares Curve Fitting (Playing the Stock Market)

In this example we will write a BASIC program for fitting a curve to a set of data using the method of least squares. We will then apply this program to the problem of fitting an appropriate "trend curve" to the set of earnings data shown in Table 7.1 for a fictitious company known as Federated Mousetraps, Incorporated. Once we have obtained such a "trend curve," we can estimate what the per-share earnings will be at some future time, say in 1988. Based upon some average price-to-earnings ratio, we can then estimate what the price of the stock will be in 1988, using the formula

$$P = R \cdot E$$

where P = estimated price of one share of stock in 1988
R = average price-to-earnings ratio
E = estimated earnings, dollars per share, in 1988

This information might be used as a guide in determining whether or not to buy stock in the company at the current price.

Table 7.1 Yearly Earnings per Share of Federated Mousetraps, Inc.

Earnings, $/Share	Year
$0.01	1967
0.02	1968
0.02	1969
0.03	1970
0.03	1971
0.04	1972
0.04	1973
0.09	1974
0.24	1975
0.38	1976
0.63	1977
0.93	1978
1.24	1979
1.48	1980
1.73	1981
2.07	1982
2.50	1983
3.12	1984
3.48	1985

The Least Squares Technique

The method of least squares is a common technique for fitting a curve

$$y = f(x)$$

to a set of data points $(y_1, x_1), (y_2, x_2), \ldots, (y_M, x_M)$. The method is based upon the concept of minimizing the sum of the square errors,

$$e_1^2 + e_2^2 + \cdots + e_M^2$$

where e_i is the ith error. That is, for a given x_i, e_i is the difference between the data point y_i and a value $y = f(x_i)$ which is read from the fitted curve. (See Fig. 7.7.)

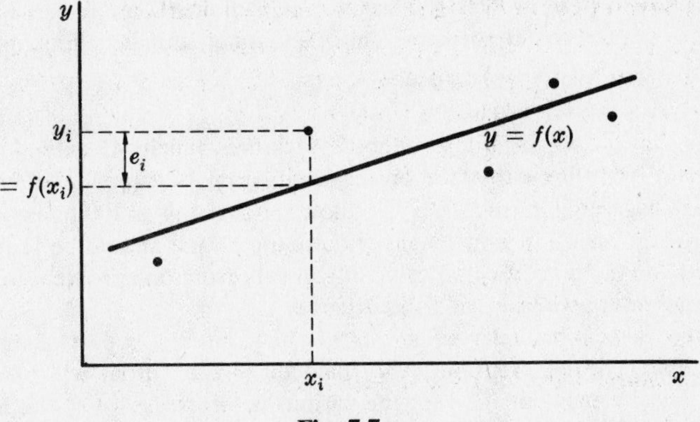

Fig. 7.7

The method is commonly applied to power functions, exponential functions and to polynomials. In each case the method requires solving a set of simultaneous, linear algebraic equations, where the unknown quantities are the *constants* in the equation for the curve.

For example, suppose we wish to pass the power function

$$y = ax^b$$

through a set of M data points. To do this we must solve the following two equations for a and b:

$$M \log a + \left\{\sum_{i=1}^{M} \log x_i\right\} b = \sum_{i=1}^{M} \log y_i$$

$$\left\{\sum_{i=1}^{M} \log x_i\right\} \log a + \left\{\sum_{i=1}^{M} (\log x_i)^2\right\} b = \sum_{i=1}^{M} (\log x_i)(\log y_i)$$

where Σ indicates summation. (For instance, $\Sigma_{i=1}^{M} \log x_i = \log x_1 + \log x_2 + \cdots + \log x_M$.) Notice that these are linear algebraic equations in terms of the unknowns $\log a$ and b. Once $\log a$ has been determined, it is, of course, very simple to obtain the constant a.

Now suppose that we wish to pass the exponential curve

$$y = ae^{bx}$$

through a set of M data points. The equations to be solved are

$$M \log a + \left\{\sum_{i=1}^{M} x_i\right\} b = \sum_{i=1}^{M} \log y_i$$

$$\left\{\sum_{i=1}^{M} x_i\right\} \log a + \left\{\sum_{i=1}^{M} x_i^2\right\} b = \sum_{i=1}^{M} x_i \log y_i$$

Again we solve two simultaneous, linear algebraic equations for $\log a$ and b.

If the curve is the polynomial

$$y = c_1 + c_2 x + c_3 x^2 + \cdots + c_{n+1} x^n$$

then we determine the coefficients $c_1, c_2, c_3, \ldots, c_{n+1}$ by solving the system of equations

$$Mc_1 + \left\{\sum_{i=1}^{M} x_i\right\} c_2 + \left\{\sum_{i=1}^{M} x_i^2\right\} c_3 + \cdots + \left\{\sum_{i=1}^{M} x_i^n\right\} c_{n+1} = \sum_{i=1}^{M} y_i$$

$$\left\{\sum_{i=1}^{M} x_i\right\} c_1 + \left\{\sum_{i=1}^{M} x_i^2\right\} c_2 + \left\{\sum_{i=1}^{M} x_i^3\right\} c_3 + \cdots + \left\{\sum_{i=1}^{M} x_i^{n+1}\right\} c_{n+1} = \sum_{i=1}^{M} x_i y_i$$

$$\cdots\cdots\cdots\cdots\cdots\cdots\cdots\cdots\cdots\cdots$$

$$\left\{\sum_{i=1}^{M} x_i^n\right\} c_1 + \left\{\sum_{i=1}^{M} x_i^{n+1}\right\} c_2 + \left\{\sum_{i=1}^{M} x_i^{n+2}\right\} c_3 + \cdots + \left\{\sum_{i=1}^{M} x_i^{2n}\right\} c_{n+1} = \sum_{i=1}^{M} x_i^n y_i$$

Since each of the above cases involves the solution of simultaneous, linear algebraic equations, we will incorporate several matrix statements in our program, in a manner similar to Example 7.19.

Design of the Program

In designing the program we will include a number of features which will extend its generality. For example, we will include a provision for fitting either the power function or the exponential curve discussed earlier, or a polynomial of up to ninth degree (10 terms). We will allow for as many as 100 pairs of data, and we will convert the values of x_i and y_i to $\log x_i$ and $\log y_i$ internally if these logarithms should be required. Since the number of data points to be entered and the type of curve to be fit will vary from one problem to another, we will make use of the variable dimension feature when writing the program.

The coefficients in the system of linear equations will be printed as a part of the output. This information may be helpful when debugging the program. Also included in the output will be the equation of the fitted curve, showing the numerical values obtained for the various constants; a list of the input values x_i and y_i, with the corresponding calculated values $y(x_i)$ (this will facilitate plotting the input data and the fitted curve); and the numerical value of the sum of the square errors. This latter quantity is useful in comparing the success of fitting several different curves to the same set of data (the smaller the sum, the better the fit).

The Program Outline

In order to outline the program let us define the following variables and arrays.

X = 100-element vector containing the input values x_i

Y = 100-element vector containing the input values y_i

A = a 10×10 matrix containing the coefficients of the unknown constants in the system of linear equations

B = the inverse of A

C = a 10-element vector containing the unknown constants in the system of linear equations

D = a 10-element vector containing the right-hand terms in the system of linear equations

M = input quantity which indicates the number of pairs of data

N = input quantity indicating the curve to be used:

N = 0 indicates the power function $y = ax^b$

N = 1 indicates the exponential function $y = ae^{bx}$

N = 2, 3, ..., 10 indicates the polynomial $y = \sum_{i=1}^{N} c_i x^{i-1}$

(For example, N = 3 indicates the second-degree polynomial $y = c_1 + c_2 x + c_3 x^2$.)

N1 = number of simultaneous, linear algebraic equations

N1 = 2 if N = 0 or N = 1

N1 = N if N = 2, 3, ..., 10

The outline of the main program proceeds as follows:

1. Read the input data:
   (*a*) Read a value for N, thus specifying the particular curve to be fit.
   (*b*) Read M values for y_i followed by M values for x_i.
2. Calculate $\log x_i$ and $\log y_i$ if N = 0, or calculate $\log y_i$ if N = 1, for $i = 1, 2, \ldots, M$.
3. Calculate the elements of the arrays A and D, using the appropriate formulas for the particular curve selected.
4. Print out the elements of A and D.
5. Solve the simultaneous, linear algebraic equations.
6. Print out the values obtained for the unknown constants (the elements of the array C), in a form that shows the equation of the curve selected.
7. Calculate $y(x_i)$ for $i = 1, 2, \ldots, M$.

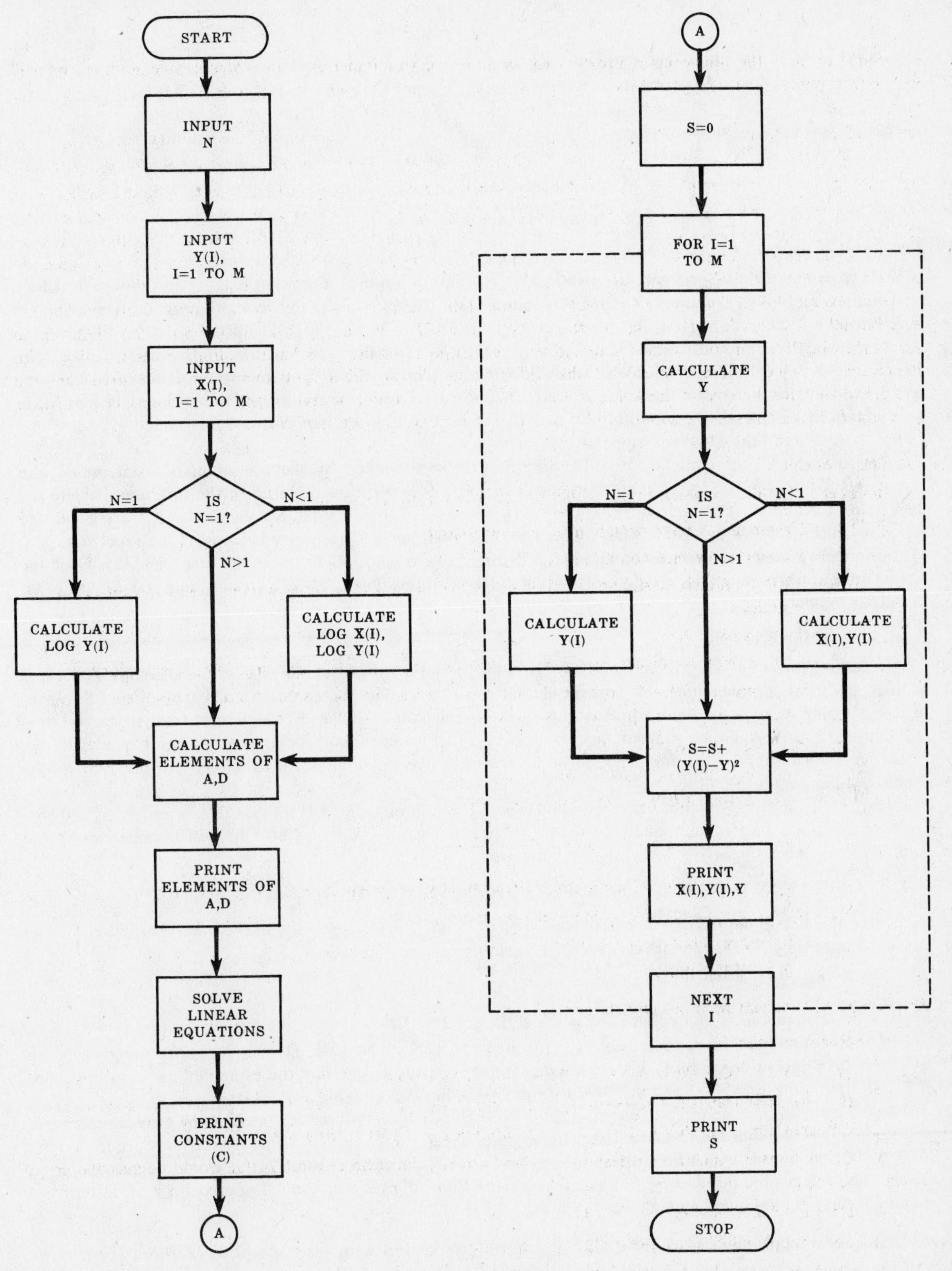
START
INPUT N
INPUT Y(I), I=1 TO M
INPUT X(I), I=1 TO M
IS N=1?
N=1
N<1
N>1
CALCULATE LOG Y(I)
CALCULATE LOG X(I), LOG Y(I)
CALCULATE ELEMENTS OF A,D
PRINT ELEMENTS OF A,D
SOLVE LINEAR EQUATIONS
PRINT CONSTANTS (C)
A
A
S=0
FOR I=1 TO M
CALCULATE Y
IS N=1?
N=1
N<1
N>1
CALCULATE Y(I)
CALCULATE X(I),Y(I)
S=S+ (Y(I)−Y)²
PRINT X(I),Y(I),Y
NEXT I
PRINT S
STOP

Fig. 7.8

8. Calculate the sum of the square errors

$$e_1^2 + e_2^2 + \cdots + e_M^2$$

9. Print out x_i, y_i and $y(x_i)$ for $i = 1, 2, \ldots$, M, and then print out the sum of the square errors. (Note that if N = 0 or N = 1, it will be necessary to convert log y_i and perhaps log x_i back to y_i and x_i.)
10. Stop.

Figure 7.8 shows a flowchart of the computational procedure.

The BASIC Program

The complete BASIC program is shown in Fig. 7.9. This program is somewhat lengthy and should therefore be examined carefully. A number of REM statements are included in order to break the program up into major logical blocks.

Notice that several matrix statements, as well as the NUM function, are included in the program (see lines 70, 75, 90, 95, 200, 205, 370 and 375). The MAT INPUT statements allow for a variable number of data points, and the MAT ZER statements cause the A-matrix and the D-vector to be redimensioned each time the program is executed. In statements 370 and 375 the B-matrix and the C-vector are *implicitly* redimensioned to correspond to the A-matrix and the D-vector, respectively.

The solution of the simultaneous equations is greatly simplified by the use of matrix statements (see statements 370 and 375). On the other hand, several FOR-TO loops are required in the program, despite the availability of the matrix statements. There are several reasons for this. First, the elements of A are generated internally (lines 185 through 285). Also, under certain conditions it is necessary to convert the input data into logarithmic form and vice versa (lines 135–145, 155–165, 510–520 and 530–540). Finally, the format in which the results are printed requires the presence of several FOR-TO loops (lines 320–350, 455–480 and 560–625) in order to output the data.

Application of the Program

Returning to our stock market problem, let us fit a curve to the earnings vs. time data for Federated Mousetraps using a power function, an exponential curve, a second-degree polynomial (N = 3) and a fourth-degree polynomial (N = 5). Before proceeding with the calculation, however, we remark that in curve-fitting calculations it is desirable to prevent the x-values and the y-values from being too far apart in magnitude. Therefore we will subtract the number 1960 from each of the x values. Thus, for example, the year 1967 will be represented as simply 7, and so on.

The results of the calculations are shown in Figs. 7.10(a) through 7.10(d) for N = 0, 1, 3 and 5 respectively. By examining the sum of the square errors in each case, we see that the best fit was obtained using the fourth-degree polynomial (N = 5), yielding the equation

$$y = -0.727783 + 0.330811x - 0.047882x^2 + 0.002563x^3 - 0.000036x^4$$

(Note that the second-degree polynomial resulted in a fit that is almost as good.) On the other hand, the worst fit was obtained using the exponential curve (N = 1), resulting in the expression

$$y = 0.000853\, e^{0.356011x}$$

Each of these equations is plotted with the original data in Fig. 7.11.

In order to estimate the per-share earnings for the year 1988, we let 1988 − 1960 = 28. Substituting this value into the fourth-degree polynomial yields a value of $y = 4.92$. Thus we see that the estimated earnings per share of Federated Mousetraps, Inc., will be $4.92 for the year 1988.

Based upon an average price-to-earnings ratio of 30 (which is not unusual for a company growing this fast), we estimate that one share of Federated Mousetraps should sell for about $147.60 in 1988. If we were to buy the stock in 1984 at a price of $75.00 (corresponding to a price-to-earnings ratio of 24), it would be reasonable to expect almost to double our money by 1988. This is equivalent to a yield of about 19 percent a year, in terms of simple interest, compounded annually.

All of the examples in this chapter have been concerned with arrays whose elements represent numeric values. The reader is reminded that BASIC will also accept string arrays and that the matrix statements can also be used to carry out legitimate string array operations. Remember, however, that some versions of BASIC do not support matrix statements. This is especially true of the newer versions of BASIC which are available for microcomputers.

```
5   REM         LEAST SQUARES CURVE FITTING
10  DIM X(100),Y(100)
15  PRINT "INPUT N=0 FOR A POWER FUNCTION, N=1 FOR AN EXPONENTIAL ";
20  PRINT "FUNCTION."
25  PRINT "FOR A POLYNOMIAL, LET N EQUAL THE NUMBER OF TERMS IN ";
30  PRINT "THE POLYNOMIAL."
35  PRINT "N=";
40  INPUT N
45
50  REM        ENTER DATA POINTS
55
60  PRINT
65  PRINT "ENTER THE Y-VALUES"
70  MAT INPUT Y
75  LET M=NUM
80  PRINT
85  PRINT "ENTER THE X-VALUES"
90  MAT INPUT X
95  IF NUM=M THEN 115
100 PRINT "THE NUMBER OF Y-VALUES DOES NOT CORRESPOND TO THE ";
105 PRINT "NUMBER OF X-VALUES"
110 STOP
115
120 REM        CALCULATE LOGARITHMS OF X- AND Y-VALUES IF NECESSARY
125
130 IF N>=2 THEN 170
135 FOR I=1 TO M
140     LET Y(I)=LOG(Y(I))
145 NEXT I
150 IF N=1 THEN 170
155 FOR I=1 TO M
160     LET X(I)=LOG(X(I))
165 NEXT I
170
175 REM         CALCULATE ELEMENTS OF A-MATRIX AND D-VECTOR
180
185 LET N1=N
190 IF N1>=2 THEN 200
195 LET N1=2
200 MAT A=ZER(N1,N1)
205 MAT D=ZER(N1)
210 FOR I=1 TO N1
215    FOR J=1 TO N1
220        IF I+J>2 THEN 235
225        LET A(I,J)=M
230        GOTO 250
235        FOR K=1 TO M
240            LET A(I,J)=A(I,J)+X(K)^(I+J-2)
245        NEXT K
250    NEXT J
255    FOR K=1 TO M
260        IF I>1 THEN 275
265        LET D(I)=D(I)+Y(K)
270        GOTO 280
275        LET D(I)=D(I)+Y(K)*X(K)^(I-1)
280    NEXT K
285 NEXT I
290
295 REM         PRINT SIMULTANEOUS LINEAR EQUATIONS
300
```

Fig. 7.9 *(Program continues on next page)*

```
305 PRINT
310 PRINT "COEFFICIENTS IN SYSTEM OF LINEAR EQUATIONS"
315 PRINT
320 FOR I=1 TO N1
325    FOR J=1 TO N1
330       PRINT A(I,J);
335    NEXT J
340    PRINT D(I)
345    PRINT
350 NEXT I
355
360 REM        SOLVE SIMULTANEOUS LINEAR EQUATIONS
365
370 MAT B=INV(A)
375 MAT C=B*D
380
385 REM         PRINT EQUATION FOR CURVE FIT
390
395 IF N>1 THEN 430
400 LET C1=EXP(C(1))
405 IF N=1 THEN 420
410 PRINT "POWER FUNCTION:  Y=";C1;"*X^";C(2)
415 GOTO 490
420 PRINT "EXPONENTIAL FUNCTION:  Y=";C1;"*EXP(";C(2);"*X)"
425 GOTO 490
430 IF C(2)>=0 THEN 445
435 PRINT "POLYNOMIAL FUNCTION:  Y=";C(1);C(2);"X";
440 GOTO 450
445 PRINT "POLYNOMIAL FUNCTION:  Y=";C(1);"+";C(2);"*X";
450 IF N=2 THEN 485
455 FOR I=3 TO N
460    IF C(I)>=0 THEN 475
465    PRINT C(I);"*X^";I-1;
470    GOTO 480
475    PRINT "+";C(I);"*X^";I-1;
480 NEXT I
485 PRINT
490
495 REM        PRINT INPUT VALUES OF X AND Y AND CALCULATED VALUES OF Y
500
505 IF N>=2 THEN 545
510 FOR I=1 TO M
515    LET Y(I)=EXP(Y(I))
520 NEXT I
525 IF N=1 THEN 545
530 FOR I=1 TO M
535    LET X(I)=EXP(X(I))
540 NEXT I
545 PRINT
550 PRINT TAB(2);"X";TAB(16);"Y (ACTUAL)";TAB(30);"Y (CALCULATED)"
555 LET S=0
560 FOR I=1 TO M
565    IF N>=2 THEN 595
570    IF N=1 THEN 585
575    LET Y1=C1*X(I)^C(2)
580    GOTO 615
585    LET Y1=C1*EXP(C(2)*X(I))
590    GOTO 615
595    LET Y1=C(1)
600    FOR J=2 TO N
605       LET Y1=Y1+C(J)*X(I)^(J-1)
610    NEXT J
615    LET S=S+(Y(I)-Y1)^2
620    PRINT X(I),Y(I),Y1
625 NEXT I
630 PRINT
635 PRINT "SUM OF SQUARE ERRORS=";S
640 END
```

Fig. 7.9 *(continued)*

```
INPUT N=0 FOR A POWER FUNCTION, N=1 FOR AN EXPONENTIAL FUNCTION.
FOR A POLYNOMIAL, LET N EQUAL THE NUMBER OF TERMS IN THE POLYNOMIAL.
N= ?0

ENTER THE Y-VALUES
 ?.01,.02,.02,.03,.03,.04,.04,.09,.24,.38,.63,.93,1.24,1.48,1.73&
 ?2.07,2.50,3.12,3.48

ENTER THE X-VALUES
 ?7,8,9,10,11,12,13,14,15,16,17,18,19,20,21,22,23,24,25

COEFFICIENTS IN SYSTEM OF LINEAR EQUATIONS

 19  51.4244 -26.0334

 51.4244  141.871 -56.6213

POWER FUNCTION:   Y= 2.26350E-7 *X^ 5.14716

  X              Y (ACTUAL)    Y (CALCULATED)
 7.              0.01          5.06560E-3
 8               2.00000E-2    1.00722E-2
 9.              2.00000E-2    1.84678E-2
 10.             3.00000E-2    3.17640E-2
 11.             3.00000E-2    5.18788E-2
 12.             4.00000E-2    8.11884E-2
 13.             4.00000E-2    0.12258
 14.             9.00000E-2    0.179506
 15.             0.24          0.256038
 16              0.38          0.356922
 17.             0.63          0.487632
 18.             0.93          0.65443
 19.             1.24          0.864418
 20.             1.48          1.1256
 21.             1.73          1.44693
 22.             2.07          1.83839
 23.             2.5           2.31103
 24.             3.12          2.87701
 25.             3.48          3.54972

SUM OF SQUARE ERRORS= 0.614177
```

(*a*)

```
INPUT N=0 FOR A POWER FUNCTION, N=1 FOR AN EXPONENTIAL FUNCTION.
FOR A POLYNOMIAL, LET N EQUAL THE NUMBER OF TERMS IN THE POLYNOMIAL.
N= ?1

ENTER THE Y-VALUES
 ?.01,.02,.02,.03,.03,.04,.04,.09,.24,.38,.63,.93,1.24,1.48,1.73&
 ?2.07,2.50,3.12,3.48

ENTER THE X-VALUES
 ?7,8,9,10,11,12,13,14,15,16,17,18,19,20,21,22,23,24,25

COEFFICIENTS IN SYSTEM OF LINEAR EQUATIONS

 19  304 -26.0334

 304  5434 -213.607

EXPONENTIAL FUNCTION:   Y= 8.53337E-4 *EXP( 0.356011 *X)

  X              Y (ACTUAL)    Y (CALCULATED)
 7               0.01          1.03137E-2
 8               2.00000E-2    1.47242E-2
 9               2.00000E-2    2.10205E-2
 10              3.00000E-2    3.00094E-2
 11              3.00000E-2    4.28422E-2
 12              4.00000E-2    6.11625E-2
 13              4.00000E-2    0.087317
 14              9.00000E-2    0.124656
 15              0.24          0.177962
 16              0.38          0.254062
 17              0.63          0.362705
 18              0.93          0.517806
 19              1.24          0.739232
 20              1.48          1.05535
 21              1.73          1.50664
 22              2.07          2.15091
 23              2.5           3.07069
 24              3.12          4.38379
 25              3.48          6.25839

SUM OF SQUARE ERRORS= 10.395
```

(*b*)

Fig. 7.10 (*continues on next page*)

```
INPUT N=0 FOR A POWER FUNCTION, N=1 FOR AN EXPONENTIAL FUNCTION.
FOR A POLYNOMIAL, LET N EQUAL THE NUMBER OF TERMS IN THE POLYNOMIAL.
N= ?3

ENTER THE Y-VALUES
?.01,.02,.02,.03,.03,.04,.04,.09,.24,.38,.63,.93,1.24,1.48,1.73&
?2.07,2.50,3.12,3.48

ENTER THE X-VALUES
?7,8,9,10,11,12,13,14,15,16,17,18,19,20,21,22,23,24,25

COEFFICIENTS IN SYSTEM OF LINEAR EQUATIONS

 19   304   5434   18.08

 304   5434   105184   394.84

 5434   105184   2151370   8773.92

POLYNOMIAL FUNCTION:   Y= 1.73884 -0.34583 X+ 1.65945E-2 *X^ 2

 X                  Y (ACTUAL)     Y (CALCULATED)
 7                  0.01           0.131157
 8                  0.02           3.42441E-2
 9                  0.02          -2.94800E-2
 10                 0.03          -6.00152E-2
 11                 0.03          -5.73615E-2
 12                 0.04          -2.15188E-2
 13                 0.04           4.75128E-2
 14                 0.09           0.149733
 15                 0.24           0.285143
 16                 0.38           0.453741
 17                 0.63           0.655528
 18                 0.93           0.890505
 19                 1.24           1.15867
 20                 1.48           1.46002
 21                 1.73           1.79457
 22                 2.07           2.1623
 23                 2.5            2.56322
 24                 3.12           2.99733
 25                 3.48           3.46463

SUM OF SQUARE ERRORS= 8.91439E-2
```

(*c*)

```
INPUT N=0 FOR A POWER FUNCTION, N=1 FOR AN EXPONENTIAL FUNCTION.
FOR A POLYNOMIAL, LET N EQUAL THE NUMBER OF TERMS IN THE POLYNOMIAL.
N= ?5

ENTER THE Y-VALUES
?.01,.02,.02,.03,.03,.04,.04,.09,.24,.38,.63,.93,1.24,1.48,1.73&
?2.07,2.50,3.12,3.48

ENTER THE X-VALUES
?7,8,9,10,11,12,13,14,15,16,17,18,18,20,21,22,23,24,25

COEFFICIENTS IN SYSTEM OF LINEAR EQUATIONS

 19   304   5434   105184   2151370   18.08

 304   5434   105184   2151370   45723424   394.84

 5434   105184   2151370   45723424   9.98814E+8   8773.92

 105184   2151370   45723424   9.98814E+8   2.22672E+10   197719

 2151370   45723424   9.98814E+8   2.22672E+10   5.04212E+11   4.50758E+6

POLYNOMIAL FUNCTION:   Y=-0.727783 + 0.330811 *X-4.78821E-2 *X^ 2 +
 2.56300E-3 *X^ 3 -3.63439E-5 *X^ 4

 X                  Y (ACTUAL)     Y (CALCULATED)
 7                  0.01           3.35158E-2
 8                  0.02           1.76392E-2
 9                  0.02           1.03749E-3
 10                 0.03          -8.32534E-3
 11                 0.03          -3.35775E-3
 12                 0.04           2.21596E-2
 13                 0.04           7.35737E-2
 14                 0.09           0.15536
 15                 0.24           0.271119
 16                 0.38           0.423584
 17                 0.63           0.614611
 18                 0.93           0.845186
 19                 1.24           1.11542
 20                 1.48           1.42456
 21                 1.73           1.77098
 22                 2.07           2.15216
 23                 2.5            2.56473
 24                 3.12           3.00446
 25                 3.48           3.4662

SUM OF SQUARE ERRORS= 6.42682E-2
```

(*d*)

Fig. 7.10 (*continued*)

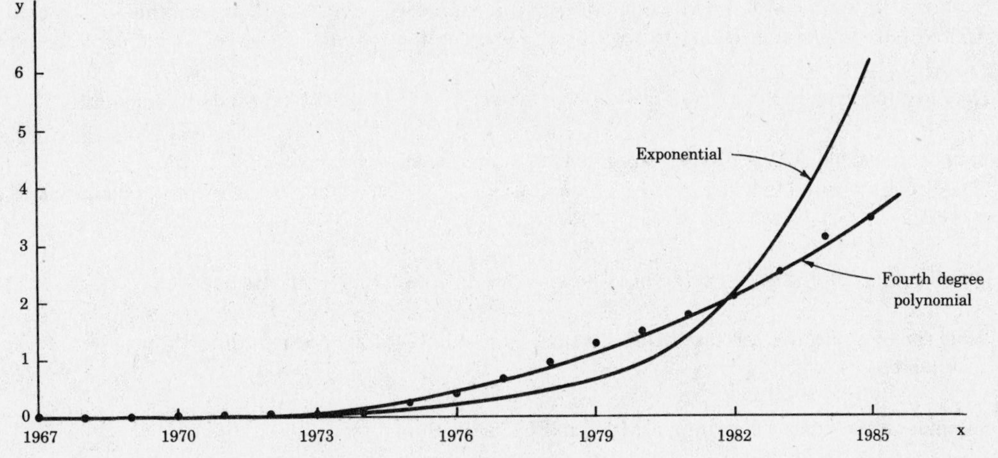

Fig. 7.11

Review Questions

7.1 What is a vector? A matrix?

7.2 Is it necessary to use matrix statements to carry out vector and matrix operations? What advantage is there in the use of matrix statements?

7.3 What is the difference between scalar multiplication and matrix multiplication? What conditions must be satisfied in order to multiply one matrix by another?

7.4 Summarize the rules for writing each of the following matrix statements.

(*a*) Assignment (*c*) Subtraction (*e*) Matrix multiplication
(*b*) Addition (*d*) Scalar multiplication

7.5 What is the purpose of the MAT READ statement? What other BASIC statement must be used in conjunction with MAT READ?

7.6 Summarize the rules for writing a MAT READ statement.

7.7 Suppose a MAT READ statement contains the name of one matrix. In what order will the values in the data block be assigned to the matrix elements?

7.8 How are the zeroth elements of a vector or matrix affected by a MAT READ statement?

7.9 Suppose a single MAT READ statement contains several array names. In what order will the values in the data block be assigned to the array elements?

7.10 What is the purpose of the MAT PRINT statement? Summarize the rules for writing this statement.

7.11 Suppose a MAT PRINT statement contains the name of one matrix. In what order will the matrix elements be printed? How can we distinguish one row of the matrix from another? How can the spacing of the matrix elements be altered?

7.12 Suppose a MAT PRINT statement contains the name of a vector. How can the vector elements be printed out in columnar form? In row form? How can the spacing of the vector elements be altered?

7.13 How are the zeroth elements of a vector or matrix affected by a MAT PRINT statement?

7.14 Suppose a single MAT PRINT statement contains several array names. In what order will the array elements be printed? How can the elements of one array be distinguished from the elements of another array?

7.15 Can formulas and function references be included in a MAT PRINT statement?

7.16 What is the purpose of the MAT INPUT statement? How does it differ from the MAT READ statement?

7.17 Summarize the rules for writing a MAT INPUT statement.

7.18 What happens when a MAT INPUT statement is executed? How are the input values transmitted to the computer?

7.19 How is the zeroth element of a vector affected by a MAT INPUT statement?

7.20 How can two or more lines of input data be read with a single MAT INPUT statement?

7.21 How can we determine the number of vector elements that have been entered by a MAT INPUT statement? Suggest a convenient place to store this number.

7.22 Can a MAT INPUT statement be used to enter matrix elements as well as vector elements? Are there any restrictions with matrices that are not present with vectors?

7.23 What is an identity matrix?

7.24 What is meant by the transpose of a matrix?

7.25 What is meant by the inverse of a matrix? Does an inverse always exist? Explain.

7.26 What relationship must exist between the number of rows and the number of columns of an identity matrix? An inverse matrix?

7.27 What relationship must exist between the number of rows and columns of a given matrix and its transpose? Can a vector have a transpose?

7.28 What is the result of multiplying a matrix by an identity matrix?

7.29 What is the result of multiplying a matrix by its inverse?

7.30 State the purpose and summarize the rules for writing each of the following matrix statements.

(*a*) MAT ZER
(*b*) MAT CON
(*c*) MAT IDN
(*d*) MAT TRN
(*e*) MAT INV

7.31 What is the purpose of the DET library function? For what kinds of matrices can the DET function be used? What matrix statement must always precede a reference to the DET function?

7.32 How can we determine whether or not a particular square matrix has an inverse?

7.33 How can we solve a system of simultaneous, linear algebraic equations using matrix statements? Is there a simple procedure to check the accuracy of the solution?

7.34 Which matrix statements allow an array to be redimensioned during program execution? How is the redimensioning accomplished?

7.35 Compare the concept of array redimensioning discussed in Section 7.4 with the variable dimension feature included in the MAT INPUT statement.

7.36 What operations can be performed on string arrays? Which matrix statements can be used for the manipulation of string arrays?

Solved Problems

7.37 Several BASIC statements, or groups of statements, are shown below. Some are written incorrectly. Identify all errors.

(*a*)
```
10 DIM P(12,20),Q(12,20),R(12,20)
   . . .
50 MAT P=(.5)*(Q+R)
```

Matrix formulas cannot appear in a matrix statement.

(*b*)
```
10 DIM P(12,20),Q(12,20)
   . . .
50 MAT P=((N+1)/2)*Q
```

Correct, provided N is an ordinary (scalar) variable.

(*c*)
```
30 MAT INPUT A,B,C
```

Most versions of BASIC allow only one vector name to appear in a MAT INPUT statement.

(*d*)
```
30 MAT INPUT N$
```

Correct, provided N$ is a string vector.

(*e*)
```
200 MAT PRINT A,B,A+B,A-B
```

Formulas cannot appear in a MAT PRINT statement.

(*f*)
```
10 DIM A(10,20),B(20,10)
   . . .
30 MAT READ A
40 MAT B=TRN(A)
```

Correct.

(*g*)
```
10 DIM P(3,6),Q(8,10),R(5,5)
  . . .
50 MAT R=P+Q
```

Matrices cannot be added if their dimensions do not correspond.

(*h*)
```
10 DIM C(6,8),D(6,8),V(12)
  . . .
60 MAT D=INV(C)
  . . .
90 MAT V=IDN
```

It is not possible to calculate an inverse for a nonsquare matrix. Also, a vector cannot appear in a MAT IDN statement.

7.38 Write one or more BASIC statements for each of the situations described below.

(*a*) Evaluate the formula

$$Y = X^T * A * X$$

where A is a 10×10 matrix, X is a 10-element vector (disregarding the zeroth row), and X^T is the transpose of X. What will be the dimensionality of Y?

```
100 MAT Z=TRN(X)
110 MAT B=Z*A
120 MAT Y=B*X
```

or

```
100 MAT Z=TRN(X)
110 MAT C=A*X
120 MAT Y=Z*C
```

Y will represent a single value (i.e., Y will be an ordinary variable, not an array).

(*b*) Evaluate the formula

$$T = (N) * F^{-1} * G + H$$

where F, G and H are 50×50 matrices, N is an ordinary (scalar) variable and F^{-1} represents the inverse of F. What will be the dimensionality of T?

```
100 MAT A=INV(F)
110 MAT B=A*G
120 MAT C=(N)*B
130 MAT T=C+H
```

T will be 50×50 matrix.

(*c*) Calculate the difference between I and $A^{-1} * A$, where A is a 10×10 matrix, A^{-1} represents the inverse of A and I is a 10×10 identity matrix. (Note that this difference should, in principle, be a matrix whose elements are zero. In reality the matrix elements may be different from zero because of numerical errors.)

```
100 MAT B=INV(A)
110 MAT C=B*A
120 MAT I=IDN
130 MAT D=I-C
```

(*d*) Print the answer obtained for part (*c*) above in matrix form, with the elements spaced as closely as possible.

```
140 MAT PRINT D;
```

(*e*) Suppose that A and B are 10×10 matrices whose elements are given in a data block. Read the elements of A, one *row* at a time, followed by the elements of B, one *column* at a time.

```
10 MAT READ A,C
20 MAT B=TRN(C)
```

(Note that A and C are each read row-by-row.)

(*f*) Suppose that X and Y are vectors whose elements are to be assigned values from the console. The number of values entered for X and Y will be stored in X(0) and Y(0), respectively.

```
10 MAT INPUT X
20 LET X(0)=NUM
30 MAT INPUT Y
40 LET Y(0)=NUM
```

(*g*) Suppose that P is a 5×12 matrix, T is a 6×6 matrix and X is a 10-element vector. Print the values of P, T and X, with X appearing in row form.

```
200 MAT PRINT P,T,X,
```

(*h*) Repeat part (*g*) above, with the array elements spaced as closely as possible.

```
200 MAT PRINT P;T;X;
```

Supplementary Problems

7.39 Several BASIC statements, or groups of statements, are shown below. Some are written incorrectly. Identify all errors.

(*a*)
```
10 DIM L$(100),M$(100)
   . . .
50 MAT INPUT M$
60 MAT L$=M$
```

(*b*)
```
35 MAT Q=(A+B)*P
```
where A, B, P and Q are 10×10 matrices.

(*c*)
```
35 MAT Q=(A+B)*P
```
where A and B are ordinary (scalar) variables and P and Q are 10×10 matrices.

(*d*)
```
60 MAT H=(3)*H
```
where H is a 6×6 matrix.

(*e*)
```
60 MAT G=H*H
```
where G and H are 6×6 matrices.

(*f*)
```
60 MAT H=G*H
```
where G and H are 6 × 6 matrices.

(*g*)
```
10 DIM X(10,20),Y(10,20),Z(10,20)
. . .
50 MAT Z=X*Y
```

(*h*)
```
10 DIM V(100)
. . .
50 MAT INPUT V(50)
```

(*i*)
```
10 DIM C(100,50),D(100,50)
20 INPUT M,N
30 MAT READ C(M,N),D(M,N)
```

(*j*)
```
10 DIM C(100,50),D(100,50)
20 INPUT M,N
. . .
100 MAT PRINT C(M,N),D(M,N)
```

(*k*)
```
10 DIM A(25,25)
. . .
50 MAT A=CON(12,24)
```

(*l*)
```
10 DIM A(20,5)
. . .
80 MAT A=ZER(10,6)
```

(*m*)
```
10 DIM F(10,20),G(10,20)
. . .
60 MAT G=INV(F)
```

(*n*)
```
10 DIM K(20,30)
. . .
50 MAT K=IDN(12,12)
```

7.40 Write one or more BASIC statements for each of the situations described below.

(*a*) Evaluate the formula

$$F=(2*N+1)*(A^T*A-I)$$

where A is a 10 × 10 matrix and A^T is its transpose, I is a 10 × 10 identity matrix and N is an ordinary (scalar) variable. What will be the dimensionality of F?

(*b*) Suppose that A, B, C and D are 10 × 10 matrices. Calculate the determinant of G, where

$$G=A*C-B*D$$

and print out its value.

(*c*) Modify part (*b*) above to print out the elements of G, followed by the inverse of G and the determinant of G. Space the matrix elements as closely as possible.

(*d*) Suppose that A is a 20 × 30 matrix. Assign zeros to the elements in the first 8 columns of the first 12 rows.

(*e*) Suppose that A and B are 20 × 30 matrices. Read the elements in the first 12 columns of the first 8 rows of A, followed by the elements in the first 15 columns of the first 6 rows of B. How must the data be arranged in the data block?

(*f*) Suppose that A and B are 20 × 30 matrices. Print the elements in the first 12 columns of the first 8 rows of A, followed by the elements in the first 15 columns of the first 6 rows of B. Compare with the solution to part (*e*) above.

Programming Problems

7.41 Modify the program given in Example 7.15 so that the transpose of F, the inverse of F and the determinant of F are calculated and printed. Explain the results that are obtained.

7.42 Modify the program given in Example 7.19 so that any system of N equations in N unknowns can be solved. Use the variable dimension feature described in Section 7.4. Include a provision for printing the determinant of the coefficient matrix.

7.43 When numerical errors are generated in solving the system of simultaneous equations C*X=D, it is often helpful to proceed as follows.

(*a*) Calculate the vector F=C*X.

(*b*) Calculate the error vector G=D−F. (If numerical errors are not present, then F will be the same as the given vector D, and the elements of G will be zeros.)

(*c*) If the elements of G are not all equal to zero, then solve the system of simultaneous equations

A*Y=G

for the values of Y(1), Y(2), . . . , Y(N).

(*d*) Add the elements of Y to the corresponding elements of X to obtain an improved solution.

Modify the program given in Example 7.19 to include this error-correction feature. Include a provision for calculating the determinant of the coefficient matrix.

Use the program to solve the following system of equations.

$$x_1+\tfrac{1}{2}x_2+\tfrac{1}{3}x_3+\tfrac{1}{4}x_4+\tfrac{1}{5}x_5=\tfrac{1}{6}$$
$$\tfrac{1}{2}x_1+\tfrac{1}{3}x_2+\tfrac{1}{4}x_3+\tfrac{1}{5}x_4+\tfrac{1}{6}x_5=\tfrac{1}{7}$$
$$\tfrac{1}{3}x_1+\tfrac{1}{4}x_2+\tfrac{1}{5}x_3+\tfrac{1}{6}x_4+\tfrac{1}{7}x_5=\tfrac{1}{8}$$
$$\tfrac{1}{4}x_1+\tfrac{1}{5}x_2+\tfrac{1}{6}x_3+\tfrac{1}{7}x_4+\tfrac{1}{8}x_5=\tfrac{1}{9}$$
$$\tfrac{1}{5}x_1+\tfrac{1}{6}x_2+\tfrac{1}{7}x_3+\tfrac{1}{8}x_4+\tfrac{1}{9}x_5=\tfrac{1}{10}$$

Compare the answers obtained with and without the error-correction feature.

7.44 Modify the program given in Example 7.22 so that several different curves can be fit to the same set of data (i.e., the program can be run several different times) *without* rereading the data each time the program is repeated.

7.45 Write a BASIC program for each of the problems described below. Include a detailed outline or a flowchart for each problem.

(*a*) Starting with the matrix A given in Example 7.18, calculate a new matrix D, where each element of D is the reciprocal of the corresponding element of A, i.e., $d_{ij}=1/a_{ij}$. Compare the elements of D with the elements of the inverse of A. (The inverse of A is shown as the matrix B in Example 7.18.)

(*b*) Calculate the inverse of the matrix B given in Example 7.18. Compare the elements of this matrix with the elements of the matrix A in Example 7.18.

(*c*) For the matrices A and B given in Example 7.15, show that A*B does not equal B*A.

(*d*) For the matrices A and B given in Example 7.6, show that $(A*B)^T = B^T*A^T$, where A^T represents the transpose of A, B^T represents the transpose of B, etc.

(*e*) Evaluate the matrix formula

$$Y=D^T*C^T*C*D$$

using the matrix C and the vector D given in Example 7.19. What will be the dimensionality of Y?

(*f*) Evaluate the matrix formula

$$P=I+A+A^2+A^3+A^4$$

using the matrix A in Example 7.18. (Note that I represents the identity matrix, $A^2=A*A$, $A^3=A*A*A$, etc.) What will be the dimensionality of P?

Chapter 8

Data Files

In computer jargon a *file* is an orderly, self-contained collection of information. Any type of information may be included. Hence a file may contain a sequence of BASIC statements, or it may consist of data values (i.e., numbers and strings). The first type of file is, of course, a BASIC program; the latter is called a *data file.*

Data files offer a convenient means of storing data sets, since data files can easily be read and updated by a BASIC program. This chapter is concerned with the creation and use of such data files.

We will see that BASIC includes a number of file manipulation statements similar to the matrix statements presented in Chapter 7. Unlike the matrix statements, however, there is considerable variation in the exact form of the file manipulation statements between one version of BASIC and another. Therefore this chapter will emphasize the *concepts* of data file manipulation rather than the details of the individual statements.

The particular file manipulation statements appearing in this chapter are a part of the BASIC language applicable to Digital Equipment Corporation's DECsystem-10 computer. They are *representative* of the file manipulation statements available in other versions of BASIC. Typical file manipulation procedures used with microcomputers are presented in Chapter 9, Section 9.4.

8.1 SEQUENTIAL DATA FILES

A *sequential file* is characterized by the fact that the individual items are arranged sequentially, one after another. Usually the items in this type of file correspond to separate lines of information on a console. Thus a BASIC program is stored as a sequential file, since each statement appears on a separate line and the statements are arranged in the order of increasing line numbers.

A sequential file can also represent sets of data. Such a file will consist of several lines of data, each line beginning with a line number. The lines will be arranged sequentially, in the order of increasing line numbers. The data items on a given line can be numbers, strings or a combination of the two, separated either by commas or by blank spaces. If a string contains a comma or a blank space, it must be enclosed in quotation marks.

EXAMPLE 8.1

A sequential data file contains the name and exam scores of each student in a computer science class. The file appears as follows.

```
10 "COMP SCI 100" "FALL, 1982"
20 "ADAMS B F" 45 80 80 95 55
30 "BROWN P" 60 50 70 75 55
40 "DAVIS R A" 40 30 10 45 60
50 "FISHER E K" 0 5 5 0 10
60 "HAMILTON S P" 90 85 100 95 90
70 "JONES J J" 95 90 80 95 85
80 "LUDWIG C W" 35 50 55 65 45
90 "OSBORNE T" 75 60 75 60 70
100 "PRINCE W F" 85 75 60 85 90
110 "RICHARDS E N" 50 60 50 35 65
120 "SMITH M C" 70 60 75 70 55
130 "THOMAS B A" 10 25 35 20 30
140 "WOLFE H" 25 40 65 75 85
150 "ZORBA D R" 65 80 70 100 60
```

We see that each line begins with a line number. The first line contains two strings, identifying the course and the term, respectively. (Notice that the strings are enclosed in quotation marks, since commas and blank spaces are included within the strings.) Each successive line contains the name of a student (a string), followed by five examination scores. Thus the file consists of 15 lines, though there are only 14 students in the class.

It should be understood that the sequencing of this data file is determined by the line numbers, not the names. The fact that the names are arranged alphabetically is immaterial.

Creating and Editing a Sequential File

Since a sequential data file is structured in the same way as a BASIC program, we can create and edit such a file in the same manner as a program. We can also print a sequential data file on the console if we wish. These functions are carried out with the system commands presented in Chapter 3 (e.g., NEW, OLD, SAVE, LIST, etc.).

The rules for naming a data file are the same as for a BASIC program—typically one to six characters, beginning with a letter.

EXAMPLE 8.2

Suppose that the sequential data file shown in Example 8.1 is to be entered into the computer via the console and saved under the name SCORES. To do so we must log in, specify that SCORES will be a new file, type the data sets line by line and then save the file. We can also list the file if we wish, after it has been entered and corrected.

```
NEW OR OLD-->NEW
NEW FILE NAME-->SCORES
>10  "COMP SCI 100" "FALL, 1982"
>20  "ADAMS B F" 45 80 80 95 55
>30  "BROWN P" 60 50 70 75 55
>40  "DAVIS R A" 40 30 10 45 60
>50  "FISHER E K" 0 5 5 0 10
>60  "HAMILTON S P" 90 85 100 95 90
>70  "JONES J J" 95 90 80 95 85
>80  "LUDWIG C W" 35 50 55 65 45
>90  "OSBORNE T" 75 60 75 60 70
>100 "PRINCE W F" 85 75 60 85 90
>110 "RICHARDS E N" 50 60 50 35 65
>120 "SMITH M C" 70 60 7%\%\5 70 55
>130 "THON\N\MAS C\C\B A" 10 25 35 20 30
>140 "WOLFE H" 25 40 65 75 85
>150 "ZORBA 65 80 70 100 60
>150 "ZORBA D R" 65 80 70 100 60
>SAVE
>LIST

SCORES

10   "COMP SCI 100" "FALL, 1982"
20   "ADAMS B F" 45 80 80 95 55
30   "BROWN P" 60 50 70 75 55
40   "DAVIS R A" 40 30 10 45 60
50   "FISHER E K" 0 5 5 0 10
60   "HAMILTON S P" 90 85 100 95 90
70   "JONES J J" 95 90 80 95 85
80   "LUDWIG C W" 35 50 55 65 45
90   "OSBORNE T" 75 60 75 60 70
100  "PRINCE W F" 85 75 60 85 90
110  "RICHARDS E N" 50 60 50 35 65
120  "SMITH M C" 70 60 75 70 55
130  "THOMAS B A" 10 25 35 20 30
140  "WOLFE H" 25 40 65 75 85
150  "ZORBA D R" 65 80 70 100 60
```

Fig. 8.1

Figure 8.1 shows the major portion of the timesharing session, beginning after the login procedure. Notice that three typing errors were made when entering the data (in lines 120, 130 and 150). These errors were corrected either through use of the DELETE key (lines 120 and 130) or by retyping the entire line (see line 150).

A complete listing of the data file is shown at the bottom of Fig. 8.1. This listing was produced in response to the LIST command, shown in the middle of the figure.

The system commands entered by the user have been underlined. It should be understood that the lines of data shown in the top half of the figure were also entered by the user, though they are not underlined.

A sequential data file can also be created directly by a BASIC program. We will see how to do this in Example 8.4.

Reading a Sequential Data File

In many applications the information stored in a data file will be read and then processed by a BASIC program. The data items in a sequential data file must be read in the same order they are stored, starting at the beginning of the data file. All of the information that is read will be preserved for subsequent use.

In order to read data from a sequential data file under program control, we will make use of the file manipulation statements FILES, INPUT and IF END. The following example illustrates how this is accomplished.

EXAMPLE 8.3

Let us return to the list of names and exam scores shown in Fig. 8.1. Suppose we want to carry out the following operations for each student in the class.

1. Read the first five exam scores from data file SCORES.
2. Enter a sixth exam score from the console.
3. Calculate an average of all six exam scores.
4. Print the average on the console.

The computation will cease when the end of the data file has been reached.

A BASIC program which will carry out these operations is shown in Fig. 8.2. The variables in this program are defined as follows.

N = line number of each line in data file SCORES
T$ = course title
Y$ = term
N$ = student name
C1, C2, C3, C4, C5 = exam scores for each student in data file SCORES
C6 = exam score to be entered from the console for each student
A = calculated average of all six exams for each student

An explanation of the file manipulation statements appearing in this program is given after the program listing.

```
10  FILES SCORES
20  INPUT #1,N,T$,Y$
30  PRINT "COURSE:";T$,"TERM:";Y$
40  PRINT
50  INPUT #1,N,N$,C1,C2,C3,C4,C5
60  PRINT N$,"SCORE=";
70  INPUT C6
80  LET A=(C1+C2+C3+C4+C5+C6)/6
90  PRINT "AVERAGE=";A
100 PRINT
110 IF END #1,THEN 130
120 GOTO 50
130 END
```

Fig. 8.2

A transfer of information between a data file and a BASIC program always takes place over a *data channel.* Statement number 10 (FILES) assigns the data file SCORES to data channel number 1. This must be done before any information can be transferred to or from the data file. All subsequent file manipulation statements will then refer to the data file by channel number, not by name.

Statement 20 reads the line number (N), the course title (T$) and the term (Y$) from the first line of the data file assigned to channel number 1 (i.e., data file SCORES). Statement 50 reads a line number, a student's name and five examination scores from a line in SCORES. (Notice that the line numbers must be read from the data file, even though they are not used.)

Statement number 110 tests for an end of the data file. If there are no more data (end of file), then control is transferred to statement 130 (END); otherwise, control passes to the next executable statement (statement 120). Thus we see that this statement is very similar to our familiar IF-THEN statement, although it is used only to test for an end-of-file condition.

The remaining statements in this program are ordinary BASIC statements, as discussed in earlier chapters of this book. Their meaning should be straightforward.

Figure 8.3 shows the output which is generated by this program and data file SCORES. (A listing of the data file is shown in Fig. 8.1.) Note that the only information entered directly from the console is a single exam score for each student. The remaining data was either transferred to the console from the data file, or else generated by the program. (The input data are underlined.)

```
COURSE:COMP SCI 100            TERM:FALL, 1982

ADAMS B F       SCORE= ?75
AVERAGE= 71.6667

BROWN P         SCORE= ?80
AVERAGE= 65

DAVIS R A       SCORE= ?55
AVERAGE= 40

FISHER E K      SCORE= ?5
AVERAGE= 4.16667

HAMILTON S P    SCORE= ?90
AVERAGE= 91.6667

JONES J J       SCORE= ?80
AVERAGE= 87.5

LUDWIG C W      SCORE= ?70
AVERAGE= 53.3333

OSBORNE T       SCORE= ?80
AVERAGE= 70

PRINCE W F      SCORE= ?100
AVERAGE= 82.5

RICHARDS E N    SCORE= ?70
AVERAGE= 55

SMITH M C       SCORE= ?75
AVERAGE= 67.5

THOMAS B A      SCORE= ?10
AVERAGE= 21.6667

WOLFE H         SCORE= ?95
AVERAGE= 64.1667

ZORBA D R       SCORE= ?95
AVERAGE= 78.3333
```

Fig. 8.3

Writing a Sequential Data File

Information can be written onto a data file by a BASIC program in much the same manner that information is read from a data file. When writing onto a sequential data file, the new information will automatically be located beyond any existing data, thus protecting whatever information may already be in the file. If the old data are to be deleted prior to writing the new data, then the file must explicitly be erased and repositioned to its starting point.

In the following example we will see how information can be read from both a sequential data file and the console, processed, and the results written out to the console and to a new sequential data file. To accomplish this we will utilize the file manipulation statements FILES, QUOTE, SCRATCH, INPUT, PRINT and IF END. The purpose of each statement will be discussed in the example.

EXAMPLE 8.4 Processing Student Examination Scores

In this example we will continue with the problem situation described in Examples 8.2 and 8.3—namely, recording and processing a set of exam scores for a class of students. Let us now develop a more comprehensive program which can perform the following operations for each student.

1. Read a set of exam scores from an existing data file (e.g., SCORES).
2. Enter a new exam score from the console.
3. Calculate an average for all of the exam scores.
4. Print the calculated average on the console.
5. Write the new set of data (i.e., the original exam scores, the new exam score and the calculated average) onto a new data file.

At the completion of the computation the new data file will contain all of the information in the original data file, plus an additional exam score and an average grade for each student.

Computational Procedure

We will write the program so that we can simply add a new exam score to each student's record, without calculating an average, if we wish. This allows us to use the program *during* the school term to record additional data (exam scores) and at the *end* of the school term to process the data (i.e., calculate an average score which will be used to determine each student's final grade).

In order that our program be as general as possible, let us enter all of the exam scores for each student into the array C. Thus C(1) will refer to the first exam score, C(2) the second exam score, etc. We will allow for as many as 15 individual exam scores for each student.

The variable K will refer to the particular exam being entered from the console; e.g., if the scores are being entered for the sixth exam, then K will be assigned a value of 6. Also, J$ will represent either "YES" or "NO", depending upon whether or not an average score is to be calculated for each student. All other variables will be as defined in Example 8.3.

The computation will proceed as follows.

1. Assign the data file SCORES to data channel 1, and UPDATE to data channel 2. (SCORES will be the input file and UPDATE the output file.)
2. Erase any old data that may appear on UPDATE and reposition the file to its starting point in preparation for writing output.
3. Read a line number (N), the course title (T$) and the term (Y$) from SCORES.
4. Print the course title and the term on the console.
5. Write the line number, the course title and the term onto UPDATE.
6. Enter a value for K (the exam number) from the console.
7. Enter a value for J$ (either "YES" or "NO") from the console, indicating whether or not an average score is to be calculated for each student.
8. Read a line number (N), a student's name (N$) and K-1 exam scores from SCORES.
9. Enter the Kth exam score from the console.

(*Continued on p. 210*)

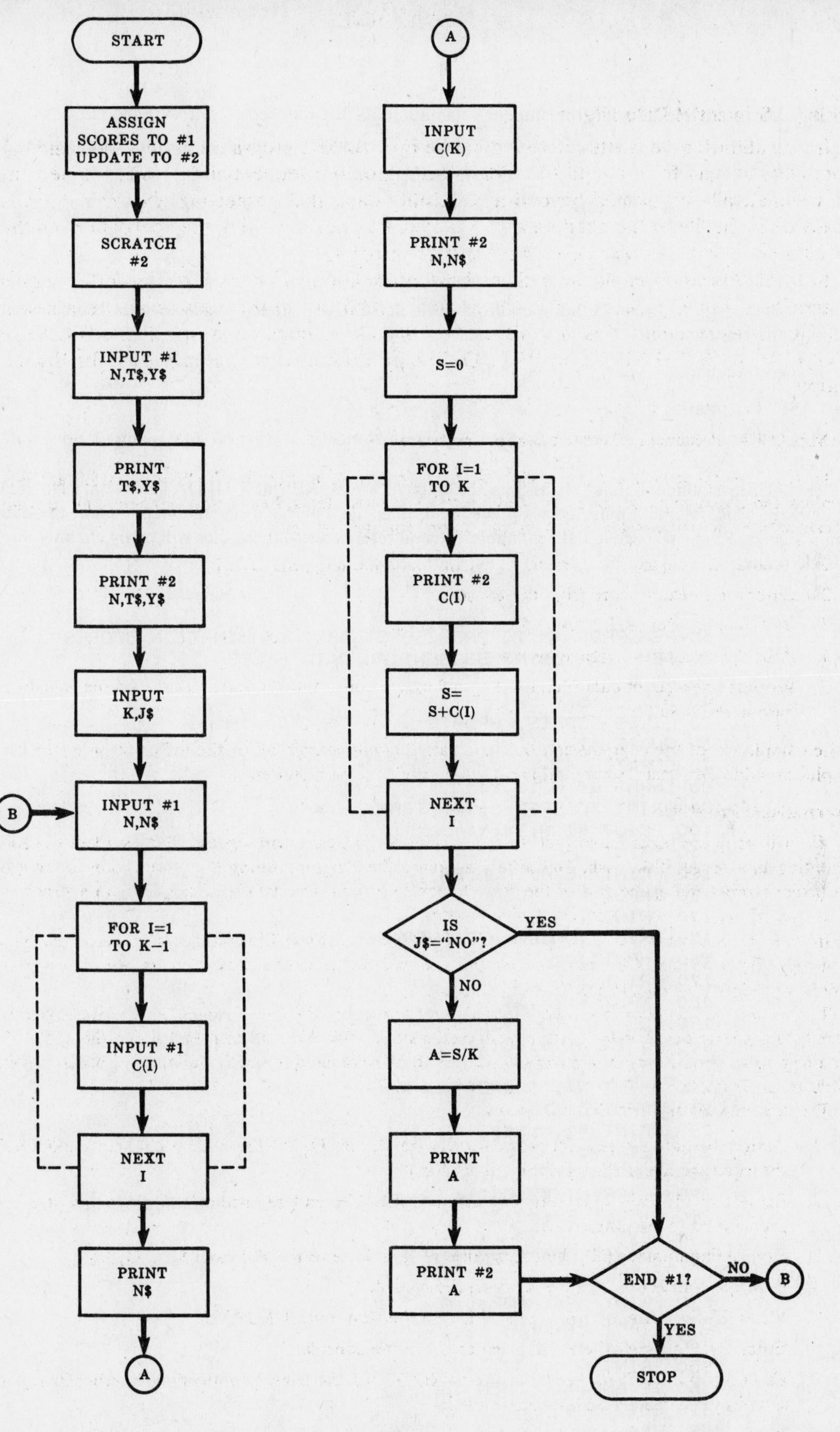
START
ASSIGN
SCORES TO #1
UPDATE TO #2
SCRATCH
#2
INPUT #1
N,T$,Y$
PRINT
T$,Y$
PRINT #2
N,T$,Y$
INPUT
K,J$
B
INPUT #1
N,N$
FOR I=1
TO K−1
INPUT #1
C(I)
NEXT
I
PRINT
N$
A
A
INPUT
C(K)
PRINT #2
N,N$
S=0
FOR I=1
TO K
PRINT #2
C(I)
S=
S+C(I)
NEXT
I
IS
J$="NO"?
YES
NO
A=S/K
PRINT
A
PRINT #2
A
END #1?
NO
B
YES
STOP

Fig. 8.4

10. Write the line number, the student's name and all K exam scores onto UPDATE.
11. If J$="NO", then proceed to step 13 below. Otherwise, calculate an average exam score, A, using the formula

$$A = \frac{C(1)+C(2)+\cdots+C(K)}{K}$$

12. Print the average score on the console and write this value onto UPDATE.
13. Test to see if there are additional data sets in SCORES. If so, return to step 8; otherwise, terminate the computation.

A corresponding flowchart is shown in Fig. 8.4.

The BASIC Program

Figure 8.5 contains the actual BASIC program. Notice that several file manipulation statements are included.

The FILES statement (line 50) assigns the data files SCORES and UPDATE to data channels 1 and 2, respectively. This statement must always precede all other file manipulation statements. Once the data files have been assigned to their respective data channels, then all references to these files will be by channel number rather than file name.

```
10 REM PROGRAM TO PROCESS STUDENT EXAMINATION SCORES
20 REM       USING SEQUENTIAL DATA FILES
30
40 DIM C(15)
50 FILES SCORES, UPDATE
60 QUOTE #2
70 SCRATCH #2
80 INPUT #1,N,T$,Y$
90 PRINT "COURSE:";T$,"TERM:";Y$
100 PRINT #2,N;T$;Y$
110 PRINT
120 PRINT "EXAM NUMBER";
130 INPUT K
140 PRINT
150 PRINT "CALCULATE AVERAGES (YES OR NO)";
160 INPUT J$
170 PRINT
180 INPUT #1,N,N$
190 FOR I=1 TO K-1
200     INPUT #1,C(I)
210 NEXT I
220 PRINT N$,"SCORE=";
230 INPUT C(K)
240 PRINT #2,N;N$;
250 LET S=0
260 FOR I=1 TO K
270     PRINT #2,C(I);
280     LET S=S+C(I)
290 NEXT I
300 IF J$="NO" THEN 340
310 LET A=S/K
320 PRINT "AVERAGE=";A
330 PRINT #2,A;
340 PRINT #2
350 PRINT
360 IF END #1, THEN 380
370 GOTO 180
380 END
```

Fig. 8.5

Statement number 60 (QUOTE) specifies that all strings that are written onto UPDATE will be enclosed in quotation marks. This is necessary if the strings are to be read by a BASIC program at some later time. The SCRATCH statement (line 70) causes UPDATE to be erased and reset to its starting point in preparation for writing data.

Data are read from SCORES at several places within the program (lines 80, 180 and 200). Similarly, data are written onto UPDATE at several places (lines 100, 240, 270, 330 and 340). Notice that the line numbers are read and written, even though they are not used by the program. Also, we see that the variables appearing in the PRINT #2 statements are followed by semicolons. This causes the data in each line of UPDATE to be spaced as closely as possible.

```
COURSE:COMP SCI 100            TERM:FALL, 1982

EXAM NUMBER ?6

CALCULATE AVERAGES (YES OR NO) ?NO

ADAMS B F        SCORE= ?75

BROWN P          SCORE= ?80

DAVIS R A        SCORE= ?55

FISHER E K       SCORE= ?5

HAMILTON S P     SCORE= ?90

JONES J J        SCORE= ?80

LUDWIG C W       SCORE= ?70

OSBORNE T        SCORE= ?80

PRINCE W F       SCORE= ?100

RICHARDS E N     SCORE= ?70

SMITH M C        SCORE= ?75

THOMAS B A       SCORE= ?10

WOLFE H          SCORE= ?95

ZORBA D R        SCORE= ?95

TIME:   0.80 SECS.
>OLD
OLD FILE NAME-->UPDATE
>LIST

UPDATE

10   "COMP SCI 100" "FALL, 1982"
20   "ADAMS B F" 45  80  80  95  55  75
30   "BROWN P" 60  50  70  75  55  80
40   "DAVIS R A" 40  30  10  45  60  55
50   "FISHER E K" 0  5  5  0  10  5
60   "HAMILTON S P" 90  85  100  95  90  90
70   "JONES J J" 95  90  80  95  85  80
80   "LUDWIG C W" 35  50  55  65  45  70
90   "OSBORNE T" 75  60  75  60  70  80
100   "PRINCE W F" 85  75  60  85  90  100
110   "RICHARDS E N" 50  60  50  35  65  70
120   "SMITH M C" 70  60  75  70  55  75
130   "THOMAS B A" 10  25  35  20  30  10
140   "WOLFE H" 25  40  65  75  85  95
150   "ZORBA D R" 65  80  70  100  60  95
```

Fig. 8.6

Finally, in line 360 we examine SCORES for an end of file. Control is transferred to line 380 (END) if an end of file is found, thus terminating the computation. Otherwise control is transferred to the next executable statement (line 370) in preparation for processing the next student's grades.

Application of the Program

In Fig. 8.6 we see how the program can be used to add an additional exam score for each student, without calculating averages. Each new exam score is entered via the console. (The user's responses are underlined.)

The new data file (UPDATE), containing six exam scores for each student, is shown at the bottom of Fig. 8.6. The data file was generated from the original data file, SCORES, which is shown in Fig. 8.1. The system command LIST was used to produce a listing of UPDATE on the console, after the program execution had been completed.

Suppose that at some later time the new data file is to be used as an *input* file for this same BASIC program. Then it will be necessary to change the name of this data file from UPDATE to SCORES. This can be accomplished by using the system commands SCRATCH (to delete the original data file SCORES) and RENAME (to change the name of UPDATE to SCORES). The procedure is shown in Fig. 8.7. (Do not confuse the BASIC *system command* SCRATCH with the *file manipulation statement* SCRATCH, e.g., SCRATCH #2.)

```
>OLD
OLD FILE NAME-->SCORES
>SCRATCH
>OLD
OLD FILE NAME-->UPDATE
>RENAME SCORES
```

Fig. 8.7

Now let us see how this program can be used to enter a new exam score and then calculate an average score for each student. The new exam scores and the calculated averages are shown in Fig. 8.8. (This output was generated using the *original* data file, SCORES, shown in Fig. 8.1.)

Notice the similarity between Fig. 8.8 and Fig. 8.3 (the latter was generated using the program in Example 8.3). Now, however, we have not only a record of each student's average exam score shown on the console but also a complete record of the individual exam scores and the averages in data file UPDATE. A listing of UPDATE is shown at the bottom of Fig. 8.8.

Sequential data files are particularly useful for storing sets of data which will be processed by a BASIC program at some later time. There are two reasons for this. First, a sequential data file can be edited using the BASIC system commands without altering the program. Furthermore, it is possible to include both strings and numeric data within a sequential data file.

On the other hand, some applications require that information be transferred to or from a data file without regard for the order in which the data are stored. The use of a sequential data file is relatively inefficient in such situations, since considerable computer time may be wasted by repeatedly searching along the data file for the desired information. In the next section we will consider a different kind of data file that is better suited for applications of this type.

8.2 RANDOM DATA FILES

Whereas a sequential data file contains data sets that are arranged in the order of increasing line numbers, a *random data file* consists of individual data items that are not arranged in any particular order. Each data item can be read directly from or written directly onto a random data file without proceeding sequentially along the data file from the beginning. Therefore it is faster to transfer information to or from a random data file than a sequential data file.

Random data files can consist of either numeric data or strings but not both. The type of file (i.e., numeric or string) is specified by placing either a percent sign (%) or a dollar sign ($) after the file name. The % sign signifies a numeric file, the $ sign a string file. A positive integer quantity

```
COURSE:COMP SCI 100          TERM:FALL, 1982

EXAM NUMBER ?6

CALCULATE AVERAGES (YES OR NO) ?YES

ADAMS B F       SCORE= ?75
AVERAGE= 71.6667

BROWN P         SCORE= ?80
AVERAGE= 65

DAVIS R A       SCORE= ?55
AVERAGE= 40

FISHER E K      SCORE= ?5
AVERAGE= 4.16667

HAMILTON S P    SCORE= ?90
AVERAGE= 91.6667

JONES J J       SCORE= ?80
AVERAGE= 87.5

LUDWIG C W      SCORE= ?70
AVERAGE= 53.3333

OSBORNE T       SCORE= ?80
AVERAGE= 70

PRINCE W F      SCORE= ?100
AVERAGE= 82.5

RICHARDS E N    SCORE= ?70
AVERAGE= 55

SMITH M C       SCORE= ?75
AVERAGE= 67.5

THOMAS B A      SCORE= ?10
AVERAGE= 21.6667

WOLFE H         SCORE= ?95
AVERAGE= 64.1667

ZORBA D R       SCORE= ?95
AVERAGE= 78.3333

TIME:  0.92 SECS.
>OLD
OLD FILE NAME-->UPDATE
>LIST

UPDATE

10  "COMP SCI 100" "FALL, 1982"
20  "ADAMS B F" 45  80  80  95  55  75  71.6667
30  "BROWN P" 60  50  70  75  55  80  65
40  "DAVIS R A" 40  30  10  45  60  55  40
50  "FISHER E K" 0  5  5  0  10  5  4.16667
60  "HAMILTON S P" 90  85  100  95  90  90  91.6667
70  "JONES J J" 95  90  80  95  85  80  87.5
80  "LUDWIG C W" 35  50  55  65  45  70  53.3333
90  "OSBORNE T" 75  60  75  60  70  80  70
100  "PRINCE W F" 85  75  60  85  90  100  82.5
110  "RICHARDS E N" 50  60  50  35  65  70  55
120  "SMITH M C" 70  60  75  70  55  75  67.5
130  "THOMAS B A" 10  25  35  20  30  10  21.6667
140  "WOLFE H" 25  40  65  75  85  95  64.1667
150  "ZORBA D R" 65  80  70  100  60  95  78.3333
```

Fig. 8.8

(ranging from 1 to 132) must follow a $ sign. This quantity specifies the maximum number of characters that may appear in each string.

EXAMPLE 8.5

A BASIC program contains the statement

```
10 FILES SALES%,MASTER%,ITEMS$20,CUSTMR$72
```

The files SALES and MASTER, assigned to data channels 1 and 2, are numeric random data files, as indicated by the % sign following each file name. ITEMS and CUSTMR, assigned to data channels 3 and 4, are string random data files with maximum string lengths of 20 and 72 characters per string, respectively.

Note that the % sign, or the $ sign followed by a positive integer, is not a part of the actual file name. Rather, it is a suffix. (Recall that each file name, exclusive of suffixes, cannot exceed six characters.)

Random data files, unlike sequential data files, cannot be listed directly on the console. Neither can they be edited using the BASIC system commands. However, we can easily write a BASIC program that will carry out either or both of these tasks. We will see how this is accomplished later in this chapter. First we must consider how the individual items in a random data file can be accessed.

Pointer Control

Although the data items in a random data file are not arranged in any special order, the *locations* of the data items are numbered sequentially from the start of the file (beginning with location number 1 and increasing by one unit for each consecutive data item). A *pointer* is used to indicate the location of the individual data items. The pointer must always be properly positioned before a data item can be transferred to or from the data file.

EXAMPLE 8.6

A random data file contains eight numeric values, arranged in the order shown below.

Location	*Value*
1	433
2	256
3	307
4	180
5	75
6	224
7	609
8	52

Suppose we want to read the fifth, the second and the seventh data items, in that order. We first position the pointer to location 5 and read a value of 75. Then we reposition the pointer to location 2 and read a value of 256. Finally, we move the pointer to location 7 and read a value of 609.

The pointer is automatically advanced one location every time a data item is read from or written onto the file. Thus it is possible to read and write data items sequentially from a random data file. We can reposition the pointer whenever we wish, however, by means of the SET statement (the RESET statement in some versions of BASIC). This statement permits us to access data items in whatever order we may desire.

Closely associated with the SET statement are the library functions LOC and LOF. The LOC function allows us to determine the position of the pointer, and the LOF function indicates the last storage location in the file. We see an illustration of the use of the SET statement and the LOC and LOF functions in the next example.

EXAMPLE 8.7

Shown below is the skeletal structure of a BASIC program that accesses data from a numeric random data file.

```
10 FILES VALUES%
   . . .
40 SET :1,K
   . . .
80 IF LOC(1)>LOF(1) THEN 200
   . . .
110 SET :1,LOC(1)+3
   . . .
150 SET :1,(1+LOF(1))/2
```

Statement 10 assigns the numeric random data file VALUES to data channel 1. In statement 40 the pointer for data channel 1 is positioned at the location indicated by the variable K (we assume that K has been assigned a positive integer value). Statement number 80 causes a transfer of control to statement 200 if the pointer for data channel 1 is positioned at any location beyond the end of the file.

In statement 110 we reposition the pointer for data channel 1 three locations beyond its present position. Finally, in statement 150 we reset the pointer to the midpoint of the file, determined as the average of the first and last locations in the file.

Notice that the pointer position in statements 110 and 150 are determined by the formulas LOC(1)+3 and (1+LOF(1))/2, respectively. A formula is permitted in a SET statement provided its value is positive but does not exceed the last location in the file. Noninteger values are automatically truncated.

Observe also that the channel number in the SET statement is preceded by a colon (:) instead of a pound sign (#). This is how we distinguish a random data file from a sequential data file. All of the file manipulation statements that refer to a channel number make use of this sign convention.

We will see a complete BASIC program that makes use of the SET statement and the LOC and LOF functions in Example 8.13.

Reading a Random Data File

We have already seen that a random data file can be read either sequentially or randomly. If the data are to be read sequentially, then the position of the pointer need not be considered, since the FILES statement places the pointer at the first location in the file and the pointer is automatically advanced one location each time a new data item is read.

EXAMPLE 8.8

The random data file STATES contains the names of the 50 states in the United States, arranged alphabetically. Figure 8.9 presents a BASIC program that will read the name of each state from the data file and then print the name on the console. The data will be read sequentially, in the same order they are stored within the file.

The FILES statement accomplishes several things in this program. First, it assigns the string random data file STATES to data channel 1, and it specifies that each string will consist of no more than 15 characters. Furthermore, it positions the pointer to the first location in the file.

Notice that we use the file manipulation statement READ rather than INPUT when reading a random data file. (In many versions of BASIC the READ and WRITE statements are used for random data files, and the INPUT and PRINT statements for sequential data files.)

The output that is generated by this program (i.e., the listing of the data file) is shown at the bottom of Fig. 8.9.

If the items in a data file are to be read randomly, then we must move the pointer to the proper location before reading each item. We use the SET statement for this purpose, as shown in Example 8.9.

```
10 FILES STATES$15
20 FOR I=1 TO 50
30     READ :1,N$
40     PRINT N$
50 NEXT I
60 END

>RUN

FILGEN          18:52          23-MAR

ALABAMA
ALASKA
ARIZONA
ARKANSAS
CALIFORNIA
COLORADO
CONNECTICUT
DELAWARE
FLORIDA
GEORGIA
HAWAII
IDAHO
ILLINOIS
INDIANA
IOWA
KANSAS
KENTUCKY
LOUISIANA
MAINE
MARYLAND
MASSACHUSETTS
MICHIGAN
MINNESOTA
MISSISSIPPI
MISSOURI
MONTANA
NEBRASKA
NEVADA
NEW HAMPSHIRE
NEW JERSEY
NEW MEXICO
NEW YORK
NORTH CAROLINA
NORTH DAKOTA
OHIO
OKLAHOMA
OREGON
PENNSYLVANIA
RHODE ISLAND
SOUTH CAROLINA
SOUTH DAKOTA
TENNESSEE
TEXAS
UTAH
VERMONT
VIRGINIA
WASHINGTON
WEST VIRGINIA
WISCONSIN
WYOMING

TIME:  0.08 SECS.
```

Fig. 8.9

EXAMPLE 8.9

Let us again consider the random data file STATES, as described in Example 8.8. We now wish to write a BASIC program that will perform the following steps.

1. Enter from the console the location of a string in STATES. (Each location will be specified by an integer constant having a value between 1 and 50.)
2. Read the string (i.e., the name of a state) contained in that location.
3. Print the string on the console.

This procedure will be repeated until a location is specified whose value is less than 1 or greater than 50.

Figure 8.10 presents the desired BASIC program. The variables L and N$ represent the specified location and the string contained in that location, respectively. Notice that the SET statement precedes the READ statement, thus placing the pointer at the proper location prior to reading each data item.

The lower part of Fig. 8.10 shows the output that is generated in response to several input quantities. Note that the names of the states are listed in the order specified by the input rather than the order in which they are stored in the data file.

```
10  FILES STATES$15
20  PRINT "LOCATION";
30  INPUT L
40  IF L<1 THEN 110
50  IF L>50 THEN 110
60  SET :1,L
70  READ :1,N$
80  PRINT N$
90  PRINT
100 GO TO 20
110 END

>RUN

EX8.9            19:02            23-MAR

LOCATION ?38
PENNSYLVANIA

LOCATION ?23
MINNESOTA

LOCATION ?50
WYOMING

LOCATION ?11
HAWAII

LOCATION ?8
DELAWARE

LOCATION ?45
VERMONT

LOCATION ?0


TIME:  0.31 SECS.
```

Fig. 8.10

Writing a Random Data File

A data item can be written onto a random file in much the same manner that it is read, except that we now use the file manipulation statement WRITE instead of READ. As before, the pointer must be positioned at the proper location before the data item is written. The new data item will replace whatever was previously stored in that location.

EXAMPLE 8.10 Inventory Control

A warehouse maintains an inventory of many different items. The quantity of each item will fluctuate from one day to another as orders are filled for customers (thus decreasing the inventory) and as shipments are received from suppliers (increasing the inventory). We wish to maintain a record of the exact inventory for each item. To do so we must adjust the inventory level after every individual transaction.

Computational Procedure

The inventory level for each item can be recorded most conveniently in a numeric random data file. We will use the data file INVTRY for this purpose.

Each item will be assigned a unique *stock number* (a positive integer) which will identify that item. The stock number will also be used to indicate the location of the inventory record in the data file. Thus if we should want to know how many units of item 86 are currently in the warehouse, we would examine the contents of storage location 86 in the data file.

The computation will proceed as follows.

1. Assign the data file INVTRY to data channel 1.
2. Print the size of the data file (i.e., the value of the last storage location) on the console.
3. Enter a value for the stock number (P) from the console.

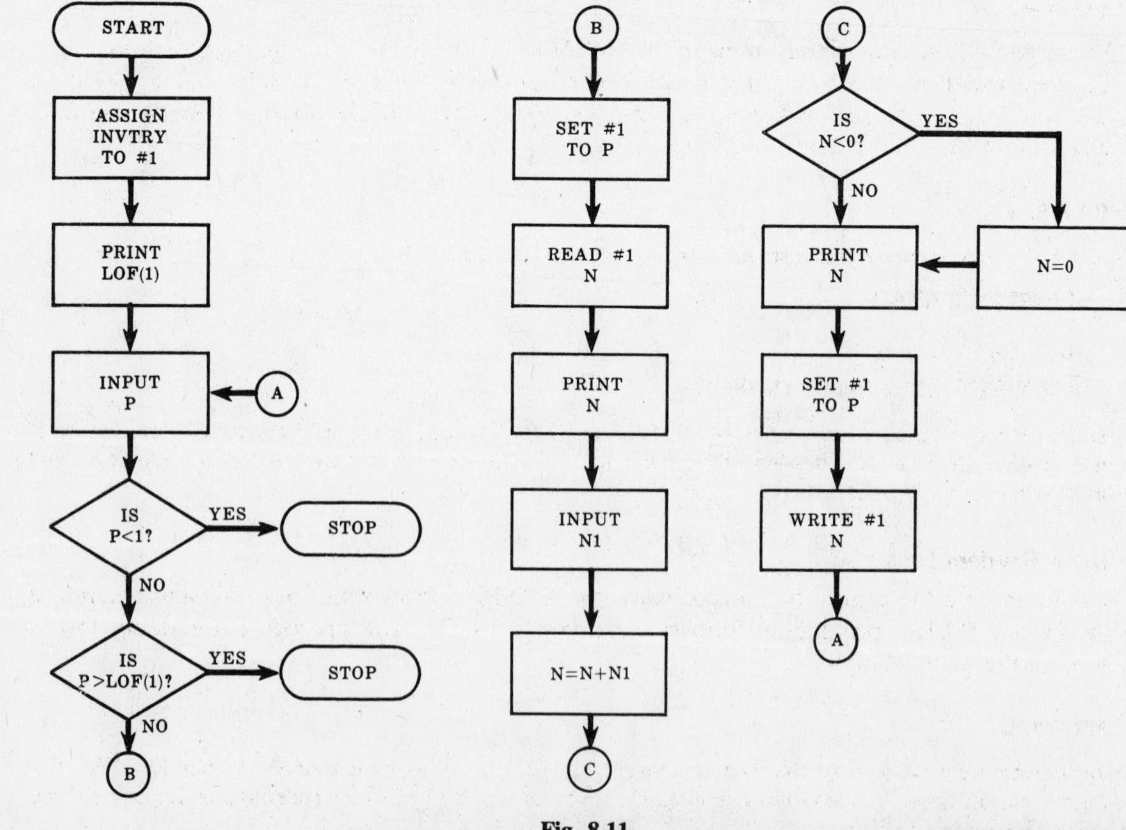

Fig. 8.11

4. If P has a value that is less than 1 or greater than the last location in the data file, then terminate the computation. Otherwise proceed with step 5 below.
5. Set the pointer for the data file to location P.
6. Read the inventory level (N) from the data file.
7. Print the current value for N on the console.
8. Enter the change in the inventory level (N1), in terms of number of units, from the console. (Note that a decrease in the inventory level must be indicated by entering a negative value for N1.)
9. Calculate a new inventory level, i.e., let

   N=N+N1

10. If the new value for N is negative (which is physically impossible), then set N equal to zero.
11. Print the new value for N on the console.
12. Reset the pointer to location P. (Note that the pointer will have advanced to location P+1 after step 6.)
13. Write the new value for N onto the data file.
14. Return to step 3.

A corresponding flowchart is shown in Fig. 8.11.

The BASIC Program

Figure 8.12 contains the actual BASIC program. We see that the program contains the file manipulation statements FILES, SET, READ and WRITE, as well as the library function LOF. Notice that the READ and WRITE statements are each preceded with a SET statement, thus positioning the pointer to the proper location before transferring information to or from the data file.

The lower portion of Fig. 8.12 shows a typical set of data resulting from execution of the program. Both input and output data are shown. Note that the program execution is terminated by entering a value of zero for a stock number.

We can include several output items in a single WRITE statement if we wish. In such cases the first data item will be placed in the location designated by the pointer, and the subsequent data items will be stored in the following consecutive locations. As with the PRINT statement, each data item can be represented by a constant, a variable, a formula or a function reference.

EXAMPLE 8.11

A BASIC program contains the statements

```
10 FILES DATA%
...
100 SET :1,P
110 WRITE :1,C1,(A+B)/2,SQR(X)
```

Suppose that P has been assigned a value of 39. Then the value assigned to C1 will be placed in location 39 of the numeric data file DATA. Location 40 will contain the value represented by the formula (A+B)/2, and location 41 will contain SQR(X).

Creating a Random Data File

A random data file cannot be created using the BASIC system commands. We must therefore write a special BASIC program to create a random data file. The procedure for doing this is presented in the next example.

EXAMPLE 8.12

Suppose that we wish to create the random data file STATES by means of the BASIC program FILGEN. The BASIC program and its associated system commands are shown in Fig. 8.13. The user-added system commands have once again been underlined.

```
10 REM INVENTORY CONTROL PROGRAM
20 FILES INVTRY%
30 PRINT "STOCK NUMBERS RUN FROM 1 TO ";LOF(1)
40 PRINT
50 PRINT "STOCK NUMBER";
60 INPUT P
70 IF P<1 THEN 220
80 PRINT
90 SET :1,P
100 READ :1,N
110 PRINT "ORIGINAL INVENTORY=";N;" ITEMS"
120 PRINT "CHANGE IN INVENTORY LEVEL";
130 INPUT N1
140 LET N=N+N1
150 IF N>=0 THEN 170
160 LET N=0
170 PRINT "NEW INVENTORY=";N;" ITEMS"
180 PRINT
190 SET :1,P
200 WRITE :1,N
210 GOTO 50
220 END


>RUN


EX8.10          19:04          23-MAR

STOCK NUMBERS RUN FROM 1 TO  2000

STOCK NUMBER ?1186

ORIGINAL INVENTORY= 346  ITEMS
CHANGE IN INVENTORY LEVEL ?-45
NEW INVENTORY= 301  ITEMS

STOCK NUMBER ?708

ORIGINAL INVENTORY= 368  ITEMS
CHANGE IN INVENTORY LEVEL ?200
NEW INVENTORY= 568  ITEMS

STOCK NUMBER ?84

ORIGINAL INVENTORY= 147  ITEMS
CHANGE IN INVENTORY LEVEL ?16
NEW INVENTORY= 163  ITEMS

STOCK NUMBER ?1400

ORIGINAL INVENTORY= 78  ITEMS
CHANGE IN INVENTORY LEVEL ?-50
NEW INVENTORY= 28  ITEMS

STOCK NUMBER ?0


TIME:  0.29 SECS.
```

Fig. 8.12

```
>NEW
NEW FILE NAME-->STATES
>SAVE
>NEW
NEW FILE NAME-->FILGEN
>10 FILES STATES$15
>20 INPUT N$
>30 IF N$="END" THEN 60
>40 WRITE :1,N$
>50 GO TO 20
>60 END
>SAVE
```

Fig. 8.13

Note that the first three lines define and save the file STATES, even though data have not yet been entered into STATES. This is required so that the file name specified in the FILES statement (line 10) will be recognized by the system.

When the program FILGEN is executed, a sequence of strings will be entered from the console and written onto STATES, beginning in location 1 and continuing in consecutive storage locations. The computation will be terminated when the word END is typed, after all of the data have been entered.

8.3 RUN TIME FILE SPECIFICATIONS

In many applications we may wish to write a BASIC program that makes use of data files but does not specify any particular file names. Rather, we would enter the required file names as input data whenever the program is executed. A program that is written in this manner will be much more general than a program that requires specific data files.

It is quite simple to enter the required file names at run time (i.e., during program execution) if we wish. To do so we must make use of the FILE statement rather than FILES. (Note that FILE and FILES are two different file manipulation statements, as we will see in the example below.)

EXAMPLE 8.13 Searching a Data File

This example presents an efficient technique for locating a particular data item in a random data file containing strings. We will assume that the strings are stored alphabetically within the file. The method, known as *binary search*, is very similar to the scheme presented in Example 6.6 for finding the maximum of a function.

Computational Procedure

Let us consider a search interval consisting of several consecutive storage locations within the file. Initially the search interval will consist of the entire file. Our overall strategy will be to compare the string at the middle of the search interval with the desired string. One of three results will be obtained.

1. The string at the midpoint will be the desired string, in which case the computation will cease.
2. The desired string will be in the first half of the search interval. Hence the second half of the search interval will be eliminated, and the desired string will be compared with the string at the middle of the remaining subinterval.
3. The desired string will be in the second half of the search interval. In this case we eliminate the first half of the search interval and compare the desired string with the string located at the middle of the remaining subinterval.

This procedure is repeated until either the desired string has been found, or it has been determined that this string is not contained within the data file.

The Program Outline

In order to outline the procedure let us define the following variables.

F$ = the name of the string random data file, including the suffix

N$ = the string which is to be located within the data file

M$ = a string which is read from the data file and compared with N$

P1 = pointer indicating the start of the search interval

P2 = pointer indicating the midpoint of the search interval

P3 = pointer indicating the end of the search interval

The computation will proceed as follows.

1. A file name is entered from the console and assigned to F$.
2. The file represented by F$ is associated with data channel 1.
3. A string is entered from the console and assigned to N$. If N$=END, then the program execution will end; otherwise the computation continues with step 4 below.
4. The pointers P1 and P3 are assigned initial values of 1 and LOF(1), respectively. This defines the initial search interval.
5. If the search interval has been narrowed down to such an extent that P1 and P3 point to adjacent locations, then a value for M$ is read from location P1 and compared with N$.
   (*a*) If N$=M$, then control is transferred to step 8 below.
   (*b*) If N$ and M$ are different, then a new value for M$ is read from location P3 and compared with N$.
   (*c*) If N$=M$, then control is transferred to step 8 below.
   (*d*) If neither value of M$ is the same as N$, then a message is printed on the console which indicates that the desired string cannot be found. We then return to step 3 above.
6. If P1 and P3 do not point to adjacent locations, then a value is determined for P2 using the formula

   P2=INT((P1+P3)/2)

7. A value for M$ is read from location P2 and compared with N$.
   (*a*) If N$=M$, the control is transferred to step 8 below.
   (*b*) If N$<M$, then we retain the first half for the search interval. Hence a new value for P3 is computed as

   P3=P2−1

   and control is transferred back to step 5 above.
   (*c*) If N$>M$, we retain the second half of the search interval. We therefore calculate a new value for P1 as

   P1=P2+1

   Control is then transferred back to step 5 above.
8. A message is printed on the console indicating that the desired string is stored in location LOC(1)−1. (Note that we use LOC(1)−1 rather than LOC(1) because the pointer will have advanced one unit when the most recent value of M$ was read.)
9. We then return to step 3 above, thus repeating the search for a new string.

A corresponding flowchart is presented in Fig. 8.14.

The BASIC Program

Figure 8.15 contains a complete BASIC program for this problem. Three file manipulation statements are included in the program—namely, FILE (line 40), SET (lines 180 and 290) and READ (lines 190, 210 and 300). The LOC and LOF statements are also present, in lines 460 and 130, respectively. Notice that the customary FILES statement, which assigns a specific data file to a data channel, is not present. Rather, the program *reads in* a file name from the console (line 30) and then assigns this file name to data channel 1 by means of the FILE statement in line 40.

The dialog that is generated by running this program is shown in Fig. 8.16. We see that the data file STATES, discussed in Examples 8.8, 8.9 and 8.12, is to be searched in this example. Notice that the suffix (i.e., $15) is entered along with the file name. (The input data are underlined.)

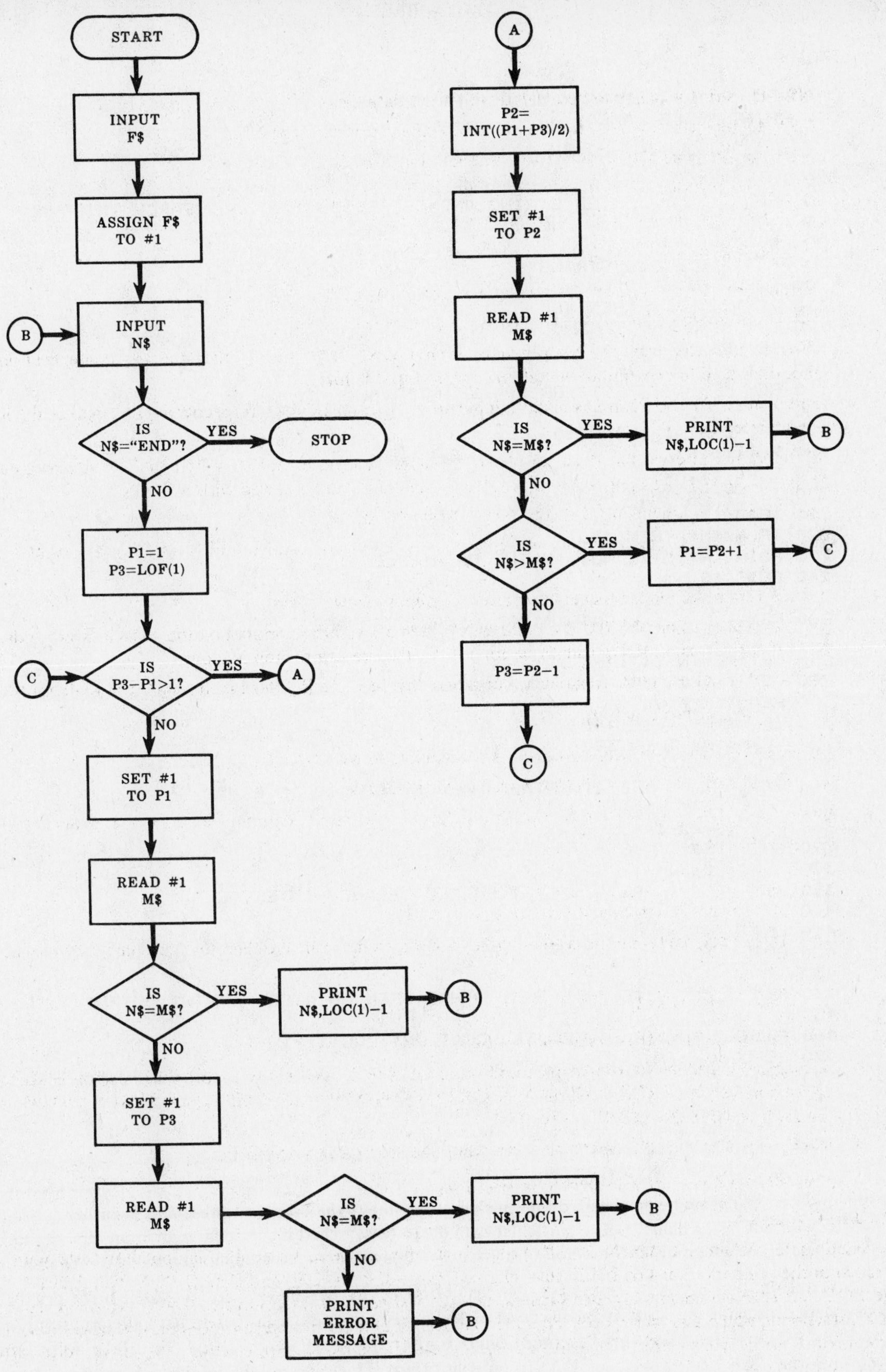
START
INPUT F$
ASSIGN F$ TO #1
B
INPUT N$
IS N$="END"?
YES
STOP
NO
P1=1 P3=LOF(1)
C
IS P3−P1>1?
YES
A
NO
SET #1 TO P1
READ #1 M$
IS N$=M$?
YES
PRINT N$,LOC(1)−1
B
NO
SET #1 TO P3
READ #1 M$
IS N$=M$?
YES
PRINT N$,LOC(1)−1
B
NO
PRINT ERROR MESSAGE
B
A
P2= INT((P1+P3)/2)
SET #1 TO P2
READ #1 M$
IS N$=M$?
YES
PRINT N$,LOC(1)−1
B
NO
IS N$>M$?
YES
P1=P2+1
C
NO
P3=P2−1
C

Fig. 8.14

```
10 REM          BINARY SEARCH PROCEDURE
20 PRINT "FILE NAME";
30 INPUT F$
40 FILE :1,F$
50
60 REM          ENTER STRING AND ESTABLISH INITIAL SEARCH INTERVAL
70
80 PRINT
90 PRINT "DESIRED STRING";
100 INPUT N$
110 IF N$="END" THEN 480
120 LET P1=1
130 LET P3=LOF(1)
140
150 REM          TEST FOR SMALL INTERVAL
160
170 IF P3-P1>1 THEN 260
180 SET :1,P1
190 READ :1,M$
200 IF N$=M$ THEN 440
210 READ :1,M$
220 IF N$=M$ THEN 440
230 PRINT N$;" IS NOT IN THE DATA FILE"
240 GOTO 60
250
260 REM          LOCATE MIDPOINT AND COMPARE
270
280 LET P2=INT((P1+P3)/2)
290 SET :1,P2
300 READ :1,M$
310 IF N$=M$ THEN 440
320 IF N$>M$ THEN 390
330
340 REM          RETAIN FIRST HALF OF SEARCH INTERVAL
350
360 LET P3=P2-1
370 GOTO 150
380
390 REM          RETAIN LAST HALF OF SEARCH INTERVAL
400
410 LET P1=P2+1
420 GOTO 150
430
440 REM          DESIRED STRING HAS BEEN LOCATED - PRINT OUTPUT
450
460 PRINT N$;" IS STORED IN LOCATION";LOC(1)-1
470 GOTO 60
480 END
```

Fig. 8.15

Finally, it should again be emphasized that this program, unlike the programs presented in earlier examples, can be run with *any* string data file. The particular data file to be searched is specified as an input quantity rather than as a part of the program. This method of file specification greatly increases the generality of the program.

Some file manipulation statements, such as RESTORE, MARGIN and PAGE, have not been discussed in this chapter. (Some versions of BASIC also include a set of matrix file manipulation statements.) The reason for this, as mentioned earlier, is the variability of the file manipulation statements between one version of BASIC and another. The reader who may wish to make use of data files should determine the exact nature of the file manipulation statements available for his or her particular computer.

```
FILE NAME ?STATES$15

DESIRED STRING ?PENNSYLVANIA
PENNSYLVANIA IS STORED IN LOCATION 38

DESIRED STRING ?FLORIDA
FLORIDA IS STORED IN LOCATION 9

DESIRED STRING ?OHIO
OHIO IS STORED IN LOCATION 35

DESIRED STRING ?ALASKA
ALASKA IS STORED IN LOCATION 2

DESIRED STRING ?PUERTO RICO
PUERTO RICO IS NOT IN THE DATA FILE

DESIRED STRING ?CALIFORNIA
CALIFORNIA IS STORED IN LOCATION 5

DESIRED STRING ?MASSACHUSETTS
MASSACHUSETTS IS STORED IN LOCATION 21

DESIRED STRING ?END

TIME:   0.45 SECS.
```

Fig. 8.16

Review Questions

8.1 What is a file? What kinds of information can be contained within a file?

8.2 What is the difference between a sequential data file and a random data file?

8.3 What are the advantages of a sequential data file compared with a random data file?

8.4 What are the advantages of a random data file compared with a sequential data file?

8.5 How are the data sets ordered in a sequential data file?

8.6 Can numbers and strings both be included in a sequential data file? A random data file?

8.7 How are the individual data items separated from one another in a sequential data file? What special rule applies to strings that contain commas or blank spaces?

8.8 Can the BASIC system commands be used to create and edit a sequential data file? A random data file?

8.9 What rule applies to naming a data file?

8.10 For which type of file must the file name be followed by a suffix? What information is provided by the suffix?

8.11 Must the data items in a sequential data file be read in any particular order?

8.12 How can we test for the end of a sequential data file?

8.13 What is a data channel? How is a particular data file assigned to a data channel?

8.14 Where on a sequential data file must new information be written?

8.15 How can a sequential data file be erased and repositioned to its starting point?

8.16 When writing a data set onto a sequential data file, how can the spacing of the individual data items be controlled?

8.17 How can a sequential data file be renamed?

8.18 How are the data items arranged in a random data file? How can a specific data item be accessed?

8.19 What is a pointer? How can the location of a pointer be established? How can a pointer be repositioned?

8.20 How are data items read from a random data file? Can a random data file be read sequentially? Explain.

8.21 How are data items written onto a random data file? Can a random data file be written sequentially? Explain.

8.22 When a data item is written onto a random data file, what happens to the information that was previously stored in that location?

8.23 How can a random data file be created?

8.24 How can a program be written so that the name of a data file can be specified during run time? Which file manipulation statements must be utilized in order to accomplish this?

8.25 When a random data file is specified at run time, must the suffix be included with the file name?

8.26 Summarize the purpose of each of the following file manipulation statements: FILES, FILE, INPUT, READ, PRINT, WRITE, IF END, QUOTE, SCRATCH, SET.

8.27 How do the file manipulation statements INPUT and PRINT differ from READ and WRITE?

8.28 How do the file manipulation statements FILES and FILE differ from one another?

8.29 What is the purpose of the library functions LOC and LOF?

Solved Problems

8.30 Several BASIC statements, or groups of statements, are shown below. Some are written incorrectly. Identify all errors.

(*a*)
```
10 FILES DATAOLD,DATANEW
```

A file name cannot exceed six characters in most versions of BASIC.

(*b*)
```
50 PRINT #3,N,N$,P+Q,LOG(T)
```

Correct, provided a sequential data file has been assigned to data channel 3.

(*c*)
```
25 READ :2,N$,M$,C1,C2
```

A random file cannot contain both strings and numeric constants.

(*d*)
```
150 IF END #1, THEN STOP
```

The word STOP must be replaced with a statement number.

(*e*)
```
10 FILES DATA1%,DATA2%
. . .
40 READ :1,C1,C2
. . .
80 WRITE :2,C1,C2
```

Correct.

(*f*)
```
10 FILES SALES
. . .
75 SET #1,P
80 INPUT #1,A,B,T$,G
```

The SET statement is used only with random data files.

(*g*)
```
60 IF P=LOF(2) THEN 175
```

Correct, provided a random data file has been assigned to data channel 2.

8.31 Write one or more BASIC statements or system commands for each of the situations described below.

(*a*) Create the sequential data file SALES. Save and list the file after it has been entered.

```
NEW OR OLD-->NEW
NEW FILE NAME-->SALES
 10...  }
 20...  }  Data file SALES
 ...    }
200...  }
SAVE
LIST
```

(*b*) Assign the sequential data file SALES to data channel 1.

```
10 FILES SALES
```

(*c*) Assign the sequential data file represented by the variable F$ to data channel 1.

```
10 INPUT F$
20 FILE #1,F$
```

(*d*) Each line in the sequential data file FILE1 consists of a line number, followed by the values for the variables A, B, P$ and Q$. For each value of A and B we wish to calculate a value for C, where

C=SQR(A*B)

and write the values for A, B, C, P$ and Q$ onto another sequential data file called FILE2. Assume that the data sets are read from channel 2 and written onto channel 4.

```
10 FILES,FILE1,,FILE2
20 QUOTE #4
30 SCRATCH #4
40 INPUT #2,N,A,B,P$,Q$
50 LET C=SQR(A*B)
60 PRINT #4,N,A,B,C,P$,Q$
70 IF END #2, THEN 90
80 GO TO 40
90 END
```

(*e*) A program reads data from the sequential data file MASTER and writes updated data onto the sequential data file REVISE. At some later time we wish to use this same program to read the data file REVISE. Since the program will not be altered, we wish to change the name of REVISE (the new output file) to MASTER (the old input file). Show how this can be accomplished.

```
OLD
OLD FILE NAME--> MASTER
SCRATCH
OLD
OLD FILE NAME--> REVISE
RENAME MASTER
```

(*f*) A program will write data onto the random data file MASTER. Show how a blank file called MASTER can be defined and saved in preparation for running the program.

```
NEW
NEW FILE NAME--> MASTER
SAVE
```

(*g*) Determine the current location of the pointer for a random data file on channel 3. Transfer control to the end of the program if the pointer is positioned at the last location in the data file.

```
100 LET P=LOC(3)
110 IF P=LOF(3) THEN 250
    ...
250 END
```

(*h*) Read a positive integer quantity from the console. Position the pointer for data channel 5 to the location indicated by the input quantity.

```
150 INPUT P5
160 SET :5,P5
```

Supplementary Problems

8.32 Determine which of the following file manipulation statements are available at your particular installation: FILES, FILE, INPUT, READ, PRINT, WRITE, IF END, QUOTE, SCRATCH, SET (or RESET), RESTORE, MARGIN, PAGE. Are other file manipulation statements also available?

8.33 Review the purpose of each of the file manipulation statements available for your particular computer. Summarize the grammatical rules for writing each statement.

8.34 Several BASIC statements, or groups of statements, are shown below. Some are written incorrectly. Identify all errors.

(*a*)
```
35 READ #1,N,A,B,C,P$,Q$
```

(*b*)
```
160 WRITE :2,X,Y,X+Y,X−Y,P$
```

(*c*)
```
80 SET :2,LOC(1)+2
90 WRITE :2,X1,X2,X3
```

(*d*)
```
10 FILES NAMES$20,ACCTS%
```

(*e*)
```
10 FILES MASTER
20 SCRATCH MASTER
30 QUOTE MASTER
```

(*f*)
```
10 INPUT F$
20 FILES F$
```

(*g*)
```
100 SET :1,LOF(1)+3
110 READ :1,L,M,N
```

(*h*)
```
10 FILES NAMES$20,ACCTS%
 . . .
75 SET :1,P1
80 READ :1,N$
85 SET :2,P2
90 WRITE :2,N$
```

8.35 Write one or more BASIC statements or system commands for each of the situations described below.

(*a*) Assign the sequential data files LIST1 and LIST2 to data channels 1 and 3, respectively.

(*b*) Assign the string random data file NAMES to data channel 1, and assign the numeric random data file ACCTS to data channel 2. Assume that each string in NAMES will consist of 25 or fewer characters.

(*c*) Assign the random data files represented by the variables F$ and G$ to data channels 2 and 5, respectively.

(*d*) Create the sequential data file TAPE1. Save and list the file after it has been entered.

(*e*) A program will write data onto the random data file ITEMS. Show how a blank file called ITEMS can be defined and saved in preparation for running the program.

(*f*) A program reads data from the sequential data files OLD1 and OLD2 and writes updated data onto the sequential data files NEW1 and NEW2. At some later time we may want to use this same program to read the data files NEW1 and NEW2. How can the names of the previous output files (NEW1 and NEW2) be changed so that they can be used as input files?

(*g*) How can the program described in part (*f*) above be rewritten so that the output files need not be renamed before they can be read? Assume that the input files will be assigned to data channels 1 and 2 and the output files to channels 3 and 4.

(*h*) Each line in the sequential data file assigned to data channel 5 consists of a line number followed by the values for the variables F$, X, Y, Z and G$. Suppose that we want to write the values of Z, F$ and G$ onto a sequential data file assigned to data channel 3. Show how this can be accomplished.

(*i*) Copy the numeric random data file assigned to data channel 5 onto the file assigned to data channel 3.

(*j*) Read a positive integer quantity from the console. Position the pointer for data channel 6 to the location indicated by the input quantity. Read a value of X from this location, and write the value of X onto the corresponding location for data channel 2.

(*k*) Determine the location of the pointer for the random data files assigned to data channels 1 and 4. Transfer control to statement number 200 if both pointers have the same value (i.e., indicate the same respective locations). Otherwise set the pointer for data channel 2 to the greater of the two values.

(*l*) Determine the last locations of the random data files assigned to data channels 3 and 5. Transfer control to statement 25 if the last locations are not the same.

Programming Problems

8.36 Modify the program given in Example 8.4 so that the file names can be entered from the console during program execution. Also, include an option which will cause the data sets to be stored in the order of decreasing class averages rather than by alphabetical order of the students' names.

8.37 Modify the program given in Example 8.10 so that any of the following options can be carried out.

(*a*) Simply print the inventory level for a given stock number.

(*b*) Define a "block" of stock numbers by reading in the first and last stock numbers in the block. Print the inventory level for each stock number within the block.

(*c*) Print the inventory level for each stock number within the data file.

(*d*) Print the stock numbers and the corresponding inventory levels for all items having less than some specified inventory level.

(*e*) Print the stock numbers and the corresponding inventory levels for all items having greater than some specified inventory level.

8.38 Modify the program given in Example 8.13 so that any of the following options can be carried out.

(*a*) The entire data file can be listed on the console.

(*b*) All of the strings beginning with a specified letter will be printed on the console.

(*c*) All of the strings which precede a specified string will be printed.

(*d*) All of the strings that are located beyond a specified string will be printed.

8.39 For each problem listed below rewrite the program so that the data are read from or written onto a data file. (*Note*: some problems will require reading the data from a data file and printing the calculated results on the console. Other problems will accept input from the console and write the output onto a data file. In a few cases it may be desirable to read the input data from one data file and write the output onto another data file.)

(*a*) Averaging of air polution data (Example 4.16)

(*b*) Generation of Fibonacci numbers and search for primes (Example 4.18)

(*c*) Compound interest with annual compounding (Problem 4.48(*e*))
(*d*) A table of functions (Example 5.5)
(*e*) Generating a table of damped sinusoidal functions (Problem 5.48)
(*f*) Four-letter word unscrambler (Problem 5.49)
(*g*) Reordering a list of numbers several different ways (Problem 5.50)
(*h*) Alphabetizing a list of names (Problem 5.51)
(*i*) Multiplying the elements in two tables (Problem 5.52)
(*j*) Generating a table of compound interest factors (Problem 5.53)
(*k*) Calculating deviations about an average (Problem 5.54)
(*l*) Calculating student grade averages (Problem 5.55)
(*m*) Matching countries with their capitals (Problem 5.56)
(*n*) Premultiplying a vector by a matrix (Problem 5.57(*a*))
(*o*) Matrix multiplication (Problem 5.57(*b*))
(*p*) Generating a table of Legendre polynomials (Problem 5.57(*c*))
(*q*) Statistical calculations (Problem 5.57(*d*))
(*r*) Lagrangian interpolation (Problem 5.57(*h*))
(*s*) A monthly payroll (Example 6.26)
(*t*) Simulation of a bouncing ball (Example 6.28)
(*u*) A weekly payroll (Problem 6.48)
(*v*) Analysis of student grade averages (Problem 6.52(*e*))
(*w*) Encoding and decoding a line of text (Problem 6.52(*j*))

8.40 Write a complete BASIC program that will create and utilize a sequential data file containing names, addresses and telephone numbers. Include a provision for each of the following features.

(*a*) Add a new record (i.e., a new name, address and telephone number) to the file.
(*b*) Find and display a particular record, based upon identifying information entered from the console (e.g., a name, an address or a telephone number).
(*c*) Delete a particular record, based upon identifying information entered from the console.
(*d*) Alphabetize the records, based upon the last name in each record.
(*e*) List (i.e., print) the entire file.
(*f*) Terminate the computation.

8.41 Repeat Problem 8.40 utilizing a random data file. Compare with the sequential data file version from a standpoint of programming ease and execution speed.

PART III: *Microcomputer BASIC*

Chapter 9

Enhancements to BASIC

Virtually all microcomputers support BASIC as a primary programming language. Some microcomputers contain a BASIC interpreter within a read-only memory (ROM), so that the language actually becomes a part of the computer's internal circuitry. Other machines read the BASIC interpreter into the computer's memory from a mass storage device (e.g., a floppy disk) when it is needed. In either case, BASIC lends itself very naturally to the microcomputer environment. In fact, the availability of BASIC has been a very significant factor in the commercial development of the microcomputer marketplace.

Most microcomputers support very sophisticated versions of BASIC, including many enhancements that are not present in the more traditional versions of the language. Moreover, these sophisticated forms of BASIC are, for the most part, variants of *Microsoft BASIC* (developed by the Microsoft Corporation, Bellevue, Washington). For example, the microcomputers marketed by Apple, AT&T, IBM, Tandy (Radio Shack), Texas Instruments, and Zenith, among others, all include some variation of Microsoft BASIC. Hence, the material presented in the next four chapters of this book will be based upon the features found in Microsoft BASIC (in particular, the version of Microsoft BASIC available on the popular IBM Personal Computers).

The material presented in this text is intended to be representative of those features that are available on a typical state-of-the-art microcomputer. The reader should understand, however, that all of these features may not be implemented on every computer. Furthermore, those features that are more universally available may be implemented somewhat differently on each computer. This material should therefore be considered to be a general overview of microcomputer BASIC rather than a precise reference document. For specific information about a particular version of the language, the reader should consult the appropriate programmer's reference manual.

The more common features of Microsoft BASIC are summarized in Appendix D of this text.

9.1 ELEMENTARY LANGUAGE EXTENSIONS

The different versions of microcomputer BASIC generally allow a greater latitude in the definition and use of variables and operators than their more traditional counterparts. Some of the more common extensions are discussed below.

Larger Variable Names

Most versions of microcomputer BASIC permit variable names that are longer than two characters. In fact, some versions of the language do not place any restriction on the maximum permissible number of characters. This is a very convenient feature, since it allows variable names to correspond more closely to the items that they represent. Usually, however, only the first several characters are significant in identifying the variable. Typical values for the number of significant characters can range from as few as 2 to as many as 40. On the IBM Personal Computer, variable names can consist of as many as 40 characters, all of which are significant.

EXAMPLE 9.1

Several typical variable names are shown below.

AREA	NAME
SIZE	ADDRESS
TABLE	PATIENT
VECTOR	PAYROLL
VELOCITY	TAX

Many versions of microcomputer BASIC will recognize each of these names as a separate variable. If only the first two characters are significant, however, then the variables VECTOR and VELOCITY, PATIENT and PAYROLL, and TABLE and TAX will be indistinguishable.

The use of BASIC keywords (e.g., PRINT, DATA, NEXT, etc.) as variable names must be avoided as this will thoroughly confuse the interpreter, most likely resulting in an error message. In particular, the programmer must be careful not to use any of the less common keywords (e.g., NAME, CHAIN, SWAP, etc.) as variable names.

Multiple Numeric Data Types

Most versions of microcomputer BASIC distinguish between *integer, real* and *double-precision* quantities.

Integer quantities are positive or negative whole numbers that typically fall within the range of −32,768 to 32,767. Such quantities are not subject to roundoff errors. Hence they are useful as counters, as subscripts for array elements, as running variables (indices) in FOR-TO loops, ON-GO TO statements, etc. Also, it may be desirable to use integer quantities when carrying out certain logical tests with the IF-THEN statement.

Real quantities are ordinary numeric values, as discussed in Chapter 2. A real quantity may or may not include a fractional (decimal) component and/or an exponent. Typically, the magnitude of a real quantity may be as small as 2.9E−39 and as large as 1.7E+38 (the value 0.0 is also an acceptable real quantity).

Within the computer's memory real quantities and integer quantities are represented differently, even if a fractional component is not included. Real quantities are imprecise (they are subject to round-off errors), whereas integer quantities are exact.

Double-precision quantities are essentially real (single-precision) quantities with a greater number of significant figures. Typically, a double-precision quantity will be represented in terms of 16 significant figures, whereas a real quantity will contain only 6 or 7 significant figures. Also, the letter D is used to represent an exponent rather than the letter E.

Many versions of microcomputer BASIC recognize other numeric data types, such as octal (base 8) and hexadecimal (base 16). The use of these data types is, however, beyond the scope of our present discussion.

EXAMPLE 9.2

Several different types of numbers are shown below.

Number	*Type*
16458	Integer or real
36.55	Real
−0.666667E−3	Real
−0.6666666666666667D−3	Double-precision

When a number is represented by a numeric variable, the number and the variable must be of the same type. Thus integer, real, and double-precision quantities must be represented by integer, real, and double-precision variables, respectively. The different variable types are generally identified by the last character of the variable name. Typically, an integer variable will end with a percent sign (%), a real variable will end with an exclamation point (!), and a double-precision variable will end with a pound sign (#). [Also, remember that a string variable must end with a dollar sign ($).] If a variable name does not end with one of these special characters, it will be interpreted as a real variable.

These special endings are sometimes referred to as *suffixes*. The different types of suffixes are summarized below.

Variable	*Suffix*
Integer	%
Real (single-precision)	! (or no suffix)
Double-precision	#
String	$

EXAMPLE 9.3

Several BASIC variables and their corresponding data types are given below.

Variable	*Data Type*
COUNT%	Integer
NAME$	String
PAY	Real (single-precision)
TAX!	Real (single-precision)
ERROR#	Double-precision

The same name with different suffixes will be interpreted as distinct variables.

EXAMPLE 9.4

Suppose that the variables

A, A$, A% and A#

all appear in the same BASIC program. They will be interpreted as separate, independent variables since they have different suffixes and therefore represent different data types.

The programmer should realize that the memory requirements for the different data types are not the same. Integer quantities require the least amount of memory (typically 2 bytes), whereas double-precision quantities require the most (8 bytes). Also, long variable names require more memory than short variable names, just as long strings require more memory than short strings. These factors should be considered when using a microcomputer, since the amount of memory available may be scarce.

Similar consideration should be given to execution time. As a rule, programs that make use of integer variables run faster than programs containing real or double-precision variables. Thus, programs that involve a great deal of numerical computation should utilize integer variables wherever practicable.

Mixed Arithmetic Operations

When arithmetic operations are carried out between different types of numerical data, the result will always be expressed at the highest possible level of precision. Thus, arithmetic operations involving integer and real data will produce a real result. Similarly, arithmetic operations involving either integer and double-precision data, or real and double-precision data, will produce a double-precision result.

EXAMPLE 9.5

In each of the following expressions, assume that I% = 4, R! = −0.2 and D# = 0.16666666D−4.

Expression	*Value*
R! + 5	4.8 (real)
I% * R!	−0.8 (real)
3 * I% * D#	0.199999992D−3 (double-precision)
(1 + R!) * D#	0.133333328D−5 (double-precision)

Now consider a numerical assignment statement (i.e., a LET statement) in which the variable on the left and the quantity on the right are of different types. The right-hand quantity will automatically be converted to the same data type as the left-hand variable. Normally, this will cause a fractional quantity on the right to be *rounded* if assigned to an integer variable on the left (some versions of BASIC will *truncate* rather than round the fractional quantity).

EXAMPLE 9.6

In each of the following assignment statements, assume that I% = 4, R! = −0.2 and D# = 0.16666666D−4.

Assignment Statement	*Result*
10 LET N% = 3 * R!	N% = −1
20 LET FRACT = 1/3	FRACT = 0.3333333
30 LET FRACT# = 1/3	FRACT# = 0.3333333333333333
40 LET ANS% = I%↑2/3	ANS% = 5
50 LET RATIO = (I% − R!)/D#	RATIO = 2.52E+5

(Notice the rounding that results from statement number 10. Truncation would have resulted in N% = 0 rather than N% = −1.)

Recall that a numerical quantity cannot be assigned to a string variable and vice versa. Also, remember that the keyword LET is optional in most versions of microcomputer BASIC.

Additional Operators

Many versions of microcomputer BASIC include two additional arithmetic operators: integer division (\) and integer remainder (MOD). In integer division, each of the two given numbers is first *rounded* to an integer, the division is carried out and the quotient is then truncated. The integer remainder operation provides the quantity that remains after an integer division has been performed.

EXAMPLE 9.7

Several integer division and integer remainder operations are presented below.

13\5 = 2	13 MOD 5 = 3
8.6\2.7 = 3	8.6 MOD 2.7 = 0
8.3\2.7 = 2	8.3 MOD 2.7 = 2
8.3\2.2 = 4	8.3 MOD 2.2 = 0

Some of the simpler versions of microcomputer BASIC recognize only integer-type numeric data. In such cases the regular division operator (/) will imply integer division (with a truncated quotient).

Most versions of microcomputer BASIC include the *logical* operators AND, OR and NOT. The first two operators (AND and OR) allow two or more logical *operands* (i.e., true-false conditions) to be combined. The third operator (NOT) is used to *negate* an operand (i.e., change true to false or false to true). These operations allow more complex conditions to be included in the IF-THEN statement.

EXAMPLE 9.8

Shown below are several IF-THEN statements that make use of complex logical conditions.

(*a*)
```
10 IF (X<10) AND (Y>0) THEN 90
20 PRINT X,Y
```

Statement number 90 will be executed next if X has a value less than 10 *and* Y has a value greater than zero. Otherwise, statement number 20 will be executed next.

(*b*)
```
50 IF (COUNT>99) OR (N$ = "END") THEN 175
60 GO TO 30
```

Statement number 175 will be executed next if the value of COUNT exceeds 99 or if "END" has been assigned to N$ (or both). If neither condition is true, then statement number 60 will be executed next.

(*c*)
```
75 IF NOT ((X<10) AND (Y>0)) THEN 200
80 PRINT X,Y
```

This is just the opposite of example (*a*). In the present case, statement number 200 will be executed if the condition

```
(X<10) AND (Y>0)
```

is false, i.e., if X>= 10 or if Y<= 0. Otherwise, statement number 80 will be executed next.

Note that the given IF statement could also have been written:

```
75 IF (X>= 10) OR (Y<= 0) THEN 200
```

As a practical matter, the NOT operator is used infrequently in actual BASIC programs.

Some versions of microcomputer BASIC include the additional logical operators XOR (exclusive OR), EQV (equivalent) and IMP (implies). Briefly, when used to connect two logical operands, XOR will result in a condition that is true only if one of the operands is true and the other false; EQV will result in a condition that is true if both operands have the same logical value (either both true or both false); and IMP will result in a true condition if both operands are true or if the first operand is false (regardless of the value of the second operand). Since these three logical operators are used relatively infrequently, we will not discuss them further in this text.

Typically, the complete hierarchy of arithmetic, relational, and logical operators is as follows:

Operation	*Operator*
1. Exponentiation	↑ or ^
2. Negation (i.e., preceding a variable or a number with a minus sign)	−
3. Multiplication and division	* /
4. Integer division	\
5. Integer remainder	MOD
6. Addition and subtraction	+ −
7. Relationals	= <> <= < >= >
8. Logical NOT	NOT
9. Logical AND	AND
10. Logical OR	OR
11. Logical XOR	XOR
12. Logical EQV	EQV
13. Logical IMP	IMP

The hierarchy may vary, however, from one version of BASIC to another. Within a given hierarchical group, the operations are carried out from left to right.

Many versions of microcomputer BASIC also include a *concatenation* operator, which is used to combine strings. This operator is usually represented by a plus sign (+), though an ampersand (&) or a comma may be used in certain versions of the language.

EXAMPLE 9.9

Suppose that the string variables A$ and B$ represent the strings MICRO and COMPUTER, respectively. Then the statement

```
10 PRINT A$+B$
```

will cause the (single) string

```
MICROCOMPUTER
```

to be printed (assuming that the concatenation symbol is the plus sign).

Similarly, the statement

```
20 PRINT "SEVEN"+"TEEN"
```

will cause the (single) string

```
SEVENTEEN
```

to appear.

Multiple Statements per Line

Most enhanced versions of BASIC allow multiple statements to appear on the same line. Typically, a colon (:) will be used to separate one such statement from another.

EXAMPLE 9.10

Several multistatement lines are shown below.

```
10 LET A=0.25 : B=0.5 : C=-0.125
20 PRINT "X="; : INPUT X
30 FOR I%=1 TO N% : READ A(I%) : NEXT I%
```

The use of this feature is convenient for two reasons. First, it allows sequences of related statements to be grouped more logically, and second, it contributes to a more efficient use of memory. The habitual use of multistatement lines may, however, result in programs that are difficult to read and to correct.

EXAMPLE 9.11 Generating Fibonacci Numbers and Searching for Primes on a Microcomputer

In Example 4.18 we saw a complete BASIC program that generates a sequence of Fibonacci numbers and determines which of them are prime numbers. Figure 9.1 shows another BASIC program, written in Microsoft BASIC, that allows the same calculations to be carried out on an IBM Personal Computer. This program makes use of several of the language extensions that have been presented earlier in this chapter. In particular, we see the use of long variable names, integer-type variables and multiple statements on several of the lines. Also, the logic used to identify prime numbers is somewhat more straightforward, since we are now able to make use of the integer remainder (MOD) operation. (Compare lines 110 to 120 in the current program with lines 140 to 160 in the original program.)

Execution of this program produces output similar to that shown in Fig. 4.10 of Example 4.18. Figure 9.2 shows a typical set of output generated by this program (though the output is normally displayed on a TV monitor rather than printed on a hard-copy terminal). The user's responses have been underlined.

It should be noted that on a microcomputer the largest value that can be assigned to N% (in line 30) is 23, since a value greater than 23 will result in a Fibonacci number that exceeds 32,767, the largest permissible integer on most micros. This restriction may limit the practical use of this particular program on a microcomputer.

Also, notice that the strings that are shown in lines 20, 30, 50, 60 and 140 include both uppercase and

```
10 REM ***** GENERATION OF FIBONACCI NUMBERS AND SEARCH FOR PRIMES *****
20 PRINT "Generation of Fibonacci Numbers and Search for Primes":PRINT
30 PRINT "How many Fibonacci numbers";:INPUT N%:PRINT
40 F1%=1:F2%=1
50 PRINT "I=";1,"F=";F1%;" (Prime)"
60 PRINT "I=";2,"F=";F2%;" (Prime)"
70 FOR INDEX%=3 TO N%
80    F%=F1%+F2%:ROOT=SQR(F%):MAX%=ROOT
90    PRINT "I=";INDEX%,"F=";F%;
100   FOR DENOM%=2 TO MAX%
110      REMAINDER%=F% MOD DENOM%
120      IF REMAINDER%=0 THEN 150
130   NEXT DENOM%
140   PRINT " (Prime)";
150   PRINT
160   F2%=F1%:F1%=F%
170 NEXT INDEX%
180 END
```

Fig. 9.1

```
Generation of Fibonacci Numbers and Search for Primes

How many Fibonacci numbers? 23

I= 1          F= 1  (Prime)
I= 2          F= 1  (Prime)
I= 3          F= 2  (Prime)
I= 4          F= 3  (Prime)
I= 5          F= 5  (Prime)
I= 6          F= 8
I= 7          F= 13  (Prime)
I= 8          F= 21
I= 9          F= 34
I= 10         F= 55
I= 11         F= 89  (Prime)
I= 12         F= 144
I= 13         F= 233  (Prime)
I= 14         F= 377
I= 15         F= 610
I= 16         F= 987
I= 17         F= 1597  (Prime)
I= 18         F= 2584
I= 19         F= 4181
I= 20         F= 6765
I= 21         F= 10946
I= 22         F= 17711
I= 23         F= 28657  (Prime)
```

Fig. 9.2

lowercase letters. The distinction between uppercase and lowercase is recognized by most microcomputers, though only in strings.

9.2 ADDITIONAL STATEMENTS

Most versions of microcomputer BASIC include a number of useful and convenient statements that are not available in the traditional versions of the language. Several of the more common additional statements are discussed below.

DEFINT, DEFSNG, DEFDBL, and DEFSTR

In some situations it is convenient to define several different variables of a particular data type. This can be accomplished with the *DEFINT, DEFSNG, DEFDBL,* and *DEFSTR statements* (for integer, single-precision, double-precision, and string data, respectively), provided all the variable names of a given type begin with the same first letter. It is also possible to specify a *range* of first letters, as illustrated below.

EXAMPLE 9.12

A BASIC program contains the following statements.

```
10 DEFINT I
20 DEFDBL X-Z
30 DEFSTR A-C,N
```

Statement number 10 states that all variables beginning with the letter I will be integer variables. Statement number 20 causes all variables beginning with X, Y and Z to be double-precision variables, and statement number 30 defines all variables beginning with A, B, C and N as string variables. (Note that suffixes are not required for any of these variables.)

It should be understood that variable names which include a suffix take precedence over those variable names that are defined by a DEF-type statement.

IF-THEN

Most versions of microcomputer BASIC include an expanded form of the *IF-THEN statement* in which one or more independent statements may appear after the keyword THEN, provided they are all on the *same line.* These statements will be executed if the given logical condition is satisfied. Otherwise, the statement beginning on the *following line* will be executed next.

EXAMPLE 9.13

A BASIC program contains the following statements.

```
50 IF ERROR>0.001 THEN PRINT ERROR
60 LET X = X1
```

The IF-THEN statement will cause the value of ERROR to be printed if it exceeds 0.001. Otherwise, control will be passed directly to line number 60.

EXAMPLE 9.14

A BASIC program contains the following statements.

```
200 IF FLAG = 1 THEN A = 10 : C$ = BLUE : GO TO 35
210 PRINT A
```

If FLAG has a value of 1, then the variables A and C$ will be assigned the values 10 and BLUE, respectively, and control will be transferred to line number 35. Otherwise, line number 210 will be executed next. (Note that the keyword THEN is followed by three separate statements.)

IF-THEN-ELSE

Some versions of microcomputer BASIC allow an *ELSE clause* to be included in the IF-THEN statement. Thus, the statement (or statements) following THEN will be executed if the given logical condition is satisfied. Otherwise, the statement (or statements) following ELSE will be executed.

EXAMPLE 9.15

A BASIC program contains the following IF-THEN-ELSE statement.

```
80 IF Z<0 THEN 50 ELSE 120
```

If the value of Z is less than zero, then the statement on line number 50 will be executed next. Otherwise, the statement on line number 120 will be executed next.

EXAMPLE 9.16

Now consider the BASIC statement

```
80 IF DIFF<0.001 THEN PRINT ANS: GO TO 300: ELSE X=X1: GO TO 35
```

The value of ANS will be printed and control will be transferred to line number 300 if the value of DIFF is less than 0.001. Otherwise, the current value of X1 is assigned to X and control is transferred to line number 35.

An IF-THEN-ELSE statement can usually be *nested* within other IF-THEN-ELSE statements, though the logic can be tricky and the results can turn out differently than the programmer may expect. The reader is referred to his or her particular programmer's reference manual for more information on nested IF-THEN-ELSE statements.

Finally, it should be mentioned that the use of the expanded IF-THEN-ELSE statements can often improve the logical clarity of a BASIC program. This is accomplished by writing the conditional branches in an orderly, sequential manner, thus reducing the number of GO TO statements that might otherwise be present. The organization of programs in this manner is referred to as *structured programming.*

ON-GOSUB

The *ON-GOSUB statement* is available in many versions of microcomputer BASIC. This statement is similar to the ON-GO TO statement except that control is transferred to a subroutine rather than to another part of the main program. Upon completion of the subroutine, control is transferred back to the statement following ON-GOSUB.

EXAMPLE 9.17

A BASIC program contains the statements

```
100 ON FLAG GOSUB 800, 1000, 1200
110 PRINT NAME$
```

The ON-GOSUB statement will result in a transfer to one of three different subroutines, depending on the value assigned to FLAG. If FLAG = 1, control will be transferred to the subroutine beginning on line 800. Similarly, control will be transferred to the subroutine beginning on line 1000 if FLAG = 2 and to the subroutine beginning on line 1200 if FLAG = 3. Note that statement number 110 (PRINT NAME$) will be executed after the subroutine, regardless of which subroutine is chosen.

ON ERROR GO TO

Most versions of microcomputer BASIC recognize a number of different types of errors that can occur while a program is being interpreted or being run. The *ON ERROR GO TO statement* is used to carry out error correction once an error has occurred. In particular, the ON ERROR GO TO statement automatically transfers control to a remote part of the program when an error has been detected, provided the error detection occurs *after* the ON ERROR GO TO statement. This is known as *error trapping.* It allows error messages or error correction routines to be included within the program. Usually, such error traps make use of the RESUME statement in conjunction with the ON ERROR GO TO statement (see below).

RESUME

The *RESUME statement* is used to indicate where execution should resume after an error has been detected and an error-correction routine has been carried out.

EXAMPLE 9.18

The error-trapping portion of a BASIC program is shown below.

```
10 ON ERROR GO TO 800
   :
50 PRINT "ACCOUNT NUMBER: ";
60 INPUT ACCTNO
   :
800 PRINT "INPUT ERROR—TRY AGAIN"
810 RESUME 50
```

Now suppose that incorrect input data is entered during execution of the program (by entering a string instead of a number in line 60, for example). This will cause a branch to line 800, resulting in the generation of an error message. Control will then return to line 50 for another attempt to read the data correctly.

We will say more about the use of the ON ERROR GO TO statement and the RESUME statement in Chapter 11. (See Section 11.3.)

WHILE and WEND

Many versions of microcomputer BASIC include a *conditional looping* feature in which a sequence of statements will be executed repeatedly as long as some particular condition remains true. The *WHILE* and *WEND statements* are used to define the beginning and end, respectively, of the conditional loop. The condition that must be satisfied (i.e., remain true) is included in the WHILE statement. Within the loop, there must be a provision for eventually changing the value of the condition; otherwise, the loop will continue indefinitely.

EXAMPLE 9.19

Shown below is a conditional loop that will add the elements of a numeric array, X, until a zero value is encountered.

```
10 DIM X(100)
   :
100 LET SUM = 0 : I = 1
110 WHILE X(I)>0
120       SUM = SUM + X(I) : I = I + 1
130 WEND
```

In this example the conditional loop begins with line number 110 and ends with line number 130. Note the use of multiple statements in lines 100 and 120. Also, notice that the keyword LET has been omitted from line 120.

It should be noted that this example will generate an error if all of the array elements are positive, since the loop will continue to execute until the array subscript (I) exceeds the upper bound (100) specified in the DIM statement.

INPUT

In many versions of microcomputer BASIC, the INPUT statement can be used to print a *prompt message* (i.e., a string) prior to entering input data. To do so, the message must follow the keyword INPUT and it must be enclosed in quotation marks. Usually a semicolon will be required after the message in order to separate the string from the list of input variables.

EXAMPLE 9.20

Consider the statement

```
10 INPUT "WHAT IS YOUR NAME"; N$
```

Execution of this statement will cause the message

```
WHAT IS YOUR NAME?
```

to appear on the terminal. The response (i.e., the string assigned to N$) is then typed on the same line, immediately after the question mark. Thus, if the user chooses to reply by typing SANTA CLAUS, the entire line appears as

```
WHAT IS YOUR NAME? SANTA CLAUS
```

(Note that the user's response has been underlined.)

In some versions of microcomputer BASIC, it is possible to suppress the question mark after the prompt message. This can usually be accomplished by placing a comma rather than a semicolon at the end of the prompt message.

EXAMPLE 9.21

Here is a variation of the INPUT statement presented in Example 9.20. In this example, the question mark following the prompt statement will be suppressed.

```
10 INPUT "PLEASE ENTER YOUR NAME: ",N$
```

Execution of this statement will cause the message

```
PLEASE ENTER YOUR NAME:
```

to appear on the terminal. If the user again responds by entering the name SANTA CLAUS, the entire line will appear as

```
PLEASE ENTER YOUR NAME: SANTA CLAUS
```

(The user's response is again underlined.)

Notice that the prompt message has been modified to appear as a statement rather than a question since there will be no question mark associated with this prompt.

INKEY$ and INPUT$

INKEY$ and *INPUT*$ are *functions* (not statements) that are used to enter single-character or multicharacter strings, respectively, from the keyboard. In order to use these functions properly, the newly entered string must be assigned to an appropriate string variable. Unlike the INPUT statement, the use of these functions does not generate a question mark requesting input data. The input string is simply entered from the keyboard without pressing the return key. The characters being entered will *not* be displayed on the terminal.

The INKEY$ and INPUT$ functions are sometimes used to create a pause in the execution of a program. Thus, program execution will temporarily be suspended when one of these functions is encountered until the required string has been entered. INKEY$ requires a single-character string, whereas INPUT$ requires a string whose length is specified as a part of the function reference.

Section 9.3 contain a more general discussion of functions in microcomputer BASIC.

EXAMPLE 9.22

A microcomputer BASIC program contains a number of PRINT statements that are intended to provide instructions for whoever uses the program. These instructions will fill an entire TV-monitor screen (and hence disappear as soon as the screen is cleared). In order to allow ample time for the user to read the instructions, the print statements are followed by a statement that makes use of the INKEY$ function. Hence, the instructions will remain on the screen until the user presses a key, thus causing a single-character string to be entered into the computer.

A portion of the program is shown below.

```
10 PRINT TAB (34); "INSTRUCTIONS"
 :
 :
190 PRINT TAB(26); "(PRESS ANY KEY TO CONTINUE)"
200 A$ = INKEY$ : IF A$="" THEN 200
```

Notice that the program will continue to loop through statement 200 until some key is pressed, thus causing the required single-character string to be entered and assigned to the string.

Here is another way to accomplish the same thing, using the INPUT$ function.

```
20 PRINT TAB (34); "INSTRUCTIONS"
   :
190 PRINT TAB(26); "(PRESS ANY KEY TO CONTINUE)"
200 A$=INPUT$(1)
```

In this case, the program will come to a standstill until a single-character string is entered from the keyboard. (The 1 that appears in parentheses following INPUT$ specifies that the input string will consist of one character.)

We will say more about these types of programming techniques in Chapters 10 and 11.

PRINT USING

The *PRINT USING statement* is included in most versions of microcomputer BASIC. It allows printed output to be *formatted*, thus specifying the appearance and location of each data item. Both string and numeric data can be formatted, though the feature is generally more useful for numeric data.

There are several different ways to format output data with the print using statement. All of them involve placing a *format string* immediately after the keyword PRINT USING and before the list of output items. A semicolon must appear between the format string and the first output item.

EXAMPLE 9.23

Here is the most common form of the PRINT USING statement.

```
100 PRINT USING "##.## ";A,B,C
```

In this example the format string is "##.## ", which specifies a numeric field containing a decimal point, with not more than two digits on each side. Fractions (decimals) extending beyond two digits will be rounded. The space at the end of the format string is required to produce a separation between the printed values of A, B and C.

Now suppose that the variables A, B and C have been assigned the values 17.667, −5.38 and 40, respectively. Then the following line of output will be generated by the above PRINT USING statement.

```
17.67     -5.38     40.00
```

EXAMPLE 9.24

Another form of the PRINT USING statement is shown below.

```
200 PRINT USING "##.###^^^^"; VALUE
```

Notice the four upward-pointing arrows at the end of the format string. They specify exponential notation. Thus, if VALUE represents the number 856.07, the above PRINT USING statement will generate the value

```
8.561E+02
```

Similarly, if VALUE has been assigned the number −856.07, then the PRINT USING statement will generate

```
-8.561E+02
```

EXAMPLE 9.25

This example illustrates how commas can be placed in an output number.

```
30 PRINT USING "########, . ##"; COST#
```

The comma preceding the decimal point in the format string will cause commas to be placed in the whole-number part of each output quantity. Thus, if the double-precision variable COST# has a value of 15673088.209, the above statement will generate the following output.

```
15,673,088.21
```

Note that the whole-number portion is broken up into groups of three digits, starting at the decimal point and moving to the left.

This feature is useful for financial reports and other types of business applications.

There are many other variations of the PRINT USING statement that are too detailed to be presented here. The reader is referred to a programmer's reference manual for more specific information.

LPRINT and LPRINT USING

Some versions of microcomputer BASIC include the *LPRINT statement*, which is used specifically to print output data onto a line printer or a hard-copy terminal (rather than a TV monitor). The statement is identical to the PRINT statement except for the use of the keyword LPRINT rather than PRINT.

Those versions of microcomputer BASIC that support the PRINT USING statement may also include an analogous *LPRINT USING statement.*

EXAMPLE 9.26

A BASIC program contains the following two print statements.

```
200 PRINT A,B,C
210 LPRINT A,B,C
```

The first statement will cause the values of A, B and C to be displayed on a TV monitor, whereas the second statement will cause these same values to be printed on a hard-copy terminal.

General Comments

The reader is reminded that the statements presented above are intended to be *representative* of the more commonly available versions of microcomputer BASIC. They may or may not be available in a particular version of the language. If they are available, the details may be somewhat different.

Most versions of microcomputer BASIC also include additional statements not discussed above. Appendix D contains a more extensive summary of the statements that are commonly available in most versions of Microsoft BASIC. The reader is again referred to the programmer's reference manual for his or her particular version of the language for more detailed information.

EXAMPLE 9.27 Search for a Maximum on a Microcomputer

Now let us return to a programming example that we considered previously in Example 6.6. Now, however, we will make use of a number of new features that are available in Microsoft BASIC as implemented on the IBM Personal Computer.

Figure 9.3 presents the microcomputer version of the program. The logic is essentially the same as that described in Example 6.6, though the variable names have been expanded, and some different program constructs are used. In particular, the variables that were formerly called X1, X2, X3 and X4 are now called LEFT, XL, XR and RIGHT, respectively. Also, Y2 and Y3 are now called YL and YR, D is now called DISTANCE, and I is now called COUNT%. These variable names have been changed so that they are more descriptive of the actual problem. The program is somewhat more general than that presented in Example 6.6 in that the maximum number of iterations is now an input variable (MAXCOUNT%) rather than a constant that is built into the program.

In addition, this program contains a number of the new statements that have just been described. Specifically, we see the use of DEFSNG (line 30), extended IF-THEN (line 160), nested IF-THEN-ELSE (line 230), a WHILE-WEND loop (lines 150 through 240), expanded use of the INPUT statement (lines 70 through 100) and the

```
10 REM     SEARCH FOR A MAXIMUM OF THE FUNCTION  Y = X * COS(X)
20 '
30 DEFSNG A-Z
40 DEF FNY(X) = X*COS(X)
50 '
60 PRINT "Search for a Maximum of the Function  y = x * cos(x)" : PRINT
70 INPUT "Left boundary : ",LEFT
80 INPUT "Right boundary: ",RIGHT
90 INPUT "Minimum distance between interior points : ",DISTANCE
100 INPUT "Maximum number of iterations : ",MAXCOUNT% : PRINT
110 COUNT% = 0
120 '
130 REM    BEGIN LOOP
140 '
150 WHILE (RIGHT - LEFT) > 3 * DISTANCE
160     IF COUNT% = MAXCOUNT% THEN PRINT "Too many iterations" : END
170     COUNT% = COUNT% + 1
180     XL = LEFT + .5 * (RIGHT - LEFT - DISTANCE)
190     XR = XL + DISTANCE
200     YL = FNY(XL)
210     YR = FNY(XR)
220     GOSUB 360
230     IF YL = YR THEN 280 ELSE IF YL < YR THEN LEFT = XL ELSE RIGHT = XR
240 WEND
250 '
260 REM   COMPUTE AND PRINT FINAL SOLUTION
270 '
280 X = .5 * (XL + XR)
290 PRINT : PRINT "Xmax = "; : PRINT USING "##.###### ";X;
300 PRINT SPC(12);"Ymax = "; : PRINT USING "##.###### ";FNY(X)
310 PRINT : PRINT "Number of iterations = ";COUNT%
320 END
330 '
340 REM   SUBROUTINE TO PRINT THE RESULTS OF EACH ITERATION
350 '
360 PRINT : PRINT ,YL,YR
370 PRINT LEFT,XL,XR,RIGHT
380 RETURN
390 END
```

Fig. 9.3

PRINT USING statement (lines 290 and 300). The use of these statements results in a program that is shorter and more concise than the program presented earlier in Fig. 6.5.

There are a few other features of this program that should be pointed out. Notice that several lines are blank except for an apostrophe. The apostrophe is another way of writing a remark in Microsoft BASIC (everything following an apostrophe is considered to be a remark). In the present example, these "empty" remarks are just a way of introducing blank lines to separate different sections of the program. (The interpreter will not accept numbered lines that are totally blank.)

In addition, notice that the END statement appears in three different places within the program (lines 160, 320 and 390). In the first two lines, the END statement is used in place of the STOP statement in order to suppress an unwanted message that is generated by STOP. In the last line, END is used in the more traditional manner. Curiously, END is not required at the (physical) end of a program in Microsoft BASIC. Hence, its appearance at the end of this program is unnecessary.

Figure 9.4 shows the output that is generated when this program is executed, using input parameters that are essentially the same as those used in Example 6.6 (though fewer iterations are allowed this time, since we already know how many will be required). Normally, this output will be seen on a TV monitor. Note that the input data have been underlined.

It is interesting to compare this output with that shown in Fig. 6.6.

```
Search for a Maximum of the Function  y = x * cos(x)

Left boundary : 0
Right boundary: 3.14159
Minimum distance between interior points : 0.0001
Maximum number of iterations : 20

             8.063497E-05                -7.647047E-05
 0           1.570745       1.570845     3.14159

             .5553565       .5553716
 0           .7853725       .7854725     1.570845

             .4508655       .4507949
.7853725     1.178059       1.178159     1.570845

             .5454382       .5454121
.7853725     .9817156       .9818156     1.178159

             .5605342       .5605293
.7853725     .8835441       .8836441     .9818156

             .5604048       .5604101
.7853725     .8344583       .8345583     .8836441

             .5610945       .5610948
.8344583     .8590012       .8591012     .8836441

             .5609718       .5609695
.8590012     .8712727       .8713727     .8836441

             .5610725       .5610713
.8590012     .865137        .865237      .8713727

             .5610933       .5610929
.8590012     .8620691       .8621691     .865237

             .5610963       .5610963
.8590012     .8605352       .8606352     .8621691

             .561096        .5610961
.8590012     .8597682       .8598682     .8606352

             .5610963       .5610964
.8597682     .8601517       .8602518     .8606352

             .5610963       .5610963
.8601517     .8603434       .8604435     .8606352

Xmax =  0.860393            Ymax =  0.561096

Number of iterations =  14
```

Fig. 9.4

9.3 ADDITIONAL LIBRARY FUNCTIONS

Most versions of microcomputer BASIC include a number of special library functions in addition to those customarily found in the more traditional versions of the language. We have already discussed two of these new functions—INKEY$ and INPUT$—in Section 9.2. Several of the more commonly used microcomputer functions are summarized below. Notice that most of these functions provide string-related capabilities.

Function	*Purpose*	*Example*
CDBL(*e*)	Converts the value of the numeric expression *e* to double-precision.	Y# = CDBL(3*X!−2*Y!)
CINT(*e*)	Converts (rounds) the value of the numeric expression *e* to integer.	Y% = CINT(3*X!−2*Y!)
CSNG(*e*)	Converts the value of the numeric expression *e* to single-precision.	Y! = CSNG(2*A#/B#)
FRE(*n*)	Returns the number of unused bytes of memory (*n* is a dummy variable).	PRINT FRE(0)
INKEY$	Returns a character from the keyboard (the character will not be displayed).	Y$ = INKEY$
INPUT$(*n*)	Returns an *n*-character string from the keyboard (the string will not be displayed).	Y$ = INPUT$(3) (Will return a three-character string)
INSTR(*s1,s2*)	Returns the position where one string (*s2*) is found within another string (*s1*).	Y = INSTR(A$,B$) (IF A$ = "BASIC" and B$ = "AS", Y = 2)
LEFT$(*s,n*)	Returns the leftmost *n* characters of the string *s*.	Y$ = LEFT$(A$,4) (If A$ = "COMPUTER", Y$ = "COMP")
LEN(*s*)	Returns the number of characters in the string *s*.	Y = LEN(A$) (If A$ = "COMPUTER", Y = 8)
MID$(*s,m,n*)	Returns a portion of string *s*, *n* characters long, beginning with character number *m*.	Y$ = MID(A$,3,5) (IF A$ = "COMPUTER", Y$ = "MPUTE")
RIGHT$(*s,n*)	Returns the rightmost *n* characters of the string *s*.	Y$ = RIGHT$(A$,4) (If A$ = "COMPUTER", Y$ = "UTER")
SPACE$(*n*)	Returns a sequence of *n* blank spaces.	PRINT X;SPACE$(5);Y (The values of X and Y will be separated by five blank spaces)
STR$(*e*)	Returns a string representation of the numeric expression *e*.	Y$ = STR$(K + 1) (Y$ = "6" if K=5)
STRING$(*m,n*)	Returns an *m*-character string of characters whose ASCII code is *n* (*n* cannot exceed 255).	Y$ = STRING$(8,42) (Y$ = "********", because CHR$(42) = "*")
VAL	Returns a numeric representation of the string *s* (assuming that *s* consists of digits, preceded by an optional sign).	Y = VAL(N$) (Y = 900 if N$ = "900")

Some additional microcomputer library functions will be discussed in later sections of this book in conjunction with other topics. Appendix D contains a summary of all commonly used library functions in Microsoft BASIC.

EXAMPLE 9.28 Generating Piglatin on a Microcomputer

In Example 6.15 we developed a BASIC program to generate piglatin from a line of English text. Let us now repeat this example using several of the functions that are unique to Microsoft BASIC.

The Program Outline

In order to best utilize these new functions, we will use a somewhat different strategy than that employed in Example 6.15. Before describing the computational scheme, however, let us introduce the following variables.

ENGLISH$ = A string representing the given line of English text

TAG$ = The first three letters in the original line of English text

POINTER(I) = An array element that represents the location of the space after the Ith word in the given line of English text

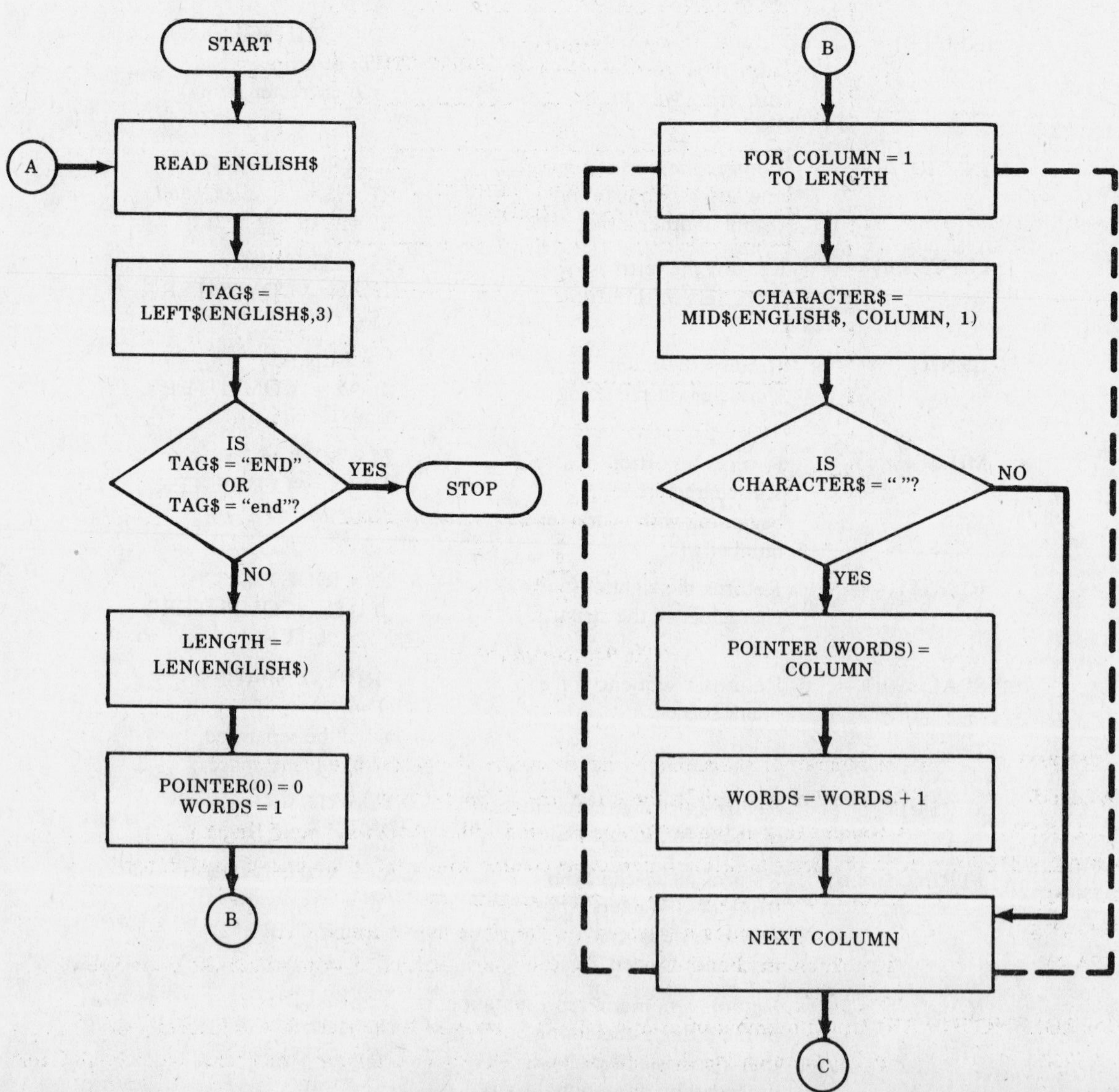

Fig. 9.5 *(continues on next page)*

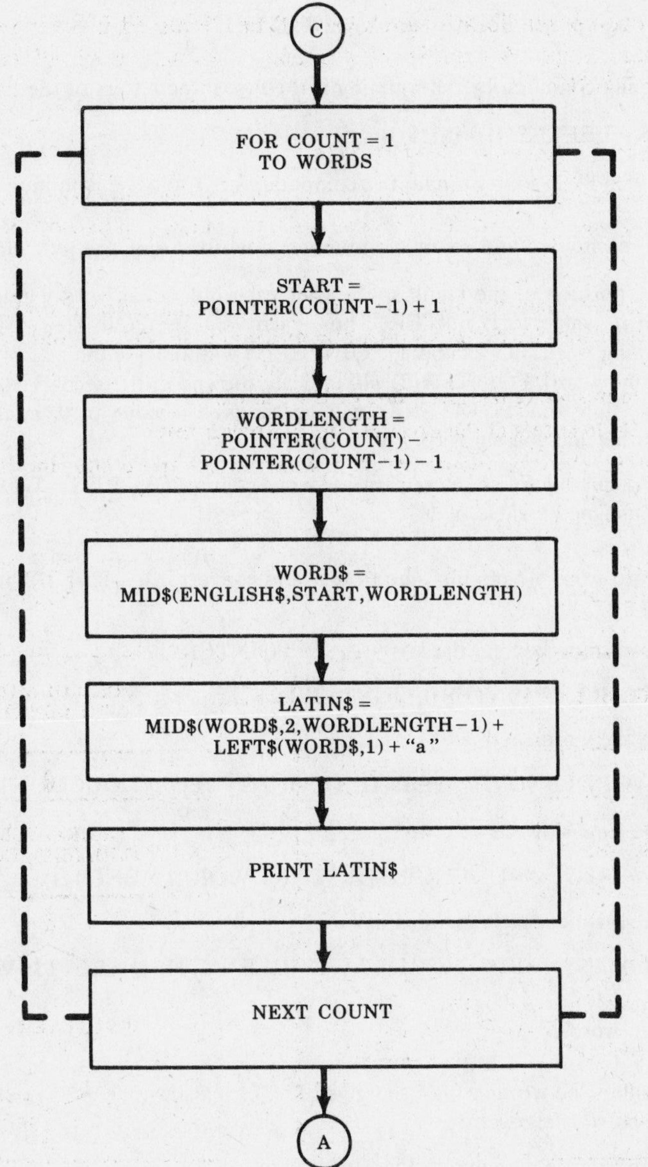

Fig. 9.5 (*continued*)

LENGTH	= The number of characters in the given line of English text
WORDS	= The number of words in the given line of English text
COLUMN	= A counter that indicates column position within the given line of English text
CHARACTER$	= The character that is in a particular column within the given line of English text
COUNT	= A word counter for the given line of English text
WORD$	= A string representing a word within the given line of English text
START	= The column number indicating the start (first letter) of a word within the given line of English text
WORDLENGTH	= The length (number of characters) of a word within the given line of English text
LATIN$	= A string representing the piglatin equivalent of a word within the given line of English text

The computation can now be described as follows.

1. Read a line of English text and assign it to ENGLISH$.

2. Test for a stopping condition by determining if the first three letters of the English text, i.e.,

   TAG$ = LEFT$(ENGLISH$,3)

   are "END" or "end". If so, terminate the computation. Otherwise, continue below.

3. Find the end of each word and count the number of words, using the following procedure.

   (*a*) Locate the position of the blank space after each individual word within the line of English text and assign its value to POINTER. Thus, each value of POINTER will identify the end of the corresponding word. For example, POINTER(1) will indicate the end of the first word (beginning of the second word), POINTER(2) will indicate the end of the second word (beginning of the third word), etc. Note that POINTER(0) will be assigned a value of 0, indicating that the first word begins just beyond column zero.

   (*b*) Each time a space is found, increment the word counter (WORDS = WORDS + 1, where WORDS is initially assigned a value of 1).

4. Extract each word from the original line of text and convert it to piglatin. This can be accomplished as follows.

   (*a*) Begin one position beyond the last value of POINTER, i.e.,

   START = POINTER(COUNT−1) + 1)

   (*b*) Determine the wordlength as

   WORDLENGTH = POINTER(COUNT) − POINTER(COUNT − 1) − 1

   (*c*) Extract the English word as

   WORD$ = MID$(ENGLISH$,START,WORLDLENGTH)

   (*d*) Form the equivalent piglatin word as

   LATIN$ = MID$(WORD$,2,WORDLENGTH−1) + LEFT$(WORD$,1) + "a "

5. Print the piglatin word.

6. Continue until all of the words within the given line of text have been converted and printed. Then go back to step 1 and start all over.

A flowchart of the procedure is shown in Fig. 9.5.

The BASIC Program

Figure 9.6 contains the actual BASIC program. Notice the use of several new library functions; namely, LEFT$ (lines 100 and 290), LEN (line 120) and MID$ (lines 180, 280 and 290). Also, notice the use of the concatenation operation in line 290. And finally, note that the program comments are all written with apostrophes rather than the REM statement (lines 10, 60, 140 and 230).

This program is about the same length as the piglatin generator written in traditional BASIC, shown in Fig. 6.9 (as a part of Example 6.15). Thus, the use of the new microcomputer features has not shortened the program significantly. The logic behind the current program is, however, more straightforward. The reader should carefully compare the two programs on this basis.

Figure 9.7 shows the output that is generated when the program is executed. Note that the English text that is entered as input is the same as in Example 6.15, except for the use of both uppercase and lowercase letters. (The input data are again underlined.) The reader should compare Figs. 9.7 and 6.10 to see the correspondence.

```
10 '*** MICROCOMPUTER PIGLATIN GENERATOR ***
20 '
30 DIM POINTER(80)
40 PRINT "Welcome to Microcomputer Piglatin" : PRINT
50 '
60 '*** READ A LINE OF ENGLISH TEXT
70 '
80 PRINT "Enter a line of text below: "
90 INPUT "",ENGLISH$
100 TAG$ = LEFT$(ENGLISH$,3)
110 IF TAG$ = "END" OR TAG$ = "end" THEN END
120 LENGTH = LEN(ENGLISH$)
130 '
140 '*** FIND THE END OF EACH WORD AND COUNT THE NUMBER OF WORDS
150 '
160 POINTER(0) = 0 : WORDS = 1
170 FOR COLUMN = 1 TO LENGTH
180    CHARACTER$ = MID$(ENGLISH$,COLUMN,1)
190    IF CHARACTER$ = " " THEN POINTER(WORDS) = COLUMN : WORDS = WORDS + 1
200 NEXT COLUMN
210 POINTER(WORDS) = LENGTH + 1
220 '
230 '*** CONVERT EACH WORD TO PIGLATIN AND PRINT
240 '
250 FOR COUNT = 1 TO WORDS
260    START = POINTER(COUNT-1) + 1
270    WORDLENGTH = POINTER(COUNT) - POINTER(COUNT-1) - 1
280    WORD$ = MID$(ENGLISH$,START,WORDLENGTH)
290    LATIN$ = MID$(WORD$,2,WORDLENGTH-1) + LEFT$(WORD$,1) + "a "
300    PRINT LATIN$;
310 NEXT COUNT
320 PRINT : PRINT
330 GOTO 80
340 END
```

Fig. 9.6

```
Welcome to Microcomputer Piglatin

Enter a line of text below:
this is a piglatin generator
hista sia aa iglatinpa eneratorga

Enter a line of text below:
WHAT SORT OF GARBLED MESSAGE IS THIS ANYHOW
HATWa ORTSa FOa ARBLEDGa ESSAGEMa SIa HISTa NYHOWAa

Enter a line of text below:
Now is the time for all good men to come to the aid of their country
owNa sia heta imeta orfa llaa oodga enma ota omeca ota heta idaa foa heirta

ountryca

Enter a line of text below:
end
```

Fig. 9.7

9.4 MICROCOMPUTER DATA FILES

One of the most important types of microcomputer applications involves the use of data files under control of a BASIC program. Most versions of microcomputer BASIC support both sequential and random data files, though there is considerable variation in the way these files are accessed from one version of BASIC to another. Moreover, the file management procedures used with microcomputers are generally not the same as the large-computer file management procedures presented in Chapter 8. (Note that the use of microcomputer data files requires some type of auxiliary mass storage device, such as a floppy disk, hard disk or solid-state memory module.)

In this section we present several simple examples illustrating the use of data files using the version of Microsoft BASIC included with the IBM Personal Computer. The reader should understand, however, that these examples are merely *representative* of microcomputer data file applications. The reader should consult the programmer's reference manual for his or her particular microcomputer to determine the appropriate file management procedures.

Sequential Data Files

With most microcomputers, a sequential data file consists of multiple sets of data items, arranged sequentially, without regard to line numbers. (This differs from the sequential data files described in Chapter 8, where line numbers were an integral part of the data.) Such files are created, read and modified under direct program control. The manner in which this is accomplished is illustrated in the following examples.

EXAMPLE 9.29 Creating a Sequential Data File

Figure 9.8 shows an IBM Personal Computer BASIC program that creates a sequential data file containing the student names and examination scores shown in Fig. 8.1. (Note that the sequential data file is now being created by a BASIC program rather than typed directly into the computer, as described in Chapter 8.)

Line 30 of this program causes a sequential data file called SCORES to be opened in the output ("O") mode and assigned to data channel number 1. Lines 40 and 50 allow two strings (TITLE$ and TERM$) to be entered from the keyboard. These strings are then written onto the data file in lines 60 and 70. Similar data transfers occur in lines 80, 100, 110 and 120. This procedure continues repeatedly until the word "END" (or "end") is entered in place of a student name. The data file is then closed and the computation terminates.

When running the program, the course title and the term (e.g., Comp Sci 141, Fall 1985) are entered on separate lines, followed by carriage returns. The same is true of the student names. Each student name is entered on one line, followed by five exam scores on another line. All five exam scores are entered on the same line, separated by commas and ending with a carriage return.

Figure 9.9 shows the contents of the data file that is produced when this program is run, using the student names and exam scores given in Fig. 8.1. This data file will be called SCORES. Compare Fig. 9.9 with the corresponding data file shown at the bottom of Fig. 8.1.

```
10 REM ****** CREATE A SEQUENTIAL DATA FILE ******
20 REM         (STUDENT EXAMINATION SCORES)
30 OPEN "O",1,"SCORES"
40 INPUT "Course title";TITLE$
50 INPUT "Term";TERM$
60 PRINT #1,TITLE$
70 PRINT #1,TERM$
80 PRINT: INPUT "Name";N$
90 IF N$="END" OR N$="end" THEN 140
100 INPUT "Exam scores";C1,C2,C3,C4,C5
110 PRINT #1,N$
120 PRINT #1,C1;C2;C3;C4;C5
130 GOTO 80
140 CLOSE
150 END
```

Fig. 9.8

```
Comp Sci 141
Fall 1985
Adams B F
 45  80   80   95   55
Brown P
 60  50   70   75   55
Davis R A
 40  30   10   45   60
Fisher E K
 0  5  5   0   10
Hamilton S P
 90  85   100   95   90
Jones J J
 95  90   80   95   85
Ludwig C W
 35  50   55   65   45
Osborne T
 75  60   75   60   70
Prince W F
 85  75   60   85   90
Richards E N
 50  60   50   35   65
Smith M C
 70  60   75   70   55
Thomas B A
 10  25   35   20   30
Wolfe H
 25  40   65   75   85
Zorba D R
 65  80   70   100   60
```

Fig. 9.9

It should be understood that this information will be written to an auxiliary storage device (e.g., a floppy disk) rather than the printer. Once the sequential data file has been created, however, its contents can be listed on a printer. This is how Fig. 9.9 was generated.

The general procedure for updating a sequential data file is to copy the contents of the old data file onto a new data file, incorporating any additions or changes in the data during the copy procedure. After the updating has been completed, the old file is deleted ("KILLed"), and the new (updated) file is given the name of the old file.

EXAMPLE 9.30 Processing Student Examination Scores on a Microcomputer

In Figure 9.10, we see an IBM Personal Computer BASIC program that allows us to update the sequential data file created in Example 9.29. (This program parallels the traditional BASIC program shown in Fig. 8.5, which has the same purpose.)

In this program, line 40 causes the old data file, called SCORES, to be opened in the input ("I") mode and assigned to data channel number 1. Similarly, line 50 causes a new file, called UPDATE, to be opened in the output ("O") mode and assigned to data channel number 2. The course title (TITLE$) and the term (TERM$) are then read from SCORES (lines 60 and 70), displayed on the TV monitor (line 80) and written onto UPDATE (line 90). Lines 100 and 110 allow the user to specify the exam number and whether or not to compute an average score for each student. We then encounter a loop, ranging from lines 120 to 240, in which the following steps are carried out for each student.

1. The student's name and previous exam scores are read from SCORES (lines 120 and 130).
2. The student's name is then displayed on the TV monitor (line 140) and a new score is entered from the keyboard (line 150).
3. The student's name and exam scores are then written onto UPDATE and an (optional) average score is computed (lines 160 through 200).
4. The calculated average is displayed on the TV monitor (line 210) and written onto UPDATE (line 220).

```
10 REM ****** PROGRAM TO PROCESS STUDENT EXAMINATION SCORES ******
20 REM ******          USING SEQUENTIAL DATA FILES           ******
30 DIM C(15)
40 OPEN "I",1,"SCORES"
50 OPEN "O",2,"UPDATE"
60 INPUT #1,TITLE$
70 INPUT #1,TERM$
80 PRINT "Course title: ";TITLE$,"Term: ";TERM$
90 PRINT #2,TITLE$: PRINT #2,TERM$
100 PRINT: INPUT "Exam number";K
110 PRINT: INPUT "Calculate averages (Y/N) ";ANS$
120 PRINT: INPUT #1,N$
130 FOR I=1 TO K-1: INPUT #1,C(I): NEXT I
140 PRINT N$,
150 INPUT "New score";C(K)
160 PRINT #2,N$
170 SUM=0
180 FOR I=1 TO K: PRINT #2,C(I);: SUM=SUM+C(I): NEXT I
190 IF ANS$="N" OR ANS$="n" THEN 230
200 AVG=SUM/K
210 PRINT "Average=";AVG
220 PRINT #2,AVG
230 IF NOT EOF(1) THEN 120
240 CLOSE
250 KILL "SCORES"
260 NAME "UPDATE" AS "SCORES"
270 END
```

Fig. 9.10

```
Course title: Comp Sci 141  Term: Fall 1985

Exam number? 6

Calculate averages (Y/N) ? y

Adams B F       New score? 75
Average= 71.66666

Brown P         New score? 80
Average= 65

Davis R A       New score? 55
Average= 40

Fisher E K      New score? 5
Average= 4.166667

Hamilton S P    New score? 90
Average= 91.66666

Jones J J       New score? 80
Average= 87.5

Ludwig C W      New score? 70
Average= 53.33333

Osborne T       New score? 80
Average= 70

Prince W F      New score? 100
Average= 82.5

Richards E N    New score? 70
Average= 55

Smith M C       New score? 75
Average= 67.5

Thomas B A      New score? 10
Average= 21.66667

Wolfe H         New score? 95
Average= 64.16666

Zorba D R       New score? 95
Average= 78.33334
```

Fig. 9.11

5. This process is continued as long as an end-of-file is not detected in SCORES (line 230). Once an end-of-file is detected, both files are closed (line 240), and the original file is deleted (KILLed, in line 250). The new file is then renamed SCORES (line 260).

Figure 9.11 shows a typical interactive session resulting from the execution of the program. In this situation, a sixth exam score is being entered for each student and a term average (for all six exam scores) is then determined. The user's responses are underlined. The exam scores are the same as those entered in Example 8.4 (see Fig. 8.8). The reader should compare the results shown in Fig. 9.11 with those obtained in Fig. 8.8.

Figure 9.12 shows the contents of the new data file containing all six exam scores and a term average for each student. Notice the similarity with the corresponding data file shown in the lower portion of Fig. 8.8. When the execution of the program is complete, this data file will automatically be renamed as SCORES, replacing the earlier data file SCORES shown in Fig. 9.9.

```
Comp Sci 141
Fall 1985
Adams B F
 45  80  80  95  55  75  71.66666
Brown P
 60  50  70  75  55  80  65
Davis R A
 40  30  10  45  60  55  40
Fisher E K
 0  5  5  0  10  5  4.166667
Hamilton S P
 90  85  100  95  90  90  91.66666
Jones J J
 95  90  80  95  85  80  87.5
Ludwig C W
 35  50  55  65  45  70  53.33333
Osborne T
 75  60  75  60  70  80  70
Prince W F
 85  75  60  85  90  100  82.5
Richards E N
 50  60  50  35  65  70  55
Smith M C
 70  60  75  70  55  75  67.5
Thomas B A
 10  25  35  20  30  10  21.66667
Wolfe H
 25  40  65  75  85  95  64.16666
Zorba D R
 65  80  70  100  60  95  78.33334
```

Fig. 9.12

Random Data Files

From a programming standpoint, random data files are somewhat more complicated than sequential data files. On the other hand, individual file components can be accessed much more rapidly in a random access file, as described in Chapter 8.

The procedures for creating, reading and updating random data files are generally different on a microcomputer than on a large computer. On the IBM Personal Computer, for example, a random data file is defined as a collection of fixed-length *records.* Individual data items are stored as *strings* within each record. Those data items that represent numerical values must be converted to actual numbers when transferred into the computer's memory. Similarly, such data items must be converted back into strings prior to being transferred to the data file. A *buffer* area, containing one record, is created within the computer's memory. The buffer is subdivided into *fields,* where each field holds one data item.

EXAMPLE 9.31 Microcomputer Inventory Control

Figure 9.13 contains a simple inventory control program that is written for an IBM Personal Computer. The overall approach to the problem is essentially the same as that outlined in Example 8.10, and the program closely parallels the large-computer version presented in Fig. 8.12. The variables have been renamed, however, to be more descriptive of the actual problem. In particular, the record number is now referred to as RECNO%, the string that represents the inventory level (i.e., number of units) is now called UNITS$, and its integer counterpart is now called UNITS%. Also, the change in the inventory level is now called CHANGE%.

```
10 REM *** Microcomputer Inventory Control Program ***
20
30 OPEN "R",#1,"INVTRY",5
40 FIELD #1,5 AS UNITS$
50 PRINT "Stock numbers run from 1 to 2000"
60 PRINT: PRINT "To end session, enter a negative stock number"
70 PRINT: INPUT "Stock number";RECNO%
80 IF RECNO% < 1 THEN 260
90 IF RECNO% > 2000 THEN PRINT: GOTO 50
100
110 REM *** UPDATE A RECORD
120
130 GET 1,RECNO%
140 UNITS%=CVI(UNITS$)
150 PRINT "Original inventory=";UNITS%;" items"
160 INPUT "Change in inventory level";CHANGE%
170 UNITS%=UNITS%+CHANGE%
180 IF UNITS% < 0 THEN UNITS% = 0
190 PRINT "New inventory=";UNITS%;" items"
200 LSET UNITS$=MKI$(UNITS%)
210 PUT 1,RECNO%
220 GOTO 70
230
240 REM *** END RECORD UPDATE
250
260 CLOSE
270 END
```

Fig. 9.13

The program utilizes a random access file called INVTRY. Line 30 causes this file to be opened in the random ("R") mode and assigned to memory buffer number 1, with a record size of 5 bytes (characters). Line 40 specifies that the string variable UNITS$ will occupy the first five characters of the memory buffer, i.e., a five-character field is reserved for UNITS$. Note that UNITS$ represents the inventory level (i.e., the number of units) in string form for record number RECNO%.

An initial message is generated on the TV display in lines 50 and 60. Line 70 allows the stock number (RECNO%, which also represents the record number) to be entered from the keyboard. A negative value closes the data file and terminates the program (lines 80, 260 and 270). Line 90 tests to see if the value of RECNO% is too large. If so, control is transferred back to line 50 (i.e., another value for RECNO% is requested). If, however, the value of RECNO% falls in the proper range, then the record number is read from the data file into the memory buffer (line 130). The string representation of the inventory level is then converted into an integer quantity (line 140), which is then shown on the TV display (line 150).

Line 160 allows a change in the inventory level to be entered, and lines 170 and 180 cause the inventory level to be updated accordingly. The new inventory level is displayed in line 190. Finally, the new inventory level is converted back to a string in line 200 and written onto the data file in line 210. The program then returns to line 70 where a new stock number (record number) is requested.

Notice that this program makes use of certain statements and library functions that are unique to random data file applications. In particular, the GET statement (line 130) and the PUT statement (line 210) are used to read data from and write data to the data file. Also, the library functions CVI (line 140) and MKI$ (line 200) are used to convert a string into an integer quantity and vice versa.

```
Stock numbers run from 1 to 2000

To end session, enter a negative stock number

Stock number? 1186
Original inventory= 346  items
Change in inventory level? -45
New inventory= 301  items

Stock number? 708
Original inventory= 368  items
Change in inventory level? 200
New inventory= 568  items

Stock number? 84
Original inventory= 147  items
Change in inventory level? 16
New inventory= 163  items

Stock number? 1400
Original inventory= 78  items
Change in inventory level? -50
New inventory= 28  items

Stock number? -999
```

Fig. 9.14

Figure 9.14 shows a typical interactive session, utilizing the same numerical values as in Example 8.10. Once again, the user's responses have been underlined. Notice the similarity in the appearance of this figure and the lower portion of Fig. 8.12.

The reader is again reminded that the programs presented in this section are specifically written in Microsoft BASIC as implemented on the IBM Personal Computer (see Appendix D for a summary of this version of Microsoft BASIC). Many microcomputers utilize these same instructions. Other microcomputers may use file management procedures that are somewhat different.

9.5 MACHINE-LANGUAGE PROCEDURES IN BASIC

Many versions of microcomputer BASIC include capabilities for carrying out certain procedures that are customarily associated with machine language. These include

1. Selecting a portion of the computer's memory
2. Examining the contents of the computer's memory
3. Altering the contents of the computer's memory
4. Accessing machine-language subroutines

A detailed discussion of the use of these features is beyond the scope of this text. Basically, however, they are used in such applications as advanced graphics, sound and music generation and the control of external devices.

The most common of these features are summarized below.

Statement or Function	*Purpose*	*Example*
DEF SEG=M	Selects a segment of memory beginning with (decimal) memory location M	10 DEF SEG=32768 (Select a segment of memory beginning with location 32768.)
PEEK(M)	Returns the contents of (decimal) memory location M	10 LET Z=PEEK(768) (The contents of location 768 are assigned to Z.)
POKE M,X	Places the value X in (decimal) memory location M	20 POKE 200,333 (Place the value 333 in memory location 200.)
CALL V	Accesses the machine-language subroutine that begins in the (decimal) memory location indicated by the variable V	20 START=1024 30 CALL START (Access the subroutine beginning in memory location 1024.)
USR(X)	Transfers the value X to a machine-language subroutine	40 PRINT USR(12) (Print a value generated by a machine-language subroutine, which accepts 12 as an input parameter.)

Note: Some versions of BASIC allow the beginning of the machine-language subroutine to be specified by a DEF statement, e.g., 50 DEF USR=1280.

The reader is reminded that *DEF SEG*, *CALL* and *POKE* are *statements*, whereas *PEEK* and *USR* are *library functions*.

EXAMPLE 9.32

Consider the BASIC statments shown below.

```
200 IF PEEK(768)>127 THEN POKE 768,127
210 CALL START
```

The first statement (line 200) causes the contents of (decimal) memory location 768 to be examined and replaced with the value 127 if the original value exceeds 127. The second statement (line 210) then accesses the machine-language subroutine that begins at the (decimal) location specified by the variable START. (We are assuming that the value stored in location 768 cannot exceed 127 if the machine-language subroutine is to be executed successfully.)

9.6 FEATURES EXCLUDED FROM MICROCOMPUTER BASIC

The reader is again reminded of the variation in the different versions of microcomputer BASIC that are currently available. Although most versions are highly sophisticated, there are a few traditional features of BASIC that are not usually found in microcomputer BASIC. These include

1. The MAT (matrix) statements (see Chapter 7).
2. Multiline functions (see Section 6.3).
3. Certain system commands (e.g., BYE, OLD, REPLACE, SCRATCH).

4. The inclusion of blank lines. (Note, however, that some versions of the language allow a line to contain a statement number followed by a delimiter, e.g., 100: or a statement number followed by an empty comment, e.g., 100 '.)

The reader is reminded, however, that BASIC is rapidly growing in popularity and becoming more sophisticated as microcomputers continue to proliferate in homes, schools and offices. New and improved features can therefore be expected in future versions of the language.

Review Questions

9.1 What advantage is there in the use of long variable names?

9.2 Can BASIC keywords (e.g., PRINT, DATA, NEXT) be used as variable names?

9.3 Name the different types of data that are available in microcomputer BASIC. How are the corresponding variable types distinguished from one another?

9.4 What type of result is obtained from an arithmetic operation involving

(*a*) Integer and real data?
(*b*) Integer and double-precision data?
(*c*) Real and double-precision data?

9.5 What happens when numerical data of one type is assigned to a numerical variable of a different type?

9.6 What happens when a real or a double-precision quantity is assigned to an integer variable?

9.7 How does integer division differ from ordinary division?

9.8 What is the purpose of the MOD operator?

9.9 What is the purpose of the AND, OR and NOT operators? In what type of statement are they used?

9.10 Summarize the hierarchy of arithmetic, logical and relational operators. Do all versions of microcomputer BASIC employ this particular hierarchy?

9.11 What is meant by concatenation? To what type of data does concatenation apply? What operator is usually used to indicate concatenation?

9.12 What advantages are there in writing two or more statements on the same line? How are such statements distinguished from one another?

9.13 What is the purpose of the DEFINT, DEFSNG, DEFDBL and DEFSTR statements? How does the use of these statements compare with the use of suffixes on variable names?

9.14 Describe the expanded use of the IF-THEN statement in microcomputer BASIC.

9.15 Describe the IF-THEN-ELSE statement and compare its use with that of the expanded IF-THEN statement. How significant is the addition of the ELSE clause?

9.16 What is meant by structured programming?

9.17 What is the purpose of the ON-GOSUB statement? How does it differ from ON-GO TO?

9.18 What is the purpose of the ON ERROR GO TO?

9.19 Describe the WHILE and WEND statements. What new type of program structure can be defined by these two statements?

9.20 Describe the expanded use of the INPUT statement in microcomputer BASIC.

9.21 Describe the use of the INKEY$ and INPUT$ functions to create pauses in program execution. Do all versions of microcomputer BASIC support these functions?

9.22 Summarize the more common features that are provided by the PRINT USING statement. How are these features implemented? How significant are these features?

9.23 What is the purpose of the LPRINT and the LPRINT USING statements?

9.24 Describe the purpose of each of the following library functions: CDBL, CINT, CSNG, FRE, INKEY$, INPUT$, INSTR, LEFT$, LEN, MID$, RIGHT$, SPACE$, STR$, STRING$ and VAL. How many arguments are required by each function? What types of arguments are required?

9.25 What is the difference between sequential and random data files as implemented in Microsoft BASIC? What are the advantages and disadvantages of each?

9.26 How does the use of sequential data files on a microcomputer differ from the use of sequential data files on a large computer (as described in Chapter 8)?

9.27 How does the use of random data files on a microcomputer differ from the use of random data files on a large computer (as described in Chapter 8)?

9.28 Describe the purpose of each of the following statements or functions: DEF SEG, PEEK, POKE, CALL, USR. Which are statements and which are functions? For what types of applications are these statements and functions used?

9.29 Name those features of traditional BASIC (as implemented on large computers) that are not available in most versions of microcomputer BASIC.

Supplementary Problems

The following "problems" are concerned with information gathering rather than actual problem solving. Answer the questions as they apply to your particular version of microcomputer BASIC.

9.30 Does your version of BASIC support long variable names? If so, what is the maximum permissible length of each variable name? How many characters are significant?

9.31 What types of numeric data are supported? What distinction is there between different types of numeric variables? Can all variables with a common first letter be defined to be of a particular data type?

9.32 Can arithmetic operations be carried out between different types of numeric data? If so, what type of result will be obtained with each combination of data types?

9.33 Can numeric data of one type be assigned to a numeric variable of another type? What type of result will be obtained?

9.34 What additional operators are available? What is the purpose of each?

9.35 What is the complete hierarchy of arithmetic, relational and logical operators?

9.36 Does your version of BASIC support concatenation? If so, what operator is used for this purpose?

9.37 Can multiple statements be placed on one line? If so, how are such statements separated from one another?

9.38 How is the IF-THEN statement implemented in your version of BASIC? Can multiple statements follow THEN on the same line? Is the ELSE clause available?

9.39 Is the ON-GOSUB statement available in your version of BASIC?

9.40 Is the ON ERROR GO TO statement available in your version of BASIC? Is the RESUME statement available?

9.41 Does your version of BASIC support a conditional looping feature? How is the conditional loop defined?

9.42 Can a prompt message be generated by an INPUT statement in your version of BASIC? Can the question mark at the end of the prompt be suppressed?

9.43 Are the INKEY$ and INPUT$ functions available in your version of BASIC?

9.44 Does your version of BASIC support the PRINT USING statement? If so, summarize the different types of output formats that are available.

9.45 Are the LPRINT and LPRINT USING statements available in your version of BASIC?

9.46 What additional library functions are available in your version of BASIC? What special capabilities are provided by these library functions?

9.47 How are sequential data files utilized in your version of BASIC? How is a sequential data file created? How is it deleted? How are sequential data files opened and closed? How are data items written onto and read from such files?

9.48 What is the general procedure for updating a sequential data file? What special BASIC instructions are available for carrying out the various sequential data file procedures?

9.49 How are random data files utilized in your version of BASIC? How are such files created and deleted? What is the procedure for defining each record?

9.50 How are random data files opened and closed? How are data items written onto and read from such files? Must numerical data be stored as strings? If so, how is the conversion accomplished? How are the strings converted back to numerical quantities?

9.51 Is a memory buffer required when using random data files? If so, is the buffer subdivided into fields? How is this accomplished?

9.52 Does your version of BASIC include the following machine-language procedures:

(*a*) Selecting a portion of the computer's memory
(*b*) Examining the contents of the computer's memory
(*c*) Altering the contents of the computer's memory
(*d*) Accessing a machine-language subroutine

If so, how is each of these procedures carried out?

9.53 Are there certain traditional features of BASIC that are excluded from your version of the language? (See Appendixes A, B and C for a summary of the traditional features of BASIC.)

9.54 What additional enhanced features are available in your particular version of BASIC?

Programming Problems

9.55 Rewrite the piglatin generator given in Example 9.28 so that it includes the following additional features.

(*a*) Accepts multiple lines of English text
(*b*) Processes punctuation marks
(*c*) Distinguishes between uppercase and lowercase letters and makes appropriate corrections (e.g., converts Washington to Ashingtonwa)
(*d*) Accommodates double-letter sounds (e.g., converts Philadelphia to Iladelphiapha)

9.56 Rewrite the programs given in Examples 9.29 and 9.30 for creating and processing student examination scores, using the sequential data file procedures included in your version of BASIC (see also Examples 8.2, 8.3 and 8.4).

9.57 Rewrite the inventory control program given in Example 9.31 using the random data file procedures included in your version of BASIC (see also Example 8.10).

9.58 Rewrite the binary search program given in Example 8.13 using the random data file procedures included in your version of BASIC.

9.59 Rewrite each of the following programs so that they fully utilize the enhanced features available in your version of microcomputer BASIC. In particular, utilize the IF-THEN, IF-THEN-ELSE, WHILE/WEND and PRINT USING features wherever practical.

(*a*) Roots of a quadratic equation (Example 2.30)
(*b*) Roots of an algebraic equation (Example 4.5)
(*c*) Calculating depreciation (Example 4.9)
(*d*) Averaging of air pollution data (Example 4.16)
(*e*) Reordering a list of numbers (Example 5.14)
(*f*) Table manipulation (Example 5.15)
(*g*) A game of chance (shooting craps) (Example 6.20)
(*h*) Simulation of a bouncing ball (Example 6.28)

9.60 Extend the word unscrambler (Example 5.9) so that it will rearrange the letters in *any* word (any number of letters) into all possible combinations. Make full use of the extended library functions that are available in your version of microcomputer BASIC.

9.61 Solve each of the following programming problems making full use of the enchanced features available in your version of microcomputer BASIC. In particular, utilize the IF-THEN, IF-THEN-ELSE, WHILE/WEND and PRINT USING features whenever it is natural to do so.

(*a*) Calculating a weighted average (Problem 4.47(*b*))
(*b*) Calculating factorials (Problem 4.48(*c*))
(*c*) Calculating the sine of *x* (Problem 4.48(*d*))
(*d*) Compound interest with annual compounding (Problem 4.48(*e*))
(*e*) Compound interest with quarterly compounding (Problem 4.48(*f*))
(*f*) Simulation of a four-function desk calculator (Problem 4.48(*g*))
(*g*) Alphabetizing a list of names (Problem 5.51)
(*h*) Matching countries with their capitals (Problem 5.56)
(*i*) Matrix multiplication (Problem 5.57(*b*))
(*j*) Statistical calculations (Problem 5.57(*d*))
(*k*) Home mortage costs (Problem 5.57(*f*))
(*l*) Lagrangian interpolation (Problem 5.57(*h*))
(*m*) Newton-Raphson iteration (Problem 5.57(*i*))
(*n*) Numerical integration using Simpson's rule (Problem 5.57(*k*))
(*o*) Solution of a differential equation (Problem 5.57(*l*))
(*p*) Computation of a weekly payroll (Problem 6.48)
(*q*) Calculating the area under a curve using a Monte Carlo technique (Problem 6.52(*d*))
(*r*) Encoding and decoding a line of text (Problem 6.52(*j*))

9.62 Solve Problem 5.57(*e*) (calculating the variance of a list of numbers using two different formulas) using real (single-precision) numbers. Then repeat the calculations using double-precision numbers. Compare the results obtained from the two sets of calculations.

9.63 Solve Problem 5.55 (computation of student exam scores, including the class average and the deviation of each student's average about the class average) using the enhanced features available in your version of microcomputer BASIC. In particular, be sure to use the PRINT USING statement.

9.64 Write a complete BASIC program that will create and utilize a sequential data file containing names, addresses and telephone numbers, as described in Problem 8.40. Use the sequential data file procedures included in your version of microcomputer BASIC.

9.65 Repeat Problem 9.64 utilizing a random data file. Use the random data file procedures included in your version of microcomputer BASIC. Also, use a binary search to find individual records (see Example 8.13). Compare with the sequential data file version from a standpoint of programming ease and execution speed.

Chapter 10

The Microcomputer Environment

In this chapter we will discuss the microcomputer environment with respect to hardware as well as software. We begin with a discussion of file designation procedures and microcomputer BASIC system commands. The unique characteristics of the TV display and the microcomputer keyboard will then be considered, along with several related features of microcomputer BASIC. Later we consider the use of some programmable input devices, and the use of color and sound. The chapter concludes with a brief discussion of built-in program editing procedures.

Again, our emphasis will be on the use of Microsoft BASIC and its accompanying operating system, MS-DOS, as implemented on the IBM Personal Computer and other microcomputers of this type. (IBM refers to this operating system as PC-DOS.) The reader should consult an appropriate reference manual for information on other types of microcomputers or microcomputer operating systems.

10.1 FILE DESIGNATIONS

Most microcomputers have at least one, and usually two or three, mass storage devices on which various kinds of files can be stored. The most common type of mass storage device is the floppy disk, but tape cassettes, hard disks, optical disks and bubble memories are also available. Any of these mass storage devices can be used to store BASIC programs, data files and other types of files (e.g., machine-language programs that are a part of the operating system). Thus, when referring to a particular file, there is a need to specify the name of the file, the type of file and the mass storage device on which it is stored.

On the IBM Personal Computer (or any other microcomputer that uses the MS-DOS operating system), a complete file designation consists of the following three items.

1. A reference to the mass storage device (a single letter followed by a colon)
2. A file name (one to eight characters)
3. A file extension, which indicates the file type (one to three characters preceded by a period)

EXAMPLE 10.1

A complete MS-DOS file designation is shown below.

A:SAMPLE.BAS

This file designation refers to a BASIC program called SAMPLE, which is stored on drive A. (Typically, the disk drives will be lettered A, B, C, etc.) Thus, the device designation is A, the file name is SAMPLE, and the extension is BAS. Notice the colon between the device designation and the file name and the period separating the file name and the extension.

When a microcomputer is in operation, one of the mass storage devices will always be designated as the "active device" (or if it is a disk drive, the "active drive"). When accessing a file that is stored on the active device, the device designation need not be specified. When accessing a file on another device, however, the device designation must be included as a part of the file specification.

EXAMPLE 10.2

A microcomputer has two floppy disk drives, designated as drive A and drive B. Suppose that drive A is currently the active drive. If we want to refer to a BASIC program on drive A called SAMPLE, we could write the file specification as

SAMPLE.BAS

On the other hand, if we should want to refer to a BASIC program on drive B called DEMO, we would have to write the entire file specification as

B:DEMO.BAS

A file (e.g., a program) that is stored on one device can easily access another file (e.g., a data file) that is stored on another device. To do so, we simply include the device designation as a part of the file designation when accessing the second file.

EXAMPLE 10.3

Consider once again a microcomputer with two floppy disk drives, A and B, with drive A active. Suppose that we are running a BASIC program that is stored on drive A and this program accesses a random-access data file on drive B called STUDENTS.DAT. Then we must refer to the random-access data file as

B:STUDENTS.DAT

from within the program.

EXAMPLE 10.4

Figure 10.1 shows a variation of the program that was developed in Example 9.30 for processing student examination scores using information stored in sequential data files. (The original program is shown in Fig. 9.10.) Now, however, the sequential data files are accessed from drive B, and each has the extension .DAT attached to the file name. Lines 40, 50, 250 and 260 reflect these changes in usage.

```
10 REM ****** PROGRAM TO PROCESS STUDENT EXAMINATION SCORES ******
20 REM ******         USING SEQUENTIAL DATA FILES            ******
30 DIM C(15)
40 OPEN "I",1,"B:SCORES.DAT"
50 OPEN "O",2,"B:UPDATE.DAT"
60 INPUT #1,TITLE$
70 INPUT #1,TERM$
80 PRINT "Course title: ";TITLE$,"Term: ";TERM$
90 PRINT #2,TITLE$: PRINT #2,TERM$
100 PRINT: INPUT "Exam number";K
110 PRINT: INPUT "Calculate averages (Y/N) ";ANS$
120 PRINT: INPUT #1,N$
130 FOR I=1 TO K-1: INPUT #1,C(I): NEXT I
140 PRINT N$,
150 INPUT "New score";C(K)
160 PRINT #2,N$
170 SUM=0
180 FOR I=1 TO K: PRINT #2,C(I);: SUM=SUM+C(I): NEXT I
190 IF ANS$="N" OR ANS$="n" THEN 230
200 AVG=SUM/K
210 PRINT "Average=";AVG
220 PRINT #2,AVG
230 IF NOT EOF(1) THEN 120
240 CLOSE
250 KILL "B:SCORES.DAT"
260 NAME "B:UPDATE.DAT" AS "B:SCORES.DAT"
270 END
```

Fig. 10.1

When accessing a BASIC program, both the device designation and the file extension can be omitted under certain conditions. We will say more about BASIC file specifications in the next section.

10.2 MICROCOMPUTER SYSTEM COMMANDS

Many versions of microcomputer BASIC contain certain system commands that are not found in the more traditional versions of the language. On the other hand, certain of the traditional system commands are not available on a microcomputer, or else they are implemented differently. We therefore give some consideration to the more common microcomputer system commands, as implemented in Microsoft BASIC.

Some microcomputers enter BASIC automatically as soon as they are turned on. It is more common, however, for a microcomputer to access its operating system after being turned on. In order to enter BASIC from the operating system, the user must type the command BASIC. (Similar commands are available for accessing other languages or other microcomputer applications, such as word processing.)

Once BASIC has been accessed, the user will see a message such as that shown below.

```
The IBM Personal Computer Basic
Version D2.10 Copyright IBM Corp. 1981, 1982, 1983
61327 Bytes free

Ok
```

The user may then load a BASIC program, run the program, list the program, etc., by entering the appropriate system commands. The most common system commands (as implemented in Microsoft BASIC for the IBM Personal Computer) are summarized below.

Command	*Purpose*	*Examples*
AUTO	Automatically numbers successive program lines. (Numbers will be 10, 20, 30, . . . , unless specified otherwise.)	AUTO AUTO 100,5 (Begin with line 100, increment by 5s.)
CLEAR	Set all numeric variables to zero; all string variables become null.	CLEAR
CONT	Resume execution after an interruption (e.g., STOP or END statement).	CONT
DELETE	Delete a block of lines from the program currently in memory.	DELETE 50–80 (Delete lines 50 through 80.)
EDIT	Enter line edit mode (see Section 10.7).	EDIT 100 (To edit line 100)
FILES	List all files that have been stored on a mass storage device (e.g., a floppy disk).	FILES FILES "B:"
KILL	Delete a file from a mass storage device (e.g., a floppy disk).	KILL "SAMPLE" KILL "B:STUDENTS.DAT"

(*continues on page 267*)

Command	*Purpose*	*Examples*
LIST	List on the console all or part of the program currently stored in memory.	LIST LIST 100–200 (List lines 100 through 200.)
LLIST	List on the line printer all or part of the program currently stored in memory.	LLIST LLIST 100–200 (List lines 100 through 200.)
LOAD	Retrieve a file from a mass storage device (e.g., a floppy disk) and store in the computer's memory.	LOAD "DEMO" (DEMO is the file name.) LOAD "B:SAMPLE.BAS"
MERGE	Merge a program stored on a mass storage device (e.g., a floppy disk) with the program currently in memory.	MERGE "TRIAL" MERGE "B:REPORT.BAS"
NAME	Rename a file that is stored on a mass storage device (e.g., a floppy disk).	NAME "SAMPLE" AS "NEWPROG" NAME "B:DEMO" AS "B:INVADERS.BAS"
NEW	Delete the program currently stored in memory.	NEW
RENUM	Renumbers program lines automatically. (Numbers will be 10, 20, 30, . . . , unless specified otherwise.)	RENUM RENUM 10,100,5 (Begin original line 10, change to line 100, increment by 5s.)
RUN	Execute the program currently in memory, or LOAD a program and then execute it.	RUN RUN "B:SAMPLE"
SAVE	Store the program currently in memory on a mass storage device (e.g., a floppy disk).	SAVE "DEMO" SAVE "B:SAMPLE"
SYSTEM	Exit from BASIC to the operating system.	SYSTEM
TRON	A debugging aid; causes program line numbers to be displayed as they are executed.	TRON
TROFF	Cancels the TRON command.	TROFF

Notice that the required file designations are enclosed in quotes. This is a characteristic of Microsoft BASIC. It should be understood that the syntactical details may be different with other versions of microcomputer BASIC. Moreover, the commands themselves may be different with other versions of the language.

EXAMPLE 10.5 Time of Day

Figure 10.2 shows a typical session involving the use of BASIC with an IBM Personal Computer. In this session we see what happens when the computer is first turned on and BASIC is accessed. We begin by loading a program called DEMO.BAS, which is stored on the active floppy disk drive (drive A). The program is then listed and run. We then alter the program by adding two additional PRINT statements (lines 35 and 65), list the new version, run the new version and then save the new version on the active drive. Finally, we exit from BASIC, returning to the operating system.

```
Current date is Tue  1-01-1980
Enter new date:  9-5-1985
Current time is  0:00:12.74
Enter new time:  19:36

The IBM Personal Computer DOS
Version 2.10 (C)Copyright IBM Corp 1981, 1982, 1983

A>BASIC

The IBM Personal Computer Basic
Version D2.10 Copyright IBM Corp. 1981, 1982, 1983
61327 Bytes free

Ok

LOAD "DEMO"
Ok

LIST
10 REM *** "Good morning" program ***
20 '
30 INPUT "Hi, what's your name? ",N$
40 HOUR = VAL(LEFT$(TIME$,2))
50 IF HOUR < 12 THEN PRINT "Good morning, "; ELSE IF HOUR < 18 THEN
   PRINT "Good afternoon, "; ELSE PRINT "Good evening, ";
60 PRINT N$
70 END
Ok

RUN
Hi, what's your name? Sharon
Good evening, Sharon
Ok

35 PRINT
65 PRINT

LIST
10 REM *** "Good morning" program ***
20
30 INPUT "Hi, what's your name? ",N$
35 PRINT
40 HOUR = VAL(LEFT$(TIME$,2))
50 IF HOUR < 12 THEN PRINT "Good morning, "; ELSE IF HOUR < 18 THEN
   PRINT "Good afternoon, "; ELSE PRINT "Good evening, ";
60 PRINT N$
65 PRINT
70 END
Ok

RUN
Hi, what's your name? Sharon

Good evening, Sharon

Ok

SAVE "DEMO"
Ok

SYSTEM

A>
```

Fig. 10.2

The program itself first reads a name, e.g., "Sharon," and then determines the current time-of-day (note that the time is entered when the computer is first turned on). The program will then print "Good morning, Sharon", "Good afternoon, Sharon", or "Good evening, Sharon" as appropriate. In this particular session the program prints "Good evening, Sharon" since we entered 19:36 (i.e., 7:36 p.m.) at the start of the session. (Note that the program makes use of several new library functions, as described in Section 9.3.)

Notice that the program (file) designations need not include the drive specification, since the program is loaded from and saved to the currently active drive. Also, note that the extension is assumed to be .BAS. Since the current program does indeed have this extension, we need not include it in the file designation.

As in previous examples of this type, the user's responses are underlined.

Remember that this example is *representative* of a microcomputer programming session with Microsoft BASIC. The details may differ from one computer to another. Furthermore, the session may be altogether different with some other version of microcomputer BASIC.

The reader is referred to Appendix D for a more extensive summary of Microsoft BASIC, including the more commonly used system commands.

10.3 THE TV MONITOR

Most microcomputers and many timesharing terminals utilize a *TV monitor* (i.e., a CRT unit) as a primary output device. These units typically display 24 or 25 lines of text, with up to 80 characters per line (though some microcomputers generate large-character output, resulting in fewer characters per line and perhaps fewer lines). Graphical displays can also be generated on these devices (see Chapter 12). Both color and monochromatic-type monitors are now in common use.

Clearing the Screen

TV monitors have certain unique characteristics that must be taken into consideration when writing BASIC programs. For example, a TV monitor can display only a finite number of lines at any one time (in contrast to a line printer, which can go on forever if there is enough paper). Therefore we must clear the screen periodically so that a new display can begin in the upper left corner of a blank screen.

On the IBM Personal Computer, the statement *CLS* (clear screen) is used to clear the screen. This command erases whatever was displayed on the screen and then positions the cursor in the upper left corner.

Moving the Cursor

Another unique characteristic of a TV monitor is the *cursor.* This is a blinking character, typically a small rectangle or a horizontal line, which is used to indicate a specific screen location (i.e., a particular line and column). The cursor has many useful purposes; for example, it can be used to draw attention to a particular screen location (to read a message, perhaps), to indicate a request for input data or to show where the next output message will appear.

When a file (e.g., a BASIC program) is being *edited,* the cursor position is controlled at the keyboard. Most microcomputer keyboards include special keys that are used to move the cursor up, down and sideways (more about this in the next section). When a program is being *executed,* however, the cursor location is determined from within the program. The ability to move the cursor in this manner is particularly important when writing interactive (conversational-style) programs. Most versions of microcomputer BASIC therefore include special statements for positioning the cursor under program control.

When a Microsoft BASIC program is being executed on the IBM Personal Computer, the position of the cursor is specified by the *LOCATE statement.* A typical LOCATE statement might appear as

```
LOCATE 5,20
```

This particular statement causes the cursor to be located on row 5 (i.e., the fifth row from the top)

and column 20 (from the left). Other row and column positions can be specified simply by changing the numerical parameters in this statement.

It is important to recognize that the cursor can be moved anywhere on the screen in this manner without erasing any of the text that may have previously been written. Thus, it is possible to move the cursor to some particular word or symbol that is already on the screen.

EXAMPLE 10.6

In order to clear the screen and then position the cursor at the center of the screen (i.e., row 13, column 40) with an IBM Personal Computer, we would write

```
10 CLS
20 LOCATE 13,40
30 ANS$ = INPUT$(1)
```

Note that the last statement causes a pause in the execution in the program, thus allowing the cursor to be seen in its new location. Program execution will resume when any key is pressed.

Some of the earlier versions of Microsoft BASIC do not include any explicit cursor-movement statements. In such cases the CLS statement can be simulated by writing PRINT CHR$(12), since 12 is the (decimal) ASCII code for a *form feed.* Also, the LOCATE statement can be simulated by printing a sequence of blank lines followed by several blank spaces within the desired line.

EXAMPLE 10.7

In order to clear the screen and position the cursor at the center of the screen (i.e., row 13, column 40) using an older microcomputer without explicit cursor-movement commands, we could write

```
10 PRINT CHR$(12)
20 FOR ROW = 1 TO 12 : PRINT : NEXT ROW
30 FOR COL = 1 TO 40 : PRINT " "; : NEXT COL
40 INPUT " ",A$
```

(compare with Example 10.6).

This method is, of course, less convenient than the method presented in Example 10.6. Hence it should not be used unless it is the only method available.

There are three functions that are used with the PRINT statement in order to position the cursor along a line. They are *TAB, SPC* and *SPACE$.* The first of these (TAB) is used to position the cursor relative to the *beginning* of the line, as discussed in Chapter 5. The second function (SPC) causes the cursor to move a specified number of spaces beyond its *last position* (which is usually adjacent to the last printed character). The last function (SPACE$) is similar to SPC; it returns a string consisting of a designated number of blank spaces.

EXAMPLE 10.8

The statement

```
10 PRINT "RED";TAB(6);"BLUE"
```

will cause the string BLUE to begin in column number 6 (which is actually the 7th column in the line), whereas the statement

```
20 PRINT "RED";SPC(6);"BLUE"
```

will cause six spaces to appear between RED and BLUE. (Hence BLUE will begin in column number 9, which is actually the 10th column in the line.)

The last PRINT statement could also be written as

```
20 PRINT "RED";SPACE$(6);"BLUE"
```

This statement will also cause six spaces to appear between RED and BLUE.

The *POS function* will return the current position of the cursor in a given line. This allows conditional branching based upon cursor location, as illustrated below. (Note that this function ignores whatever value is specified for the required argument.)

EXAMPLE 10.9

Consider the following two statements.

```
10 PRINT NAME$;
20 IF POS(1)<20 THEN PRINT TAB(20); ADDRESS$
   ELSE PRINT SPC(2); ADDRESS$
```

The second string (ADDRESS$) will start in column number 20 (actually the 21st column) if the first string (NAME$) is less than 20 characters long. Otherwise the second string will start three columns beyond the end of the first string (two blank spaces will separate the two strings).

Vertical Scrolling

Another special characteristic of a TV monitor is the *vertical scrolling* feature. This refers to the vertical movement of the screen display when a new line of text is generated at the bottom of a screen that is already full. When this happens, the line that was formerly at the top of the screen will be lost; all other lines move up one position, and the new line appears at the bottom of the screen.

Vertical scrolling can sometimes be used advantageously to create certain special effects, as illustrated in Example 10.10 below. It can also be an annoyance, since it may cause a display of text to disappear before it can be read. This problem can usually be eliminated (or at least minimized), however, by utilizing special programming techniques, such as empty FOR-TO loops to generate time delays, the use of the INKEY$ or INPUT$ functions to create pauses (see Example 9.22), vertical repositioning of the cursor or the use of a line printer to display lengthy text.

A closely related problem is that of the screen being cleared (by the CLS statement) before a displayed text message can be read. This problem can also be eliminated through the use of empty FOR-TO loops or the INKEY$ or INPUT$ functions.

```
10  REM  *** TV-DISPLAY DEMO (IBM Version 1) ***
20  '
30  CLS : LOCATE 11,28
40  PRINT "WELCOME TO THE WONDERFUL"
50  LOCATE 14,28
60  PRINT "WORLD OF MICROCOMPUTERS!"
70  FOR I=1 TO 3000 : NEXT I
80  CLS: LOCATE 11,18
90  PRINT "Just relax, enjoy yourself and remember that"
100  LOCATE 14,25
110  PRINT "NOTHING CAN POSSIBLY GO WRONG!"
120  FOR I = 1 TO 3000 : NEXT I
130  LOCATE 24
140  FOR I = 1 TO 24
150    FOR J = 1 TO 8
160        PRINT "GO WRONG! ";
170    NEXT J
180    PRINT : PRINT
190  NEXT I
200  CLS: LOCATE 11,37
210  PRINT "DARN!"
220  LOCATE 15,30
230  PRINT "Something went wrong!"
240  LOCATE 23
250  END
```

Fig. 10.3

EXAMPLE 10.10 Programming a TV Display (Nothing Can Go Wrong, Go Wrong, Go Wrong, . . .)

In Fig. 10.3 we see a short, entertaining program that is written in Microsoft BASIC for an IBM Personal Computer. This program illustrates the use of time delays, cursor movement and deliberate vertical scrolling. The program is designed to cause the message

```
GO WRONG! GO WRONG! GO WRONG! GO WRONG! GO WRONG! GO WRONG! GO WRONG!
```

to fill an 80-character screen and scroll vertically, thus creating the obviously false impression that the trustworthy microcomputer, which presumably never goes awry, has indeed done so!

This program contains a number of CLS instructions (lines 30, 80 and 200) and several LOCATE instructions (lines 30, 50, 80, 100, 130, 200, 220 and 240). These statements allow the programmer to control the appearance of the screen, particularly the location of the various printed messages. The program also includes two empty FOR-TO loops (lines 70 and 120) which create time delays. The net effect is a dynamic, animated display with considerable visual impact.

The reader is urged to run this program in order to observe the actual vertical scrolling. This will greatly enhance the reader's appreciation for the program. It is also interesting to execute the program on a line printer or a hard-copy terminal and compare the impact with that of a TV display.

10.4 THE KEYBOARD

Most microcomputer keyboards contain considerably more than the standard "typewriter-style" keys. Two or three additional groups of keys are quite common. These additional keys may include a set of cursor- and screen-movement keys, a "numeric pad" (i.e., a set of numeric keys that duplicates the numeric typewriter keys but has a calculator-type arrangement) and a set of special function keys. Certain of these keys can be programmed to perform special tasks during the execution of a BASIC program.

Fig. 10.4

Consider, for example, the keyboard used with the IBM Personal Computer, shown in Fig. 10.4. Notice that the typewriter keys are located in the center of the keyboard. To the right is a group of keys that serve two different functions; they are usually used as cursor- and screen-movement keys, though they can become numeric keys if the "NumLock" key (located in the upper-right corner) is depressed. The left side of the keyboard contains a group of function keys, labeled F1 through F10.

The advanced version of Microsoft BASIC that is supplied with the IBM Personal Computer (called BASICA) contains several special commands that allow the computer to determine if any of the function keys or certain of the cursor-movement keys have been pressed.* The computer can then respond in any way the programmer may wish, through special subroutine calls (i.e., through a special form of the ON-GOSUB statement). We will see how this is accomplished in the next example.

EXAMPLE 10.11 Programming the Function Keys

Figure 10.5 presents a simple BASIC program, written in advanced Microsoft BASIC (i.e., BASICA), for the IBM Personal Computer. This program contains a loop that displays the consecutive positive integers 1, 2, 3, . . . , 32767 on the screen, one integer per line. Since the screen can only display 24 lines at any one time, the numbers scroll vertically upward once the screen becomes filled.

The program contains a provision for terminating the computation any time the user may wish, simply by pressing function key F2. Also, the screen colors can be "reversed" (i.e., changed from white characters on a black background to black characters on a white background, and vice versa) at any time by pressing function key F1 while the program is executing.

```
10 REM *** FUNCTION KEY DEMO ***
20 '
30 ON KEY(1) GOSUB 160
40 ON KEY(2) GOSUB 200
50 KEY(1) ON : KEY(2) ON
60 '
70 CLS : FLAG = 1
80 PRINT "FUNCTION KEY DEMONSTRATION" : PRINT
90 PRINT "Press F1 to REVERSE the screen, F2 to STOP" : PRINT
100 PRINT "Press any other key to begin"
110 DUMMY$ = INPUT$(1)
120 FOR COUNT = 1 TO 32767 : PRINT COUNT : NEXT COUNT
130 END
140 ,
150 REM *** SUBROUTINE TO REVERSE THE SCREEN ***
160 IF FLAG = 1 THEN COLOR 0,7 : FLAG = 0 ELSE COLOR 7,0 : FLAG = 1
170 RETURN
180 '
190 REM *** SUBROUTINE TO TERMINATE THE COMPUTATION ***
200 END
```

Fig. 10.5

Now let us examine this program in detail. Lines 30 and 40 associate each function key with a particular subroutine, and line 50 activates these associations. Line 70 clears the screen and then assigns a value of 1 to FLAG, indicating white characters on a black background. An initial message is then provided in lines 80 through 110. The consecutive integers are generated and printed in the FOR-TO loop which appears on line 120, and line 130 represents the end of the main part of the program.

Lines 150 through 170 comprise the first subroutine (associated with F1), which reverses the colors. The principal part of the subroutine is the IF-THEN-ELSE statement on line 160. The color reversals are carried out with the COLOR statement. Thus if FLAG = 1, indicating white on black, the colors are reversed by specifying COLOR 0,7 (the 0 indicates black characters, and the 7 indicates a white background). FLAG is then set equal

* The IBM Personal Computer actually supports three different versions of Microsoft BASIC, called Cassette BASIC, Disk BASIC and Advanced BASIC, respectively.

to 0. Similarly, if FLAG is not equal to 1, the colors are reversed by specifying COLOR 7,0 (white characters, black background) and FLAG is reset to 1. The RETURN statement in line 170 causes control to be returned to the statement following the point where the function key was depressed.

The second subroutine consists simply of an identifying remark and an END statement. A RETURN statement is not required here since the purpose of this subroutine is to terminate the computation.

We will say more about the COLOR statement later in this chapter (see Section 10.6). It should be apparent, however, that this statement is used to produce colored text against different colored backgrounds. It can also be used to generate color graphics, as we shall see in Chapter 12.

Finally, the reader should see this program in operation to appreciate what it does and how it works. If an IBM-type personal computer is available, the reader is strongly encouraged to type in the program and then run it, pressing F1 several times during the program execution, and then pressing F2 to stop the program execution.

10.5 OTHER PROGRAMMABLE INPUT DEVICES

Microcomputers are able to make use of several different types of programmable input devices in addition to the keyboard. Two commonly used devices are the *light pen* and the *joystick*. The light pen is a pointing device that can be programmed to sense a location on the screen and then activate some function. Similarly, the joystick is a positioning device that can be programmed to position the cursor and then activate a function by depressing a button. Microsoft BASIC allows these devices to be programmed in much the same manner as the keyboard function keys, as described in Section 10.4.

Consider, for example, the light pen, the use of which is illustrated in Fig. 10.6. This is a

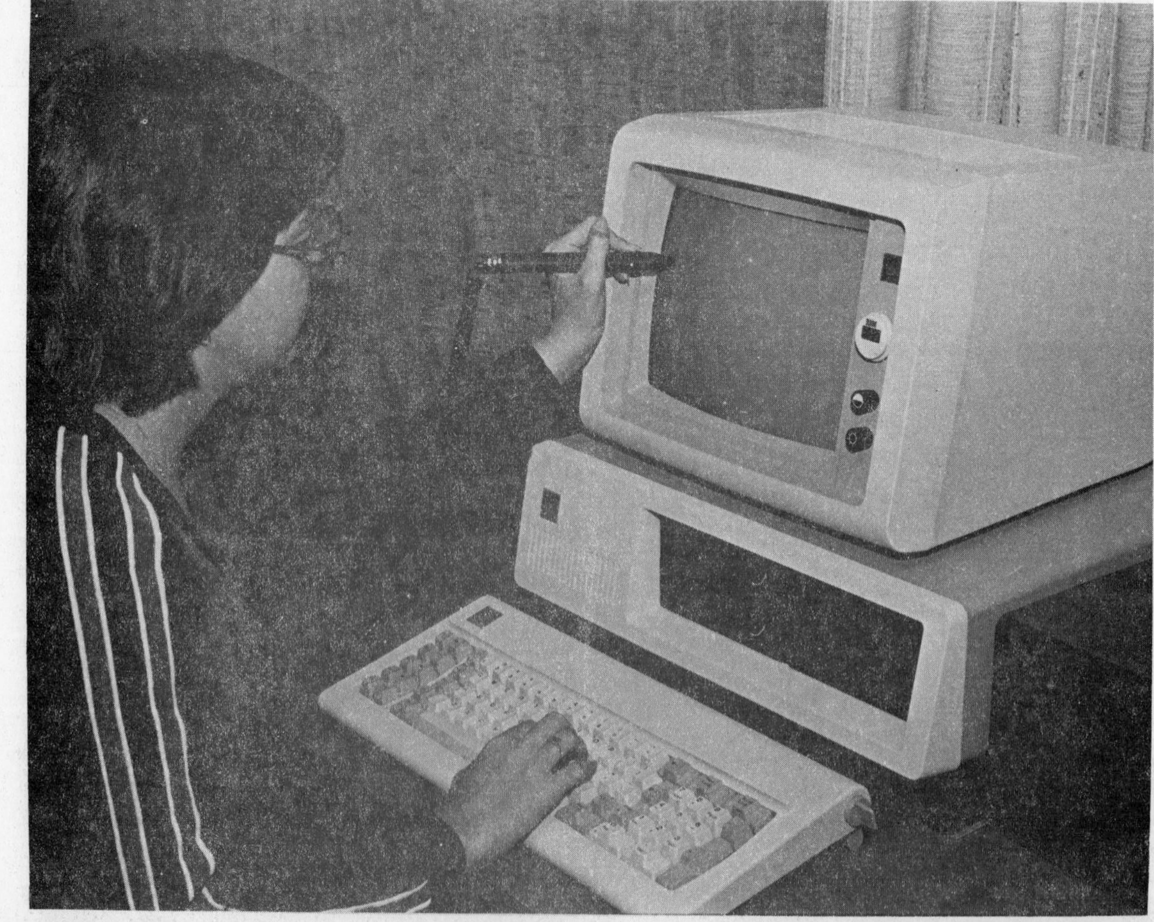

Fig. 10.6

light-sensitive device with a switch built into its tip. The switch is actuated by pressing the light pen against a light source on the TV monitor. The location of the light source (row and column) can then be determined by the computer.

Advanced Microsoft BASIC contains several special statements and functions that are designed to be used with a light pen. Use of these special features is illustrated in the next example.

EXAMPLE 10.12 Programming a Light Pen

In Fig. 10.7 we see an advanced BASIC program, written for the IBM Personal Computer, that allows the user to select one of several items displayed in the form of a "menu" on the TV monitor. The selection is made with a light pen. Once an item has been selected, an action is taken which is specific to that selection.

```
10 REM *** LIGHT PEN DEMO ***
20 '
30 ON PEN GOSUB 240
40 PEN ON
50 SQUARE$=CHR$(219)+CHR$(219)
60 '
70 REM *** MAIN LOOP ***
80 '
90 CLS : PRINT "Multi-lingual greetings"
100 LOCATE 4,1 : PRINT "Please select a language"
110 LOCATE 6,4 : PRINT SQUARE$;SPC(4);"English"
120 LOCATE 8,4 : PRINT SQUARE$;SPC(4);"French"
130 LOCATE 10,4 : PRINT SQUARE$;SPC(4);"German"
140 LOCATE 12,4 : PRINT SQUARE$;SPC(4);"Hawaiian"
150 LOCATE 14,4 : PRINT SQUARE$;SPC(4);"Hebrew"
160 LOCATE 16,4 : PRINT SQUARE$;SPC(4);"Italian"
170 LOCATE 18,4 : PRINT SQUARE$;SPC(4);"Japanese"
180 LOCATE 20,4 : PRINT SQUARE$;SPC(4);"Spanish"
190 LOCATE 22,4 : PRINT SQUARE$;SPC(4);"END"
200 GOTO 200
210 '
220 REM *** SUBROUTINE TO PRINT 'HELLO' ***
230 '
240 ROW=PEN(6)
250 IF ROW=22 THEN LOCATE 23,1 : END
260 LOCATE ROW,20
270 IF ROW=6 THEN PRINT "Hello" : GOTO 350
280 IF ROW=8 THEN PRINT "Bonjour" : GOTO 350
290 IF ROW=10 THEN PRINT "Guten tag" : GOTO 350
300 IF ROW=12 THEN PRINT "Aloha" : GOTO 350
310 IF ROW=14 THEN PRINT "Shalom" : GOTO 350
320 IF ROW=16 THEN PRINT "Buon giorno" : GOTO 350
330 IF ROW=18 THEN PRINT "Konichihua" : GOTO 350
340 IF ROW=20 THEN PRINT "Buenos dias"
350 FOR COUNT=1 TO 1000 : NEXT COUNT
360 LOCATE ROW,20 : PRINT SPACE$(15)
370 RETURN
380 END
```

Fig. 10.7

In particular, the program will generate a list containing the names of eight different languages, each preceded by a square block of light. The user presses the point of the light pen against the block corresponding to the language of his or her choice. An appropriate greeting, in the chosen language, will then appear adjacent to the language name. The greeting will remain on the screen for a second or two (long enough for it to be read comfortably) and then erased. The user may then choose another language, and the process will be repeated. This will continue until the user selects the last menu item (END), which causes the program to stop.

Now let us examine the actual program in some detail. Line 30 associates a signal coming from the light pen with a subroutine, and line 40 activates this association. Line 50 defines a string consisting of a block of light.

The menu is generated by lines 90 through 190. Line 200 simply loops back to itself an indefinite number of times, causing the computer to wait for a signal from the light pen.

Once a signal has been detected from the light pen (caused by the light pen being pressed against one of the blocks of light, thus triggering its switch), program control automatically jumps to line 240. This statement makes use of the PEN function. The argument 6 causes the function to return the number of the row where the light pen was activated. This value is then assigned to the variable ROW. Line 260 then positions the cursor, in preparation for displaying the appropriate greeting, and lines 270 through 340 select the appropriate greeting and cause it to be displayed. A time delay is generated by the empty FOR-TO loop in line 350. Finally, the greeting is erased (overwritten by blank spaces) in line 360 and control is returned to line 200. This process continues until row 22 is selected, causing the program to stop (line 250).

Execution of the program causes a menu, similar to that shown in Fig. 10.8, to appear on the screen. (Note that the dark blocks will appear as blocks of light on the TV monitor.) The user presses the light pen against one of the blocks, and the appropriate greeting will occur to the right of the current menu selection. For example, if the light pen is pressed against the second block, the greeting "Bonjour" will appear to the right of the word "French." The greeting will disappear after a short time delay. The user may then make another selection. Notice that the program can be ended at any time simply by selecting the last block.

```
Multi-lingual greetings

Please select a language

■    English

■    French

■    German

■    Hawaiian

■    Hebrew

■    Italian

■    Japanese

■    Spanish

■    END
```

Fig. 10.8

Now consider a typical joystick, such as that illustrated in Fig. 10.9. This device has a handle (i.e., a "stick") that can be moved in two different directions (up/down and left/right). The position of the handle is described by a pair of integer values representing x and y coordinates (e.g., each coordinate might typically be represented by an integer ranging from 0 to 127). These values are continuously transmitted to the computer, where they can be transformed into a cursor position (i.e., row and column numbers). If the joystick handle is moved, the cursor position will change correspondingly. Hence, the computer can be programmed to move the cursor around the screen in response to the movement of the joystick handle.

The joystick also has two buttons (switches) that can be used to transmit individual signals to the computer. Thus, it is possible to position the cursor to a desired location by moving the joystick handle and then activate some function by pressing one of the buttons. Each button can be programmed separately to activate its own unique function.

Advanced Microsoft BASIC includes several special statements and functions that can be used to program a joystick. The manner in which this can be accomplished is illustrated in the example shown below.

Fig. 10.9

EXAMPLE 10.13 Programming a Joystick

Figure 10.10 contains an advanced BASIC program that allows an IBM Personal Computer to operate under control of a joystick. The program begins by blanking out the entire screen. The user can then position the cursor to any desired position by moving the handle of the joystick. At any cursor position the user can cause an asterisk (*) to be displayed by pressing button 1 (the button closest to the handle in Fig. 10.9). Also, an existing asterisk can be "erased" by pressing button 2.

```
10 REM *** JOYSTICK DEMO ***
20 '
30 CLS
40 ON STRIG(0) GOSUB 170
50 ON STRIG(4) GOSUB 200
60 STRIG(0) ON : STRIG(4) ON
70 '
80 REM *** MAIN LOOP ***
90 '
100 X=STICK(0) : Y=STICK(1)
110 ROW=23*(Y/127) + 1
120 COL=79*(X/127) + 1
130 LOCATE ROW,COL,1
140 GOTO 100
150 '
160 REM *** SUBROUTINE TO PRINT AN ASTERISK ***
170 PRINT "*"; : RETURN
180 '
190 REM *** SUBROUTINE TO PRINT A BLANK SPACE ***
200 PRINT " "; : RETURN
210 END
```

Fig. 10.10

The program begins by clearing the screen (line 30). Lines 40 and 50 associate signals coming from buttons 1 and 2 with subroutines that print an asterisk or a blank space, respectively. Line 60 then activates these associations.

Lines 100 through 140 define a loop which forms the heart of the program. Line 100 detects numerical values for the variables X and Y, depending on the position of the joystick handle. Each of these values will fall within the interval 0 to 127. Thus, the point X=0, Y=0 refers to the upper left corner, and the point X=127, Y=127 refers to the lower right corner. Lines 110 and 120 then convert these values into a row number (ranging from 1 to 24) and a column number (ranging from 1 to 80). Line 130 positions the cursor at this new location. Finally, line 140 closes the loop (thus detecting new values for X and Y in response to a movement of the joystick handle) and repositions the cursor accordingly.

Line 170 defines a simple subroutine that prints an asterisk (*) at the current cursor position. This subroutine is activated whenever joystick button 1 is pressed during execution of the main loop. Similarly, line 200 defines a subroutine that prints a blank space at the current cursor position (thus erasing whatever else may have been at this position). This subroutine is activated by pressing button 2 during execution of the main loop.

Notice that this program continues to execute indefinitely, or until the computer breaks out of BASIC by some command from the user. The program could be improved by adding a routine that would end the computation whenever a function key is pressed, as in Example 10.11.

Though the light pen and the joystick are popular microcomputer input devices, they are by no means the only such devices available. Modern microcomputers also support digitizers, speech recognition devices, and several other types of input devices.

Of particular importance is the growing interest in the use of a device known as a *mouse*. This is a positioning device, similar to a joystick. The mouse is easier to control, however, because the cursor is positioned by sliding the mouse along a broad flat surface (typically an area about one square foot) rather than by making delicate adjustments to the small, sensitive handle of a joystick.

Figure 10.11 shows a photograph of a typical mouse. Notice that two buttons are located on the front of the mouse. (Some mice have three buttons; others have only one.) Like the joystick, the mouse permits various functions to be activated at any time simply by pressing one of these buttons.

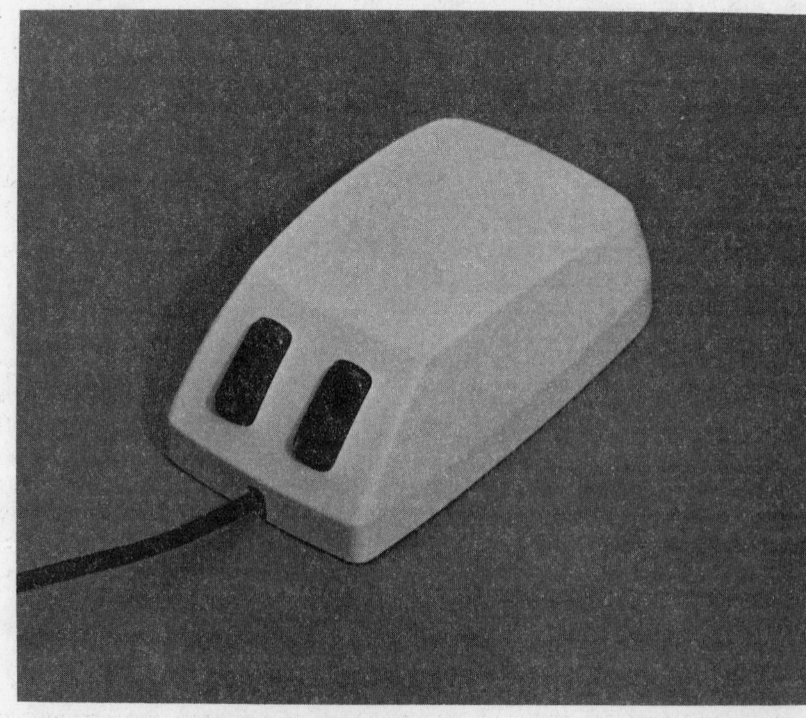

Fig. 10.11

The use of a mouse is becoming popular for certain office automation applications, particularly word processing and applications that make extensive use of graphics. Some versions of microcomputer BASIC now support the use of a mouse (with a group of instructions similar to those used with a joystick), and others do not. The inclusion of "mouse commands" in microcomputer BASIC should become increasingly common, however, in future years.

10.6 USE OF COLOR AND SOUND

Some microcomputers support the use of color TV monitors, thus allowing text of one color to be displayed against a background of a different color. The use of colored text displays can provide an effective form of program enhancement, particularly if the program is highly interactive.

For those microcomputers that support the use of color, BASIC allows colors to be selected by means of the *COLOR statement.* This statement generally includes three parameters, specifying the foreground (text) color, the background color and the "border" (i..e., the background area along the outer edges of the screen). On the IBM Personal Computer, for example, the following foreground colors may be selected.

0	black	8	gray
1	blue	9	light blue
2	green	10	light green
3	cyan	11	light cyan
4	red	12	light red
5	magenta	13	light magenta
6	brown	14	yellow
7	white	15	high intensity white

Any of the first eight colors (0 through 7) may also be selected for the background or the border. Thus, the statement COLOR 7,0,0 indicates white text on a black background and a black border; COLOR 0,7,7 selects black text against a white background and a white border; COLOR 14,1,4 indicates yellow text against a blue background with a red border, and so on. The value of the parameters can be modified at any time during the execution of a program, thus causing the colors to change as desired.

Use of the COLOR statement is generally preceded by the *SCREEN statement,* which specifies the mode (text vs. graphics) and color status (enabled or disabled). Thus, on the IBM Personal Computer, the statement SCREEN 0,1 specifies text mode, with color enabled.

EXAMPLE 10.14 Multicolored Text

To illustrate the use of colored text on the IBM Personal Computer, we present a program written in Microsoft BASIC that displays the same line of text repeatedly but with different color parameters. This will result in vertical scrolling on the screen, with each line displayed in a different color. Initially, the background and border will be black. However, the program includes a provision for changing the background and border colors at any time simply by pressing function key F1. Also, function key F2 is used to stop the computation.

The complete program is shown in Fig. 10.12. The program begins with the SCREEN command in line 30, which specifies text mode with color enabled. Line 40 removes the display of any previous function key definitions from the bottom line of the screen. Lines 50 through 70 generate a message at the bottom of the screen which describes the current use of the function keys; i.e.,

F1: Change background color   F2: End

This last group of instructions requires some additional explanation. On the IBM Personal Computer, the bottom line displayed on the screen (i.e., line 25) is a nonscrolling line which is normally used to display prompts and messages of this type. Such messages are often displayed in inverse color (black text on white background)

```
10 REM *** COLOR TEXT DEMO ***
20 '
30 SCREEN 0,1
40 KEY OFF
50 LOCATE 25,1 : COLOR 0,7
60 PRINT "F1: Change background color    F2: End ";
70 COLOR 7,0 : LOCATE 1,1
80 ON KEY(1) GOSUB 210
90 ON KEY(2) GOSUB 250
100 KEY(1) ON : KEY(2) ON
110 FOREGROUND=1 : BACKGROUND=0
120 '
130 REM *** MAIN LOOP ***
140 '
150 COLOR FOREGROUND,BACKGROUND,BACKGROUND
160 PRINT "Programming with BASIC is lots of fun! "
170 FOREGROUND=(FOREGROUND+1) MOD 16
180 GOTO 150
190 '
200 REM *** SUBROUTINE TO CHANGE BACKGROUND COLOR ***
210 BACKGROUND=(BACKGROUND+1) MOD 8
220 RETURN
230 '
240 REM *** SUBROUTINE TO TERMINATE THE COMPUTATION ***
250 COLOR 7,0,0
260 END
```

Fig. 10.12

to distinguish them from whatever else may appear on the screen. Hence, line 50 positions the cursor at the lower left corner of the screen and specifies inverse color. Line 60 generates the actual message across the bottom line, and line 70 restores the normal color (white text on black background) and then repositions the cursor to the upper left corner of the screen.

Lines 80 through 100 set up the use of the function keys, as described in Example 10.11. The initial color scheme (blue text on black background) is then set up in line 110.

The scrolling text is generated by a loop consisting of lines 150 through 180. Each pass through the loop generates one line of text, and each line of text will be displayed in a different color. Thus, line 150 selects the current colors in accordance with the values that are assigned to the parameters FOREGROUND (for the color of the text) and BACKGROUND (for the background and borders). Line 160 generates the actual line of text, i.e.,

```
Programming with BASIC is lots of fun!
```

and line 170 generates a new value for the parameter FOREGROUND in preparation for the next pass through the loop. (Note that FOREGROUND takes on sequential integer values between 0 and 15 due to the use of the MOD operator.) Finally, line 180 closes the loop by returning to line 150.

Lines 210 and 220 define the subroutine that is activated by function key F1. This subroutine causes the value of BACKGROUND to be increased by 1 whenever F1 is pressed. (Note that BACKGROUND takes on sequential integer values between 0 and 7.) This in turn causes the background and border color to change as soon as control is returned to the main loop.

Similarly, lines 250 and 260 define the subroutine that is activated by function key F2. This subroutine simply restores the standard color scheme (white text, black background, black border) and ends the computation.

Once execution begins, the program will remain in the main loop indefinitely, until function key F2 is pressed. Each line of text will appear in a different color, but the colors will repeat themselves every 16 lines, since there are only 16 different foreground colors. One line in each group of 16 will be unreadable because the foreground color will be the same as the background color. The background color will change every time F1 is pressed. The sequence of background colors will begin to repeat after eight different colors, however, since only eight background colors are available.

The reader should actually run this program on an IBM-type computer equipped with a color monitor if at all possible. This will provide the reader with a greater appreciation of the effect that is created.

If the computer is equipped with a monochromatic TV monitor (e.g., black and white, or black and green) rather than a color monitor, the COLOR statement may be interpreted somewhat differently. In particular, certain of the parameters may be used to specify text attributes, such as underlined, high intensity or flashing text. We will see an example of this in Example 10.17.

Let us now turn our attention to the use of sound in a BASIC program. Most microcomputers include an internal speaker that can be activated under program control. Though these speakers are typically small, they are capable of producing a remarkable variety of sounds. Many BASIC programs can be enhanced through the use of such program-generated sounds.

On the IBM Personal Computer, for example, there is a *BEEP statement* that simply "beeps" the speaker, producing a short, high-pitched sound of constant frequency. Such beeps are useful for drawing the user's attention to some specific event that may occur during program execution. The beep is often used in conjunction with an error-trapping routine (see Chapter 11), though there are other uses for it as well.

EXAMPLE 10.15

Let us modify the Microsoft BASIC program shown in the last example so that the speaker beeps whenever the background color is changed (i.e., whenever function key F1 is pressed). This can be accomplished very easily by adding a BEEP statement to the subroutine defined by lines 210 through 220. Thus, the subroutine may be written as

```
200 REM *** SUBROUTINE TO CHANGE BACKGROUND COLOR ***
210 BACKGROUND=(BACKGROUND+1) MOD 8
215 BEEP
220 RETURN
```

(Note the addition of line 215.) The reader should make this change and execute this program, if at all possible, to experience the effect that is created.

Microsoft BASIC also includes the *SOUND statement*, which is used to create a sound with a variable frequency and duration. The higher the frequency, the higher the pitch of the sound. Similarly, the greater the duration, the longer the sound. For example, the statement SOUND 5000,1 will produce a relatively high-pitched, short sound whereas SOUND 100,2000 generates a low, long tone. (The first parameter represents frequency, and the second represents duration.)

A certain amount of experimentation with the SOUND statement can be very revealing, as many interesting sounds can be produced by the creative use of this statement. This is particularly true if the statement is included within a FOR-TO loop with variable values for the parameters. Some of these effects are illustrated in the next two examples.

EXAMPLE 10.16 Programming the Speaker (A Siren)

Figure 10.13 presents a Microsoft BASIC program, written for the IBM Personal Computer, that causes the internal speaker to generate a siren sound. Essentially, the program consists of a FOR-TO loop that is repeated an indefinite number of times. Each complete execution of the loop produces one "wail" of the siren. This characteristic siren sound is repeated every time the entire loop is executed. The siren will continue indefinitely, until function key F1 is pressed.

Now let us examine the program in detail. Line 30 removes the display of any previous function key definitions from the bottom of the screen, and lines 40 and 50 generate the message

```
Press F1 to STOP
```

at the center of the screen. Line 60 associates function key F1 with a subroutine to end the computation, and line 70 activates this association. The length of each individual sound is then established by assigning the value 0.02 to DURATION in line 80. (Note that each individual sound will be short.)

Lines 120 through 150 produce the actual siren sound. In lines 120 through 140 we see a FOR-TO loop that creates one wail of the siren. Each pass through this loop generates a short tone whose frequency is determined by the running index (FREQUENCY). Notice that the tone will increase in frequency during each pass through the loop. Since the tones are short, the effect will be that of creating a continuously rising siren sound, even

```
10 REM *** SOUND DEMO (SIREN) ***
20 '
30 KEY OFF
40 CLS : LOCATE 12,32
50 PRINT "Press F1 to STOP";
60 ON KEY(1) GOSUB 180
70 KEY(1) ON
80 DURATION=.02
90 '
100 REM *** MAIN LOOP ***
110 '
120 FOR FREQUENCY=400 TO 1000 STEP 5
130     SOUND FREQUENCY,DURATION
140 NEXT FREQUENCY
150 GOTO 120
160 '
170 REM *** SUBROUTINE TO TERMINATE THE COMPUTATION ***
180 END
```

Fig. 10.13

though the individual tones have separate, discrete frequencies. Finally, line 150 causes the loop to start over, thus generating the repeated siren sound.

The entire process will continue until function key F1 is pressed. This immediately transfers control to the END statement in line 180, causing the program to stop.

Once again, the reader is urged to actually run this program in order to appreciate what happens.

The next example illustrates the combined use of the COLOR, BEEP and SOUND statements to enhance a BASIC program that generates a simple display of text. The program is intended to be run on a monochrome TV display. Hence the COLOR statement is used to select various text attributes, such as flashing and high intensity, rather than actual colors.

EXAMPLE 10.17 Programming a TV Display (Nothing Can Go Wrong, Go Wrong, Go Wrong . . .)

Figure 10.14 shows a variation of the program originally presented in Example 10.10, which causes the message

```
GO WRONG! GO WRONG! GO WRONG! GO WRONG! GO WRONG! GO WRONG! GO WRONG!
```

to fill an 80-character screen and scroll vertically. The logic is essentially the same as the program presented earlier (see Fig. 10.3). However, this version of the program is enhanced by several additional COLOR statements and several BEEP and SOUND statements.

For example, the statement COLOR 15,0 in line 40 causes the introductory message

```
WELCOME TO THE WONDERFUL
WORLD OF MICROCOMPUTERS!
```

to be displayed in high intensity, thus providing special emphasis on this message. Similarly, the COLOR 15,0 statement in line 230 causes the word

```
DARN!
```

to appear in high intensity, again providing special emphasis. (Note that the high intensity text is turned off by the COLOR 7,0 statement in lines 90 and 280.)

A somewhat different effect is achieved by the COLOR 16,7 statement in line 150. This statement causes the lines containing the message

```
GO WRONG! GO WRONG! GO WRONG! GO WRONG! GO WRONG! GO WRONG! GO WRONG!
```

to be displayed as flashing black letters against a white background (i.e., as a flashing inverse display), thus adding a dramatic touch as the lines scroll up the screen.

The program is further enhanced by the two BEEP statements, in lines 40 and 90 and the SOUND statements in lines 210 and 260. The BEEP statements cause the speaker to beep when each of the opening

```
10  REM  *** TV-DISPLAY DEMO (IBM Version 2) ***
20  '
30  KEY OFF
40  CLS : COLOR 15,0 : LOCATE 11,28 : BEEP
50  PRINT "WELCOME TO THE WONDERFUL"
60  LOCATE 14,28
70  PRINT "WORLD OF MICROCOMPUTERS!"
80  FOR I=1 TO 3000 : NEXT I
90  CLS : COLOR 7,0 : LOCATE 11,18 : BEEP
100  PRINT "Just relax, enjoy yourself and remember that"
110  LOCATE 14,25
120  PRINT "NOTHING CAN POSSIBLY GO WRONG!"
130  FOR I = 1 TO 3000 : NEXT I
140  LOCATE 24
150  COLOR 16,7
160  FOR I = 1 TO 16
170     FOR J = 1 TO 8
180        PRINT "GO WRONG! ";
190     NEXT J
200     PRINT
210     SOUND 500,5 : SOUND 32767,5 : PRINT
220  NEXT I
230  COLOR 15,0
240  CLS : LOCATE 11,37
250  PRINT "DARN!"
260  FOR I=1 TO 18 : SOUND 50,1 : SOUND 32767,1 : NEXT I
270  LOCATE 15,30
280  COLOR 7,0 : PRINT "Something went wrong!"
290  LOCATE 23
300  END
```

Fig. 10.14

messages is first displayed, thus drawing attention to these messages. Similarly, the two SOUND statements in line 210 create a lower pitch, longer beep that accompanies each of the scrolling lines of text. (The first SOUND statement generates the actual sound. The second SOUND statement produces a pause, i.e., a sound of very high frequency, which is inaudible. Without this pause, the sounds produced by the first SOUND statement would run together during successive passes through the FOR-TO loop, thus producing one long, continuous tone.)

In line 260 we see two consecutive SOUND statements, as in line 210, contained within a FOR-TO loop. Now, however, the only purpose of the FOR-TO loop is to execute these SOUND statements repeatedly. The overall effect is a sequence of short, low-pitched sounds, somewhat like a frog's croak. This croaking sound is intended to enhance the word DARN! which is generated in the previous line.

We again encourage the reader to actually run this program in order to appreciate fully the various visual and sound effects that are created.

10.7 PROGRAM EDITING

Most versions of microcomputer BASIC offer much more flexibility in editing a program than the older, traditional versions of the language. In Microsoft BASIC, for example, a BASIC program can be edited three different ways: with the *EDIT statement,* with the full-screen edit feature and with a conventional text editor or word processor.

The EDIT statement is best suited for making occasional, single-line changes in different parts of a program. To use this statement, the programmer simply types EDIT, followed by the appropriate line number, e.g.,

EDIT 50

This causes the line to be displayed on the monitor, with the cursor situated at the beginning of the line. The desired editing function (i.e., cursor movement, insertion, deletion, etc.) can then be initiated by pressing the appropriate key.

Interested readers are referred to the BASIC programmer's reference manual for their particular computer for more information on this useful feature.

EXAMPLE 10.18

Consider the BASIC program presented in Example 10.17 (see Fig. 10.14). Suppose that line 150 had been incorrectly entered as

150 COLLR 16,7

(Note that COLLR has been entered instead of COLOR.) To make the necessary correction, the programmer simply types

EDIT 150

followed by a carriage return. This causes the original (incorrect) line to appear on the TV monitor, with the cursor situated beneath the 1 in 150, i.e.,

<u>1</u>50 COLLR 16,7

The cursor is then moved to the incorrect character, i.e.,

160 COL<u>L</u>R 16,7

and the L is replaced with an O. Once the change has been made the programmer presses the carriage return, thus replacing the original line with the edited line.

If several successive lines must be changed within the program, it may be more convenient to list the entire block of lines on the screen rather than edit each line individually. Each of the required changes can then be made by moving the cursor to the appropriate place within each line and then retyping as necessary. Pressing the carriage return after each change causes the newly edited line to replace the original line. The cursor will then automatically be positioned at the start of the next line. This is referred to as *full-screen editing.*

EXAMPLE 10.19

Consider once again the BASIC program presented in Example 10.17. Suppose that lines 160 through 220 are known to contain several errors. One way to correct these errors is to edit each line individually, as in the preceding example. It may be easier, however, to type

LIST 160–220

This will produce the following display on the TV monitor (note that each line contains at least one error):

```
160 FUR I=1 TO 16
170     FOR J=1 TO 16
180     PRUNT "GO WRING! ";
190     NEXT I
200     PRNT
210     SOUND 500 : SOUND 32767 : PRINT
220 NEXT J
```

To edit this block of statements, first move the cursor to the appropriate place in line 160, correct the error (FUR should be FOR) and press the carriage return. This will automatically position the cursor at the beginning of line 170. Move the cursor and correct the error in line 170, press the carriage return, then correct the errors in line 180, etc., until all the changes have been made. At the end of this process, lines 160 through 220 will appear as

```
160 FOR I=1 TO 16
170     FOR J=1 TO 8
180     PRINT "GO WRONG! ";
190     NEXT J
200     PRINT
210     SOUND 500,5 : SOUND 32767,5 : PRINT
220 NEXT I
```

Note that it has not been necessary to type EDIT 160, EDIT 170, etc., for each of the lines requiring editing.

A BASIC program can also be edited with a conventional text editor or word processor provided it has first been saved as an ASCII file rather than an encoded, compressed file. To save a program in this manner when using Microsoft BASIC, the user must type

SAVE "*program name*",A

The program can then be recalled by a text editor and altered as necessary.

EXAMPLE 10.20

Suppose that the "GO WRONG!" program presented in Example 10.17 has been entered into the computer for the first time, and it is suspected that numerous typing errors have been made throughout the program. These errors may be corrected using either of the methods described in the last two examples. It may be easier, however, to save the program as an ASCII file and then make the corrections using a text editor.

To store the program as an ASCII file on disk drive B with the name DEMO.BAS, we must type

SAVE "B:DEMO",A

We can then access the text editor, load the file DEMO.BAS from drive B and make the necessary corrections. Once all the corrections have been made, the new file can again be stored on drive B as DEMO.BAS and later executed.

Review Questions

10.1 Determine what operating system is available for the microcomputer at your home or office. Determine how files are designated with this particular operating system.

10.2 What is the difference between a file name and a file extension? What useful purpose is served by a file extension?

10.3 How can a program that is stored on one mass storage device access a file (e.g., a data file) that is stored on another mass storage device?

10.4 Describe the purpose of each of the following microcomputer system commands: AUTO, CLEAR, CONT, DELETE, EDIT, FILES, KILL, LIST, LLIST, LOAD, MERGE, NAME, NEW, RENUM, RUN, SAVE, SYSTEM, TRON, TROFF.

10.5 What system commands are available on the microcomputer that is used at your particular home or office? Compare each of these commands with those listed in Question 10.4.

10.6 How much text (how many rows and columns) can be displayed on a typical microcomputer TV monitor?

10.7 How can the screen be cleared during execution of a BASIC program?

10.8 How can the cursor be positioned while a program is being edited? How can it be positioned during program execution?

10.9 When a BASIC program is being executed, is it possible to move the cursor to a position on the screen that already has text displayed? If so, will this destroy the previous text display?

10.10 What is the difference between the BASIC functions TAB, SPC and SPACE$? When can each function best be used?

10.11 What is meant by vertical scrolling? How can vertical scrolling be controlled?

10.12 Why are time delays useful in a microcomputer BASIC program? How can such time delays be generated?

10.13 Compare the use of finite time delays (i.e., time delays that last for some specified period of time) with untimed delays (interruptions that remain in effect until the user presses a key, etc.). Under what circumstances is each type of time delay most suitable?

10.14 Describe the major groups of keys on a typical microcomputer keyboard. What is the purpose of each major group?

10.15 Does the version of BASIC available on your particular microcomputer include a provision for programming the function keys? If so, how is this accomplished?

10.16 What is a light pen? For what kind of applications is this device useful?

10.17 Does the version of BASIC available on your particular microcomputer include a provision for programming a light pen? If so, how is this accomplished?

10.18 What is a joystick? For what kinds of applications is this device useful?

10.19 Does the version of BASIC available on your particular microcomputer include a provision for programming a joystick? If so, how is this accomplished?

10.20 What is a mouse? For what kinds of applications is this device useful? (Compare with a joystick.)

10.21 Does the version of BASIC available on your particular microcomputer include a provision for programming a mouse? If so, how is this accomplished.

10.22 What is the purpose of the COLOR statement when in the text mode (in contrast to the graphics mode)? What is each parameter used for?

10.23 How is the COLOR statement interpreted by a microcomputer that is equipped with a monochromatic TV monitor?

10.24 What is the purpose of the SCREEN statement? What is each parameter used for when in the text mode?

10.25 Does your particular microcomputer include the COLOR and SCREEN statements? If not, are there other statements that accomplish the same thing?

10.26 What is the purpose of the BEEP statement?

10.27 What is the purpose of the SOUND statement? What is the purpose of each parameter?

10.28 How can the COLOR, BEEP and SOUND statements be used to enhance a BASIC program that is nongraphical in nature?

10.29 Describe the use of the EDIT command. For what types of editing situations is this command well suited?

10.30 Describe how editing can be accomplished using the full-screen editing feature found in many versions of microcomputer BASIC. Under what circumstances is full-screen editing preferable to the repeated use of the EDIT command?

10.31 Does your particular version of microcomputer BASIC include the EDIT command (or a comparable command)? Does it support full-screen editing?

10.32 Compare the use of a text editor with the use of the full-screen editing feature that is available in many versions of microcomputer BASIC. Which is better, and under what circumstances?

10.33 How can a BASIC program be saved as an ASCII file with your particular version of microcomputer BASIC?

Supplementary Problems

The following "problems" are concerned with information gathering rather than actual problem solving. Answer the questions as they apply to your particular version of microcomputer BASIC.

10.34 How are complete file designations written for your particular microcomputer? How are multiple disk drives distinguished from one another?

10.35 What system commands are available in your version of BASIC? How do these system commands differ from the traditional system commands described in Chapter 3?

10.36 What is the maximum number of lines that can be displayed on your TV monitor? What is the maximum number of characters per line?

10.37 How can the screen be cleared within your version of BASIC?

10.38 How can the cursor be positioned when a program is being edited? How can the cursor be positioned within your version of BASIC?

10.39 How can vertical scrolling be initiated and controlled within your version of BASIC?

10.40 How can a timed pause (i.e., a pause for a definite time period) be generated during program execution with your version of BASIC? How can an untimed pause (i.e., a pause for an unspecified time period) be generated?

10.41 How can output be diverted from a TV monitor to a printer? Does this include formatted output?

10.42 Does your microcomputer keyboard include cursor movement keys and/or function keys? If so, are there special BASIC statements that allow these keys to be programmed?

10.43 Does your microcomputer support the use of special peripheral devices, such as a light pen, joystick or mouse? If so, are there special BASIC statements that allow these devices to be programmed?

10.44 Does your microcomputer support colored text? If so, how is the color specified in BASIC? Can the background color be specified separately? Is there a separate border color?

10.45 Is there a special command to "beep" the speaker in your version of BASIC?

10.46 Does your version of BASIC allow various sounds to be generated under program control? If so, what command is used to do this? How are the frequency and the duration specified?

10.47 Does your version of BASIC include a line-editing capability? If so, how is the cursor moved within the line being edited? How are characters inserted and deleted?

Programming Problems

Most of the problems given below require the use of color. If you do not have a color monitor, substitute different monochrome attributes (e.g., high intensity, inverse or flashing text) for different colors.

10.48 Modify the program given in Example 10.14 to include the use of the function keys F1 through F4. Utilize the function keys in the following manner.

F1—select the foreground color
F2—select the background color
F3—select the border color
F4—end the computation

Have the computer "beep" whenever a color is changed.

You may wish to replace the message

Programming with BASIC is lots of fun!

with a message of your own chice.

10.49 Modify the inventory control program (Example 9.31) so that zero inventories appear in a different color (e.g., red) than the other text displayed on the screen.

10.50 Modify the program for generating Fibonacci numbers and searching for primes (Example 9.11) so that the prime numbers appear in a color that is different than the remaining text. Have the computer "beep" whenever a prime number is printed.

10.51 Problem 9.63 asks you to solve Problem 5.55 (computation of student exam scores, including the class average and the deviation of each student's average about the class average) using the enhanced features available in your version of microcomputer BASIC. Solve Problem 9.63, adding the use of color to the display of the output data.

In particular, display all the text in the same color except the class average and the deviation of each student's average about the class average. Display the class average in some other color, and the deviations in a third color.

10.52 Problem 9.55 asks you to rewrite the piglatin generator given in Example 9.28 so that it can accommodate several additional features, such as multiline text, punctuation marks and double-letter sounds.

Rewrite the piglatin generator as indicated in Problem 9.55. In addition, however, add a provision so that the English text (i.e., the input data) is shown on the TV monitor in one color and the piglatin (the corresponding output) is shown in another color. Utilize three different functions keys to change the colors of the English text, the piglatin text and the background, respectively. Have the computer "beep" at the start of each piglatin translation (each new block of output). Utilize a function key to switch the beeping on and off.

10.53 Rewrite the program for calculating depreciation (Example 4.9) so that each column of numbers is shown on the TV monitor in a different color.

Utilize the advanced features offered by your version of microcomputer BASIC wherever it is practical to do so. In particular, use the function keys to select the method used to calculate the depreciation (e.g., use F1 to select straight-line depreciation, F2 to select the double declining balance method, F3 to choose sum-of-the-years'-digits and F4 to end the computation). Display a brief "menu" at the top of the screen, indicating the purpose of each function key. Show the results of each calculation on a separate screen (i.e., clear the screen between calculations).

10.54 Modify the "hello" program given in Example 10.12 (Programming a Light Pen) to include the use of color. Specifically, display the list of languages in one color and the corresponding greeting in another. Have the computer "beep" whenever a greeting is displayed.

10.55 Rewrite the program given in Example 10.12 so that a language can be selected with the function keys rather than a light pen. Include the use of color, as described in Problem 10.54.

10.56 Rewrite the program given in Example 10.12 so that a language can be selected with a joystick rather than a light pen. Include the use of color, as described in Problem 10.54.

10.57 Rewrite the program given in Example 10.12 so that a language can be selected with a mouse rather than a light pen. Include the use of color, as described in Problem 10.54.

10.58 Solve Problem 5.56 (matching countries with their capitals) using the function keys to select either a country or a capital. Be sure to use the enhanced features included in your version of microcomputer BASIC wherever it is practical to do so. Also, utilize color and sound, as described in Problem 10.54.

10.59 Repeat Problem 10.58 using each of the following programmable input devices to select either a country or a capital.

(*a*) Light pen (*b*) Joystick (*c*) Mouse

Be sure to enhance your program through the effective use of color and sound.

10.60 Modify the program given in Example 10.13 (Programming a Joystick) so that the function keys can be used to select different foreground and background colors. Design the program in such a manner that different colored asterisks can be displayed against a uniform background. Allow the background color to be changed at any time.

10.61 Repeat Problem 10.60 using a mouse rather than a joystick.

10.62 Modify the program given in Example 10.16 so that an "up-and-down" siren sound is generated. Include a provision that automatically changes the foreground and background colors each time the siren sound is generated.

10.63 Write a BASIC program that will generate a musical scale in the key of C. Include provisions for selecting an ascending scale, a descending scale or both (i.e., a scale that goes up and then down). Allow the choice to be made by selecting an appropriate function key. Display a "menu" in the upper left portion of the screen indicating the purpose of each available function key. (Your programmer's reference manual may tell you what frequencies to specify in order to generate musical tones.)

10.64 Write a BASIC program that will play a simple melody on your computer's speaker. (Your programmer's reference manual may indicate how musical notes can be generated in BASIC with your particular computer.)

Chapter 11

User-Friendly Programming

The highly interactive microcomputer environment encourages the use of user dialogs in many BASIC programs. These dialogs usually involve some form of question-answer interaction where the computer asks the questions and the user provides the answers. This technique works very well when the questions are simple and few in number. In some applications, however, the questions may be numerous, complicated or repetitious, resulting in possible confusion, frustration or distraction on the part of the user. Data-input errors are much more likely to occur under such conditions. Moreover, the user may conclude that the program is too difficult or too irritating to use comfortably and may therefore avoid its use in the future.

Such problems can often be eliminated by including user-friendly features, such as *prompts, menus, error-checks* and *user verification,* within the program. These features generally simplify the use of the program, though their adoption usually requires more work on the part of the programmer.

We will discuss the use of several user-friendly techniques in this chapter.

11.1 PROMPTS

A *prompt* is a brief instruction or explanation that is generated by the computer prior to a request for information. Thus, a prompt may explain what kind of information is requested or what answers are permitted. The creation of a dialog between the user and the computer is largely accomplished through the intelligent use of such prompts.

We have already encountered the use of prompts in several of the examples presented in earlier chapters of this book. For the most part, however, these prompts have been very brief. We now consider the use of more detailed prompts, accompanied by error-checking routines that test the validity of the input data.

EXAMPLE 11.1

Suppose that a microcomputer BASIC program is required to prompt the user for a student examination score, whose value will be between 0 and 100 percent. The program might include the following INPUT statement, which includes an acceptable prompt.

```
100 INPUT "Exam score (0-100): ",SCORE
```

The prompt tells the user what information is required, and it indicates the range of permissible values. The program does not, however, check to determine if the value actually entered by the user (i.e., the value assigned to SCORE) falls within the required range.

Here is a similar prompt, which is accompanied by an error check for incorrect numerical input values.

```
100 LOCATE 3,1: INPUT "Exam score (0-100): ",SCORE
110 IF SCORE < 0 OR SCORE > 100 THEN BEEP: LOCATE 3,1:
    PRINT SPACE$(30): GOTO 100
```

Now if SCORE is assigned a numerical value which is outside the permissible range, the computer will beep (indicating an error), the previous value will be erased from the screen (actually, the entire line will be written over by 30 blank spaces) and the prompt will appear again in its original location. The program will continue this looping procedure until the user enters an acceptable value for SCORE.

The two statements shown above are adequate for trapping incorrect numerical values, but there is still the possibility that the user might enter a letter or some other nonnumerical character rather than a number. Here is a prompt accompanied by a more comprehensive error check which includes a test for unwanted characters as well as a test for inappropriate numbers.

```
100 LOCATE 3,1: INPUT "Exam score (0-100): ",ANS$
110 IF LEFT$(ANS$,1)="0" THEN SCORE=0: GOTO 130
    ELSE SCORE=VAL(ANS$)
120 IF SCORE <= 0 OR SCORE > 100 THEN BEEP: LOCATE 3,1:
    PRINT SPACE$(30): GOTO 100
130 . . . next statement . . .
```

Now the user's response is initially entered as a string (ANS$) rather than a numerical value. If the user deliberately enters the value 0, the program recognizes this in line 110, assigns a value of 0 to SCORE and then transfers out of the loop to line 130. If anything else is entered, however, the value of ANS$ is converted directly to a numerical value and assigned to SCORE. Any nonnumerical character will automatically be converted to 0, which will now be unacceptable because of the test in line 120. Thus, we are now able to detect unwanted nonnumerical characters as well as numerical values that do not fall within the acceptable range.

EXAMPLE 11.2 Entering Student Examination Scores

In Example 9.29 we encountered a BASIC program that creates a sequential data file containing a group of student examination scores. The actual program, written in Microsoft BASIC for the IBM Personal Computer, is shown in Fig. 9.8.

Let us now alter this program to make it more conversational, and consequently easier to use, by adding some additional prompts with corresponding error checks. The new program is shown in Fig. 11.1. The overall

```
10 '****** CREATE A SEQUENTIAL DATA FILE ******
20 '
30 '****** (ENTER STUDENT EXAMINATION SCORES - VERSION 2) ******
40 '
50 DIM SCORE(12)
60 OPEN "O",1,"SCORES"
70 KEY OFF: CLS: WIDTH 80
80 LOCATE 1,1: INPUT "Course title: ",TITLE$
90 LOCATE 3,1: INPUT "Term: ",TERM$
100 LOCATE 5,1: INPUT "How many exam scores per student? (1-12) ",ANS$
110 N=VAL(ANS$)
120 IF N < 1 OR N > 12 THEN BEEP: LOCATE 5,1: PRINT SPACE$(60): GOTO 100
130 PRINT #1,TITLE$
140 PRINT #1,TERM$
150 COUNT=1
160 '
170 '*** BEGIN LOOP ***
180 '
190 CLS: PRINT "Student number";COUNT
200 LOCATE 3,1: INPUT "Student name (Type END to end data entry): " ,N$
210 IF N$="END" OR N$="end" THEN 330
220 PRINT #1,N$
230 FOR I=1 TO N
240    LOCATE I+4,1: PRINT "Exam number";I;" (0-100): ";: INPUT "",ANS$
250    IF LEFT$(ANS$,1)="0" THEN SCORE(I)=0: GOTO 270 ELSE SCORE(I)=VAL(ANS$)
260    IF SCORE(I) <= 0 OR SCORE(I) > 100 THEN BEEP: LOCATE I+4,1:
       PRINT SPACE$(60): GOTO 240 ELSE PRINT #1,SCORE(I);
270 NEXT I
280 PRINT #1,""
290 COUNT=COUNT+1: GOTO 190
300 '
310 '*** END LOOP ***
320 '
330 CLOSE
340 END
```

Fig. 11.1

program logic is similar to that used in the earlier program. Now, however, we have added prompts and corresponding error checks for each of the numerical input quantities. In particular, notice that lines 100 through 120 prompt for the number of exam scores per student and then check the values that are entered. Similarly, lines 240 through 260 primpt for the value of each exam score and then check the values that are entered. The error-checking procedures are very similar to the prototype presented in Example 11.1.

In addition, this program makes use of a number of screen-control features, and it is more general in the sense that it can accommodate from 1 to 12 examinations per student. Observe the use of a FOR-TO loop (lines 230 to 270) to enter each student's exam scores from the keyboard and write them to the sequential data file.

Figures 11.2 and 11.3 illustrate a typical user dialog that occurs when the program is executed. Figure 11.2 shows the initial dialog that prompts for the course title, the term and the number of exams per student. The user's responses have been underlined.

```
Course title: Comp Sci 141

Term: Fall 1985

How many exam scores per student? (1-12) 5
```

Fig. 11.2

```
Student number 1

Student name (Type END to end data entry): Adams B F

Exam number 1   (0-100): 45
Exam number 2   (0-100): 80
Exam number 3   (0-100): 80
Exam number 4   (0-100): 95
Exam number 5   (0-100): 55
```

Fig. 11.3

Figure 11.3 shows the dialog requesting the name and exam scores of the first student. Again, the user's responses are underlined. This same dialog will be repeated for each successive student until the word END is entered for the student name.

Unfortunately, these figures are not able to illustrate the effects of the error checks. The reader is therefore encouraged to actually run this program and enter incorrect information in order to gain some insight into the way the error checks work.

11.2 MENUS

Some programs require that the user select one of several different options that may be available. Usually, the selection is best accomplished by choosing from a *menu*, i.e., a display which lists all the options, with a distinct number or letter corresponding to each option. The user can then make his or her selection simply by typing the appropriate number or letter. This menu-selection process is very simple and tends to minimize the likelihood of errors.

EXAMPLE 11.3

Suppose that a Microsoft BASIC program, written for the IBM Personal Computer, includes a provision for selecting one of four different background colors. The program might include the following statements, which generate a menu and allow the user to choose accordingly.

```
100 CLS
110 LOCATE 1,1: PRINT "Background Colors:"
120 LOCATE 3,1: PRINT "  1 - Blue"
130 LOCATE 4,1: PRINT "  2 - Green"
140 LOCATE 5,1: PRINT "  3 - Red"
150 LOCATE 6,1: PRINT "  4 - White"
160 LOCATE 8,1: INPUT "Please enter your selection: ",ANS$
170 CHOICE=VAL(ANS$)
180 IF CHOICE < 1 OR CHOICE > 4 THEN BEEP: LOCATE 8,1:
    PRINT SPACE$(60): GOTO 160
190 ON CHOICE GOTO 200,300,400,500
```

When the program is executed, the following menu will appear on the screen:

```
Background Colors:

  1 - Blue
  2 - Green
  3 - Red
  4 - White

Please enter your selection:
```

The user will respond by entering 1, 2, 3 or 4. The program would then select the correct background color, presumably by branching to line 200, 300, 400 or 500 as directed by the ON-GOTO statement in line 190.

Notice that lines 160 through 180 contain a prompt and a corresponding error check that will cause any input value other than 1, 2, 3 or 4 (including nonnumeric characters) to be rejected. Thus, the user is allowed to respond only by entering one of the given menu choices.

In this particular example we could have used letters rather than numbers for menu choices. A logical choice would be to use the first letter of each color. Thus, the menu might appear as follows:

```
Background Colors:

  B - Blue
  G - Green
  R - Red
  W - White

Please enter your selection: _
```

This would work well for this particular group of colors, since each of the colors begins with a different letter. If two or more colors began with the same letter, however (e.g., if black were also available), then the use of first letters as menu items would not be possible. It would, of course, be possible to choose other letters so that each menu item would have a unique letter. This might create confusion on the part of the user, however, and would therefore be undesirable.

Some programs may include both a main menu and one or more submenus. In such situations it may be desirable to use both letters and numbers as menu choices. For example, numbers might be used in the main menu and letters in the submenus. An illustration of this technique is shown in the next example.

EXAMPLE 11.4 Personal Finance (Compound Interest Calculations)

Many problems in consumer economics are concerned with compound interest calculations. In particular, we often wish to know how much money will accumulate in a savings account or how much it will cost to repay a loan for a give time period, a given interest rate and a given frequency of compounding.

In this example we consider three calculations of this type. They are

1. Future value of a given amount of money
2. Future value of a series of monthly deposits
3. Monthly loan repayments

We will develop a single menu-driven program that will allow all of these calculations to be carried out on an IBM Personal Computer. The program will be written in Microsoft BASIC.

The necessary equations for each type of calculation are given below. These equations make use of the following symbols.

P = present sum of money, either deposited or borrowed
F = future accumulation of money
A = uniform monthly deposit or uniform monthly payment
i = annual interest rate (expressed as a decimal)
m = number of interest periods per year
n = number of years

Here are the actual equations.

1. Future value (F) of a given amount of money (P)

   (*a*) Annual, semiannual, quarterly, monthly or daily compounding (m = 1, 2, 4, 12 or 365, respectively)

   $$F = P(1 + i/m)^{mn}$$

   (*b*) Continuous compounding

   $$F = Pe^{in}$$

2. Future value (F) of a series of monthly deposits (A)

   (*a*) Annual, semiannual, quarterly or monthly compounding (m = 1, 2, 4 or 12, respectively)

   $$F = \left(\frac{12A}{m}\right)\left[\frac{(1 + i/m)^{mn} - 1}{i/m}\right]$$

   (*b*) Daily compounding (m = 365)

   $$F = A\left[\frac{(1 + i/m)^{mn} - 1}{(1 + i/m)^{m/12} - 1}\right]$$

   (*c*) Continuous compounding

   $$F = A\left[\frac{e^{in} - 1}{e^{i/12} - 1}\right]$$

3. Monthly repayments (A) of a loan (P)

   (*a*) Annual, semiannual, quarterly or monthly compounding (m = 1, 2, 4 or 12, respectively)

   $$A = \left(\frac{mP}{12}\right)\left[\frac{(i/m)(1 + i/m)^{mn}}{(1 + i/m)^{mn} - 1}\right]$$

   (*b*) Daily compounding

   $$A = P(1 + i/m)\left[\frac{(1 + i/m)^{m/12} - 1}{(1 + i/m)^{mn} - 1}\right]$$

   (*c*) Continuous compounding

   $$A = Pe^{in}\left[\frac{e^{i/12} - 1}{e^{in} - 1}\right]$$

Design of the Program

Let us design a program that is conversational in nature and as general as possible, within practical limits. The program will begin by displaying a main menu which allows the user to select one of the three different types of calculations or to end the computation. The screen will then clear and the program will prompt for the required input data. A submenu will be used to assist the user in specifying the frequency of compounding.

Once the data have been supplied, the appropriate calculations will be carried out and the answer displayed at the bottom of the screen. The screen will remain unchanged until the user presses any key, which will then return the user to the main menu.

The Program Outline

In order to outline the program, let us define the following variables.

P = present sum of money

F = future accumulation of money

A = uniform monthly deposit (or payment)

RATE = annual interest rate, expressed as a *percentage*

I = annual interest rate, expressed as a *fraction* (note that I = 0.01*RATE)

M% = number of interest periods per year (e.g., M% = 12 for monthly compounding)

N% = number of years

CHOICE = a variable which determines which type of calculation will be carried out (CHOICE will be assigned a value of 1, 2, 3 or 4)

F$ = a variable which determines the frequency of compounding (F$ will be assigned "A", "S", "Q", "M", "D" or "C" for annual, semiannual, quarterly, monthly, daily or continuous compounding)

The program will proceed as follows.

1. Display the main menu.
2. Read a value for CHOICE.
3. Branch to an appropriate subroutine, as determined by the value assigned to CHOICE.

(*a*) CHOICE = 1 (future value of a given amount of money).

(i) Read a value for P.

(ii) Read values for N% and RATE and calculate a value for I using the formula I = .01*RATE.

(iii) Display the submenu.

(iv) Read a value for F$.

(v) Assign an appropriate value to M%.

(vi) Calculate a value for F, using the appropriate formula.

(vii) Display the value of F.

(viii) Return to the main menu.

(*b*) CHOICE = 2 (future value of series of monthly payments).

(i) Read a value for A.

(ii) Read values for N% and RATE and calculate a value for I using the formula I = .01*RATE.

(iii) Display the submenu.

(iv) Read a value for F$.

(v) Assign an appropriate value to M%.

(vi) Calculate a value for F, using the appropriate formula.

(vii) Display the value of F.

(viii) Return to the main menu.

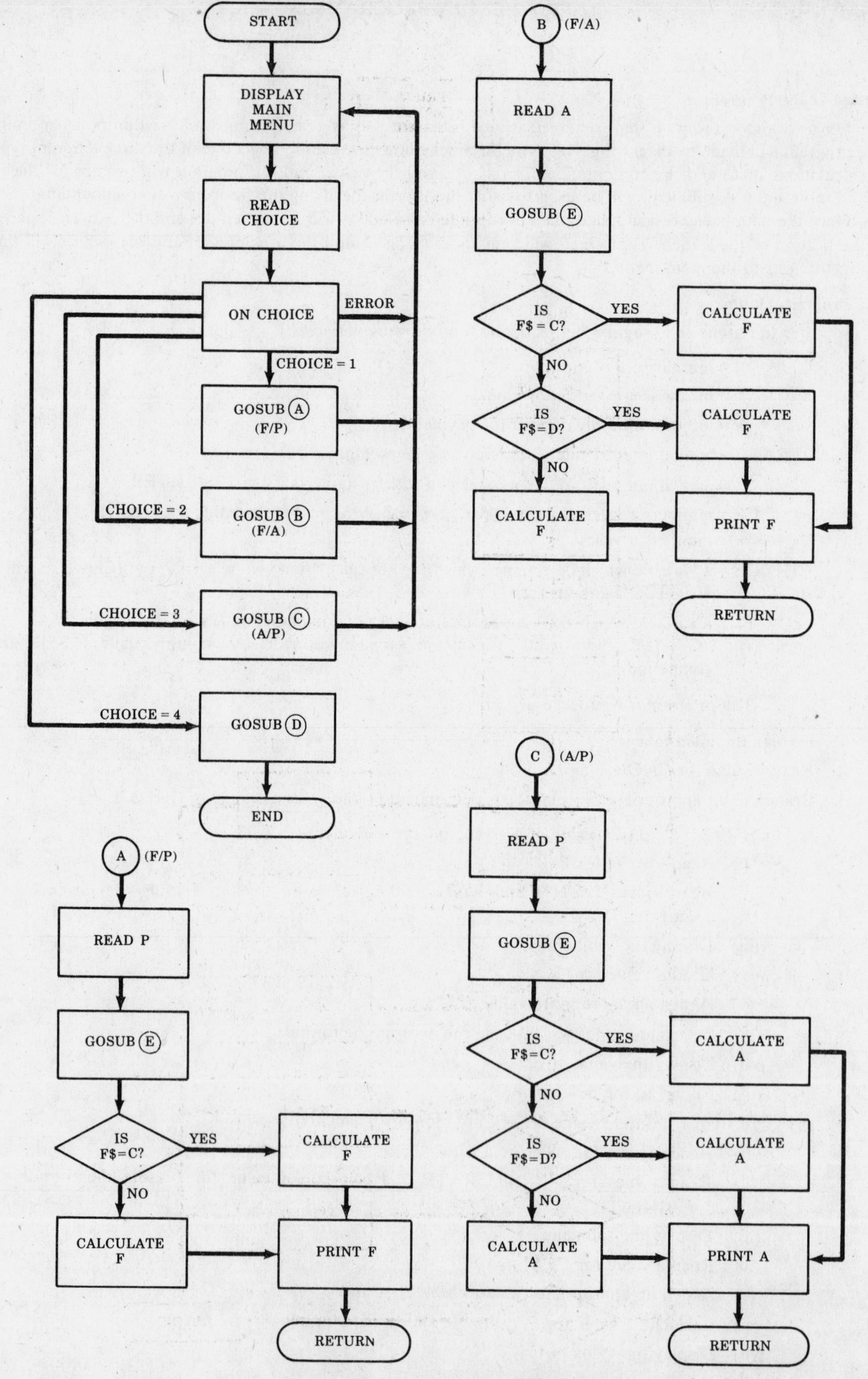

Fig. 11.4 (*Continues on next page*)

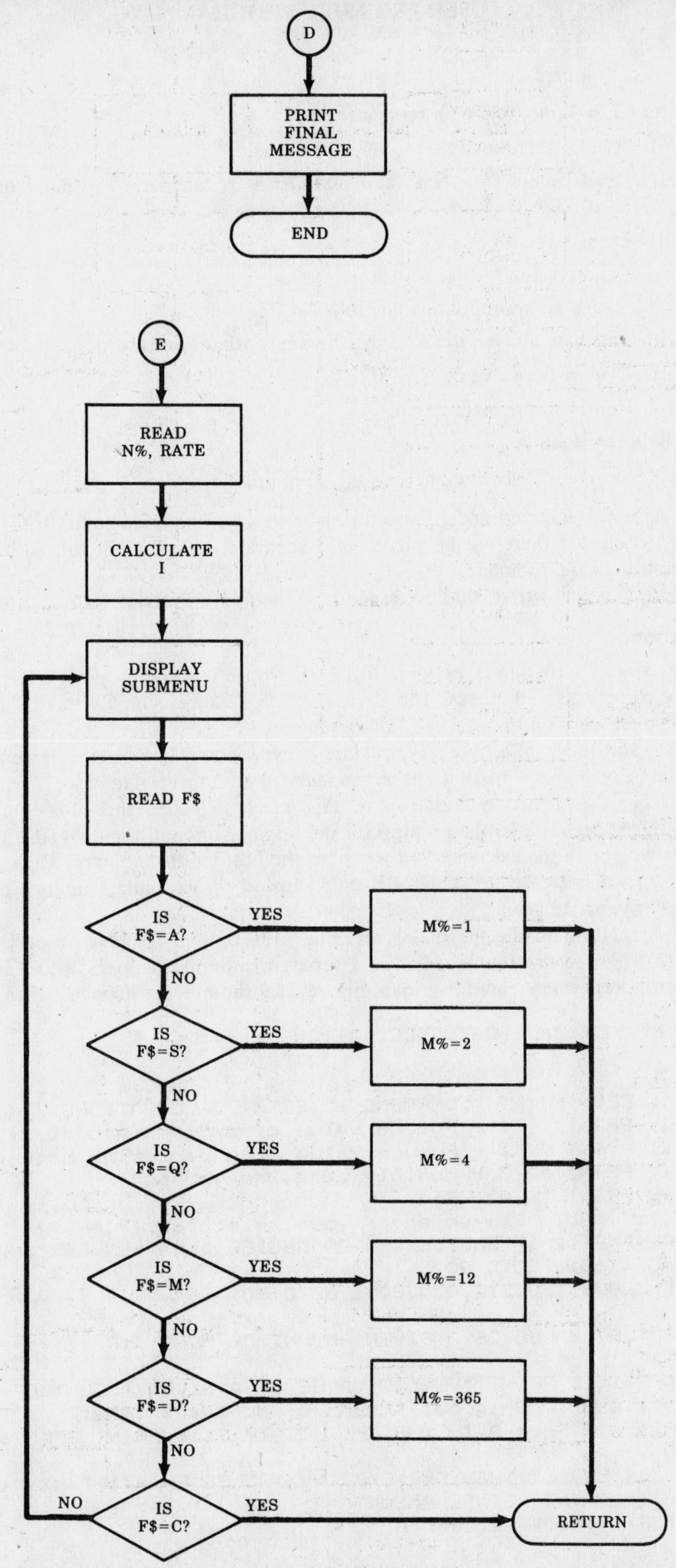

Fig. 11.4 *(continued)*

(*c*) CHOICE = 3 (monthly loan repayments).

(i) Read a value for P.

(ii) Read values for N% and RATE and calculate a value for I using the formula I = .01*RATE.

(iii) Display the submenu.

(iv) Read a value for F$.

(v) Assign an appropriate value to M%.

(vi) Calculate a value for A, using the appropriate formula.

(vii) Display the value of A.

(viii) Return to the main menu.

(*d*) CHOICE = 4 (end).

Display a sign-off message and end the computation.

Notice that steps (ii), (iii), (iv) and (v) are the same in parts 3(*a*), 3(*b*) and 3(*c*). The instructions for this portion of the program will therefore be placed in a separate, independent subroutine. This subroutine will include the generation of the submenu.

Figure 11.4 presents a flowchart that corresponds to the above outline.

The BASIC Program

The complete BASIC program is shown in Fig. 11.5. Notice that the program is somewhat long, due to the use of prompts, error checks and menus. These user-friendly features simplify the use of the program, though they require additional work on the part of the programmer.

Figures 11.6(*a*) and 11.6(*b*) illustrate a typical interactive session. In Fig. 11.6(*a*) we see the main menu with the user's selection (shown underlined) of option number 1 (i.e., future value of a given amount of money). The dialog resulting from this selection is shown in Fig. 11.6(*b*). Notice the submenu, titled "Frequency of Compounding," which appears after the prompts for the original amount of money, the number of years and the interest rate. Finally, we see the calculated answer near the bottom of the figure. Thus, we see that an original investment of $1000 will increase to $3262.04 if it is allowed to accumulate interest at 12 percent per year, compounded quarterly, for 10 years.

Figures 11.7 and 11.8 illustrate the dialog resulting from options 2 and 3, respectively. Specifically, Figs. 11.7(*a*) and 11.7(*b*) refer to the future value of a series of monthly deposits, and Figs. 11.8(*a*) and 11.8(*b*) illustrate the monthly repayment rate for a loan. Figure 11.9 shows what happens when the program is ended.

```
10 '****** COMPOUND INTEREST CALCULATIONS ******
20 '
30 KEY OFF: CLS
40 LOCATE 1,1: CLS: PRINT "COMPOUND INTEREST CALCULATIONS"
50 LOCATE 3,1: PRINT "  1 - Future Value of a Given Amount of Money"
60 LOCATE 5,1: PRINT "  2 - Future Value of a Series of Monthly Deposits"
70 LOCATE 7,1: PRINT "  3 - Monthly Loan Repayments"
80 LOCATE 9,1: PRINT "  4 - End"
90 LOCATE 11,1: INPUT "Please enter your selection: ",ANS$
100 CHOICE=VAL(ANS$): IF CHOICE < 1 OR CHOICE > 4 THEN BEEP: LOCATE 11,1:
    PRINT SPACE$(60): GOTO 90
110 ON CHOICE GOSUB 150,270,420,840: GOTO 30
120 '
130 '****** FUTURE VALUE OF A GIVEN AMOUNT OF MONEY (F/P) ******
140 '
150 CLS: LOCATE 1,1: PRINT "FUTURE VALUE OF A GIVEN AMOUNT OF MONEY"
160 LOCATE 3,1: INPUT "Original Amount of Money: $",ANS$
170 P=VAL(ANS$): IF P <= 0 THEN BEEP: LOCATE 3,1: PRINT SPACE$(60): GOTO 160
180 GOSUB 570
190 IF F$="C" OR F$="c" THEN F=P*EXP(I*N%) ELSE F=P*(1+I/M%)^(M%*N%)
200 LOCATE 18,1: PRINT "FINAL AMOUNT =";
210 PRINT USING "$$########,.##";F
220 GOSUB 790
230 RETURN
```

Fig. 11.5 (*Program continues on next page*)

```
240 '
250 '****** FUTURE VALUE OF A SERIES OF CONSTANT MONTHLY DEPOSITS (F/A) ******
260 '
270 CLS: LOCATE 1,1: PRINT "FUTURE VALUE OF A SERIES OF MONTHLY DEPOSITS"
280 LOCATE 3,1: INPUT "Amount of Each Payment: $",ANS$
290 A=VAL(ANS$): IF A <= 0 THEN BEEP: LOCATE 3,1: PRINT SPACE$(60): GOTO 280
300 GOSUB 570
310 IF F$="C" OR F$="c" THEN F=A*(EXP(I*N%)-1)/(EXP(I/12)-1): GOTO 350
320 FACTOR=(1+I/M%)^(M%*N%)-1
330 IF F$="D" OR F$="d" THEN F=A*FACTOR/((1+I/M%)^(M%/12)-1): GOTO 350
340 F=(12*A/M%)*FACTOR/(I/M%)
350 LOCATE 18,1: PRINT "FINAL AMOUNT =";
360 PRINT USING "$$########,.##";F
370 GOSUB 790
380 RETURN
390 '
400 '****** MONTHLY LOAN REPAYMENTS (A/P) ******
410 '
420 CLS: LOCATE 1,1: PRINT "MONTHLY LOAN REPAYMENTS"
430 LOCATE 3,1: INPUT "Amount of Money Borrowed: $",ANS$
440 P=VAL(ANS$): IF P <= 0 THEN BEEP: LOCATE 3,1: PRINT SPACE$(60): GOTO 430
450 GOSUB 570
460 IF F$="C" OR F$="c" THEN A=P*(EXP(I*N%)*(EXP(I/12)-1))/(EXP(I*N%)-1):
    GOTO 500
470 FACTOR=(1+I/M%)^(M%*N%)-1
480 IF F$="D" OR F$="d" THEN A=P*(FACTOR+1)*((1+I/M%)^(M%/12)-1)/FACTOR:
    GOTO 500
490 A=(M%*P/12)*(I/M%)*(FACTOR+1)/FACTOR
500 LOCATE 18,1: PRINT "MONTHLY PAYMENT =";
510 PRINT USING "$$#######,.##";A
520 GOSUB 790
530 RETURN
540 '
550 '****** OBTAIN INPUT INFORMATION ******
560 '
570 LOCATE 4,1: INPUT "Number of Years: ",ANS$
580 N%=VAL(ANS$): IF N% <= 0 THEN BEEP: LOCATE 4,1: PRINT SPACE$(60): GOTO 570
590 LOCATE 5,1: INPUT "Annual Interest Rate (Percent): ",ANS$
600 I=.01*VAL(ANS$): IF I <= 0 THEN BEEP: LOCATE 5,1: PRINT SPACE$(60): GOTO 590


610 LOCATE 7,1: PRINT "Frequency of Compounding:"
620 LOCATE 9,1: PRINT "  A - Annual"
630 LOCATE 10,1: PRINT "  S - Semiannual"
640 LOCATE 11,1: PRINT "  Q - Quarterly"
650 LOCATE 12,1: PRINT "  M - Monthly"
660 LOCATE 13,1: PRINT "  D - Daily"
670 LOCATE 14,1: PRINT "  C - Continuous"
680 LOCATE 16,1: INPUT "Please enter your selection: ",F$
690 IF F$="A" OR F$="a" THEN M%=1: RETURN
700 IF F$="S" OR F$="s" THEN M%=2: RETURN
710 IF F$="Q" OR F$="q" THEN M%=4: RETURN
720 IF F$="M" OR F$="m" THEN M%=12: RETURN
730 IF F$="D" OR F$="d" THEN M%=365: RETURN
740 IF F$="C" OR F$="c" THEN RETURN
750 BEEP: LOCATE 16,1: PRINT SPACE$(60): GOTO 680
760 '
770 '****** PAUSE ******
780 '
790 LOCATE 22,1: PRINT "(Press any key to continue)";
800 ANS$=INPUT$(1): RETURN
810 '
820 '****** SIGNOFF ******
830 '
840 LOCATE 13,1: PRINT "GOODBYE, COME AGAIN!"
850 END
```

Fig. 11.5 *(continued)*

```
COMPOUND INTEREST CALCULATIONS

   1 - Future Value of a Given Amount of Money

   2 - Future Value of a Series of Monthly Deposits

   3 - Monthly Loan Repayments

   4 - End

Please enter your selection: 1
```

(*a*)

```
FUTURE VALUE OF A GIVEN AMOUNT OF MONEY

Original Amount of Money: $1000
Number of Years: 10
Annual Interest Rate (Percent): 12

Frequency of Compounding:

  A - Annual
  S - Semiannual
  Q - Quarterly
  M - Monthly
  D - Daily
  C - Continuous

Please enter your selection: Q

FINAL AMOUNT =    $3,262.04

(Press any key to continue)
```

(*b*)

Fig. 11.6

```
COMPOUND INTEREST CALCULATIONS

   1 - Future Value of a Given Amount of Money

   2 - Future Value of a Series of Monthly Deposits

   3 - Monthly Loan Repayments

   4 - End

Please enter your selection: 2
```

(*a*)

```
FUTURE VALUE OF A SERIES OF MONTHLY DEPOSITS

Amount of Each Payment: $100
Number of Years: 7
Annual Interest Rate (Percent): 8.5

Frequency of Compounding:

  A - Annual
  S - Semiannual
  Q - Quarterly
  M - Monthly
  D - Daily
  C - Continuous

Please enter your selection: M

FINAL AMOUNT =   $11,424.37

(Press any key to continue)
```

(*b*)

Fig. 11.7

```
COMPOUND INTEREST CALCULATIONS

  1 - Future Value of a Given Amount of Money

  2 - Future Value of a Series of Monthly Deposits

  3 - Monthly Loan Repayments

  4 - End

Please enter your selection: 3
```

(*a*)

```
MONTHLY LOAN REPAYMENTS

Amount of Money Borrowed: $5000
Number of Years: 5
Annual Interest Rate (Percent): 12.5

Frequency of Compounding:

  A - Annual
  S - Semiannual
  Q - Quarterly
  M - Monthly
  D - Daily
  C - Continuous

Please enter your selection: C

MONTHLY PAYMENT =      $112.66

(Press any key to continue)
```

(*b*)

Fig. 11.8

```
COMPOUND INTEREST CALCULATIONS

  1 - Future Value of a Given Amount of Money

  2 - Future Value of a Series of Monthly Deposits

  3 - Monthly Loan Repayments

  4 - End

Please enter your selection: 4

GOODBYE, COME AGAIN!
```

Fig. 11.9

11.3 ERROR CHECKING

We have already seen several examples of error checking in the earlier sections of this chapter. All these error checks were concerned with data-input errors. There are, however, other types of errors that can occur within a BASIC program. These include syntax errors (e.g., FOR without NEXT, subscript out of range, missing operand, etc.), run-time errors (e.g., division by zero, numerical overflow), disk I/O errors (e.g., file not found, disk full) and hardware errors (e.g., device unavailable, printer out of paper).

Most versions of microcomputer BASIC include special error-trapping statements that can detect specific errors when they occur and then transfer control to an error correction routine within the program. This is usually accomplished by means of the ON ERROR–GOTO statement (e.g., ON ERROR GOTO 200), as described in Section 9.2.

The errors themselves are usually encoded in a numerical format (e.g., error number 11 might be *division by zero*). It is then possible to write an IF statement that takes remedial action once a specific type of error has been detected (e.g., IF ERR=11 THEN PRINT "Division by zero").

EXAMPLE 11.5

Presented below is a portion of a Microsoft BASIC program that enters two numbers, calculates the square root of their difference and displays the result. The routine is error-trapped to generate a message and then repeat the data entry routine if the difference in the numbers is negative.

```
200 ON ERROR GOTO 500
210 INPUT "X=";X
220 INPUT "Y=";Y
230 Z=SQR(X-Y)
240 PRINT "Z=";Z
250 ON ERROR GOTO 0
    .
    .
    .
500 IF ERR=5 AND ERL=230 THEN PRINT "Attempt to take square root
    of negative number": PRINT "Please enter data again": PRINT:
    RESUME 210
```

The ON ERROR statement in line 200 causes a transfer of control to line 500 if an error (*any* error) is detected during program execution. The IF-THEN statement in line 500 tests for error number 5 (illegal function call) in line 230. If an error is detected, an error message is generated and control is transferred back to line 210, thus allowing the user to reenter the data.

Note that the last transfer of control is carried out via a RESUME statement rather than GOTO. RESUME is a special statement that is intended for use at the conclusion of an error-trapping routine (see Section 9.2).

Finally, notice the ON ERROR–GOTO 0 statement in line 250. This statement disables any subsequent error checking within the program. In other words, the ON ERROR GOTO 0 statement effectively negates any error trap that may have been defined previously.

EXAMPLE 11.6 Processing Student Examination Scores

Figure 11.10 contains a Microsoft BASIC program for processing student examination scores using a sequential data file. This program is a variation of the program presented in Example 9.30 (see Fig. 9.10).

The current program differs from the earlier program in several respects. For example, the current program allows the user to specify whatever file name he or she may wish. (In the earlier version, the file name was required to be SCORES.) Thus, line 80 prompts the user for the file name, and line 350 causes the newly updated file (UPDATE) to be assigned this name at the conclusion of the program.

In addition, the current program contains several prompts and error checks that were not present in the earlier version. Line 160, for example, indicates the permissible values for the exam number, and line 250 indicates the permissible values for each exam score. These input statements are accompanied by error checks (line 170, and lines 260 and 270) so that the input values supplied by the user fall within the indicated ranges.

The error checks are similar to those shown in Example 11.2 (Fig. 11.1). Now, however, we make use of the statement LOCATE CSRLIN-1,1 in several places. This statement repositions the cursor to the beginning of the previous line. (Note that lines 160 and 250 do not include LOCATE statements; hence any repositioning of the cursor must be included within the error-checking routines.)

```
10 '****** PROGRAM TO PROCESS STUDENT EXAMINATION SCORES ******
20 '******          USING SEQUENTIAL DATA FILES          ******
30 '
40 KEY OFF: CLS
50 DIM C(15)
60 PRINT "UPDATING STUDENT EXAMINATION SCORES"
70 ON ERROR GOTO 390
80 PRINT: INPUT "File name: ",F$
90 OPEN "I",1,F$
100 OPEN "O",2,"UPDATE"
110 ON ERROR GOTO 0
120 INPUT #1,TITLE$
130 INPUT #1,TERM$
140 PRINT: PRINT "Course title: ";TITLE$;SPC(10);"Term: ";TERM$
150 PRINT #2,TITLE$: PRINT #2,TERM$
160 PRINT: INPUT "Exam number (1-15): ",ANS$: K=VAL(ANS$)
170 IF K < 1 OR K > 15 THEN BEEP: LOCATE CSRLIN-1,1: PRINT SPACE$(40):
    LOCATE CSRLIN-2,1: GOTO 160
180 PRINT: INPUT "Calculate averages (Y/N) ";ANS$
190 '
200 '*** BEGIN LOOP ***
210 '
220 PRINT: INPUT #1,N$
230 FOR I=1 TO K-1: INPUT #1,C(I): NEXT I
240 PRINT N$,
250 INPUT "New score (0-100): ",ANS$
260 IF LEFT$(ANS$,1)="0" THEN C(K)=0: GOTO 280 ELSE C(K)=VAL(ANS$)
270 IF C(K) <= 0 OR C(K) > 100 THEN BEEP: LOCATE CSRLIN-1,1: PRINT SPACE$(40):
    LOCATE CSRLIN-1,1: GOTO 240
280 PRINT #2,N$
290 SUM=0
300 FOR I=1 TO K: PRINT #2,C(I);: SUM=SUM+C(I): NEXT I
310 IF ANS$="N" OR ANS$="n" THEN 350
320 AVG=SUM/K
330 PRINT "Average =";AVG
340 PRINT #2,AVG
350 IF NOT EOF(1) THEN 220 ELSE CLOSE: KILL F$: NAME "update" AS F$: END
360 '
370 '*** ERROR TRAP FOR INPUT FILE NAME ***
380 '
390 IF ERR=53 AND ERL=90 THEN PRINT: PRINT "File does not exist": RESUME 80
400 END
```

Fig. 11.10

There is also a check to determine if the specified data file is present on the current diskette (line 390). If the data file is not present, an error message is displayed and the user is again prompted for the name of the data file. Notice that this error check is activated by the ON ERROR statement (line 70), in contrast to the other error checks which check the input data directly. Notice also that this error check ends with a RESUME statement which transfers control back to line 80. And finally, notice that the error check for the file name is deactivated in line 110 by the statement ON ERROR GOTO 0.

The current program also contains a few additional comments and screen displays that are somewhat better organized.

Figure 11.11 shows a typical interactive session, using the same set of input data (student exam scores) as in Example 9.30. Again, the user's responses are underlined.

It is interesting to compare the current interactive session with that shown in Fig. 9.11. In the current session, notice that the user initially specified a nonexistent file name (in the second line). The error trap then generated the message "File does not exist" and again prompted the user for another file name. The remainder of the interactive session is similar to the earlier session, except for the greater separation between the course title and the term and the extended prompts. What is not apparent, however, is the effect of the error checks for the exam number and the individual scores. The user must actually run the current program to see the effects of these features.

```
UPDATING STUDENT EXAMINATION SCORES

File name: score

File does not exist

File name: scores

Course title: Comp Sci 141            Term: Fall 1985

Exam number (1-15): 6

Calculate averages (Y/N) ? y

Adams B F       New score (0-100): 75
Average = 71.66666

Brown P         New score (0-100): 80
Average = 65

Davis R A       New score (0-100): 55
Average = 40

Fisher E K      New score (0-100): 5
Average = 4.166667

Hamilton S P    New score (0-100): 90
Average = 91.66666

Jones J J       New score (0-100): 80
Average = 87.5

Ludwig C W      New score (0-100): 70
Average = 53.33333

Osborne T       New score (0-100): 80
Average = 70

Prince W F      New score (0-100): 100
Average = 82.5

Richards E N    New score (0-100): 70
Average = 55

Smith M C       New score (0-100): 75
Average = 67.5

Thomas B A      New score (0-100): 10
Average = 21.66667

Wolfe H         New score (0-100): 95
Average = 64.16666

Zorba D R       New score (0-100): 95
Average = 78.33334
```

Fig. 11.11

11.4 USER VERIFICATION

Everyone makes an occasional mistake when entering input data. Usually, the consequences of erroneous input data are not serious. The user can simply run the program with the bad data, then reenter the input data correctly and run the program again.

Sometimes, however, the consequences of data-input errors are more severe. This is especially true of programs involving lengthy data entry procedures, programs that require extensive execution time or programs that store data in data files. With such programs, the need to reenter the data and rerun the problem can be both time-consuming and annoying.

Data input errors can often be detected and then corrected prior to program execution simply by requiring that the validity of the current data be verified. This is generally accomplished by prompting for some subset of the required input parameters (e.g., enough to fill the screen comfortably) and then asking if these input values are correct. If the user indicates that the data are correct, the program prompts for any additional data that may be required or else it proceeds to process the data. If the user indicates that the data are not correct, however, then the user is asked to reenter the data and again verify its correctness. This procedure continues until all the required data have been entered and verified.

EXAMPLE 11.7 Storing Laboratory Data

A research chemist has written a Microsoft BASIC program for storing the data taken from numerous coal samples in a random data file. For each coal sample, the following information must be entered into the computer.

1. Sample number (an integer ranging from 1 to 9999)
2. Rank of the coal (There are only four permissible entries: anthracite, bituminous, lignite and peat. A single letter, i.e., A, B, L or P, will therefore be sufficient to characterize the rank of the coal.)
3. Percentage "ash" (i.e., noncombustible impurities)
4. Percentage sulfur
5. Percentage moisture
6. Heating value (calories per gram)

For each sample, the data entry procedure will begin with the heading

```
COAL SAMPLE DATABASE SYSTEM
```

appearing at the top of an otherwise empty screen. Individual prompts will then appear, one at a time, for each of the required data items. After all the data have been entered, the user will be asked to verify whether or not the data are correct. (Presumably, the user will examine the information that has just been entered and is still displayed on the screen.)

If the data have been entered correctly, the user will respond by pressing either Y (uppercase or lowercase) or the carriage return. This will cause the input data to be stored in a random data file called SAMPLES, with the sample number interpreted as the record number. The program will then move on to the next coal sample.

If the data have been entered incorrectly, however, the user will respond by pressing N (or any other character other than Y or a carriage return) when asked to verify. The screen will then clear, and the message

```
Please reenter the data for this sample
```

will appear. The series of prompts will then be repeated, thus allowing the user to reenter (and again verify) the data for the same sample. This entire procedure will continue until the user verifies that the current data are correct.

The actual BASIC program is shown in Fig. 11.12. Line 50 removes any previous display of function key definitions and clears the screen, and line 60 opens the random data file. (Notice that the OPEN statement is written in a somewhat different form than in the previous examples that made use of random data files.) The composition of each record is defined in line 70. The screen heading is then generated in line 80.

Lines 100 through 120 prompt for the sample number. The prompt instructs the user to enter a value of 0 in

```
10 '****** COAL SAMPLE DATABASE SYSTEM ******
20 '
30 '**** READ INPUT DATA FOR EACH SAMPLE ****
40 '
50 KEY OFF: CLS
60 OPEN "SAMPLES" AS #1 LEN=20
70 FIELD #1, 1 AS R$, 4 AS A$, 4 AS S$, 4 AS M$, 7 AS C$
80 LOCATE 1,1: PRINT "COAL SAMPLE DATABASE SYSTEM"
90 '
100 LOCATE 3,1: INPUT "Sample number (0 to end, otherwise 1-9999): ",ANS$
110 IF LEFT$(ANS$,1)="0" THEN END ELSE N=VAL(ANS$)
120 IF N <= 0 OR N > 9999 THEN BEEP: LOCATE 3,1: PRINT SPACE$(78): GOTO 100
130 '
140 LOCATE 5,1: INPUT "Rank:  A)nthracite, B)ituminous, L)ignite, P)eat: ",ANS$
150 IF ANS$="A" OR ANS$="a" THEN RANK$="A": GOTO 210
160 IF ANS$="B" OR ANS$="b" THEN RANK$="B": GOTO 210
170 IF ANS$="L" OR ANS$="l" THEN RANK$="L": GOTO 210
180 IF ANS$="P" OR ANS$="p" THEN RANK$="P": GOTO 210
190 BEEP: LOCATE 5,1: PRINT SPACE$(78): GOTO 140
200 '
210 LOCATE 7,1: INPUT "Percent ash (0-100): ",ANS$
220 IF LEFT$(ANS$,1)="0" THEN A=0: GOTO 250 ELSE A=VAL(ANS$)
230 IF A <= 0 OR A > 100 THEN BEEP: LOCATE 7,1: PRINT SPACE$(78): GOTO 210
240 '
250 LOCATE 8,1: INPUT "Percent sulfur (0-100): ",ANS$
260 IF LEFT$(ANS$,1)="0" THEN S=0: GOTO 290 ELSE S=VAL(ANS$)
270 IF S <= 0 OR S > 100 THEN BEEP: LOCATE 8,1: PRINT SPACE$(78): GOTO 250
280 '
290 LOCATE 9,1: INPUT "Percent moisture (0-100): ",ANS$
300 IF LEFT$(ANS$,1)="0" THEN M=0: GOTO 330 ELSE M=VAL(ANS$)
310 IF M <= 0 OR M > 100 THEN BEEP: LOCATE 9,1: PRINT SPACE$(78): GOTO 290
320 '
330 LOCATE 10,1: INPUT "Heating value (cal/gm): ",ANS$
340 IF LEFT$(ANS$,1)="0" THEN C=0: GOTO 370 ELSE C=VAL(ANS$)
350 IF C <= 0 THEN BEEP: LOCATE 10,1: PRINT SPACE$(78): GOTO 330
360 '
370 LOCATE 12,1: INPUT "Is everything ok? (Y/N) ",ANS$
380 IF ANS$="Y" OR ANS$="y" OR ANS$="" THEN 440
390 CLS: PRINT "Please reenter the data for this sample"
400 GOTO 100
410 '
420 '**** STORE THE DATA ****
430 '
440 LSET R$=RANK$
450 LSET A$=MKS$(A): LSET S$=MKS$(S): LSET M$=MKS$(M): LSET C$=MKS$(C)
460 PUT #1, N
470 CLS: GOTO 80
480 END
```

Fig. 11.12

order to end the program and a value between 1 and 9999 otherwise. Lines 110 and 120 comprise an error trap for any input values that do not fall within this range.

Lines 140 through 190 prompt for the rank of the coal. Since there are only four permissible replies (A, B, L or P), this prompt is displayed in the form of a brief menu. Notice that the user may respond with either uppercase or lowercase letters.

Lines 210 through 230 prompt for the percentage of ash. This group of statements includes an error trap for numerical values that fall outside of the indicated range of 0 to 100 percent. Similar prompts are then generated for the percentage of sulfur (lines 250 through 270), the percentage of moisture (lines 290 through 310) and the heating value of the coal, in calories per gram (lines 330 through 350).

Finally, the user verification is generated in line 370. If the user indicates that the data are correct, the input values are stored in the random data file (lines 440 through 460). The screen is then cleared and control is transferred to line 80, thus initiating the data input procedure for the next sample. If the user indicates that the data are not correct, however, then the "Please reenter" message appears (line 390) and control is transferred to line 100. Notice that the input data are not stored unless they are verified as being correct.

```
COAL SAMPLE DATABASE SYSTEM

Sample number (0 to end, otherwise 1-9999): 1330

Rank:  A)nthracite, B)ituminous, L)ignite, P)eat: B

Percent ash (0-100): 14.8
Percent sulfur (0-100): 7.0
Percent moisture (0-100): 4.2
Heating value (cal/gm): 6818

Is everything ok? (Y/N) N
```

(*a*)

```
Please reenter the data for this sample

Sample number (0 to end, otherwise 1-9999): 1330

Rank:  A)nthracite, B)ituminous, L)ignite, P)eat: B

Percent ash (0-100): 14.8
Percent sulfur (0-100): 7.0
Percent moisture (0-100): 4.2
Heating value (cal/gm): 6188

Is everything ok? (Y/N) Y
```

(*b*)

Fig. 11.13

Figure 11.13(*a*) illustrates the data-input procedure for a typical coal sample. The user's responses are underlined, as usual. Note that the user has indicated that these values are not correct. Thus, the program will ignore the current data and repeat the data-input procedure for this sample.

Figure 11.13(*b*) shows the entry of the corrected data. Note that the heating value is different than in Fig. 11.13(*a*). This time the user indicates that the data are correct, causing the data items to be stored in the random data file.

Review Questions

11.1 Summarize the four user-friendly features that are described in this chapter. What is the purpose of each?

11.2 What kind of information is transmitted to the user by a prompt for input data?

11.3 Describe the use of error checking in conjunction with data-input prompts. In what way do these two features complement one another?

11.4 How do menus differ from ordinary prompts? For what kinds of situations are menus well suited?

11.5 Under what conditions might it be desirable to include a main menu and one or more submenus in the same program?

11.6 Describe the use of the ON ERROR GOTO statement and the RESUME statement to carry out error checks. How do these error checks differ from those used in conjunction with data-input prompts?

11.7 Are the ON ERROR GOTO and RESUME statements available on your particular microcomputer? If not, are similar statements available?

11.8 Determine the method used for encoding errors with your particular microcomputer. Are the ERR and ERL functions available?

11.9 Describe the manner in which user verification is carried out. For what kinds of programs is user verification helpful?

Supplementary Problems

The following "problems" are concerned with information gathering rather than actual problem solving. Answer the questions as they apply to your particular version of microcomputer BASIC.

11.10 Section 11.1 describes a type of error checking in which a numerical input quantity is tested to determine whether it falls within an acceptable range of values. This type of error checking makes use of the following Microsoft BASIC statements and functions:

LOCATE	PRINT
INPUT (including a prompt)	SPACE$
IF-THEN	GOTO
BEEP	

Determine whether all these statements are available in your version of microcomputer BASIC and whether they are interpreted in the same manner as in Section 11.1. If not, how can this type of error checking be carried out using your version of microcomputer BASIC?

11.11 Section 11.2 shows how to generate a menu using the following Microsoft BASIC statements and functions:

CLS	IF-THEN
LOCATE	BEEP
PRINT	SPACE$
INPUT	GOTO
ANS$	ON-GOTO
VAL	

Determine whether all these statements are available in your version of microcomputer BASIC and whether they are interpreted in the same manner as in Section 11.2. If not, how can such menus be generated using your version of microcomputer BASIC?

11.12 Section 11.3 describes another type of error checking which includes tests for syntax errors, run-time errors, disk I/O errors and hardware errors. This type of error checking makes use of the following Microsoft BASIC statements and functions:

ON ERROR GOTO	IF-THEN
RESUME	PRINT
ERR	ERL

Determine whether all these statements are available in your version of microcomputer BASIC and whether they are interpreted in the same manner as in Section 11.3. If not, how can this type of error checking be carried out using your version of microcomputer BASIC?

How does this type of error check differ from the error check presented in Section 11.1?

Programming Problems

11.13 Modify the program given in Example 9.11 (generation of Fibonacci numbers and search for primes) so that the prompt includes a display of the permissible range; i.e.,

How many Fibonacci numbers? (1–23)

Add an error check that will test for the following error conditions:

(*a*) Numerical values out of range
(*b*) Nonnumerical characters

11.14 Modify the program given in Example 9.27 (search for a maximum) so that the prompts include displays of the permissible range of each input value. Add appropriate error checks that test for numerical values out of range and for nonnumerical characters.

11.15 Modify the piglatin generator shown in Example 9.28 so that it can either translate English into piglatin or piglatin into English. Include a simple menu that will allow the user to choose either feature.

11.16 Rewrite the program given in Example 4.9 (calculating depreciation) so that it can be used with a TV monitor. Begin each calculation with a menu indicating which types of calculations are available. Generate the input dialog and the calculated output beneath the menu. Clear the screen between calculations. Be sure to include error checking for all the input data, including the menu choices.

11.17 Rewrite the program given in Example 10.12 (multilingual "hello") so that a particular language can be selected via a conventional menu rather than a light pen. Include error checks for the menu choices entered by the user.

11.18 Solve Problem 5.56 (matching countries with their capitals), using a menu to determine whether a capital will be found for a specified country or a country will be found for a specified capital. Use the function keys to make your menu selection. Be sure to include prompts and error checks with the menu selections.

11.19 Write a complete microcomputer BASIC program that will create and utilize a random data file containing names, addresses and telephone numbers, as described in Problem 9.65 (see also Problems 8.40 and 9.64). Include a provision for each of the following features.

(*a*) Add a new record (i.e., a new name, address and telephone number) to the file.
(*b*) Find and display a particular record.
(*c*) Delete a particular record.
(*d*) List the entire file.
(*e*) End the computation.

Use a binary search to find individual records (see Example 8.13).

Have the program generate a menu which will allow the user to select any one of the above features. Be sure to clear the screen and return to this menu after each of the requested features has been carried out. Include appropriate prompts and error checks with each menu selection.

Chapter 12

Microcomputer Graphics

Most microcomputers allow information to be displayed graphically as well as textually. Such displays permit the generation of many different kinds of graphs and drawings. Some microcomputers support multicolored graphical displays, and some allow certain types of graphical objects to be animated. The ability to generate colored, animated displays, enhanced with sound effects, provides the foundation for the wide variety of computer games that have become so popular in recent years.

Virtually all versions of microcomputer BASIC now include special graphics instructions that allow graphics displays to be created easily. For example, individual instructions are available for generating a number of common shapes, such as dots, lines, rectangles, circles and ellipses. These shapes can be used to create a variety of sophisticated graphics displays which may include the use of color and sound. Special instructions are also available to generate animated displays. Moreover, the animation can be controlled by auxiliary input devices, such as joysticks and mice. This chapter illustrates the use of these special BASIC instructions for a number of representative graphics applications.

As in previous chapters, our emphasis will be on the advanced version of Microsoft BASIC (i.e., BASICA) that is implemented on the IBM Personal Computer. Many other microcomputers utilize Microsoft BASIC, however, and therefore support features that are identical to or similar to those described in this chapter.

12.1 GRAPHICS FUNDAMENTALS

We have already seen that text displays are made up of words, which are made up of individual characters (i.e., letters, symbols, etc.). Therefore we can think of characters as the fundamental elements of text displays. A similar situation exists with graphics displays, where the fundamental elements are small dots called *pixels* (*picture elements*). These pixels can be combined to form more complex shapes, just as characters are combined to form words, sentences and paragraphs.

The level of detail (i.e., the *resolution*) of a graphics display is measured in terms of the largest number of horizontal and vertical pixels that can be displayed at any one time. These values will be determined by the computer's hardware. Personal computers typically support graphics displays of 640 (horizontal) by 200 (vertical) pixels, or perhaps 720 by 350 pixels. These values will vary from one computer to another. Higher resolutions (e.g., 1024 by 1024, or 4096 by 4096) can be obtained with more expensive equipment.

The maximum available number of colors is also determined by the computer's hardware. Personal computers usually do not support more than 16 colors, and some support less. A larger number of colors can be obtained with more expensive equipment. If multiple levels of resolution are available, then the higher the resolution, the fewer the colors.

For example, the IBM Personal Computer in its most basic form can support two graphics modes. These are referred to as medium resolution (320 by 200, with four colors) and high resolution (640 by 200, in black and white), respectively. The choice of a mode is accomplished with the *SCREEN statement.* Thus, SCREEN 1 invokes the medium-resolution graphics mode, and SCREEN 2 invokes the high-resolution mode. (Recall also that SCREEN 0 invokes the text mode, as described in Section 10.6.)

If medium-resolution graphics is selected by the SCREEN statement, then the choice of colors can be specified by the *COLOR statement.* This statement is interpreted differently than in the text mode, as described in Section 10.6. In particular, the COLOR statement can include two parameters, the first of which specifies the *background* color (recall that the first parameter specifies foreground color when in the text mode). This can be any integer value between 0 and 15, thus providing a choice of 16 different background colors. The individual colors and their corresponding numerical parameters are

0	black	8	gray
1	blue	9	light blue
2	green	10	light green
3	cyan	11	light cyan
4	red	12	light red
5	magenta	13	light magenta
6	brown	14	yellow
7	white	15	high intensity white

The second parameter in the COLOR statement specifies the "palette." This is a group of three colors which, together with the background color, provides a total of four colors that can be utilized in a graphics display at any one time. Only two different palettes are available. They are designated by the numerical values 0 and 1, respectively. Thus COLOR 0,0 will select a black background (first parameter) and palette 0 (second parameter), whereas COLOR 0,1 will select a black background and palette 1.

The individual colors within each palette are as follows.

Palette 0		*Palette 1*	
0	background color	0	background color
1	green	1	cyan
2	red	2	magenta
3	brown	3	white

The choice of a particular color from within the palette is accomplished with one of the graphics shape statements, e.g., PSET for a point (pixel), LINE for a line or a rectangle and CIRCLE for a circle or an ellipse. We will say more about color selection later in this chapter.

EXAMPLE 12.1

Suppose we wish to generate a medium-resolution graphics display on an IBM Personal Computer, with the colors green, red and brown displayed against a white background. Then our BASIC program must contain the following instructions.

```
10 SCREEN 1 : COLOR 7,0
```

The first instruction (SCREEN 1) specifies medium-resolution graphics (i.e., 320 horizontal pixels, 200 vertical pixels). The second instruction (COLOR 7,0) first specifies white as a background color and then selects palette 0 for the foreground colors. From the above table, we see that this palette comprised the colors red, green and brown.

EXAMPLE 12.2

Now consider a BASIC program that will generate a high-resolution graphics display on the IBM Personal Computer. If the program begins by clearing the screen, the following instructions will be required.

```
10 KEY OFF : CLS
20 SCREEN 2
```

In this situation the COLOR statement is not required, since high-resolution graphics displays (i.e., 640 horizontal pixels, 200 vertical pixels) can only be generated in black and white (i.e., white shapes against a black background).

12.2 POINTS AND LINES

The version of Microsoft BASIC that is used with the IBM Personal Computer includes two statements, *PSET* and *PRESET*, that generate single points at any specified location on the screen and in any color. The first of these, PSET, is intended to be used with a color selected from the current palette when in the medium-resolution graphics mode.

To use this statement, the word PSET must be followed by a pair of parameters, enclosed in parentheses and separated by a comma, e.g., PSET (160,100). These parameters indicate the x and y coordinates of the point. In the medium-resolution mode, the first parameter may range from 0 to 319 and the second parameter from 0 to 199. Point (0,0) represents the upper left corner of the screen, and the point (319,199) represents the lower right corner.

Following the pair of coordinates is an optional third parameter which indicates the color of the point, e.g., PSET (160,100),2. This parameter may range from 0 to 3. In the medium-resolution graphics mode, the value of this parameter will be interpreted as one of the colors from the currently active palette (see Section 12.1). If this last parameter is not explicitly included in the PSET statement, then color number 3 will automatically be selected.

EXAMPLE 12.3

A Microsoft BASIC program, written for the IBM Personal Computer, contains the following statements.

```
10 SCREEN 1 : COLOR 0,1
20 PSET (160,100),2
```

Line 10 specifies medium-resolution graphics, with a black background and color palette number 1 (colors cyan, magenta and white). Line 20 causes a magenta point to be generated at the center of the screen.

EXAMPLE 12.4

Figure 12.1 contains a Microsoft BASIC program, written for the IBM Personal Computer, that generates 100 different points at random locations on the screen. Medium-resolution graphics is used. Each point is displayed in a color selected at random from palette number 1 (except that the background color will not be selected since such a point would be invisible).

```
10 KEY OFF : CLS
20 SCREEN 1 : COLOR 0,1
30 FOR I=1 TO 100
40     X=INT(320*RND)
50     Y=INT(200*RND)
60     CLR=1+INT(3*RND)
70     PSET(X,Y),CLR
80 NEXT I
90 END
```

Fig. 12.1

Line 10 removes any previous display of function key definitions and then clears the screen. Line 20 specifies medium-resolution graphics, with a black background and color palette number 1.

The individual points are generated by the FOR-TO loop that comprises lines 30 through 80. Lines 40 and 50 generate a random pair of coordinates. Line 40 generates a random integer whose value lies between 0 and 319, and line 50 generates a random integer between 0 and 199. The color is selected randomly in line 60, where a random integer is generated whose value lies between 1 and 3. Finally, each point is actually generated in line 70, using the current randomly generated values.

The reader is encouraged to run this program and observe what happens. (The displays that are generated by graphics programs must be seen to be appreciated.)

Now consider the use of the PSET statement in the high-resolution graphics mode. The x and y coordinates may now range from 0 to 639 and 0 to 199, respectively. Thus point (0,0) represents the upper left corner of the screen, and point (639,199) represents the lower right corner.

The color parameter will be interpreted differently than in the medium-resolution mode. An even value (i.e., 0 or 2) will indicate black, and an odd value (i.e., 1 or 3) will indicate white. If the color parameter is not included, then color number 1 (white) will be selected.

EXAMPLE 12.5

A Microsoft BASIC program, written for the IBM Personal Computer, contains the following statements.

```
10 SCREEN 2
20 PSET (320,100)
```

Line 10 specifies high-resolution graphics (with white color against a black background). Line 20 causes a white point to be generated at the center of the screen.

It is interesting to compare this group of statements with the comparable group of statements in Example 12.3. Notice that the present example does not include the COLOR statement. Also, note that a color parameter is not included in the PSET statement.

EXAMPLE 12.6

Figure 12.2 shows a variation of the program presented in Example 12.4. Now, however, the 100 random points are generated in high-resolution graphics. The logic is essentially the same as that presented earlier, with small variations in some of the statements in order to accommodate the high-resolution graphics mode. (Notice the omission of the COLOR statement from the present program.)

```
10 KEY OFF : CLS
20 SCREEN 2
30 FOR I=1 TO 100
40     X=INT(640*RND)
50     Y=INT(200*RND)
70     PSET(X,Y)
80 NEXT I
90 END
```

Fig. 12.2

The reader is encouraged to run this program and compare the graphical display with that generated in Example 12.4.

Let us now turn our attention to PRESET, which is the second of the Microsoft BASIC statements that will generate a single point. This statement is identical to PSET except in the interpretation of the default color (i.e., the color that is automatically selected if the color parameter is not explicitly shown). Whereas the PSET statement will automatically select color number 3 by default, the PRESET statement will automatically select the background color. Thus, in some applications it may be convenient to use PSET to generate points, and PRESET to "erase" the points (by regenerating the points in the background color).

EXAMPLE 12.7

Consider the following statements which are included in a Microsoft BASIC program written for the IBM Personal Computer.

```
10 SCREEN 1 : COLOR 2,0
   :
   :
100 PSET (160,100),2
110 FOR I=1 TO 2000 : NEXT I
120 PRESET (160,100)
```

Line 10 specifies medium-resolution graphics, with a green background and color palette number 0 (colors green, red and brown). Line 100 causes a red point to be generated at the center of the screen. A brief time delay is then generated by the empty FOR-TO loop in line 110. Following this time delay, the red point is erased (i.e., it is regenerated in the background color) in line 120.

EXAMPLE 12.8 Dots in Space

In Fig. 12.3 we see a more comprehensive Microsoft BASIC program for the IBM Personal Computer which draws upon some of the ideas presented in earlier examples. This program generates 200 different points at random locations on the screen, using medium-resolution graphics. The color of each point is selected at random from palette number 1. The points remain visible, however, for only a limited period of time. Eventually, each point disappears (is "erased") and is replaced by a new point, at some other location on the screen. The net effect is a screen which is always filled with colored, randomly spaced points, but which is constantly changing as old points vanish and new ones appear.

```
10 REM *** DOTS ***
20 '
30 SCREEN 1 : COLOR 0,1
40 DIM X(200),Y(200)
50 RANDOMIZE
60 KEY OFF : CLS
70 I=1
80 '
90 '*** begin main loop ***
100 '
110 PRESET(X(I),Y(I))
120 X(I)=INT(320*RND) : Y(I)=INT(200*RND)
130 CLR=1+INT(3*RND)
140 PSET(X(I),Y(I)),CLR
150 I=I+1
160 IF I > 200 THEN I=1
170 GOTO 110
180 END
```

Fig. 12.3

Now let us consider on a line-by-line basis how this program works. Line 30 specifies medium-resolution graphics, with a black background and color palette number 1 (cyan, magenta and white). The DIM statement in line 40 provides for the storage of 200 pairs of coordinates (the coordinates of all points being displayed at any one time). Line 50 initializes the random number generator, and line 60 removes any previous display of function key definitions and clears the screen. The loop is then initialized in line 70.

The main loop consists of lines 110 through 170. Line 110 causes the current point (i.e., the Ith point) to be erased. We then obtain a new set of coordinates for the Ith point in line 120 and a new color in line 130. Line 140 causes this "new" Ith point to be generated.

Note that the new coordinates will be stored in the X and Y arrays. This allows the current point to be recalled and erased at some later time. The erasure will not occur, however, until an additional 199 points have been generated.

Finally, the counter is incremented in line 150 and its value reset to 1, if necessary, in line 160. This procedure allows the loop to continue indefinitely.

We again urge the reader to actually run this program and observe what happens, in order to gain a heightened appreciation for the dynamic effect that is created.

The version of Microsoft BASIC that is available for the IBM Personal Computer includes the *LINE statement*, which allows a straight line to be drawn between two points on the screen. The points can both be specified explicitly, or one of them can be the last point referenced by a previous graphics statement.

In its first form, the word LINE must be followed by two pairs of parameters, where each pair represents the x and y coordinates of one of the points. The coordinates are enclosed in parentheses and separated by a comma. The two points must be separated by a dash (minus sign), e.g., LINE (20,50) – (300,150). The permissible values of the coordinates are dependent upon the particular graphics mode (medium- or high-resolution), as described earlier in this section.

The coordinates can be followed by an optional parameter which indicates the color of the line, e.g., LINE (20,50) – (300,150),1. The value assigned to this parameter may range from 0 to 3. It is interpreted in the same way as the value of the color parameter in the PSET statement.

EXAMPLE 12.9

A Microsoft BASIC program, written for the IBM Personal Computer, contains the following statements.

```
10 SCREEN 1 : COLOR 4,1
20 LINE (20,50) – (300,150),3
```

Line 10 specifies medium-resolution graphics, with a red background and color palette number 1 (colors cyan, magenta and white). Line 20 generates a white diagonal line running from upper left, i.e., point (20,50), to lower right, i.e., point (300,150).

Note that the last parameter could have been omitted from the LINE statement, i.e.,

```
20 LINE (20,50) – (300,150)
```

since color number 3 is automatically selected if a value is not shown explicitly.

The second form of the LINE statement allows the initial pair of coordinates to be omitted; e.g., LINE –(300,150). This statement causes a line to be drawn from the point that was last referenced (in a previous statement) to the point currently specified. This form of the LINE statement is useful when drawing a sequence of interconnected lines.

EXAMPLE 12.10 A Lightning Bolt

Figure 12.4 presents a short Microsoft BASIC program, written for the IBM Personal Computer, that causes a red "lightning bolt" to be displayed on the screen.

```
10 '************ LIGHTNING BOLT ************
20 '
30 KEY OFF : CLS
40 SCREEN 1 : COLOR 0,0
50 LINE (20,20)-(120,80),2 : LINE -(80,80),2
60 LINE -(220,180),2 : LINE -(140,100),2
70 LINE -(190,100),2 : LINE -(110,20),2
80 LINE -(20,20),2
90 END
```

Fig. 12.4

Line 30 clears the screen and line 40 selects medium-resolution graphics with a black background and palette number 0 (green, red and brown). Lines 50 through 80 contain seven LINE statements, thus generating the seven interconnected lines that form the lightning bolt. Notice that both forms of the LINE statement are used. The first form must be used to generate the first line. Once an end point is established, however, the second form of the LINE statement is used to generate the remaining lines.

When the program is executed, the object shown in Fig. 12.5 is generated on the screen, with red lines against a black background.

Some microcomputers support other forms of the LINE statement which allow such features as the specification of a line *relative* to a previous point rather than from one absolute point to another, or the generation of a dashed line. We will not discuss these features, since they are used less often than the features described above. Interested readers are referred to the BASIC programming manuals that accompany their particular computers for additional information on these features.

A single LINE statement can also be used to generate a complete rectangle rather than a single line. We shall see how this is accomplished in Section 12.3.

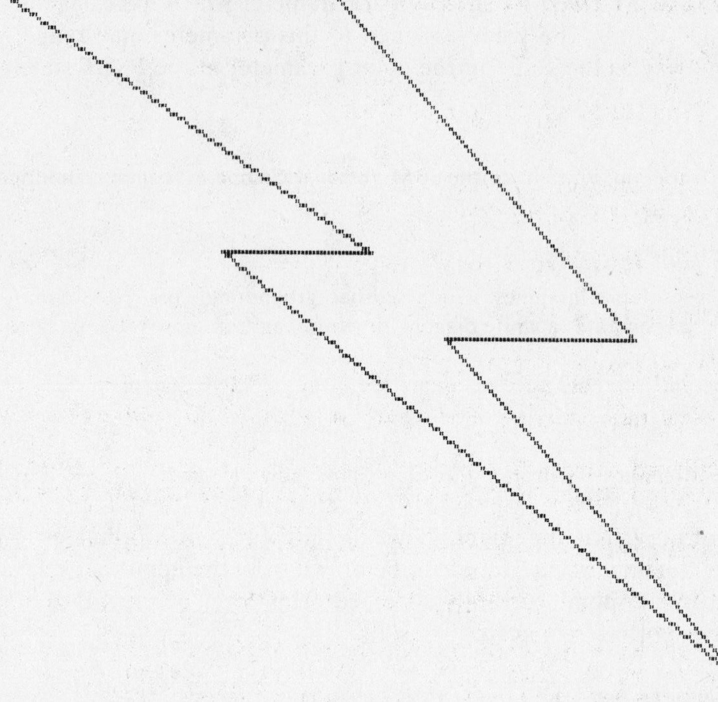

Fig. 12.5

EXAMPLE 12.11 Moving Lines (Kinetic Art)

Let us now turn our attention to a Microsoft BASIC program based upon the same general idea as the program shown in Example 12.8, but which generates displays that are much more dramatic.

We wish to generate a sequence of colored lines, in medium-resolution graphics, located randomly about the screen. However, the successive lines will not be generated independently of one another. Rather, their respective end points will differ by small displacements. Groups of consecutive lines will be displayed in a single color, selected randomly from color palette number 1. Both the magnitudes of the displacements and the color will periodically change as the program continues to execute.

The program will always display the same number of lines on the screen, but each line will eventually be erased and a new line generated. Thus the lines will appear to move around the screen in a random but related pattern, and in different colors. Moreover, interesting moiré patterms will sometimes be created as new lines intersect existing lines. The net effect is one of surprisingly spectacular beauty.

Figure 12.6 contains the actual program. Line 30 invokes medium-resolution graphics and then selects a black background and color palette number 1 (colors cyan, magenta and white). Line 40 defines all the program variables to be integer-type variables, and line 50 provides for the storage of 150 lines (i.e., 150 pairs of end points). The random number generator is initialized in line 60, and the screen is cleared in line 70. Line 80 provides an initial pair of end points (i.e., (X1,Y1) and (X2,Y2), respectively) for the first line.

Line 90 provides initial values for the counters COLORCOUNT, POINTCOUNT and I. The last of these, I, is simply a loop counter which is incremented during each pass through the loop. This counter ranges from 1 to 150 and is reset to 1 when its value exceeds 150. The other two counters require some additional explanation.

COLORCOUNT, for example, is a counter that determines when (which pass through the loop) a different color will be selected from the palette. COLORCOUNT is initially set to zero, in line 90, so that a new, nonzero value will be generated randomly during the first pass through the loop (in line 190). This is accompanied by a new, randomly generated value for the color (also in line 190). During each pass through the loop, COLORCOUNT will be decreased by 1. When COLORCOUNT has again become equal to zero, a new value will be generated and a new color selected, and so on.

Similarly, POINTCOUNT is a counter that determines when different values are selected for altering the displacement of successive lines. POINTCOUNT is initially set to zero, in line 90, so that a new, nonzero value will be generated during the first pass through the loop (in line 200). In addition, a new set of values for DX1,

```
10 REM ************ LINES ************
20 '
30 SCREEN 1: COLOR 0,1
40 DEFINT A-Z
50 DIM X1(150),Y1(150),X2(150),Y2(150)
60 RANDOMIZE
70 KEY OFF: CLS
80 X1=120: Y1=70: X2=200: Y2=130
90 COLORCOUNT=0: POINTCOUNT=0: I=1
100 '
110 '************ BEGIN MAIN LOOP ************
120 '
130 '*** erase old line ***
140 '
150 LINE (X1(I),Y1(I))-(X2(I),Y2(I)),0
160 '
170 '*** generate new values for counters if required ***
180 '
190 IF COLORCOUNT=0 THEN COLORCOUNT=5*(1+INT(10*RND)): CLR=1+INT(3*RND)
200 IF POINTCOUNT=0 THEN POINTCOUNT=5*(1+INT(10*RND)): DX1=INT(9*RND)-4:

    DY1=INT(9*RND)-4: DX2=INT(9*RND)-4: DY2=INT(9*RND)-4
210 '
220 '*** generate end points for new line ***
230 '
240 X1=X1+DX1: IF X1 < 0 OR X1 > 319 THEN X1=X1-2*DX1
250 Y1=Y1+DY1: IF Y1 < 0 OR Y1 > 199 THEN Y1=Y1-2*DY1
260 X2=X2+DX2: IF X2 < 0 OR X2 > 319 THEN X2=X2-2*DX2
270 Y2=Y2+DY2: IF Y2 < 0 OR Y2 > 199 THEN Y2=Y2-2*DY2
280 '
290 '*** display new line, then save end points ***
300 '
310 LINE (X1,Y1)-(X2,Y2),CLR
320 X1(I)=X1: Y1(I)=Y1: X2(I)=X2: Y2(I)=Y2
330 '
340 '*** adjust counters and repeat ***
350 '
360 I=I+1
370 IF I > 150 THEN I=1
380 COLORCOUNT=COLORCOUNT-1: POINTCOUNT=POINTCOUNT-1
390 GOTO 150
400 END
```

Fig. 12.6

DY1, DX2 and DY2 will be determined in line 200; these four parameters determine the displacement of the successive pairs of end points, which in turn define the locations of successive lines. During each pass through the loop, POINTCOUNT will be decreased by 1. When POINTCOUNT again becomes equal to zero, a new value will be generated and a new set of displacements will be determined.

The repeated part of the program ranges from lines 150 to 390. Line 150 causes the line defined by the Ith set of end points, which is currently stored in the array elements X1(I), Y1(I), X2(I) and Y2(I), to be erased. (During the first 150 passes through the loop, however, there will be no such end points.) Line 190 tests to see if COLORCOUNT is equal to zero. If so, a new value, ranging from 5 to 50, is selected randomly and a new value for the color, ranging from 1 to 3, is randomly generated. The color will remain unchanged until COLORCOUNT again becomes equal to zero.

Line 200 contains a similar test for POINTCOUNT. If POINTCOUNT equals zero, a new value, ranging from 5 to 50, is generated randomly and a new set of values is selected for the displacement parameters. Each of these parameters will be assigned a separate value, ranging from -4 to $+4$. The displacement parameters will remain unchanged until POINTCOUNT again becomes equal to zero.

Lines 240 through 270 calculate a new pair of end points for the current line in relation to the end points for the previous line. Each of the new coordinates is checked to determine if its new value is too large or too small (thus causing the end point to be located beyond the bounds of the screen). If so, the value of the coordinate is adjusted accordingly.

Line 310 causes the new line to be displayed, and line 320 caused the end points of this line to be stored in the arrays. This allows the current line to be recalled and erased at some later time. The erasure will not occur, however, until an additional 149 lines have been generated.

Lines 360 through 390 complete the loop by adjusting the values of the parameters and then returning to line 150 to begin another pass. Notice that the loop will continue to execute indefinitely since there is no specified stopping condition.

When the program is executed, patterns similar to that shown in Fig. 12.7 are generated in a display that continuously moves about the screen. The reader should actually observe the program in execution on a color monitor in order to appreciate fully the striking effects that are created.

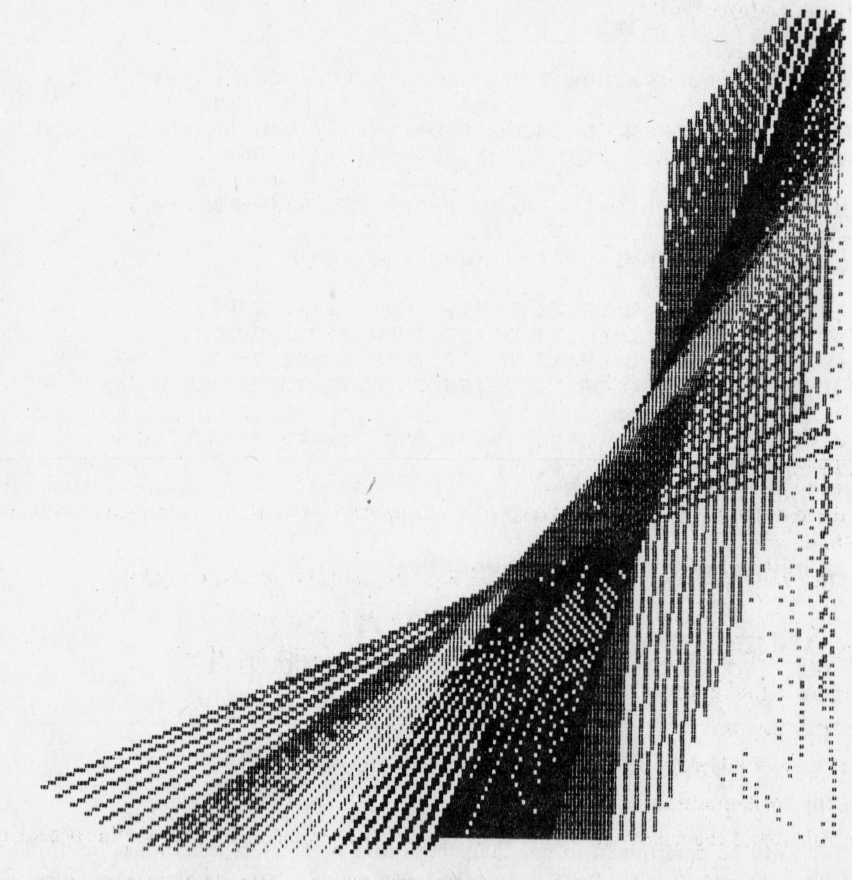

Fig. 12.7

The examples presented in this chapter so far have been oriented toward the use of graphics to produce effects that are entertaining or artistic. However, graphics can also be used very effectively to generate displays that are useful in business and technical applications. This is illustrated in the next example.

EXAMPLE 12.12 Linear Regression with Graphical Display

Let us now consider the problem of fitting a straight line to a given set of data points using the method of least squares, as described in Example 7.22. (This problem is often referred to as *linear regression.**) We will

---

* Actually, the term *linear regression* applies to curve fits involving several different types of curves, including exponential functions, logarithmic functions and polynomials (see Example 7.22).

present a Microsoft BASIC program, written for the IBM Personal Computer, that first carries out the necessary mathematical calculations and then generates a graphical display of the individual data points and the regression line. The graphical display will be scaled so that all the data points are shown and the entire screen is filled, regardless of the magnitudes of the given data. We will use the medium-resolution graphics mode to generate the display.

Essentially, the problem is that of fitting the linear equation

$$y = ax + b$$

to a set of data points $(y_1, x_1), (y_2, x_2), \ldots, (y_M, x_M)$ by minimizing the sum of the square errors, as discussed in Example 7.22. The unknown quantities are the values of the coefficients a and b. These values are obtained using the following formulas.

$$a = (Md_2 - c_1d_1)/(Mc_2 - c_1^2)$$
$$b = (d_1 - ac_1)/M$$

where

$$c_1 = \sum_{i=1}^{M} x_i$$

$$c_2 = \sum_{i=1}^{M} x_i^2$$

$$d_1 = \sum_{i=1}^{M} y_i$$

$$d_2 = \sum_{i=1}^{M} x_iy_i$$

Hence, the overall procedure will be as follows.

1. Read in the data points $(y_1, x_1), (y_2, x_2), \ldots, (y_M, x_M)$ and generate the cumulative sums c_1, c_2, d_1 and d_2, as defined above.
2. Solve for the unknown coefficients a and b, using the formulas presented above.
3. Determine the largest and smallest values of x and y, in preparation for step 4 below.
4. Scale the data points so that they will fill the entire graphics display area.
5. Generate the actual graphical display, in three phases:
   (*a*) Plot the axes.
   (*b*) Plot the individual (scaled) data points.
   (*c*) Plot the corresponding (scaled) regression line.
6. Print the calculated regression equation at the top of the screen above the graphical display.

The actual BASIC program is shown in Fig. 12.8. Lines 30 through 110 clear the screen, generate a program heading, define the required arrays and initialize key variables. The data input routine is provided by lines 150 through 200. Notice that the program allows an unspecified number of data points to be entered. The data entry procedure continues until the user presses the RETURN key when prompted for Y(I), thus entering an empty (null) string.

The slope (a) and the y-intercept (b) of the desired regression line are determined in lines 240 and 250. The individual data points are then scanned to determine the largest and smallest values of Y(I) and X(I), in lines 290 through 350. The actual scaling of the data points is carried out in lines 390 through 420. Lines 430 through 450 generate scaled end points for the calculated regression line.

The actual graphical display is generated in lines 490 through 590. Line 490 invokes medium-resolution graphics, with a black background and color palette number 1 (colors cyan, magenta and white). This is followed by the graphics output commands, which are grouped into three different sections: lines 500 through 520, which generate the axes; lines 540 through 570, which cause the individual data points to be plotted; and line 590, which generates the plot of the calculated regression line. (Notice that each data point is enclosed in a small triangle so that it is clearly visible on the screen. Hence, the PSET and LINE statements are both used.)

```
10 '************** LINEAR REGRESSION WITH GRAPHICAL DISPLAY *************
20 '
30 KEY OFF: CLS
40 WIDTH 80: SCREEN 0: COLOR 7,0
50 DIM X(100),Y(100)
60 LOCATE 1,20: PRINT STRING$(40,"*")
70 LOCATE 2,20: PRINT "*        LINEAR REGRESSION ROUTINE          *"
80 LOCATE 3,20: PRINT "*";TAB(59);"*"
90 LOCATE 4,20: PRINT "*  Press RETURN after last data point  *"
100 LOCATE 5,20: PRINT STRING$(40,"*"): PRINT
110 I=0: C1=0: C2=0: D1=0: D2=0
120 '
130 '**************** ENTER DATA AND GENERATE COEFFICIENTS **************
140 '
150 I=I+1
160 PRINT "Y(";I;") = ";: INPUT "",ANS$
170 IF ANS$="" THEN M=I-1: GOTO 240 ELSE Y(I)=VAL(ANS$)
180 LOCATE CSRLIN-1,20: PRINT "X(";I;")= ";: INPUT "",X(I)
190 C1=C1+X(I): C2=C2+X(I)^2: D1=D1+Y(I): D2=D2+X(I)*Y(I)
200 GOTO 150
210 '
220 '******************* SOLVE FOR UNKNOWN CONSTANTS *******************
230 '
240 A=(M*D2-C1*D1)/(M*C2-C1^2): IF ABS(A) < 1E-08 THEN A=0
250 B=(D1-A*C1)/M: IF ABS(B) < 1E-08 THEN B=0
260 '
270 '**************** FIND LARGEST AND SMALLEST X AND Y ****************
280 '
290 XMAX=-100000!: YMAX=-100000!: XMIN=100000!: YMIN=100000!
300 FOR I=1 TO M
310     IF X(I) > XMAX THEN XMAX = X(I)
320     IF Y(I) > YMAX THEN YMAX = Y(I)
330     IF X(I) < XMIN THEN XMIN = X(I)
340     IF Y(I) < YMIN THEN YMIN = Y(I)
350 NEXT I
360 '
370 '*********************** SCALE THE X'S AND Y'S **********************
380 '
390 FOR I=1 TO M
400     X(I)=29+INT(280*(X(I)-XMIN)/(XMAX-XMIN))
410     Y(I)=189-INT(150*(Y(I)-YMIN)/(YMAX-YMIN))
420 NEXT I
430 X1=29: X2=309
440 Y1=189-INT(150*((A*XMIN+B)-YMIN)/(YMAX-YMIN))
450 Y2=189-INT(150*((A*XMAX+B)-YMIN)/(YMAX-YMIN))
460 '
470 '******************* PLOT THE GRAPHICAL DISPLAY ******************
480 '
490 SCREEN 1,1: COLOR 0,1
500 LINE (19,29)-(19,199): LINE -(319,199)
510 FOR IY=59 TO 179 STEP 20: LINE (19,IY)-(23,IY): NEXT IY
520 FOR IX=39 TO 299 STEP 20: LINE (IX,199)-(IX,195): NEXT IX
530 '
540 FOR I=1 TO M
550     PSET(X(I),Y(I)): LINE (X(I),Y(I)-2)-(X(I)-4,Y(I)+2)
560     LINE -(X(I)+4,Y(I)+2): LINE -(X(I),Y(I)-2)
570 NEXT I
580 '
590 LINE (X1,Y1)-(X2,Y2)
600 '
610 '**************** PRINT THE REGRESSION EQUATION *****************
620 '
630 LOCATE 1,5: PRINT "Y =";A;"* X ";
640 IF B >= 0 THEN PRINT "+";B ELSE PRINT "-";ABS(B)
650 END
```

Fig. 12.8

Finally, the equation for the calculated regression line is displayed at the top of the screen. Lines 630 and 640 generate this display. (Note that this is a *text* display, though it is being generated in the graphics mode.)

Figures 12.9 and 12.10 illustrate the appearance of the screen when the program is executed. The data-entry phase, which occurs in the text mode, is illustrated in Fig. 12.9 for the following set of data. (The input data have been underlined in Fig. 12.9.)

i	y_i	x_i
1	225	10
2	287	20
3	429	30
4	542	40
5	587	50
6	744	60
7	831	70
8	880	80

Notice the position of the flashing cursor following the prompt for Y(9). Since all of the data have been entered at this point, the user simply presses the carriage return in response to the prompt. This ends the data-entry phase.

```
*******************************************
*         LINEAR REGRESSION ROUTINE        *
*                                          *
*  Press RETURN after last data point      *
*******************************************

Y( 1 ) = 225          X( 1 )= 10
Y( 2 ) = 287          X( 2 )= 20
Y( 3 ) = 429          X( 3 )= 30
Y( 4 ) = 542          X( 4 )= 40
Y( 5 ) = 587          X( 5 )= 50
Y( 6 ) = 744          X( 6 )= 60
Y( 7 ) = 831          X( 7 )= 70
Y( 8 ) = 880          X( 8 )= 80
Y( 9 ) = _
```

Fig. 12.9

Figure 12.10 (page 322) shows the corresponding graphical display. We see that the equation for the calculated regression line is

$$y = 9.875x + 121.25$$

The line that is shown passing through the given data points is generated by this equation, though the displayed line has been scaled to fill the screen.

The graphical display illustrates the accuracy with which the calculated regression line represents the given data points.

12.3 SHAPES

Most versions of microcomputer BASIC include statements that allow simple shapes to be drawn. For example, Microsoft BASIC includes a special form of the LINE statement that will generate rectangles and a CIRCLE statement that can generate circles and ellipses. These objects can be filled with an available color if desired. Many interesting graphical effects can be created by combining these objects in different ways.

Consider, for example, the LINE statement discussed in the last section. If the statement ends with the letter B, e.g., LINE (20,50) – (300,150),3,B, then the two pairs of coordinates will be

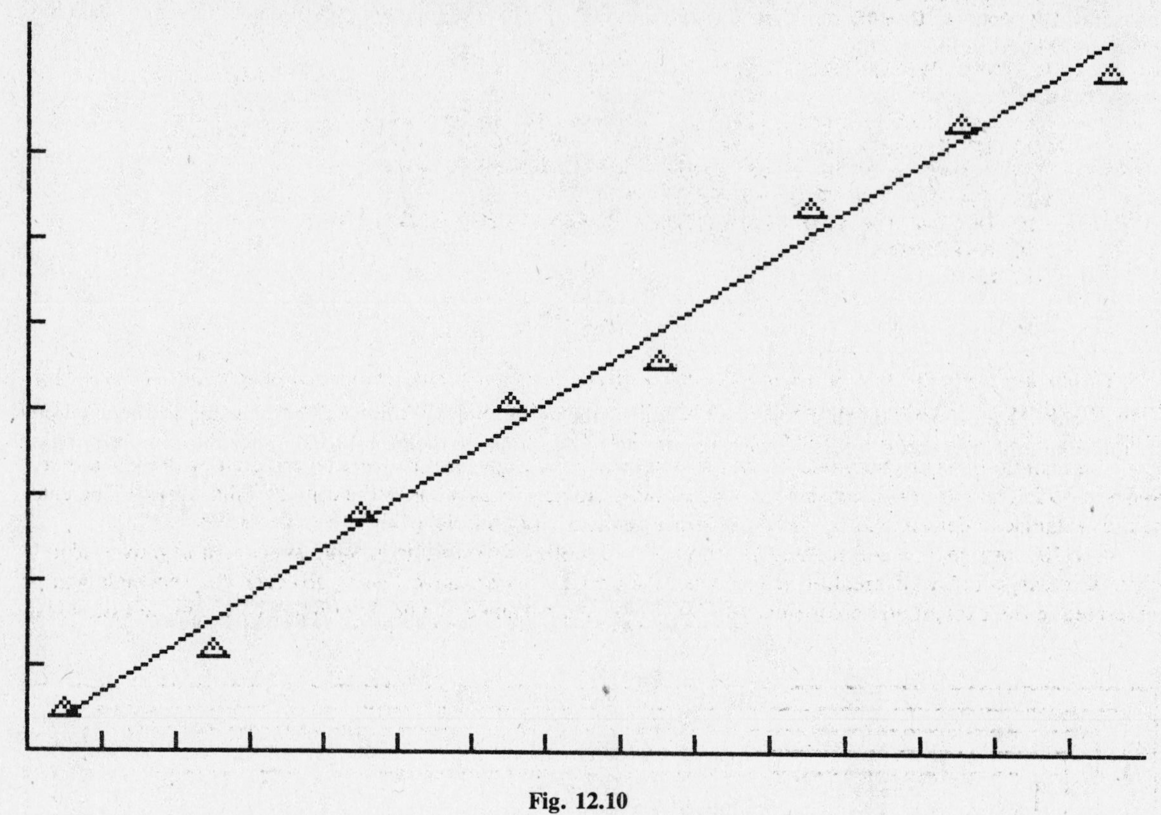

Fig. 12.10

interpreted as the opposite corners of a rectangle (i.e., a "box"). Hence, a rectangle whose diagonal connects these two points will be drawn in the indicated color.

EXAMPLE 12.13

A Microsoft BASIC program, written for the IBM Personal Computer, contains the following statements.

```
10 SCREEN 1 : COLOR 4,1
20 LINE (20,50) - (300,150),3,B
```

Line 10 specifies medium-resolution graphics, with a red background and color palette number 1 (colors cyan, magenta and white). Line 20 generates a white rectangular outline whose diagonal connects points (20,50) and (300,150), against the red background. (Compare with Example 12.9.)

The next example illustrates a complete BASIC program in which the generation of rectangles is utilized more creatively.

EXAMPLE 12.14 Expanding Rectangles

Figure 12.11 contains a complete Microsoft BASIC program, written for the IBM Personal Computer, which causes a sequence of rectangles to move from the center of the screen to the outer edges. Groups of rectangles are generated in alternating foreground and background colors, creating the illusion of "pulses" of rectangular shapes originating at the center of the screen. The program also utilizes sound to enhance the graphical effects.

```
10 '************ EXPANDING RECTANGLES ************
20 '
30 KEY OFF : CLS
40 SCREEN 1 : COLOR 0,1 : C=3
50 P=0 : Q=-45
60 '
70 '*** BEGIN MAIN LOOP ***
80 '
90 LINE (160-1.6*P,100-P)-(160+1.6*P,100+P),C,B
100 IF Q >= 0 THEN LINE (160-1.6*Q,100-Q)-(160+1.6*Q,100+Q),0,B
110 P=P+5 : IF P > 95 THEN P=0 : C=1+INT(3*RND)
120 Q=Q+5 : IF Q > 95 THEN Q=0
130 IF P=0 OR Q=0 THEN SOUND 20+INT(1000*RND),10
140 GOTO 90
150 END
```

Fig. 12.11

Within the program, line 30 clears the screen. Line 40 invokes medium-resolution graphics, with a black background, color palette 1 (colors cyan, magenta and white), and foreground color 3 (white). The program utilizes two counters, P and Q, which are initialized in line 50.

The main loop begins with line 90, which generates a rectangle whose size is determined by the value that is assigned to P. (Initially P=0, causing the first rectangle to appear as a dot at the center of the screen.) The color of the rectangle is determined by the value that is assigned to C (initially white).

Line 100 also generates a rectangle, provided Q is not negative. (Q is initially assigned a negative value in order to create a delay. Thereafter, it increases and remains nonnegative.) Now, however, the rectangle will be generated in the background color (black). The size of this rectangle will be determined by the value assigned to

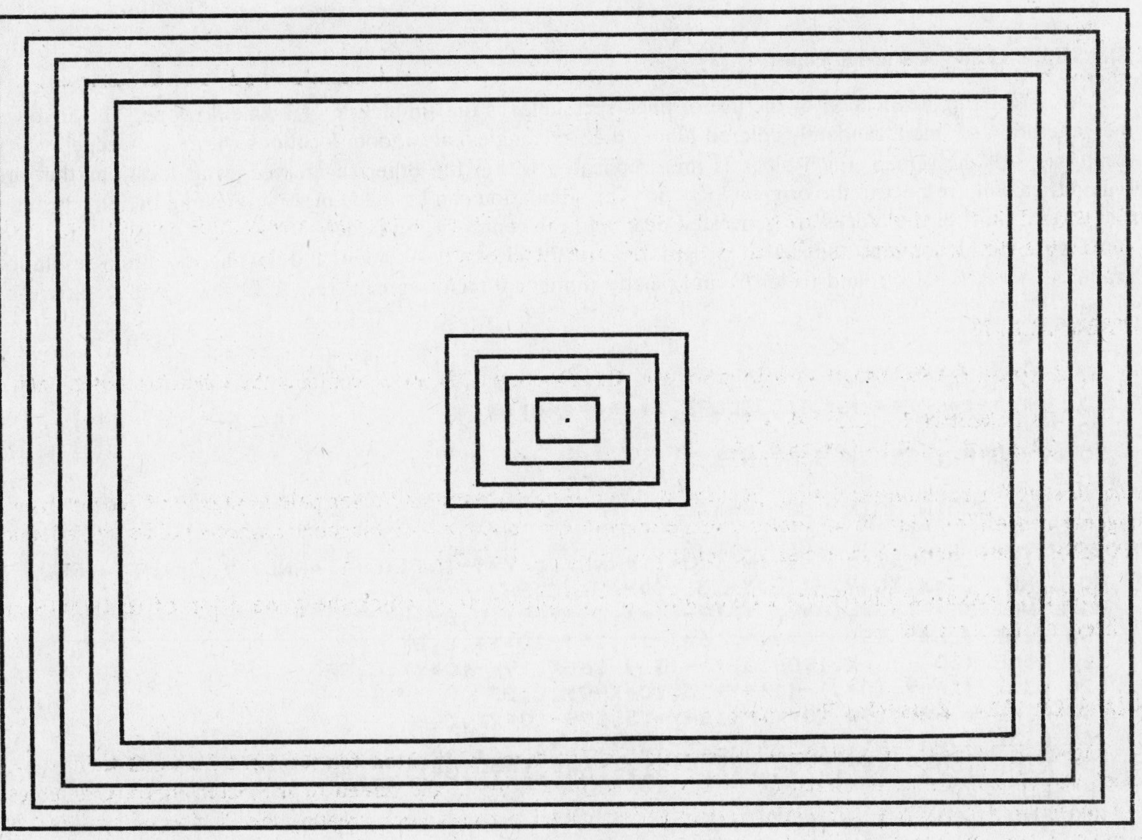

Fig. 12.12

Q. Since P and Q will always differ in magnitude, this rectangle will not coincide with the rectangle generated in line 90. The effect will be to erase one of the rectangles drawn earlier.

Lines 110 and 120 increment P and Q, respectively, resetting each parameter to zero if its value exceeds 95. Also, a new foreground color is generated randomly whenever P is reset to zero.

Line 130 generates a random sound whenever a new sequence of rectangles begins at the center of the screen (i.e., whenever P or Q is reset to zero). Line 140 then returns control to line 90 for another pass through the loop. Note that the loop will continue to execute indefinitely.

Figure 12.12 indicates the type of graphical display that is generated once the program begins to execute. As with other programs of this type, however, the reader is encouraged to actually run the program in order to fully appreciate the dynamic effects that are created.

Now suppose that a LINE statement ends with the letters BF rather than simply B, e.g., LINE (20,50) – (300,150),3,BF. The last letter, F, represents "fill." This parameter causes the rectangle (generated by the parameter B) to be filled with the specified foreground color.

EXAMPLE 12.15

Consider once again a Microsoft BASIC program, written for the IBM Personal Computer, which contains the statements

```
10 SCREEN 1 : COLOR 0,0
20 LINE (20,50) – (300,150),1,BF
```

Line 10 invokes medium-resolution graphics, with a black background and color palette number 0 (colors green, red and brown). Line 20 causes a solid green rectangle to be generated whose diagonal connects the points (20,50) and (300,150). This rectangle will be displayed against a black background. (Compare with Examples 12.9 and 12.13.)

EXAMPLE 12.16 A Kaleidoscope

An interesting application of the use of filled rectangles is the simulation of a kaleidoscope. This involves the generation of small, randomly colored blocks (i.e., rectangles) at random locations within a "wedge" which comprises $\frac{1}{8}$ of the screen. Each block is then replicated within the other seven wedges at locations that are symmetrical with respect to the original location. The simulation can be made more interesting by introducing a bias so that most of the blocks are generated nearer to the center of the screen.

Figure 12.13 contains the actual program. Line 30 clears the screen and invokes medium-resolution graphics. A black background (color 0) and palette number 0 (colors green, red and brown) will be active by default.

```
10 '************ KALEIDOSCOPE ************
20 '
30 KEY OFF : CLS : SCREEN 1
40 '
50 '*** BEGIN MAIN LOOP ***
60 '
70 U=INT(10*RND) : X=9-INT((U+1)*RND) : Y=9-INT((U+1)*RND) : C=INT(4*RND)
80 LINE (16*X,10*Y)-(16*X+15,10*Y+9),C,BF
90 LINE (304-16*X,10*Y)-(319-16*X,10*Y+9),C,BF
100 LINE (16*X,190-10*Y)-(16*X+15,199-10*Y),C,BF
110 LINE (304-16*X,190-10*Y)-(319-16*X,199-10*Y),C,BF
120 LINE (16*Y,10*X)-(16*Y+15,10*X+9),C,BF
130 LINE (16*Y,190-10*X)-(16*Y+15,199-10*X),C,BF
140 LINE (304-16*Y,10*X)-(319-16*Y,10*X+9),C,BF
150 LINE (304-16*Y,190-10*X)-(319-16*Y,199-10*X),C,BF
160 GOTO 70
170 END
```

Fig. 12.13

The repeated generation of the randomly colored blocks occurs in the main loop, which comprises lines 70 through 160. Each pass through the loop generates eight blocks, which are located symmetrically with respect to one another, with one block in each of the wedges. Each group of blocks will be the same color. Thus line 70 establishes the location of the first block and the color of all eight blocks. Notice that the values of the coordinates X and Y are dependent on the randomly generated parameter U. This causes the pairs of coordinates to be clustered toward the center of the screen.

Lines 80 through 150 each generate one of the blocks. Each block will be 16 pixels wide and 10 pixels (10 scan lines) high. The end points are chosen in such a manner that the blocks will create a symmetric pattern on the screen. It is this symmetry that simulates the action of the kaleidoscope.

Figure 12.14 illustrates a typical pattern. Again, however, the reader is urged to actually run the program to appreciate the dynamic patterns that are created.

Fig. 12.14

Some versions of Microsoft BASIC include a *CIRCLE statement*, which permits circles, arcs and ellipses to be drawn. In its simplest form, this statement consists of the word CIRCLE, followed by a pair of coordinates enclosed in parentheses and separated by a comma. The coordinates must be followed by a value for the radius, e.g., CIRCLE (160,100),80.

An integer indicating the choice of color may appear after the radius as an option, e.g., CIRCLE (160,100),80,3. If the color is not specified in this manner, color number 3 will automatically be selected from the current palette.

EXAMPLE 12.17

The following statements are included in an advanced Microsoft BASIC program (BASICA), written for the IBM Personal Computer.

```
10 SCREEN 1 : COLOR 4,1
20 CIRCLE (160,100),80,3
```

Line 10 specifies medium-resolution graphics, with a red background and color palette number 1 (colors cyan, magenta and white). Line 20 generates a white circular outline whose center is at the middle of the screen, i.e., point (160,100), and whose radius is 80 pixels.

EXAMPLE 12.18 Expanding Circles

Figure 12.15 contains an advanced Microsoft BASIC program, written for the IBM Personal Computer. This program causes repeated groups of concentric circles to be generated, with each group starting at the center of the screen and moving radially outward toward the edge. Each group of circles will be drawn in a single color which is selected randomly. As successive groups of circles are generated, however, the new circles will create interference patterns with the previous circles, thus forming interesting and colorful patterns.

```
10 '****** CIRCLES ******
20 '
30 KEY OFF : CLS
40 SCREEN 1 : COLOR 0,1
50 LINE (39,0)-(279,199),3,B
60 CLR=1
70 '
80 '*** BEGIN LOOP ***
90 '
100 FOR R=5 TO 120 STEP 5
110     CIRCLE (160,100),R,CLR
120 NEXT R
130 CLR=CLR+1 : IF CLR > 3 THEN CLR=1
140 GOTO 100
150 END
```

Fig. 12.15

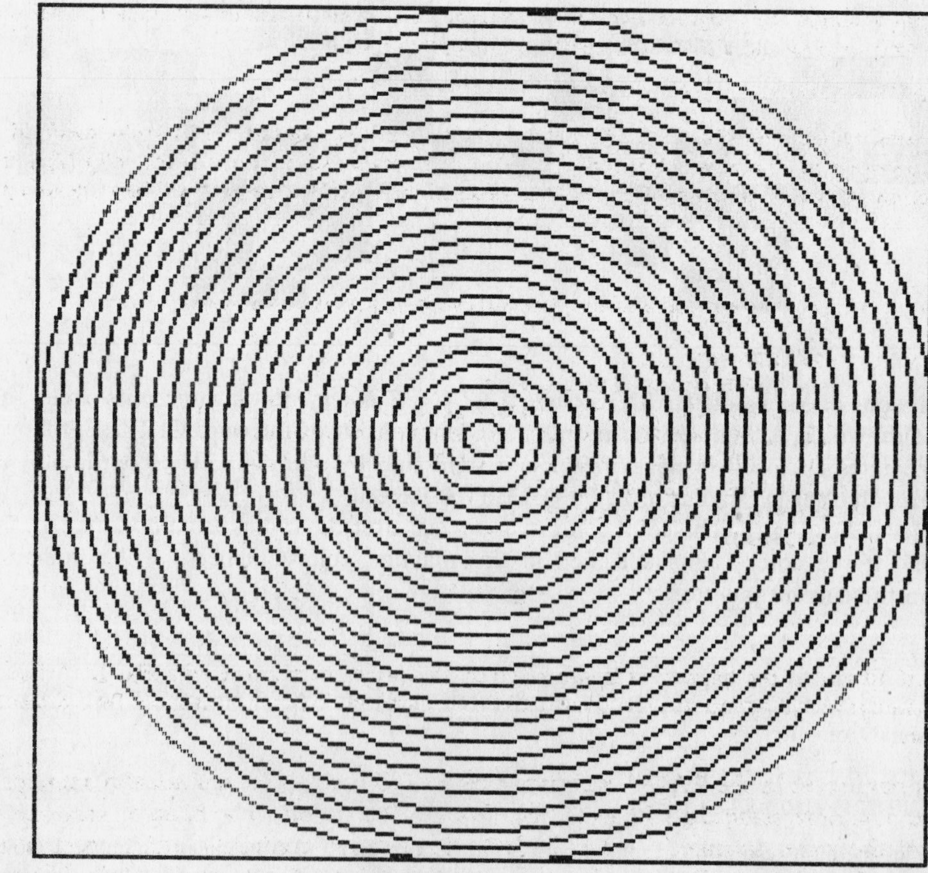

Fig. 12.16

Let us consider this program in detail. Line 30 removes any previous display of function key definitions and clears the screen, whereas line 40 specifies medium-resolution graphics, with a black background and color palette number 1 (colors cyan, magenta and white). Line 50 generates a white square around the outer edges of the screen. A color (cyan) for the first group of circles is then specified in line 60.

The repeated portion of the program begins with line 100 and continues through line 140. Lines 100 through 120 make up a FOR-TO loop that generates a group of concentric circles whose color is specified by the parameter CLR. The value of the color parameter is then changed in line 130. (Note that the value of this parameter will always be either 1, 2 or 3.) Line 140 returns control to the FOR-TO loop, thus generating another group of circles, and so on.

Figure 12.16 indicates the type of patterns that are generated by this program. It should be understood, however, that the patterns include interesting color variations and that they are in constant motion. Thus, the reader should observe the program in execution in order to appreciate what happens.

The CIRCLE statement does not include a provision for filling the circle with any color other than the background color. However, most versions of Microsoft BASIC that include the CIRCLE statement also include the *PAINT statement,* which allows any closed shape (including circles, ellipses and rectangles) to be filled with other colors. This statement consists of the word PAINT, followed by a pair of coordinates enclosed in parentheses and separated by a comma, e.g., PAINT (160,100). The coordinates can represent any enclosed point within the shape that is to be filled.

The coordinates may be followed by an integer which specifies the color, e.g., PAINT (160,100),3. If the color is not specified, then color number 3 will automatically be selected from the current palette.

EXAMPLE 12.19 A Filled Lightning Bolt

Let us again examine the program given in Example 12.10, which generates a "lightning bolt" (see Fig. 12.4). Suppose that we now add a PAINT statement to this program; i.e.,

90 PAINT (100,40),2

The complete program is shown in Fig. 12.17. Notice that the coordinates (100,40) specified by the PAINT statement refer to a point which is contained within the figure. Also, note that the color (2) is the same as that specified by the LINE statements. Hence, the effect of the PAINT statement will be to generate a solid red figure.

```
10 '************ LIGHTNING BOLT ************
20 '
30 KEY OFF : CLS
40 SCREEN 1 : COLOR 0,0
50 LINE (20,20)-(120,80),2 : LINE -(80,80),2
60 LINE -(220,180),2 : LINE -(140,100),2
70 LINE -(190,100),2 : LINE -(110,20),2
80 LINE -(20,20),2
90 PAINT (100,40),2
100 END
```

Fig. 12.17

Figure 12.18 illustrates the figure that is generated by this program (compare with Fig. 12.5). Remember, however, that the figure will appear in red against a black background if the program is run on a computer with a color monitor.

The color parameter in the PAINT statement can be followed by an additional parameter which represents the *boundary color,* e.g., PAINT (160,100),3,2. The object to be filled in must match this color. Thus, if the point specified by the PAINT statement is contained within more than one object and each object has a different color, the boundary color will determine which object will be filled.

Fig. 12.18

EXAMPLE 12.20

Now suppose that an advanced Microsoft BASIC program contains the following four statements.

```
10 SCREEN 1 : COLOR 4,1
20 CIRCLE (160,100),80,2
30 CIRCLE (160,100),60,3
40 PAINT (160,100),3,2
```

These statements cause two concentric circles to be generated. The outer circle (defined by line 20) will be magenta with a radius of 80, and the inner circle (line 30) will be white with a radius of 60. The PAINT statement in line 40 will cause the *outer* circle to be filled with color number 3 (white), since the boundary color in line 40 (i.e., color number 2) coincides with the color specified in line 20.

The CIRCLE statement can be used to generate not only full circles but also portions of circles (arcs). To do so, the color parameter must be followed by two additional parameters: a starting angle and an ending angle. These angles are measured in the traditional geometric sense, increasing in the counterclockwise direction from the right half of the horizontal axis (i.e., the right half of the abscissa). Both angles must be expressed in radians and therefore must fall within the range of 0 to 2π, e.g., CIRCLE (160,100),80,1,0,3.14.

If a value for the color parameter is not included in the CIRCLE statement but the starting and ending angles are included, then the value for the radius must be followed by two commas, e.g., CIRCLE (160,100),80,,0,3.14. The two consecutive commas denote an empty color parameter.

EXAMPLE 12.21

The following statements are included in an advanced Microsoft BASIC program (BASICA), written for the IBM Personal Computer.

```
10 SCREEN 1 : COLOR 0,0
20 CIRCLE (160,100),80,1,0,3.14
```

Line 10 specifies medium-resolution graphics, with a black background and color palette number 0 (colors green, red and brown). Line 20 then generates the top half of a green circle with radius 80. (Note that the starting and ending angles are 0 and π, respectively.)

If line 20 were replaced with

```
20 CIRCLE (160,100),80,1,3.14,0
```

then the bottom half of a green circle would be generated, since the starting and ending angles are π and 2π, respectively. This same effect could be achieved by writing

```
20 CIRCLE (160,100),80,1,3.14,6.28
```

Now suppose that the original version of line 20 is replaced with

```
20 CIRCLE (160,100),80,,0,3.14
```

This statement will generate the top half of a circle, but in brown rather than green. (Since a value for the color parameter is not explicitly specified, the default value of 3 will apply; hence the color brown.)

The starting and ending angles in the CIRCLE statement can be negative as well as positive, e.g., CIRCLE (160,100),80,1,−3.14,−6.28. Negative angles will still be interpreted as though they were positive, in the geometric sense. The effect of a negative angle, however, is to connect the corresponding end point to the center of the circle.

EXAMPLE 12.22

Now suppose that the advanced Microsoft BASIC program described in the last example contained the statements

```
10 SCREEN 1 : COLOR 0,0
20 CIRCLE (160,100),80,1,-3.14,-6.28
```

Line 20 will now generate the bottom half of a green circle, with a horizontal line connecting the two end points.

EXAMPLE 12.23

The following statements will generate a figure that is familiar to many video-game buffs.

```
10 SCREEN 1 : COLOR 0,1
20 PI=3.141593
30 CIRCLE (160,100),40,2,-PI/4,-2*PI
40 CIRCLE (170,78),5,0
50 PAINT (150,100),2,2
```

Note that the figure will be filled with magenta.

EXAMPLE 12.24 A Piechart Generator

A "piechart" is a circular graph that is generally used to represent data which is expressed in the form of percentages. Each piece of information (i.e., each percentage) is represented in terms of a "pie-shaped" circular sector. The circumference of each sector is proportional to the value of the corresponding data point. Hence, the value *40 percent* would be represented by a circular sector whose circumference is 40 percent of the entire circle.

Figure 12.19 shows a complete BASIC piechart generator, written in advanced Microsoft BASIC for the IBM Personal Computer. Each piece of data is assumed to consist of a title and a numerical value for the percentage. Hence each sector within the piechart will be accompanied by an appropriate label.

This program will generate a piechart containing as many as six sectors. The program consists of four main sections: a heading and initialization section, a data-entry section, a high-resolution graphics section that generates the actual piechart, and a concluding section that labels each of the sectors.

Let us consider the individual instructions in some detail. Line 30 removes any previous function key definitions and clears the screen. Line 40 specifies text mode, white characters against a black background. The required program arrays are defined in line 50, and an initial screen display is generated by lines 60 through 100.

Lines 140 through 230 make up the data input section. Line 140 prompts for the number of sectors. This

```
10 '************** PIECHART GENERATOR *************
20 '
30 KEY OFF: CLS
40 WIDTH 80: SCREEN 0: COLOR 7,0
50 DIM TITLE$(6),PERCENT(6),A(6)
60 LOCATE 1,20: PRINT STRING$(40,"*")
70 LOCATE 2,20: PRINT "*";TAB(59);"*"
80 LOCATE 3,20: PRINT "*           PIECHART GENERATOR           *"
90 LOCATE 4,20: PRINT "*";TAB(59);"*"
100 LOCATE 5,20: PRINT STRING$(40,"*"): PRINT
110 '
120 '**************** ENTER DATA FOR EACH SECTOR **************
130 '
140 LOCATE 8,1: INPUT "Enter number of sectors (1-6): ",N: PRINT
150 IF N < 1 OR N > 6 THEN BEEP: LOCATE 8,32: PRINT SPACE$(6);: GOTO 140
160 SUM=0
170 FOR I=1 TO N
180     PRINT "Sector";I;SPC(8);
190     INPUT "Title: ",TITLE$(I)
200     LOCATE CSRLIN-1,40: INPUT "Percent: ",PERCENT(I)
210     SUM=SUM+PERCENT(I)
220 NEXT I
230 IF SUM < 99.9 OR SUM > 100.1 THEN BEEP: CLS: LOCATE 23:

    PRINT "Percentages do not sum to 100 - Please try again": GOTO 60
240 '
250 '************ GENERATE THE PIECHART ************
260 '
270 SCREEN 2
280 PI=3.14
290 A1=0
300 FOR I=1 TO N
310     A2=A1+2*PI*PERCENT(I)/100
320     A(I)=(A1+A2)/2
330     CIRCLE (320,100),150,1,-A1,-A2
340     A1=A2
350 NEXT I
360 '
370 '************ LABEL THE SECTORS ************
380 '
390 FOR I=1 TO N
400     C1=(320+75*COS(A(I)))\8+3
410     IF A(I) > PI/2 AND A(I) < 3*PI/2 THEN C1=C1-6
420     R1=(100-30*SIN(A(I)))\8+1
430     IF A(I) < PI THEN R1=R1-1 ELSE R1=R1+1
440     LOCATE R1,C1: PRINT PERCENT(I);"%"
450 '
460     C2=(320+150*COS(A(I)))\8+5
470     IF A(I) > PI/2 AND A(I) < 3*PI/2 THEN C2=C2-LEN(TITLE$(I))-8
480     R2=(100-62.5*SIN(A(I)))\8+1
490     IF A(I) < PI THEN R2=R2-1 ELSE R2=R2+1
500     LOCATE R2,C2: PRINT TITLE$(I);
510 NEXT I
520 END
```

Fig. 12.19

value must be greater than zero, but it cannot exceed six. Line 150 performs an error check on the specified number of sectors and returns to line 140 if the value supplied is out of range (try again). The cumulative sum of all percentages is initialized in line 160. Lines 170 through 220 then prompt for each of the data items (first the title of each sector, then the corresponding percentage). The percentages are accumulated as they are entered. Finally, line 230 checks to see if all the percentages sum to 100 (or very nearly so). If not, the initial screen display is regenerated, and the entire data input portion of the program is repeated.

The actual piechart is generated in lines 270 through 350. Line 270 causes the program to switch to high-resolution graphics, clearing the screen in the process. Lines 280 and 290 assign numerical values to the variables PI and A1 (the starting angle for the first sector). Lines 300 through 350 then generate the individual sectors of the piechart. The starting angle will always be known. Hence, the ending angle is calculated in line 310, and a representative average angle is determined in line 320. This last value is stored in an array for later use when the piechart is labeled. The sector itself is then generated in line 330. (Note the use of the CIRCLE statement with negative starting and ending values.) Finally, the value for the starting angle is reassigned in line 340 in preparation for the next sector.

Lines 390 through 510 cause the piechart to be labeled. Note that this is carried out while the program remains in the high-resolution graphics mode. In lines 400 through 440, the location of each percentage is determined, making use of the average angles calculated in the previous section, and the percentage is then displayed. (The details of these individual statements need not be discussed except to mention that each text character has a height of 8 pixels; hence the need for the integer division by 8.) Similarly, the location of each title is determined and then displayed in lines 460 through 500. The entire piechart will have been generated, with appropriate labels, upon completion of this loop.

Now suppose that the program is executed using the following set of input data:

Source of Revenue	*Percentage*
Tuition	45
State aid	25
Research	15
Gifts	8
Other	7

The input dialog is illustrated in Fig. 12.20. (Note that the user's responses are underlined.) Figure 12.21 shows the resulting piechart.

```
*****************************************
*                                       *
*           PIECHART GENERATOR          *
*                                       *
*****************************************


Enter number of sectors (1-6): 5

Sector 1        Title: Tuition        Percent: 45
Sector 2        Title: State aid      Percent: 25
Sector 3        Title: Research       Percent: 15
Sector 4        Title: Gifts          Percent: 8
Sector 5        Title: Other          Percent: 7
```

Fig. 12.20

There is one additional parameter associated with the CIRCLE statement which has not been discussed. This is the *aspect* parameter. It is used to create ellipses and elliptical arcs rather than circles and circular arcs.

The aspect parameter must follow the starting and ending angles in the CIRCLE statement, e.g., CIRCLE (160,100),80,1,0,3.14,2. It must be a positive number (not necessarily an integer) or an expression resulting in a positive numerical value. A value of 1 results in a figure which is circular, or very nearly so. (The value required to produce a perfect circle may vary somewhat from one computer to another.) A value less than 1 will generate a horizontal ellipse, whereas a value greater than 1 will generate a vertical ellipse. The more the aspect parameter differs from 1, the greater the eccentricity.

When the CIRCLE statement is used to generate an ellipse or an elliptical arc, the radius parameter refers to the length of the major (largest) axis.

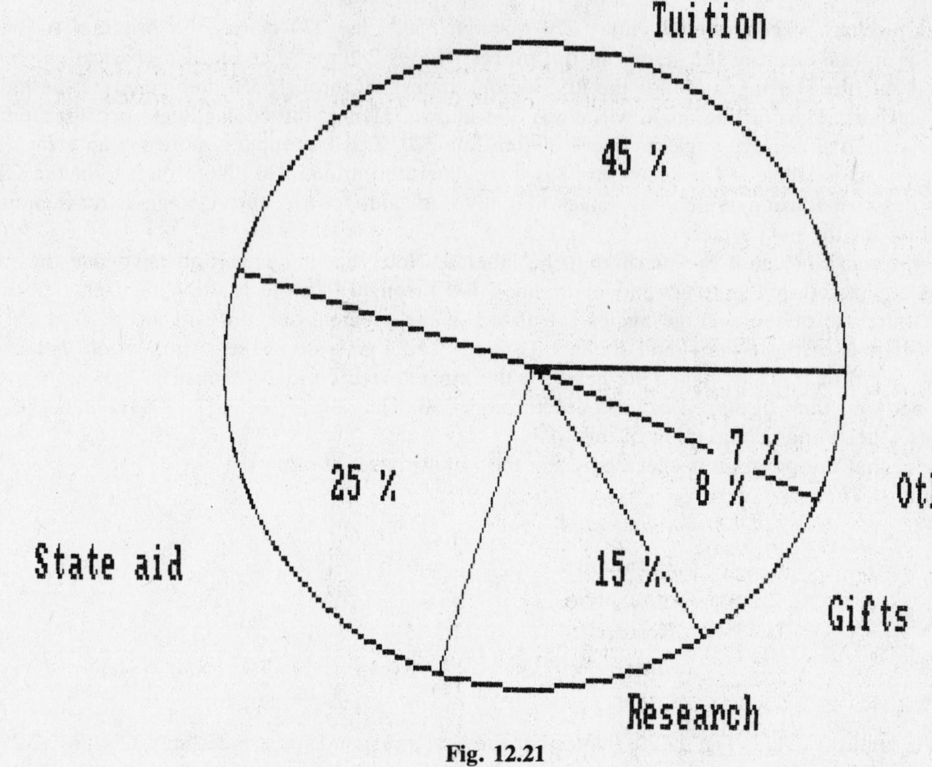

Fig. 12.21

EXAMPLE 12.25

The following statements are included in an advanced Microsoft BASIC program (BASICA), written for the IBM Personal Computer.

```
10 SCREEN 1 : COLOR 0,0
20 PI=3.141593
30 CIRCLE (160,100),80,1,0,PI,.5
```

Line 10 specifies medium-resolution graphics, with a black background and color palette number 0 (colors green, red and brown). Line 20 assigns a value to the parameter PI, and line 30 generates a green elliptical arc that ranges from 0 to π. Note that the value of the aspect parameter is less than 1; hence, the major axis of the elliptical arc will be horizontal. Moreover, the length of the major axis will be 160 pixels since the radius is assigned a value of 80.

EXAMPLE 12.26

Now suppose that an advanced Microsoft BASIC program contains the following statements.

```
10 SCREEN 1 : COLOR 0,1
20 CIRCLE (160,100),50,,,,.5
```

Line 10 specifies medium-resolution graphics, with a black background and color palette number 1 (colors cyan, magenta and white). Line 20 causes a white horizontal ellipse to be generated at the center of the screen (note that white is the default color, corresponding to a value of 3). The major axis will be 100 units long, since the value of the radius is 50.

If line 20 were changed to

```
20 CIRCLE (160,100),50,,,,2
```

then the ellipse would be vertical rather than horizontal.

EXAMPLE 12.27 Blimp with Animated Text

Figure 12.22 contains an advanced Microsoft BASIC program, written for the IBM Personal Computer, that generates a drawing of a blimp. At the center of the blimp is an area that displays an animated message (in this case, SCHAUM'S OUTLINES).

```
10 '************ BLIMP ************
20 '
30 KEY OFF : CLS
40 TEXT$="                S C H A U M ' S   O U T L I N E S   "
50 SCREEN 1 : COLOR 0,1
60 '
70 '*** DRAW THE BLIMP ***
80 '
90 CIRCLE (150,100),150,3,,,.4
100 CIRCLE (150,100),150,3,,,.3
110 CIRCLE (150,100),150,3,,,.2
120 LINE (260,60)-(270,40)
130 LINE -(320,40) : LINE -(300,100)
140 LINE (260,140)-(270,160)
150 LINE -(320,160) : LINE -(300,100)
160 LINE (260,99)-(300,99)
170 LINE (260,100)-(300,100)
180 LINE (118,160)-(125,170)
190 LINE -(175,170) : LINE -(182,160)
200 CIRCLE (135,165),3
210 CIRCLE (150,165),3
220 CIRCLE (165,165),3
230 LINE (80,90)-(225,110),3,B
240 '
250 '*** GENERATE THE MESSAGE ***
260 '
270 FOR I=1 TO 52
280     LOCATE 13,12 : PRINT MID$(TEXT$,I,16);
290     FOR COUNT=1 TO 200 : NEXT COUNT
300     LOCATE 13,12 : PRINT SPACE$(16);
310 NEXT I
320 GOTO 270
330 END
```

Fig. 12.22

The structure of this program is quite simple. Line 30 clears the screen, and line 40 assigns the message to the variable TEXT$. Line 50 specifies medium-resolution graphics, with a black background and color palette number 1 (colors cyan, magenta and white).

The blimp itself is generated by lines 90 through 230. In particular, lines 90, 100 and 110 generate three concentric ellipses that make up the overall shape of the blimp. Lines 120 through 170 generate the tail section, and lines 180 through 230 generate the undercarriage and the outline of the display area.

The animated message is generated by lines 270 through 320. Note that this group of statements involves the use of the MID$ function within a FOR-TO loop. The essential idea is to display 16 characters of the text at any one time. However, each pass through the loop will result in the group of characters being shifted one character to the right. Following the printing of each group of characters there is a short time delay. Then the display area is cleared in preparation for the next group of characters. Notice that line 320 causes the loop to be repeated, thus causing the animated message to continue indefinitely.

Figure 12.23 illustrates a typical display, though the reader should remember that the display is constantly in motion when the program is being executed.

Some versions of microcomputer BASIC also include the *DRAW statement*, which allows a complex shape to be defined in terms of a string. For example, the statement DRAW "R100 D50 L100 U50" defines a horizontal rectangle by moving right 100 units, down 50 units, left 100 units and then up 50 units. Execution of this statement will automatically generate the rectangle.

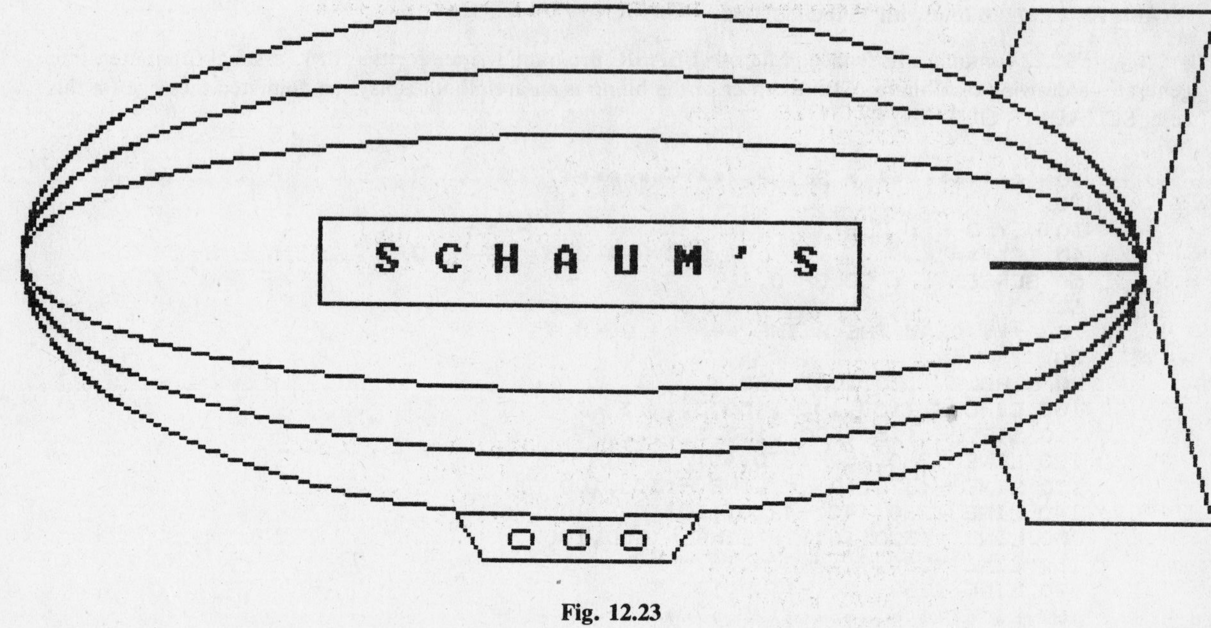

Fig. 12.23

We will not discuss the DRAW statement in any detail within this book, as the rules for defining the shape strings are somewhat complex. For more information on this subject, the reader is referred to the BASIC reference manual that is available for his or her particular microcomputer.

12.4 ANIMATIONS

One of the most interesting and entertaining applications of microcomputers is that of animated displays. Such applications provide a basis for many computer games, and they are an important part of many educational and artistic programs.

We have already encountered some simple animations in Examples 12.8 (dots in space), 12.11 (kinetic art), 12.14 (expanding rectangles), 12.18 (expanding circles) and 12.27 (blimp with animated text). All these animations are based upon the same idea: namely, display an object or a line of text, create a brief time delay and erase the object. Then move to a nearby location and repeat the sequence.

This section is concerned with animations that involve the movement of filled objects. We will first see how this is accomplished using now-familiar statements such as CIRCLE and PAINT. An alternative approach, based upon two new statements—GET and PUT—will then be presented. We shall see that the second approach offers some distinct advantages over the first one.

EXAMPLE 12.28 Simulation of a Bouncing Ball

Let us now consider a simple animation in which a ball is allowed to move freely within a confined space. The animation is created by first displaying the ball at some particular location, filling it with a color, pausing briefly and then erasing the ball (i.e., redisplaying the ball using the background color). We then move to a nearby location and repeat the entire procedure. Whenever a barrier (i.e., a "wall") is encountered the ball will change direction, thus appearing to bounce off the wall.

A complete program, written in advanced Microsoft BASIC for the IBM Personal Computer, is shown in Fig. 12.24. This program utilizes high-resolution graphics and therefore does not involve the use of multiple colors. (The IBM Personal Computer supports only black and white in the high-resolution mode.) In this program the initial location of the ball and the distance between successive locations will be generated randomly.

```
10 '************ BOUNCING BALL ************
20 '
30 KEY OFF : CLS
40 DEFINT A-Z
50 RANDOMIZE : CLS
60 SCREEN 2
70 LINE (0,0)-(639,199),,B
80 LINE (10,5)-(629,194),,B
90 PAINT (5,2)
100 X=20+INT(600*RND) : Y=20+INT(160*RND)
110 DX=5*(INT(4*RND)+1) : DY=5*(INT(4*RND)+1)
120 '
130 '*** BEGIN LOOP ***
140 '
150 CIRCLE (X,Y),10,0
160 PAINT (X,Y),0
170 X1=X+DX : Y1=Y+DY
180 IF X1 < 21 THEN X1=21 : DX=-DX : GOTO 200
190 IF X1 > 618 THEN X1=618 : DX=-DX
200 IF Y1 < 10 THEN Y1=10 : DY=-DY : GOTO 220
210 IF Y1 > 189 THEN Y1=189 : DY=-DY
220 CIRCLE (X1,Y1),10
230 PAINT (X1,Y1)
240 X=X1 : Y=Y1
250 GOTO 150
260 END
```

Fig. 12.24

Let us consider this program in detail. Line 30 removes any previous display of function key definitions and clears the screen. Line 40 defines all variables to be integer-type variables, line 50 initializes the random number generator and then clears the screen, and line 60 specifies high-resolution graphics. Lines 70 through 90 generate a solid rectangle around the outer edges of the screen, thus providing the barrier that will contain the ball's motion. A random starting point is then generated in line 100, and a set of values for incrementing each move is randomly generated in line 110.

The repeated portion of the program involves lines 150 through 250. Lines 150 and 160 cause the ball to be erased from the current location (i.e., the ball is displayed in black, the background color, at the current location). Line 170 then generates a new location. In lines 180 through 210, the new point is tested to determine if the ball will go beyond the confines of the walls. If so, the direction of motion is altered, creating the illusion that the ball bounces off the walls and back into the confined interior space.

Lines 220 and 230 cause the ball to be displayed at the new location and then filled with white. The values of the new coordinates are then assigned to the variables X and Y in line 240. These two variables will be used to erase the ball during the next pass through the loop.

Figure 12.25 illustrates the type of output that is created when the program is run. The reader should remember, however, that the ball appears to be in constant motion when the program is actually executing.

Though the preceding animation technique works reasonably well, the animation is relatively slow and it is sometimes accompanied by an annoying flicker. With some versions of microcomputer BASIC it is possible to generate faster, flicker-free animations through the use of the *GET* and *PUT statements.* With this method, the object to be animated is generated only once. The GET statement then transfers the object from the screen to an array. Thereafter, the PUT statement will transfer the object from the array back to the screen at a selected location. If the object is placed directly over itself, it will appear in a color that is opposite to the previous color (e.g., black replacing white). Thus, by executing a pair of PUTs at the same location, the object can automatically be displayed and then erased. (*Note*: the GET and PUT statements, when used in this manner, should not be confused with the GET and PUT statements that are used in conjunction with random data files, as described in Section 9.4, Example 9.31.)

The general procedure, then, is to generate the object that will move about the screen and place it in an array, using the GET statement. This is carried out only once. The program then enters a

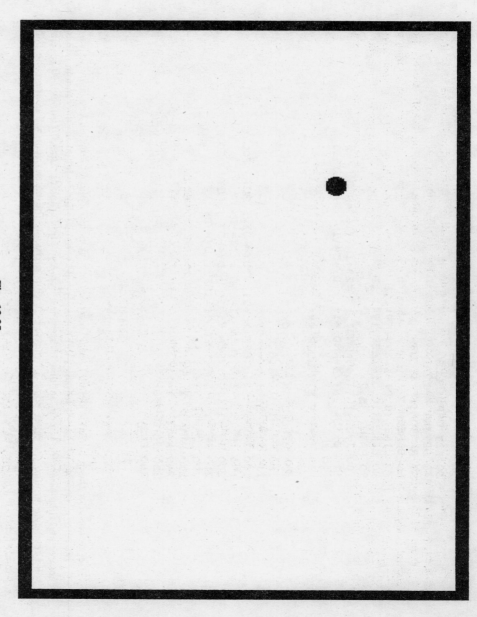

Fig. 12.25

loop in which the object is erased from its old location (via the PUT statement), a new location is determined and the object is redisplayed at this new location (again via PUT). The animation is created by repeated passes through the loop.

The GET statement consists of the word GET, followed by two pairs of coordinates. Each pair of coordinates must be enclosed in parentheses and separated by a comma. These coordinates define the opposite corners of a rectangle which contains the object. A dash (minus sign) separates the two pairs of coordinates. The second pair of coordinates is then followed by the name of the array that will contain the object, e.g., GET (X,Y) – (X+20,Y+20),FIGURE.

The dimensionality of the array depends on both the size of the object (actually, the size of the enclosing rectangle) and the level of resolution. There is a rather involved formula for calculating the required dimensionality that makes use of these two factors. The reader is referred to the user's reference manual for his or her particular computer for more information on this topic.

Once the object is stored in the required array, it is redisplayed by means of the PUT statement. This statement consists of the word PUT, followed by a single pair of coordinates enclosed in parentheses and separated by a comma. These coordinates represent the upper left corner of the rectangle which contains the object. The coordinates are then followed by the name of the array, e.g., PUT (X,Y),FIGURE.

EXAMPLE 12.29 The Bouncing Ball Revisited

Let us again consider the animation of a ball within an enclosure, as described in Example 12.28. Now, however, we will generate the animation by means of the GET and PUT statements.

Figure 12.26 contains the complete program, again written in advanced Microsoft BASIC for the IBM Personal Computer. This program is similar to that shown in Fig. 12.24. There are, however, some important differences. Notice the addition of the DIM statement in line 70, which defines BALL to be a 34-element array. Also, note that the distance between successive locations (generated in line 120) has been decreased in order to smooth out the ball's motion. This was not practical in the earlier version because the animation was too slow.

```
10 '************ BOUNCING BALL ************
20 '
30 KEY OFF : CLS
40 DEFINT A-Z
50 RANDOMIZE : CLS
60 SCREEN 2
70 DIM BALL(34)
80 LINE (0,0)-(639,199),,B
90 LINE (10,5)-(629,194),,B
100 PAINT (5,2)
110 X=20+INT(600*RND) : Y=20+INT(160*RND)
120 DX=1+INT(10*RND) : DY=1+INT(10*RND)
130 CIRCLE (X,Y),10
140 PAINT (X,Y)
150 GET (X-10,Y-10)-(X+10,Y+10),BALL
160 '
170 '*** BEGIN LOOP ***
180 '
190 PUT (X-10,Y-10),BALL
200 X1=X+DX : Y1=Y+DY
210 IF X1 < 21 THEN X1=21 : DX=-DX : GOTO 230
220 IF X1 > 618 THEN X1=618 : DX=-DX
230 IF Y1 < 10 THEN Y1=10 : DY=-DY : GOTO 250
240 IF Y1 > 189 THEN Y1=189 : DY=-DY
250 PUT (X1-10,Y1-10),BALL
260 X=X1 : Y=Y1
270 FOR C=1 TO 5: NEXT C
280 GOTO 190
290 END
```

Fig. 12.26

The CIRCLE and PAINT statements appear only once in the current program, in lines 130 and 140, respectively. These two statements provide an initial shape definition of the ball. The GET statement in line 150 then causes this shape definition to be stored in the array called BALL.

The loop portion of the program is also somewhat different than the earlier version. The pairs of CIRCLE and PAINT statements are now replaced by PUT statements in lines 190 and 250. The first of these, in line 190, erases the ball from its previous location; the second displays the ball at its new location. Finally, notice the empty FOR-TO loop which has been added in line 270. This loop is intended to slow down the animation so that it is more pleasing to the eye.

When the program is executed, the screen will again appear as shown in Fig. 12.25, but the motion will now be considerably faster and smoother. The reader is urged to actually run both programs in order to better appreciate the differences in the resulting animations.

Animations that are created in this manner need not be limited to a single moving object. Multiple objects can also be moved about the screen by means of multiple pairs of PUT statements. Each object must, however, be stored in a separate array. The technique is illustrated in the next example.

EXAMPLE 12.30 A Game of Paddleball

Here is a simple version of a popular video game, commonly referred to as "paddleball." A ball is enclosed by three walls. A small, movable "paddle" is located where the fourth wall would normally be placed. This paddle can move up and down in response to the setting of some control device, such as a joystick (we are assuming that the missing wall is vertical). The ball will be deflected back into the playing area if it is hit by the paddle; otherwise, the ball will pass through the opening and disappear.

The object of the game is to anticipate the ball's trajectory as it moves toward the open area and to position the paddle so that it hits the ball, knocking it back into the playing area. The player will receive one point for each hit and lose one point for each miss. The ball will automatically reappear at some random location within the playing area after each miss.

Figure 12.27 contains a complete BASIC program for this game. The program is written in advanced Microsoft BASIC for the IBM Personal Computer. It includes the use of medium-resolution graphics, joystick control statements and sound enhancements to accompany the movement of the ball. Thus, the program contains several of the features described in Chapter 10, as well as an animation technique.

Let us now consider the principal features of this program. Line 30 removes any previous function key definitions and clears the screen, and line 40 declares all variables to be of type integer. Lines 50 through 70 generate an introductory text display, and line 80 initializes the random number generator. Line 90 associates the signal coming from button 1 of the joystick with a subroutine and then activates this association (button 1 will be used to stop the program). Line 100 calls for medium-resolution graphics, with a black background and color palette number 1 (colors cyan, magenta and white).

The arrays containing the shape definitions of the ball and the paddle are introduced in line 110, and some program parameters are assigned their initial values in line 120. (Note that DX and DY determine the horizontal and vertical velocity of the ball, as in the previous two examples. The paddle position is determined by P.)

Lines 160 through 180 generate the three walls, and lines 190 and 200 cause brief text displays to be generated at the bottom of the screen, beneath the graphical display area. The text consists of the score and a prompt indicating how the game is ended.

Line 240 causes the initial ball location to be generated randomly. The shape of the ball and the shape of the paddle are then generated and stored in their respective arrays in lines 250 and 260.

The main loop, in which the animation is created, consists of lines 300 through 440. Line 300 determines the new positions of the ball and the paddle. Lines 310 and 320 adjust the paddle location if the paddle is too high or too low. Lines 330 and 340 test the position of the ball to see if it falls within the path of the paddle. If so, one of two different subroutines will be accessed. The choice will depend on whether or not the paddle hits the ball, as determined by the test in line 340.

Lines 350 through 370 test the location of the ball relative to the three fixed walls. If the computed location of the ball overlaps the location of a wall, an adjustment is made in the ball's location and its velocity is reversed, creating the illusion that the ball bounces off the wall. The bounce is accompanied by a short, high-pitched sound.

Lines 380 and 390 cause the animated objects to be erased from their old locations, and lines 400 and 410 cause them to be redrawn at their new locations. The values of the old locations are then initialized in line 420, and a short time delay is introduced in line 430, primarily to avoid excessive flickering. Line 440 returns control to line 300, thus initiating another pass through the loop.

Lines 480 and 490 make up a subroutine that is accessed when the paddle hits the ball. Essentially, this subroutine creates a bouncing effect similar to that produced when the ball touches one of the walls. The cumulative score is also increased by 1, and the new value is displayed at the bottom of the screen.

Lines 530 through 570 make up a subroutine that is accessed when the paddle misses the ball. Line 530 simply displays the ball near the left edge of the screen if that is its calculated position, thus preventing the ball from disappearing from view prematurely. In line 540, however, we simulate the effect of the ball disappearing from view. Both the ball and the paddle are erased by this line. Line 550 causes the velocities to be reset to their initial positive values, causing the ball to travel to the lower right corner of the screen when it reappears at some new random location.

The cumulative score is also decreased by 1, and a brief, low-pitched sound is generated. (Notice that a high-pitched sound is produced when the ball bounces off a surface, but a low-pitched sound is heard when the paddle misses the ball.) The new score is then displayed at the bottom of the screen (line 560), and a short time delay is generated (line 570) before control is returned to line 240, causing a new ball to be placed in play.

Finally, the END statement in line 610 is actually the subroutine which is accessed whenever button 1 is pressed on the joystick. This is the association that was activated in line 90.

```
10 '************ PADDLEBALL GAME ************
20 '
30 KEY OFF : CLS
40 DEFINT A-Z
50 LOCATE 4,1 : PRINT "Welcome to PADDLEBALL"
60 LOCATE 8,1 : PRINT "Rules: 1 point for each hit, "
70 LOCATE 10,7 : PRINT "-1 point for each miss"
80 LOCATE 14,1 : RANDOMIZE : CLS
90 ON STRIG(0) GOSUB 610 : STRIG(0) ON
100 SCREEN 1 : COLOR 0,1
110 DIM BALL(34),PADDLE(22)
120 DX=10 : DY=10 : P=8 : SCORE=0
130 '
140 '****** DRAW THE BORDER ******
150 '
160 LINE (0,0)-(319,5),1,BF
170 LINE (0,178)-(319,183),1,BF
180 LINE (314,6)-(319,177),1,BF
190 LOCATE 25,1 : PRINT "Score:";SCORE;
200 LOCATE 25,20 : PRINT "To stop, press B1";
210 '
220 '****** DRAW THE INITIAL FIGURES ******
230 '
240 X=10+INT(300*RND) : Y=10+INT(164*RND)
250 CIRCLE (X,Y),5 : PAINT (X,Y) : GET (X-5,Y-5)-(X+5,Y+5),BALL
260 LINE(0,P)-(6,P+20),3,BF : GET (0,P)-(6,P+20),PADDLE
270 '
280 '****** MAIN LOOP ******
290 '
300 X1=X+DX : Y1=Y+DY : DUMMY=STICK(0) : P1=199*STICK(1)/100
310 IF P1 < 6 THEN P1=6 : GOTO 330
320 IF P1 > 157 THEN P1=157
330 IF X1 >= 12 THEN 350
340 IF Y1 >= P1-2 AND Y1 <= P1+22 THEN GOSUB 480 ELSE GOSUB 530
350 IF X1 > 308 THEN X1=308 : DX=-DX : SOUND 1000,2
360 IF Y1 < 11 THEN Y1=11 : DY=-DY : SOUND 1000,2 : GOTO 380
370 IF Y1 > 172 THEN Y1=172 : DY=-DY : SOUND 1000,2
380 PUT (X-5,Y-5),BALL      'erase ball
390 PUT (0,P),PADDLE        'erase paddle
400 PUT (X1-5,Y1-5),BALL  'redraw ball
410 PUT (0,P1),PADDLE       'redraw paddle
420 X=X1 : Y=Y1 : P=P1
430 FOR C=1 TO 10: NEXT C
440 GOTO 300
450 '
460 '****** PADDLE HIT THE BALL ******
470 '
480 X1=12 : DX=-DX : SCORE=SCORE+1 : SOUND 1000,2
490 LOCATE 25,7 : PRINT SCORE;: RETURN 360
500 '
510 '****** PADDLE MISSED THE BALL ******
520 '
530 IF X1 >= 5 THEN RETURN 360
540 PUT (X-5,Y-5),BALL : PUT (0,P),PADDLE
550 DX=10 : DY=10 : SCORE=SCORE-1 : SOUND 50,2
560 LOCATE 25,7 : PRINT SCORE;
570 FOR I=1 TO 1000 : NEXT I : RETURN 240
580 '
590 '****** END THE GAME ******
600 '
610 END
```

Fig. 12.27

When the program is executed, the text display shown in Fig. 12.28 first appears. Once a value is provided for the random number generator, however, the screen switches to medium-resolution graphics, showing cyan walls, a white ball and a white paddle. The ball appears at some random location on the screen and remains in constant motion, bouncing off whatever surface it happens to touch. Figure 12.29 illustrates the appearance of the screen as the ball approaches the paddle from the upper right.

```
Welcome to PADDLEBALL

Rules: 1 point for each hit,

      -1 point for each miss

Random number seed (-32768 to 32767)? 12345
```

Fig. 12.28

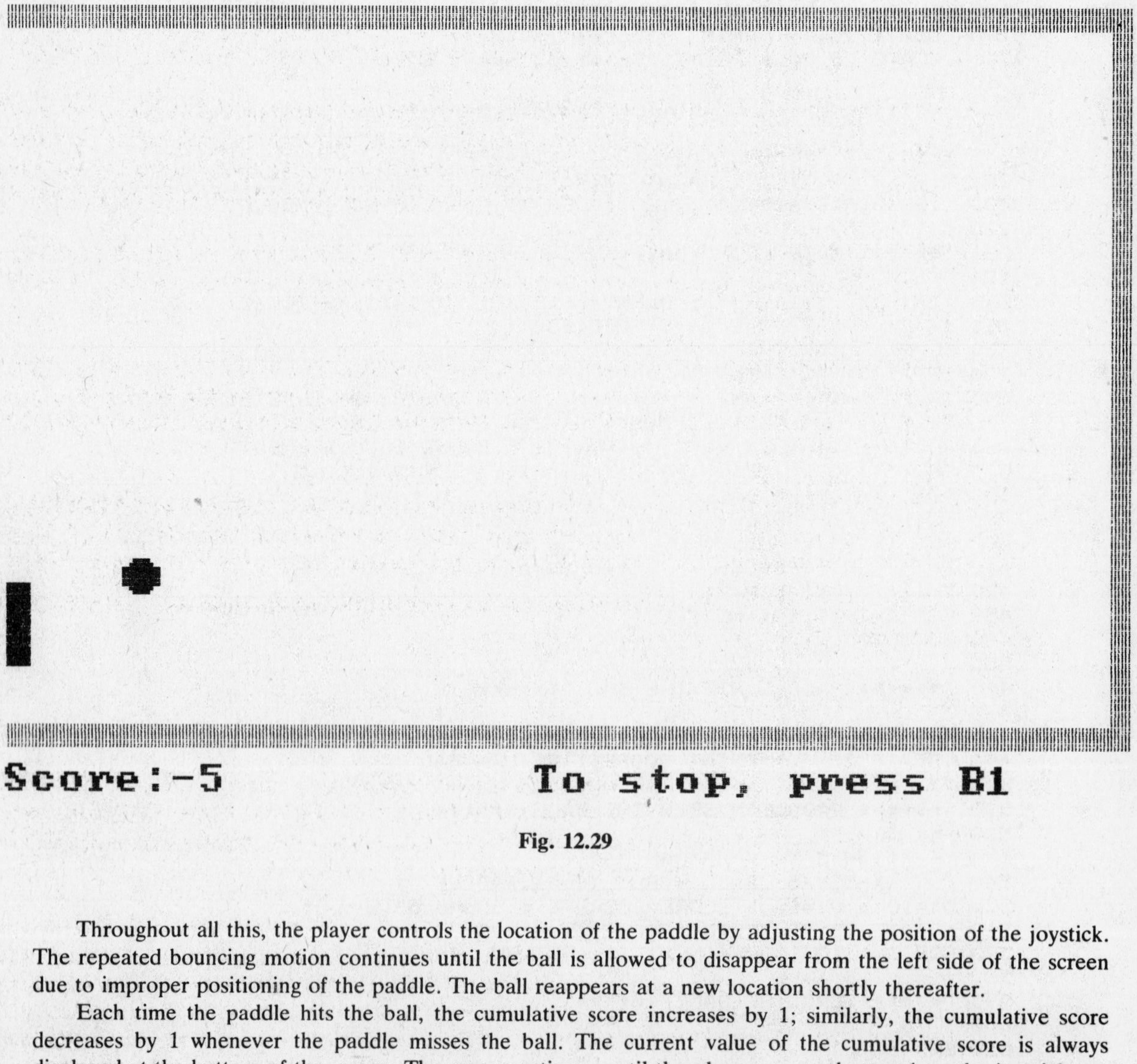

```
Score:-5            To stop, press B1
```

Fig. 12.29

Throughout all this, the player controls the location of the paddle by adjusting the position of the joystick. The repeated bouncing motion continues until the ball is allowed to disappear from the left side of the screen due to improper positioning of the paddle. The ball reappears at a new location shortly thereafter.

Each time the paddle hits the ball, the cumulative score increases by 1; similarly, the cumulative score decreases by 1 whenever the paddle misses the ball. The current value of the cumulative score is always displayed at the bottom of the screen. The game continues until the player presses button 1 on the joystick.

The reader is urged to run this program, if at all possible, in order to appreciate what actually happens. This, of course, is highly desirable for all programs of this type.

12.5 CHARACTER GRAPHICS

Certain graphical effects can often be achieved through the clever manipulation of text characters. Such effects include animated message displays and the creation of simple graphs and shapes. We have already seen some examples of animated message displays with vertical scrolling in Examples 10.10 and 10.17 and a horizontal animation included as a part of Example 12.27.

The bouncing ball program shown in Example 6.28 illustrates a simple but effective way to utilize character graphics on a line printer. And the program shown in Example 10.13 allows a joystick to be used to create various shapes as clusters of asterisks. As a rule, graphical effects that are created in this manner are less effective than those created in a graphics mode. Nevertheless, such graphical effects do serve a purpose, particularly for those microcomputers that do not support separate text and graphics modes.

The following example illustrates the use of character-type graphics to represent numeric data.

EXAMPLE 12.31 A Barchart Generator

Suppose we have a group of numerical values that we wish to display in graphical form, emphasizing the discrete nature of each value. This can often best be accomplished by means of a barchart, in which each value is represented by a rectangle whose height is directly proportional to its corresponding value. The rectangles are normally displayed horizontally, with all of them visible at the same time.

Figure 12.30 contains a Microsoft BASIC program, written for the IBM Personal Computer, that causes a barchart to be generated for as many as 12 numerical values. Each value is assumed to be nonnegative (i.e., greater than or equal to zero). The values will be displayed above each of their respective rectangles (i.e., above each "bar"). Each value will have a corresponding label which will be displayed at the bottom of the bar. The bars themselves will be made up of clusters of asterisks.

Let us examine this program in some detail. Lines 30 through 110 clear the screen, define the arrays LABEL$ and Y, generate an initial heading and initialize YMAX. Lines 150 through 250 generate a series of interactive prompts for input data.

The first item requested is a title for the barchart (line 150), followed by a request for the number of data items to be entered (lines 160 and 170). Notice that this last request includes an error trap (line 170) which requires the user's response to be a positive value between 1 and 12.

Lines 180 through 250 make up a FOR-TO loop which prompts the user for each of the data items and its accompanying label. The loop includes an error trap (lines 210 and 220) which prevents some character other than a number from being entered for the requested value. Also, the largest input value is tagged in line 240.

The actual bars are generated in lines 290 through 370. Line 290 clears the data-entry portion of the screen and calculates the width of each bar. (The greater the number of bars, the narrower each bar will be.) Lines 300 through 370 make up a triple loop that is used to generate the bars. The outermost loop causes successive bars to be generated. (Notice that the top row of each bar, which is computed in line 310, is based upon the ratio of the given value to the maximum value.) The middle loop (lines 320 through 360) generates the rows that make up each bar, and the inner loop (lines 330 through 350) generates the columns within each row.

Lines 410 through 490 label the barchart. The FOR-TO loop (lines 410 through 470) cause each data value to be displayed on the line above each bar and the corresponding label to appear beneath each bar. Lines 480 and 490 then cause the title of the barchart to be displayed at the bottom, centered horizontally.

Now suppose that the program is executed using the following set of input data:

Annual Sales Increases

Increase (%)	*Year*
5.2	1985
7.8	1986
8.2	1987
6.7	1988
10.6	1989
12.3	1990

```
10 '*************** BAR CHART GENERATOR **************
20 '
30 KEY OFF: CLS
40 WIDTH 80: SCREEN 0: COLOR 7,0
50 DIM LABEL$(12),Y(12)
60 LOCATE 1,20: PRINT STRING$(40,"*")
70 LOCATE 2,20: PRINT "*";SPC(38);"*"
80 LOCATE 3,20: PRINT "*";SPC(9);"BAR CHART GENERATOR";SPC(10);"*"
90 LOCATE 4,20: PRINT "*";SPC(38);"*"
100 LOCATE 5,20: PRINT STRING$(40,"*")
110 YMAX=0
120 '
130 '****** ENTER DATA AND FIND LARGEST Y ******
140 '
150 LOCATE 7,1: INPUT "Title: ",TITLE$
160 LOCATE 9,1: INPUT "How many data items? (1-12) ",ANS$: N=VAL(ANS$)
170 IF N < 1 OR N > 12 THEN BEEP: LOCATE 9,29: PRINT SPACE$(6): GOTO 160
180 FOR I=1 TO N
190     LOCATE I+10: PRINT "I =";I
200     LOCATE I+10,15: INPUT "Value: ",ANS$: Y(I)=VAL(ANS$)
210     IF LEFT$(ANS$,1)="0" THEN 230
220     IF Y(I) <= 0 THEN BEEP: LOCATE I+10,21: PRINT SPACE$(6): GOTO 200
230     LOCATE I+10,35: INPUT "Label: ",LABEL$(I)
240     IF Y(I) > YMAX THEN YMAX=Y(I)
250 NEXT I
260 '
270 '****** GENERATE AND DISPLAY THE BAR CHART ******
280 '
290 CLS: W=60\N
300 FOR I=1 TO N
310     R=20-18*Y(I)\YMAX: IF R=20 THEN 370
320     FOR ROW=R TO 20
330         FOR COL=(I-1)*W+11 TO I*W+8
340             LOCATE ROW,COL: PRINT "*"
350         NEXT COL
360     NEXT ROW
370 NEXT I
380 '
390 '****** LABEL THE BAR CHART ******
400 '
410 FOR I=1 TO N
420     R=19-18*Y(I)\YMAX
430     C=9 + (I-1)*W + (W-LEN(STR$(Y(I))))/2
440     LOCATE R,C: PRINT Y(I)
450     C=10 + (I-1)*W + (W-LEN(LABEL$(I)))/2
460     LOCATE 21,C: PRINT LABEL$(I)
470 NEXT I
480 C=10 + (N*W-LEN(TITLE$))/2
490 LOCATE 23,C: PRINT TITLE$;: LOCATE 23,1
500 END
```

Fig. 12.30

The dialog generated by the data-input portion of the program is shown in Fig. 12.31. (The user's responses are underlined.) Figure 12.32 shows the corresponding barchart.

Some microcomputers include a special graphics character set in addition to the 128 standard ASCII characters shown in Appendix E. For example, the IBM Personal Computer supports 256 different characters, including 128 special characters. Several of these are graphics characters (as well as mathematical symbols and characters used in foreign languages). We have already used one of these graphics characters to create blocks of light—in Example 10.12 (see line 50 in Fig. 10.7). The

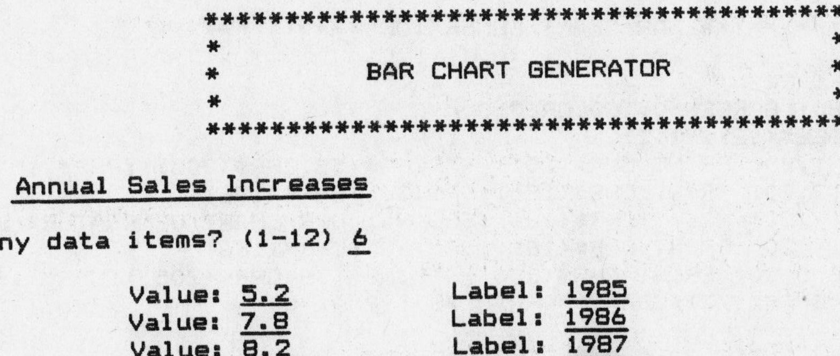

BAR CHART GENERATOR
Title: Annual Sales Increases
How many data items? (1-12) 6
I = 1 Value: 5.2 Label: 1985
I = 2 Value: 7.8 Label: 1986
I = 3 Value: 8.2 Label: 1987
I = 4 Value: 6.7 Label: 1988
I = 5 Value: 10.6 Label: 1989
I = 6 Value: 12.3 Label: 1990

Fig. 12.31

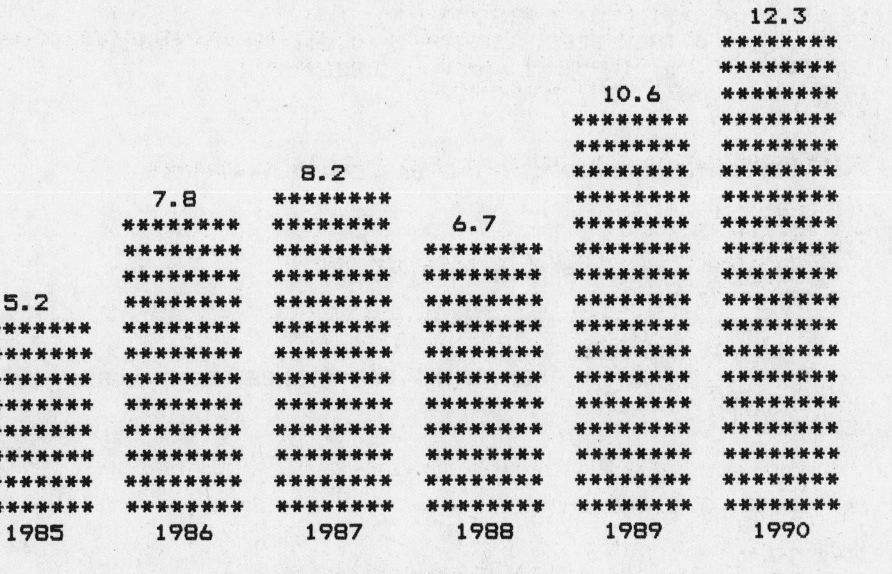

Fig. 12.32

use of these graphics characters offers the possibility of a significant improvement in character-graphic displays.

EXAMPLE 12.32 An Improved Barchart Generator

Figure 12.33 contains another Microsoft BASIC program, written for the IBM Personal Computer, for generating a barchart as described in Example 12.31. This program is similar to the program presented in Fig. 12.30. Now, however, we see reference to the special graphics characters available on the IBM Personal Computer. Notice, for example, that lines 60 through 100 include the function calls CHR\$(201), CHR\$(205), CHR\$(187), CHR\$(186), CHR\$(200) and CHR\$(188) within the various PRINT statements. These function calls cause the title "BAR CHART GENERATOR" to be framed within a double rectangle, as shown in Fig. 12.34. Also, line 110 assigns the characters CHR\$(177) and CHR\$(178) to the variable BAR1\$ and BAR2\$, respectively. These characters are printed in line 350, thus causing the rectangular bars to be composed of

```
10 '************** BAR CHART GENERATOR *************
20 '
30 KEY OFF: CLS
40 WIDTH 80: SCREEN 0: COLOR 7,0
50 DIM LABEL$(12),Y(12)
60 LOCATE 1,20: PRINT CHR$(201);STRING$(38,CHR$(205));CHR$(187)
70 LOCATE 2,20: PRINT CHR$(186);SPC(38);CHR$(186)
80 LOCATE 3,20: PRINT CHR$(186);SPC(9);"BAR CHART GENERATOR";SPC(10);CHR$(186)
90 LOCATE 4,20: PRINT CHR$(186);SPC(38);CHR$(186)
100 LOCATE 5,20: PRINT CHR$(200);STRING$(38,CHR$(205));CHR$(188)
110 BAR1$=CHR$(177): BAR2$=CHR$(178): YMAX=0
120 '
130 '****** ENTER DATA AND FIND LARGEST Y ******
140 '
150 LOCATE 7,1: INPUT "Title: ",TITLE$
160 LOCATE 9,1: INPUT "How many data items? (1-12) ",ANS$: N=VAL(ANS$)
170 IF N < 1 OR N > 12 THEN BEEP: LOCATE 9,32: PRINT SPACE$(6): GOTO 160
180 FOR I=1 TO N
190     LOCATE I+10: PRINT "I =";I
200     LOCATE I+10,15: INPUT "Value: ",ANS$: Y(I)=VAL(ANS$)
210     IF LEFT$(ANS$,1)="0" THEN 230
220     IF Y(I) <= 0 THEN BEEP: LOCATE I+10,21: PRINT SPACE$(6): GOTO 200
230     LOCATE I+10,35: INPUT "Label: ",LABEL$(I)
240     IF Y(I) > YMAX THEN YMAX=Y(I)
250 NEXT I
260 '
270 '****** GENERATE AND DISPLAY THE BAR CHART ******
280 '
290 CLS: W=60\N
300 FOR I=1 TO N
310     R=20-18*Y(I)\YMAX: IF R=20 THEN 380
320     FOR ROW=R TO 20
330        FOR COL=(I-1)*W+11 TO I*W+8
340           LOCATE ROW,COL
350           IF I MOD 2 = 0 THEN PRINT BAR1$ ELSE PRINT BAR2$
360        NEXT COL
370     NEXT ROW
380 NEXT I
390 '
400 '****** LABEL THE BAR CHART ******
410 '
420 FOR I=1 TO N
430     R=19-18*Y(I)\YMAX
440     C=9 + (I-1)*W + (W-LEN(STR$(Y(I))))/2
450     LOCATE R,C: PRINT Y(I)
460     C=10 + (I-1)*W + (W-LEN(LABEL$(I)))/2
470     LOCATE 21,C: PRINT LABEL$(I)
480 NEXT I
490 C=10 + (N*W-LEN(TITLE$))/2
500 LOCATE 23,C: PRINT TITLE$;: LOCATE 23,1
510 END
```

Fig. 12.33

partially shaded rectangular blocks rather than asterisks. The effect is shown in Fig. 12.35. Notice that alternate bars are shown in different shadings.

It is interesting to compare Figs. 12.31 and 12.34. The special graphics characters used to generate Fig. 12.34 clearly improve the appearance of the display. Even more striking, however, is the comparison between Figs. 12.32 and 12.35. (Figure 12.35 will appear better on a TV monitor since the individual block characters within each bar will touch one another, forming a solid rectangle.) Thus, we see that a small amount of additional programming effort results in a much better-looking display.

```
BAR CHART GENERATOR

Title: Annual Sales Increases

How many data items? (1-12) 6

I = 1        Value: 5.2       Label: 1985
I = 2        Value: 7.8       Label: 1986
I = 3        Value: 8.2       Label: 1987
I = 4        Value: 6.7       Label: 1988
I = 5        Value: 10.6      Label: 1989
I = 6        Value: 12.3      Label: 1990
```

Fig. 12.34

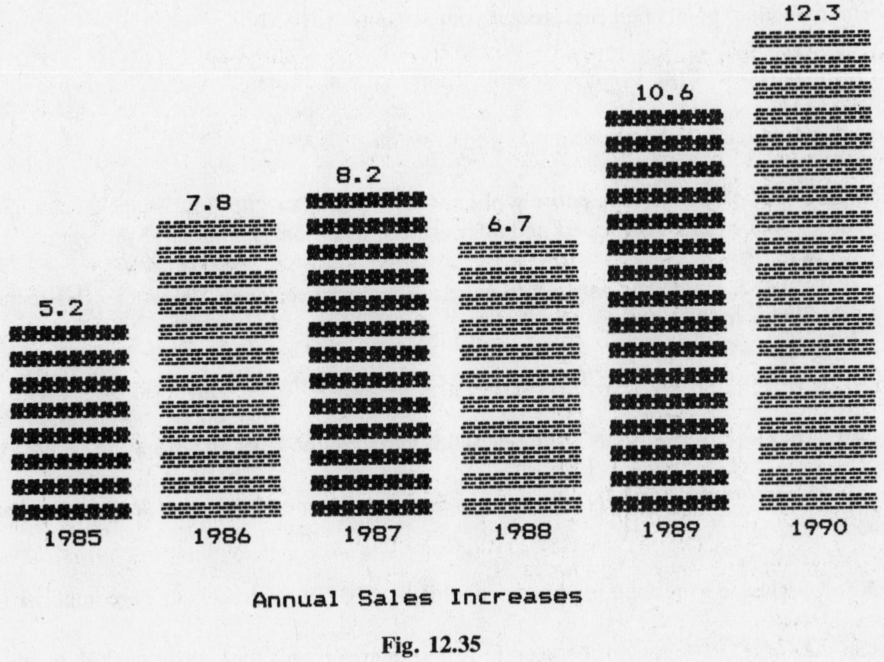

Fig. 12.35

Review Questions

12.1 Determine whether or not the version of BASIC available for your particular microcomputer includes special graphics statements. If so, are they the same as those described in this chapter?

12.2 What level of resolution is provided by the graphics features on your particular microcomputer? Are multiple graphics modes available?

12.3 Is color available on your particular microcomputer? If so, how many different colors are available in the text mode? How many are available in the graphics mode?

12.4 What is a pixel? What are pixels used for?

12.5 What is the purpose of the SCREEN statement? Summarize the rules that apply to its use.

12.6 What is the purpose of the PSET statement? Summarize the rules that apply to its use.

12.7 What is the purpose of the PRESET statement? How does it differ from the PSET statement? Summarize the rules that apply to its use.

12.8 How can individual points be generated in your version of BASIC?

12.9 What is the purpose of the LINE statement? Summarize the rules that apply to its use.

12.10 How can individual lines be generated in your version of BASIC?

12.11 Explain how a display consisting entirely of individual points or lines (not shapes) can be animated; i.e., how points or lines can be displayed and later erased, as in the "kinetic art" program.

12.12 How can the LINE statement be used to generate a closed rectangle? How can this rectangle be filled with a specified color?

12.13 What is the purpose of the CIRCLE statement? Summarize the rules that apply to its use.

12.14 What is the purpose of the PAINT statement? Summarize the rules that apply to its use.

12.15 How can the CIRCLE and PAINT statements be used to generate circular shapes that are filled with a specified color?

12.16 Can closed circles be generated in your version of BASIC? If so, how is this accomplished?

12.17 How can the CIRCLE statement be used to generate arcs rather that entire circles? How can these arcs be connected to the origin, thus creating "pie-shaped" objects?

12.18 How can the CIRCLE statement be used to generate ellipses? How can the size and orientation (i.e., horizontal or vertical) of an ellipse be specified?

12.19 Can closed elliptical shapes be generated in your version of BASIC? If so, how is this accomplished?

12.20 Explain how a text display can be animated in the horizontal direction within a fixed, confined space.

12.21 How can simple shapes be animated in your version of BASIC?

12.22 What is the purpose of the GET statement when used in the graphics mode? Summarize the rules that apply to its use.

12.23 What is the purpose of the PUT statement when used in the graphics mode? Summarize the rules that apply to its use.

12.24 When creating an animation, what is the advantage in using the GET and PUT statements rather than simply generating the shape in alternate colors (first foreground, then background)?

12.25 What is meant by character graphics? How does the quality of character-type graphics compare with other types of graphic displays?

12.26 Does your version of BASIC include special graphics characters? If so, what are they? What are their ASCII codes?

Supplementary Problems

The following "problems" are concerned with information gathering rather than actual problem solving. Answer the questions as they apply to your particular version of microcomputer BASIC.

12.27 Does your microcomputer include a graphics capability? If so, can graphical displays be created within a BASIC program? How many graphics modes are available? What level of resolution is available with each mode?

12.28 Is color available? If so, how many colors can be displayed at any one time within each graphics mode? What are these colors? Is there a distinction between foreground and background colors?

12.29 Determine how each of the following features can be implemented in BASIC.

(*a*) How is each graphics mode accessed?

(*b*) How are individual colors specified?

(*c*) How are individual points generated? How are they erased?

(*d*) How are lines generated?

(*e*) Can rectangles be generated with a single statement? If so, can the rectangles be filled with a solid color?

(*f*) Can circles be generated with a single statement? If so, can the circles be filled with a solid color?

(*g*) Can ellipses be generated with a single statement? If so, can the ellipses be filled with a solid color?

(*h*) Can circular or elliptical arcs be generated with a single statement?

(*i*) Are special statements available for carrying out animations? If so, what are they and how do they work?

(*j*) Can text be generated within the graphics modes?

(*k*) Are there other special graphics features that were not described in this chapter? If so, what are they and how do they work?

(*l*) Does your microcomputer include special graphics characters? If so, what are they? How are these characters accessed in BASIC?

Programming Problems

12.30 Modify the following programs so that the palette and the background color can be changed at any time by pressing appropriate function keys (e.g., F1 to change the palette and F2 to change the background color).

(*a*) Dots in space (Example 12.8)

(*b*) Moving lines (kinetic art) (Example 12.11)

(*c*) A kaleidoscope (Example 12.16)

(*d*) Expanding circles (Example 12.18)

12.31 Alter some of the numerical values included in the kinetic art program given in Example 12.11. Experiment with different values until you find a set of values that you like particularly well.

12.32 Modify the program given in Example 12.16 (kaleidoscope) so that the screen is filled with a larger number of rectangles. Be sure to reduce the size of the rectangles to compensate for the greater number.

12.33 Modify the program given in Example 12.16 (kaleidoscope) so that the randomly generated coordinates are spread uniformly over the entire wedge rather than being clustered near the center of the screen. Which effect do you prefer?

12.34 Modify the program given in Example 12.12 (linear regression with graphical display) so that the x and y axes are labeled. Include a provision for generating a title near the top of the graph.

12.35 Expand the program given in Example 12.12 so that power functions, exponential equations and polynomials can be fitted to a set of input data and then plotted. Use closely spaced points to represent curves when plotting the graphs. (Example 7.22 gives the appropriate equations for fitting each type of curve, based upon the method of least squares.) Include a menu that will allow the user to select the desired type of curve. Be sure to include appropriate prompts and error checks for both the numerical data and the menu selections.

12.36 Modify the piechart generator given in Example 12.24 so that each circular segment is filled with some color other than the background color. Make sure that adjacent segments do not have the same color.

12.37 Modify the barchart generator given in Example 12.32 so that one, two or three different data sets can be displayed simultaneously, provided all the data sets have the same number of bars. Place the corresponding bars next to one another, with no intervening space (i.e., place the first bar for each data set in one cluster, then the second bar for each data set, etc.). Use either a different color or a different pattern for each data set.

12.38 Write a single microcomputer BASIC program that will allow a set of data to be entered into the computer and will then generate either a piechart or a barchart (see Examples 12.24 and 12.32). Include a menu that will allow the user to select the desired type of graph. Be sure to include appropriate prompts and error checks for both the numerical data and the menu selections.

12.39 Modify the program given in Example 12.27 (blimp with animated text) so that the user may specify the message that moves across the display area. Include a prompt for the desired message at the start of the program, before the blimp is drawn.

12.40 Alter some of the numerical values included in the bouncing ball program given in Example 12.29. Experiment with different values until you find a set of values that you like particularly well. Compare the program's performance with that obtained using the original values.

12.41 Modify the paddleball game given in Example 12.30 so that the user may specify the degree of difficulty before the game begins. For a more difficult game, make the paddle smaller and make the ball move faster. Include a menu, with appropriate prompts and error checks, to assist the user in selecting the desired degree of difficulty.

12.42 Extend the program given in Example 10.13 (programming a joystick to generate character graphics) so that several different graphics characters can be utilized. Include a menu which allows the user to select the graphics characters. Also, allow the user to change the color of the background or the color of each new character by pressing an appropriate function key. Include the function key choices in the menu. (*Suggestion*: reserve the rightmost 20 columns of the screen for the menu. Allow the remainder of the screen to be used as the graphics area.)

12.43 Solve Problem 12.42 utilizing a mouse rather than a joystick.

12.44 Write a microcomputer BASIC program, similar to the one given in Example 10.13, that will allow a joystick or a mouse to generate individual pixels in the graphics mode. Include a provision for changing the color of the background or the color of each new pixel by pressing an appropriate function key. Provide a small menu at the bottom of the screen explaining the use of the function keys.

12.45 Extend the program described in Problem 12.44 so that lines, rectangles and circles can be drawn in addition to individual pixels. Include a provision for filling each solid shape with a color which the user can choose from a menu. Also, allow the user to change the color of the background or the color of each new object by pressing an appropriate function key.

12.46 Write a microcomputer BASIC program that will generate a full-screen display of your school emblem or company logo. Include color if it is available.

12.47 Write a microcomputer BASIC program that will generate a full-screen display of the flag of each of the following countries (listed in the order of increasing difficulty).

(*a*) Japan
(*b*) France
(*c*) Denmark
(*d*) Norway
(*e*) United States
(*f*) United Kingdom
(*g*) Canada
(*h*) Saudi Arabia

12.48 Write a microcomputer BASIC program that will generate an x-axis and a y-axis, thus dividing the screen into four equal quadrants. Then display a graph of the equation

$$y = c_1 + c_2x + c_3x^2 + c_4x^3 + c_5x^4$$

using values of your own choice for c_1, c_2, c_3, c_4 and c_5. (Note that it is possible to plot straight lines, quadratics, cubics, etc., by setting certain of these constants equal to zero.)

Write the program in such a manner that it can be executed repeatedly, with different values for c_1, c_2, c_3, c_4 and c_5 entered from the keyboard at the beginning of each run.

12.49 Write a microcomputer BASIC program that will generate a graphical display of the equation

$$y = 2e^{-0.1x} \sin(0.5x + c)$$

for values of x varying from 0 to 60, and $c=0$. Include the x- and y-axes in the graphical display. Label the axes.

12.50 Extend Problem 12.49 so that the generation of the graphical display occurs within a loop, with a different (increasing) value assigned to c during each pass.

12.51 A variety of interesting graphical displays can be generated by the equations that represent *Archimedes' spiral*; namely,

$$x = ar \cos r$$
$$y = br \sin r$$

where a and b are positive constants and r represents an angle, in radians.

Write a microcomputer BASIC program that will generate a graphical display of Archimedes' spiral. Let the constants a and b be input parameters. Generate a sequence of values for r (and hence a sequence of x and y values) by embedding the above formulas within a FOR-TO loop which includes a STEP parameter. Enter the value of the STEP parameter from the keyboard, along with the values of a and b, at the start of each run. (*Note*: many different graphical displays can be generated by specifying different values for a, b and the STEP parameter.)

12.52 Extend the craps game given in Example 6.20 to include a graphical display of the dice after every throw. (Note that this problem can be solved using either pixel-type graphics or character graphics.)

12.53 Write a microcomputer BASIC program that will allow a person to play a game of tic-tac-toe against the computer. Include a graphical display showing both players' moves with the customary X's and O's (see Problem 6.52(*g*)).

12.54 Extend the Roulette program described in Problem 6.52(*i*) to include a graphical display of the roulette wheel (in color, if possible). Show where the marble comes to rest after each spin.

12.55 Extend the BINGO program described in Problem 6.52(*k*) to include a graphical display of the master BINGO card. (This card will contain all 75 possible letter-number combinations in five columns, labeled B, I, N, G, O, respectively. The first column will contain the numbers 1–15, the second column will contain 16–30, etc.) Use character graphics to generate the display. Identify each letter-number combination as it is drawn (e.g., shade in the location on the card, or change the color).

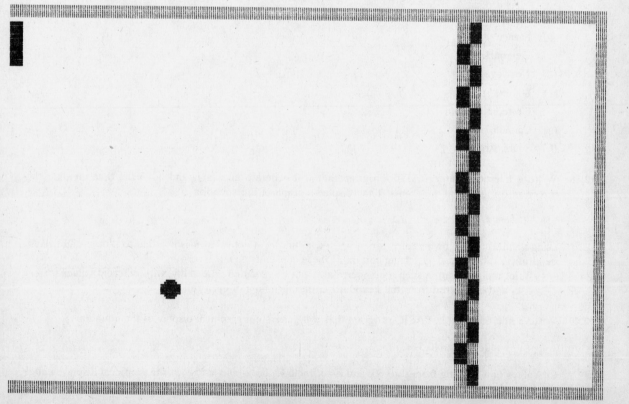

Fig. 12.36

12.56 One of the earliest of the popular video games is a game called *brickout.* This game is similar to the paddleball game described in Example 12.30 except that there is a "brick wall" located near the right side of the playing area, as illustrated in Fig. 12.36.

If the ball hits a brick, the ball bounces as it normally would but the brick disappears and the player receives one point. If the ball passes through a channel created by missing bricks, then the ball can continue to bounce within the right portion of the playing area, hitting and removing bricks, until it again passes through a channel to the left portion of the playing area. The play continues until all the bricks are gone or until the player misses the ball with the paddle. The player is allowed five balls during each game.

Write a microcomputer BASIC program to play successive games of brickout. Make each successive game more difficult by making the paddle smaller and making the ball move more rapidly. Begin a new score for each game, but maintain a record of the highest score.

Appendix A

Summary of Standard BASIC Statements

Statement	*Example*	*Reference*
CHANGE	10 CHANGE N$ TO N	Section 6.4
DATA	10 DATA 12,SEVENTEEN,−5	Section 5.5
DEF	10 DEF FNR(A,B,C)=SQR(A↑2+B↑2+C↑2)	Section 6.1
DIM	10 DIM A(10,20),X(20),F$(60)	Section 5.4
END	10 END	Section 2.11
FNEND	10 FNEND	Section 6.3
FOR-TO	10 FOR J=1 TO 99 STEP 2	Section 4.5
GO TO	10 GO TO 50	Section 2.14
GOSUB	10 GOSUB 300	Section 6.9
IF-THEN	10 IF I>=100 THEN 80	Section 4.2
INPUT	10 INPUT A,B,C,M$,N$	Section 2.9
LET	10 LET A=3.141593*R↑2	Section 2.8
NEXT	10 NEXT I	Section 4.6
ON-GO TO	10 ON K GO TO 15,40,25,40,60	Section 4.3
PRINT	10 PRINT "X=";X,"Y=";Y	Section 2.10
RANDOMIZE	10 RANDOMIZE	Section 6.7
READ	10 READ K,N$,Z(1)	Section 5.5
REM	10 REM AREA OF A CIRCLE	Section 2.13
RESTORE	10 RESTORE	Section 5.6
RETURN	10 RETURN	Section 6.8
STOP	10 STOP	Section 4.4
MAT =	10 MAT C=A	Section 7.1
MAT +	10 MAT C=A+B	Section 7.1
MAT −	10 MAT C=A−B	Section 7.1
MAT (K)*	10 MAT C=(10)*A	Section 7.1
MAT *	10 MAT C=A*B	Section 7.1
MAT CON	10 MAT B=CON	Section 7.3
MAT IDN	10 MAT C=IDN	Section 7.3
MAT INPUT	10 MAT INPUT A	Section 7.2
MAT INV	10 MAT B=INV(A)	Section 7.3
MAT PRINT	10 MAT PRINT A	Section 7.2
MAT READ	10 MAT READ A	Section 7.2
MAT TRN	10 MAT B=TRN(A)	Section 7.3
MAT ZER	10 MAT A=ZER	Section 7.3
FILE	10 FILE :1,F$	Section 8.3
FILES	10 FILES SCORES	Section 8.1

Statement	*Example*	*Reference*
IF END-THEN	10 IF END #1, THEN 130	Section 8.1
INPUT	10 INPUT #1,N,T$,Y$	Section 8.1
PRINT	10 PRINT #2,N;N$	Section 8.1
QUOTE	10 QUOTE #2	Section 8.1
READ	10 READ :1,L	Section 8.2
SCRATCH	10 SCRATCH #2	Section 8.1
SET (RESET)	10 SET :1,L	Section 8.2
WRITE	10 WRITE :1,N	Section 8.2

Arithmetic Operators:	+	−	*	/	↑	
Relational Operators:	=	<>	<=	<	>=	>

Note: ↑ appears as ˆ on some terminals.

Appendix B

Summary of Standard BASIC Library Functions

Function	*Example*	*Reference*
ABS	10 LET Y=ABS(X)	Section 5.1
ATN	10 LET Y=ATN(X)	Section 5.1
ASC	10 LET N=ASC(T)	Section 6.5
CHR$	10 LET N$=CHR$(N)	Section 6.5
COS	10 LET Y=COS(X)	Section 5.1
COT	10 LET Y=COT(X)	Section 5.1
DET	10 LET X=DET	Section 7.3
EXP	10 LET Y=EXP(X)	Section 5.1
INT	10 LET Y=INT(X)	Section 5.1
LOC	10 LET N=LOC(1)	Section 8.2
LOF	10 LET N1=LOF(3)	Section 8.2
LOG	10 LET Y=LOG(X)	Section 5.1
NUM	10 LET N(0)=NUM	Section 7.2
RND	10 LET X=RND	Section 6.6
SGN	10 LET Y=SGN(X)	Section 5.1
SIN	10 LET Y=SIN(X)	Section 5.1
SQR	10 LET Y=SQR(X)	Section 5.1
TAB	10 PRINT TAB(N);X	Section 5.1
TAN	10 LET Y=TAN(X)	Section 5.1

Appendix C

Summary of Standard BASIC System Commands

Command	*Purpose*
BYE	Terminates timesharing session.
CATALOG	Lists names of all files being saved.
GOODBYE	Same as BYE.
LIST	Produces a listing of the current file.
NEW	Specifies that a new file will be created.
OLD	Accesses an existing file.
RENAME	Allows the name of the current file to be changed.
REPLACE	Causes the current file to be saved (stored) in place of the file previously stored with the same name. (The old file will be deleted.)
RUN	Causes the current program to be compiled and executed.
SAVE	Causes the current file to be saved (stored).
SCRATCH	Removes the current file from the computer's memory.
SYSTEM	Transfers control from BASIC to the system monitor.
UNSAVE	Cancels permanent storage of a file.

Appendix D

Summary of Microsoft BASIC

Statements

Statement	*Purpose*	*Example*
BEEP	Beeps the speaker	10 BEEP
BLOAD	Loads a binary memory image	10 BLOAD "SAMPLE"
BSAVE	Saves a binary memory image	10 BSAVE "SAMPLE",0,&H8000
CALL	Calls a machine language subroutine	10 CALL START
CHAIN	Passes control to another program	10 CHAIN "PROGRAM2"
CIRCLE	Generates circles, arcs and ellipses (graphics mode)	10 CIRCLE (160,100),30,2
CLOSE	Closes a file for input/output operations	10 CLOSE #1
CLS	Clears the screen and "homes" the cursor	10 CLS
COLOR	Sets colors or other screen attributes	10 COLOR 7,0,0
COMMON	Defines a common storage area, for passing variables to a chained program	10 COMMON A,B,C,T$
DATA	Provides values for variables listed in READ statement	10 READ A,B,C,T$ 20 DATA 2.3,−0.1,6,RED
DATE$	Sets the date	10 DATE$="12/29/82"
DEF FN...	Defines a function	10 DEF FNA(X)=A*X^2+B
DEF (type)	Defines variable types (types can be INT, SNG, DBL or STR)	10 DEFINT I-N,X 20 DEFSTR P
DEF USR	Defines starting address for machine language subroutine	10 DEF USR=8000
DIM	Defines (dimension) arrays	10 DIM X(100),Z$(20,100)
END	End of program	99 END
ERASE	Erases (eliminates) individual arrays	10 ERASE Z$
ERROR	Simulates the occurrence of an error	10 X=13 20 ERROR X
FIELD	Defines field length (random files)	10 FIELD 1,20 AS CUST$
FOR and NEXT	Define the start and end of a FOR-TO loop	10 FOR COUNT=1 TO 100 : 60 NEXT COUNT
GET (text mode)	Reads a record from a random file to a memory buffer	10 OPEN "R",#1,"DATA" 20 FIELD 1,20 AS CUST$ 30 GET 1

Statement	*Purpose*	*Example*
GET (graphics mode)	Stores portion of graphics screen display in an array	10 GET (10,10)–(80,50),SHAPE
GOSUB	Transfers control to a subroutine	10 GOSUB 200
GOTO	Transfers control to a remote statement	10 GOTO 200
IF-THEN	Conditional execution	10 IF X>0 THEN 200
IF-THEN-ELSE	Conditional execution	10 IF X>0 THEN 200 ELSE X=0
INPUT	Enters data from the keyboard	10 INPUT A,B,C,T$ 20 INPUT "X=",X
INPUT #	Enters data from a sequential file or device	10 OPEN "I",#1,"NAMES" 20 INPUT #1,N$
KEY OFF	Turns off function key display	10 KEY OFF
KEY ON	Turns on function key display	10 KEY ON
KILL	Deletes an entire file	10 KILL "SAMPLE"
LET	Assignment statement (optional)	10 LET X=A+B+C
LINE	Generates lines and rectangles (graphics mode)	10 LINE (0,0)–(319,199) 20 LINE (10,5)–(50,80),2,BF
LINE INPUT	Reads an entire line from the keyboard, as a string	10 LINE INPUT T$ 20 LINE INPUT;"Ans:";A$
LINE INPUT #	Reads an entire line from a sequential file as a string	10 OPEN "I",#1,"NAMES" 20 LINE INPUT #1,N$
LOCATE	Specifies the current cursor position (row and column)	10 LOCATE 12,40
LPRINT	Prints data on the printer	10 LPRINT A,B,C,T$ 20 LPRINT "X=";X
LPRINT USING	Prints formatted data on the printer	10 LPRINT USING "#.##";X
LSET	Places data into a random file buffer, left-justified	10 OPEN "R",#1,"DATA" 20 FIELD 1,20 AS CUST$ 30 LSET CUST$=NAME$
NAME	Renames a file	10 NAME "SAMPLE" AS "DATA"
ON ERROR GOTO	Transfers control if an error occurs	10 ON ERROR GOTO 500
ON-GOSUB	Transfers control to one of several subroutines	10 ON FLAG GOSUB 100,200,300
ON-GOTO	Transfers control to one of several destinations	10 ON K GOTO 80,120,160
ON KEY( ) GOSUB	Associates a function key with a subroutine	10 ON KEY(3) GOSUB 200 (refers to function key F3)
ON PEN GOSUB	Associates light pen activation with a subroutine	10 ON PEN GOSUB 300
ON STRIG( ) GOSUB	Associates a joystick button with a subroutine	10 ON STRIG(0) GOSUB 400
OPEN	Opens a file for input/output operations	10 OPEN "I",#1,"NAMES"

Statement	*Purpose*	*Example*
OUT	Sends a byte to an output port	10 OUT 127,3 (127 is the port no.)
PAINT	Fills an enclosed graphics shape with color	10 CIRCLE (160,100),10,2 20 PAINT (160,100),2,2
PEN OFF	Turns off light pen read function	10 PEN OFF
PEN ON	Turns on light pen read function	10 PEN ON
POKE	Places a value in a specified memory location	10 POKE(32155,65) (memory location is 32155, value is 65)
PRESET	Erases a point (graphics mode)	10 PRESET (25,40)
PRINT	Displays data on the screen	10 PRINT A,B,C,T$ 20 PRINT "X=";X
PRINT #	Writes data to a sequential file	10 PRINT #1,A;B;C;T$
PRINT USING	Displays formatted data on the screen	10 PRINT USING "#.##";X
PRINT # USING	Writes formatted data to a sequential file	10 PRINT #1, USING "#.##";X
PSET	Generates a point (graphics mode)	10 PSET(25,40),1
PUT (text mode)	Writes a record from a memory buffer to a random file	10 PUT#1,22 (22 is the record no.)
PUT (graphics mode)	Displays graphics image stored in an array	10 PUT (120,80),SHAPE
RANDOMIZE	Initializes the random number generator	10 RANDOMIZE
READ	Assigns values in DATA statement to listed variables	10 READ A,B,C,T$ 20 DATA 2.3,−0.1,6,RED
REM	Places remarks in the program	10 REM *** PROGRAM 1 ***
RESTORE	Initializes the pointer in a DATA statement	10 RESTORE 20 20 DATA 2.3,−0.1,6,RED
RESUME	Continues program execution after error correction routine	10 RESUME 100
RETURN	Used at end of subroutine; returns control to statement following GOSUB	10 GOSUB 80 . 80 REM BEGIN SUBROUTINE . 100 RETURN
RSET	Places data into a random file buffer, right-justified	10 OPEN "R",#1,"DATA" 20 FIELD 1,20 AS CUST$ 30 RSET CUST$=NAME$
SCREEN	Specifies current mode (text or graphics)	10 SCREEN 0
SOUND	Generates a sound with a fixed frequency and duration	10 SOUND 800,100 (800=frequency, 100=duration)

Statement	*Purpose*	*Example*
STOP	Terminates program execution	10 STOP
STRIG OFF	Deactivates joystick buttons	10 STRIG OFF
STRIG ON	Activates joystick buttons	10 STRIG ON
SWAP	Exchanges the values of two different variables	10 SWAP X,Y
TIME$	Sets the current time	10 TIME$="13:07:42"
WAIT	Suspends program execution until a specified bit pattern is detected in an input port	10 WAIT 16,6 (input port=16)
WHILE and WEND	Define the start and end of a conditional loop	10 COUNT=1 20 WHILE COUNT<10 30 PRINT "COUNT=";COUNT 40 COUNT=COUNT+1 50 WEND
WIDTH	Specifies the number of characters per line	10 WIDTH 80
WRITE	Displays data on the screen (similar to PRINT)	10 WRITE A,B,C,T$
WRITE #	Writes data to a sequential file (similar to PRINT #)	10 WRITE #1,A,B,C,T$

Library Functions

Function	*Purpose*	*Example*
ABS	Returns absolute value	10 Y=ABS(X)
ASC	Returns ASCII code	10 Y=ASC(X$)
ATN	Returns arctangent	10 Y=ATN(X)
CDBL	Converts to double precision	10 Y#=CDBL(X)
CHR$	Returns character represented by given ASCII code	10 Y$=CHR$(X)
CINT	Converts to an integer	10 Y%=CINT(X)
COS	Returns the trigonometric cosine function	10 Y=COS(X)
CSNG	Converts to single precision	10 Y=CSNG(X#)
CSRLIN	Returns the vertical cursor position (line number)	10 Y=CSRLIN
CVD	Converts string to double precision value	10 Y#=CVD(X$)
CVI	Converts string to integer value	10 Y%=CVI(X$)
CVS	Converts string to real value	10 Y=CVS(X$)
DATE$	Returns the date	10 Y$=DATE$
EOF	Indicates an end-of-file	10 IF EOF(1) THEN 100
ERL	Returns the line number where an error occurred	(see next example)

Function	*Purpose*	*Example*
ERR	Returns an error code	10 PRINT ERR, ERL
EXP	Returns the exponential function	10 Y=EXP(X)
FIX	Converts to an integer (truncates)	10 Y%=FIX(X)
FRE	Returns the number of unused bytes of memory	10 Y=FRE(0)
HEX$	Converts from decimal to hexadecimal	10 Y$=HEX$(X)
INKEY$	Returns a character from the keyboard	10 Y$=INKEY$
INP	Returns a byte from an input port	10 Y=INP(127)
INPUT$	Returns a multicharacter string from the keyboard	10 Y$=INPUT$(3)
INSTR	Returns the position where one string (X$) is found within another string (T$)	10 Y=INSTR(T$,X$)
INT	Returns the largest integer that does not exceed the specified value	10 Y%=INT(X)
LEFT$	Returns the leftmost *n* characters of a string	10 Y$=LEFT$(X$, 3)
LEN	Returns the number of characters in a string	10 Y=LEN(X$)
LOC	Returns the current record number	10 Y=LOC(1)
LOF	Returns the file length, in bytes	10 Y=LOF(1)
LOG	Returns the natural logarithm	10 Y=LOG(X)
LPOS	Returns the column number of the current print-head position (for a printer)	10 IF LPOS>40 THEN PRINT "*"
MID$	Returns an *n*-character string, starting at location *m*	10 Y$=MID$(X$,5,3) (*m*=5, *n*=3)
MKD$	Converts a double-precision value to a string	10 Y$=MKD$(X#)
MKI$	Converts an integer value to a string	10 Y$=MKI$(X%)
MKS$	Converts a real value to a string	10 Y$=MKS$(X)
OCT$	Converts from decimal to octal	10 Y$=OCT$(X)
PEN	Returns information associated with a light pen	10 X=PEN(1):Y=PEN(2)
PEEK	Returns the contents of a specified memory location	10 Y=PEEK(32155)
POINT	Returns the color of a point on the screen	10 Y=POINT(3,12)
POS	Returns the column number of the current cursor position	10 Y=POS(0)

Function	*Purpose*	*Example*
RIGHT$	Returns the rightmost *n* characters of a string	10 Y$=RIGHT$(X$, 3)
RND	Returns a random number between 0 and 1	10 Y=RND
SCREEN	Returns ASCII code for the character at the designated location	10 Y=SCREEN(5,12)
SGN	Returns an integer that indicates the sign of a value	10 Y=SGN(X)
SIN	Returns the trigonometric sine function	10 Y=SIN(X)
SPACE$	Returns a sequence of blank spaces	10 PRINT X;SPACE$(5);Y
SPC	Generates blank spaces in a PRINT statement	10 PRINT X;SPC(5);Y
SQR	Returns the square root of a value	10 Y=SQR(X)
STICK	Returns joystick coordinates	10 X=STICK(0):Y=STICK(1)
STRIG	Returns information associated with joystick buttons	10 Y=STRIG(0)
STR$	Converts a numerical value to a string	10 Y$=STR$(1000)
STRING$	Returns an *n*-character string of repeated characters	10 Y$=STRING$(8,42) (*n*=8, ASCII char=42)
TAB	Tabs to a specified position in a print statement	10 PRINT X;TAB(18);Y
TAN	Returns the trigonometric tangent	10 Y=TAN(X)
TIME$	Returns the current time	10 Y$=TIME$
USR	Accesses a machine-language subroutine	10 Y=USR(X)
VAL	Converts a string to a numerical value	10 Y=VAL(X$)
VARPTR	Returns the memory address of a variable	10 Y=VARPTR(X)

System Commands

Command	*Purpose*	*Example*
AUTO	Automatic line numbering	AUTO 100,10
CLEAR	Clears values assigned to numeric and string variables	CLEAR
CONT	Resumes program execution after a break	CONT
DELETE	Deletes program lines	DELETE 180–230
EDIT	Accesses a line for editing	EDIT 100
FILES	Displays names of all files	FILES
KILL	Deletes an entire file	KILL "SAMPLE"
LIST	Lists the program, or parts of the program, on the screen	LIST

Command	*Purpose*	*Example*
LLIST	Lists the program, or parts of the program, on a printer	LLIST LLIST 100–160
LOAD	Loads a program into memory	LOAD "SAMPLE"
MERGE	Merges a program file into the program now in memory	MERGE "TRIAL"
NAME	Renames a file	NAME "SAMPLE" AS "NEWPROG"
NEW	Deletes the program currently in memory	NEW
RENUM	Renumbers program lines automatically	RENUM
RESET	Closes all files and clears the memory buffer	RESET
RUN	Initiates program execution	RUN
SAVE	Saves the program currently in memory	SAVE "SAMPLE"
SYSTEM	Exits from BASIC to the operating system	SYSTEM
TRACE ON (TRON)	Activates tracing of program statements during program execution	TRACE ON TRON
TRACE OFF (TROFF)	Discontinues tracing of program statements during program execution	TRACE OFF TROFF

Operators (listed hierarchically)

Operation	*Operator*	*Operation*	*Operator*
1. Exponentiation	↑ or ^	8. Logical NOT	NOT
2. Negation	−	9. Logical AND	AND
3. Multiplication and division	* /	10. Logical OR	OR
4. Integer division	\	11. Logical XOR (exclusive OR)	XOR
5. Integer remainder	MOD	12. Logical EQV (equivalence)	EQV
6. Addition and subtraction	+ −	13. Logical IMP (implication)	IMP
7. Relationals	= <> <= < >= >		

Other Punctuation

Colon (:) Used to separate statements on the same line.
Example: 10 CLS : KEY OFF

Apostrophe (') Used to designate comments on a statement line.
Example: 10 CLS 'clear the screen

NOTES:

1. Many specific implementations include additional commands.
2. Some statements can also be used as system commands (e.g., CLS).
3. Some statements or functions may have different interpretations or multiple interpretations (e.g., GET, PUT).

Appendix E

The ASCII Character Set

<table>
<tr><th>ASCII Value</th><th>Character</th><th>ASCII Value</th><th>Character</th><th>ASCII Value</th><th>Character</th><th>ASCII Value</th><th>Character</th></tr>
<tr><td>000</td><td>NUL</td><td>032</td><td>blank</td><td>064</td><td>@</td><td>096</td><td>‘</td></tr>
<tr><td>001</td><td>SOH</td><td>033</td><td>!</td><td>065</td><td>A</td><td>097</td><td>a</td></tr>
<tr><td>002</td><td>STX</td><td>034</td><td>”</td><td>066</td><td>B</td><td>098</td><td>b</td></tr>
<tr><td>003</td><td>ETX</td><td>035</td><td>#</td><td>067</td><td>C</td><td>099</td><td>c</td></tr>
<tr><td>004</td><td>EOT</td><td>036</td><td>$</td><td>068</td><td>D</td><td>100</td><td>d</td></tr>
<tr><td>005</td><td>ENQ</td><td>037</td><td>%</td><td>069</td><td>E</td><td>101</td><td>e</td></tr>
<tr><td>006</td><td>ACK</td><td>038</td><td>&</td><td>070</td><td>F</td><td>102</td><td>f</td></tr>
<tr><td>007</td><td>BEL</td><td>039</td><td>’</td><td>071</td><td>G</td><td>103</td><td>g</td></tr>
<tr><td>008</td><td>BS</td><td>040</td><td>(</td><td>072</td><td>H</td><td>104</td><td>h</td></tr>
<tr><td>009</td><td>HT</td><td>041</td><td>)</td><td>073</td><td>I</td><td>105</td><td>i</td></tr>
<tr><td>010</td><td>LF</td><td>042</td><td>*</td><td>074</td><td>J</td><td>106</td><td>j</td></tr>
<tr><td>011</td><td>VT</td><td>043</td><td>+</td><td>075</td><td>K</td><td>107</td><td>k</td></tr>
<tr><td>012</td><td>FF</td><td>044</td><td>,</td><td>076</td><td>L</td><td>108</td><td>l</td></tr>
<tr><td>013</td><td>CR</td><td>045</td><td>-</td><td>077</td><td>M</td><td>109</td><td>m</td></tr>
<tr><td>014</td><td>SO</td><td>046</td><td>.</td><td>078</td><td>N</td><td>110</td><td>n</td></tr>
<tr><td>015</td><td>SI</td><td>047</td><td>/</td><td>079</td><td>O</td><td>111</td><td>o</td></tr>
<tr><td>016</td><td>DLE</td><td>048</td><td>0</td><td>080</td><td>P</td><td>112</td><td>p</td></tr>
<tr><td>017</td><td>DC1</td><td>049</td><td>1</td><td>081</td><td>Q</td><td>113</td><td>q</td></tr>
<tr><td>018</td><td>DC2</td><td>050</td><td>2</td><td>082</td><td>R</td><td>114</td><td>r</td></tr>
<tr><td>019</td><td>DC3</td><td>051</td><td>3</td><td>083</td><td>S</td><td>115</td><td>s</td></tr>
<tr><td>020</td><td>DC4</td><td>052</td><td>4</td><td>084</td><td>T</td><td>116</td><td>t</td></tr>
<tr><td>021</td><td>NAK</td><td>053</td><td>5</td><td>085</td><td>U</td><td>117</td><td>u</td></tr>
<tr><td>022</td><td>SYN</td><td>054</td><td>6</td><td>086</td><td>V</td><td>118</td><td>v</td></tr>
<tr><td>023</td><td>ETB</td><td>055</td><td>7</td><td>087</td><td>W</td><td>119</td><td>w</td></tr>
<tr><td>024</td><td>CAN</td><td>056</td><td>8</td><td>088</td><td>X</td><td>120</td><td>x</td></tr>
<tr><td>025</td><td>EM</td><td>057</td><td>9</td><td>089</td><td>Y</td><td>121</td><td>y</td></tr>
<tr><td>026</td><td>SUB</td><td>058</td><td>:</td><td>090</td><td>Z</td><td>122</td><td>z</td></tr>
<tr><td>027</td><td>ESC</td><td>059</td><td>;</td><td>091</td><td>[</td><td>123</td><td>{</td></tr>
<tr><td>028</td><td>FS</td><td>060</td><td><</td><td>092</td><td>\</td><td>124</td><td>|</td></tr>
<tr><td>029</td><td>GS</td><td>061</td><td>=</td><td>093</td><td>]</td><td>125</td><td>}</td></tr>
<tr><td>030</td><td>RS</td><td>062</td><td>></td><td>094</td><td>↑</td><td>126</td><td>~</td></tr>
<tr><td>031</td><td>US</td><td>063</td><td>?</td><td>095</td><td>—</td><td>127</td><td>DEL</td></tr>
</table>

Note: The first 32 characters and the last character are control characters; they cannot be printed.

Answers to Selected Supplementary Problems

1.28 (*a*) Calculate the area of a triangle whose base and height are given.

(*b*) Calculate the circumference of a rectangle whose length and width are given.

(*c*) Evaluate

$$w = u + v$$
$$x = u - v$$
$$y = uv$$
$$z = u/v$$

where u and v are specified.

(*d*) Evaluate

$$y = 1 + x + \frac{x^2}{2} + \frac{x^3}{6}$$

where x is specified.

1.29 (*a*)

```
10 INPUT R
20 LET C=2*3.141593*R
30 PRINT R,C
40 END
```

Statement number 20 can also be written as

```
20 LET C=6.283186*R
```

(*b*)

```
10 INPUT B,H
20 LET L=(B↑2+L↑2)↑.5
30 PRINT B,H,L
40 END
```

(*c*)

```
10 INPUT U,V
20 LET W=(U−V)/(U+V)
30 PRINT U,V,W
40 END
```

(*d*)

```
10 INPUT X
20 LET Y= 100*(1+X+2*X↑2+3*X↑3)
30 PRINT X,Y
40 END
```

1.30 The following errors are present.

1. The second line contains two statements. (Only one statement is allowed per line.)
2. The third line does not contain the keyword LET. (This is permitted in some versions of BASIC.)
3. The numbers of the successive program statements do not increase. (The fourth line should have a statement number that is greater than 35 but less than 40.)

2.43 (*a*) 5 (*e*) −7328500 or −7.3285E+6
(*b*) 8000 or 8E+3 (*f*) 2851 or 0.2851E+4
(*c*) −1.8033E−9 (*g*) 0.2851E+10 or 2851E+6, etc.
(*d*) 0.33333333 (*h*) −16752.47 or −1.675247E+4

2.44 (*a*) Correct.
(*b*) Correct.
(*c*) Correct.
(*d*) Exponent cannot contain a decimal point.
(*e*) Correct.
(*f*) Commas not allowed.
(*g*) Exponent is too large in magnitude.
(*h*) Correct.
(*i*) Too many significant figures.
(*j*) Correct.
(*k*) Letter E must be followed by a numerical exponent.
(*l*) Exponent is written incorrectly (should read E−2).

2.45 (*a*) Correct.
(*b*) Correct.
(*c*) Too long for some versions of BASIC.
(*d*) Correct.
(*e*) Quotation marks are not allowed.
(*f*) Correct.

2.46 (*a*) Numeric (correct).
(*b*) Numeric (correct).
(*c*) String (correct).
(*d*) The dollar sign cannot be followed by an integer.
(*e*) The first character must be a letter.
(*f*) Some versions of BASIC do not allow an integer to be included in a string variable
(*g*) Too many characters.
(*h*) Too many integers.
(*i*) Too many letters.
(*j*) String (correct).
(*k*) The first character must be a letter.
(*l*) Second character, if present, must be an integer or a dollar sign.
(*m*) Numeric (correct).
(*n*) Numeric (correct).

2.47 (*a*) T↑(N+1)
(*b*) (X+3)↑(1/K)
(*c*) 2*(A/B)↑.33333333 or 2*(A/B)↑(1/3)
(*d*) 1.87*(U+V)−5.088*(X/Y+2*Z↑2)

(*e*) 1+X+X↑2/2−X↑3/6+X↑4/24−X↑5/120

(*f*) (2*(P/Q)↑(K−1))/((R−3*T)↑(1/M))

(*g*) (I+J−1)↑2/5 or 0.2*(I+J−1)↑2

(*h*) (((X1+X2)↑M*(Y1+Y2)↑N)/((X1/Y1)↑(M+N)*(X2/Y2)↑(M−N)))↑(1/(M*N))

2.48 Each variable that appears on the right side of the equal sign in a LET statement must previously have been assigned an appropriate numerical or string value.

2.49 (*a*) 10 LET P=758.33

(*b*) 20 LET B=A

(*c*) 30 LET F$="PITTSBURGH, PA."

(*d*) 40 LET N$=M$

(*e*) 50 LET Y3=X/(A+B−C)

(*f*) 60 LET K=K−2

(*g*) 70 LET C5=2*C5

(*h*) 80 LET B=C=(A↑2+B↑2)↑.5

2.50 (*a*) 10 LET W=((A+3)*B↑N)/(2.7*(C−D/B)+1)

(*b*) 20 LET F=(((A/B)↑N/(C−D)↑M)/(D/(B−A)↑(N+M)))↑(1/(N+M))

(*c*) 30 LET Y=(A1−A2*X+A3*X↑2−A4*X↑3+A5*X↑4)/(C1−C2*X+C3*X↑2−C4*X↑3)

(*d*) 40 LET P=R*A*(1+R)↑N/((1+R)↑N−1)

2.51 (*a*)
```
10 LET W1=(A+3)*B↑N
15 LET W2=2.7*(C−D/B)+1
20 LET W=W1/W2
```
(*b*)
```
50 LET F1=(A/B)↑N/(C−D)↑M
55 LET F2=D/(B−A)↑(N+M)
60 LET F=(F1/F2)↑(1/(N+M))
```
(*c*)
```
100 LET Y1=A1−A2*X+A3*X↑2−A4*X↑3+A5*X↑4
105 LET Y2=C1−C2*X+C3*X↑2−C4*X↑3
110 LET Y=Y1/Y2
```
(*d*)
```
200 LET Q=(1+R)↑N
205 LET P=R*A*Q/(Q−1)
```

2.52 (*a*) $f = a + 2b/\sqrt{c}$

(*b*) $f = a + \sqrt{2b/c}$

(*c*) $f = (a+2)\sqrt{b/c}$

(*d*) $f = \sqrt{(a+2)b/c}$

(*e*) $g = (pq/r)(s/t)$

2.53 If (Y − Z) represents a negative quantity, then difficulty will be encountered since a negative quantity cannot be raised to a fractional power in BASIC.

2.54 P=−(2↑4)=−16

2.55 P=(−2)↑4=16

2.56 (*a*) 10 INPUT A,B,C,M$,N$

(*b*) 10 INPUT A,N$,B
15 INPUT M$,C

(*c*) 10 INPUT A
12 INPUT B
14 INPUT C
16 INPUT M$
18 INPUT N$

(*d*) 10 PRINT "ENTER VALUES FOR A,B,C,M$ AND N$";
20 INPUT A,B,C,M$,N$

(*e*) 10 PRINT "ENTER VALUES FOR A,B,C,M$, AND N$"
20 INPUT A,B,C,M$,N$

(*f*) 100 PRINT A,B,C,M$,N$

(*g*) 100 PRINT A;B;C;M$;N$

(*h*) 120 PRINT A;B;C;

(*i*) 200 PRINT A;B;C;(A+B+C)/3;(A*B*C)↑(1/3);(A↑2+B↑2+C↑2)↑.5
210 PRINT
220 PRINT M$,,,,N$

(*j*) 300 PRINT "A=";A,"B=";B,"C=";C

or

300 PRINT "A=";A;"B=";B;"C=";C

(*k*) 500 PRINT ,,"NAME: ";M$
510 PRINT
520 PRINT ,,"SOCIAL SECURITY NUMBER: ";N$

2.57 (*a*) ?6.2E−6,27.5E−12,−1000
?SHARON,GAIL

The first line of data can also be typed as

?.0000062,.275E−10,−1000

(*b*) ?−743.08,.00987,SUSAN

or

?−.74308E+3,.987E−2,SUSAN

(*c*) ?"NEW YORK","CHICAGO","SAN FRANCISCO"

(The quotation marks are required around NEW YORK and SAN FRANCISCO because of the inclusion of a blank space. In the case of CHICAGO, the quotation marks are optional.)

(*d*) ?2770543,"DECEMBER 29, 1963",48.8E+9,"ELEVEN O' CLOCK"

(The strings must be enclosed in quotation marks because of the blank spaces and the comma.)

2.58 (*a*)
```
6.20000E-6   2.75000E-11 -1000   2770543 -743.08   9.87000E-3
4.88000E+10
```

(*b*)
```
6.20000E-6      2.75000E-11    -1000           2770543        -743.08
9.87000E-3      4.88000E+10
```

(*c*)
```
6.17250E-6      5.67734E-5     -75286.7
```

(*d*)
```
SHARON          DECEMBER 29, 1963              ELEVEN O'CLOCK
```

2.59 (*a*) 10 REM AVERAGING OF AIR POLLUTION DATA
(*b*) 250 REM BEGIN LOOP TO CALCULATE CUMULATIVE SUM
(*c*) 80 LET A=S/N 'CALCULATE AVERAGE VALUE
(*d*) 20 INPUT X,T 'READ A DATA POINT

2.60 (*a*) Correct.
(*b*) The statement number to which control is transferred must be a positive integer, not a formula.
(*c*) A GO TO statement cannot transfer control to itself.
(*d*) Correct.
(*e*) The quotation marks cannot appear.

2.61 The flowchart is shown in Fig. P-2.61.

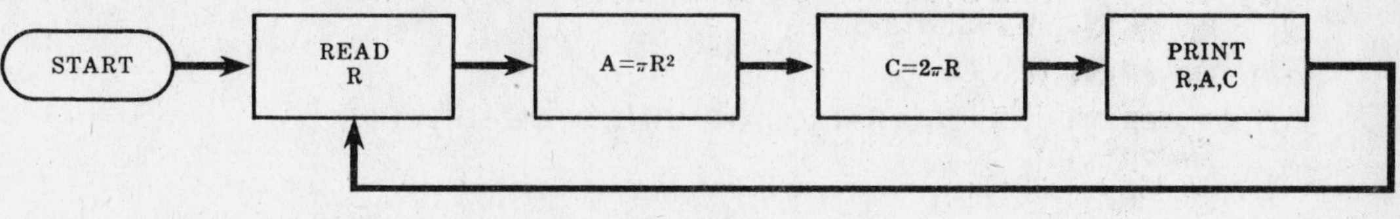

Fig. P-2.61

2.62 (*a*)
```
10 REM HELLO!
20 PRINT, , "HELLO!"
30 END
```
(*b*)
```
10 REM WELCOME!
20 PRINT "HI, WHAT'S YOUR NAME";
30 INPUT N$
40 PRINT
50 PRINT
60 PRINT "WELCOME "; N$; "!"
70 PRINT "LET'S BE FRIENDS!"
80 END
```

2.63 (*a*)
```
10 REM TEMPERATURE CONVERSION PROBLEM
20 PRINT "TEMPERATURE IN DEGREES FAHRENHEIT=";
30 INPUT F
40 LET C=5*(F-32)/9
50 PRINT "DEGREES F=";F,"DEGREES C=";C
60 END
```
(*b*)
```
10 REM PIGGY-BANK PROBLEM
20 PRINT "NUMBER OF HALF-DOLLARS=";
30 INPUT N1
40 PRINT "NUMBER OF QUARTERS=";
50 INPUT N2
60 PRINT "NUMBER OF DIMES=";
70 INPUT N3
80 PRINT "NUMBER OF NICKELS=";
90 INPUT N4
100 PRINT "NUMBER OF PENNIES=";
110 INPUT N5
120 LET S=.5*N1+.25*N2+.1*N3+.05*N4+.01*N5
130 PRINT "TOTAL AMOUNT OF MONEY=";S;" DOLLARS"
140 END
```

Note that the END statement can be replaced with an appropriate GO TO statement in each of the above problems. This will allow each program to process multiple sets of data in succession.

2.64 Presented below is a complete BASIC program for each problem. It should be understood, however, that the actual programming should not begin until a detailed outline or flowchart has been prepared. Each program is written in such a manner that multiple sets of data can be processed sequentially.

(*a*)

```
10 REM VOLUME AND AREA OF A SPHERE
20 LET P=3.1415927
30 PRINT "RADIUS=";
40 INPUT R
50 LET V=4*P*R↑3/3
60 LET A=4*P*R↑2
70 PRINT "R=";R,"V=";V,"A=";A
80 PRINT
90 GO TO 30
100 END
```

(*b*)

```
10 REM COMPUTATION OF MASS OF AIR IN A TIRE
20 PRINT "P=";
30 INPUT P
40 PRINT "V=";
50 INPUT V
60 PRINT "T=";
70 INPUT T
80 LET M=P*V/(.37*(T+460))
90 PRINT "M=";M
100 PRINT
110 GO TO 20
120 END
```

(*c*)

```
10 REM GEOMETRIC PROPERTIES OF A TRIANGLE
20 PRINT "A=";
30 INPUT A
40 PRINT "B=";
50 INPUT B
60 PRINT "C=";
70 INPUT C
80 LET S=(A+B+C)/2
90 LET A0=(S*(S-A)*(S-B)*(S-C))↑.5
100 LET R1=A0/S
110 LET A1=3.14159*R1↑2
120 LET R2=A*B*C/(4*A0)
130 LET A2=3.14159*R2↑2
140 PRINT "AREA OF TRIANGLE=";A0
150 PRINT "AREA OF LARGEST INSCRIBED CIRCLE=";A1
160 PRINT "AREA OF SMALLEST CIRCUMSCRIBED CIRCLE=";A2
170 PRINT
180 GO TO 20
190 END
```

(*d*)

```
10 REM COMPOUND INTEREST PROBLEM
20 PRINT "P=";
30 INPUT P
40 PRINT "I=";
50 INPUT I
60 PRINT "N=";
70 INPUT N
80 LET F=P*(1+I)↑N
90 PRINT "F="; F
100 PRINT
110 GO TO 20
120 END
```

If the interest is compounded quarterly rather than annually, statement number 80 must be changed to read

```
80 LET A=P*(1+I/4)↑(4*N)
```

(*e*)

```
10 REM GROWTH OF A BACTERIA POPULATION
20 PRINT "T=";
30 INPUT T
40 LET C=.0289*T
50 LET F=1+C+C↑2/2+C↑3/6+C↑4/24+C↑5/120+C↑6/720+C↑7/5040+C↑8/40320
60 LET F=F+C↑9/362880
70 PRINT "P/P0=";F
80 PRINT
90 GO TO 20
100 END
```

Notice that the computation of the multiplication factor (F) requires two statements because a single statement could exceed a single line (depending on its length).

4.32 (*a*) Correct.

(*b*) This condition can never be satisfied.

(*c*) Correct.

(*d*) Correct.

(*e*) A numeric variable cannot be compared with a string variable.

(*f*) Correct.

4.33 The string represented by P$ must come earlier in alphabetical order than the string represented by Q$.

4.34 (*a*) Correct.

(*b*) Incorrect grammatical structure (THEN can be followed only by a statement number).

(*c*) Not all versions of BASIC allow use of GO TO in place of THEN.

(*d*) Correct.

(*e*) The statement number to which control is transferred must be a positive integer, not a variable.

(*f*) Correct.

(*g*) The condition can never be satisfied.

4.35 (*a*)

```
40 IF K<15 THEN 50
```

(*b*)

```
100 IF N$="OPTION A" THEN 70
110 GO TO 150
```

(*c*)

```
60 ...
...
150 IF X>=100 THEN 200
160 LET J=J+1
170 INPUT X
180 GO TO 60
...
200 ...
```

(*d*)

```
20 ...
...
80 IF J=0 THEN 150
90 LET S=S+J
100 GO TO 20
...
150 ...
```

4.36 (*a*) Correct.

(*b*) The loop will continue indefinitely, since the value of J will always be reset to 1. (If statement number 80 is changed to

```
80 GO TO 40
```

then the loop will be executed correctly.)

(*c*) Control will always be transferred to statement 200.

(*d*) The loop will continue indefinitely since the value of X will never exceed 100.

(*e*) Correct.

4.37 (*a*) A string variable cannot appear in an ON-GO TO statement.

(*b*) Correct.

(*c*) An ON-GO TO statement cannot transfer control to itself.

(*d*) The statement numbers to which control is transferred must be positive integers, not variables.

(*e*) Correct.

(*f*) Not all versions of BASIC allow use of THEN in place of GO TO.

(*g*) Incorrect grammatical structure (ON must precede GO TO).

4.38 (*a*) An error message will result (execution cannot proceed because J−K=−1).

(*b*) Control will be transferred to statement number 20.

(*c*) Control will be transferred to statement number 50.

(*d*) An error message will result (execution cannot proceed because J−K=5).

(*e*) Control will be transferred to statement number 100.

4.39 (*a*) Correct.

(*b*) A formula cannot appear in place of a running variable.

(*c*) String variables cannot appear in a FOR-TO statement.

(*d*) Correct. (Note that V(1), V(2) and V(3) are subscripted variables, which are discussed in Chapter 5.)

(*e*) Correct.

(*f*) Illogical statement (the running variable is required to decrease in value, but cannot do so because of the positive STEP size).

4.40 (*a*)

```
10 FOR I=1 TO 200
...
70 NEXT I
```

(Statement numbers are arbitrary.)

(*b*)

```
10 FOR I=1 TO 200
      ...
50    IF X<.001 THEN 175
      ...
70 NEXT I
...
175 ...
```

(*c*)

```
10 FOR I=1 TO 73 STEP 3
...
70 NEXT I
```

(*d*)

```
10 FOR C=.5 TO A↑3−10 STEP A+B
...
70 NEXT C
```

4.41 (*a*) The value of the running variable is altered within the loop.

(*b*) Correct.

(*c*) The loops overlap.

(*d*) The inner and outer loops use the same running variable (X). Also, both loops end with the same NEXT statement.

(*e*) Correct, provided numerical values have been assigned to the variables T and T1.

(*f*) The running variable in the NEXT statement (C) is not the same as the running variable in the FOR-TO statement (X).

5.40 (*a*) 10 LET Y=SQR(SIN(X)−COS(X))

(*b*) 10 LET P=Q*EXP(−Q*T)

(*c*) 10 LET C=LOG(SQR(ABS(A+B)))+LOG(SQR(ABS(A−B)))

(*d*) 10 LET W=ABS(ABS(U−V)−ABS(U+V))

(*e*) 10 LET Z=COS(X+ATN(Y))

5.41 (*a*) 10 ON SGN((A*B−C*D)/(F+G))+2 GO TO 135,260,75

(*b*) 100 PRINT TAB(4);"X=";X;TAB(28);"Y=";Y;TAB(52);"Z=";Z

(*c*) 100 IF (N/2)=INT(N/2) THEN 200

Control will be transfered to statement number 200 if N is even-valued.

(*d*) Control will continue to be transferred to statement number 200 if N is even.

5.42 (*a*) N$ is a string list.

(*b*) A is a numeric table, A$ a string table, B a numeric list and C$ a string list.

(*c*) P$ is a string list, P is a numeric table.

(*d*) Z is a numeric table.

5.43 (*a*) Correct.

(*b*) Correct.

(*c*) The quantities enclosed in parentheses in the DIM statement must be positive integers; variables are not allowed.

(*d*) A DIM statement cannot contain nonsubscripted variables (in this case, the variables C1 and C2).

(*e*) A subscript cannot have a negative value.

(*f*) Correct.

5.44 (*a*)
```
10 LET S=0
20 FOR I=1 TO 199 STEP 2
30     LET S=S+X(I)↑2
40 NEXT I
50 LET S1=SQR(S)
```

(*b*)
```
10 FOR I=1 TO 8
20     FOR J=1 TO 12
30         LET H(I,J)=1/(I+J-1)
40     NEXT J
50 NEXT I
```

(*c*)
```
100 FOR I=1 TO N
110     IF K(I)>15 THEN 130
120     PRINT TAB(8);"I=";I;TAB(44);"K=";K(I)
130 NEXT I
```

(*d*)
```
100 LET P=1
110 FOR I=1 TO K
120       LET P=P*W(I,I)
130 NEXT I
```
(*e*)
```
100 FOR I=1 TO M
110       PRINT TAB(10);M$(I,4)
120 NEXT I
```
(*f*)
```
100 FOR I=1 TO M
110       PRINT M$(I,4);" ";
120 NEXT I
```
(*g*)
```
100 FOR J=1 TO N
110       PRINT M$(5,J);" ";
120 NEXT J
```

5.45 (*a*)
```
10 READ L$(1),L$(2),L$(3),L$(4),P,Q,R,H$
20 READ T(1,1),T(1,2),T(1,3),T(1,4),T(2,1),T(2,2),T(2,3),T(2,4)
   . . .
200 DATA WHITE, YELLOW, ORANGE, RED
210 DATA 2.25E+5,6.08E-9,-1.29E+12,RESTART
220 DATA 1,-3,5,-7,-2,4,-6,8
```
The READ and DATA statements can be combined or expanded if desired.

(*b*)
```
10 FOR I=1 TO 4
20      READ L$(I)
30 NEXT I
40 READ P,Q,R,H$
50 FOR I=1 TO 2
60      FOR J=1 TO 4
70           READ T(I,J)
80      NEXT J
90 NEXT I
```
The DATA statements will be the same as in part (*a*).

(*c*)
```
10 FOR I=1 TO 4
20      READ L$(I)
30 NEXT I
40 READ P,Q,R,H$
50 FOR I=1 TO 2
60      FOR J=1 TO 4
70           READ T(I,J)
80      NEXT J
90 NEXT I
   . . .
150 RESTORE*
160 READ P1,Q1,R1
```
The DATA statements will be the same as in part (*a*).

(*d*) The solution is the same as in part (*c*), except that statement number 150 must be replaced by either

```
150 RESTORE
```
or
```
150 RESTORE$
```
and statement number 160 must be replaced by
```
160 READ A1$,A2$,A3$,A4$
```

6.41 (*a*)
```
10 DEF FNY(A,B,X)=A*X↑B
```

(*b*)
```
10 DEF FNQ(R)=C0+C1*R+C2*R↑2+C3*R↑3+C4*R↑4
```

The values for C0 through C4 must be specified elsewhere in the program, before the function is referenced.

(*c*)
```
10 DEF FNI(J,K)=(J+K)↑(J+K)
```

(*d*)
```
10 DEF FNR(A,B,C)
20 IF B↑2<4*A*C THEN 50
30 LET FNR=SQR(B↑2-4*A*C)
40 GO TO 60
50 LET FNR=SQR(4*A*C-B↑2)
60 FNEND
```

6.42 (*a*)
```
10 DEF FNZ(Z)=INT(Z+.5)
```

(*b*)
```
10 DEF FNP(N)
20 LET P=1
30 FOR I=1 TO N
40      LET P=P*T(I)
50 NEXT I
60 LET FNP=P
70 FNEND
```

(*c*)
```
10 DEF FNR(A,B)
20 LET FNR=0
30 FOR I=1 TO 5
40      LET X=A+(B-A)*RND
50      IF X<=R THEN 70
60      LET FNR=X
70 NEXT I
80 FNEND
```

(*d*)
```
10 DEF FNW$(X)
20 ON SGN(X)+2 GO TO 30,50,70
30 LET FNW$="NEGATIVE"
40 GO TO 80
50 LET FNW$="ZERO"
60 GO TO 80
70 LET FNW$="POSITIVE"
80 FNEND
```

(*e*)
```
10 DEF FNL$(N$)
20 CHANGE N$ TO L
30 LET N=90
40 FOR I=1 TO L(0)
50      IF N<=L(I) THEN 70
60      LET N=L(I)
70 NEXT I
80 LET FNL$=CHR$(N)
90 FNEND
```

Note that the constant 90 is equivalent to the letter Z in the 7-bit ASCII code (see Table 6.1, page 130).

6.43 (*a*)
```
100 LET T=FNY(C1+C2,3,X+Y)
```

[See the solution given for Problem 6.41(*a*).]

(*b*)
```
100 LET Q=FNQ(LOG(X))
```

[See the solution given for Problem 6.41(*b*).]

(*c*)
```
100 PRINT FNI(A-B,C)
```
[See the solution given for Problem 6.41(*c*).]

(*d*)
```
100 LET D=ABS(X-FNZ(X))
```
[See the solution given for Problem 6.42(*a*).]

(*e*)
```
10 FOR I=1 TO 60
20      IF FNP(I)>1000 THEN 40
30 NEXT I
40 PRINT "N"; I
```
[See the solution given for Problem 6.42(*b*).]

(*f*)
```
10 FOR I=1 TO 20
20      PRINT "I=";I,"LARGEST R=";FNR(2,5)
30 NEXT I
```
[See the solution given for Problem 6.42(*c*).]

6.44 (*a*) The number of arguments in the function reference does not agree with the number of arguments in the function definition.

(*b*) This example contains two errors:

(i) The function name (FNC) is not assigned a value within the function.

(ii) A RETURN statement cannot appear in a function definition.

(*c*) This example contains two errors:

(i) Control cannot be transferred into a subroutine by a GO TO statement.

(ii) An FNEND statement cannot appear in a subroutine.

(*d*) This example contains two errors:

(i) The function is named incorrectly.

(ii) Formulas cannot appear as dummy arguments.

(*e*) Arguments are not present in the function reference.

(*f*) Control cannot be transferred out of a subroutine by means of an IF-THEN statement.

(*g*) The program logic is incorrect. (The function references the subroutine, which in turn references the function.)

7.39 (*a*) Correct.

(*b*) Matrix formulas cannot appear in a matrix statement.

(*c*) Correct.

(*d*) Correct.

(*e*) Correct.

(*f*) A matrix cannot be updated by means of matrix multiplication.

(*g*) Matrix multiplication cannot be carried out unless the number of columns of the first matrix (X) is the same as the number of rows of the second matrix (Y). In this example X has 20 columns but Y has only 10 rows.

(*h*) The MAT INPUT statement should be written
```
50 MAT INPUT V
```

(*i*) Correct, provided M and N are assigned positive integer values not exceeding 100 and 50, respectively.

(*j*) The variable dimension feature cannot be used with a MAT PRINT statement.

(*k*) Correct.

(*l*) One of the dimensions specified in the MAT ZER statement exceeds the corresponding dimension in the DIM statement.

(*m*) A nonsquare matrix cannot have an inverse.

(*n*) Correct.

7.40 (*a*)
```
100 MAT I=IDN
110 MAT B=TRN(A)
120 MAT C=B*A
130 MAT D=C-I
140 MAT F=(2*N+1)*D
```
F will be a 10 × 10 matrix.

(*b*)
```
100 MAT E=A*C
110 MAT F=B*D
120 MAT G=E-F
130 MAT H=INV(G)
140 LET D1=DET
150 PRINT "DETERMINANT OF G=";D1
```

(*c*) Add the statement
```
145 MAT PRINT G;H;
```
to part (*b*) above.

(*d*)
```
100 MAT A=ZER(12,8)
```

(*e*)
```
100 MAT READ A(8,12),B(6,15)
```
The data block must contain the elements of A, in a row-by-row order, followed by the elements of B, row-by-row.

(*f*)
```
100 FOR I=1 TO 8
110     FOR J=1 TO 12
120         PRINT A(I,J);
130     NEXT J
140     PRINT
150 NEXT I
160 PRINT
170 FOR I=1 TO 6
180     FOR J=1 TO 15
190         PRINT B(I,J);
200     NEXT J
210     PRINT
220 NEXT I
```
The FOR-TO loops are required because the variable dimension feature is not available with the MAT PRINT statement.

8.34 (*a*) Most versions of BASIC make use of the INPUT statement rather than the READ statement when reading a sequential data file.

(*b*) A random data file cannot contain both strings and numeric constants.

(*c*) Correct, provided random data files have been assigned to data channels 1 and 2.

(*d*) Correct.

(*e*) The SCRATCH and QUOTE statements must include data channel numbers, not file names.

(*f*) The FILES statement must include a file name, not a string variable.

(*g*) A pointer cannot be positioned beyond the end of the file.

(*h*) A string cannot be written onto a numeric random data file.

8.35 (*a*)
```
10 FILES LIST1,,LIST2
```

(*b*)
```
10 FILES NAMES$25,ACCTS%
```

(*c*)
```
10 FILE :2,F$
20 FILE :5,G$
```

(*d*)
```
NEW OR OLD-->NEW
NEW FILE NAME-->TAPE1
10 ...  }
20 ...  }
...     }  Data file TAPE1
300 ... }
SAVE
LIST
```

(*e*)
```
NEW OR OLD-->NEW
NEW FILE NAME-->ITEMS
SAVE
```

(*f*)
```
OLD
OLD FILE NAME-->OLD1
SCRATCH
OLD
OLD FILE NAME-->OLD2
SCRATCH
OLD
OLD FILE NAME-->NEW1
RENAME OLD1
OLD
OLD FILE NAME-->NEW2
RENAME OLD2
```

(*g*) Presumably, the program described in Problem 8.35(*f*) will contain the statement

```
10 FILES OLD1,OLD2,NEW1,NEW2
```

This statement should be replaced by the following sequence of statements.

```
10 INPUT A$,B$,C$,D$
20 FILE #1,A$
30 FILE #2,B$
40 FILE #3,C$
50 FILE #4,D$
```

When the program is executed, the names of the input files will be assigned to A$ and B$, and the names of the output files to C$ and D$.

(*h*)
```
10 INPUT A$,B$
20 FILE #5,A$
30 FILE #3,B$
40 QUOTE #3
50 SCRATCH #3
60 INPUT #5,N,F$,X,Y,Z,G$
70 PRINT #3,N,Z,F$,G$
80 IF END #5, THEN 100
90 GO TO 60
100 END
```

(*i*)
```
10 INPUT A$,B$
20 FILE :5,A$
30 FILE :3,B$
40 READ :5,X
50 WRITE :3,X
60 IF LOC(5)=LOF(5) THEN 80
70 GO TO 40
80 END
```

(*j*)
```
50 INPUT P
60 SET :6,P
70 READ :6,X
80 SET :2,P
90 WRITE :2,X
```

(*k*)
```
100 LET P1=LOC(1)
110 LET P4=LOC(4)
120 IF P1=P4 THEN 200
130 LET P2=P1
140 IF P4<=P1 THEN 160
150 LET P2=P4
160 SET :2,P2
```

(*l*)
```
100 IF LOF(3)<>LOF(5) THEN 25
```

Index